VIRGINIA

Vital Records

$\mathcal{V}$IRGINIA

Vital Records

From The Virginia Magazine of History and Biography,
the William and Mary College Quarterly,
and Tyler's Quarterly

Indexed by Judith McGhan

CLEARFIELD

Reprinted for
Clearfield Company, Inc. by
Genealogical Publishing Co., Inc.
Baltimore, Maryland
2000

Excerpted and reprinted from *The Virginia Magazine of History
and Biography,* the *William and Mary College Quarterly Historical
Magazine,* and *Tyler's Quarterly Historical and Genealogical
Magazine,* with added Publisher's Note, Contents, and Index, by
Genealogical Publishing Co., Inc., Baltimore, 1982.
Copyright © 1982 by Genealogical Publishing Co., Inc.
Baltimore, Maryland, all rights reserved.
Library of Congress Catalogue Card Number 82-80464
International Standard Book Number 0-8063-0984-9
Made in the United States of America

Note

VIRGINIA VITAL RECORDS is composed of articles which have been excerpted in facsimile from *The Virginia Magazine of History and Biography*, the *William and Mary College Quarterly Historical Magazine*, and *Tyler's Quarterly Historical and Genealogical Magazine*. It is primarily a collection of articles containing lists of births, marriages, and deaths, with information drawn for the most part from church and parish registers, tombstone inscriptions, and obituary notices—vital records in the very broadest sense of the term. Also drawn on are the revealing records of birth, marriage, and death inscribed in family Bibles (see especially Appendix C).

The articles collected here represent virtually everything in the way of vital records ever published in the above-named periodicals (with the exception of an independent grouping of marriage lists in *Virginia Marriage Records,* the first volume in this series of source record extracts). They constitute the best efforts of an army of researchers and provide, in the aggregate, one of the largest bodies of Virginia source material ever published. No matter that some of the articles have been superseded, that some are fragmentary and incomplete, while others beg as many questions as they answer; what remains are the highlights of a great era of achievement in genealogical research, and their appearance here in a single, comprehensive volume will save the researcher long and tedious hours of library work.

Genealogical Publishing Company

Contents

Hanover County

Henrico County

xi

Northumberland County

Orange County

Pittsylvania County

Prince George County

Prince William County

Richmond County

APPENDIX C: Bible Records from The Virginia Magazine of History and Biography

VIRGINIA

Vital Records

INSCRIPTIONS ON TOMBS AT BOWMAN'S FOLLY, ACCOMAC.

CONTRIBUTED BY CHARLES H. RUSSELL.

Mrs. Mary Anne Cropper, only child of Major John Cropper and Elizabeth Savage Cropper, and wife of Dr. John Washington Cropper, of Accomac County, Eastern Shore of Virginia. Born October 1, 1814, died December 23, 1837.

Coventon Carbon Cropper, son of Sebastin and Sabra, his wife. Died at Washington Academy, Maryland, March 12, 1786, aged 18 years, 4 months, 6 days.

Sabra Cropper, wife of Sebastin Cropper, daughter of Coventon Cropper and Barbara, his wife. Died December 28, 1776, aged 38 years.

Sebastin Cropper, son of Bowman Cropper and Tabitha, his wife. Died March 20, 1776.

Louisa Anne Joyner, daughter of Thomas R. Joyner, of Accomac County, Virginia. She was the wife of Dr. George Robertson Dennis, of Kingston, Somerset County, Maryland. Born MDCCCXXII, died MDCCCLII.

General John Cropper, oldest son of Sabra and Sebastin Cropper. Was born at Bowman's Folly, in the county of Accomac, Eastern Shore of Virginia, December 23, 1755. He was an officer in the Revolution and did continue until the end. He died January 18, 1821, leaving a loving wife, seven children and seven grandchildren.

Margaret Cropper, wife of John Cropper, daughter of William Pettitt and Mary, his wife, of Northampton. Died June 3, 1784.

Mrs. Catherine Cropper, wife of General John Cropper. Born 1772, died on her birthday, 18th of June, 1855. She was the excellent of the earth.

TOMBSTONES AT HILL'S FARM, IN ACCOMAC COUNTY.
COMMUNICATED BY MARGARET SEYMOUR HALL.

Sacred to the memory of Thomas Bayly, Son of Edmund Bayly, Grandson of Edmund Bayly, and great-grandson of Richard Bayly, of Craddock. His mother was Rose, the daughter of Maddox Fisher, of Northampton. He was born March 14th, 1737-'8, O. Stile and died ———— (illegible).

In memory of Anne Bayly, wife of Thomas Bayly, Daughter of Richard Drummond and grand-daughter of Major Richard Drummond by his wife Patience, who was the daughter of Richard Hill, the proprietor and patentee of this plantation (Hill's Farm) in the year 1666. Her mother was Catharine, the daughter of Thomas Harmanson, of Northampton. She was born February 26th, 1742-'3, Old Stile, and died Sept. 8th, 1801, N. Stile. On her left lie her Father, sister and six of her children. Her second son was lost at sea, and left living Three sons and two daughters.

Edmund Bayly, son of Thomas Bayly and Ann his wife. He was married to the daughter of John Upshur, of Northampton. He was the clerk of the district and county courts held at Accomac Court House, and was born Aug. 27th, 1763, and died Nov. 18th, 1805.

Sacred to the memory of Col. Thomas M. Bayly, 3[d] son of Col. Thomas Bayly and Anne Drummond his wife. He was born March 26, 1775. On the 24th of March, 1802, he was married to Margaret P. Cropper, daughter of Gen. John Cropper. On the 21st of Dec., 1826, he was married to Jane O. Addison, the Widow of Colonel Kendall Addison, and the daughter of Samuel Coward. On the 7th of January, 1834, he died. Devotedly attached to his country he spent the best years of his life in her service. Col. Bayly entered into public life in 1798, and continued in it, with the intermission of a few years, until 1830, during which time he discharged the respective duties of a Member of the House of Delegates of Virginia, of the Senate of Virginia, of the Congress of the United States, of the late Convention of Virginia which formed her new Constitution, and of the important session of the Legislature succeeding it. Col. Bayly's highest eulogy as a public man is to be found in the continued confidence of his constituents, which he enjoyed during all the aggravated times and amid all the mutation of parties through which he passed. It is a fact as honourable as singular in his history that he never lost an election, and very rarely ever had one closely contested. Col. Bayly as a politician was ever found on the side of popular rights. This monument is erected to his memory by his widow.

2

NOTES.

Lieut.-Col. Edmund Scarbrough had issue: Tabitha Scarbrough married Col. William Smart, who had issue: Tabitha Scarbrough Smart married Richard Hill of Hill's Farm, who had issue: Patience Hill married Major Richard Drummond, who had issue: Richard Drummond married Catharine Harmanson (daughter of Thomas Harmanson), who had issue: Ann Drummond married Thomas Bayly, who had issue: Edmund Bayly married Rachel Upshur, who had issue: Ann Upshur Bayly married William Digby Seymour, who had issue: Ann Upshur Bayly Seymour married Rev. Alfred Henno Ames, who had issue: Anne Seymour Ames, George Christian Ames.

Tabitha Scarbrough, widow of Col. William Smart, afterwards married Col. Edward Hill, of Shirley. Richard Hill was brought to Northampton by Col. Scarbrugh (spelled thus in old record), and was for some time his business manager. Mary Persey (daughter of Abraham Persey and of Frances West, daughter of Nathaniel West, nephew of Lord De la Ware) married Thomas Hill in 1638, and had two children. (See *Virginia Magazine of History and Biography*, Vol. I., p. 188.) The widow, Mary Hill, married Col. Thomas Bushrod, of "Essex Lodge," York county, and John Hill was living on his farm at death. Catharine Harmanson was daughter of Thomas Harmanson, who was born in Brandenburg, Germany, 1631. See notice of Thomas Harmanson, aged 22, in an Act of Assembly naturalizing Thomas Harmanson, "a German, born in the Dominion of Brandenburg but now an inhabitant of Northampton county, professing the Protestant Religion."—WILLIAM AND MARY QUARTERLY, Vol I., p. 192.

Rachel Upshur, the wife of Edmund Bayly, was daughter of John Upshur and Anne Emerson. 1763–1805.

In Hotten's list is William Bayly of West-Shirley Hundred, born in 1583. Mary, born 1600, was his wife They came to Virginia in 1617, and had son Thomas, born 1620.

TOMBSTONES AT MT. AIR, NEAR SCOTTSVILLE, ALBEMARLE CO., VA.

"OUR MOTHER,"
Maria J. Adams,
Died   13th, 1852.

John Baker Gilmer,
Son of Thomas W. and Anne E. Gilmer.
Died April 25th 1859.
Aged 30 yrs.
Erected by his mother.

Ellen Tapscott Gilmer,
Daughter of Thos. W. & Anne E. Gilmer.
Died Dec. 13th 1857,
Aged 25 yrs.
Erected by her mother.

In memory of Virginia Douglas,
Daughter of Thos. W. & Annie E. Gilmer.
Born Feb. 4th 1842.
Died June 4th 1844.

Sacred to the memory of Francis Robert.
Son of Thos. W. & Annie E. Gilmer.
Born July 13th 1838.
Died July 6th 1839.

In memory of
Thos W. Gilmer,
Born April 6th 1802,
Gov. of Va. 1840.
Member of Congress, 1842.
Sec'y of U. S. Navy 1844.

Killed by the explosion of a gun on board of U. S. Man-of-war
steamer, Princeton, Feb. 6th 1844.

Gifted with genius, swayed by honors, he ever sought noble ends
by noble means; constant in friendship, firm in virtue, in deeds of
patriotism faithful to the end.

Humble in piety, abundant in good works, with his harness on
he met the summons of an untimely death. Honored by his Country,
esteemed by the just and good, and most esteemed by those who
new him best.

Erected by his widow.

Anne Elizabeth Gilmer,
Wife of Hon. T. W. Gilmer.
Born Nov. 9th 1809.
Died April 10th 1874.
Worthy helpmeet of an honored husband;

Widowed at the early age of 35, with a large and helpless family, she assumed the responsibility and discharged it with unflagging
zeal. Guided by christian wisdom, fortitude and temperance. Eminent for enlarged culture and wit, a bright ornament of the social
circle; abounding in charity and good works, she was above all an
humble follower of the Lord Jesus.

4

She sleeps with those she loved so well, awaiting with them a glorious resurrection.

Erected by her surviving children.

Scottsville, Va. March 27, —93.

REVOLUTIONARY SOLDIERS BURIED AT BETHEL CHURCH, AUGUSTA COUNTY, VIRGINIA

Contributed by Fannie B. King.

1. David Hamilton. Died March, 1820, aged 69.
2. James Hamilton. Died March 29, 1831, in 79th year.
3. John Hamilton. Died March 27, 1826, in 80th year.
4. Andrew McClure. Died Dec. 30, 1847, aged 80.
5. Samuel Doak. Died 1826, in 80th year.
6. Col. Robert Doak. Died March 12, 1832.
7. Robert Tate. Died July 9, 1932, aged 79.
8. John Logan. Died Jan. 9, 1837.
9. Thomas Sharp. Died Jan. 28, 1826, aged 65.
10. David Carlisle Humphreys. Died 1826, aged 85.
11. James Frazier. Died 1818.
12. John Frazier. Died July 11, 1832, in 82d year.
13. Joseph Sharp. Died Oct., 1828, aged 75.
14. William McCutcheon. Died June 29, 1848.
15. Thomas Mitchell. Died Dec. 30, 1806, aged 74.
16. James Mitchell. Died 1806, aged 66.
17. William Mitchell. Died?
18. Alexander Hamilton. Died 1831, aged 72.
19. James McClure. Died Sept. 13, 1799.
20. John Tate. Died Aug. 6, 1836.
21. John Nelson. Died June 2, 1818, Aged 62.
22. Robert Mitchell. Died 1834.
23. Jacob Bumgardner. Died 1857, aged 91.
24. William Kerr. Died July 16, 1828.

Daughters of Revolutionary Soldiers Buried at Bethel Church, Augusta County, Va.

1. Margaret Alexander married Tate.
2. Isabella Mitchell married Doak.
3. Rebecca Baxter married Tate.
4. Hannah Humphreys married McClure.
5. Margaret Moore married Humphreys.
6. Mary Tate married Wallace.
7. Margaret Finley Humphreys married Blackwood.
8. Matilda Scott married Sproul.
9. Peggy Tate, unmarried.
10. Margaret Blackwood married Donald.
11. Mary Mitchell married McClure.
12. Polly Doak, unmarried.
13. Isabelle Doak, unmarried.
14. Dorcas Doak, unmarried.
15. Rachel McPeeters married Logan.

TOMBSTONE OF MARTHA MARTIN.

Major Lewis Burwell had two daughters Martha, one by Abigail Smith, who married Henry Armistead, and was the young lady who so infatuated Governor Nicholson, and the other Martha, called "Martha, Junior," by his second wife, Martha Lear, daughter of Col. John Lear, of Nansemond county. It is seen from this tombstone that she married Col. John Martin, of Caroline county. This inscription was communicated by Mr. and Mrs. R. E. DeJarnette, of Norfolk. The stone lies at Clifton, Caroline county, seven miles from Bowling Green:

> Interred beneath this stone
> lyes the Body of Mrs.
> Martha Martin, Wife of Col.
> John Martin, of Caroline
> County, and daughter of
> Lewis Burwel Esq., of Gloff-
> ter County, who departed this
> Life the 27th of May 1738 in
> the 36 year of her Age & left
> three sons & four daughters.

OLD INSCRIPTIONS AT PORT ROYAL, VA.

> Here lyes the Body of
> Catherine Gilchrist
> late the Wife of Robert Gilchrist
> of Port Royal, Merchant.
> She died the 4th of May 1769
> Aged 54 years.
> This Stone is inscribed as a
> Monument to her Memory
> by her disconsolate Husband.

6

Here Lyes the Body
of Robert Gilchrist, Esq.
of Port Royal, Merch.
Died the 16th July 1790
Aged 69 Years.
This Stone is Inscribed a
Monument to his Memory
By His Executors.

Beneath this humble stone a Youth doth lie
Most too Good to live too Young to dye
Count his few Years how short the scanty Span
But count ——— his Virtues, and he dy'd a Man.

Sacred to the Memory of Younger,
The Son of William & Anne Fox
of Port Royal, Who was born the
10th of September 1754 and dyed
the 25th of May 1763.

Beneath this stone lies
Elizabeth Hill
Wife of
James Dunlop
Merchant in Port Royal.
Who died the 8th of May 1780.
Aged 31 Years.

Sally S. Lightfoot
Wife of
Philip Lightfoot
of Port Royal, Va.
Born 7th. March 1790.
Died 22nd August 1859.

Philip Lightfoot
of Port Royal, Va.
Born
September 24th 1784
Died
July 22nd 1865.

John Lightfoot, the son of the above Philip and Sally, is buried in the Church-Yard of St. Peters Episcopal Church, Port Royal. By his side rests the remains of his wife, Hariet, son George, and daughter Sally. A son Howard is burried in Danville (or Lynchburg). They are survived by daughter Mrs. Hariet Broooke, of Richmond, and two sons. Wm. L. & John B.

W. B. CRIDLIN.

EPITAPH OF JOHN BATTAILE.

"Here lies the Body of Mr. John Battaile,
of Caroline County,
and Sarah Battaile his wife.
He was born December, 1695,
and died 2nd March, 1732-3.
She was born 16th October, 1695,
and died 7 August, 1768."

From family grave-yard, Caroline county.

8

EARLY RECORDS OF CHARLES CITY COUNTY.[1]

County Commissioners or Justices of the Peace.

June 4th 1655.—

Coll° Edd. Hill } Esqrs.
Capt. Henry Perry }

Mason A^bm Wood   Ca. John Bishopp
Mr Thomas Drewe   Capt. John Epes.
Mr Antho. Wyatt   Mr John Gibbs
Mr Rice Hoe.   Capt. Daniel Peibles.

Aug. 3, 1655, Capt Richard Tye
Sept. 17, 1655, Mr War. Horsmanden
Mch. 3, 1655 [1656], Mr Charles Sparrow
Sept. 1, 1656, Capt Tho. Stegge
Oct. 3, 1656, Capt Robert Wynne
Feb. 3, 1657, Capt Abra. Wood
April 20, 1658, Mr James Barber
Aug. 3, 165?, Mr Steph. Hamlin
Feb. 3, 1658, Mr John Holmwood

April 1, 1657 (8?)—

Mr Richd Cock   Mr Xtofer Branch
Mr Richd Ware   Capt Wm Farrar.
Mr Henry Isham   Mr Wm Worsham

June 1, 1657, Maj Wm Harris
Aug. 1, 1657, Mr Wm Baugh,   Mr Thos Ligon
Aug. 3, 1659, Coll° Edwd Hill Esqr   Mr Edward Hill
Jan'y 2, 1659, Mr Francis Epes
April 3, 1660, Capt Edward Hill
June 3, 1660, Capt ffranc Gray
June 3, 1663, Capt Otho Southcott
Aug. 3, 1663, M^r Wm Bird
Aug. 3, 1664, Theodorick Bland Esq

---

[1] Kindly furnished by Mr. R. A. Brock.

Feb. 2, 1665, Capt John Barker.

Militia, Sept 17, 1655—
Coll⁰ Edd Hill Esqʳ
Lᵗ Coll Walter Aston
Ca Richᵈ Tye
Ca Daniel Peibles
Capt Wᵐ Harris
Capt Daniel Lewellin

Militia, July 2, 1661—
Coll Abraham Wood Esq.   Capt. Edward Hill
Lᵗ Coll Thomas Drewe   Capt ffrancis Grey
Major Miller Harris ⎰ Capt Thomas Stegge
Capt John Epes   ⎱ Comander of Horse

Vestry held at Westover and for that parish June 4th 1655—
Messrs Hill, Perry ,Drewe, Hooe, Bishop, Peibles, as above and·
Mʳ John Waradine   Mʳ Joseph Parsons
Lᵗ John Banister   Mʳ Edd. Mosby.

Children Baptized in the P'ish of Martins Brandon in Ao 1660.

Maurice yᵉ son of Richᵈ Hamlet..................Apr. 4.
Mary yᵉ daughter of Walter Housworthy..........May 16.
Wᵐ the son of Walter Lucas .... " 26.
Elias the son of Benjamin Waid ....Aug. 12
Sara the daughter of Thomas Stevenson...........Sept. 29.
ffrancis the son of ffrancis Hogwood..............9ber. 14.
Elizab. the daughter of Thomas Mudgett..........January 9.
Mary, the daughter of Theophilus Beddingfield.....ffeb. 6.

Marriages of Anno 1660.

John Cunliffe & John Mountain..................Aug. 7.
Daniel Kigan & Phebe Banks....................Aug. 8.
Wᵐ Rawlinson & Jane Sparrow..................September 16.
Walter Horldsworthy & Naomie Davis.............October 11.

Burialls in Anno 1660.

Lawrence the son of Lawrence Seares.............May 7.
Mary the wife of Walter Horldsworthy............May 11.
Charles Sparrow................................September 11.
Margaret Bottle.................................Aug. 11.
Ellinor the daughter of Ralph Poole..............October 19.
Naomie the wife of Ben. Waid ....October 22.
Hugh Grubbins.................................October 11.
Wᵐ Doelittle............................ ....May 1.

10

John Cunliffe..................................May 14.
Ellinor the wife of Thomas Mudgett..............May 15.
Mary Minter................................May 15.
    record: May 3, 1661.

OLD TOMBSTONES IN CHARLES CITY COUNTY.

COLLECTED BY THE EDITOR.

I.

SANDY POINT.

[*Arms.*[1]]

Philip Lightfoot
son of John Lightfoot, Esq,
Barister at Law, son of John
Lightfoot Minister of Stoke
Bruain in Northamptonshire

[*Arms.*[2]]

This Tomb is Sacred to the Memory
of the Honourable Philip Lightfoot Esquire.
In various Employments of Public Trust
An Example
of Loyalty to his King, of Affection to his Country
In the several Regards of Private Life
A Pattern
Worthy of Imitation
An Equanimity which few are (cap)able of
Conducted him with success
Through the [less] elevated Scenes of Life
And continued to be the Ornament
Of the most Exalted.
Not arrogant with Prosperity
He graced a superiour Fortune

11

Acquired by his own Industry, and honesty.
Not imperious with advancement
He rose to almost the highest honours of his Country
His Rank & Fortune made him more Extensively * *
He was descended from an Ancient Family in England
Which came over to Virginia in a Genteel and Honble Character
On the 30th Day of May, 1748, in the 59th Year of his [Age]
His Spirit returned to God who gave it
And his Body reposes Here
In sure and certain Hopes of a joyfull resurrection

[*An upright tomb—one side.*]
Francis Lightfoot, son of
William & Mildred Lightfoot
Born the 13th Day of May 1747
Died the 24th March 1748-9

[*Another side.*]
Sacred
to the Memory of
William only son of
William H and
Sarah S. Lightfoot
Who departed this Life
On the 27th of October
1831
Aged 25 years and 27 days

[*Arms.*³]
Here Lieth Interred the Body of
Mrs Elizabeth Lightfoot
Wife of Mr Francis Lightfoot Gent
who departed this Life December
the 31st 1727 in the Thirty Fourth
Year of his Age
Also ye above Mr Francis Lightfoot
Who departed this Life January ye 7th
1727 in the Forty First Year of his Age
Also the Body of Francis Lightfoot
Son of the abovesaid Mr Francis and

Mrs Elizabeth Lightfoot who
Departed this Life May the 14, 1730
In the Eight Year of his Age.
[On another part of Sandy Point are headstones with these inscriptions without date.]

Here Lyes the Body of
Francis Gibson

Here Lyes the Body of
Gibby Gibson

Here Lyes the Body of
Thomas Gibson

II.

BACHELORS' POINT.

Here Lyeth Interred ye Body
of William Hunt⁴ Senr who
Departed this Life Novemb y^e
11th An° Dmi 1676 Aged 77
Yeares.

Here lyeth Interred the Body
of William Hunt Eldest son of
William Hunt who departed
this life September the 9th
day Anno Domini 1694 aged
11 yeares 8 months and 28 dayes
Whose Birth was Joy But the
day of his death was sorrowfull.

III.

WESTOVER CHURCH.
Richard Weir, Merchant
Erected this monument to the
dear Memory
of his pupil and friend
He died the 17 of June 1748.

13

NOTES BY THE EDITOR.

[1] This is the tomb of Major Philip Lightfoot, the immigrant, who married Alice Corbin, daughter of Hon. Henry Corbin, September 28, 1679.—*Middlesex* (Christ Chnrch) *Parish Register.* The arms are: Lightfoot impaling Corbin; the crest, a griffin's head. In this coat the lines are raised, the space between on the level. For LIGHTFOOT Family, see QUARTERLY, Vol. II., 91, 204, 259; Vol. III., 104, 137.* The tombstone errs in giving John Lightfoot as minister of Stoke Bruain. It was Rev. Richard Lightfoot.

[2] The arms are Lightfoot, and the crest the same as above, save that the ears of the animal are pressed forward, and that the tongue protrudes further.

[3] Same crest as in the others, and Lightfoot arms.

[4] This was probably William Hunt, "a principal aider and abettor of Nathaniel Bacon, who died before the rebels were reduced to their allegiance,' and whose property was confiscated for his conduct. Hening's Statutes, II., page 375.

---

*See *Genealogies of Virginia Families: From the William and Mary College Quarterly Historical Magazine* (Baltimore: Genealogical Publishing Co., Inc., 1982), Vol. III, pp. 409-430.

OLD TOMBSTONES IN CHARLES CITY COUNTY.

COLLECTED BY THE EDITOR.

IV.

WESTOVER.[1]

Here lies the body of
RALPH DAVIS
Died July 22[d] 1751.

Here Lyeth Interred the
Body of M[r] Will[m] Willabe
who Departed this Life
the 7th day of June 1723
In the 30th Year of his Age.

Here Lyes interred the Body of
Rev. Charles Anderson[2] who was
Minister of this Parish 26 yeares
and dyed the 7th of April 1718
in the 49th year of his Age.

[*Arms.*[3]]
S. M.
Prudentis & Eruditi Theodorici
Bland[4] Armig qui obijt Aprilis
23[d] A D, 1671 Ætatis 41
Cujus vidua Moestissima Anna
Filia Richard Bennett Armig:
hoc Marmor Posuit.

15

Here Lyeth interred the body of leftenant
Colo^{nell} Walter Aston [5] who died the 6th
April 1656.   He was Aged
49 years And
Lived in this country 28 yeares
Also here lyeth the Body of Walter Aston
the son of Leftenant Collonel Walter Aston
who departed this life ye 29th of Ianuari 1666
Aged 27 Yeares and 7 Monthes.

———————

Here lyeth the body of Captaine
Wm Perry [6] who lived neere
Westovear in this Collony
who departed this life the 6th day of
August Anno Domini 1637.

———————

Hic reconduntur cineres Gulielmi
Byrd [7] Armigeri et regii huj
Provinciæ Qaestoris qui hanc Vitam
Cum Eternitate commutavit 4to Die
Decembris 1701 postquam vixisset
52 annos.

———————

Here Lyeth the Body
of Mary Byrd Late wife of William
Byrd, Esq. and Daughter of Warham
Horsmanden [8] Esq.
Who Dyed the 9th
Day of November
1699 in the 47th
Year of Her Age.

———————

[On the North Side]

[Arms]

Here lyeth [9]
the Honorable William Byrd Esq.
Being born to one of the amplest fortunes in this country
He was sent early to England for his education;

16

Where under the care and direction of Sir Robert Southwell,
And ever favored with his particular instructions,
He made a happy proficiency in polite and various learning;
By the means of the same noble friend,
He was introduced to the acquaintance of many of the first persons
of that age
For knowledge, wit, virtue, birth, or high station,
and particularly contracted a most close and bosom friendship
with the learned and illustrious Charles Boyle, Earl of Orrery.
He was called to the bar in the Middle Temple,
studied for some time in the Low Countries,
visited the court of France,
and was chosen Fellow of the Royal Society.

[On the south side is the inscription:]

Thus eminently fitted for the service and ornament of his country,
He was made Receiver General of his Majestey's revenues here,
was thrice appointed publick agent to the Court and ministry of
England,
and being thirty-seven years a member,
at last became President of the Council of this colony.
To all this were added a great elegancy of taste and life,
the well bred gentleman and polite companion,
the splendid œconomist, and prudent father of a family,
with-all the constant enemy of all exorbitant power,
and hearty friend to the liberties of his country.
Nat: Mar. 28, 1674, Mort. Aug. 26, 1744, An. Aetat. 70.

Here in the Sleep of Peace
Reposes the Body of Mrs Evelyn Byrd[10]
Daughter
of the Hon^{le} William Byrd Esqr.
The various & excellent Endowments
of Nature Improved and perfected
by an accomplished Education
Formed her
For the Happyness of her Friends:
For an Ornament of her Country;
Alas Reader!

One can detain nothing however valued
From unrelenting Death:
Beauty, Fortune, or exalted Honour!
See here a Proof!
And be reminded by this awfull Tomb
That every worldly Comfort flees away
Excepting only what arises
from imitating the Virtues of our Friends
And the contemplation of the Happyness,
To which
God was pleased to call this Lady
On the 13th Day of Novemb 1737,
In the 29th Year of Her Age.

———

[*Arms.*[11]]

Under this marble [12] rests
[the] Body of Mrs Elizabeth Harrison
Relict [of] Benjamin Harrison
of Ber[keley] and second Daughter of
Col° Lewis Burwell of
Gloster county   She Departed
[th]is Life on Monday the 30th of
[De]cember 1734 in the Fifty-Seventh
[Year of her] Age
* * * aven * * r only one son
* and * * * d children.

———

Memoriæ Sacrum.
Hic situs est in Spem Resurectionis
Benjaminus Harrison [13] de Berkeley
Benjamini Harrison de Surrey Filius Natu,
Maximus Uxorem Duxit Elizabetham Lodovici
Burwell Glocestriensis Filiam E Qua Filium
Reliquit Unicum Benjamin et unam Filiam
Elizabetham. Obijt Apr x Anno Dom MDCCX
Ætatis xxxvii,
Plurimum Desideratus
Prolocutor Domus Burgentium
Causidicus Ingenio, Doctrinâ, Eloquentiâ Fide et
αφιλαργυρια Insignis

18

Viduarum Orphanorum omniumque Pauperum
Oppressorum Patronus Indefessus
Controversarum Et Literum Arbiter et Diremptor
Auspicatus Et Pacificus,
In Administratione Iustitiæ Absque Tricis Et
Ambagibus Comitatus Hujus Iudex
Æquissimus Ibidemque Impietatis Et
Nequitiæ Vindex Acerrimus,
Libertatis Patriæ Assertor Intrepidus Et
Boni Publici Imprimis Studiosus,
Hunc Merito Proprium Virginia Iactet Alumnum
Tam Propere Abreptum, sed Querebunda Dolet.
Publicus Hic Dolor Et Nunquam Reparabile Damnum
Det Deus Ut Vitæ sint Documenta Novæ.

V.
SHIRLEY.

[*Arms.*[14]]

Here lyeth Intered the Body of
Edward Hill Esq. one of his Maj[tyes]
Honble Councell of State Collonel and
Comander in chiefe of the County[s]
of Charles Citty and Surrey Judge of
his Majestyes high court of Admiralty
and Sometime Treasurer of Virginia who
dye[d] the 30th day of Nov[r] in the 63[d]
year of his age Anno Dom 1700.

VI.
WILKINSON'S GRAVEYARD.

Sacred to the Memory
of Anne B. Southall who
died the 8th day of Oct
1820 in the 74th year of
her age.

VII.
SANDY POINT.[15]

Here Lieth the Body of
Dorothy Farrell who
Deceased the 18th of
January 1673.

VIII.

WEYANOKE.

Here lyeth y^e
Body of William
Harris ^{16} who departed
this life y^e 8 day
of March 168$\frac{7}{8}$
Aged 35 years.

NOTES.

[1] The church and churchyard of Westover Parish were at Westover till about 1731, when the present church was built. The history of this celebrated colonial home is given in another place.

[2] See page 127 (last magazine) for an account of Rev. Charles Anderson. His daughter Frances, by her marriage with Captain Ellyson Armistead, of York county, was grandmother of President John Tyler's mother, Mary Marot Armistead, daughter of Robert Booth Armistead, of York county.

[3] These arms represent Bland impaling Bennett: on a bend three pheons for Bland; three demi-lions for Bennett. This Richard Bennett mentioned in the inscription was Richard Bennett, Governor of Virginia under the Commonwealth. In a letter in 1666 Thomas Ludwell informed the Earl of Arlington that his arms were similar to the Earl's. See *Virginia Magazine of History and Biography*, July, 1895, for an account of the Bennett family.

[4] Theodorick Bland bought Westover from Sir John Pawlett in 1666. He left it to his son Theodorick Bland, who took into joint occupancy his brother Richard, and together they sold the estate to William Byrd in 1688. For *Bland Family* see *Familæ Gentium Minorum*, and *Richmond Critic*, July 9, 1888, etc.

[5] On August 12, 1646, Walter Aston patented one thousand and forty acres, near Shirley Hundred, on Kimage's Creek, two hundred acres of which, known as "Cawsey's Care," were purchased, in 1634, by Aston of John Causey, being the same land patented by Nathaniel Causey (probably his father), 10th December, 1620. (*Land Register.*) Nathaniel Causey was an old soldier, who came in with the first supply in 1608. Walter Aston's wife is named in the land patents Warbow or Narbow. He represented Shirley Hundred Island in 1629-'30; both Shirley Hundreds, Mr. Farrar's and Chaplain's, in February, 1631-'32; Shirley Hundred Maine and "Cawsey's Care," in September, 1632, and February, 1632-'33, Charles City county in 1642-'43. He was Justice of the Peace and Lieutenant-colonel. He married, secondly, Hannah ——, who appears to have married after his death Colonel Edward Hill. Lieutenant-colonel Walter Aston had issue: 1, Susannah, relict, in 1655, of Lieutenant-colonel Edward Major, deceased; 2, Walter; 3, Mary, m. Richard Cocke, deceased before 1666; 4, Elizabeth, m. —— Binns. In Byrd's *Book of Title Deeds* is the will of Walter Aston, of "Cawsey's Care": To Hannah Hill, his mother, he gives that parcell of land called the "Level"; to godson

20

John Cocke, the son of Richard Cocke, dece'd, 4,000 pds. of tobacco to be paid in 1668; to godson Edward Cocke, son of the abovesaid Cocke, 6,000 pds. of tobacco, to be paid in 1669; survivor to have the whole 10,000, and in case both die, to the rest of the children; to sisters Mary Cocke and Elizabeth Binns 20 shillings apiece for a ring; gun called Pollard to servant John Mitten, and a young white sow shoat that is with pig; to my Irish boy Edward a sow; to Mr. George Harris, merchant, all my dividend at Cawsey's Care and the land at Canting Point and all the residue of my estate. Dated 21 Dec., 1666; Prov'd Feb. 4, 1666–'67.

The testator before his death had sold two hundred acres of the land, above mentioned, to William Edwards, and one hundred more to Hannah Hill. But both these parcels were purchased by George Harris, of Westover, merchant, who dying seized of the entire tract and leaving no children, it all fell to his brother, Thomas Harris, merchant tailor, of London, who sold the same to Col. Thos. Grendon, Jr., of Cawsey's Care, who by his will (Feb. 23, 1683–'84—Dec. 3, 1684) devised the same to William Byrd, Jr., son of William Byrd, Sr.; whereupon it became absorbed into the Byrd estate. (*Byrd's Book of Title Deeds.*)

Brown says that Walter Aston, the immigrant, was cousin of Sir Walter Aston, Ambassador to Spain, 1620–1625 and 1635–1638, created a baronet in 1611, and Lord Aston, of Forfar, in the Scottish Peerage, Nov. 28, 1627. We have the following pedigree from the *Visitation*, of London, 1634:

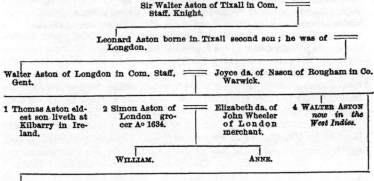

Virginia was often called "the West Indies," and thus Walter Aston was one of four brothers, sons of Walter Aston, of Longdon, Stafford county, and great-grandsons of Sir Walter Aston (knighted in 1560—see Metcalfe's *Book of Knights*). Lord Aston was descended from the elder line as follows: Sir Walter[1] Aston, knighted in 1560; Sir Edward[2] Aston, eldest son, knighted in 1570; Sir Walter[3] (Lord) Aston, born July 9, 1584, died August 13, 1639.

Arms of Aston: *Argent a fess and in chief three lozenges sable.*

⁶ Between the tombstones of Walter Aston and of Theodorick Bland is a stone from which the incription is entirely worn away. This was probably the tombstone of Captain William Perry, which Campbell, the historian, says r e, in his day, the inscription given in the text.

21

[7] This is the tombstone of the first William Byrd. For Byrd pedigree, see *Richmond Critic*, December 16, 1688.

[8] Mary Byrd's father, Colonel Warham Horsmanden, was the son of Rev. Daniel Horsmanden, removed by Parliament as a cavalier minister in 1643. See Brown's *Genesis* for an account of the St. Legers and Horsmandens. (Vol. II., p. 990.)

[9] The monument of Colonel William Byrd, the second, is not in the old graveyard, but in the garden at Westover. It has suffered some mutilation, and the handsomely carved escutcheon, bearing the family arms, was broken off and carried away when the county was in the Federal occupation during the war. This has since been replaced, however, by an exact copy.—W. G. Stanard in *Richmond Critic* for December 16, 1888.

[10] The portrait of Evelyn Byrd, with those of a number of others of the family, as well as of the English friends of the second Colonel Byrd, is at Brandon. This young lady has been the frequent subject of magazine articles.

[11] The arms on the tomb of Elizabeth Harrison stand for Burwell: A saltire between four eagles' heads, erased; crest, an eagle's head erased, with a branch in its beak. The tomb of James Burwell, at King's Creek, York county, and Lewis Burwell, at Carter's Creek, Gloucester county, have griffins instead of eagles. (See QUARTERLY, Vol. II., p. 231.) *

[12] The marble is very much shattered, but I gathered the pieces together with the above result.

[13] Benjamin Harrison, clerk of the council, was in Virginia as early as 1634. He was father of Benjamin Harrison, of Surry, a distinguished lawyer, whose tombstone is at Cabin Point; born 20th September, 1645, died 30th January, 1712-'13. This tomb at Westover is that of the third Benjamin Harrison. He was the father of the fourth Benjamin Harrison, who was father of Benjamin Harrison, of Berkeley, the signer, the fifth of the name. With the exception of the Lees, there is no family in the United States which has exhibited a similar heredity of talent as the Harrison family, holding for two hundred and sixty years the very first offices. See *Richmond Critic*, June 23, 1889, for Harrison family, and Keith's *Ancestry of Benjamin Harrison*.

[14] The arms of Colonel Edward Hill, of Shirley, of whose family an account is given by Mr. Stanard in *Virginia Historical Magazine* (Vol. III., p. 149), appear from the picture in *The Century Magazine* to be a lion passant, and the crest, a demi-lion rampant. This splendid colonial homestead, "Shirley," is well described by Mr. Charles Washington Coleman in his article, *Along the Lower James*, published in *The Century*. (Vol. XLI., p. 326.)

[15] The tombstone of Dorothy Farrell was taken from Sandy Point (not Weyanoke, as elsewhere stated), and is now in the outside of the walls of St. Paul's Church, Norfolk. Dorothy Farrell was the daughter of Colonel Thomas Drew, of Charles City county. She married Captain Hubert Farrell, of James City county, who was killed in 1676 in an attack at King's Creek on Major Thomas Whaley. Sandy Point was, until the eighteenth century, in James City county. There is a tomb of Daniel Farrell at St. Peter's Church in New Kent. He died in 1786.

[16] This tombstone of William Harris was moved from Weyanoke to Norfolk, and also placed in the walls of St. Paul's Church. Major William Harris, of Henrico, had a son of that name.

*Page 71, this volume.

TOMBSTONE AT KETTEWAN

On the north shore of Kettiwan creek, near its mouth, in Charles City Co., Va. is a tombstone which has the following inscription:

Here Lyeth the Body of
Elizabeth Hollings—
Horst, the widow of
Thomas Hollinghorst
Shipmaster, and the
Daughter of Mr Peter
Gordon of the Family of
Tilleangus in Aberdeenshire
In Scotland who dyed
November 30th, 1728

Dr. Armistead C. Gordon, of Staunton, sends the following as a note on the Gordons of Tillyangus to which Mr. Peter Gordon named above belonged.

THE GORDONS OF TILLYANGUS

(Cadets of Craig)

The Gordons of Tillyangus traced descent from William Gordon of Tillytermont, second son of "Jack" Gordon of Scurdargue by Elizabeth Maitland.

I. *William Gordon of Tillytermont* (died 1481) married a lady named Rutherford, sister of Sir John Rutherford. Knight, owner of the lands of Tarland, Aberdeenshire. By her he had two sons; the elder, George, was ancestor of the Gordons of Lesmoir, from whom the family of Colonel James Gordon of Lancaster, Virginia, and his brother, John Gordon, of Middlesex, Virginia, trace descent. (See Armistead C. Gordon's "Gordons in Virginia", published by Wm. M. Clemens, Hackensack, N. J. 1918).

23

II. *Patrick* Gordon, son of William Gordon of Tillytermont, was *first laird of Craig,* or Auchindoir (1510)

III. *William Gordon,* son of Patrick (II), was the *second laird of Craig.* He "either built or more properly completed the building of the Castle of Craig." We find him with the designation "of Auchindore" a witness to the surrender of the lands of Kincraigie, 1519-20.

IV. *James Gordon, first laird of Tillyangus,* was the second son of William Gordon, second laird of Craig (III) by Elspet Stewart, daughter of the laird of Laithers. James Gordon, first of Tillyangus, married Christian Leith of Harthill. He took part in the battle of Corrichie, and was forfeited in consequence. His name does not occur in the remission granted in 1567; but in 1568 his name is found in the "Band for the Queen's service, and to concur with and assist the Earl of Huntlie, her majestys Lieutenant in the North of Scotland," immediately following that of George Gordon of Lesmoir.

V. *William Gordon, second laird of Tillyangus,* married in 1576 Elizabeth Gordon, eldest daughter of Alexander Gordon, of Knockespock.

VI. *James Gordon, third laird of Tillyangus,* got sasine of the lands of Tillyangus in 1638. He married Magdalen Gordon, daughter of Patrick Gordon of Auchmenzie.

VII. *William Gordon, fourth laird of Tillyangus,* was probably son (possibly brother) of the third laird, James, (VI). He married Marjorie Gordon, daughter of Sir James Gordon of Knowes. In 1640 this laird was 'listing men for the Covenant."

The lands of Tillytermont, Craig and Tillyangus were in Aberdeenshire, Scotland. Another prominent Gordon family "of Craig" was seated in Kirkcudbrightshire, Galloway, and belonged to the "Border Gordons", as distinguished from the "Gordons of the North." There is a tombstone in old Blandford Churchyard, Petersburg, Virginia, bearing the inscription: "Here lies the corps of Mr. Samuel Gordon, son of David Gordon, Esq., of Craig, in the stewartry, Kirkcubright, North Britain, who died the 14th. of April 1771, aged 54 years". (Gordons in Virginia," p. 141).

The foregoing account of the family of Gordon of Tillyangus, has been obtained from the privately printed volume, "Memorials of the Family of Gordon of Craig, collected by Captain Douglas Wimberley, sometime of the 79th. or Cameron Highlanders", in 1904, and from the second volume of "The House of Gordon," edited by Mr. J. M. Bulloch, editor of the London "Graphic", and published by the New Spalding Club, Aberdeen, Scotland, 1907.

ASHBURN.

William Ashburn
of Liverpool
Who traded to this province
for many years Died the 25th
Day of October 1773 Aged 43 Years
and was burried beneath
this Stone.

Recently I was shown this inscription on a slab covering a grave located near the site of old Ware church in Chesterfield county, near old Osborn landing and on or near the Howlett farm on the James River.

A broken slab covered another grave alongside of this one. Thinking this might be of some interest to you I copied it.

Trees nearly one hundred years old, I judge, have grown up around these graves and they seemingly have long since passed out of the care of any one.

Sterling Boisseau.

OLD BLANDFORD TOMBSTONES.

AN EXACT TRANSCRIPT OF THE EPITAPHS ON ALL THE TOMBSTONES NOW
EXISTING WITHIN THE ORIGINAL ENCLOSURE OF OLD BLANDFORD
CHURCH YARD, NEAR PETERSBURG, VA.

Collected by C. G. Chamberlayne (1896).

Take holy earth all that my soul held dear
Take that best gift which heaven so lately gave.

JAMES WRIGHT
A native of Weathersfield
State of Connecticut.
Born August 25th A. D. 1779:
Departed this life September 16th 1811.
This tomb
the last tribute of affection,
is rear'd to his memory
by his disconsolate widow,
LUCY WRIGHT.

SACRED
to the Memory
of
EDWARD HOLMES
Son of
SAMUEL HOLMES
of Mecklenburg County
Aged 26 Years.
Thus Merit & Worth in Youth combined,
Are to an untimely Tomb consigned.

(Arms and Crest.)
Here Lyeth Interred the Body of
IOHN HERBERT [1] Son of Iohn Herber(t)
Apothecary and Grandsonn of
RICHARD HERBERT Citizen & Groce(r)
of LONDON who departed this Life
the 17th day of March 1704 in the
46th year of his Age

Underneath this Stone are deposited
The Remains of
Mrs A. W. M^cCONNICO,
the affectionate
and
beloved Wife
of
CHRISTOPHER M^cCONNICO,
in whom
R e l i g i o n
With every amiable Virtue
was adorned
by
a genuine benevolence of Temper,
and
a Native sweetness of Manners.
Her Heart
formed for Friendship
was
humane & Charitable,
She died
in the twenty seventh Year of her Age
on the tenth of February 1786.
Sincerely lamented
by all who knew her.
The Loss
can never be retrieved
by
Her Parents,
Her Children,
Her Brothers, Sisters,
or
Her Husband,
by whom
This monument of the tenderest affection
is
erected
to her Memory.

Sacred
to the memory of
Mᵣˢ NANCY ANN ROE
who died
the 10ᵗʰ of Janʸ 1800
after a painful and lingering
illness which she bore with
christian fortitude.

———————

TO THE MEMORY
OF ANDREW JOHNSTON ESQ.
OF GLASGOW IN SCOTLAND,
MERCHANT IN PETERSBURG:
WHO RESIDED MANY YEARS IN THIS STATE,
WHERE HE ACQUIRED A FORTUNE
BY HONEST INDUSTRY,
AND
DIED REGRETTED.
THIS STONE IS ERECTED
IN TESTIMONY OF AFFECTIONATE REGARD,
BY HIS SISTER
OB: 5ᵗʰ MAY 1785. ÆTA: 43.

———————

Sacred
to the memory
of
JOHN STUART
Native of GLASGOW,
SCOTLAND,
And for many years
An eminent Merchant
of this TOWN.
Died 1ˢᵗ of February 1814.
Aged 60 Years.
This Monument
is caused to be erected
By his Daughter
MARY ANN
in testimony
of
Her affectionate regard.

(RIC)HARD
(YA)RBROUGH[2]
1702
Aged 87

WILLIAM CORLING
Departed this life
Nov. 16. 1852
In the 84 year
of his age.

ELIZABETH CORLING
Wife of Wm. Corling
Departed this life
May 19. 1839.
In the 84 year
of her age.

IN
MEMORY OF
CHARLES CORLING
Native of Ashford
COUNTY OF KENT
ENGLAND
Came to VIRGINIA 1783
Died January 14 1814,
AGED 43 YEARS,
Leaving an affectionate
Wife and three Children
Viz. William—Charles—&
Eliza, to deplore the
loss of a kind Husband
and tender Father.

MRS. ELIZA LEVERING
Daughter of
Charles & Ann Corling
Consort of
W. W. Levering
Departed this life
July 20. 1855
In the 48. year
of her age.

HERE LYES
The Body ^{of} A McConnald
Who Departed this Life
The 29 of oct^{br} in th Year
1788 in the 49th ^{year} of his age
(A)lso The Body of Jane
(Mc)Connald Who Depa^{td}
(t)his Life the 1st November
In the 30th Year of her age
And Daniel McConnald
Who departed this life the
12 of Jun^e 1790 the 2th year of
His Age

IN MEMORY
of
Mrs SARAH TAYLOR
who died July 21st 1801
aged 54 years
and
Mr ALEXR TAYLOR
who departed this life
June 26th 1805 aged 68 years
While o'er their dust their children still shall grieve
and still this spot the soft affections move
Their spotless souls in paradise shall live
Blessd and united in the realms above

This stone is erected as a record
of their virtues by their children

30

IN MEMORY
OF
W:ᴹ WILSON LEVERING.
who departed this life
July 17ᵗʰ 1829,
in the 29ᵗʰ year of his age.

SACRED
to the memory of
LUKE W.
Son of
Wᴍ J. & ANN H. UZZELL
Born Feb. 6, 1848
Died Nov. 17, 1856.
Weep not for those who are
gathered early to there
Heavenly Father

SACRED
To the memory of
ANDREW F. P.
son of
Wᵐ J. & Aɴɴ H. Uᴢᴢᴇʟʟ
Born May 30, 1855
Died Jan. 21, 1861.
A breathing form of beauty
encasing a gentle spirit, claimed
by a Father's hand ere earth's cares
had touched or spoiled

HERE LIES THE BODY OF
DAVID LANG SHIPMASTEʀ
SON TO WILLIAM LANG
IN INNERKIP WHO DIED IN
VIRGINIA THE 21 OF MAY
1762 AGED 31 YEARS.

Underneath this Stone are deposited
the Remains of
Mrs KATHERINE ROSE
the affectionate
and
Beloved Wife
of
ALEXANDER ROSE,
in whom
every amiable Virtue was adorned
and native sweetness of manners,
She died
on the 2nd Day of February 1801
in the 43rd Year of her Age;
Sincerely lamented by all who knew her.
The loss
can never be retrieved
by
her Children
or
her Husband
by whom
This Monument of the tenderest affection
is
erected
to her Memory.
On the South side lies her five Children.

In memory of
HELEN *daughter* of EBENEZR and ELIZABETH STOTT,
who departed this life sep^t 5th 1797 aged one year and three weeks.
of another *daughter* born 1st June 1798. who died three days after
her birth.
and of five others of their infants still born,
and in memory of HARIET PHILE sister of ELIZABETH STOTT.
who died in July 1797
aged twenty one years.

SACRED
TO THE MEMORY
of
M^{rs} E Pegram who
DEparteD this life
Feby 16th 1804
aged 29 years

SACRED
to the Memory of
ROBERT DONALDSON
late of
Fayetteville
NORTH CAROLINA
Merchant;
Born
on the 4th of March 1764
Obiit
on the 1st of July 1808
Aged 44 Years

Here lye
the Bodies of
MARGARET, ADAM, AND
IOHN=ADAM Ruſsels
The first died june 23^d
1787 aged 2 years 7 months
& 3 days the second died
jan^r 12th 1788 aged 7 weeks
the third died augst 9th 1799
aged 11 months 2 weeks & 2 days,
the beloved Children of
ROBERT and jANET Ruſsel(s)

Here lyes the Body of John
Mackie Son to Patrick Mackie
merch^t. and late provest of
Wigton in Scotland who
Dyed at Petersburgh Octr the
11th 1750 aged Ninteen years

Joseph the son of ye late
Mr Joseph Littledale Merch^t,
In Whitehaven died Nov^{br}, 3^d 1754
Aged 16 Years.

This monument is erected
in memory of
MATTHEW MABEN,
A native of Dumfries SCOTLAND
And for many years
A respectable Merchant,
of this place;
Died 8th of January 1822,
Aged 45 Years.

Here Lies in hopes of a Blessed Resurrection
the body ^{of} Mrs Lucy Williams.   Wife of
Mr Thomas Williams, She was ye daughter
of Mr James Boisseau & Mary his wife
Born february ye 8th 1730.   Married novemb^r
the 27th 1746. who died ye 25th of July 1747
Aged 16 years five months & two weeks &
3 days. who was very much beloved and lamente^d
Young men & women, all & standers by
That on these tombs do cast a wandering eye
Call on ye Lord whilst in your health & youth
For die you must, it is a certain truth
Your life a Shadow is more pris'd than gold
As for Example here you may behold
Beneath these mournful tombs there lyeth three
Which maketh eight out of one Familey
Two loving virtuous wives and child most dear
All died within two days & one whole year
Whose patience quitted not their silent breast
But lull'd them into an eternal rest
To wait in peace, until that glorious day
The trumpet sounds, to call them hence away

HERE LYES INUR'D THE BODY
OF THOMAS WILLIAMS BORN
IN S̲ᵀ IAMES PARISH LONDON
IN THE YEAR ONE THOUSAND
SEVEN HUNDRED AND TWO
AND DEPARTED THIS LIFE THE
9T̲H̲ DAY OF NOV̲ᴿ 1763.

MOURN NOT FOR ME MY FRIENDS AND
CHILDREN DEAR
I AM NOT DEAD BUT ONLY SLEEPING
HERE
FROM SIN AND WORLDLY CARES I
AM FREE AND BLIST
WHERE WEARY SOULS RETIRE AND
ARE AT REST
MY DEBT IS PAID BEHOLD MY GRAVE
YOU SEE
WAIT GODS APPOINTED TIME
YOU'LL COME TO ME

———————

(H)ere lyes in hopes of a Blessed Ressurrection
the body of Mᵣˢ Rachell Williams, wife of
Mᵣ Thomas Williams, she was yᵉ Daughter
of Mᵣ John Freeman, and Mary his wife
of Willesy in Glouster, born April yᵉ 15ᵗʰ
1718, married August 28ᵗʰ 1735. who died the
23 of July 1746. Aged 28 Years, 3 months &
ten days, Leaving Issue one Son & 2 Daughters
She was Exceedingly Beloved & Lamented
Sweet natur'd kind, giving to all their due
Supremely good, & to her Consort true
She'd differ not, but to his will agree
With condesending, sweet humility
Tender and loveing to her children dear
And to her servants not at all sevear
She feared not, nor strove at all with death
But patiently, Resigned her willing bre(a)th
Her Soul so silent, from her body we(n)t
They seem'd as if they parted by consent
To meet in glory at yᵉ last of days
And sing with Joy her blessed Saviour's prais(e)

Here Lyes also ye body of Hannah
Williams, daughter of Thomas Williams
and Rachell his wife, who died July ye 14
1747 aged 3 Years & seven weeks

NOTES.

1. JOHN HERBERT.—Within the past eighteen months this tombstone was, under the direction of relatives, removed from Puddledock, in Prince George Co., Va., and placed in Blandford churchyard. The *Virginia Gazette* for August 7, 1752, has an advertisement inquiring for "the descendants of Mr. John Herbert, late merchant on James River, who formerly married Miss Frances Anderson of said place, and died in the year 1704 or 1705, and what arms he bore is said to be cut on his tombstone. He left two sons, Butler and Richard, and one daughter, named Martha, who married Mr. James Powell Cocke about the year 1718."

2. RICHARD YARBROUGH.—In connection with this stone the following note, taken from Slaughter's *Bristol Parrish* (first edition, 1846), may prove of interest :

Richard Yarbrough 1702 – aged 87.

The above inscription is on a soft, free-stone slab. There is a trace above the cypher, making it read 1762. From my knowledge of this stone, and acquaintance with engraving, I think 1702 was the original inscription.

J. DAVIDSON, *Keeper of Graveyard.*

(*To be continued.*)

OLD BLANDFORD TOMBSTONES.

IN
memory of
Cameron,
Anderson,
Son of D. & M. R.
Anderson, was
born 15th Sept^r
1803, & died on
the 24th aged
9 days.

IN
memory of
Duncan Cameron,
Anderson, Son of
D. & M. R. Anderson,
was born Novr 3rd
1799, & died May
22nd 1800.

IN
memory of
William Cameron,
Anderson,
Son of D. & M. R.
Anderson,
was born July 8th
1798, & died July
16th 1799.

In Memory of
M^R. DANIEL ANDERSON,
Merchant
who died January 25th, 1813,
Aged 64 Years.

SACRED
to the memory of
DAVID ANDERSON,
a native of SCOTLAND,
and for many years a respectible
merchant of this place
who departed this life
June the 18th 1812,
aged 52 years.
He was long a member of the Common Hall
And
Chamberlain of the Town of Petersburg
Upright honerable kind & benevolent
And
The muniffecent FOUNDER
of
The Anderson Seminary
THE
CORPORATION OF PETERSBURG
Have inscribed this record
Rather
To mark their gratitude for his beneficence
THAN

To commemorate his virtues
BELIEVING
That when this stone
Shall have mouldered into dust
The Institution which he founded
Will still preserve his name
AS
A BENEFACTOR OF PETERSBURG
AND
A FRIEND OF MAN.

———————

SACRED
to the memory of
JAMES FRAME
A native of ALLOA
SCOTLAND
who departed this life
October the 26th 1803.
Aged 37 years.

———————

SACRED
to the memory of
ROBERT POLLOCK,
Merchant
Born in
GLASGOW,
SCOTLAND,
12th March 1775,
Died in
PETERSBURG
19th May 1811.

———————

Here rests the Body of
MARY DOUGLAS,
A Native of London-Derry.
Insatiate Death could not *one* suffice
Thrice you drew your shaft and *thrice* my peace destroyed.

Memento Mori
In remembrance of
SUSANNA MAITLAND
the affectionate wife of David Maitland,
merchant in Blandford;
who departed this life the 9th
of February 1799, aged 33 years.
She was daughter of Joshua &
Mary Poythress, of Flower de Hundred.

MARY CURRIE MAITLAND,
daughter of David and Susanna,
died the 27th January 1795,
aged 4 years.

IN
Memory
OF
RICHARD RYLAND
RANDOLPH
Only Son of
RYLAND &
ELIZABETH RANDOLPH
Died Oct 8 1834
In the
39th Year of his
Age.

In Memory of
ELIZABETH MILLS
RANDOLPH. Wife of
RYLAND RANDOLPH
who died the 9th of march
1798. in the 21st Year
of her Age.

HERE LYES THE CORPSE
OF SARAH POYTHRESS [1]
DAUGHTER OF COLLONE(L)
FRANCIS EPPES AND WIF(E)
TO COLLONEL WILLIAM
PO(YTH)RESS WHO DIED
TH(E   ) OCTOBER 1750
AGED 48 YEARS.

(3.)

Here lies the Corpse
of
COL. WILLIAM POYTHRESS
Son of
IOHN POYTHRESS
Who died
the 18 Jan 1763
Aged 68 years

(Arms and Crest)
HERE LIES THE CORPS OF MR. SAMUEL GORDON
SON OF DAVID GORDON ESQ^R OF CRAIG
IN THE STEWARTRY OF KIRKCUDBRIGHT
NORTH BRITAIN
who DIED THE 14th of APRIL 1771
AGED 54 YEARS.

SACRED
to the memory of
MRS. ELIZABETH S. MALLORY,
wife of
ROGER MALLORY,

---

[1] In the WILLIAM AND MARY COLLEGE QUARTERLY (Volume I.. p. 118) the Poythress family is included in the list of Virginia families entitled to bear arms. As a proof of this right, reference is made to a Poythress tombstone (first name not given) in Blandford churchyard. There are only two Poythress tombstones there (Sarah Poythress and Col. William Poythress), neither of which has a coat-of-arms. The tomb next to these (that of Mr Samuel Gordon) has a coat-of-arms on it, and possibly the mistake may have arisen from this fact.

who departed this life
on the 14th day of April 1815,
In the 21st year of her age.
Leaving a disconsolate Husband and one child
to deplore the loss of an affectionate wife and
tender Mother.
"Blessed are the dead which die in the Lord;
they may rest from their labors and their
works do follow them."
Also her only child who lies in the same grave.
WILLIAM KEEN MALLORY,
who died september th: 5 1816 in the
2nd year of his age.
but jesus said suffer little children and forbid them
not to come unto me for of such is the
kingdom of heaven.

Here rest the mortal remains of
Miss Martha Wills Cole,
who departed this life
on the 2nd of September Anno Domino 1817,
at the early age of 16 years and 1 month
words could but faintly delineate her
virtures, her worth was known to her friends
who loved her as the life pulse of their own
hearts she was beloved by all, who knew
her but by one more than all, who has caused
this tomb to be erected as a
token of his affection.

Oh: She was good and She was fair,
But for a moment given;
The Angels came to claim their own
And bare her soul to Heaven.

Sacred to the Memory,
of ELIAS PARKER;
who departed this Life
Decr 8th, 1799,
Aged 39 Years.

Here lies entomb'd
the Remains of
MR JACOB PARKER
a Native of Boston,
in Massachusetts.
who departed this Life
July 27th, 1789.
Anno Ætatis 17.

IN MEMORY OF
The Rev. JOHN URQUHART,
WHO DIED DEC. 8. 1816,
AGED 50 YEARS.

SACRED
to the memory of
GRAHAM BELL
who departed this life
on the 4th Day of May 1817,
aged 56 Years
This stone is erected by his son peyton bell
Adieu dear friends i take my leave,
Farewell my loving wife
Our children dear your guardians be,
And bless your widowed life,
When from this world you are releas'd
Its sorrows, toils and cares,
In everlasting Joy we'll meet,
To sing our maker's praise.

SACRED
to the memory
of
M^{RS} ELIZABETH KID^D
who died
APRIL 29th 1801
Æ 66

BENEATH
this Marble rest
the Remains of
M^{RS} ELIZABETH GEDDY,
who departed this Life
December the 7th, 1799
in the 65th Year of her age.
Her disconsolate Husband
(who with so worthy a Partner
upwards of 17 Years
enjoyed every Felicity
the connubial state can afford)
erected this TOMB
in commemoration of her
VIRTUES.

In commemoration of
Captain JOHN JEFFERS
late of the Petersburg Troop of Horse
whose untimely Death was deservedly.
Regretted by all who had the pleasure
of his acquaintance
He was a Useful Magistrate a Sincere Friend
and a Worthy member of Society,
He died November 14th 1795.
Aged 34 Years.

Also DOMINICK JEFFERS Merchant.
who departed this life the 31st December 1793.
Aged 32 Years.

This Stone is erected to their Memories
by their Surviving Relatives
to whom they were endeared
in the highest degree.

HERE
rest the remains of
EDWARD JEFFERS
Late Merchant of this Town,

who departed this Life
April 14ᵗʰ Anno Domini 1802,
Aged 34 years.
Mild & affectionate in his disposition,
Alike humane & charitable,
He was esteemed by all who knew him.
His life was devoted to the service
of his Maker, and his friends:
Tho' short, it was well spent:
May our lives resemble his, then shall we
meet death with like serenity.

———

Sacred
to the memory of
SAMUEL MYERS
a native of Baltimore
he fell a victim to the
memorable fire in Petersburg
on the 16ᵗʰ July 1815.

———

Sacred
to the memory of
JOHN NIBLO
Son of
JOHN & ELIZA NIBLO,
Born 14ᵗʰ of May 1824
Departed this life
14ᵗʰ of July 1829.

———

In
Memory of
JOEL PAULSON
Newport Delaware, State
who Departed this Life
at Petersburgh, June 12ᵗʰ
1799.
Aged 21, Years, 5. Months,
8 Days.

45

Here lies the remains of
BENNIT ALDRIGE
Son of
PETER & ELIZABETH ALDRIGE,
Born in Dinwiddie, Co. Va.,
Jan. 8. 1777,
Died Oct. 23. 1858.

TOMB STONES IN DINWIDDIE CO, VA

Communicated by Rev. S. O. Southall.

About 2 miles west of "Old Reams" and (3 miles west of the "New Reams") station on the Atlantic Coast Line R. R., at a place owned in 1870 by Mr More, and among numerous other graves, there is a solitary slab "Erected to the memory of Burwell Brown—a native of Virginia born in the year 1777, son of Hezekiah Brown and Sarah his wife [no date of his death] Epitaph:

Here lies the Body of an old Tar Where is he now? God knows where"

Davidson Fecit
Petersb'g"

[Note. Davidson was the ''keeper of Graves in Petersburg some time near 1830-40]

At "Jones' Hole", apparently at the sight of the old colonial ("Jones' Hole") church are erected two slabs, viz.

Sacred to the memory of Mary Ann, daughter of William and W. Wilkerson born Nov. 29 1815 died March 22 1836"
Davidson Fecit

Sacred to the memory of Winnyford, wife of William Wilkerson born Sept 17 1793 died Jan'y 26 1818

[Note Jones' Hole is 2 miles East of "Old Reams" station—and on East side of the Rail Road]

At what was Billups Tavern—also known as Ellis—2 miles west of "Reams," A. C. L station are two slabs (very difficult to read), viz.

"Sacred to the memory of Capt. Augustine Ellis, merchant of Pe'tersb'g Died March 16 1826 in the 32 year of age. Erected by his Faithful wife"

"Erected to the memory of Augustine Billups died the 18th of June 1826 aged 69 years * * * * * * Mary Billups * * * * * *

About 2½ miles of Pool's siding on the N & W R. R. is this solitary stone

"To the memory of "Doratha P. daughter of John and Martha Boisseau, and wife of Bennett Alridge. born 1786 died June 20 1840

At "Swenden" an old Goodwyn place about 3 miles south of Sutherland station of N. & W. R R. are the following:

"Amey Eppes Allen, wife of Daniel Allen and daughter of Col Peterson and Elizabeth Goodwyn died Feb 1st 1829"

"Daniel E Allen who died at "Mayfield near Petersburg this county Oct 24 1847 aged 62 Erected by his daughter Eliza Ann Eppes Allen—

47

"Erected by Flectcher H. Archer, in memory of his rife Eliza Ann Eppes Archer who died in Petersburg Tuesday Aprıl 22 1851 aged 24 years and 11 days—leaving an infant daughter—.

"Peterson Goodwyn, son of Col. Peterson Goodwyn, late of Greensville, Co. died Oct 15. 1856 aged 56 years

"Martha T. Goodwyn, wife of Albert T. Goodwyn, and daughter of Major Elijah and Judith King died March 12 1831 aged 24 years."

"Albert Thweatt Goodwyn died April 18, 1845, aged 47

In a Vault are the following:

"Thomas Whitworth consort of E. H. Whitworth born Jan'y 4th 1794 died June 24 1874

Also, Infant grandson Thos. W Willson died June 18, 1866

Eliza H. Whitworth, wife of Thomas Whitworth and daughter of Col Peterson Goodwyn died Dec 29 1847

Also Mary A Willson, infant grand daughter died July 1 1875"

At the "old Smith place" near Dinwiddie C. H., among many graves there is a solitary shaft with two inscriptions
On one side of which is:

Captain John Hill, son of Col Larkin Smith, born March 14 1782 died March 28 1843

On the other side

"Mary Cary daughter of Col. John Ambler and wife of Hon. John Hill Smith died Sept 25 1843

In Old Saponey Church,

A Shaft to

"Rev. Devereux Jarratt. Rector of this (Bath) Parish Nat 17— ob. Jan'y 1800.

A Plate in the wall To

Martha Jarratt, wife of Rev. D. Jarratt, Nat 1744— ob March 9, 1826.

Memorial Windows:

"Elizabeth Grammer Withers Born March 16 1785, died Sept 30 1861"

"Rev. E. B. Jones, M. D. Rector of this Church May 1876—Feb 1893. Born Oct 31 1823 died Feb 11 1893"

Susan A Hardaway (afterwards Mrs Heartwell) Born Sept. 3 1823, died Sept 5 1887.

Note. The Rev. Devereux Jarratt, says in his Autobiography that he was born in New Kent County Jan'y 1732-3, O. S., and that he became Rector of Bath Parish on the 28th of August 1763

Note. Saponey Church dates from 1725— In that year a committee of the Vestry of Bristol Parish agreed with Mr Calwell to build a chapel—"a good substantial building upon the lands of John Stith upon Sapponey convenient to the upper Nottoway River road"— About the year 1870 this old church had a dramatic and almost tragic ending—

According to eye Witnesses a large congregation had assembled that Sunday, and the services being finished, were leaving the church, when bits of plaster were seen to fall from the ceiling. Mrs Lucinda W. Cutler, one of the oldest and most influential communicants was the last to leave. She was still on the steps of the church, when it collapsed.

In about two years mainly through her influence the church was restored. The same old furniture—Pulpit, Lectern, and pews were put in the restored church— In fact, they used much of the timber of the old church in building the new. At this time the remains of Rev Devereux Jarratt and his wife were removed from the old residence and placed in the church under the Pulpit, and the above shaft and Plate were erected in the church.

McCarthy Family.

Inscriptions on tombstones in Fairfax County, contributed by Mrs. Carrie White Avery:

Sacred
to the memory of
DANIEL McCARTY
who departed this life
March 1st, 1801,
in the 43d year of his age.
He was at 16 years of age a Lieut.
in the Revolutionary War and was
in the battles of Brandywine
and Germantown.

In
memory of
MAJOR
DENIS McCARTY
who died March 25th
A. D. 1742
in the 38th year of his age.

Sacred
to the memory of
MRS. SARAH McCARTY
daughter of George Mason of 76
and wife of Daniel McCarty.
She departed this life Sept. 11th,
1823, in the 63d year of her age.

EPITAPH OF MRS. WILLIAM B. GILES.

While in Fincastle some weeks ago I visited the Presbyterian Cemetery one evening and among the tombs saw a slab with the following inscription:

UNDER THIS STONE
REMOTE FROM ALL WHO KNEW AND LOVED HER
LIES THE BODY OF
MARTHA PEYTON GILES
LATE WIFE OF WILLIAM B. GILES
A SENATOR IN THE CONGRESS OF THE UNITED STATES.
SHE WAS BORN OCTOBER 1777, AND DIED JULY 1808.

In the midst of every earthly blessing
    Beloved by Rich and Poor
        She Died!!!
Her mind adorned with every virtue;
Her person in the full Bloom of beauty;
The Darling of a Fond Mother;
The Pride of affectionate relations;
The Delight of adoring Friends—
        She Died!!!
She left behind her a husband who adored her
    and Three lovely children
        Reader!!
Mourn for them and for their disconslate Father:
        Mourn!!!
For Virtue and Beauty both Lie Buried here!!
    Lost to this World forever!!!!!

William B. Giles and Martha Peyton Tabb were married in Amelia County, Virginia. Date of marriage bond 6 March, 1797.

AUGUSTA B. FOTHERGILL.

SOME EXTRACTS FROM THE REGISTER OF KINGSTON PARISH.

BIRTHS.

James, son of James & Letitia Ransone, born June 28, 1755.

Frances, daughter of William & Elizabeth Gwyn, born June 26, 1755.

Mary, daughter of Thomas & Elizabeth Winder, born July 3, 1755.

George Reade, son of Israel & Martha Christian, born Aug. 20, 1755.

John, son of Humphrey & Frances Gwyn, born March 27, 1756.

Thomas, son of Thomas & Sarah Jervis, born May 7, 1756.

James, son of Henry & Mary Bernard, born July 16, 1756.

John, son of Francis & Elizabeth Jervis, born July 18, 1756.

Ann, daughter of Robert & Catherine Armistead, born Sept. 12, 1756.

Armistead, son of Thomas & Dorothy Smith, born Dec. 1, 1756.

Ann, daughter of James & Letitia Ransone, born Dec. 26, 1756.

Mary, daughter of William & Lucy Jervis, born April 20, 1757.

Bailey, son of Israel & Martha Christian, born Dec. 25, 1757.

Frances, daughter of Humphrey & Frances Gwyn, born Dec. 5, 1757.

John, son of Anthony & Ann Singleton, born July 2, 1758.

William, son of Rev. John & Lucy Dixon, born Oct. 12, 1758.

William, son of Gwyn & Dorothy Reade, born Oct. 25, 1758.

Robert, son of James & Letitia Ransone, born Dec. 29, 1758.

Thomas William, son of Francis & Elizabeth Jervis, born March 1, 1759.

William, son of William & Lucy Jervis, born May 9, 1759.

John, son of Thomas & Dorothy Smith, born May 10, 1759.

Elizabeth, daughter of Robert & Elizabeth Tabb, born June 3, 1759.

Mildred, daughter of Humphrey & Frances Gwyn, born Nov. 23, 1759.

Sarah, daughter of James & Letitia Ransone, born March 15, 1760.

Thomas, son of Rev. John & Lucy Dixon, born Dec. 26, 1760.

Susanna, daughter of Robert & Elizabeth Tabb, born April 28, 1761.

John, son of Israel & Martha Christian, born Oct. 16, 1761.

Lucy, daughter of William & Lucy Dixon, born Nov. 10, 1761.

Mildred, daughter of Robert & Caty Armistead, born Feb. 11, 1762.

Pemmy, daughter of Henry & Pemmy Singleton, born March 7, 1762.

Letitia, daughter of James & Letitia Ransone, born April 13, 1762.

Bailey Seaton, son of Robert & Elizabeth Tabb, born Aug. 10, 1762.

William, son of Richard & Averilla Singleton, born Oct. 2, 1762.

Gwyn Reade, son of Nathaniel & Lucy Palmer, born Oct. 10, 1763.

Robert, son of Robert & Elizabeth Tabb, born Nov. 29, 1763.

Edward, son of Francis & Elizabeth Jervis, born Oct. 18, 1763.

Betty, daughter of John & Elizabeth Power, born Dec. 5, 1763.

Lucy, daughter of James & Letitia Ransone, born April 20, 1764.

Israel, son of Israel & Martha Christian, born Aug. 30, 1764.

Bannister, son of Wm. & Lucy Jervis, born Aug. 31, 1764.

William, son of Robert & Elizabeth Tabb, born June 6, 1766.

Martha Peyton, daughter of Humphrey & Frances Gwyn, born Feb. 2, 1766.

Mildred, daughter of Harry & Lucy Gwyn, born March 6, 1766.

Peter, son of Mr. John & Mary Robinson, born Sept. 23, 1766.

Francis, son of William & Lucy Jervis, born July 3, 1767.

Mary, daughter of Robert & Elizabeth Tabb, born Feb. 20, 1768.

Humphrey, son of Humphrey & Frances Gwyn, born Feb. 9, 1769.

Judith, daughter of Mathew ——— Whiting, born Feb. 26, 1770.

John, son of Francis & Ann Jervis, born April 17, 1770.

Ralph, son of Richard & Elizabeth Armistead, born May 4, 1770.

William, son of William & Mary Armistead, born May, 5, 1770.

Dorothy Clack, daughter of James & Sarah Reade, born Aug. 12, 1770.

Betty, daughter of Francis & Ann Jervis, born Dec. 24, 1770.

Armistead, son of Robert Ballard Dudley & Ann his wife, born Jan. 27, 1771.

Mariana, daughter of John Tabb, Esq., & Frances, his wife, born Jan. 27, 1771.

Hannah, daughter of Henry Whiting & Humphrey Frances, his wife, born April 7, 1771.

Francis, son of Currel & Margaret Armistead, born 1772.

Gwyn, son of John & Judith Reade, born March 22, 1772.

Elizabeth Toye, daughter of Humphrey & Frances Gwyn, born April 25, 1772.

John, son of Francis & Ann Jervis, born March 22, 1773.

Gawin, son of William & Lucy Jervis, born June 27, 1773.

John Dixon, son of Lindsay & Elizabeth Jervis, born August 21, 1773.

Elizabeth, daughter of Richard & Betty Armistead, born Aug. 22, 1773.

Franky, daughter of Nelson & Dorothy Waller, born Sept. 11, 1773.

Robert, son of John & Ann Armistead, born Sept. 26, 1773.

Anna, daughter of William Armistead, Esq., & Mary, his wife, born Oct. 2, 1773.

Matthew James, son of Richard & Ann Ransone, born Dec. 25, 1773.

Letitia Hunly, daughter of John & Dorothy Gwyn, born May 12, 1774.

Mary Tabb, daughter of Humphrey & Frances Gwyn, born Aug. 22, 1774.

Patty Reade, daughter of Francis & Ann Jervis, born Aug. 20, 1774.

Judith Carter, daughter of William Armistead & Mary, his wife, born Dec. 30, 1774.

Mary, daughter of William & Elizabeth Buckner, born April 24, 1775.

Anna, daughter of William & Elizabeth Dixon, born June 4, 1775.

Elizabeth, daughter of John & Sally Jervis, born July 27, 1775.

Sarah, daughter of William Armistead, Esq., & Mary, his wife, born Feb. 22, 1776.

Elizabeth, daughter of John & Mary Jervis, born March, 1776.

William, son of Francis & Ann Jervis, born Aug. 1, 1776.

Susanna, daughter of Richard & Elizabeth Armistead, born Aug. 26, 1776.

Lucy, daughter of John & Dorothy Gwyn, born Nov. 10, 1776.

James, son of James & Sarah Reade, March 27, 1777.

Elizabeth, daughter of James & Lucy Jervis, born Nov. 15, 1776.

Thomas, son of Thomas & Dorothy Smith, b. February, 1778.

MARRIAGES.

John Gordon & Lucretia Singleton, Nov. 8, 1751.

Mathew Whiting & Martha Peyton, Nov. 22, 1751.

Augustine Ransone & Catherine Hill, April 18, 1753.

Henry Singleton & Letitia Hunley, February 16, 1754.

Anthony Singleton & Ann Smith, Nov. 19, 1754.

Humphrey Gwyn & Frances Peyton, February 21, 1755.

Robert Billups & Ann Ransone, June 14, 1755.

John Mayo & Mary Tabb, December 3, 1755.

Peter Wiat & Sarah Billups, January 30, 1756.

Humphrey Toy Tabb & Mary Peyton, Nov. 24, 1756.

Peter Bernard & Frances Dudley, Sept. 7, 1758.

Joseph Mayo & Martha Tabb, September 3, 1761.

William Bohannon & Mary Gordon, May 9, 1761.

Henry Whiting & Humphrey Frances Toye, November 11, 1762.

Nathaniel Palmer & Lucy Reade, December 30, 1762.

Mathew Whiting & Elizabeth Toye, February 26, 1763.

Nathaniel Gwyn & Dorothy Reade, July 2, 1763.

William Thomas & Judith Armistead, August 13, 1764.

Mr. Mordecai Buckner & Mrs. Mary Tabb, January 10, 1765.

James Reade & Sarah Tompkins, September 6, 1765.

Rev. Mr. Thomas Price & Mrs. Mary Armistead, September 15, 1765.

Francis Armistead & Dorothy Reade, February 2, 1766.

—— Cully & Mary Armistead, February 5, 1766.

Gwyn Reade & Harry Ann Whiting, June 5, 1766.

Humphrey Davis & Martha Christian, January 2, 1768.

William Darricot, of Hanover, & Catherine Finch, of Pets-worth, 1768.

John Reade & Judith Plummer, May 16, 1769.

Sterling Thornton & Ann Cary, November 30, 1769.

Francis Jervis & Ann Christian, December 23, 1769.

Mr. John Tabb & Frances, daughter of Sir John Peyton, 1770.

Richard Armistead & Elizabeth Jervis, February 11, 1770.

George Armistead & Lucy Palmer, widow, December 12, 1770.

Currell Armistead & Margaret Michen, December 29, 1770.

Richard Ransone & Ann Whiting, March 21, 1770.

Capt. Thomas Smith & Ann Plater, December 26, 1771.

Isaac Davis & Rebecca Armistead, January 9, 1772.

Lindsay Jarvis & Elizabeth Dixon, November 2, 1772.

Mr. John Gwyn & Miss Dorothy Ransone, February 6, 1773.

Mr. John Dixon & Mistress Elizabeth Peyton, February 6, 1773.

Mr. Starky Armistead & Miss Mary Tabb, June 19, 1773.

Mr. Mordecai Throgmorton & Miss Mary Peyton, December 11, 1773.

Mr. Josiah Dean of the Co. of Norfolk & Miss Rosanna Lilly of this parish, February 26, 1773.

John Reade & Susanna Peak, April 14, 1774.

William Dixon & Elizabeth ——, October 27, 1774.

Capt. Thomas Dixon & Miss Sarah Hawkins, December 8, 1774.

Dudley Cary & Lucy Tabb, November 11, 1775.

George Fitzhugh & Frances Tabb, November 25, 1775.

Thacker Washington & Miss Harriet Peyton, October 12, 1775.

Ralph Cully & Mary Singleton, November 6, 1775.

Robert Gwyn & Ann Ransone, Jan. 25, 1778.

Edward White & Pemmy Singleton, February, 1778.

DEATHS.

Mary, wife of John Jervis, Jan. 1, 1750.

Perin Smith, Jan. 30, 1752.

Ann Smith, Jan. 5, 1752.

Israel, son of Israel Smith, April 7, 1752.

Mary Plummer, April 26, 1752.

Robert, son of Robert Reade, October 26, 1759.

Mary, daughter of Capt. Gwyn Reade, November 6, 1759.

Capt. Thomas Machen, December 22, 1759.

Letitia Ransone, Jan. 11, 1760.

William Dudley, Jan. 15, 1760.

Lucy, daughter of Humphrey Gwyn, died March 16, 1771.

Thomas Dawson, clerk of the New Church, died July 28, 1770.

John, son of Humphrey Gwyn, was drowned in Milford Haven, 1770.

INSCRIPTIONS ON OLD TOMBS IN GLOUCESTER CO., VIRGINIA.

COLLECTED BY THE EDITOR.

I.

ABINGDON PARISH.[1]

[Arms.[2]]

Here Lyeth the Body of
M[r] Jeffrey Flower
Who departed this Life Sept[br] y[e] 2d 1726
Aged 38 Years.

Under this Stone lyes the Body
of Capt. William Blackburne[3]
Who was born in the Town of
New Castle on Tyne in Great
Britain on the 17th of Septemb[r]
1653   He departed this Life
the 18th day of October in the Year
of our Lord 1714
In hopes of a Joyful Resurrection

In Memory of
Mildred Thruston
Daughter of
John and Sarah Thruston[4]
*   *   *   *   *   *   *   *   *   October 1756
*   *   *   *   *   *   *   *   *   *   *   1758

At Dr. Walker Jones's Residence.

Here lies the body of Sarah Timson
Wife of Samuel Timson of York County
And daughter of Thomas & Ann Thornton
Of this County. She was a dutiful
Child, obedient wife, Tender Mother
And kind Mistress. She departed this
Life the 28th of February 1763 in the
21st year of her Age.[5]

III.

Carter's Creek or Fairfield.

To the lasting memory of Major Lewis Burwell[7]
Of the County of Gloucester, in Virginia,
Gentleman, who descended from the
Ancient family of the Burwells, of the
Counties of Bedford and Northampton,
In England, nothing more worthy in his
Birth than virtuous in his life, exchanged
This life for a better on the 19th day of
November in the 33d year of his age A. D. 1658 (?)

[*Arms.*[8]]

[In per]petual memory of yᵉ virtuous
[Lucy B]URWELL[9] the Loveing and Beloved
[Wife of] Major Lewis Burwell of yᵉ County
[of Glos]ter in Virginia (long since deceased)
[She was de]cended from the Ancient family
[of the H]igginsons. She was yᵉ only Daughter
[of the v]alliant Capt Robert Higginson
[One of th]e first comandʳˢ that subdued
[the cou]ntry of Virginia from the power of
[the heat]hen who not being more worthy in her
[birth th]an Vertuous in her life Exchanged this
[World for] a Better one on the 6th November, in
[the ———] yeare of her Age, Anno Domini 1675.
* * * buried on the * * ght hand of her
* * * d * * her M * * * * * * ll of her owne
Grand Children.

[*Arms.* [10]]

Here Lyeth the Body of
Hon[ble] Lewis Burwell [11] Son of
Maj Lewis Burwell & Lucy his wife
Of the County of Gloucester who first Married
Abigail Smith of y[e] family of y[e] Bacons
by whom he had four Sons and Six Daughters
and after her Death to Martha [12] the Widow
of y[e] Hon[ble] William Cole by whom he
also had two Sons and three Daughters and
Departed this Life the 19th Day of December
Anno Domini 1710 Leaveing behind him
three Sons and Six Daughters. [13]

[*Arms.* [14]]

To the Sacred Memory of Abigail the
Loveing & Beloved Wife of Maj Lewis
Burwell of the County of Gloster in
Virginia Gent who was Descended of the
illustrious Family of the Bacons and
Heiress of the Hon Nathaniel
Bacon Esq President of Virginia, who
Not Being more Honorable in her Birth
Than Vertuous in her Life Departed
this World the 12th day of November
1692 aged 36 years having Blessed her
Husband with four sons & six Daughters.

Sacred to the memory of the dearly beloved
* * * Martha, daughter of * * * Nansemond
County in Virginia, married to Col
William Cole by whom she had no [two] sons and
No [two] daughters. Afterwards married to
Major Lewis Burwell, by whom she had
Six [two] sons and three daughters; resigned
This mortal life the 4th day of Aug., 1704. [15]

Here lyeth the Body of
Lewis, son of Lewis Burwell and Abigail

61

His wife, on the left hand
Of his brother, Bacon, and
Sister, Jane.   He departed
This life yᵉ 17th day of
September 1696, [16] in the 15th year of his age.

Here lyeth the body of Mary, the daughter
Of Lewis and Martha, his wife.   She departed
This life in the first year of her age
On the 20th of July. [17]

[*Arms.* [18]]

Beneath this Tomb
Lies the Body of Major
Nathaniel Burwell
Eldest son of Major Lewis
Burwell who by A well
regulated Conduct and firm Integrity
Justly Established a good Reputation
He died in the forty & first Year of
His Age leaving behind him three
Sons & one Daughter [19] by
Elizabeth Eldest Daughter
of Robert Carter Esq
In yᵉ year of our Lord Christ
MDCCXXI.

IV.

JARVIS'S FARM ON WARE RIVER.

[*Arms.* [20]]

Underneath this loanly Tomb lieth yᵉ
Body of Mary Booth the wife of
Thomas Booth Gent deceased
Who lieth near her.   She was daughter
Of Mordecai Cooke Gent of Ware Parish
Gloucester County in Virginia Who de-
parted this life January 21st 1723.

This Monument is erected by the
Sons and Daughters of the Said
Thomas and Mary Booth in memory
Of our Dear and tender Mother.

[*Arms.* [21]]

Here lieth interred ye Body of Thomas
Booth [22] Gent who was born in Lanca-
shire but lived most of his days in Gloucester county Ware parish in Virginia
Where he departed this life on the 11 of
October Ann° Dom 1736 in the 74th year
of His Age.
This monument is erected as the last
Duty paid to the memory of a tender and
loving Father by the Sons and Daughters
of the said deceased and by memento
for us to follow the steps he trod knowing we all must die so saith ye Lord.

But death or the loanly cave why need we fear
If we but live and die as He that lyeth here
Who only waits his Saviour's call
To rise again as he did fall
And then receive the glorious crown
So let us his example follow
And fear not if we die to-morrow.

Underneath this Lonely
Tomb[23] Lieth the Remains of
John Booth Late Commander
of the Ship Mermaid who
Departed this Life May 13 1748,
In the 34th Year of his Age
Erected by Mordecai Booth.

Whilst on this variant stage he rov'd
From Port to port on Ship board drove

63

Sometimes the wished for haven reached
But twice his bark was stranded on the beach
No other coffin but the ship the Sea his grave
But God the merciful and just
Has brought him to the haven safe in dust
O to this haven do I say
Yes near his father and Mother to lay
The Port he long in illness craved
O blessed Lord into this Grave
His sailes unfurled his voyage tis oer
His anchors gone hes safe on shore.

V.

Wareham.[24]

Here lieth the body of Mrs Ann
Cooke the wife of Mr John Cooke
and Eldest daughter of Capt Thomas
and Elizabeth Todd   She was Born
in this Parish of Ware on the 9th day
of November Anno 1682 and died
the 18th day of July 1720 in hopes of
A joyfull Resurrection to Eternal life
which God grant her for her Blessed
Redeemer's Sake.   Amen.

Here lies the Body of Mrs Mary
Cooke the wife of Mr John Cooke
and Eldest daughter of John Smith, Esq [25]
and Elizabeth Smith   She was Born
in this Parish of Ware on the 14th day
of April Anno 1691 and died the 15th
of March 1724 in hopes of a Joyfull
Resurrection to Eternal Life
Which God grant her for her blessed
Redeemer's Sake.   Amen.

Here lieth the Body of Elizabeth Cooke
Wife of Mr. Mordecai Cooke
And eldest daughter of
Francis and Mary Whiting
Who was born in the Parish of Ware
On the Seventeenth of Decr Anno 1713
And died the 8th day of December 1762
in hopes of a Joyfull Resurrection
To Eternal Life
Which God grant her for her Blessed
Redeemer's Sake   Amen.

In Joyfull hopes of a Glorious Resurrection
to Life Eternal Mordecai Cooke
Son of John & Ann Cooke
After a conscientious discharge of every
social and every Religious Duty on Earth
Chearfully resigned his soul to God
his Body to this silent Grave 5th April
in the year of our Lord 1751
of his Age 43.

VI.

HIGH GATE.

[*Arms.* [20]]

Underneath this Stone lyeth Interred
the Body of Mrs Catharine Washington
Wife of Major John Washington [27]
and Daughter of Coll Henry Whiting by
Elizabeth his Wife   Born May the 22d 1694
She was in her several Stations
a Loving and Obedient Wife a tender
and ever Indulgent Mother a kind and
Compassionate Mistress and above all
an Exemplary Christian
She departed this Life February ye 7th 1743
Age 49 Years
to the Great loss of all that had ye Happiness
of her Acquaintance.

In a Well grounded Certainty of an
Immortal Resurrection
Here lyes the Remains of Elizabeth
the Daughter of
John and Catharine Washington
She was a Maiden
Virtuous without Reservedness
Wise without Affectation
Beautiful without Knowing it
She left this life on the Fifth day of
Feb[r] in the Year MDCCXXXVI in the
Twentieth Year of her age.

Here lies the Body of
Ariana M. Kemp
(late Consort of Peter Kemp Jun[r29])
Who departed this life April 30th 1811,
Aged 30 Years
She was the daughter of
Maj[r] John Grymes and Susannah his wife
of London
Regretted by all who knew her

Here rests the Body of
William Curtis
Who departed this life April 22d 1806
Aged 49 Years.

VII.

WARNER HALL.

Augustine Warner [30] Deceased
y[e] 24th of December 1674,
Aged 63 Yeares 2 M[th] 26D[s].

Tho dead whilest most men live he canot dy
His name will live fresh in their memory
True worth is highly shown in liveing well
When future ages of his praise shall tell

Mary Warner y⁰ wife of Augustine Warner Esq. was Born
15th of May 1614 And Dyed y⁰ 11th Day
of August 1662.

Here Lyeth the Body of
Co¹¹ Augustine Warner[21]
who was born y⁰ 3d of
June 1642 and Died
y⁰ 19th of June 1681.

Here Lyeth interred
Augustine Warner
son of Co¹¹ Augustine &
Mildred Warner, born y⁰
17th of January, 166$\frac{6}{7}$, And
deceased y⁰ 17th of March, 168$\frac{6}{7}$.

Here Lyeth Interred
the Body of Coll⁰ John Lewis[22]
son of John and Isabella Lewis,
and one of his Majestys Honble
Council for this Colony who was
born y⁰ 30th of November 1669 & departed
this Life on y⁰ 14th of November 1725.

Here Lyeth Interr'd y⁰ Body
of Elizabeth Lewis the
Daughter of Col Augustine
Warner and Mildred his
Wife and late wife of John
Lewis Esq   She was Born at
Chesake the 24th of November,
1672   Aged 47 year^s 2 Month^s
and 12 Day^s, and was a Tender
Mother of 14 children   She
Departed this Life the 5th
Day of February 17$\frac{19}{20}$.

Sacred to the Memory
of Caroline Barrett wife of Charles Barrett Esq and eldest
Daughter of Warner Lewis by his
Second wife Mary Fleming.
She was born June 28 1783,
and Departed this vale of tears April 6th 1811.
No language can explain what she was
Her Eulogium is where she still liveth,
In the heart of her sorrowing h * *.

Warner Lewis
Eldest son of Warner Lewis Esq
and Eleanor Gooch
Widow of William Gooch [33]
and Daughter of
James Bowles Esq of Maryland.
Died the 30th of December 1791
Aged 24 years.

Mary Lewis first Wife of Warner Lewis Esq
Daughter of John Chiswell [34]
of Williamsburg.
and Elizabeth Randolph
of Turkey Island
Died the first of November 1776.
Aged 28 Years.

[*Arms* [35].]

Hic Subter Suae Sunt reliquae D.
Thomas Clayton M. B. Johannis Clayton
Arm. Filii natu minimi Aulae pembrochianae
Cambrigiensis olim Alumni qui studiis
et labore professionis fractus postquam
aetatis suae annum XXXVIII * * * * XVII
die Octobris anno nostrae salutis a Christo
MDCCXXXIX pie et suaviter in Domino
obdormivit cujus vidua Isabella pientissima
hoc marmor pro munere extremo uberibus
cum lachrymis devotissime posuit.

Magnificas nullas cernes hic suae columnas.
Saxa nec artificis vivere jussa manu
Pyramides celsa laetor nec surgere in
illis in campis Isidis arte pares.
Scilicet hanc speciem mentorum quaerat
famam qui metitus conciliare nequit.

Here Lyes the Remains of
Juliana Clayton yᵉ only Daughter
of Thomas Clayton and Isabella his
Wife   She was born May yᵉ 17th 1731
* * * * * *   yᵉ 12th of May 1734
* * * * * * *

[*Arms* ³⁶.]
Here Sleeps the Body
of Isabella Clayton While
her Soul is gone in Triumph to
meet the best of Husbands
and never more to be Devorced
by him to be taught to Sing
Eternal Praises of God & yᵉ Lamb
For Ever.

This is to the Memory of
James J. McLanahan
Eldest son of
John and Elizabeth McLanahan
of Franklin County
Pennsylvania
Born November 15, 1791
Died October 16, 1831.

[TO BE CONTINUED.]

NOTES BY THE EDITOR.

[1] Last summer the editor spent several delightful weeks in Gloucester, visiting the old homesteads. He tried to take down as literally as possible the inscriptions upon the old tombstones, which are rapidly disappearing. Gloucester county was divided originally into Ware, Abingdon, Petsworth, and Kingston parishes, the last being cut off with Mathews in 1790. A register and vestry book of Abingdon parish and a vestry book of Petsworth are at the Episcopal seminary at Alexandria. Abingdon Church is a handsome square brick building, standing on the road to Gloucester Point. Upon the arch of the door have been cut the figures 1765. The building is probably the last of a series of similar structures on the same spot. The silver service, which is kept by Mrs. Selden of "Sherwood," bears the inscription, "The gift of L. B. to Abingdon Parish." One of the leading parishoners in 1700 was Lewis Burwell.

[2] The arms are those of Flower of Chilton, Co. Wilts : Sa. a unicorn pass., or on a chief ar. Jeffrey Flower died "intestate," Peter Whiting administrator. (Ludwell MSS.)

[3] At the lower church in Middlesex are tombs of Dorothy and Thomas (children of William and Elizabeth Blackburne), who died respectively in 1726 and 1727. Capt. William Blackburn, J. P. and Burgess, died in Middlesex in 1738. (Va. Gazette.)

[4] This Thruston tomb is a fragment, placed for preservation in the vestry room at Abingdon Church.

[5] This Timson inscription was furnished the editor by Dr. Walker Jones, of Gloucester county. Samuel Timson was a descendant of Samuel Timson, formerly a merchant of London, and Mary Juxon, his wife and sister of William Juxon, merchant of London. See *Virginia Historical Society Collections*, XI., pp. 99–100 for the immigrant's inscription. From various contemporary sources, William Thornton was guardian of John Liptrott, in York Co. (1646). He patented land in Gloucester Co., Petsworth parish in 1665–'66, and was vestryman. He had issue—William, Jr., Francis, and Rowland—from whom many of the Thornton name in the United States are descended. From an old book-plate (I have seen a photograph of it) of William Thornton, of Virginia, the family arms are: A chevron betw. three hawthorn trees, agreeing in Burke with Thornton of counties Cambridge, Norfolk, and York. I purpose to give a full account of the Thorntons and Timsons in some future number of this QUARTERLY.[*]

[6] "Carter's Creek," the old seat of the Burwells, is situated on a creek of that name and not far back from York River. On the high triple chimney are cut the letters L B A. Besides the tombstones mentioned in this paperof the Burwell family there are extant the tombstone (badly injured) of Elizabeth (Burwell) Harrison, of "Westover," and her brother, James Burwell, of King's Creek, York county (inscription published in *Virginia Historical Papers*, Vol. XI.).

[7] Ancestor of Burwell family. Inscription taken from Meade; tomb missing or shattered now. Had grant in 1648 for head rights Roger Wingate, the minister his son, the Lady Clifton and her two maids, William Burwell, etc. Mrs. Eliz. Hull had grant in 1643 for William, George, Elizabeth, and Lewis Burwell. [She (Elizabeth Hull) perhaps married 2dly Robert Vaulx, called "brother" by Lewis B.] Francis Hammond, brother of Gen. Mainwaring

[*]For Thornton see *Genealogies of Virginia Families: From the William and Mary College Quarterly Historical Magazine* (Baltimore: Genealogical Publishing Co., Inc., 1982), Vol. V, pp. 19–65; for Timson see *ibid.*, pp. 144–148.

Hammond, had in 1654 head-rights Robert, Eliz., Susan, and Humphrey Vaulx, Francis and Mana. Hammond, John Woodington, &c. Robert Vaulx's brothers were Thomas, James, and Humphrey Vaulx. John Woodington, a kinsman. James Vaulx went to Dorchester Co., Md. Lewis Burwell was son of Edward Burwell, of Bedfordshire, and Dorothy, d. of William Bedell, of Catsworth, who had, 1, Edward; 2, Dorothy, perhaps m. —— Woodington; 3, Elizabeth, probably married, 1st, Hull, 2d, Vaulx; 4, Lewis, bapt. at Ampthill Mch. 5, 1621, the immigrant; 5, George; 6, Edward. An Edward Burwell was living in York Co. in 1648. The date of Lewis Burwell's death was probably 1653, not 1658, as Meade makes the tomb read. See Keith's *Ancestry of Benjamin Harrison*, etc., York Co. Records, and Land-Office Register.

[8] Arms too worn for the Editor to make out.

[9] Lucy, Higginson married, 1st, Major Lewis Burwell; 2d, Col. William Bernard, and 3d, Col. Philip Ludwell. Her father, Capt. Robert Higginson, commanded at Middle Plantation in 1646, and as a reward for valiant service received from the Colony 100 acres of land (York Co. Records). This tombstone is much injured, and the portion of the inscription in brackets is supplied from Campbell (*Southern Literary Mess.*, xiii., p. 464). The last lines (Campbell does not give them) were doubtless: "She was buried on the right hand of her husband. Erected to her memory by several of her own grandchildren."

[10] I found this tomb intact. The crest is a human bust, the crest of Abigail Smith, Burwell's first wife. The arms are, *dexter*, a saltire between four griffins' heads erased; *sinister*, three roses in bend; the former for Burwell, the latter doubtless for Smith. The Burwell shield, as represented at this place and on James Burwell's tomb at King's Creek, is not charged with eagles' heads, as commonly represented. The last has for crest a griffin's claw with three talons grasping a twig with four leaves.

[11] I found Lewis Burwell's will (proved Feb. 19, 1710) on record in York Co. He mentions sons, Nathaniel, James, and Lewis; grandson, Lewis, son of Nathaniel; son-in-law, Henry Seaton; daughters, Joanna, Elizabeth, Lucy, Martha, Jane, and Martha, jun.; godson, William Burwell, about 4 years old, living with William Davis and Ellinor his wife, whom he directs to be educated at William and Mary College, in style "becoming a gentleman's son," and to have 65 pds. worth of plate "that hath his mother's coat-of arms upon it"; [Matthew Burwell, probably the father of William, and William Davis were witnesses to Lewis Burwell's deed in 1700;] brother Philip Ludwell; £30 to the poor of Abingdon parish, and £30 for mourning-rings. Should his children die without issue, his property in York, James City, King William, etc., to go for establishing free schools, and a chair of Law, Medicine, or Divinity in William and Mary College. Mr. Keith was probably unaware of this will.

[12] Lewis Burwell, the second of the name, had, by Martha Lear, two sons and three daughters, but Meade says *eight daughters*, which is certainly wrong. (See Note 15.)

[13] Burwell had, by his first marriage, four sons and six daughters. In March, 1691-'92 (date of the proof of Col. Bacon's will), there were living three sons, Nathaniel, Lewis, and James, and four daughters named in the will in this order: Joanna, Elizabeth, Lucy and Martha. Bacon and Jane, two others not mentioned in the will, must have died before 1691-'92. Lewis died in 1696. Henry Seaton probably married a daughter, also deceased. By the second

71

marriage after 1694 (date of Col. Wm. Cole's death), he had two sons and three daughters. Of this number Mary, who died in 1704, was one; Lewis, Jane, and Martha jun., mentioned last in the order of his children in 1710, were doubtless three others. One I have no knowledge of. There must have been two daughters of the name of Martha living in 1710, one by Abigail Smith, and the other by Martha Lear, else the whole number of surviving children called for by Lewis B's tomb would not be the number named in his will. It also follows that in 1704, when Governor Nicholson was wild about one of the Burwell girls, the children of the second marriage were of tender age. Martha, as being the only child of the first marriage unmarried, must have been the object of his attentions.

Mr. Keith suggests only two sons for John Armistead, of Hesse, Henry and William, and makes the lady whom James Burwell in his will (1718) calls "sister Martha Armistead," the wife of Henry Armistead. James Burwell married Mary Armistead, and speaks also of "brother John Armistead," and Mr. Keith says that this John was brother of his wife, and a son of William Armistead, who married Anna Lee, a fact evidenced by Burwell mentioning his "mother, Ann Armistead." This is contrary to the account given to me by several correspondents, and to Mr. Brock's Armistead pedigree in the *Standard*, but is perhaps correct, except as to the first particular.

In support of the views of the last, Barradall's Reports (MSS. in Virginia Historical Society and Law Library) show that in 1737, Burwell Armistead and one Dudley sued in behalf of John[4] Armistead, then an infant, who was eldest son and heir of John[3] Armistead deceased, who was eldest son and heir of John[2] Armistead deceased, who was eldest son and heir of John[1] Armistead, who in 1680 bought land with Robert Beverley, in Gloucester county. Robinson, the plaintiff, was eldest son and heir of John Robinson, Esq., who married Catharine, daughter of Robert Beverley. Other facts may be added to Mr. Keith's account of the Burwells. Col. Bacon's old homestead at King's Creek, descended under Major Lewis Burwell's will, to his son James, who is buried there (see Virginia Historical Society Papers, Vol. XI., for inscription on tomb). James married Mary Armistead (she married secondly Philip Lightfoot) and had Captain Nathaniel Burwell and Lucy Burwell.

Captain Nathaniel Bacon Burwell (Inventory £1669 rec. 1749) married, and had James, who married Anne Jones (b. Feb. 15, 1739, d. 1779) sister of Dr. Walter Jones, of the Revolution ; issue, 1, Nathaniel Bacon; 2, James; 3, Ann; 4, Rachel; 5, Bacon. "Descendants of Roger Jones" mentions another, Lucy, the reputed wife of Bishop Ravenscroft; but she is not mentioned in Ann Burwell's will. In 1790 Nathaniel Bacon Burwell, Jr., and Elizabeth, his wife, sold Kings Creek plantation, of 1800 acres, "on which he now lives, and his late father, James Burwell lived," to John Tayloe Corbin, of King and Queen county. Elizabeth, his wife, was daughter of John Smith, brother of Dr. Augustine Smith, and (in 1793 of Richmond county, but formerly of York) and left a son, James Bacon Burwell, infant in 1793.

I think a daughter of Capt. Nathaniel Bacon Burwell must have married John Reade (son of Robert, son of Col. George), as Elizabeth, his daughter, is called granddaughter in Mary Armistead Lightfoot's will (pr. 1775). She, Elizabeth, first married Rev. Richard Hewitt, of Hungar's Parish, Northampton county (he died before 1779). She had by him, 1, Elizabeth Burwell; 2,

Mary; 3, Ann; 4, Dorothy; 5, Sarah. Of these, Elizabeth, who married Henry Lee, Sarah, who married Littleton Kendall, and Dorothy, alone survived in 1798. The widow, Elizabeth (Reade) Hewitt, married secondly Col. Edward Harwood, son of William Harwood, of Warwick county. (York Records, Chancery papers, &c.)

[14] Abigail Burwell, née Smith, was the heiress of Col. Nathaniel Bacon, and the arms on her tomb are Burwell impaling Bacon. The crest is a human bust, representing, probably, Smith. Meade says that Mrs. Elizabeth Bacon was daughter of Richard Kingsmill, and her tombstone at Norfolk is confirmatory, bearing as it does the arms of Tayloe (her first husband was William Tayloe, of the Council) impaling Kingsmill, as in Burke.

[15] The tomb of Martha (Lear) Burwell is shattered. This inscription is taken from Meade, but is erroneous in stating her children. At Bolthorpe are tombstones to three children by her marriage with Col. William Cole. And in the York records is a deed by Lewis Burwell, dated December 2, 1700, conveying certain negroes "in trust for William Cole, son of Col. William Cole, late of Warwick county, deceased, by his wife Martha, and now the wife of me, the said Lewis Burwell, to be delivered to him when he shall attain the age of 18"; "and in event of his death, to the surviving children of said Lewis and Martha Burwell." The inscription probably read, "two sons and two daughters," instead of "no sons and no daughters." In like manner, instead of "six sons and three daughters" by Lewis Burwell, Martha's tombstone doubtless read, "two sons and three daughters," a correction agreeing with the tombstone, still intact, of Major Burwell himself.

[16] Meade says, Lewis Burwell, son of Major Lewis and Abigail (Smith) Burwell, died in 1676, but Campbell says 1696, which, as Keith shows, is undoubtedly correct.

[17] This inscription is taken from Meade; tombstone now missing.

[18] The arms on the tombstone of Nathaniel Burwell are the same as on that of James, his brother, at King's Creek. The crest seems to be also the same.

[19] The children of Nathaniel Burwell were: Lewis, President of the Virginia Council, Carter, of the Grove in James City county, Elizabeth, wife of William Nelson, and mother of Gen. Nelson.

[20] The arms are enclosed in a lozenge, and represent in Burke "the later arms" of Booth of Barton, county Lancaster, impaling Cooke, of Whitefield, county Suffolk.

[21] The arms as above, enclosed in a shield, bearing as *crest:* A demi St. Catharine, ppr. couped at the knees, in the *dexter* hand a Catharine wheel, in her *sinister* a sword, the point downwards.

[22] Robert Bristow of London, merchant, son of Major Robert Bristow, formerly of Gloster county, Virginia, made a power of attorney in 1709, to Thomas Booth of Gloster county, to sell his property and plantations in Virginia. (York county Records.) One Thomas Booth still controlled the Bristow estate in 1772, when William Nelson solicited the agency for Col. Robert Tucker, of Norfolk, who had suffered heavily from a great fire. (Nelson MSS. Letter Book at Episcopal Theological Seminary.) The Bristow estate was shortly after confiscated by the Virginia goverment on the ground that the Bristows were aliens. (See QUARTERLY II., July Number for an account of the Bristow family and arms.) An elaborate chart pedigree of the

73

family, prepared at much cost, shows that Thomas Booth, the immigrant, was son of St. John Booth, son of John Booth, son of George Booth, whose son William was father of George first Lord Delamere, which last was father of Henry, first Earl of Warrington.

Thomas[1], the immigrant, married Mary Cooke and had George[2], Thomas[2], Mordecai[2], John[2], William[2], and 4 daus.

Mordecai[2] mar. —— and had George[3] and two daus., one of whom married twice.

George[3] mar. Mary Wythe Mason, and had George Wythe[4], Mary[4], Fanny[4].

George Wythe[4] mar. Lucy Jones, issue, Mary[5], Fanny[5], Lucy[5].

Mary[4] mar. James H. Roy, issue, William H., James, Mary, Laura. William H. Roy mar. 1st Anne Seddon; issue, Thomas S., William, James H. (all died young), Anne S., Susan S.; mar. 2nd Euphan W. Macrae, issue, Fanny W., Mary M., Ellen D.

Mary[5], daughter of George Wythe, died unmarried.

Fanny[5], d. of Geo. Wythe, mar. Warner T. Taliaferro, issue: General William Booth Taliaferro[6] (1894).

Lucy[5], d. of George W., died unmarried.

Thomas[2], son of the immigrant Thomas[1], mar. Anne Buckner and had George[3], Thomas[3], John[3], and Mordecai[3], and one married daughter.

George[3], son of Thomas[2], mar. ——, and had Thomas,[4] Sarah,[4] and six married sisters.

Sarah[4] mar. Thomas Baytop, and had James Baytop, who mar. Lucy Taliaferro Catlett, and had Ann Walker Carter Baytop, who mar. Jeff. W. Stubbs, of Gloucester county, and had Prof. T. J. Stubbs, of William and Mary, J. N. Stubbs, State Senator (1894), Prof. W. C. Stubbs, of Louisiana, &c. The Booths, of Nottoway, trace to Gilliam Booth, a reputed descendant of the Gloucester family. See Goode's "Virginia Cousins."

There was a prominent family of Booths in York Co. Robert[1] Booth was clerk, burgess, etc., from about 1640 till his death (1657); mar. Frances —— had perhaps Robert[2], J. P., who mar. Anne, dau. of James Bray, Esq., of the Council, and Angelica —— his wife. Robert[2] died in 1692, and his widow mar. Capt. Peter Temple (died 1695), son of Peter Temple, minister of York parish. After Peter Temple's death, she married, 3dly, Mungo Inglis, grammar master of William and Mary College, and had children. William[2] Booth, J. P. (will proved 13 May, 1692), was perhaps another son of Robert[1], and mar. Margaret ——, and had Elizabeth, who married, 1st, Dr. Peter Plovier (d. 1677-'78); married, 2d, John Griggs; 3d, Captain Thomas Nutting, J. P., whose dau. Katherine married, 1st, Capt. William Sheldon; 2d, Capt. Robert Armistead, son of Major Anthony Armistead, of Elizabeth City. The York records say that Elizabeth[2] was a daughter of Robert[1] Booth, clerk of York Co., and married Dr. Patrick Napier. Her children were Robert[3] (under 21 in 1672) and Frances[3], and lived in New Kent. Robert[3] had Booth[4] Napier (b. Feb. 1, 1692) and other children. (See St. Peter's Parish Register.)

[23] This is a splendid tomb, highly ornamented. Gen. William B. Taliaferro has a handsome funeral ring with the engraving on the inside: "John Booth obiit —— 1748, Æt. 36"; as also a ring, evidently in memory of his father, on which all that can be made out is, "Tho: . . . . . . 73" [Thomas Booth obiit, etc., æt. 73].

[24] This is a quaint old brick house, near the Pianketank, the early residence of the Cookes. Mordecai Cooke patented 1174 acres at the head of Ware River in Mockjack Bay.

[25] John Smith was member of the Council, and eldest son of Major Laurence Smith. See arms and account of his family, in QUARTERLY, July, 1893; paper entitled "Temple Farm."

[26] The arms are, apparently: On a chevron between three wolves' heads erased, three trefoils,—presumably Whiting. Crest, a wolf's head (?) erased.

[27] Major John Washington was eldest son of Lawrence Washington and Mildred Warner. Lawrence was son of Colonel John Washington, who with his brother Lawrence came to Virginia about 1655. Major John was great-uncle of General George Washington. See Sparks's *Life of Washington*, I., page 548.

[28] This tomb bears the arms used by General Washington. (Spark's *Washington*, Vol. I., p. 542.)

The crest on the tombstone is, "out of a ducal coronet a raven, wings addorsed ppr."

[29] Peter Kemp, Jr., was the son Peter Kemp, vestryman of Petsworth parrish.

[30] Col. Augustine Warner came to Virginia about 1628, was justice of York county, and finally settled in Gloucester county, on the estate still known as Warners Hall. (For description of this house see *Virginia Magazine of History and Biography*, Vol. I., No. 3, p. 351, n. 11.) Was burgess for York in 1652, and for Gloucester, 1655; member of the Council 1659-1667, married Mary ——, and had 1, Sarah married Lawrence Townley, and was ancestress of General Robert E. Lee, 12, Col. Augustine.

[31] Col. Augustine Warner, eldest son of the preceding, married Mildred, daughter of Col. George Reade, of York county. He studied at the Merchant Taylor's School, in London, and was Councillor, Speaker of the House of Burgesses, etc. For details as to his descendants, see Richmond *Critic*, October 5, 1889; Richmond *Standard*, iii., 23, 38, 52; iv., 23.

[32] John Lewis, Esq., member of the Council, etc., was son of Robert Lewis, who settled in Gloucester county. Mrs. William Reynolds writes that it was established through the researches of Capt. Henry Howell Lewis of Baltimore, "who had every statement verified from the old English and Welsh records," that Robert was the son of Sir Edward Lewis, of Van and Erdington. It would be interesting to know the exact evidence by which this important fact was established.

[33] William Gooch was the son of Governor William Gooch of Virginia. The Lady Rebecca, his mother, presented to the College a gilt sacrament cup and patten, and Bible (Samuel Athawes MSS. 29 July, 1775). And a cup and patten answering this description are in the custody of Bruton church in Williamsburg.

[34]. John Chiswell, of Hanover, clerk of the General Court, died in April 1737, in his sixtieth year (*Virginia Gazette*), had a son, Col. John Chiswell, who married Elizabeth, daughter of William Randolph, of Turkey Island (she died, aged fifty-four, in February, 1776), and had, issue, 1, Susanna, married John Robinson, the speaker; 2d, William Griffin, 2 Mary, married Warner

Lewis ; 3, Elizabeth, married Charles Carter, of Ludlow, Stafford county; 4, Lucy, born August 3, 1752, died April 4, 1810, married Col. William Nelson. Col. Chiswell, their father, discovered in 1757 the New River lead mines (now known as the Wythe Lead and Zinc Works); and Fort Chiswell, within a few miles thereof, was named for him. In 1766 he killed a Scotch gentleman named Robert Routlidge, probably a refugee and supporter of the Pretender, as Chiswell called him "a rebel Presbyterian." The county court refused to bail Chiswell, but on his way to jail he was bailed by three of the General Court, John Blair, Presley Thornton, and William Byrd. They were said to be relatives of Chiswell, and were bitterly attacked for their interference. His prosecutor was chosen in the prevailing custom by lot, and it fell to John Blair, Jr., an intimate friend, to conduct the case, but the suicide of the accused ended the proceedings. (See Richmond *Times*, March 4, 1894; *Virginia Gazette*, by Purdie, for 1766; Call's *Reports*, Vol. IV; and the letter of John Camm in this number.)

[35] The arms on the tomb of Dr. Thomas Clayton are: A cross engrailed between four tortoaux; crest, a leopard's gamb erased and erect, grasping a pellet, or torteau. From Mr. Stanard's carefully prepared pedigree, based on Le Neve, Wills at Somerset House, &c., printed in Wallace's *Historical Magazine*, for October, 1891:

Thomas,[1] of Clayton Hall, Lancaster, England, m. Agnes, d. of John Thornell, issue, William[2] "2d son but heir," d. 1627. William[2] m. —— Cholmeley, issue, 1, John[3] 2, Sir Jasper[3] of St. Edmunds, Lombard St., Mercer, Alderman, &c., knighted 1600. Sir Jasper[3] m. Mary Thompson, d. of William Thompson, "late citizen and haber-dasher of London," issue 1 Sir John[4] 2, George,[4] 3, Mary[4], 4, Prudence[4], 5, Rebecca[4].

Sir John[4] m. Alice Bowyer, d. of Sir William Bowyer, of Denham, Bucks, boronet, and relict of William Buggins, of North Crey, Eng. Issue 1, John,[5] born 1665, died Nov. 18, 1737; studied at the university, probably Cambridge, and at Inner Temple; and in 1705 was appointed attorney-general of Virginia; was judge of the Court of Admiralty, member of the House of Burgesses, recorder of Williamsburg, &c. Married, not known whom, and had 1, John,[6] the eminent botanist, and author of "Flora Virginia." (See Chalmers' Biographical Dictionary.) 2. Arthur,[6] clerk "of a county on the upper part of James River." 3. Dr. Thomas,[6] educated at the University of Cambridge, and completed his medical studies in London, returned to Virginia, where he married, in 1728, Isabella Lewis, of Warner Hall, and died October 17, 1739. He had one child, Juliana, born May 17, 1731, died 12th May, 1734. The descendants of John[6] are numerous in Virginia.

William Pryor was an early justice of York county; made his will, proved 25th January, 1646-'47, and appointed his brother-in-law, Jasper Clayton, executor of his English estate, and Capt. Thomas Harwood and Capt. Thomas Harrison, Gent., formerly of Ratcliffe, Middlesex county, Eng., executors of his Virginia estate. He left two daughters, Mary, and Margaret who married Thomas Edwards, of the Inner Temple, London. (York county, Va, Records.) William Bernard, of Purton, in Gloucester, purchased Pryor's estate in York county, just above Yorktown, and his wife, Anna, sold it to Robert Baldrey, who left it to Thomas Ballard, of the Council. (*Ibid.*)

Inscriptions on old Tombs in Glouces-ter Co., Virginia.

COLLECTED BY THE EDITOR.

VIII
OLD UPTON [1]

In Memory of
Fanny Wiatt
Died Sept 8 1838
Aged 67 Years

In Memory of Peter Wiatt
Born Aug. 1, 1799
Died Sept 25th 1824.

IX
OAKLEY
[On the "Dragon Swamp," boundary between Gloucester and Middlesex Counties

Here lies the Body of
Peter Wiatt
Who departed this Life
on the 26th December, 1815
Aged forty-seven years.

Here lies the Body of
Frances L. Wiatt
Wife of
Peter Wiatt
who departed this life 13th February
1817
Æt. 47.

X
VIOLET BANKS. [2]
Here lieth the Body of Edward Porteus
of Petsworth Parish Gloucester County
Merchant Departed this life the——

169——, in the——Yeare of his Age
leaveing one only son Robert to
Succeed him.

XI
ROBINS' NECK [3]
In remembrance of Frances Robins
daughter of Thomas &
Mildred Stubbs born the
14 February 1745 & departed
this life the 18th of July 1800

In remembrance of Tho-
mas Robins son of Wil-
liam & Elizabeth Rob-
ins born the 11th February
1745 & departed this Life
the 8th November 1808

XII
GLOUCESTER COURT-HOUSE.
[Arms]
Under this Marble are Reposed
until yᵉ Day of General Resurrection
the Remains of Tho Reade [4] Gent
Eldest son
to Tho Reade gent of this place
He was suddenly taken away
By the hand
of Divine Providence
From this to a Far better Life
on the XVII Day of April
Ann: Dom MDCCXXXIX.
Aetate XLII
To whose Dear Memory
His loving And Disconsolate
Wife
Hath Erected this Monument

Here lies Mʳˢ Lucy the wife of
Mʳ John Dixon of Bristol Daughter
of Mʳ Thoˢ Reade of this place with

78

two of their children Died Nov 22d
1731 Aged 30 years;
Near her is Mrs Elizabeth Dixon
his sister Died Sept 8 1732
Aged 13 Years.

————

Here quietly reposes the body of
William Smart
Born in England of William & Mary Smart
on the 20th of July 1784
In early life he emigrated to the United States
and after sustaining an irreproachable reputation
and a life of unexceptionable piety he died
in certain hope of the resurrection
of the just and eternal life
on the 1th of February 1840
Let me die the death of the Righteous
and let my last end be like his

————

In memory of Louisa
The wife of William Smart
Who departed this Life October 7th 1828
in the 34th year of her age
She found redemption through Blood of the Lamb
Reader—hast thou?

————

XIII

MT. PLEASANT.

To the Memory of
Doct.
John Dixon
only son of
John Dixon &
Sally Throckmorton
of Airville
Died June 24
1835
In the 23d yr
of his Age

————

John Dixon
only son of
John Dixon and
Elizabeth Peyton
of Mount Pleasant
who died Sept. 5th, 1830,
in the 53d year
of his age.

His memory will long be
cherished by all who knew
him   In him the widow
and Fatherless always
found a friend,

This Tomb is erected by his
daughter Harriet P. Sheldon in
token of her ardent effection,
He died in the full hope
of a joyful resurrection
He was the last male descendant
of the Dixon family

XIV.

PETSWORTH CHURCH. [5]

[Skull and cross bones]

Heie lyeth the   *   *   *   *
   Edward Sinclair   *   *   *
who departed   *   *   *   *
16 Nov   *   *   *   *   *

Here Lies the Body of the Rev.

Mr Emanuel Jones [6]
the Husband of Mrs Anne Jones,
who departed this Life the 29th day
of January in the year of our Lord Christ
1739 and in the 72d year of his Age.

[Arms]

Here Lies the Body of John Jones
The Eldest son of the late
Reverend Emanuel and Anne Jones

80

who departed this Life
the 12th day of August
1715 (?)
In the 27th year of his age

Here lieth
the Body of John Wood
who departed this life Jan^{ry}
26, 1769 Age 56 years.

XV.

WARE PARISH CHURCH.(7)

[Her]e lyeth the Body of
[Jame]s Clack(8) son of William and Mary Clack
[who wa]s born in the Parish of Marden
*   *   *   * Miles from the Devizes
[In] the county of Wilts
[He] Came out of England in August
[16]78, Arrived in Virginia upon
New Years day following came
into the Parish of Ware [on] Easter
Where he continued Minister near
forty five years till he Dy^ed
He departed this life on the 20th
day of December in the year of
our Lord God 1723 in hopes of
a joyful Resurection to Eternal Life
which God grant him for his Blessed
Redeemer's Sake, Amen.

Underneath this stone(9) lyeth the body of Amy
    Richards, the
most dearly-beloved wife of John Richards, min-
    ister of this parish, who
departed this life 21st of November, 1725, aged
    40 years
"Near her dear mistress lies the body of Mary Ades,

81

her faithful and beloved servant, who
departed this life the 23^d of November, 1725, aged
28 years.

Here lyeth the body of Mrs. Ann Willis, the wife
of Col. Francis(10)
Willis, who departed this life the 10th of June,
1727, in the (32^d) year of her age
Also the body of A., daughter of the
abovesaid aged 7 days

Underneath this stone lyeth the body of Mr. John Richards
late rector
of Nettlestead and vicar of Teston in the county of
Kent, in the Kingdom
of England, and minister of Ware, in the county of
Gloucester and colony
of Virginia, who, after a troublesome passage
through the various changes
and chances of this mortal life, at last reposed
in this silent grave in ex-
pectation of a joyful resurrexion to eternal life,
He died the 12th day
of November, in the year of our Lord MDCC
*   *   *   V, aged 46.

Here lyeth the body of Isabel, daughter of Mr. Thomas
Booth, wife
of Rev. John Fox, minister of this Parish; who
with examplary patience
having borne various afflictions, and with equal
piety discharged her several
duties on earth, cheerfully yielded to mortality,
exchanging the miseries
of this life for the joys of a glorious eternity
on the 13th day of June, in
the year of our Lord MDCCXLI I, of her age 38.

Here also lie the bodies of Mary and Susannah,
    daughters of the
above mentioned John and Isabel.   The one depart-
    ed this life on the 5th
day of September 1742 in the 4th year of her age;
    the other on the
7th of October, in the 3^d year of her age, MDCCXLIII.

XVI.

TIMBER NECK.

Here lyeth ye Body of
John Mann ⁽¹¹⁾ of Gloucester County
in Virginia Gent Aged 63 years
who Departed this life ye 7th Day
of January Anno Domini 1694

[Arms]
Here lyeth Interred the Body
of Mrs Mary Mann, of the
County of Gloucester in the
Collony of Virginia Gentle Wom
who Departed this life the 18th
day of March 170 ¾ Aged 56 yeares.

[Arms] (12)
Here Lyeth ye Body of
Elizabeth Page Daughtar
of mathew page of ye Colony
of Virginia Gentle man Aged
three years who departed
this life ye 15th day of march
Anno Domino 1693.

Notes By the Editor.

(1) "Old Upton" is portion of an elder tract called "Boxley," long the home of the Virginia Wiatts. The last is named after "Boxley Parish" in Kent Co., England, famous chiefly for three things,—1st, its ancient Abbey, where the blessed "Rood of Grace" wrought miracles, in the popular fancy only second to those of St. Thomas of Canterbury; 2nd, Penenden Heath, where the Norman Bishops met to try Odo, the half-brother of William the Conqueror, and Wat. Tyler rallied his Kentish mal-contents; and 3rd the Wiat family, who had their seat there for centuries, becoming possessors of the Abbey, after it was confiscated by the crown. The pedigree of Francis Wiat, Governor of Virginia from 1621 to 1626, and from 1639 to 1642, is Adam[1], William[2], Robert, Geoffrey[4], Richard[5], Sir Henry[6], Sir Thomas[7], Sir Thomas[8] the younger, George[9], Francis.[10] Of these, two names previous to our Francis, shine out conspicuously.—The first is Sir Henry, who for his friendship to Henry VII underwent, at the hands of Richard III, severe imprisonment and was saved from starvation by a cat which brought him food. The monumental inscription in Boxley Church to the Wiat family states this fact, and so does one of the "Wiat MSS." in possession of Lord Romney, the present representative of the Wiat family in England. The latter says: "He was imprisoned often; once in a cold and narrow Tower, where he had neither bed to lie on, nor clothes sufficient to warm him, nor meat for his mouth; he had starved there had not God * * sent * * a cat both to feed and warm him * * It was his own relation from whom I had it. A cat came one day down into the dungeon unto him, and, as it were, offered herself unto him; he was glad of her, laid her in his bosome, to warm him, and by making much of her won her love. After this she would come every day unto him diverse times; and when she could get one, bring him a pigeon * * * and * * the keeper * * dressed for him from time to time such pigeons as his *Acater*, the cat, provided for him. Sir Henry in his prosperity would ever make much of a cat and perhaps you will never find a picture of him anywhere, but—like Sir Christopher Hatton with his dog—with a cat beside him." After the usurper Richard fell on Bosworth field Sir Henry Wiat was raised to the highest honors—Knight of the Bath, Knight Banneret, Privy Councillor etc., and was executor of King Henry. The second great representative of the Wiat family was Sir Thomas Wiat, the younger, grandson of Sir Henry. He attempted to raise a rebellion against Queen Mary in order to prevent her alliance with Philip of Spain, was captured and beheaded. His estates were confiscated, but Queen Elizabeth granted a revocation of the bill of attainder in favor of George, Sir Thomas' eldest son and the representative of the house, and restored to him a portion of the old estate and the reversion of the Abbey house and land. Sir Thomas Wiat, Jr. married Jane, daughter of Sir William Hawte or

84

Haute of Bourne, and George, his only son that lived to age, married Jane, daughter of Sir Thomas Finch and had Sir Francis, Hawte and Eleanor, [This is according to the Wiat monument and the"History of Boxley *Parish*," by Rev. J.Cave-Brown, M. A., vicar of Detling, Kent, 1892. According, however, to Wiat pedigree from Vincent's *Kent* 116 p. 73, printed in *Works of Surrey and Wiat*, edited by G. F. Nott, D.D. London, 1816, vol. I I, there were also three younger sons, Henry, George and Thomas]. Sir Francis Wiat changed the spelling to "Wyat," and died in 1644 leaving the Boxley property to his eldest son, Henry. Henry was succeeded by his eminent brother Edwin, Chief Justice of the grand sessions for the counties of Carmarthen, Pembroke and Cardigan, Member of Parliament for Maidstone, etc. His sons, Francis and Richard, died without issue. The old site of the Abbey is now owned by Major Mawdestly G. Best, of Park House; and another portion of the ancient possessions, called *Boxley House* estate, which was bequeathed by Richard Wyat to his relative Robert, Lord Romney was recently purchased by Albert F. Style, great-grandson of the second Lord Romney. In the church, besides the monumental tablets to the Wiats, may be mentioned a tablet to George Sandys, who translated the Iliad in Virginia and a tablet to the Athawes family, placed there in 1799 by Samuel Athawes, "son and successor of Edward Athawes, a Virginian merchant of London."

The Wiat tablet, after stating that George Wiat was succeeded by "his eldest son, Sir Francis Wiat, twice governor, and married Margaret, daughter of Sir Samuel Sandys" [elder brother of the poet George] says that he, George, "left also Haute Wiat who died vicar of this parish and hath issue living in Virginia." The following is from Rev. J. Cave-Brown himself, who is fully informed on the Wiat pedigrees:

"Detling Vicarage, Maidstone [Kent Co.]. The Boxley Register imply that Haute Wiat married his first wife, Elizabeth, *before he was ordained*, and had by her a son Thomas—his wife dying 14 days after the child's baptism and the child himself on the 10th of the following April. By his 2d wife, Anne, he had a daughter, Anna; this wife died 12 days after the birth of the child. From the family pedigree I find he had by his first wife two other sons, George and Edward, and by his 2d wife a son, John. These must have been the "fons et origo of the Virginian Wiats."

The tradition in the Gloucester Co., Va. family is that they derive descent from Rev. Hawte or Haute Wiatt, and the name of their old home is "Boxley." When their ancestry is traced, we find that their progenitor was Edward Wyat, who is found first with George Wyat, living together at this place (then called Middle Plantation) as early as 1645 (York records—Land Register.) Edward Wyat was administrator in 1644 of John Clarke dec'd (who had also lived here), son of Sir John Clarke of Wrotham in Kent Co., England, the younger and only brother of Sir William Clarke of that place. In 1652 "Mr. Wiat"

85

represented Hannah Clarke, [doubtless the widow of John Clarke dece'd] as the executrix of Sir Dudley Wyatt, whose will, dated 29th March 1650, was recorded at Jamestown 25 7 ber, 1651, and devises land near the "Middle Plantation" to her. Hannah sold the same to Dr. Jeremiah Harrison, of Queen's Creek. [In 1654 Mrs. Frances Harrison, widow, patented 1000 acres in Westmoreland, headrights Dr. Jeremy Harrison, Frances Harrison etc. John Harrison, patented 1000 acres in Westmoreland, failing his heirs to "his sister," Mrs. Frances Harrison,and failing her heirs to Giles Brent of "Peace",Westmoreland Co.(Land Register). Dr. Jeremiah Harrison married Frances, sister of Thomas Whitgreave of Mosely in Stafford County, England, who saved the life of Charles II after the battle of Worcester in 1651. (Burke's "Landed Gentry.") In 1652 Mrs. Clarke patented lands near Williamsburg adjoining the lands of Col. Philip Honiwood, who came with Sir Thomas Lunsford, and the lands of Joseph Croshaw, whose daughter Unity had married John West, nephew of Lord Delaware. Sir Dudley Wyat had also served in the army of Charles I.—See Clarendon's History. He was one of the grantees of the Northern Neck from Charles II, dated at "St, Germains" in France, Sept. 18, 1650, and he came to Virginia at once.]

In 1663 "Edward Wyat, gentleman" patented John Clarke's land at "Middle Plantation,"as an escheat, and subsequently, with his wife Jane, sold it in 1667 to George Poindexter and Otho Thorpe,of Middle Plantation. But the General Court decided 22 March, 1675-6 that the property belonged to John Clarke of Wrotham, in England. (York Co., General Court, and Land Records) In 1662 he patented lands in Gloucester, and subsequently hailed from there. In 1665 he was security for Edward Conquest, to serve James Miller of Surry "in sea affairs," for two years of his term assigned by "Capt. John Scott, Esq., of the Long Island." In 1672 Conquest Wyat, "son and heir" of Edward Wyat, patented lands on Hoccadie's Creek, near his old Plantation. Conquest was vestryman (1690), sheriff (1705) etc. Petsworth Vestry book shows that the following Wyats were vestrymen there: Francis from 1710 to 1728, Conquest 1727. Capt. Edward 1740, Capt. John 1753; Peter 1763; Capt. John 1775; James 1787. From this parish a steady stream has been sent out all over the State. Rev. William E. Wiatt, pastor of Newington and Petsworth Baptist churches, is descended from Captain John Wiatt of Gloucester, who married Miss Mary Todd and had Dr. William E. Wiatt, sheriff of Gloucester Co. in 1802. He married Mary, daughter of John Graham of Prince William Co., and had 1. John who m Cecelia Dabney 2. Dr. W. G. Wyatt who m . Louisa dau. of John S. Stubbs 3. Eliza who m. Walker Jones 4. Eleanor who m. Col. Scott of Petersburg 5. Col. Thomas Todd 6. Col. Hawte.

George Wyat, "Coop" (Cooper) lived at "Middle Plantation" as early as 1645, had in 1660 a wife Susannah; in 1671 his son and heire", Henry of Gloucester, sold his land here to John Page (York records.) Henry was born in 1647, and lived with wife Alice in New Kent Co.; vestryman of St. Peters in 1686. In 1705 Richard Wyat's son Henry of New Kent, was legatee of Henry W. dece'd. In 1728 Henry of Prince George released a mill in New Kent. (Henrico Co. records, Adams MSS.)

Other early Wiatts in Virginia were (1) *Ralph* who leased land on Appomattox river in 1636; wife was widow of Capt. William Button (2) *Richard* patented in Gloucester in 1645, and ordered by York Court to pay a hogshead of tobacco to Dr. Thomas Eaton of London, "cururgeon," His son and heir, *Thomas*, patented in Gloucester in 1665. (3) *William*, evidently a kinsman of Edward Wyat, was witness to a deed in 1655 to "Mr. Edward Wyat"from the "Chiscoyake"Indians; major and sheriff of New Kent in 1671, married before 1674 Anna "the mother of Anna Jackson" (York records); had a son William jun. who patented in 1670.(4.)*Anthony* was burgess from Charles City in 1645, '55, '56, was called Major, and had son, Capt. Nicholas, active in Bacon's Rebellion, who patented in 1686 "Chaplin's Choice" etc. (5) *Christopher*, 26 in 1672 (York records,) probably a son of one of the preceding. (6,) *Thomas* patented in 1643. [For notices of later Wyats in Virginia see W. G. Stanard's Paper in Richmond *Critic*, Dec. 10, 1889 and R. A. Brock's notes in New Eng. Hist. and Gen. Register, vol. 40, p. 43, and Virginia Hist. Soc. Coll. VIII, p. 102. The following in addition may not be without value:

From *Abingdon Parish Register*: Mr. Francis Wyatt married to Miss. Lucy Row, Oct. 30, 1742
Mary dau^r. of Mr Francis and Lucy Wyatt,
Anne dau^r. of Mr Francis and Lucy Wyatt
From *St. Peters Parish Register*: Peyton son of Joseph and Dorothy Wyatt born Nov. 15, 1763,

The Wyatt arms are: Party perfesse, azure and gules, a barnacle argent.

The Hawte arms are: Or a cross engrailed gules.

The name of the Wiatt family is variously spelled in our records, but the spelling of the Gloucester branch seems now to be "Wiatt."]

(2) "Violet Banks" is the modern name of the house of Edward Porteus, the emigrant. It is an old square brick building, two stories and a half, with four rooms to a floor. Though abandoned, it still retains the fine panelling and interior carving of the long past. It fronts York River and on the west is Poropotank Creek. Robert Porteus, his, son lived at "New Bottle," subsequently called "Concord." In 1693 Edward Porteus was recommended by the Governor of Virginia for appointment to the Council (Sainsbury MSS.), vestry man of Petsworth Parish in 1681 (vestry book). He married "the Relict of Robert Lee," who left in his will seven pounds to the poor of Petsworth (Ibid).

His only son, Robert Porteus, Esq. was vestryman in 1704, member of the Council and removed to York, England; and in the Cathedral at Rippon is an inscription on the walls to his memory. (Spotswood's *Letters*, II. 54.) He had nineteen children, the youngest of whom but one, Beilby Porteus, was born at York, May 8, 1731, and died May 14, 1808. He became bishop of Chester and of London, (Chalmer's Biographical Dictionary.) This College, however, owes him no thanks, for he boasts of having induced Lord Thurlow to exclude it from all share in the fund of the Honble Robert Boyle long used for the education of Indians and diverted after the Revolution, at the suggestion of Porteus, to the conversion and religious instruction of the Negroes in the British West Indies (5 Versey jr's Reports; Brown's "History of the Propagation of Christianity," II p. 625). What a contrast this action to the splendid conduct of the English Court in 1867, when the Mary Whaley fund for the establishment of a free-school in York and James City Counties, after lying forgotten of men in the Bank of England for 136 years, was turned over to the control of the College for the purpose indicated. Robert Porteus married the daughter of Edmund Jennings, Esq., son of Sir Edmund of Rippon, England. One of his places in Gloucester county was called "New Bottle," after a place of similar name in Scotland owned by him. The Bishop, his son, had "a singular picture which though not in the best style of coloring was yet thought valuable by Sir Joshua Reynolds as a specimen of the extent to which the art of painting had at that time reached in America, and he himself very highly prized it as exhibiting a faithful and interesting representation of his father's residence." (See "Life of Bishop Porteus," by Rev. Robert Hodgson.)

The neighborhood of the Porteuses in Virginia was certainly respectable. At an interval of a mile along the York River shore, or up the numerous creeks were well built brick houses, some few of which still remain. Going down the river from the Porteus mansion, one passed successively the lands of the Smiths of Purton, the family of Capt. John Stubbs, the Burwells of Carter's Creek, the Warners, of Warner Hall, the Pages of Rosewell, the Manns of Timberneck, the Perrins of Sarah's creek, etc., while on the opposite shore, were the houses of Edmund Jenings, Nathaniel Bacon, Dudley Digges, the Ballards, the Reades, the Smiths, Chismans, Calthorpes etc.—families of first consequence in the colony, having good libraries, most of them of proved descent from respectable English gentlemen, and all of them displaying coats-of-arms of undoubted authenticity.

(3) For an account of the Robins family see Richmond *Critic* Aug. 14, 1889. The imigrant was John Robins of Elizabeth City, whose son, Dr. Thomas Robins, married Mary, sister of Major Thomas Hansford, the first Virginian born ever hanged; and settled in Robins.

Neck, Gloucester county, where his descendants resided until the present time.

(4) Col. George Reade was brother of Robert Reade, private Secretary to Windebank, Secretary of State to Charles I. and married Elizabeth, daughter of Capt. Nicholas Martian and had 1. Mildred, who married Augustine Warner, 2. George, living in 1655, 3. Robert, who married Mary, daughter of John Lilly (who married the heiress of Edward Malson, a cooper of York county living in 1657,) 4. Francis who married 1st, Jane Chisman, daughter of Capt. Thomas Chisman and had Mary who m. Edward Davis of K. and Q.,and Elizabeth who married Paul Watlington before 1707. He married 2dly Anne—, before 1693. He had also George and Anne. He died about 1694, leaving a son Benjamin living in 1715. 5. Benjamin married Lucy before 1692. In 1691 he sold fifty acres for the site of Yorktown, and after living about forty years later died, and in 1738 his eldest son Gwyn Reade, who married Dorothy—, sold five acres as a commons for the citizens of Yorktown. 6. Thomas Reade married Lucy Gwyn, daughter of Edmund Gwyn, and had Thomas (tombstone) died without issue, and Rev. John of King and Queen, dead before 1769, leaving an only daughter Sarah who married John Rootes. 7. Elizabeth who married Capt. Thomas Chisman.

Robert, the eldest son, died in 1712, and had John of St. Stephen's parish K. & Q. Co., Robert, George, Samuel, Francis, Thomas, Margaret married Thomas Nelson and Mildred married 1st James Goodwin 2d Capt. Lawrence Smith. Robert had Robert who had Elizabeth who married 1st Rev. Richard Hewitt 2. Col. Edward Harwood. Samuel, another son of Robert Reade, married Mary. Nutting, and had Frances who married Major Anthony Robinson.

There were other Reades in York county contemporaneous with George Reade Esq. Thomas Reade, called in the records his "kinsman," lived in Warwick and married Elizabeth, daughter of John and Ruth (Beale) Tiplady. According to the will of Mrs. Alice Beale, wife of Col. Thomas Beale of the Council, and mother of Ruth Tiplady, he had living in 1702 two sons, John and Thomas Reade. Benjamin Reade, probably a brother of Col. George Reade,(will proved in York Co. Jan. 24, 169⅔) calls "Mr. Robert Reade and Mr. Francis Reade" kinsmen" and their sons "nephews;" calls Elizabeth, daughter of Capt. Thomas Chisman "niece" and makes his two kinsmen, "Mr. Robert and Mr. Francis Reade" executors. Other persons mentioned in will are "niece Anne Cary, daughter of Mr. Henry Cary," "James Manders brother of my deceased wife,""Mrs. Elizabeth Flowers, mother of my deceased wife," "aunt" Mary Myhill, Ralph Flowers jr. and Samuel Flowers. Gives 20 £ to the poor of Mulberry Islands parish, and has lands in England and Merchants' Hundred, James City Co. [Hening's Statutes V. 68; VIII. 483; wills of Elizabeth Reade, widow of Col. George, pr. Jan. 24, 1686-7, of Robert Reade (1712), of

Mary Reade (1722,), of Samuel Reade, 1758 etc.]

(5) Petsworth was probably pronounced "Petsoe" as the vestry book calls the parish by the last name. The parish was probably named for the Bernard family who came from Petsworth, Buckinghamshire. Mr. W. G. Stanard writes:

"From Chester's London Marriage Licences, license Nov. 24, 1634, to Richard Bernard, of Petsoe, Bucks, Gent. widower, 26 [years]. and Anna Corderoy spinster, 22, dau. of Mr. [blank] Corderoy Esq. decd. [to be married] at St. Andrews–in–the–wardrobe.

There is a pedigree of Bernard in Lipscomb's History of Bucks I. 519, 521 and of "Cordray" in the visitation of Wiltshire, 1623."

There is a grant to Mrs. Anna Bernard in which Richard Bernard, Mrs. Anna B., Cordery B., Edward Cordery, etc., are head-rights. From a deed [1653] found in Westmoreland it appears that Mrs. Bernard had a daughter, Ann Smith; probably in this way Purton came to the Smiths. In York records Richard Bernard purchased Pryor's plantation in 1647. The clerk makes a drawing of his arms on the scroll in the Record Book, which is clearly a bear rampant and common to families of the name in Bucks, Lincoln, Northants etc. "Anna Barnard of Purton" in 1662 sold Pryor's Plantation to Capt. Robert Baldrey. In Westmoreland Co. records, Richard Bernard of Petsoe parish, Gloucester Co. empowers in 1689 William Buckner of Stafford to receive 400 acres granted to Ann Bernard and assigned to said Richard. Barradall's Reports (1738) show that in 1651 and 1654 Anna Bernard obtained patents for land, which on her death descended to her son Richard, who died in 1691, leaving the land by his will to sons Philip and John. John had the whole by survivorship and died in 1709, devising the land to his son Richard, his heir, aged 25 when the suit was brought.—Legan, lessee of Richard Bernard plt vs. Washington Parish, Dishman, Weeden, John and William Brown defts.

Hening shows that William Bernard of Gloucester (will made 1704) had son Robert alive 1734. [Bernard, Balnard, Barnett were the same.] Richard Barnard was vestryman of Petsworth in 1677 (vestry book.) Mr. William Barnard was churchwarden in 1695. Peter Bernard of Gloucester was Captain in the Revolution. His brother and heir, John Bernard of Buckingham, was sheriff there in 1781, and married Heningham dau. of Col. George Carrington. Capt. Peter B. had a sister, Margaret, who married in 1764 George Carrington. There have been numerous representatives of the Bernard name in Virginia.

Col. William Bernard, of the Council, had a son George living in 1653, and was then husband of Lucy, widow of Lewis Burwell. Col. William died in 1662. Capt. Thomas Bernard was burgess for Warwick in 1642, 1643, and 1645.

Nothing now remains of old Petsworth church, of which Meade

gives an interesting account. There is near by a famous spring of cool water.

6. See Jan. Quarterly, 1894, for notice of the Jones tombs.*

7. Ware Parish church is built on land granted to the church by the Throckmorton family. It is a rectangular brick building and is in good repair. Rev. Mr. Lee now officiates here, and at Abingdon church, and York church.

8. Meade prints the name James Black, which is a mistake. William Thornton Sen. (William[1] Thornton, William[2], Franciss[3]) married Jane Clack, of Brunswick Co., born June 9, 1721 (Family Bible.) She was perhaps a grand-daughter. James Clack was living in Gloucester in 1740 (York records), guardian of Charlotte, d. of Robert Ballard, dec'd, of York.

9. This and the three subsequent inscriptions are taken from Meade, the original stones being concealed under the church floor.

10. Francis Willis was an early settler in York county, Virginia in which he had a patent for land in 1642. In 1640 he was removed from his office as clerk, for abusing the governor and council and burgesses, and punished by having to stand at the court-house door with a paper in his hat and disabled from being a clerk or attorney in any court, pay a fine etc. In 1645 he was Justice of York county, and in 1652 burgess for Gloucester Co. The will of Richard Simons (dated 13 July, 1647), who was brother and heir of Thomas Simons deceased, mentions his eldest son Richard in England and his brother, Francis Willis, and makes Mr. Thomas Curtis, of the new Pawquosin parish, supervisor of his will etc. The will of Francis Willis, his son, shows that he left 1. Francis, died in 1691, 2. Henry who had Susannah, Mary Herren, Alice, Francis, William 3. William who had William (New Eng. and Hist. Gen. Register, Vol. 41, 257.)

York records mention in 1732 Henry Willis of Spotsylvania and Mildred his wife, (late widow of John Brown, dec'd in 1726); that Francis son of Francis, of Gloucester Co., married Elizabeth, daughter of John Perrin of Gloucester about 1767.

Abingdon Parish Register shows that "Mr. Francis Willis married Elizabeth Carter Sept. 30, 1742."

11 Mary Mann was widow of Edmund Berkeley, deceased, before 1674. The will of John Mann, her second husband, was proved in, Gloucester County court 13 Feb.,1694,and the original paper preserved bears date 6 Jan., 1694-5, gives his cousin Mary Hampton 500 £ sterling, son–in–law Edmund Berkeley 50 £ sterling; god. dau. Ann Booker 20 £ sterling; ⅓ of the rest of his real and personal estate to his wife, Mary, and the balance to his daughter, Mary Page, and for want of heirs to go equally to my son-in-law Edmund Berkeley and my cousin Mary Hampton, and for want of heirs to go to my two grandchildren Joseph and Edmund Ring, and for want of heirs then to the College "for ye maintenance of Poor children"; mentions

*Pages 80-81, this volume.

Mr. John Williams, son-in-law Matthew Page; Mr. Stephen Ford and Capt. Richard Booker to see this will performed, Witnesses Richard Booker, George Jonson, Willock Bostock. P. Beverly cl. cur. Joseph Ring's will was proved in York Co. May 24, 1703—he was justice, burgess, and recommended to the council; five children Edmund, Joseph, Elizabeth, Sarah and Mary, legacy of 100£ to Isaac Sedgwick, and appoints his loving brothers, Capt. Matthew Page and Mr. Edmund Bartlet (Berkeley is often spelt this way) exors. [Isaac Sedgwick was a lawyer and brother of William Sedgwick, clerk of York county, who in his will calls himself of Burlen Hall, in Lincolnshire. Hottens' "Immigrants" has John Mann, aged 21, transported to Barbadoes in 1635. Feb. 1, 13 Charles II, John Mann, gent. appointed chief surveyor of Jamaica.]

For description of the arms on Mary Mann's tomb see "Coats-of Arms" in last Quarterly.

1£. This tomb has arms different from the usual Page arms; being within a lozenge a cross engrailed, in the right hand corner a conch shell.

———

OLD TOMBSTONES IN GLOUCESTER COUNTY, VA.

COLLECTED BY THE EDITOR.

XVII.

Toddbury,[1] on North River.

Here Lyes Interred
The Body of Frances Todd[2]
who was born April 12, 1692
And departed this Life
November the 5th 1703.

Here Lyes the Body of
Capt. Christopher Todd
who was born the 2d Day of April in the
Year of our Lord 1690 and Departed
This Life the 26th of March 1743.

Here lyes the Body of
Capt. Thomas Todd, Sen.,
who was Born in the Year of our Lord
1660 and Departed this Life the 16th
day of January 172½

Here lies the Body of
George Wythe Booth
who departed this Life
Decr 20th 1808
in the 36th year of his age.

Here lies the body of
James H. Roy
who departed this life
On the 18th March 1825
in the 49th year of his age.

Here lies the body of
Mrs. Elizabeth Roy
wife of
James H. Roy
who departed this life
On the 15th of April 1813
in the 41st year of her age.

Here lies the body of
Mary Jones,
Relict of
the Rev'd Emanuel Jones
who departed this life
April 18th 1820
in the seventy-first year of her age.

Here lies the Body of
Mary E. Booth
Daughter of
George W. and Lucy B. Booth
who departed this Life
On the 12th of September, 1818
in the eighteenth year of her age.

Here lies the body of
Philip A. Smith
second son of the
Rev'd Armistead Smith
And Martha Smith
who
after a lingering and painful illness
which he bore with uncommon
Christian fortitude
departed this life
the 1st day of October 1813
in the 25th year of his age
universally lamented by his numerous
relations, friends and acquaintances.

In memory of
Thomas Smith
Eldest son of
The Rev'd Armistead and Martha Smith,
of Mathews County, Virginia.
Born March 5th, 1785
Died April 13th 1841.

In Memory of
Thomas Todd Tabb
Eldest son of
Philip and Mary
who was born
The 4th of Dec. 1782
And departed this Life
The 20th of June, 1835.

Here lies the Body
of Lucy Armistead Tabb
Daughter of
The Rev. Armistead Smith
And the Wife
of Thomas Todd Tabb
who departed this life
Nov. 14th, 1821
in the 39th year of her age.

———————

Within this Tomb
rest the mortal remains of
Frances A. Taliaferro [3]
late wife of
Warner Taliaferro
and Daughter to
George and Lucy Booth.
In the full tide of youth, beauty and
all the external Blessings of friends
and fortune she sunk to an early, not
untimely grave
For the beauty of holyness illumined
her path and she was ripe for eternity.
She departed this life
April 3d 1824
Aged 22 years.

———————

Sacred to the memory of the
Rev. Armistead Smith
of Mathews county
Who after having faithfully served God
in the Gospel of his Son
departed this life
Sept'r 12, 1817,
aged 60 years 9 months & 12 days
If sincerity in friendship, a heart glowing
with true piety, benevolence & charity
have a claim to lasting regard the memory
of the deceased will be fondly cherished.

Here lies the Body of
Martha Smith
Relict
of the Rev. Armistead Smith
and daughter
of Edward & Mary Tabb
who was born Oct'r 21st, 1757
and departed this life
Sept'r 16th, 1821.

Philip Tabb
Son of
Edward & Lucy Tabb
Born 6th day of November, 1750
Departed this life 25th day of Feb'y
1822.

Edward Tabb
son of
John Tabb & Martha his wife
born the 3d day of February 1719
departed this life
29th day of January, 1782

Here lies the body of
Pauline Booth
daughter of
Edward and Lucy Tabb
and wife of
George W. Booth
who departed this life
on the 6th of April 1794
in the 29th year of her age.

Lucy Tabb
daughter of
Christopher and Elizabeth Todd.
Born November 20, 1721.
Departed this Life
18th day of February, 1791.[4]

XVIII.—ABINGDON PLACE.

In Memory of
Richard Coke,[5]
Born Nov. 16, 1790.
Died March 31st 1851.
Beloved in life, lamented in death,
The best consolation of his friends
is their hope of his
Immortality.

NOTES BY THE EDITOR.

[1] Toddbury is now occupied by the Mott family, having passed out of the Todd family, to which it belonged for generations. The building upon the place is of brick, and upon the chimney on one side I have read, carved in the brick, the year 1722. It probably suggests some repairs made in that year, as the tombstones indicate a much earlier origin. The house is not large, but is beautifully panelled within, and dispensed a princely hospitality. The scenery of the North river is exquisite. Every half mile or so, some handsome residence decorates the shore—Newstead, Toddbury, Exchange, Elmington, Dunham Massie, Green Plains, Auburn, Isleham, etc.

[2] There is one tomb at Toddbury so worn as to be undecipherable. It is supposed to be that of the father of Capt. Thomas Todd, Sen.

[3] Mother of General William B. Taliaferro.

[4] TABB.—The first of this family in Virginia was Humphrey Tabb, who appears from the Land-Books to have settled in Elizabeth City county about 1637, and was a justice of that county in 1652. In 1662 there is a grant to Thos. Tabb, son and heir of Humphrey Tabb, deceased. From these descended the families of the name in Elizabeth City, York, Gloucester, Mathews, Amelia, Norfolk, Mecklenburg, etc. Among the prominent representatives of the name before and during the Revolution were Thos. Tabb, Sheriff of Elizabeth City, 1708 and 1709; Thos. Tabb, Sheriff of Amelia, 1741, and many years Burgess, who died Nov. 27, 1709; John Tabb, Burgess for Amelia from about 1753 to 1774, member of the Convention of 1774, and of the Colonial Committee of Safety, 1775–'6; John Tabb, Burgess for Elizabeth City, 1748–'58; and Augustine Tabb, captain in the State line during the Revolution.

TODD.—Several of the name appear early in the seventeenth century. Robert Todd is mentioned in the York records in 1642, and bought land in Gloucester in 1652. In 1666 there is a grant of land in Gloucester to Wm. Todd, "son and heir of Robert Todd, deceased," Thos. Todd patented land in Elizabeth City in 1647, and in Gloucester in 1664. Branches of the family were long resident in Gloucester and in King and Queen. The most prominent man of the name was Thos. Todd, of Kentucky, Justice of the United States Supreme Court, who was born in King and Queen county, Va. The History of Baltimore County, Md., states that a Major Thomas Todd came from Virginia, patented land at North Point in 1664, and left a son Thomas.

[5] Richard Coke was a distinguished Virginia politician and Member of Congress, uncle of the present Senator Coke, of Texas.

97

OLD TOMBSTONES IN GLOUCESTER COUNTY.

COLLECTED BY THE EDITOR.

WARE CHURCH. [1]

XVIII.
[Arms [2].]

Here lyeth the body of M[rs]
Ann Willis the wife of Col[ll] Francis
Willis who departed this life y[e]
10th of June, 1727 in the 32[d] year of her age
Also the Body of Ann Willis
Daughter of y[e] above said aged 7 days

———

Underneath this Stone
Lieth Interred the Body of
Amy Richards the most
Dearly Beloved wife of
John Richards minister
of the Parish who

98

Departed this life the 21ˢᵗ
of November 1725
Aged 40 years.
Near
Her dear Mistris lies the
Body of Mary Ades Her
Faithful and Beloved
Servant who Departed
this life the 23ᵈ of Nov.
1725 Aged 28 years

[Arms ².]
Underneath this stone lyeth the Body of
Mʳ John Richards
late Rector of Nettlestead and Vicar of Teston
in the County of Kent in the kingdom of
England and Minister of Ware in the County
of Gloucester and Colony of Virginia who after
a troublesome passage thro' the various changes
and chances of this Mortal life is at last reposed
in this silent Grave in expectation of a joyful
Resurrection to Eternal Life.   He departed the twelfth
Day of Novembʳ in the year of our Lord
MDCCXXXV Aged XLVI years.

[Arms ⁴.]
Here lieth the Body of Isabella the
Daughter of Mʳ Thomas Booth
wife of the Revᵈ Mʳ John Fox
Minister of this Parish
who with exemplary patience
having borne various afflictions
and with equal Piety
discharged her Several Duties
on Earth
Chearfully yielded to Mortality
exchanging the miseries of this life
for the joys of a glorious Eternity
on the 13ᵗʰ day of June in the year
of our Lord MDCCXLII of her Age XXXVIII

Here also lie the Bodies of Mary
and Susannah Daughter of the
above mentioned John and Isabella
the one departed this life
on the 5th day of Sept. 1742
in the 4th year of her age
the other on the 8th of October in the 3d year
of her age MDCCXLIII

XIX.

WAVERLEY.

In memory of Doctor
Richard Edwards
who departed
This Life the 8
Day of March in
The Year 1721
Having had two
Wives and at the
Time of his Death
Nine children
Living
[Skull and cross bones.]

---

*   *   *   *   *   *   *
*   *   *   *   Richard
Edwards[5] who departed
this Life the
*   *   *   March
In the Year 170[7]

XX.

EXCHANGE [6].

Here lies the body of
Mary Anderson
born 27th Aug. 1749
and
died on 12th June 1820.

Here lies the body of
Mathew Anderson Esq
born 6th Decemb. 1743
and
died on 24 Decr 1806.

Here lies the Body of
George Dabney Anderson
son of
Mathew & Mary Anderson
who was born October 8th 1760
and departed this Life
Septemb 9, 1771.
Snatched in his Dawn (how Swift our Blessings fly)
Here the fond hopes of his grieved Parents lye
But cease to weep, look up ye mournful pair
Behold your Darling a bright Seraph there
See how he beckons from yon distant sphere
Here fix your Hopes, he cries, your
Treasure's here.

XXI.
ROSEWELL. [7]
[Arms [8].]
Here lieth interred ye Body of ye Honourable
Collonell Mathew Page Esqr one of her Maj^{tes}
most Honourable Councell of the Parish of
Abington in the county of Gloucester in the
Collony of Virginia
Son of the Honourable Collonell John & Alice
Page of the Parish of Bruton in the County
of Yorke in ye aforesaid Collony, who Departed
this life in the 9th day of January Ann^o
Dom. 1703 in ye 45 year of his Age.

[Arms [9].]
Here lyeth Interr'd the Body
of Mary Page wife of the
Honble Mathew Page Esq.
one of Her Majestyes Councel
of this Collony of Virginia and

101

Daughter of John and Mary
Mann of this Collony, who
Departed this life y⁰ 24ᵗʰ Day
of March in y⁰ year of our
Lord 1707 in y⁰ Thirty Sixᵗʰ
year of her age.

———

Near this Place lye interred the Body of
Mathew Page Son of y⁰ honourable Collonᵉˡˡ
Mathew Page Esqʳ. and Mary his wife
who Departed this life y⁰ 31ˢᵗ day of December
Anñ Dom 1702 in y⁰ 5ᵗʰ month of his Age.
Allso the Body of Mary Page Daughter
to Collonᵉˡˡ Matthew Page Esqʳ & Mary
his wife who Departed this life y⁰ 14ᵗʰ day of
Jañ: Anñ Dom 170⅔ in the 7ᵗʰ yeare of her Age

———

[Arms [10].]
Here lie the remains of the Honourable Mann Page Esq [11]
One of his Majesties Council of this Collony
of Virginia
who departed this Life the 24ᵗʰ Day of January 1730
In the 40ᵗʰ Year of his Age.
He was the only Son of the Honourable Mathew Page Esqʳ.
who was likewise a Member of his Majesties Council.
His first wife was Judith Daughter of Ralph Wormeley Esq.
Secretary of Virginia;
By whom he had two sons and a Daughter.
He afterwards married Judith Daughter of the Honᵇˡ Robert
Carter Esqʳ.
President of Virginia
with whom he lived in the most tender reciprocal affection
For twelve Years.:
Leaving by her Five Sons and a Daughter
His publick Trust he faithfully Discharged
with
Candour and Discretion
Truth and Justice.
Nor was he less eminent in His Private Behaviour
For he was

102

A tender Husband and Indulgent Father
A gentle Master and a faithfull Friend
Being to All
Courteous and Benevolent Kind and Affable
This Monument was Piously Erected to His Memory
By His mourfully Surviving Lady.

Sacræ et Piæ Memoriæ
Hoc monumentum positum doloris,
ab Honorato Mann Page armigero
Charissimæ suæ conjugis
Judithæ,
In ipso ætatis flore decussæ,
Ornatissimi Ralphi Wormeley
de Agro Middlesexiæ
Armigeri
Nec non Virginiani Secretarii quondam Meritissimi
Filiæ dignissimæ
Lectissimæ delectissimæque fœminæ
Quæ vixit in Sanctissimo matrimonio
quatuor annos totidemque menses
Utriusque Sexus unum Superstitem
reliquit
Ralphum et Mariam
vera Patris simul et Matris ectypa
Habuitque tertium Mann nominatum
vix quinque dies videntem
Sub hoc Silenti Marmore Matre sua inclusum
Post cujus partum tertio die
Mortalitatem pro immortalitate
commutavit
Proh dolor!
Inter uxores amantissima
Inter Matres fuit optima
Candida Domina
Cui summa comitas
Cum venustissima suavitate morum et sermonam
Conjuncta
Obiit duodecimo die Decembris
Anno Milessimo Septingessimo decimo Sexto
Aetatis Suæ vicessimo Secundo.

Here lies the Body of Mrs Alice Page
Wife of Mann Page Esq.
She departed this life on the 11th Day of January [1746]
In child bed of her second Son
in the 23rd year of her age
Leaving
Two Sons and one Daughter
She was the third daughter
of the Honourable John Grimes Esq.
of
Middlesex County
one of his Majesty's Council in this Colony
of Virginia
Her personal Beauty
and the uncommon Sweetness of her Temper
Her affable Deportment and Exemplary Behaviour
Made her respected by all who knew
The Spotless Innocency of her Life
and her singular Piety
Her constancy & Resignation at the Hour of death
Sufficiently testified
Her firm & certain Hopes of a joyfull Resurrection
To her Sacred Memory
This Monument is piously erected.

Here lieth interr'd the Body of
Tayloe Page
Third Son of Mann and
Ann Corbin Page
who departed this life
the 29th Day of November 1760
in the 5th year of his Age.

NOTES.

---

[1] WARE CHURCH.—These inscriptions as given by Bishop Meade were published in the July QUARTERLY, pp. 32–34. September 20, 1894, the chancel which concealed them was taken up, and the copies now printed are from the originals which had been concealed since several years before the war.

[2] These arms represent Wyllys impaling Rich. It appears from the Sainsbury MSS. that the Francis Willis who died in 1691 was the original emigrant and not his son, as I was inclined to think. (See page 42.) He was clerk of

York county, burgess, councillor. There is a mention in the Sainsbury MSS. about 1680, that Col. Francis Willis, of the Council, had gone to England, where it seems he died in 1691 at an advanced age. To the information contained in the note, p. 42, add: "Henry, son of Francis and Elizabeth Willis, born November 8, 1760."—*Abingdon Parish Register*. In 1712 Francis Willis, of London, merchant, Katharine Bristow and Robert Bristow executors of Robert Bristow, deceased, are mentioned.—*York County Records*. Investigations in England would, no doubt, produce interesting results in reference to this family.

[3] See *Ante* for a description of these arms.

[4] These arms represent the Fox family.

[5] This inscription is much worn, but I have been informed it honored the memory of one of the wives of Dr. Edwards.

[6] There are some interesting portraits at Exchange by the Gloucester County, painter, Huberd: Portraits of Thomas Todd Tabb, of Elizabeth Foreman his wife, of Martha Tompkins who married Dr. Henry Wythe Tabb, and of Dr. James Dabney.

[7] The inscriptions at "Rosewell" have been published in the "Page Family," but as printed above they were by me compared in the book with the originals. Some verbal inaccuracies were found to exist. Rosewell was built by Hon. Mann Page. The main building has two large halls (out of each hall three good-sized rooms may be made), nine passages, fourteen large rooms, nine small rooms, basement, an attic, and a cupola. It had two wings (now pulled down), which contained six rooms apiece. They formed the court; and the front of the original building and wings was two hundred and thirty-two feet. The main building is three stories and a basement. The large rooms are at least twenty feet square, and the small ones fourteen by seven.

[8] The arms on this tomb are the usual Page arms, with crescent for difference.

[9] Same arms as [8].

[10] The arms are Page impaling Carter.

[11] The tombstone of Hon. Mann Page is sadly wrecked, but all its parts are preserved. It is in form an oblong octagon, and the figures on the sides represent an allegory. The first side represents a cherub weeping, with fist to his eye and torch reversed, a forget-me-not at his feet. The second side, the pall looped with scalloped shells. The third side has a cherub representing immortality; his left foot is on a skull, left hand holds a cherry branch, his right foot on a thigh bone, his right hand points to a lamp with flame, a forget-me-not at his feet. The fourth side, which is the head of the tomb, has a cherub's head between two wings, underneath a wreath. The fifth side has a cherub, with hand raised, holding a serpent which has its tail in its mouth—representing eternity—the forget-me-not as in the others. The sixth side has the pall again. The seventh has a cherub, with hands folded on its breast, and a forget-me-not at its feet—representing resignation. And the eighth side, which is the foot of the tomb, has the crown of the saints, and underneath, the trumpets of the archangels crossed, surrounded by a wreath of cherry branches.

For many courtesies and attentions at "Rosewell" I am indebted greatly to its occupants, Judge Fielding Lewis Taylor and his wife, who was Miss Nellie Deans.

OLD TOMBSTONES IN GLOUCESTER COUNTY.

COLLECTED BY THE EDITOR.

XXII.

Sarah's Creek.[1]

Here Lyeth y° Body of
M[rs] Mary Perrin Daughter
of M[r] John and M[rs] Mary
Perrin died Sep[r] y° 18th
1738   Aged three years
One month & five Days.

Here lies the Body of
John Perrin son of Thomas
and Elizabeth Perrin
Who departed this life Nov[br] 2[d] 1752
Aged 63 years 1 month and 2 Days.

XXIII.

Goshen.

Here lies the body
of
Hannah
widow of Morgan Tomkies [2] of
Gloucester C[y] daughter of Benj[a]
& Hannah Robinson of King & Queen
C[y] who departed this life the 20th
Jan[y] 1825, aged 43 years, 8 months
& 20 days.

XXIV.

SHACKELFORD'S FARM.[3]

Here lyeth interred the body of
Annie Byfield daughter of
William Byfield who departed
this life — July 1700, in the
11th month of her age.

* * * *
Richard Byfield
* * * * *

NOTES.

[1] Sarah's Creek flows into York River on the east side of Gloucester Point. At its mouth was the favorite harborage of the British men-of-war. On the east side of the mouth stood the Perrin mansion, still in good condition, and of the style of architecture so usual in Virginia during the reigns of the Georges— a large brick building, two stories high and four rooms to a floor, wainscoated and panelled. The house is in full view of Yorktown. The Perrin family have intermarried with many of the leading families of Virginia. In the York records I found the following quaint letter from the anxious mother to the immigrant youth, John Perrin:

SON JOHN: My love to yo^u, and I was very glad to heare of yor health, but very sorry to heare of ye accident wch befell yo^u by fire. I have sent yo^u a boy wch I desire that you would have as much care of as if he was yor owne alsoe. I have sent yo^u some things, so much as I am able at this tyme, and if God shall enable me to live another yeare I shall send yo^u more. Yo^r father hath departed this life, and hath left you a little house in ye South-gate streete in burg worth the matter of 40℔, there is a noate in ye barrell it lieth at ye topp in ye new blankett, and I have sent yo^u by Tho : a small peece of gould for yor wife alsoe I have pd for ye boy his passage, his name is Backer yor uncle Christopher lives at Ascamack at Cheryston creeke, & as yo^u desire my blessing have a care of ye boy, and learn him his trade, and not to pt from him *
* * my love to yo^u & yor wife desiring of God to keepe * * *
Your loveing mother,
SUSAN PERRIN.

[This letter which is without date is entered in the proceedings of the court for 1648.]

[2] In the Virginia *Gazette* of May 20, 1737 is the notice of the death of Charles Tomkies, at his house in Gloucester county, practitioner in physic, skilful in his profession, for many years justice of the peace.

[3] These Byfield tombstones lie about three miles from York River, and seven miles from the Court-house. Tradition has it that these little children wandered off from home and were lost in the woods and died, and were buried on the spot where found.

ERROR : On page 31 of this volume (Vol. III. No. 1) the four last lines of the inscription of "John Dixon, only son of John Dixon and Elizabeth Peyton," etc., were transposed from the inscription of Doct. John Dixon his son (page 30). It was the latter "who died" etc., and was "the last male descendant of the Dixon family." *

*Pages 80-81, this volume.

REGISTER OF ST. JAMES NORTHAM PARISH, GOOCHLAND COUNTY.

(This register, which was kept by Rev. William Douglas, is the property of R. Lee Traylor, Esq., of Memphis, Tennessee, and the following notes were taken by me from his very full manuscript:)

I came to Goochland Dec. 12, 1750. Preached 1st. at Dover Church Sept. 15, 1750. Received by the vestry as parish minister by the then vestry following viz: Stephen Sampson, Will Holman, Will Lewis, John Hopkins, Archer Payne.

List of the Vestry for the year 1756 when I got this book:

Capt. Will Burton.
Col. Arthur Hopkins. } Churchwardens 1756.

Col. Charles Lewis, Col. Henry Wood, Col. John Payne, Major John Smith, Major Josias Payne, Capt. James Holman,

George Payne, William Miller, Charles Jordan, John Woodson, Robert Burton, Oct., 1756, James Cole, Oct., 1756, Capt. William Pryor, 1758, Capt. William Stamp, 1758, Joseph Pollard, 1757, Capt. Noel Burton, 1761, Tho: Mann Randolph, 1763, Tho: Bolling, 1764, (all dead) John Bolling, George Payne, Jun., Tho: Underwood, Joseph Woodson.

MARRIAGES.

1751, Oct. 12. John Martin & Mary Rogers, both of this parish.

1751, Dec. 20. Alexander Grant & Agnes Jarrett, in this parish.

1751, Dec. 27. Thomas Woodson & Mary Woodson, both in Goochland.

1751. Nov. 23. Guy Smith & x x Hopkins.

"   "   " Drury Christian & Lucy Williams.

"   "   " Alexander Trent & —— Scott, in Manikin.

1753, Aug. 24. Abraham, Sallé & Elizabeth Woodson.

"   Sept. 25. Will Banks & Elizabeth Martin.

"   Sept. 25. Will Groom & Dorothy Madison, both in this parish.

1754, July 23. James Woodson & Elizabeth Whitelock.

"   Dec. 24. John Woodson & Elizabeth Bailey, both in this parish.

1775, Mar. 6. Will Payne & Mary Barret, both in this parish.

"   Sept. 15. John Lee & Betty Page.

"   Sept. 21. Sylvanus Stokes & Cat: Hicks, in this parish.

"   Oct. 15. John Hancock & Elizabeth Maddox, both in this parish.

"   Oct. 27. Jac: Flournoy & Elizabeth Burner, in Manakin Town.

1756, April 15. George Webb & Mrs. Hannah Fleming, in his parish, but Mr. Webb, in Hanover.

1756, May 6. Jer. Doss and Wesley Taylor, both in this county.

1756, Jan. 24. Charles Carter, of Cumberland, & Judette Carter, of Lickinghole.

Feb. 29. John Woodward & Susannah Tilman, both in this parish.

1756, Oct. Sylvanus Massie and Hannah Raglin, both in this
" Oct. 27. Jac: Flournoy & Elizabeth Burner, in Manikin town.

1756, Dec. 23. Peter Walker & Eliz. Harris, both in Cum^d parish.

1756, Oct. 13. Robert Burton & ——— Laferce, both in this parish.

1756, Dec. 30. Perrin Ferrar, in this parish, & Sarah Lacy, in St. Martin's Parish, Hanover County.

1758, Jan. 5. William Roberts and Eliz Lewis, both in this parish.

1758, Mar. 25. Thomas Hancock & Mary Shoemaker, both in this parish.

1758, March 25. John Gordon in this & Judith Moracet, in Manikintown Prh.

1758, May 9. Stephen Woodson & Lucy Ferran, both in this parish.

1758, June 1. Thomas Lewis & Susannah Ellis, both in Henrico.

1758, Dec. 1. Mr. William Walton & Elizabeth Tilmon, both in this parish.

1758, Dec. 21. Antony Martin & Sarah Holman, both in Manikin Town.

1759, Jan. 1. Josiah Leek in this parish & Ann Fenton, in Henrico.

1759, Sept. 16. Richard Clopton and Mary Davis, both in this parish.

1759, July 22. Benjamin Johnson & Susannah Peace, both in this parish.

1760, Jan. 22. John Wales, in Charles City, & Eliz. Lomax, in this parish.

1760, Feb. 20. Mr. Robert Lewis & Jean Woodson, both in this parish.

1760, Feb. 20. John Hales, in Henrico, & Eliz. Mutler, in this parish.

1760, Mch. 20. John Woodson, in Albemarle, & Mary Minns, in this parish.

1760, Aug. 27. Samuel Pryor, of Amelia County, & Frances Morton, of this parish.

1760, Sept. 2. Robert Sims of Louisa & Frances Lewis, of this parish.

1760, Nov. 9. Carter Henry Harrison, in Cumberland, & Susana Randolph, in this parish.

1760, Dec. 27. Alexander Moss & Ann Thurman, both of this parish.

1761, Jan. 1. William Harrison, in this psh, & Mary Cobbs, in Albemarle County.

1760, July 22. Robert Payne & Nan Burton in this parish.

1762, Mar. 17. William Ferran & Eliz. Bib, both in this parish.

1762, July 22. Andrew Jamison & Martha Stephenson, both in this parish.

1762, July 1. Pleasants Cocke & Eliz. Forden, both in this parish.

1762, July 22. Edward Radford and Ann Curd, both in this parish.

1762, Aug. 22. John Lewis & Judith Crouch, both of this parish.

1762, Sept. 10. James Meriwether and Eliz. Pollard, in this parish.

Joseph Curd, in this parish, & Mary Warrin, in St. Paul's.

1762, Apl. 6. John Ware, in Manikin Town, & Mary Watson, in Henrico.

1762, Jan. 1. Gideon Moss & Susannah Richerson, both in this parish.

1762, Sept. 28. Joseph Curd, in this parish, & Mary Warrin, in St. Paul's.

1762, Oct. 26. Joseph Pace and Mary Ann Page, both in this parish.

1762, Dec. 29. Henry Mullens & Frances Walton, both in this parish.

1763, Jan. 6. George Hancocke & Mary Whitloe, both in this parish.

1763, Jan. 20. Thomas Pollard & Sarah Hardine, both in this parish.

1763, Mch. 9. Jesse Ellis, in Henrico, & Sarah Woodson, in this parish.

1763, Mch. 9. Julius Burton, in Henrico, & Rebecca Clayton, in this parish.

1763, Mch. 17. Peyton Smith, in Henrico, & Judith Wadley, both in this parish.

1763, April 7. John Dudley, in Albemarle, & Sarah Bromfield, in this parish.

1763, Aug. 7. John Martin & Barbara Lewis, both in this parish.

1763, Aug. 19. John Cobbs & Judith Cobbs, both in Albemarle County.

1763, Oct. 1. Mathew Jordan & Mary Stogdill, both in this parish.

1764, Mch. 18. Edmund Curd & Mary Curd, both in this parish.

1764, Aug. 16. Edmund Pendleton & Milly Pollard, both in Goochland.

1764, Dec. 23. Richard Johnson & Ann Nicholls, both in this parish.

1765, March 21. Jacob Michaux & Sarah Neville in Cum^d.

1765, March 28. Rene Napier, of this parish, & Rebecca Hart, in Drisdale parish.

1764, April 1. Robert Bowman, in Chesterfield, & Elizabeth Craigwald, in this parish.

1765, June 11. Robert Wingfield & Frances Jordan, both of this parish.

1765, Oct. 1. John Goode & Frances Loftis, both in this parish.

1765, Dec. 31. George Payne & Betty McCarthy Morton, in James City parish.

1766, March 6. Benjamin Johnson & Martin Hughes in St. Martin's Psh.

1766, May 20. Thomas Massie, in this p'sh, & Mary Williams, in Louisa.

1766, Aug. 14. Shadrach Woodson in Bkg. & Sus. Walker, in this parish.

1766, Aug. 26. Turner Rountree & Sarah Woodson, both of Goochland.

1766, Nov. 6. Peter Walker & Sarah Wadley both in this parish.

1766, Nov. 20. James Curd & Mary Graves, both in this parish.

1766, Dec. 25. Milner Redford & Sarah Lewis, both in this parish.

1767, Jan. 22. Stephen Letcher & Elizabeth Perkins, both in this parish.

1767, Jan. 23. Moses Taylor & Obedience Smith, both in this parish.

1767, May 14. Barnard Markham & Mary Harris, both in Manikintown.

1768, May 25. John Glass & Sally Martin, both in this parish.

1768, June 4. Capt. Hugh Moss & Jeannie Ford, both in this parish.

1768, June 23. Benjamin Cocke & Mary Johnson, both in this parish.

1768, Oct. 11. Julius Allen, in Henrico, & Mary Biggar, in Henrico.

1768, Oct. 12. John Perkins, in Goochland, & Ursley Richardson, in Henrico.

1768, Nov. 2. George & Martha Meriwether.

1768, Dec. 13. Fisher Rice Bennett & Judith Hanson, in Albemarle.

1768, Dec. 18. Benj. Perkins & Mary Curd.

1768, Dec. 25. George Underwood & Elizabeth Curd.

1769, Jan. 27. Benjamin Anderson & Judith Mims, of this parish.

1769, March 23. George Anderson & Susannah Mims, of this parish.

1769, July 21. Mr. Archibald Bryce & Mary Mitchell.

1770, Feb. 22. Spencer Norvil & Frances Hill, both of this parish.

1770, June 2. Joseph Winston & Lucy Cobb.

1770, June 19. Shadrach Vaughan & Mary Meriwether.

1770, Nov. 14. Richard Johnson & Polly Powers.

1770, July 2. Burgess Ball & Mary Chichester.

1770, Oct. 13. David Walker & Eliz Gilbert.

1770, Nov. 10. Leonard Price & Judith Elldridge.

1770, Dec. 19. James Grason & Mary Christian.

1771, April 28. Robert Smith & Eliz. Carroll.

1771, May 9. John Christian & Judith Leek.

1771, July 4. Sam Martin & Ann Pleasants.

1771, Aug. 25. Sally Graves, in Goochland, & Barret Price, in Henrico.

1771, Nov. 7. Richard Sampson & Ann Curd, both in Goochland.

1772, Mar^ch 19. Will Miller & Maria Laprade.

1772, Apl. 23. Joseph Pleasants & Mary Gerrand.

1772, July 6. Will Bolding & Ann Burgess, both from Albemarle Co.

1772, July 9. John Robards & Sarah Marshall, both in Goochland.

1773, Jan: 1. Joseph Mayo & Jeannie Richardson in Goochland.

1773, Mar. 25. Clayburn Rice & Molly Smith in Goochland.

1773, March 23. Thomas Glass & Martha East.

1773, May 4. Mathew Payne & Sally Pryor.

1773, Aug. 1. Walter Leek & Winifred Johnson.

1773, Sept. 7. Ben Anderson & Sarah Johnson, both of Louisa.

1773, Oct. 23. Charles Clark & Sarah Cooke, both in Goochland.

1773, Dec. 22. Robert Burton Payne & Margaret Sydenham Morton, both in Goochland.

1774, Jan. 3. Will Roberts & Eliz. Pleasants Cocke, both in Goochland.

1774, Jan. 27. Sam Jordan & Frances Periere, of Henrico.

1774, Mar. 6. Ambrose Edwards & Olive Martin, both in Louisa.

1774, Feb. 24. Will Lewis & Sally Mason, both of Goochland.

1774, May 1. John Ellis & Patty Wood, both in Henrico.

1774, June 30. James Gordon, in Lancaster, & Ann Payne, in Goochland.

1774, July 28. Charles Lacy & Eliz. Hudson, in Louisa.

1774, Sept. 6. Jesse Lacy & Mary Johnson, in Louisa.

1774, Oct. 25. Ben Lacy & Judith Christian, both in Goochland.

1774, Nov. 4. Charles Rice & Mary Tony, both in Albemarle.

1775, Jan. 26. Devreux Jerrat & Joanna Wade, both of this parish.

1775, Feb. 2. Rene Woodson, in Albemarle, & Martha Johnson, in Louisa.

1775, Apl. 27. William Pledge & Ursley Woodson, both of Y^s. parish.

1775, June 9. Thomas Diggs, in Louisa, & Ann Kent, in Albemarle.

1775, Aug. 5. Archibald Pleasants & Jean Woodson, both of Y^s. parish.

1775, Sept. 8. John Curd in Y^s. & Ann Underwood, in Louisa.

1776, Jan. 3. Samuel Moss & Susannah Harris.

1776, May 16. Will Pryor in Y^s parish & Eliz. Hughes, in Cumberland.

1776, June 26. Thomas & Elizabeth Massie, both of Y^s parish.

1776, Aug. 24. Natt Massie, in Y^s parish, & Ann Clark, in Albemarle.

1776, Sept. 29. Patrick Napier & Eliz. Woodson in this parish.

1776, Oct. 5. James Cole & Fanny Cheesman Wills, both in Albemarle.

1776, Dec. 8. Tho. Pope, in Y^s parish, & Mary Snead, of Albemarle.

1777, Feb. 22. Christopher Johnson & Elizabeth Dabney, both of Hanover.

1777, June 19. Samuel Woodson & Elizabeth Payne, both of Y⁸ parish.

1777, March 16. Joseph Lewis & Ann Porter, both in Y⁸. parish.

1778, Feb. 4. Da. Bullock & Susannah More in Louisa.

1778, Nov. 29. Malachi Chiles & Eliz Garton, both in Orange.

1779, Jan. 8. Jesse Payne & Sally Lewis, both in Goochland.

1779, March 14, Ben Woodson & Sally Johnson, both in Goochland.

1779, March 16. Will Jordan Morton & Martha Pryor, both of Goochland.

1779, July 20. Macon Biggars & Christian Poindexter, both of Goochland.

1779, Aug. 3. Nath. West Dandridge & Jean Pollard, in Goochland.

1779, Sept. 23. Rich'd Clough & Jean Woodson, in Goochland.

1779, Nov. 24. Joseph Woodson in G'd, & Sarah Hughes, in Cumberland.

1780, Feb. 3. Charles Slaughter in Culpeper & Eliz^a Poindexter, in Louisa.

1780, April 24. Col. Richard Anderson & Catherine Fox, both of Louisa.

1780, April 28. Liner Gooch & Rhode Turner, both of Louisa.

1780, Sept. 28. Will Lee, in Northumberland, & Jean Payne, in Goochland.

1781, Sept. 7. Will Robards & Eliz. Lewis, both of Goochland.

1781, Oct. 4. Tho. Mallory & Constance Davis, both in Louisa.

1781, Dec. 26. John Poindexter & Eliz. Thornton Johnston, both in Louisa.

1781, Dec. 27. Henry Mallory & Lucy Long, both in Orange.

1782, Feb. 12. David Bullock & Jane Terry, both in Louisa.

1782, Feb. 20. Tho. Shelton & Cecelly Dabney, both of Louisa.

1782, Apl. 25. Richmond Terrill & Cecelia Darracott, both in Louisa.

1782, June 27. Garland Cosby & Molly Poindexter, both of Louisa.

1782, Aug. 22. Joseph & Jean Pleasants.

1782, Oct. 15. Will: Clayton & Mary Rose, both of Spottsylvania.

1783, Feb. 6. Stephen Mayo & Ann Isabel, both of Goochland.

1783, Feb. 18. Ben: Robinson & Catharine Parker, both of Spotsylvania Co.

1783, Mch. 13. Clayborn Gooch & Mildred Thomson, both of Louisa.

1783, June 4. George Quissenbury & Jeanie Daniel, both of Orange.

1783, June 18. John Hughes & Ann Meriwether in Louisa.

1783, Sept. 11. George Morris & Sally Biggars, both of Louisa.

1783, Sept. 9. John Trice & Pattie Smith.

1783, Nov. 19. Robert Cobb & Ann Gizzage Poindexter in Louisa.

1783, Nov. 20. Charles Smith & Nancy Johnson, both of Louisa.

1783, Nov. 26. Umphrey Gooch & Mary Wagstaff, in Louisa.

1784, July 28. Will Smith, in Louisa, & Sarah Pryor, in Goochland.

1784, Sept. 21. Edward Pace & Susannah Johnson, both in Goochland.

1785, Mch. 10. Caleb Lindsay & Sally Stephens, both in Orange.

1785, Nov. 20. Capt. Rich. Phillips & Eliz. Waddy, both of Louisa.

1785, Dec. 29. Rich. Cole & Sarah Sansum, both of Louisa Co.

1787, May 22. Spencer Coleman & Eliz. Goodwin, of Louisa Co.

1788, Jan. 24. Thornton Mead & Mary Garland, both of Louisa.

1788, Jan. 18. Robert Green & Eliz Bibb, both in Louisa.

1788, June 24. Thomas Lewis & Eliz. Meriwether, both in Albemarle.

1788, Nov. 20. John Durrett & Martha Bibb, both of Louisa.

1789, Julius Curle & Mary Curd in Goochland.

1788, June 26. David Hutson & Mary Clopton, in Louisa.

1789, June 15, Will Cole & Sally Byers, in Louisa.

1789, March 28. John Slaughter & Ann Lewis Johnson, of Louisa.

1789, May 31. Josel Graves & Sarah Graves, in Orange.

John Garland & Lucy Gordon, both in Louisa.

1791, March 27. Tho. Meriwether & Ann Minor.

1791, March 12. Dr. Joseph Duke & Mary Quarles, both in Spotsylvania.

1795, Nov. 1. Fortunatus Cosby & Mary Anne Fontane, in Louisa.

1783, Feb. 20. Chiles Tyrell & my Peggie were married.

1791, March 29. Francis Quarles & Mary Garrett Brooke, of Louisa.

BIRTHS.

James Bates & Winifred Hix had issue: Fleming b. Nov. 22, 1747; William Nov. 23, 1749; Samuel C. May 29, 1752; Stephen C. March 4, 1754.

Capt. Ish. Randolph & Jane Rogers, Susannah b. Sept. 25, 1736.

Capt. James Cole & Mary Wills, Mary b. Dec. 19, 1747, Janey b. Sept. 26, 1751, William b. May 31, 1753, Catharine b. May 2, 1755.

Noel Burton & Lucy Barret, son Robert b. Ap. 9, 1756.

James Bates & Winifred Hix, Daniel b. July 6, 1756.

Capt. Tho. Stark & Joan Williams, daughter Joan, b. Feb. 15, 1757.

Jan. 27, 1756. Julius Saunders & Jemima Woodward in Albemarle, a son, born Oct. 1755, named Clayburn. Capt. John Raley & Eliz. Randolph in Cumberland, a dau. b. Jan. 25, Susannah.

April 11, 1756. Will Miller & Mary Heath, Mary b. March 6, 1756.

Oct. 10, 1756. Ralph Graves & Judith Womack, dau. Sally, b. Sept. 1, 1756.

Mar. 20, 1757. Benjamin Clopton & Agnes Morgan, son Walter b. Dec. 26, 1756.

April 11. Capt. William Pryor & Sarah Wood, dau. Elizabeth b. Feb. 10, 1757.

Capt. Wm. Stamps & Elenor Brent, dau. Catherine, b. Oct. 17, 1757.

Noel Burton & Lucy Barrett, dau. Priscilla b. Dec. 26, 1757.

Drury Christian & Lucy Williams, James b. April 23, 1758.

Capt. Will Burton & Rebecca Cobbs, son John Cobbs b. Jan. 27, 1758.

Benjamin Woodson & Rebecca Cocke, Booth b. Dec. 4, 1757.

Capt. Robert Burton & Judith La Force, Sarah b. July 16, 1758.

Nov. 19. William Miller & Mary Heath, Henry b. Sept. 25, 1758.

Obadiah Smith & Mary Burks, Charles b. Nov. 13, 1758.

James Gregory & Sarah Thompson, William b. Aug. 11, 1758.

John Lewis & Eliz. McBride, Joseph b. Dec. 31, 1758.

Capt. Will Pryor & Sarah Wood, John b. Feb. 21, 1759.

René Woodson & Mary Thomson dec'd, dau. Eliz. Booth b. Feb. 16, 1759.

David Cosby & Mary Johnson, William b. Feb. 14, 1759.

George Anderson & Frances Woodson, Susannah b. Sept. 22, 1758.

John Curd & Lucy Brent, son James b. June 24, 1759.

Capt. Tho. Stark & Jean Williams, Reuben b. Aug. 10, 1759.

Capt. William Stamps & Helen Brent, James b. Dec. 25, 1759.

Capt. James Cole & Mary Wills, dau. Susannah, b. Mch. 23. 1760.

Benjamin Woodson & Rebecca Cox, Frances b. Dec. 17, 1759.

Valentine Mayo & Ann Patterson, Mary b. June 2, 1759.

James Woodson, & Eliz. Whitlock, Jennie b. May 2, 1760.

Richard Clopton & Mary Davis, dau. Susannah b. June 27, 1760.

Mr. Tho. Bolling & Elizabeth Gay, John b. Jan. 31, 1761.

John Lewis & Elizabeth McBride, John b. April 5, 1761.

Capt. Robert Burton & Judith La Force, Priscilla b. May 29, 1761.

Will Pryor & Sarah Wood, Patty b. April 6, 1761.

John Woodson & Mary Mims, Jennie Booth b. Oct. 25, 1760.

Mary Woodson, spouse to Thomas Woodson on Janito was baptized.

Thomas & Mary Woodson, a son named Jacob, born Mch 29, 1761.

Benjamin Clopton & Aggie Morgan, Elizabeth b. May 5, 1760.

Capt. John Really & Eliz. Randolph, William b. Dec. 26, 1760.

Obadiah Smith & Mary Burks, Joseph b. Nov., 1761.

David Cosby & Mary Johnson, Jeremiah b. Oct. 11, 1761.

William Miller & Mary Heath, son named Heath-Jones Miller b. Dec. 19, 1761.

Sam Pryor & Frances Morton, Samuel b. Jan. 12, 1762.

James Cole & Mary Wills, Roscow b. Mar. 9, 1762.

Alex^r Moss & Ann Thurmond, Joan b. Nov. 24, 1761.

John Bolling & Mary Jefferson, John b. Mch 24, 1762.

William Roberts & Eliz. Lewis, Jesse b. Apl 7, 1762.

John Curd & Lucy Brent, Elizabeth b. Feb. 25, 1762.

John Really & Eliz. Randolph, James b. April 16, 1762.

Thomas Smith & Jean Williams, John b. May 15, 1762.

Richard Curd & Sarah Downer, Nannie Williams b. July 11, 1762.

(To be continued.)

REGISTER OF ST. JAMES NORTHAN PARISH, GOOCHLAND COUNTY.

BIRTHS.

Tarlton Fleming and Mary Randolph, son Tarlton, b. July 18, 1763.

Alexander Moss and Ann Thurman, son Philip, b. May 21, 1763.

Mr. Thomas Bolling and Elizabeth Gay, Rebecca, b. Aug. 19, 1763.

Tho. Stark and Martha Price, Mary, b. April 27, 1763.

Benj. Woodson and Rebecca Cocke, Tabetha, b. July 11, 1763.

Peyton Smith and Judeth Wadley, Sally, b. Dec. 17, 1763.

Mr. Tho. Randolph and Mrs. Ann Cary, of Tuckahoe, Henry Cary, b. Jan. 8, 1764.

Mr. Tho. Randolph and Mrs. Ann Cary, of Tuckahoe, Mary, b. Aug. 9, 1762.

Major Will Pryor and Sarah Wood, Mary, b. Feb. 4, 1764.

Col. John Payne and Joan Smith, Smith, b. Jan. 18, 1764.

Tho. Woodson and Elizabeth Woodson, Susannah, b. Nov. 19, 1763.

Mr. John Bolling and Mary Jefferson, Thomas, b. Feb. 11, 1764.

Drury Christian and Lucy Williams, Ann, b. Mch. 3, 1764.

John Martin and Anna Barbour Lewis, Peter, b. Mch. 16, 1764.

Carter Henry Harrison and Susannah Randolph, Betty, b. Mch., 1764.

John Curd and Lucy Brent, Nannie, b. March 5, 1764.

Tyree Glenn and Sarah Shelton, Jeannie, b. May 17, 1763.

James Glass and Eve Williams, David, b. Sept. 21, 1764.

Thomas Walker, Surgeon and Mildred Thornton, son Francis, b. June 22, 1764.

Richard Pryor and Mary Mooney, Richard, b. Dec. 11, 1763.

Benjamin Clopton and Agnes Morgan, dau. Olive Judith, b. July 5, 1762; another dau. Mary, b. April 27, 1764.

John Woodson and Mary Mims, Eliz., b. May 22, 1764.

Col. Nathaniel West Dandridge and Dorothea Spotswood, Elizabeth, b. Sept. 12, 1764.

Will Curd and Mary Watkins, Susannah, b. Oct. 11, 1764.

Mr. Thomas Bolling and Betty Gay, Mary, b. Jan., 1764.

James Woodson and Eliz. Whitlock, Gillie b. Jan. 13, 1763.

William Pryor and Martha Wood, Mathew, b. Feb. 16, 1765.

Joseph Royal Ferrar and Phoebe Harris, Sarah, b. Feb. 10, 1765.

Will Robards and Eliz. Lewis, Sally, b. Jan. 25, 1765.

John Pace and Susanna Houchins, Francis, b. Nov. 25, 1764.

Robert Burton and Judeth Laforce, Jean, b. Mch. 29, 1765.

Noel Burton and Lucy Barret, William Barret, b. April 2, 1765.

Tarleton Fleming and Mary Randolph, son William, b. April 14, 1765.

Turner Southall and Martin Vandeval, William, b. April 27, 1765.

John Lewis and Eliz. McBride, Mary, b. Mch. 21, 1765.

David Cosby and Mary Johnson, James, b. March 28, 1765.

Gideon Moss and Susanna Richardson, John. b. March 10, 1764.

Alexander Moss and Ann Thurmond, Fleming, b. April 20, 1765.

Edmund Curd and Mary Curd, Jeanie, b. July 12, 1765.

Thomas Cocke and Ann Johnston, Agnes, b. March 29, 1765.

Richard Johnston and Ann Nichols, William, b. ———, 1765.

Benjamin Johnston and Susannah Pace, Susannah, b. Oct. 17, 1765.

Thomas Underwood and Ann Taylor, William, b. Oct. 2, 1765.

Edward Willis and Catherine Barker, Eliz., b. Nov. 6, 1765.

Booth Napier and Christian Terril, Will Parsons, b. Oct. 19, 1765.

John Curd and Lucy Brent, Catherine, b. Jan. 30, 1766.

John Bolling, and Mary Jefferson, Jane, b. Sept. 17, 1765.

Benjamin Woodson and Rebecca Cocke, Rebecca, b. Mch. 29, 1766.

James Glass and Eve Williams, John, b. Dec. 22, 1765.

Major William Pryor and Sarah Wood, Ann, b. June 5, 1764.

Capt. William Harrison and Ann Payne, Robert, b. June 29, 1766.

James Cole and Mary Willis, Susannah, b. Aug. 19, 1766.

Thomas & Elizabeth Woodson, Mary, b. June 15, 1766.

Drury Christian and Lucy Williams, Drury, b. Aug. 16, 1766.

Benjamin Clopton and Agnes Morgan, Susannah, b. July 23, 1766.

Tucker Woodson and Mary Netherland, John Pleasants, b. May 21, 1766.

Capt. John Really and Eliz. Randolph, Charles, b. Nov. 24, 1766.

Pleasants Cocke and Eliz. Fowler, William, b. Dec. 21, 1765.

Thomas Underwood and Ann Taylor, John, b. Feb. 22, 1767.

Tarleton Fleming and Mary Randolph, Thomas Mann, b. Feb. 15, 1767.

Edward Rice and Ann Ryan, Elizabeth, b. Jan. 27, 1767.

Valentine Wood and Lucy Henry, Sarah, b. Mch. 1, 1767.

James Woodson and Elizabeth Whitlock, Thomas, b. Feb. 28, 1767.

Turner Richardson and Ann Allen, Nathaniel, b. Nov. 28, 1768.

Edmund Curd, a daughter named Peggie, b. Jan. 22, 1767.

John Bolling and Mary Jefferson, Ann, b. July 18, 1767.

John Curd and Lucy Brent, Newton, b. Nov. 21, 1767.

René Napier and Rebecca Hurt, Skelton, b. May 29, 1767.

James Curd and Mary Graves, Jesse, b. Dec. 7, 1767.

Stokes McCawl and Agnes Williamson, Mary, b. Dec. 29, 1767.

William Pryor and Sarah Wood, Valentine Wood, b. Jan. 18, 1768.

John Saunders and Eliz. Hancocke, Mary, b. June 13, 1767.

Bernard Markham and Mary Harris, Martha, b. Jan. 13, 1768.

Noel Burton and Lucy Barret, daughter, b. Feb. 20, 1768.

Thomas Underwood and Ann Taylor, son Thomas, b. March 31, 1768.

Edw'd Rice and Ann Ryan, daughter Patty, b. May 24, 1768.

John Tolliver and Eliz. Sydnor, Lucy, b. May 23, 1768.

Dabney Ker and Martha Jefferson, twins named Mary and Lucy, b. Mch. 7, 1768.

Jesse Payne and Frances Morton, George Morton, b. June 28, 1768.

Meredith Price and Eliz. Fox, Nathaniel West, b. Oct. 25, 1768.

William Massie and Frances Adams, Benjamin, b. July 13, 1768.

John Harris and Obedience Turpin, son Francis, b. May 7, 1768.

Gideon Moss and Susanna Richardson, son Gideon, b. March 19, 1768.

Benjamin Clopton and Aggie Morgan, Ben Michaux, b. Aug. 19, 1768.

William Curd and Mary Watkins, Mary, b. Oct. 10, 1768.

Thomas Mann Randolph and Nancy Cary, Tho. Mann, b. Oct. 1, 1768.

James Glass and Eve Williams, Molly, b. June 11, 1768.

Benjamin Woodson and Rebecca Cocke, Sarah, b. July 6, 1768.

John Pace and Susanna Houchins, son Charles, b. Oct. 24, 1768.

Benjamin Johnson and Martha Hughes, Jean, b. Oct. 14, 1768.

Benjamin Johnson and Susanna Peirce, William, b. Dec. 16, 1768.

Pleasants Cocke and Elizabeth Fowler, Robert, b. Feb. 14, 1769.

René Napier and Rebecca Hurt, Thomas, b. Nov. 1, 1768.

John Payne and Anne Chichester, Anne Ball, b. Feb. 16, 1769.

Jeremiah Doss and Ursley Taylor, Israel, b. Dec. 15, 1768.

Hugh Moss and Jennie Ford, Sallie Wain, b. Apl. 17, 1769.

George Underwood and Betty Curd, Richard, b. Apl. 5, 1769.

John Hanson and Eliz. Pace, son Joseph, b. March 20, 1769.

Thomas Hord and Eliz. Fitzpatrick, Abraham, b. Feb. 26, 1769.

Edmund and Mary Curd, a son Edward, b. May 20, 1769.

Valentine Wood and Lucy Henry, Mary, b. May 8, 1769.

William Pryor and Sarah Wood, son Luke, b. June 25, 1769.

Benjamin Cocke and Mary Johnson, dau. Ann, b. May 24, 1769.

George Richardson and Eliz. Miller, William Miller. b, May 2, 1769.

James Woodson and Eliz. Whitlock, dau. Sally, b. May 25, 1769.

John Glass and Sally Martin, David, b. May 27, 1769.

David Cosbie and Mary Johnson, son Pleasants, b. 1769.

John Bolling and Mary Jefferson, Martha, b. 1769.

John Curd and Lucy Brent, Mary, b. Sept. 10, 1769.

Jesse Payne and Frances Morton, Richard Baylie, b. Sept. 10, 1769.

Stokes McCawl and Agnes Williamson, son Richard, b. Dec. 13, 1769.

Col. Thos. Randolph and Ann Cary, son William, b. Jan. 16, 1770.

John Martin and Barbara Lewis, John, b. Dec. 26, 1769.

Dabney Carr and Martha Jefferson, Peter, b. Jan. 2, 1770.

Tucker Woodson and Mary ————, Henry Macon, b. Mch. 22, 1770.

Thos. Massie and Mary Williams, Martha, b. April 1, 1770.

John Railey and Eliz. Randolph, Randolph, b. May 14, 1770.

Meredith Price and Eliz. Fox, John Fox, b. June 1, 1770.

James Holman and Sarah Miller, Peg. Martin, b. July 26, 1770.

John Woodson and Sarah Mims, Sam Tucker, b. Sept., 1769.

Charles Christian and Sarah Duke, son Charles Hunt, b. Nov. 18, 1770.

Ben. Clopton and Aggie Morgan, Anthony, b. June 28, 1770.

Jan. 3, 1771. Archer Payne and Martha Dandridge, John Dandridge, b. Nov. 20, 1770.

Robert Mayo and Mary Richardson, Sally Thomson, b. Jan. 30, 1771.

Lyddal Bacon and Anne Apperson, Anne Apperson, Mch. 19, 1771.

Thomas Randolph and Jane Cary, twins, viz., Isham, Thomas, b. Mch. 27, 1771.

Arch. Bryce and Mary Mitchell, Mary Gildchrist, b. July 31, 1770.

René Napier and Rebecca Hurt, Sarah Garland, b. Jan. 22, 1771.

John Lewis and Eliz. McBride, Eliz. b. April 20, 1771.

Will Massie and Francis Adams, Betty, b. June 22, 1771.

Jesse Payne and Frances Morton, Jesse Burton, b. June 27, 1771.

Ben. Fitzpatrick and Mary Perkins, Constantine Perkins, b. June 23, 1771.

John Curd and Lucy Brent, Price b. Aug. 14, 1771.

Thos. Mann Randolph and Ann Cary, Archibald Cary, b. Aug. 24, 1771.

Thomas Woodson and Mary Woodson, Judith, b. Mch. 7, 1771.

Jeremiah Blacklock and Eliz. Gentry, Hezekiah, b. May 2, 1771.

Dabney Carr and Martha Jefferson, Samuel, b. Oct. 9, 1771.

David Copland and Susan Skeleton, Susan Skeleton, b. Jan. 7, 1772.

Nath. West Dandridge and Dorothea Spotswood, Mary Clayburn, b. Jan. 14, 1772.

Valentine Wood and Lucy Henry, son Valentine, b. — —, —.

Joseph Curd and Mary Warran, Martha, b. Sept. 5, 1771.

Burgess Ball and Mary Chichester, Eliz. Burgess, b. Mch. 16, 1772.

James Glass and Eve Williams, Janey, b. June 14, 1772.

Will Glass and Eliz. McGaw, Nancy, b. Nov. 4, 1771.

John Glass and Sally Martin, John, b. June 8, 1771.

Archy Payne and Martha Dandridge, dau. Anne Spottswood, b. April 19, 1772.

Nathaniel Massie and Eliz. Watkins, Thomas, b. June 2, 1772.

Tarlton Fleming and Mary Randolph, Judith, b. July 4, 1769.

Clayborn Rice and Mary Rice, Susannah, b. Oct. 6, 1771.

John Payne, Sr., and Jean Smith, Eliz. Woodson, b. 1772.

Tho. Mann Randolph and Ann Cary, Judith, b. Nov. 24, 1772.

Ben. Johnson and Martha Hughes, dau. Frances Anderson, b. Sept. 23, 1772.

Meredith Price and Eliz. Fox, Katie, b. Dec. 5, 1772.

John Bolling and Mary Jefferson, Edward, b. Sept. 17, 1772.

John Pace and Susannah Huchins, James, b. Nov. 25, 1772.

James Holman and Sarah Miller, Will Miller, b. Nov. 15, 1772.

Rich. Johnson and Dolly Powis, Reuben Powis, b. Oct. 7,

Edward and Mary Curd, Elizabeth, b. March 5, 1773.

Robert Mayo and Margaret Richardson, James, b. Mch. 11, 1773.

Dabney Carr and Martha Jefferson, Dabney, b. April 27, 1773.

William Miller and Joanna Laprade, John, b. May 1, 1773.

William Jordan and Eliz. Woodson, Woodson, b. Dec. 27, 1772.

John Woodson and Mary Mims, son Booth, b. Aug. 28, 1771.

John Curd and Lucy Brent, Daniel, b. Oct. 14, 1773.

Arch. Payne and Martha Dandridge, Martha, b. Nov. 6, 1773.

Will Robards and Eliz. Lewis, son Robert, Dec. 7, 1773.

Milner Radford and Sarah Lewis, Mary, b. Dec. 27, 1773.

Valentine Wood and Lucy Henry, Lucy, b. Jan. 7, 1774.

Joseph Mayo and Jennie Richardson, Patty, b. Feb. 21, 1774.

Will Massie and Frances Adams, Frankie, b. Feb. 5, 1774.

Tho. Massie and Mary Williams, Suckie, b. Ap. 30, 1774.

James Curd and Mary Graves, Nancy, b. June 12, 1774.

John Payne and Mary Chichester, Molly, b. April 3, 1774.

Will Lewis and Hannah Underwood, John Underwood, b. Nov. 4, 1774.

Tho. Mann Randolph and Ann Cary, Ann Cary, b. Sept. 16, 1774.

Tucker Woodson and Sarah Knolling, Charles Woodson, b. Dec. 29, 1774.

Charles Cosbie and Elizabeth Sydnor, James Overton, b. Oct. 20, 1774.

Garret Minor and Mary Overton Terrill, Rebecca, b. Feb. 2, 1774.

Jacob Mayo and Susannah Isabel, George, b. Dec., 1774.

James Cocke and Jane Johnson, Elizabeth, Feb. 3, 1775.

Wm. Lewis and Sally Mann, Jesse, b. Dec. 28, 1774.

George Underwood and Eliz. Curd, James, b. Feb. 6, 1774.

Wm. Heath Miller and Joanna Laprade, John Heath, b. Mch. 10, 1775.

Tho. Underwood and Ann Taylor, Francis, b. Mch. 18, 1775.

Robert Payne and Margaret Sydenham Morton, Lucy, Morton, b. 1775.

Will Massie and Frances Adams, Mary, b. June 16, 1775.

Waddy Thomson and Mary Lewis, Mildred, b. Sept. 21, 1775.

Obadiah Smith and Lucy Poor, Betsy, b. Aug. 30, 1775.

John Todd and Mary Williams, John, b. Aug. 7, 1775.

John Saunders and Eliz. Hancocke, Benj., b. Sept. 16, 1775.

John Curd and Lucy Brent, Woodford, b. Dec. 15, 1775.

William Cole and Sarah Clayborn, Mary, b. Nov. 10, 1775.

Archer Payne and Martha Dandridge, Archer, b. Nov. 29, 1775.

Valentine Wood and Lucy Henry, John, b. Jan. 18, 1776.

William Miller and Joanna Laprade, Betsy, b. July 6, 1776.

Garrett Minor and Mary Overton, Eliz. Lewis, b. Aug. 27, 1776.

Tho. Mann Randolph and Ann Cary, Jane Cary, b. Dec. 17, 1776.

Stokeley Towles and Elizabeth Downman, Porteus, b. Jan. 3, 1776.

Tho. Eldridge and Winifred Miller, Winifred, b. Feb. 20, 1776.

John Glass and Sally Martin, William, b. Oct. 20, 1776.

Will Lewis and Sally Mann, William, b. Jan. 19, 1776.

Edmund and Mary Curd, Charles, b. Feb. 18, 1777.

Meredith Price and Eliz. Fox, Jean Ballard, b. Feb. 27, 1777.

George Underwod and Eliz. Curd, Edmund, b. April 1, 1777.

James Dabney and Judith Anderson, Mary, b. Jan. 27, 1777.

George Richardson and Eliz. Miller, Betsy Jones,, b. Mch. 25, 1777.

Wil Lewis and Hannah Underwod, Ann, b. May 8, 1777.

George Payne and Betty McCarthy Morton, Lucy Hubard, b. May 14, 1777.

Archer Payne and Martha Dandridge, Dorothea Dandridge, b. July 10, 1777.

Robert Payne and Margaret Sydenham Morton, Richard Beckwith, b. Aug. 9, 1777.

Tho. and Eliz. Massie, David, b. May 17, 1777.

Jas. Cocke and Martha Parin, (?) William, b. Aug. 1, 1777.

Nath. Massie and Ann Clark, Rebekah, b. Aug. 28, 1777.

Tho. and Eliz. Massie, Elizabeth Watkins, b. March 29, 1781.

Will Cole and Sarah Woodson, Sarah, b. Jan. 10, 1781.

Ja: Cole and Fanny Willis, Lucy, b. June 3, 1781.

Tunstall Quarles and Susannah Edwards, Tunstall, b. May 11, 1781.

René Woodson and Martha Johnson, Fanny, b. Aug. 23, 1780.

Turner Christian and Anna Payne, Billie Payne, Jan. 17, 1781.

Garrett Minor and Mary Terrill, Sarah b. Aug. 14, 1781.

Pat. Woodson and Nanny Cloof, (?) Molly, b. Sept. 17, 1771.

Sam Dabney and Jean Meriwether, Francis, b. July 1, 1781.

George Underwod and Eliz. Curd, George, b. Nov. 21, 1781.

Hen: Chiles and Judith Daniel, James, b. Sept. 3, 1781.

Lewis Barret and Jane Price, Mary, b. Nov. 23, 1781.

Jo: Dickeson and Mary Cole, Ja: Cole, b. Dec. 24, 1781.

George and Elizabeth Watkins, Fielding Lewis, b. Feb. 13, 1782.

Sam Newton and Agnes Chiles, Henry, b. July 3, 1781.

Aaron Laurie and Maple Holland, Overton, b. Feb. 23, 1782.

Will Robinson and Agnes Smith, Agnes, b. Oct. 28, 1781.

Jo: Nelson and Lucy Robinson, Agnes, b. Feb. 6, 1782.

Will Pryor and Eliz. Hughes, Martha, b. Mch. 31, 1782.

Archer Pledge and Ann Woodson, Archer, b. Jan. 1, 1782.

Rich: Clough and Jane Woodson, Mary, b. Mch. 9, 1782.

Will Macon and Sally Woodson, Henry, b. Mch. 8, 1782.

Nathaniel Massie and Ann Clark, Ann, b. March 5, 1779, Sarah, b. May, 1781.

Arch. Bryce and Mary Mitchell, Elizabeth, b. Mch. 19, 1781.

George Richardson and Eliz. Miller, Marg. Frizel, b. Oct. 23, 1782.

Will Poindexter and Marg't Daniel, child, b. June 9, 1782.

Hickerson Cosby and Nancy Harris, Mary, b. June 23, 1782.

Will Bigger and Martha Richardson, Polly, b. Oct. 13, 1781.

Rich. Anderson and Ann Meriwether, Ann Meriw^r, b. Aug. 3, 1782.

Armistead Brown and Sally Daniel, Betty, b. Sept. 5, 1782.

Rich. Johnson and Ann Nicholson, Rhoda, b. June 18, 1782.

Turner Christian and Anne Payne, Jesse George, ——, 1782?

Tho. Cosbie and Elizabeth Cosbie, William, b. July 16, 1782.

Richard Taliferro and Ann Taliferro, Lucy, b. Aug. 6, 1782.

Samuel Woodson, and Sarah Mills; twins, Will. Fontain and Jo: LeVillain, Jan. 30, 1785.

Jo: Poindexter and Eliz. Johnson, Tho. Poindexter, b. Dec. 31, 1782.

Archer Payne and Patty Dandridge, Elizabeth, b. Oct. 29, 1782.

Stokeley Towles and Eliz. Downman, Mildred b. Oct. 13, 1782,
Da: Bullock and Jane Terry, Sally Terry, b. Dec. 2, 1782.
Garret Minor and Mary Overton Terrill, Peter, b. Jan. 30,
1782.
Cha: Cosbie and Eliz. Sydnor, Lucy Hawkins, b. Mch. 5, 1783.
William Bibb and Eliz. Biggars, Biggars, b. May 2, 1783.
Winkfield Cosbie and Ann Baker, Ann Winkfield, b. Aug. 10,
1783.
Ja: Cole and Fanny Wills, Roscow, b. Jan. 28, 1783.
Will Christian and Martha Evans, John, b. Aug. 28, 1783.
Jos: Woodson and Sarah Crouch, La Fayette, b. Aug. 12,
1783.
Will Gooch and Lovinah Clements, Sally, b. Feb. 16, 1769.
Tho: Johnson and Eliz. Meriwether, Thomas, b. Nov. 14, 1783.
Clayborne Gooch and Mildred Thomson, Thomson, b. Jan.
28, 1784.
Jo. Curd and Ann Underwood, b. June 5, 1783.
Lewis Barret and Jane Price, Lewis, b. Jan. 17, 1784.

REGISTER OF ST. JAMES NORTHAM PARISH, GOOCHLAND COUNTY, VIRGINIA.
Extracts.

BIRTHS.

Will Smith and Mary Rhodes, Clifton Rhodes, b. April 12, 1784.
Will Pryor and Elizabeth Hughes, William, b. Jan. 21, 1784.
Stephen Yancey and Jean Bond, John, b. May 29, 1784.
Edward Herndon and Betty Minor, George, b. Sept. 12, 1784.
Pomphrey Gooch and Mary Thomas, John, b. Nov. 2, 1784.
Aaron Fontain and Barbara Terrell, Patsy Minor, b. March 14,
1785.

Ben Robinson and Catherine Parker, Ann Parker, b. March 22, 1785.

Col. Garret Minor and Mary Terrell, son James, b. April 18, 1785.

Major Thomas Johnson and Ursillia Row, Lucy, b. July 14, 1781.

Macon Biggars and Christian Gissage, Huldah, b. May 17, 1783, and Betsie Smith, b. April 22, 1785.

Joseph Nelson and Lucy Tate, Sarah, b. April 1, 1785.

Will Jordan Morton and Martha Pryor, Sarah, b. Nov. 10, 1781; Rebecca, b. May 21, 1783, Frances, b. March 9, 1785.

George Underwood and Elizabeth Curd, William, b. January 23, 1784.

Joseph Nelson and Agatha Winston, Catherine Winston, b. Sept. 30, 1785.

Garland Cosbie and Molly Poindexter, Nicholas, b. Feb. 22, 1785.

Stephens Thomson and Mary Armistead, Armistead Thomson, b. Aug. 4, 1785.

Robert Cobb and Ann Given Poindexter, Jo: Poindexter, b. May 27, 1785.

Jo: Nelson and Lucy Robinson, Elizabeth, b. Oct. 18, 1785.

Richard Anderson and Caty Fox, Charles, b. May 7, 1781, Susanna, b. Oct. 1, 1782; Joseph, b. Aug. 17, 1784; Nancy, b. Nov. 22, 1785.

Isham Railey and Susanna Woodson, John, b. July 18, 1785.

Jo: Maddison and Mary Biggars, Nancy, b. August 6, 1785.

Will Biggar and Martha Richardson, Landie, b. Sept. 20, 1785.

Col. Jo: Anderson and Susannah Daniel, Jo: Daniel. b. May 3, 1786.

Armistead Brown and Sally Daniel, Henry, b. May 10, 1786.

Edmund Curd and Elizabeth Crogwell, Sám Hawes, b. July 10, 1796.

Jos. Nelson and Rebecca Wooduffe, John, b. May 4, 1786.

Thos. Johnson and Betsy Merriwether, Ann Merriwether, b. Oct. 10, 1786.

Jo: Poindexter and Elizabeth Thornton Johnson, Nicholas, b. Sept. 17, 1786.

Aaron Fontaine and Barbara Terrill, Sarah, b. March 17, 1787.

Richard Cole and Sarah Sansum, William, b. Oct. 5, 1786.

Ch. Barret and Elizabeth Clough, Will Torrence, b. Feb. 29,1787.

Richard Johnson and Susanna Garret, Kitty, b. Dec. 18, 1786.

Chas. Thomas and Frances Armistead, James, Nov. 13, 1786.

Stephen Southall and Martha Wood, Mary Wood, b. April 9,1787.

Archer Payne and Martha Dandridge, America, b. Nov. 5, 1786.

George Underwood and Eliza Curd, John Curd, b. Jan. 25, 1786.

George Quisenbury and Jane Daniel, George, b. Sept. 23, 1786.

Col. Garret Minor and Mary Overton Tyrrhill, Louisa, b. Aug. 13, 1787.

James Chiles and Susanna Graves, Jeanie, b. January 29, 1788.

Will Armistead and Mary Knuckles, Rebecca, b. January 11, 1788.

Sam Cole and Elizabeth Cosby, Lydia, b. Oct. 22, 1787.

Pumphrey Gough and Mary Thomson, Rolling, b. Oct. 31, 1787.

Claiborn Googe and Milly Thomson, Unie, b. Sept. 14, 1787.

Caleb Lindsay and Sally Stevens, Sally Montague, b. June 2, 1787.

Ed. Dudley and Roxanna Smith, Ballard Smith, b. Sept. 11,1789.

Armistead Brown and Sally Daniel, Sally Beverley, b. Oct. 3, 1792.

Benjamin Robinson and Catharine Parker, Eliz. Winston Parker, b. June 6, 1789.

Jo: Poindexter and Elizabeth Hunter Johnson, Lucy Jones, b. Feb. 2, 1789.

Caleb Lindsay and Sally Stevens, Landon, b. May 25, 1789.

Col. Garret Minor and Mary Overton Terrill, Sam Overton, June 13, 1790.

Robt. Cobb and Nancy Poindexter, Dec. 25, 1789.

Samuel Newton and Agnes Chiles, Samuel, b. Oct. 7, 1789.

Ed. Dudley and Roxanna Smith, Ann Meriwether, Sept. 27,1792.

Aaron Fontaine and Barbara Terrill, William Maury Fontaine, b. Jan. 16, 1793.

Oct. 5, 1792, Richard Terrell and Lucy Carr married.

July 17, 1793, Richard Terrell and Martha Jefferson, married.

Aaron Fontaine and Barbara Terrell, Barbara Carr, b. Dec. 25, 1794; Ann "Overton," b. April 19, 1796.

Armistead Brown and Sally Daniel, Edwin Jones, b. July 23, 1794.

Funeral Sermons.

June 12, 1759, Capt. Holman; April 23, 1770, Booth Napier; May 29, 1755, Tho: Massie; July 18, 1760, Mr. Goodwin; May 5, 1763, Mrs. Tilman in Albemarle; May 31, 1769, Noel Burton; July 23, 1773, Rev. Mr. McLaurin's in Cumberland, once my scholar for many years. Nov. 4, 1774, Mrs. Massie's; Dec. 12, 1775, Mrs. Woodson's; June 9, 1777, Col. Pryor's; Booth Napier, Jr., April 23, 1770; Dec. 12, 1775, Mrs. Tucker Woodson; Nov. 4, 1774, Nat Massie; Sept. 19, 1782, Col. Anderson's wife (Louisa county); March 13, 1772, Mrs. Cobbs; July 18, 1760, Mrs. Goodwin's, in Albemarle; May 29, 1755, Tho: Massie's wife; May 5, 1763, Tho. Tilman's wife in Amherst; July 5, 1773, died Rev. Mr. McLaurin of Cumberland; Dec. 21, 1761, Rev. Mr. Will Proctor of Amelia, my most serious companion. Col. Jo: Smith, in Goochland, died 1775; Capt. Jo: Watts in Westmoreland died May 19, 1753; Mrs. Grayson, Col. Monroe's sister died Nov., 1752.

Jan. 20, 1758, Col. Turner and Harry Ashton died last Fall.

Feb. 5, 1767, Jo: Monroe ye Colonel's son died, a pious young man.

Dec. 2, 1789, Col. Jo: Woodson in Goochland died.

Jan. 2, 1790, Col. Jo: Wilson died aged 47 in Louisa.

Dec. 2, 1791, Mr. Joseph Pollard died.

Dec. 19, 1790, Mr. Robt. Armistead died aged 60; July 27, 1790, Rev. Jo: Todd died; July 12, 1793, Col. Beverly Winslow died aged 60; Nov. 20, 1793, Mr. Tho: Randolph of Tuckahoe died; July 29, 1784, Col. Jo: Payne in Goochland died; Dec. 2, 1789, Col. Jo: Woodson in Goochland died; Feb. 2, 1794, Dorothea Randolph his wife died; Oct. 23, 1794, Mat. Woodson died; Dec. 2, 1795, Dr. George Gilmer died; Jan. 7, 1758, Allan Ramsay died; Aug. 28, 1788, Rev. Charles Wesley, Methodist, died; May 2, 1791, Rev. John Wesley, his brother, died; Sept. 30, 1770, Mr. George Whitfield died, aged 56; Jan. 2, 1790, Col. Jo: Nelson deid in Louisa, aged 48; Feb. 2, 1794, Mrs. Bethia Woodson died; Oct. 23, 1794, Matt Woodson died.

Col. Tho. R(andolph) of Tuckahoe and Ann Carey,
William, b. June 15, 1770,
Archibald, b. Aug. 24, 1771.

Judith, b. Nov. 24, 1772,

Ann, b. July 25, 1774,

Jean, b. Dec. 17, 1776

Tho. Mann, b. Oct. 1, 1778

Archibald Bryce and Mary Mitchell married July 21, 1769:

July 31, 1770, Mary Gilchrist, baptized by Douglas.

Jan. 3, 1773, Agnes, baptized by Mr. Coats, died.

Mch. 14, 1775, Will, baptized by Mr. Selden, died.

Feb. 3, 1780, Ann.

March 9, 1782, Elizabeth.

May 3, 1784, John, baptized by Mr. Buchanan.

June 15, 1796, Charlotte, baptized by Mr. Buchanan.

Dec. 19, 1742, Capt. Jo: Cole & Mary Wills had a child called
Margaret.

George Barclay and Mary Cole were married Aug. 7, 1766, Issue:
Patrick, born October 18, 1770; Catie, born July 22, 1772;
Lucy Martin, born Mar. 15, 1776.

Capt. Ja: Cole died, aged 42, Mar. 1767.

July, 1770, Mrs. Mary Cole died.

Feb., 1778, Ja: Dickerson & Mary Cole als. Barclay married.
Issue:

Susanna Robinson, born March 21, 1779; Nancy Roscow, born
May 31, 1780;

James, born Dec. 24, 1781.

Oct. 5, 1767, Geo. Barclay & Mary Cole had Mary, who married
John Boxley, April 18, 1789.

Mr. Sam Cole & Eliz. Cosbie's children:—Barbara, Elizabeth,
John, Richard, Mary, William, Lydia, Sally, Thomas,
Rebecca, Louisa, Samuel.

Charles Cosbie & Eliz. Sydnor married Dec. 14, 1759. (Once
here in Louisa, now in Georgia). Issue:

Sydnor, born Oct. 7, 1762; Robert, born Sept. 26, 1765; Fortunatus, born Dec. 30, 1767; Richmond, born Dec. 14, 1772;
James, born Oct. 20, 1774; David, born ——; Charles Scott;
Patsy, born Feb. 13, 1764; Judith, born Oct. 12, 1769; Polly
his 3d. daughter, born March 16, 1771; Barbara, 4th. daughter; Lucy, 5th. daughter, born March 5, 1783.

Christopher Clark, once in Louisa, now in Georgia, an account
of his family, June, 1791:

Milly Tyrell his wife; Micajah, oldest son married; Christopher age 30; David aged 28; Morning, aged 26—has five
daughters; Judith, married aged 24—one child; Rachel
about 22, has 3 boys—a widow now; Agathy about 20; Molly
about 18 married; Samuel, 16; Joshua, 14; Milley, 12;
Chiles Tyrell died aged 2 months; Suckie, 9; Lucy, 5.

Register of Henry Bibb & Sarah Meed, his wife:

Robert, Mary, John, Minor, Ann, Susannah, Henry, Hartwell,
Sarah, David, Patsy & Elizabeth.

Mrs. Barbara Tyrel Mrs. Fountain, was born Sept. 3, 1756.

Nov. 30, 1756, Mr. Aaron Fountaine born, & Married May 19,
1772.

Register of their children: Peter, born Dec. 15, 1774; James
Tyrel, born Nov. 19, 1776; Mary Ann, born Oct. 14, 1778;
Elizabeth, born Sept. 15, 1780; Matilda, born Sept. 13,
1782; Patsie Minor, born March 14, 1785; Sallie Sarah,
born March 17, 1787; Moriah, born Feb. 16, 1789; America,
born March 10, 1791; Will Maury, born Jan. 16, 1793; Barbara Ker, born Dec. 25, 1794; Ann Overton, born April 19,
1796.

Col. Jo: Nelson's Family, Feb. 18, 1789:

Jo: Nelson & Fanny Armistead were married; Sept., 1765,
Frances Anderson y^r daughter was born.

Jo: Nelson & Rebecca Woodley were married. Issue: Sarah,
Philip, Ann, Hephzibah, Rebecca Woodley, Mary, Elizabeth,
Mary, now dead, Lucy Eppes, William, Catherine Griffin,
John, Solmon Hughes.

Sept. 1753, Old Stephen Sampson & Sarah Johnson were married. Jan., 1757, Sarah Sampson was born; Sept., 1759,
Eliz. Sampson was born; June 11, 1763, Ann Sampson was
born; Jan. 13, 1765, Will Sampson was born; Feb. 7, 1768,
Jean Sampson was born; Oct. 8, 1769, Stephen Sampson
was born; Jan. 9, 1772, James Johnson was born; Dec. 12,
1773 Their old very honest grandfather, Stephen Sampson,
was buried, &c.

March, 1753, Jo: Atkins & Sarah Brockman in Orange were married: April 4, 1754, their son Frankie was born; May 27, 1755, Joseph was born; Feb. 4, 1757, John was born; March 3, 1759, Susannah was born; Sept. 18, 1760, Jonathan was born; July 4, 1762 Ann was born; May 17, 1764 Hezekiah was born; May 12, 1767 Mary was born; May 11, 1769 Sarah was born; May 17, 1771 Martha was born; June 27, 1773 Sarah Lydia was born; July 4, 1775 Rhodie was born; Aug. 23, 1778 Rebecca was born; In all 13 children.

REGISTER OF ST. JAMES-NORTHAM PARISH.

Goochland Co. Va.

Extracts made by the late R. A. Brock, late Secretary of the Virginia Historical Society, and copied for this magazine by his daughter, Elizabeth Brock:

FUNERAL SERMONS PREACHED.

John Anderson's funeral in Louisa, Apr 8, 1781
Col Anderson's wife's funeral in Louisa Sept 19, 1782

Sept 20, 1753, Stephen Sampson and Sarah Johnson

Sept 23, 1754, John Johnston and Helen Thomson

Feb 4, 1755, Will Johnson and Elizabeth Mills

Dec 15, 1755, Jas Johnson in St Pauls & Rachel Hadden in this parish

Mch 19, 1756, Wm Edwards and Elizabeth Johnson

Feb 26, 1759, Benj Johnson and Susanna Peace

Feb 20, 1760, John Johnson and Martha Perry

Apr 20, 1760, Samuel Perry and Agnes Johnson

Apr 13, 1762, David Johnson in this parish and Lucy Ellis in Henrico

Nov 13, 1763, Barthm Turner and Mary Johnson

Dec 23, 1764, Richard Johnson and Anne Nichols

Oct 1, 1765, Stephen Johnson and Susannah Pace

Feb 27, 1766, James Johnson and Rachel Martin

Mch 6, 1766, Benj Johnson and Martha Hughes in St. Martin's parish

June 23, 1768, Benj Cocke and Mary Johnson

Oct 18, 1768, Chas. Johnson & Elizabeth Edwards in Goochland County

Nov 3, 1768, Jas Johnson and Sarah Parish, both in Goochland

Nov 14, 1769, Richard Johnson and Dolly Powers

Sept 8, 1770, Wm Rogers and Mary Johnson, both in Goochland Co.

Nov 7, 1771, Phil Johnson of Caroline County and Elizabeth Taylor in Goochland

Dec 8, 1771, Chas Johnson and Keziah(?) Henley in Goochland

Dec 10, 1771, Wm Johnson and Anne Smith in Goochland

Aug 1, 1773, Walter Leek and Winifred Johnson in Goochland

Sept 7, 1773, Ben Anderson and Sarah Johnson in Louisa

Oct 30, 1773, Jas Cocke and Jane Johnson in Goochland

Dec 21, 1773, Walter Johnson & Margaret Johnson in Goochland

Jan 31, 1774, Chas Goodman & Rebecca Johnson of Albemarle

Sept. 6, 1774, Jesse Lacy and Mary Johnson, both in Louisa

Sept 6, 1774, Peter Fitzgerald and Lucy Johnson, both in Goochland

Nov 29, 1774, Wm Powers of Goochland and Elizabeth Johnson in Hanover County

Feb 2, 1775, Rene Woodson in Albemarle and Martha Johnson in
  Louisa
Oct 27, 1775, Wᵐ Johnson and Judith Johnson
Oct 31, 1775, Wᵐ Hahn (?) and Nancy Johnson, both in Albe-
  marle
Dec 25, 1775, Jacob Johnson and Sarah Knowling
Jan 27, 1776, John Johnson and Anne Webber
Sept 17, 1776, Wᵐ Johnson and Eleanor Dipp (or Depp), both
  of Manikin Town
Nov 3, 1776, Jas Johnson and Elizabeth Glass
Dec 8, 1776, Henry Gray and Phoebe Johnson
Feb 22, 1777, Christopher Johnson and Elizabeth Dabney, both
  of Hanover
Feb 22, 1777, John Johnson and Judith Martin
Feb 20, 1777, Jerʰ Johnson and Elizabeth Thomson
Jan 28, 1779, Jas Johnson and Elizabeth Clarkson, both of Louisa
Mch 14, 1779, Benj Woodson & Sally Johnson, both in Goochland
Aug 3, 1779, John Price and Mary Johnson, both in Goochland
Sept 23, 1779, Abm. Davis and Ann Johnson, both in Louisa
Oct 21, 1779, Benj Johnson and Mary Johnson, both in Gooch-
  land
Apr 18, 1780, Jas Houchens and Margaret Johnson, both in Gooch-
  land
Dec 7, 1780, John Winston and Mary Johnson, both in Louisa
Dec 31, 1780, Nathˡ Moss and Joanna Johnson both in Gooch-
  land
Dec 26, 1781, John Poindexter and Elizabeth Thornton Johnston
  in Louisa
June 20, 1782, Wᵐ Porter and Sarah Johnson in Louisa
Nov 24, 1782, Wᵐ Fairis and Sally Johnston in Louisa
Mch 15, 1783, Jas Johnson and Sarah Butterworth(?) in Louisa
Nov 20, 1783, Chas Smith and Nancy Johnson in Louisa
Sept 21, 1784, Edwᵈ Pace and Susannah Johnston in Goochland
Jan 5, 1785, Powers Johnson and Barbara Garland in Louisa Co.
June 25, 1785, Joseph Johnson and Sarah Freeman in Louisa Co.
Sept 18, 1751, Timothy Rich and Mary Johnston
Oct 14, 1751, Drury Johnson and Hannah Clark
Oct 14, 1751, Jas Johnson and Mildred Mims

Mch 22, 1790, Nathaniel McAllister and Martha Johnson, both of Louisa

FUNERAL SERMONS.

Aug 12, 1761, Joseph Johnson's child
May 29, 1773, David Johnson's child
Feb 16, 1773, Mrs John Johnson
Dec 12, 1773, Stephen Sampson, Sr
Feb 26, 1775, Mrs Jas Johnson, Jr
Apr 15, 1775, Aggie Johnson
June 16, 1782, James Johnston

BAPTISMS BEFORE THE BOOK WAS USED AS A REGISTER.

Wm Johnson and Christian Leek, a daughter Judith born Apr 13, 1751
Wm Johnson and Christian Leek, a son William born June 18, 1753
Wm Johnson and Christian Leek, a son Walter born Sept 23, 1755
Wm Johnson and Christian Leek, a son Samuel born Nov 17, 1757
Wm Johnson and Christian Leek, a son Mansah born July 13, 1759
Wm Johnson and Christian Leek, a son Jeremiah born Feb 14, 1762
Wm Johnson and Christian Leek, a son Stephen born Sept 20, 1763
Wm Johnson and Christian Leek, a daughter Christian, born Feb 15, 1767
Wm Johnson and Christian Leek, a son Jonah born Apr 24, 1769

REGISTER OF BIRTHS AND CHRISTENINGS IN GOOCHLAND COUNTY.

Mch 16, 1756, Jas Johnson and Mildred Mims a daughter Sarah born Aug 27, 1755
Aug 22, 1756, Drury Johnson and Hannah Clark, a son, Jacob, born May 15, 1752
Apr 28, 1756, Thos Coke and Ann Johnson, a son John, born July 27, 1756
Dec 26, 1756, Drury Johnson and Hannah Clarke, a son Elijah born Oct 30, 1756

Jan. 16, 1757, Wm Johnson & Elizabeth Hutchison, a son, Thomas, born Oct 7, 1756 (Thos Minor)

Feb 27, 1757, David Johnson & Hannah Edwards, a daughter, Martha, born Nov 25, 1756

Mch 6, 1757, Drury Johnson & Hannah Clark, a daughter, Jennie, born June 1, 1754

Apr 9, 1757, Henry Turner & Susanna Johnson, a son, Benjamin, born Oct 4, 1756

May 8, 1757, Chas Johnson and Agnes Thomson a daughter, Agnes, born Mch 30, 1757

May 8, 1757, David Cosby & Mary Johnson, a daughter Winifred, born Jan 26, 1757

May 22, 1757, Wm Edwards & Elizabeth Johnson, a son Thomas, born Nov 2, 1756

May 29, 1757, Stephen Sampson & Sarah Johnson, a daughter, Sarah, born June 10, 1757

July 7, 1757, Wm Johnson & Elizabeth Mills, a son, Jeremiah, born June 15, 1757

Sept 26, 1757, John Johnson and Hellender Thomson a daughter, Winifred, born Sept 19, 1757

Mch 25, 1758, Dan Johnson and Jane Woodie, a son Stanhope, born Feb. 27, 1758

July 23, 1758, Drury Johnson and Hannah Clark, a daughter, Ann, born July 23, 1758

July 30, 1758, James Johnson and Rachel Street, a son Charles, born June 30, 1758

Aug 13, 1758, Wm Johnson and Elizabeth Mills, a daughter, Judith, born July 2, 1758

Aug 13, 1758, Wm Johnson and Elizabeth Hutchison, a son William, born June 23, 1758

Nov. 19, 1758, Henry Turner and Susanna Johnson, a daughter, Mary, born May 16, 1758

Feb 14, 1759, Thos. Coke and Ann Johnston a daughter, Mary, born Oct 24, 1758

Feb 18, 1759, Jas. Johnson and Mildred Mims, a daughter, Martha, born Aug 2, 1758

Feb 25, 1759, Wm Edwards and Elizabeth Johnson, a son William, born July 25, 1758

May 6, 1759, David Cosby and Mary Johnston, a son William, born
Feb 14, 1759

May 6, 1759, John Johnston and Hellinder Thomson, a daughter,
Hellinder, born Apr 14, 1759

Sept 9, 1759, David Johnson and Hannah Edwards, a son Jesse,
born July 23, 1759

Dec 3, 1759, Stephen Sampson and Sarah Johnson, a daughter,
Elizabeth, born Sept 17, 1759

June 8, 1760, Benj Johnson and Susannah Pace, a daughter, Margaret, born May 13, 1760

June 24, 1760, John Johnson and Pattie Perrie, a daughter, Mary,
born June 19, 1760

June 24, 1760, Wᵐ Johnson and Elizabeth Hutchison, a daughter,
Betty, born May 17, 1760

Aug 23, 1760, Drury Johnson and Hannah Clark, a son Clayborn,
born June 17, 1760

Sept 7, 1760, Wᵐ Edwards and Elizabeth Johnson, a son Robert,
born May 10, 1760

Mch 22, 1761, Jas Johnson and Rachel Haden, a daughter, Anne,
born Nov 29, 1760

Mch 29, 1761, Jas Johnson and Mildred Mims, a daughter, Mary,
born July 26, 1760

Apr 12, 1761, Chas Johnson and Hannah Thomson, a son Benjamin, born Feb 16, 1761

May 31, 1761, Jas Johnson and Rachel Street, a daughter Elizabeth, born Sept 29, 1761

June 6, 1761, Thos Cocke and Ann Johnston, a daughter, Nancy,
born Oct 1, 1760

June 28, 1761, Wᵐ Johnson and Elizʰ Mills, a son, William, born
May 23, 1761

July 12, 1761, Joseph Johnson and Sarah Harris, a son David, born
Aug 13, 1760

Sept 8, 1761, Daniel Johnson and Jane Woodie, a son Edward,
born June 28, 1760

Dec 23, 1761, David Johnson and Hannah Edwards, a daughter,
Ann, born Oct 23, 1761

Dec 25, 1761, Benj. Johnson and Susannah Pace, a son, Joseph,
born Nov 9, 1761

Feb 5, 1762, John Johnson and Martha Perry, a daughter, Margaret, born Jan 4, 1762

Feb 7, 1762, David Cosby and Mary Johnson, a son, Jeremiah, born Oct 11, 1761

Apr 4, 1762, Stephen Sampson and Sarah Johnson, a daughter, Judith, born Nov 21, 1761

Apr 11, 1762, James Johnson and Mildred Mims, a son David, born Mch 17, 1762

May 25, 1763, James Johnson and Rachel Haden, a daughter Mary, born Apr 19, 1763 .

June 10, 1763, David Johnson and Lucy Ellis, a daughter, Sarah, born Mch 16, 1763

July 25, 1763, Stephen Sampson and Sarah Johnson, a daughter, Ann, born June 11, 1763

Aug 21, 1763, James Johnston and Rachel Street a son, William, born July 17, 1763

Sept 14, 1763, Thos. Johnston and Elizabeth Meriwether, a daughter, Elizabeth, born Aug 30, 1763

Nov 7, 1763, John Johnson and Martha Perry, a daughter, Violette, born Oct 15, 1763

Nov 20, 1763, Wm Johnson and Christian Leek, a son, Stephen, born Sept 20, 1763

Jan 1, 1764, Benjamin Johnson and Susannah Pace, a son, Benjamin, born Nov 18, 1763

May 17, 1764, Wm Edwards and Elizabeth Johnson, a son, Benjamin, born Mch 29, 1764

June 5, 1764, James Johnson and Mildred Mims, Twins, Joseph & Benjamin, born Apr 17, 1764

June 10, 1764, Wm Strong and Frances Johnson, a son, Isham, born Apr 22, 1764

July 19, 1764, Drury Johnson and Hannah Clark, a daughter, Mary, born Nov 23, 1762

Aug 12, 1764, David Johnson and Hannah Edwards, a son, Thomas, born June 15, 1764

Sept 30, 1764, Samuel Perry and Agnes Johnson, a son Thomas, born Sept 3, 1764

Dec 23, 1764, David Johnson & Lucy Ellis, a daughter Ann, born Oct 19, 1764

Mch 8, 1765, Stephen Sampson and Sarah Johnson, a son, William, born Jan 13, 1765

May 17, 1765, David Cosby and Mary Johnston, a son, James, born Mch 28, 1765

Sept 5, 1765, Thos Cocke and Ann Johnston, a daughter, Agnes, born Mch 29, 1765

Dec 25, 1765, Benj. Johnson and Susanna Pace, a daughter, Susannah, born Oct 17, 1765

Jan 1, 1766, Richard Johnson and Ann Nichols, a son William, born —— — 1765

Mch 29, 1766, John Johnson and Martha Perry, a son, William, born Sept 16, 1765

May 11, 1766, Wm Edwards and Elizabeth Johnson, a daughter, Mary, born Feb 29, 1766

Aug 24, 1766, James Johnson and Rachel Street, a son, Jeremiah, born July 25, 1766

Feb 15, 1767, Stephen Johnson and Susannah Pierce, a son John, born Oct 18, 1766

Apr 5, 1767, Bartholomew Turner, and Mary Johnson, a son Charles, born Dec 11, 1766

Apr 5, 1765, David Johnson and Lucy Ellis, a son, William, born Dec 11, 1766

INSCRIPTIONS ON STONES IN THE CHAMBLISS CEMETERY AT EMPORIA, VIRGINIA. —The grave of Col. John R. Chambliss, member of the Secession Convention of 1861 from Greensville County, Virginia, is marked by an obelisk. [East side] "My husband/ Sacred/ to the memory of/ Col. J. R. Chambliss./ Born March 4, 1809/ Died April 3, 1875/ Aged 66 years/ The Lord gave, and the/ Lord hath taken away/ Blessed be the name of/ the Lord. Job 1,21/ My task is finished. I'll join/ thee when the Master calls— [North side] My father/ My son despise not the/ chastening of the Lord/ neither be weary of his/ correction. For whom the/ Lord loveth he correcteth/ even as a father the son/ in whom he delighteth./

Prov. III, 11, 12.—[South side] Our grandfather/ The poor committeth/ himself unto thee, thou/ art the helper of the/ fatherless. Ps. X, 14.—[West side] Loveable, openhearted/ freehanded he will long/ be remembered and/ long lamented./ An affectionate husband/ A tender father/ A loving grandfather."

Col. John R. Chambliss was born at Glen View, Sussex County. The house is on Route 301, a few miles south of Stony Creek. A description and photograph may be found in Stephenson: *Old Homes of Surry and Sussex*. Col. Chambliss graduated from William and Mary College in 1830. Some of his books, among them Adam Smith's *Wealth of Nations*, which he used at college, are now in the library of Mrs. Robert Mason Mallory, of Emporia, a connection. Col. Chambliss was a charter member of the Hicksford Baptist Church in 1839. He, with three other persons, Joseph Turner, Joseph Fisher and Rebecca Goodwyn, organized the church, now the Main Street Baptist Church, Emporia, when there was no other church organization in Hicksford. A leading citizen of Greensville County, he was its representative in the Virginia Secession Convention of 1861. The grave of Col. Chambliss' son is marked by a stone with this inscription:

"To the memory of/ John R. Chambliss, Jr./ Brigadier General CSA/ Born Jan. 23, 1833/ Killed in battle on the 16th of Aug., 1864/." (The stone is broken here, and the rest of the inscription cannot be read.)

General John R. Chambliss graduated from West Point in the class of 1853. He resigned from the Army and lived in Greensville County. He was a planter until the outbreak of the War Between the States, when he joined the Confederate Army. A complete account of his war career may be found in Eliot: *West Point in the Confederacy*. General Chambliss built the house which still stands three miles west of Emporia on route 58. It is occupied by his descendants, Mrs. William Hood Chambliss and her son, William Hood Chambliss, Jr. A highly interesting account of life at this home during the War Between the States is given in Avary: *A Virginia Girl in the Civil War*.

Other inscriptions are: "Mrs. Winifred Chambliss/ Born/ January 27, 1788/ Died/ December 17, 1859/ Aged/ 72 Years."

"Roberta Chambliss/ Born/ January 9, 1840/ Died/ January 26, 1842/ Aged/ 2 years and 17 days."

"Sacred to the memory/ James William Chambliss/ Born/ October 16, 1837/ Died/ February 19, 1842/ Aged/ 4 years and/ 4 months."

"Our children/ Ida Dove Chambliss/ Born/ December 28, 1842/ Died/ November 8, 1843/ Aged/10 months and/ 11 days/ Sallie Louisa Chambliss/ Born/ Sept. 22, 1835/ Died/ May 11, 1847/ Aged/ 11 years and/ 7 months."

The Chambliss burying ground, marked by several specimens of fine boxwood, is in the heart of Emporia, not far behind the residence of Mrs. W. C. Weaver, on South Main Street.—Contributed by Herbert Clarence Bradshaw, Rice, Virginia.

TOMBSTONES.

Communicated by Rev. S. O. Southall, Dinwiddie, Va.

New Castle, Hanover County

Sacred to the Memory of
Mr. Isaac Brown. He was
a Native of Derby in the
Island of Great Britain
But settled a merchant
in this place.
In the prime of Life,
* * * in the very moment of anxious
expectation,
* * * arrival of a beloved
* * * an infant family,
* * * pleased the Almighty
* * * take him to himself
* * * the Augt, 1785
* * * and Disconsolate widow
* * * token of her affection

On the old Smith Place half a mile east of Dinwiddie C. H.

Capt John Hill,
Son of Col. Larkin Smith
Born May 14, 1783,
Died March 28, 1843

"Old Church," Hanover Co.,
Here lies the corpse of Alexander
Mathy, son of Gabriel Mathy
Mercht in Greenoch who died
of his age.
30 of July, 1752, in the 20th year

146

INSCRIPTIONS ON GRAVESTONES IN THE OLD CEMETERY AT "BREMO" IN HENRICO—AND A CORRECTION

By W. Cabell Moore, Washington, D. C.

In the William and Mary Quarterly, January 1895, Vol. III, p. 204, are published copies of the inscriptions on two gravestones found in the ancient graveyard at "Bremo" in Henrico County, one over the grave of Richard Cocke (1639-1706), the other over the grave of Ann Bowler Cocke (1675-1705). Recently my brother, Capt. Charles E. Moore, of Richmond, and I visited this spot and with some difficulty located the site of the graveyard and found several broken and mutilated gravestones. After scraping off considerable dirt and trash with a hoe and cleaning the stones with a stiff wire brush the inscriptions were distinctly legible and we discovered that your former contributor reported erroneously the spelling of the word "Bremo" in the third line of the inscription on the gravestone of Ann Bowler Cocke. He reported it as being spelled "B R E M O R," but we found it spelled "B R E M O," with no "R" on the end. This would seem to be the correct spelling, for in Richard Cocke's will, dated October 4, 1665, a copy of which may now be seen in the Archives Division of the State Library, in Richmond, the word is spelled "Bremo," and Gen. John H. Cocke, considerably over a hundred years ago, named his home in Fluvanna for the old home place of his ancestors in Henrico and called it "Bremo."

While except for the spelling of the word "Bremo," both inscriptions were reported accurately in the main in your issue, January 1895, we found several words in addition to those recorded by your former correspondent, and we found a third gravestone which has not heretofore been described that I know of, and which though not so old as the other two still may be of some interest. In the inscription on this stone the word "Bremo" is spelled incorrectly, but this was evidently a mistake of the engraver.

The graveyard is one of the oldest, if not the oldest, private family burying ground, still recognizable as such, in Virginia. The two older gravestones are both broken into three large pieces, and the edges of the oldest stone have been badly chipped off. Above the inscription to Ann Bowler Cocke in a circle about eighteen inches in diameter is what appears to be a pair of wings spread out over a skull and cross bones, rather badly mutilated. This is a large, heavy stone. The third stone, which was found only by accident, for it was entirely covered with dirt except at one corner, is in perfectly good condition. There is every evidence of many other graves nearby, and many pieces of broken gravestone are scattered about, but we did not have time to look further. There is a movement on foot now to restore these graves and build a wall around them.

The three inscriptions as we found them several weeks ago are as follows:

—1—

HERE LYES INTERRD THE BO
RICHARD COCKE
ON OF RICHARD COCKE OF B
HE WAS BORN THE 10th DA
ECEMBER 1639 AND D PARTE
IFE THE 20th OF NOVEMBER 17

147

HERE LYETH INTER'D THE BODY
OF ANN, THE WIFE OF RICHARD COCKE
THE YOUNGER OF BREMO IN THIS COUNTY
AND DAUGHTER OF THOMAS BOWLER LATE
OF THE COUNTY OF RAPPAHANNOCK ESQ
SHE WAS BORNE THE 23d DAY OF JAN.,
1675 AND DEPARTED THIS LIFE THE 24
DAY—APRIL 1706, AGED
30 YEARS, 3 MONTH, 1 DAY.

—3—

IN MEMORY OF
MRS. LETITIA PROSSER
SPOUSE OF
MR. WILLIAM PROSSER
OF BREME
AND ELDEST DAUGHTER OF
MAJ. NATH'L FOX
OF HANOVER COUNTY
SHE WAS BORN FEB. 9, 1784
AND DEPARTED THIS LIFE
MARCH 8, 1817.

FORGET BLEST SHADE THE TRIBUTARY TEAR
THAT MOURNS THY EXIT FROM A WORLD LIKE THIS
FORGIVE THE WISH THAT WOULD HAVE KEPT YOU
HERE
AND STAY'D THY PROGRESS TO THE SEAT OF BLISS.

LIST OF OBITUARIES.

From Richmond, Virginia, Newspapers.*

Virginia Independent Chronicle.

Name	Date of Death	Date of Paper
Mrs. Margaret Cleland	June 5, 1786	Aug. 16, 1786.
Mrs. Ann Beall	Sept. 10, 1786	Sept. 20, 1786.
Chevalier de Laville Brune	Lately	Sept. 20, 1786.
George Harmer	Tuesday, last	Wed. Sept. 20, 1786.
Peter V. B. Livingston, Jr.	Sept. 23, 1786	Sept. 27, 1786.
Mrs. Ann Nicholas	Nov. 5, 1786	Nov. 6, 1786.
Abner Nash	Dec. 2. 1786	Dec. 27, 1786.
James Cross	Jan. 10, 1787	Jan. 24, 1787.
William Coutts	Thur. evening, 1787	Wed., Jan. 24, 1787.
Mrs. Elizabeth Hay	May 14, 1787	May 27, 1787.
James Baron, [Barron]	May 16, 1787	May 27, 1787.
John Hunter Holt	Friday, May 16, 1787	Wed., June 13, 1787.
William Adams	June 2, 1787	June 13, 1787.
Mrs. Ann Price	Wed. last, 1787	Wed., June 13, 1787.
William Eaton	Saturday, 1787	Wed., June 20, 1787.
Gerrard Banks	Friday, 1787	Wed., June 20, 1787.
Mrs. Formicola	Monday, 1787	Wed., June 20, 1787.
Mrs. Anna Harrison	Yesterday, 1787	Wed., Aug. 29, 1787.
Henry Lee	Aug. 15, 1787	Aug. 29, 1787, and Sept. 5, 1787.
Mrs. Elizabeth Wythe	Aug. 18, 1787	Aug. 29, 1787.
Mrs. Margaret Hunter	Friday, 1787	Oct. 3, 1787.
Mrs. Jane Williams	Monday, 1787	Oct. 3, 1787.
John Thoroughgood	Lately	Oct. 24, 1787.
William Alsop	Jan. 7, 1788	Jan. 16, 1788.
Mrs. Susanna Sheilds		Jan. 30, 1788.
Bolling Stark	Friday, 1788	Wed., Jan. 30, 1788.
Mrs. Tucker, wife of St. Geo. Tucker	Saturday, 1788	Wed., Jan. 30, 1788.
Robert Murray	Sunday	Wed., March 5, 1788.
Joseph Davenport		March 12, 1788.
William Haywood	April 6, 1788	April 16, 1788.
Mrs. Mary Davenport	Lately	April 16, 1788.
Mrs. Mary Moore		April 16, 1788.

*This list is believed to be complete, as far as it goes. It was prepared some years ago.

Name	Date of Death	Date of Paper
James Cross	Wednesday, 1787	Jan. 25, 1787.
Mrs. Page, wife of John Page		Feb. 1, 1787.
Mrs. Taylor, wife of Col. Jno. Taylor [Tayloe]		Feb. 1, 1787.
John Lomax		Feb. 1, 1787.
Mrs. Roper, wife of Jesse Roper	Thursday, 1787	March 22, 1787.
Mrs. Rebecca Stith	Saturday, 1787	April 5, 1787.
James Honey	Sunday Se'nnight night, 1787	April 11, 1787.
William Adams	Tuesday, 1787	June 7, 1787.
Jesse Key	Sunday, 1787	Aug. 23, 1787.
Mrs. Harrison, wife of Benj. Harrison, Jr	Tuesday, 1787	Aug. 30, 1787.
John Greenhow	Last Week, 1787	Sept. 6, 1787.
Mrs. Farquharson, widow of Jno. Farquharson		Sept. 6, 1787.
Beverley Dickson, Jr.		Sept. 6, 1787.
Mrs. Margaret Hunter		Oct. 4, 1787.
Mrs. Jane Williams, wife of Thomas Williams	Monday, 1787	Oct. 4, 1787.
James Buchanan	Oct. 3, 1787	Oct. 11, 1787.
George Wright	Aug. 7, 1787	Oct. 11, 1787.
Robert Murray	Sunday, 1788	March 6, 1788.
William Haywood		April 17, 1788.
Mrs. Sarah Ronald		May 29, 1788.
—— Drewidz		
John Banister		Oct. 16, 1788.
William Calder		Oct. 16, 1788.
Gabriel Galt		Oct. 30, 1788.
Mrs. Lettice Ball		November 6, 1788.
George Carter		November 6, 1788.
Alexander Skinner		November 20, 1788.
Humphrey Harwood		November 27, 1788.
Mrs. Orr, widow of Hugh Orr		December 4, 1788.
Miles Hunter		December 18, 1788.
Mrs. Sarah Trebell		February 12, 1789.
Mrs. Harwood, widow of Humphrey		February 19, 1789.
John Shackleford		February 19, 1789.
Alexander Strachan		February 26, 1789.
James Cocke		February 26, 1789.
Mrs. Ann Randolph, wife of Thos. M. Randolph		March 12, 1789.
Philip Johnson, [Johnston]		March 19, 1789.

Name	Date of Paper
James Murray	April 9, 1789.
Mrs. Jane Cringhan, wife of Dr. John Cringhan	April 30, 1789.
Littleton Eyre	May 21, 1789.
John McLean	May 28, 1789.
Richard Kello	June 4, 1789.
James Swaine	June 11, 1789.
George Richards	July 16, 1789.
David Griffith	August 27, 1789.
Robert Rawlings	September 24, 1789.
Williiam Trebell	October 15, 1789.
Mrs. McKeand, wife of John McKeand	November 12, 1789.
Richard Cary	November 19, 1789.
William Dawson	November 19, 1789.

EXAMINER.

Mrs. Sarah Wilkinson	October 10, 1800.
Thomas Bell	October 17, 1800.
Thomas Bell	October 24, 1800.
Willis Riddick	October 24, 1800.
William Nelson	January 13, 1801.

VIRGINIA ARGUS.

John Blair	September 9, 1800.
Otway Byrd	September 9, 1800.
William Bowyer	September 9, 1800.

VIRGINIA GAZETTE AND GENERAL ADVERTISER.

Abner Crump	January 15, 1802.
John Hay	January 26, 1802.
Elizabeth Skipwith	March 26, 1802.
Mrs. Alice Marshall, wife of William Marshall	April 24, 1802.
Andrew Dunscomb	May 1, 1802, May 8, 1802, (and Examiner, May 5, 1802).
James Price	May 8, 1802.
Mrs. Washington, wife of George Washington	May 29, 1802.
George Nicolson	June 19, 1802.
William Nicolson	June 19, 1802.
Bernard Markham	July 17, 1802.
Daniel Morgan	July 17, 1802.
John Tompkins	July 21, 1802.
Lewis Littlepage	July 21, 1802.
George W. Hoomes	July2 8, 1802, (and Examiner July 28, 1802).

Name	*Date of Paper*
Mrs. Judith Taylor, wife of Thomas Taylor	July 31, 1802.
Mrs. Harriet McRae, wife of Alexander McRae	August 18, 1802.
Mrs. Foushee, wife of Dr. William Foushee	September 29, 1802.
Mrs. Currie, wife of Dr. James Currie	November 27, 1802.
William Norvell	November 27, 1802.
Mrs. Cockran, relict of David Cockran	November 27, 1802.
Mungo Roy, Jr.	December 8, 1802.

THE EXAMINER.

Percy Smith Pope	December 17, 1799.
George Washington	December 20, 1799. December 24, 1799. February 28, 1800. March 4, 1800.
Robert Brooke	March 7, 1800.

RECORDER.

James Price	May 19, 1802.
Gill Armistead Selden	June 9, 1802.
John Calland	February 9, 1803, (and Gazette Jan. 9, 1803).

EXAMINER.

John Willis	June 9, 1802.
Stephens Thompson Mason	May 21, 1803, (and Examiner May 21).

GAZETTE.

William Ludwell Lee	January 29, 1803.
Mrs. Judith Lyons, wife of Peter Lyons	March 9, 1803.
Daniel Dunscomb	March 19, 1803, (and Exami'r Mar. 19).
Mrs. Rachel Brooke, wife of Robert Brooke	March 26, 1803.
William Harris	March 26, 1803.
William Radford	April 6, 1803.
Archibald Timberlake	April 30, 1803.
Mrs. Martha Shore, wife of Henry S. Shore	May 25, 1803.
Wyndham Grymes	April 16, 20, 1803.
Mrs. Elizabeth Rootes, wife of Edmund W. Rootes.	July 9, 1803.
Samuel Edens	July 23, 1803.
Edmund Pendleton	October 29, 1803. November 2, 1803.
Nathaniel Carrington	November 2, 1803.
Mrs. Jenny Pope Cousin, wife of Gerard B. Cousin.	November 16, 1803.

EXAMINER

William Booker	Oct. 16, 1802.

	Date of Paper
Name	*Date of Paper*

Mrs. Kitturah Kean, wife of Dr. Andrew Kean....March 12, 1803.
Mann Page...April 6, 1803.
Roscow Lipscombe.............................June 22, 1803.
Mrs. Ann Countes Semple, wife of James Semple....June 29, 1803.
John Thomson Callender..... ....July 20, 1803.
Simon Shultz................................... {July 20, 1803.
                                                 {July 27, 1803.
Mrs. Mildred Courtney, wife of Thomas Courtney.August 27, 1803.
Mrs. E. Whiting... ....January 3, 1804.

Gazette.

Mrs. Catherine Hare, wife of Thomas N. Hare....February 16, 1804.
Mary Hoye...February 29, 1804.
Mrs. Mary Gooseley, wife of George Gooseley.....March 17, 1804.
John Chiswell Barret ....March 24, 1804.
Robert Sydnor................................March 28, 1804, and
                                                     Apr. 7.
Anne G. C. Goodson............................August 18, 1804.
Mrs. Anna Maria Riddick.... ....August 29, 1804.
Christopher L. Smith...........................September 22, 1804.
Josiah Hatcher................. ....September 22, 1804.
Samuel Scherer............... ....September 28, 1804.
William Ross....... ....September 28, 1804.
James Hayes ....Oct. 10, 1804, (and
                                                     Enquirer).
Mrs. McGraw, wife of Samuel McGraw...........October 10, 1804.
Smith Blakey....................................October 13, 1804.
Liston Temple................. ....October 13, 1804.
Patrick Henry, Jr. ....October 24, 1804.
Mrs. Ann Randolph.............................November 3, 1804.
Mrs. Martha Banks, wife of Henry Banks.........December 5, 1804.
John Lester. ....Dec. 22, 1804, (and
                                                  Enquirer Dec. 22).

Enquirer.

Philip Pendleton..................................August 8, 1804. (and
                                                   Gazette, Aug. 6).
Mrs. Ester Cohen, wife of Jacob I. Cohen ....August 25, 1804.
Thomas H. Ellis...............................September 19, 1804.
Alexander White..............................October 17, 1804.
Mrs. Elizabeth Claiborne, wife of W. C. C. Claiborne.November 17, 1804.
Dr. John Brockenbrough.... .. ..December 1, 1804.
Martha Royall Banks, wife of Henry Banks.......Dec. 8, 1804, (and
                                                   Gazette, Dec. 5).
James Henry......................... ....January 18, 1805.
Mrs. West Jr....................................January 22, 1805.

Name	*Date of Paper*
Dr. John K. Read, Jr........ .... ⎤	
Dr. John K. Read, Sr.......................... ⎬ March 5, 1805.	
Mrs. Martha K. Banks....... .... ⎦	
Mrs. Ogilvie, wife of James Ogilvie................March 12, 1805.	
George Gairdner.................... ....March 12, 1805.	
Mrs. Polly Brainham, wife of James W. Brainham.April 2, 1805.	
Dr. Daniel Wilson........ ....April 19, 1805.	
William Winston................................April 19, 1805.	

GAZETTE.

Mrs. Ann Lightfoot, wife of William Lightfoot ....May 29, 1805.
Jane Cary............ ....July 24, 1805.
William Wiseham..... .... { August 7, 1805. August 10, 1805.
Nathaniel Thomson..........................….August 17, 1805.
Mrs. Paine, wife of Orris Paine........ ....October 2, 1805.
Sir Peyton Skipwith......................... …...Oct. 26, 1805, (and Argus, Oct. 19).
Joseph Jones............................ ....Nov. 2, 1805, (and Enquirer, Nov. 5, and Argus Nov. 2).
Mrs. Harrison, wife of Jacob Harrison...........November 6, 1805.
Dr. Jordan Anderson........ ....November 9, 1805.
Leonard Wilson ....November 13, 1805.
Mrs. Mary Anderson, wife of Dr. Jordan Anderson..November 20, 1805.
Dr. Robert Carter..............................November 27, 1805.
James Blagrove............................December 7, 1805.
John Hoomes..................................December 21, 1805.
Elizabeth Cary..............................December 21, 1805.
Robert Andrews ....…............ February 4, 1804.
Henry Randolph.................... ....February 4, 1804.
John Day.... ....April 4, 1804.
Mrs. Frances Lynch, wife of James Head Lynch...July 21, 1804.
Madame Cornillon.............................July 21, 1804.
Hastings Lynch.................... ....October 20, 1804.
John Fox .. ..December 12, 1804.
Francis Trouin........................... ....December 12, 1804.

IMPARTIAL OBSERVER.

George Wythe...............................June 14, 1806, (and Enquirer, June 10).
Meriwether Jones..............................August 23, 1806.
John Davis.....................................September 20, 1806.
Mrs. Brough, wife of Robert Brough ....September 20, 1806.
John L. Price................................... October 11, 1806.

Name	Date of Paper
Mrs. Sarah Smith, wife of George W. Smith.....	.October 11, 1806.
Dr. James Blamire...	..October 18, 1806.
Lewis Harvie......................................	April 25, 1807.

ENQUIRER.

Stewart Bankhead...........................	.May 14, 1805.
John Dixon..............	May 24, 1805.
Lunsford Lomax	June 7, 1805.
Mrs. Elizabeth Jones Dunn, wife of Washington V. Dunn..................	July 16, 1805.
Alexander Pope Price...........................	July 19, 1805.
Catherine Storke.......	August 2, 1805.
John Booker......	August 6, 1805.
James Waddell	October 4, 1805.
Mrs. Susan Field, wife of Thomas Field..........	October 4, 1805.
Joseph Shelton Watson.........................	October 8, 1805.
Elias Wills	Oct. 8, 1805, (and Argus, Oct. 9).
George Richardson....	October 18, 1805.
C. D. Hopkins.................................	November 5, 1805.
Austin Derbigny	November 19, 1805.
Beverley Stanard..............................	November 19, 1805.
Leonard Willson...............	November 19, 1805.
Henry Benskin Lightfoot	November 19, 1805.
David Patteson, Jr.....	January 2, 1806.
John Napier.........	February 18, 1806, (and Argus).
Robert H. Woodson......	March 18, 1806.
Mrs. Susanna Walford, wife of Edward Walford...	March 18, 1806.
Mrs. Mary Price, relict of John Price	March 18, 1806.
Mrs. Ann Yancey, wife of David Yancey.........	March 28, 1806.
Mrs. Maria Cocke, wife of Bowler F. Cocke... ...	April 1, 1806.
Mrs. Mary B. Randolph, wife of Thomas Randolph.	April 22, 1806.

ARGUS.

William Walker	March 21, 1804.
Mrs. Rebecca E. Tucker....	March 31, 1804.
Henry Royster	March 31, 1804.
Mrs. Eppes, wife of John W. Eppes.............	May 2, 1804.
Thomas Pleasants..............	May 9, 1804.
Jacob Bockius	June 2, 1804.
William Jones	June 9, 1804.
Dr. Wray.......................................	July 11, 1804.
John Trigg	July 14, 1804.
Jacob Wheaton	July 21, 1804.

Name	Date of Paper
Dr. Ashley Adams	August 8, 1804.
Mrs. Martha Gordon, relict of James Gordon	September 7, 1804.
Daniel Boyce	September 12, 1804.
Mrs. Allen, wife of Jedediah Allen	September 26, 1804.
Joseph Watkins	September 26, 1804.
Thomas Lewis	September 26, 1804.
Col. William Finnie	October 24, 1804.
Mrs. Frances Brooking	October 27, 1804.
John Caldwell	November 28, 1804.
John Woodger	December 22, 1804.
Mrs. Ann Dobie	January 30, 1805.
Archibald Lang	February 6, 1805.
Quin Morton	February 16, 1805.
Dr. John K. Read, Sr.	February 16, 1805.
James Johnson	March 15, 1805.
William Winston	April 20, 1805.
William Webb	May 1, 1805.
Francis Scott	May 29 1805.
Mrs. Mary Jordan, wife of Edward Jordan	June 19, 1805.
Mrs. Jane Fairfax, relict of Bryan (Lord) Fairfax	July 6, 1805.
James West	July 20, 1805.
Mrs. Mary Guerrant, wife of Peter Guerrant	August 3, 1805.
Mrs. Margaret Rowland	August 10, 1805.
John Royall	August 28, 1805.
William Worrock	Sept. 21, 1805.
Andrew McCombe	September 25, 1805.
Mrs. Janet Russell	September 28, 1805.
Thomas Fearn	October 12, 1805.
Edward Johnson	October 16, 1805.
Mrs. Ann Sheilds, wife of David Sheilds	October 19, 1805.
William Webster	October 30, 1805.
John Baker	November 6, 1805.
Dr. William Wilkinson	November 23, 1805.
Moses Tredway	November 27, 1805.
Thomas Lewis	November 30, 1805.
John Syme	December 4, 1805.
Mrs. Elizabeth Walker, wife of Dr. David Walker	December 14, 1805.

ENQUIRER.

Name	Date of Paper
William Bryan	February 6, 1806.
Robert Burton	February 15, 1806.
Lyne Shackleford	May 20, 1806.
Mrs. Sarah Bruce, wife of James Bruce	May 30, 1806.
Edward P. Chamberlayne	June 17, 1806.

Name	*Date of Paper*
Mrs. Elizabeth H. Clarke, wife of John Clarke.....July 15, 1806, (and Argus, July 16.)
Mary Elliott...July 22, 1806.
Charles Carter...July 22, 1806.
James Upshaw...July 22, 1806.
James Tompkins..August 1, 1806.
Mrs. Ambler...August 5, 1806.
Mrs. Francis Gantier ....August 5, 1806.
John Davis..September 16, 1806.
Dr. William Johnson.....................................October 21, 1806.
Octavia St. Clair Dandridge...........................October 24, 1806.
Gabriel Jones..October 31, 1806.
Mrs. Jane Tredway, wife of Thomas Tredway.....October 31, 1806.
William Lawrence.......................................November 21, 1806.
Nathaniel Pope...December 2, 1806.
Joseph Selden...Janruary 31, 1807.
Thomas Burke...February 6, 1807.
John Harvie...February 13, 1807.
Samuel Roane..February 27, 1807.
William Guy...March 17, 1807.
Mrs. Rebecca Hay, wife of George Hay...........March 24, 1807.
Muscoe Garnett..March 24, 1807.
Samuel Richardson.......................................April 7, 1807.
John Beckley..April 14, 1807.
Dr. James Currie..April 24, 1807, (and Gazette, Apr. 25,) (and Argus, April 24.)
William Austin..May 1, 1807.

ARGUS.

| Mrs. Susanna Pierce, wife of Godwin Pierce.......October 19, 1810. |
| John Prosser...October 30, 1810. |
| Edward Carrington.......................................{ October 30, 1810. / November 2, 1810. } |
| John Brown...November 2, 1810. |
| Samuel Barron...November 6, 1810. |
| John Heath...November 20, 1810. |
| Dr. Watts..November 20, 1810. |
| Abraham Judah..November 20, 1810. |
| Joseph Scott..December 14, 1810. |
| Mrs. Anne Craig...December 21, 1810. |
| William Terry...December 25, 1810. |
| Cyrus Griffin...{ December 25, 1810. / December 28, 1810. } |

Name	Date of Paper
Henry Lee	April 9, 1818.

ENQUIRER.

Name	Date of Paper
Christopher McRae	December 31, 1808.
General Martin (Henry county)	January 10, 1808.
Mrs. Gilly Stevens, relict of General Edward Steves	January 27, 1821.
James Baytop	Jan. 22, 1821. (Torn, see another copy.)
Thomas Jeffries	May 31, 1822.
John W. Semple	May 31, 1822.
Mrs. Lucy Davis, wife of Arthur L. Davis	October 31, 1823.
Nicholas Cobbs	October 31, 1823.
Mathew Branch	October 31, 1823.

FAMILY VISITOR.

Name	Date of Paper
Mrs. Ann Gresham, wife of William Gresham	Februrary 1, 1823.
John C. Lawrence	February 1, 1823.
Hiram Blackwell	February 8, 1823.
John Buchanan	December 21, 1822.
Samuel Wydown	March 1, 1823.
William Nott, Jr	" "
Mrs. Susanna L. Pleasants, wife of Daniel G. Pleasants	" "
David Watkins	" "
John Livingston	October 11, 1823.
Edmund Taylor	" "
William Dickinson	" "
Mrs. Mary Poore	" "
Pinkethman D. Booker, Sr	" "
Thomas Holes	" "
Lorenzo White	" "
Mrs. Susanna Moore	" "
Mrs. Ann Allison	" "
Mrs. Elizabeth Green	" "
Mary Pierce	" "
John M. Ryan	" "
Rebecca Thornton	" "
Grace Hall	" "
Matthew Harvey	" "
John Christian	" "
Mrs. Margaret Priddy, relict of John Priddy	" "
John T. Ford	July 10, 1824.
Mrs. Johannah Semple, wife of James Semple	" "
Julia Ann Moss	" "

(TO BE CONCLUDED.)

LIST OF OBITUARIES.

From Richmond, Virginia, Newspapers.

(CONCLUDED)

COMPILER

Name	Date of Paper
J. B. Littlepage	August 23, 1825.

ARGUS.

Name	Date of Paper
Robert Biscoe	March 4, 1806.
John Anderson	March 7, 1806.
Rev. David Patteson (Buck.)	March 14, 1806.
Mrs. Mary relict of Captain John Price	March 14, 1806.
Isaiah Isaacs	April 8, 1806.
The wife of Edmund Jameson	April 25, 1806.
Nelson Cogbill	May 9, 1806.
George Wythe	June 10, 1806.
James Upshaw	July 12, 1806.
Mrs. Hannah Dudley	July 16, 1806.
Richard S. Pleasants	July 16, 1806.
Benj. Dabney	July 19, 1806.
John Williamson	July 19, 1806.
Ann wife of Mathew Clay	July 19, 1806.
Mary Elliott	July 19, 1806.
Mrs. Ambler	August 6, 1806.
Mrs. Frances Gautier	August 6, 1806.
James Lyle, Jr	August 6, 1806.
William Powers	August 6, 1806.
Judith wife of William Powers	August 6, 1806.
Mrs. Mary wife of John Morris	August 16, 1806.
Joseph Bondurant	August 16, 1806.
Mrs. Judith Bingley	August 16, 1806.
Mrs. Polly wife of Thos. Courtney	September 10, 1806.
Joel Tucker	September 17, 1806.
Abner Waugh	September 20, 1806.
Elisha Leake	October 29, 1806.
David Bell	November 8, 1806.
Robert Jennings	November 8, 1806.

Name	Date of Paper
John M'Credie	February 7, 1807.
Thos. L. Lee	March 25, 1807.
William Heth	April 1, 1807.
Elizabeth E. Hay	April 1, 1807.
Samuel Cohen	April 18, 1807.
Lewis Harvie	{ April 18, 1807. { April 29, 1807.
Walter Irvine	April 25, 1807.
Mrs. S. Goode wife of Robert Goode	May 27, 1807.
Mrs. Frances Pynes	July 4, 1807.
John Henry	August 26, 1807.
Thomas Blackburn	August 29, 1807.
Archibald Bryce	September 12, 1807
Mrs. Mary Ann Clarke	September 12, 1807.
William F. Ash	September 26, 1807.
Nathan Bell	Oct. 7 (and Argus), 1807.
Mrs. Sally Peyton, wife of John Peyton.	October 10, 1807.
Mrs. Taylor	October 10, 1807.
John Knott	October 10, 1807.
Lady C. Stuart Griffin	October 10, 1807.
Joseph Moxley	October 24, 1807.
Mrs. Harriet Whitlocke, wife of John Whitlocke	November 24, 1807.
William Nelson	December 1, 1807.

ARGUS

Mrs. Catherine S. Greenup, wife of Chas. Greenup.	December 4, 1807.
Wilson Davenport	January 27, 1807.
Samuel Ege	February 13, 1807.
Mrs. Jane S. Ferguson, wife of James B. Ferguson	February 27, 1807.
Mrs. Elizabeth Wagner	March 6, 1807.
James Anderson	March 17, 1807.
Reuben Turner	May 16, 1807.
James Otey, Sr.	June 10, 1807.
James Cowland	{ September 26, 1807. { October 3, 1807.
Alexander George	September 9, 1807.
Thomas Newton, Sr.	September 16, 1807.
Argyle Williamson	October 3, 1807.
Charles Burton	October 7, 1807.
Philip Moody	October 10, 1807.
Archibold McRobert	October 16, 1807.
Mrs. Susanna C. Palmer, wife of Charles	October 16, 1807.

Name	Date of Paper
Wm. Stanard	October 23, 1807.
John Crew, Jr.	October 27, 1807.
Wilson Price	December 11, 1807.
Nat. Wilkinson	December 22, 1807.
Mrs. Sarah Dixon, relict of John Dixon	December 22, 1807.

GAZETTE

Name	Date of Paper
Matthew Timberlake	February 9, 1808.
Francis Timberlake	March 15, 1808.
Mrs. Sarah, wife of Wm. Wardlow	April 11, 1808.
Wm. Christian	May 6, 1808.
Marcus Elcan	May 10, 1808.
Mrs. Ann Henry, wife of LaFayette Henry	May 10, 1808.
Adam Craig	May 13, (and Enquirer 14), 1808.
Robert Means	May 17, 1808.
John M. Galt	June 21, 1808.
Wm. G. Allen	July 19, 1808.
Samuel Pointer	July 19, 1808.
Mrs. Giles, wife of Wm. G. Giles	August 16, 1808.
Mrs. Caroline M. Randolph, wife of Henry Randolph	September 30, 1808.
Mrs. Fenwick, wife of Wm. Fenwick	October 7, 1808.
Wm. Moseley	Oct. 7,(and Enqui'r October 7, 1808).
John Page	October 14, (and Argus and Enquirer Oct. 14), 1808.
Dr. Jno. Cringan	November 8, 1808.
Thomas Nicolson	November 15, 1808.
Mrs. Martha, wife of Mathew Hobson	November 29, 1808.
Samuel Calland	December 2, 1808.

ARGUS

Name	Date of Paper
Obadiah Smith	February 2, 1808.
Jane B., wife of Francis Walker	March 1, 1808.
Jane, wife of John Price	March 1, 1808.
Jane, wife of John Courtney	March 22, 1808.
Judah, wife of Robt. Metchell	March 25, 1808.
Wm. Webber	April 5, 1808.
Joseph Mosby	April 5, 1808.
James Gunn	April 12, 1808.
Anthony Tucker Dixon	May 3, 1808.
Martin Hoyle	May 27, 1808.
Anderson Royster	June 3, 1808.
Charles F. Bates	June 3, 1808.

Name	Date of Paper
Marks Vandewall	June 14, (and Enquirer), 1808.
Mrs. Ann Warren, wife of Wm. Warren	July 8, 1808.
John Addison	July 29, 1808.
Robert P. Guerrant	July 29, 1808.
Micajah Clark	July 29, 1808.
Gregory O'Neale, Sr.	August 26, 1808.
Leroy Hipkins	October 14, 1808.
Samuel D. Leake	November 8, 1808.
Pleasant Younghusband	December 20, 1808.

VIRGINIAN

Mrs. E. McCraw, wife of Samuel McCraw [and daughter Col. John Harvie]	March 29, 1808.
John D. Burk	April 15, 1808.
Anderson Royster	June 3, 1808.
Robert B. James	June 14, 1808.
John Seaton	July 22, (Enquirer, July 19, 1808).

ENQUIRER

James De Sear	May 12, 1808.
Joseph Donnison	May 14, 1808.
John Goodrich	June 14, 1808.
Wm. Lyne	September 27, 1808.
George McCarty	September 27, 1808.
Thomas H. Pays	October 7, 1808.
Mrs. Phebe, wife of Henry Gray	October 14, 1808.
Ann D. Godfrey	October 18, 1808.
Wm. Price	October 18, 1808.
Alexander Pope	October 25, 1808.
Robert B. Cabell	October 28, 1808.
Richard Crouch, Jr.	October 28, 1808.
Wm. King	November 8, 1808.
George Wythe Booth	January 7, 1809.
Mrs. Phebe Shields, wife of Alexander Shields	February 7, 1809.
Mary, wife of Robt. H. Saunders	February 10, 1809.
Philip Courtney	February 24, 1809.
Mrs. Magaret Daniel, wife of John M. Daniel	March 17, 1809.
Henry Marks	March 17, 1809.
Hardin Burnley	March 17, 1809.
John Strobia	March 17, 1809.
Nathaniel Pope	March 24, 1809.
Carter Braxton	April 14, 1809.
Mrs. Ann, relict of Chas. Carter	April 28, 1809.

Name	Date of Paper
John Southgate	May 2. 1809.
John Heveningham	December 30, 1809, [4th page.]
Wm. Chambers	January 27, 1810.
Charles Porterfield	January 27, 1810.
Joseph W. Lewis	February 10, 1810.
Elizabeth, wife of Edward Randolph	March 13, 1810.
Bathurst Jones	April 6, 1810.
Wm. Washington	April 6, 1810.
Robert Gamble	April 17, 1810.
Ann, wife of George Turner	April 27, 1810.
Peter Tinsley	July 24, 1810.
Mrs. Mary Sackrider, wife of Dr. Sackrider	July 24, 1810.
Mrs. Martha Roane, wife of Wm. Roane	August 17, 1810.
Mrs. Eliz. Winston, wife of Isaac Winston	August 17, 1810.
Wm. Fontaine	October 12, 1810.
Tarlton Hines	October 26, 1810.
Rebecca, widow of Richard Taleferro	October 30, 1810.
John Prosser	October 30, 1810.
Edward Carrington	October 30, 1810.
John Heth	November 2, 1810.
Mrs. Sarah Syme	November 23, 1810.
Mrs. Mary, wife of John Swann	November 30, 1810.
Joseph Scott	December 4, 1810.
Samuel Griffin	December 4, 1810.
Gurdon Bacchus	December 25, 1810.

COMPILER

Name	Date of Paper
Wm. Gardner	November 23, 1819.
Edward B. S. Cary	November 28, 1819.
Mrs. Mary Blair Andrews	January 14, 1820.
John Nicholas	January 18, 1820.
Robert Cowley	February 10, 1820.
Mrs. Mary Hewlett	February 29, 1820.
Charles C. Gay	March 1, 1820.
Eliz., wife of W. Scott	March 10, 1820.
Mrs. Elizabeth Barker	March 24, 1820.
Samuel Parsons	March 25, 1820.
Martha, wife of James Taliaferro	March 27, 1820.
Mrs. Susanna Simpson	March 29, 1820.
Charles K. Mallory	April 22, 1820.
Mrs. Nicholas, wife of Philip N. Nicholas	April 28, 1820.
John Bray	June 6, 1820.

Name	Date of Paper
James Entwisle	June 6, 1820.
Robt. Starbuck	June 13, 1821.
Daniel Sinclair	June 13, 1821.
Moses Nunus	June 14, 1821.
Jesse Smith	June 15, 1821.
Sarah Whitlocke	June 18, 1821.
Robert Robinson	June 19, 1821.
Frances Sheppard	June 20, 1821.
Mrs. Elizabeth Rawlings	June 30, 1821.
Wm. M. Richardson	July 11, 1821.
Samuel Travis	July 13, 1821.
Martin Baker, Sr.	July 13, 1821.
Samuel G. Adams	July 16, 1821.
Lucy, wife of Chas. Horwell	July 24, 1821.
Peter Copland	July 24, 1821.
Sterling Mann	August 6, 1821.
Thos. Gibbs	August 3, 1821.
Captain Meader	August 6, 1821.
Ebenezer Macnair	August 8, 1821.
Jane McKim	August 11, 1821.
Ann Pleasants	August 13, 1821.
Eleanor L. Richardson	August 14, 1821.
James S. Smithers, Jr.	August 18, 1821.
Leah Levy	August 23, 1821.
Seth Storer	August 27, 1821.
Joseph Timberlake	September 3, 1821.
Mrs. Frances Samuels	September 4, 1821.
Benj. P. Holmes	September 7, 1821.
C. B. Dwight	
Thomas Doing	September 15, 1821.
John Bullard, Jr.	September 18, 1821.
Wm. Robins	October 4, 1821.
Andrew Allen	October 4, 1821.
Jno. B. Harding	October 9, 1821.
Joseph Sowden	October 11, 1821.
Nathaniel White	October 13, 1821.
Benjamine Ficklin	October 15, 1821.
Aaron Burton	October 16, 1821.
John Murchie Brander	October 16, 1821.
Isaac Tucker	October 22, 1821.
John Watson	October 23, 1821.
Wm. T. Niveson	October 24, 1821.
Sidney H. Burrough	October 26, 1821.
George Pickett, Sr.	November 10, 1821.

Name	Date of Paper
Wm. H. Dulaney	February 11, 1809.
John Harris	February 11, 1809.
Mrs. Mary Saunders	February 11, 1809.
Mrs. McLane	February 11, 1809.
Tayloe Braxton	February 25, 1809.
Philip Courtney	February 25, 1809.
Mrs. Mary Logan	March 11, 1809.
Henry Marks	March 11, 1809.
John Strobia	March 11, 1809.
Mrs. Margaret Daniel	March 25, 1809.
Thos. Gholson	March 25, 1809.
Wm. Gary	March 25, 1809.
Harden Burnley	March 25, 1809.
Nathaniel Pope	March 25, 1809.
Elisha Price	April 8, 1809.
John Madison	April 8, 1809.
Gideon Wanton	May 6, 1809.
Carter Braxton	May 6, 1809.
Robert Goode	May 6 1809.
Braxton Harrison	May 6, 1809.
Mrs. Ann Carter	May 6, 1809.
Miss Jane Bledso	May 6, 1809.
John Lackland	May 20, 1809.
Wm. Davidson	May 20, 1809.
John F. Wiatt	June 3, 1809.
Wm. Richardson	June 17, 1809.
John McRae	June 17, 1809.
Joseph Prentis	July 1, 1809.
Richard Smyth	July 1, 1809.
Robert Davis	July 1, 1809.
Jno. Murray, Earl of Dunmore	July 1, 1809.
Mrs. Judith Saunders	July 29, 1809.
Peter Lyons	August 12, 1809.
Robert Nicolson	August 12, 1809.
Walter McClurg	August 26, 1809.
Eli Vickery	August 26, 1809.
Wm. Lithgow	August 26, 1809.
Edward Mason	August 26, 1809.
Archibald Moore	September 9, 1809.
David Organ	September 9, 1809.
Thomas Baldwin	September 9, 1809.
James Wilson	September 9, 1809.
John Peyton	September 9, 1809.

Name	*Date of Paper*
Wm. Claiborne	October 7, 1809.
Wm. Armistead	Gctober 7, 1809.
Mrs. Lucy Singleton	October 7, 1809.
Geo. W. Nicholas	October 7, 1809.
Alexander Frazer	October 21, 1809.
Peter Price	October 21, 1809.
John Banks	October 21, 1809.
Mrs. Eliz. Adams	October 21, 1809.
Mrs. Nancy Call Wilder	October 21, 1809.

Enquirer

Col. John Beale	October 31, 1809.
Mrs. Charlotte S. Gamble	November 3, 1809.
J. I. Peers	November 7, 1809.
Overton Anderson	December 12, 1809.
Edmund Eggleston	December 23, 1809.
Mrs. Marianne Saunders	December 28, 1809.
Peter Kemp	December 30, 1809.
John Walker	January 2, 1810.
Mrs. Mildred Timberlake	January 30, 1810.
Joseph Woodson	February 8, 1810.
Minor M. Cosby	February 23, 1810.
Mrs. Lucy Du Val	March 6, 1810.
Mrs. Eliz. Randolph	March 9, 1810.
Jno. Kirke	March 20, 1810.
Josiah Parker	March 27, 1810.
Mrs. Ann C. Hoomes	March 27, 1810.
Mrs. Preston, (wife of Genl. J. Preston)	March 30, 1810.
Bathurst Jones	April 6, 1810.
Robt. Gamble	April 13, 1810.
Mrs. Lucy Nelson	April 20, 1810.
Mrs. Ann Turner	April 24, 1810.
Jno. Roane, Jr,	April 24, 1810.
Theoderick Goode	May 8, 1810.

OBITUARIES FROM THE *FAMILY VISITOR*

April 6, 1822–April 3, 1824

Edited by PATRICIA P. CLARK*

DURING the brief existence of the *Family Visitor*, published in Richmond from 1822 to 1826, obituaries appeared regularly. These death notices, transcribed and arranged alphabetically, are here offered to the genealogist and the historian. All sentimental laudation of the deceased has been omitted, but any mention of family, war record, or occupation has been included. Unusual causes of death and interesting epitaphs are likewise reprinted. In a few cases more than one announcement of a death was published and, since discrepancies exist, both announcements appear here.

The marriage notices which were published in the *Family Visitor* during this same period were edited and printed in the July 1959 issue of the *Virginia Magazine of History and Biography* (LXVII, 318-331).**

The file of the *Family Visitor* belonging to the Virginia Historical Society has been used in transcribing the obituaries. The date following each notice is the date of the newspaper in which the obituary appears. "Ult." (abbreviation for ultimo) indicates the death occurred in the month preceding that in which the newspaper was published, and "inst." (abbreviation for instant) indicates that the death occurred during the month in which the newspaper was published. "Æt." (abbreviation for ætalis suae) means in the year of his (or her) age; therefore, Æt. 70 indicates that a person was sixty-nine years old and in his seventieth year. "Of this city" refers to Richmond.

[Died] — In Belfield, Dr. A. Abernathy, 22. — *September 13, 1823.*

[Died] — In Prince William Mr. Benjamin Adie, 38. — *November 8, 1823.*

[Died] — In Hanover Co. Mrs. Martha Adkins, consort of Mr. Thomas Adkins, of this city, 23. — *November 15, 1823.*

[Died] — At Saguina, Michigan, Lieut. James B. Allen, son of Hon. Samuel C. Allen, of Mass. — *November 15, 1823.*

Died, in the City, on Thursday morning last [October 24], aged 37, Mr. John Allen, Tobacco Merchant, a native of England. . . . In his death, his afflicted Widow (who has lately buried a brother and both her children) has lost her last relative in a foreign land. — *October 26, 1822.*

---

*Mrs. Clark, of Oak Ridge, Tennessee, was formerly a member of the staff of the Virginia Historical Society.

**Virginia Marriage Records* (Baltimore: Genealogical Publishing Co., Inc., 1982), pp. 630-643.

[Died] — In Buckingham Co. William Allen. — *March 20, 1824.*

[Died] — In James City Co. Mr. William S. Allen, 61. — *October 25, 1823.*

[Died in Fairfax Co. Va.] Mrs. Ann Allison, 53. — *October 11, 1823.*

[Died in Richmond] Mrs. Elizabeth Alvis. — *August 30, 1823.*

Died — In the City of Washington, on the 19th ult. James H. Ancrum, Esq. of South Carolina. — *February 1, 1823.*

[Died] — In Cherry Point, Izates Anderson, Esq. — *September 20, 1823.*

[Died at Alexandria] Mr. James Anderson, sen. — *October 4, 1823.*

[Died] . . . the Rev. Peyton Anderson . . . departed this life on Wednesday the 27th ult. at Culpeper Courthouse. . . . He was born and raised in Chesterfield county, about 25 miles from this city. . . . He has left an aged father and mother, five brothers and four sisters. . . . — *September 6, 1823.*

[Died] — In Williamsburg, Robert Alfred, son of Leroy Anderson, 6. — *September 20, 1823.*

[Died] — At Berwick, Maine, Mr. Hawley Applebee, aged 89 — his descendants are, 16 children, 100 grandchildren, and 69 great-grandchildren. — *April 3, 1824.*

[Died] — At Youngstown, Pa. Mrs. Margaret Armor. When bereft of her reason, she terminated her own existence. — *September 20, 1823.*

[Died] At Red-Hook, N. York, on the 24th Dec. [1822] Mrs. Aliba Armstrong, wife of Gen. John Armstrong, late Secretary of War, and sister of the late Chancellor Livingston. — *February 8, 1823.*

[Died] — In St. Louis, Lieut. and Adjutant Thomas Jefferson Ayre, of the 1st Regiment U. S. Infantry, in the 22d year of his age. — *October 25, 1823.*

[Died in this city] Mrs. Margaret Ayres, in the 86th year of her age. . . . — *March 20, 1824.*

[Died] — near New-Baltimore, same [Fauquier] Co. Mrs. Bailey, 60. — *November 29, 1823.*

[Died] — At the Warm Springs, in Bath, Mr. John Bailey, 26. — *September 13, 1823.*

Died, In Richmond, Mr. John Baird. — *December 20, 1823.*

[Died] — At Philadelphia, Benjamin G. Baker. His death is noticed as *a caution to venders of medicine;* he died by taking tincture of rhubarb, in which laudanum had by some unknown means been mixed. — *August 30, 1823.*

[Died] — At Shepherdstown, John Baker, Esq. Attorney at Law, and formerly a Representative in Congress. — *August 30, 1823.*

[Died] — At Shepherdstown, Miss Julia W. Baker. — *October 4, 1823.*

[Died] — At his lodgings in Washington, the Hon. William Lee Ball, aged about 45, for several years past and at the time of his death, a Representative in Congress from the state of Virginia. — *March 6, 1824.*

[Died] — At Elizabethtown, N. J., Jeremiah Ballad, Esq. a hero of the revolution, 75. — *September 13, 1823.*

[Died] — At Dighton, Mass. Mrs. Elizabeth Baylies, aged 63 years. — *August 9, 1823.*

[Died in Jefferson Co.] Mr. Jeremiah Beckman. — *October 4, 1823.*

[Died] — In Berkeley Co. Geo. Beddo, a distiller, was scalded to death. — *November 8, 1823.*

[Died] — Near Parkersburg, Va. Jacob Beeson, Esq. — *September 27, 1823.*

[Died in Richmond] Mr. Nathan Curtis Benjamin, a native of Connecticut. — *October 4, 1823.*

Died — In this city, yesterday morning, the Rev. Charles Bennet.... — *December 7, 1822.*

[Died] — In Frederick county, Mr. James Bennet. — *August 9, 1823.*

[Died] — In Hanover Co. Mr. Thomas Nelson Berkeley, son of Nelson Berkeley, Esq. of King William Co. — *September 27, 1823.*

[Died] In Albemarle county, on the 30th August, Mrs. Elizabeth Bernard, consort of Mr. John Bernard, in the 80th year of her age. — *September 14, 1822.*

Died — On the 20th ult. at his residence in the county of Campbell, George Beverley, Esq. in the 56th year of his age. — *January 4, 1823.*

[Died] — In Campbell Co. Mrs. Judith Beverly, relict of Mr. George B. 44. — *September 20, 1823.*

[Died] — At West Liberty, Brig. Gen. Benjamin Biggs, Æt. 71. — *January 10, 1824.*

[Died] — In New-York, Mr. Danforth Billings, a student in the General Theological Seminary of the Protestant Episcopal Church in the United States, 28. — *February 7, 1824.*

[Died in Prince George Co.] — Miss Susan Bishop, daughter of Charles Bishop, dec. formerly of Petersburg, 14. — *November 8, 1823.*

[Died] — At Columbia, S. C. George Blackburn, formerly Professor of Mathematics in the South Carolina College. — *August 30, 1823.*

Died — At the residence in Northumberland, Col. Hiram Blackwell, one of the Delegates to the Assembly from this County. — *February 8, 1823.*

The death of the Rev. John D. Blair, late pastor of the Presbyterian

Church on Shockoe Hill, in this city, has been announced. . . . having entered the 64th year of his age, he was on the 10th instant numbered with the dead. . . . — *January 18, 1823.*

[Died] — In Burlington, N. J. Gen. Joseph Bloomfield. — *October 11, 1823.*

[Died] — In South Reading, Mass. Col. Amos Boardman, 68. — *August 23, 1823.*

[Died] — In Ohio, whither he had gone on business, Hon. Elijah Boardman, a Senator of the United States from Connecticut. — *September 6, 1823.*

[Died] — In Chesterfield Co. Mr. Daniel Boisseau. — *February 7, 1824.*

[Died] — In Petersburg, . . . Mr. James Boisseau, . . . of that place. — *April 3, 1824.*

[Died] — In Amelia Co. Pinkethman D. Booker, Sen. 70. — *October 11, 1823.*

[Died] — In New-York city, Rev. Christian Bork, late Pastor of the Dutch Reformed Church, Franklin-street. — *October 11, 1823.*

[Died] — In Charlotte Co. Mrs. Ann B. Bouldin, wife of Judge Thomas T. Bouldin. — *January 10, 1824.*

[Died] — In Westmoreland Co. Mr. Thomas Bouldin, of Danville on the Roanoke. — *November 1, 1823.*

[Died] In Tennessee the Rev. Ambrose Bourne, a most valuable Minister of the church of Christ, in the Baptist denomination. — *January 17, 1824.*

[Died] — In Tennessee, Rev. Ambrose Bourne, of the Baptist denomination. — *February 28, 1824.*

[Died] — In New-York, Benj. F. Bourne, Esq. of the United States' Navy, only son of the late Honourable Judge Bourne, of Bristol, R. I. — *November 29, 1823.*

[Died] — In Hanover Co. Mr. John Bowe, 22. — *October 25, 1823.*

[Died] — At his residence in Isle of Wight county, Mr. Wm. I. Boykin, aged 23 years. — *August 9, 1823.*

[Died] — In Petersburg, Mrs. Betsey C. Brame. — *September 20, 1823.*

[Died] — In Powhatan Co. Mr. Matthew Branch, 58. — *November 1, 1823.*

[Died] — In Frankfort, Ky. Joseph Cabell Breckenridge, Esq. Secretary of State of Ky. — *September 20, 1823.*

[Died] — In Dearfield, Mass. Mr. Willard Bridges. . . . *November 22, 1823.*

[Died] — In the 73d of his age Richard Brien, Esq. late consul general of the United States to the Barbary powers. — *February 21, 1824.*

[Died] — In Wellington, Mass. widow Mary Briggs, aged one hundred and two years, leaving 9 children aged 79, 77, 73, 72, 70, 68, 63, 60, 57. — The ages of the mother and children 721. She also left 56 grand-children, and 47 great-grand-children. — *January 3, 1824.*

[Died] — In North Haven, Conn. Mrs. Sarah Brochet, aged 71, wife of Mr. Isaiah B. She was the first who died of a family of six sisters, the average of whose age is 72, and whose husbands are all yet living. — *February 28, 1824.*

[Died] — In Alexandria, D. C. Mrs. Anne Brooke, relict of the late Com. B. 65. — *October 18, 1823.*

[Died] On the 18th July, at the residence of Dr. Campbell, Miss Catharine Brown, daughter of Mr. J. Brown, of the Cherokee nation. . . . — *September 6, 1823.*

[Died] — In Winchester, Mr. Thomas Brown. — *August 23, 1823.*

[Died in Frederick Co.] Thomas Brown. — *September 20, 1823.*

Died — In Fredericksburg, in the 22d year of her age. . . . Mrs. Louisa S. B. Bryce, consort of the Rev. John Bryce. She left an infant aged eight days. — *January 18, 1823.*

Died — In this City, on the morning of the 19th inst. the Rev. John Buchanan of the Protestant Episcopal Church, in the 78th year of his age. — *December 21, 1822.*

[Died] — In Shenandoah County, Mr. Charles Buck, 74. — *August 16, 1823.*

[Died] — On the 24th of April, at Sierra Leone, Mr. Bunner, schoolmaster at Freetown. — *October 25, 1823.*

[Died] In Albemarle, Va. on the 12th ult. the Rev. Benjamin Burger, a minister of the Baptist Church. Aged 77 years. — *December 7, 1822.*

[Died at City Point] Capt. Thomas Burruss, of Caroline Co. 52. — *March 20, 1824.*

[Died] — In Botetourt Co. Mrs. Sarah Butt, of the Methodist Church. — *January 31, 1824.*

[Died] — In Savannah, Ga. Gen. William Byne, a native of King & Queen Co. Va. aged 66. — *April 3, 1824.*

Miss Elizabeth N. Cabell, died of a Consumption on the 17th of July last, at the Salt Sulphur Springs. . . . She was an only daughter, about whom centered the warmest affections of a widowed mother. . . . — *September 21, 1822.*

[Died] — At his residence near Lynchburg, Dr. George Cabell, 57. — *December 27, 1823.*

[Died] On the 2d Nov. in the 63d year of his age, Col. William Cabell, of Union Hill in the County of Nelson. — *December 14, 1822.*

[Died] — Near Trenton, N. J. Col. Lambert Cadwallader. — *September 27, 1823.*

[Died] At his late residence, near Lexington, Rowan county, N. C. a short time since, in the 77th year of his age, Andrew Caldcleugh, Esq. He served his country . . . during the Revolutionary war. . . . — *July 13, 1822.*

[Died] — In Norfolk, Col. George Washington Camp. — *December 13, 1823.*

[Died] — In Orange Co. Col. William Campbell, a Patriot of the Revolution, 69. — *November 15, 1823.*

[Died] — In Andover, Mass. Mr. Parker Carlton, an indigent youth, aged 23 years. . . . — *January 10, 1824.*

[Died] — In Fluvanna Co. Mr. Wilson Jefferson Cary, 45. — *October 4, 1823.*

[Died] In King William Co. Miss Caroline Catlett. — *October 18, 1823.*
Deacon Cauldwell . . . finished his holy course on the 4th of last month. — *April 13, 1822.*

[Died] — At Abingdon, Mrs. Cawood, wife of Mr. Benjamin Cawood. A villain approached the house and shot her with a rifle. Four persons are in custody on suspicion. — *November 15, 1823.*

[Died] — In Louisa Co. Mrs. Eliza R. Chandler, consort of Mr. Leroy Chandler, formerly of this city. — *February 21, 1824.*

[Died] — In Lexington, Va. Mr. Samuel Chandler, Sen. — *February 28, 1824.*

[Died] — In the District of Columbia, Mrs. Amelia Chapman, consort of the late Geo. Chapman, Esq. of Va. and mother of Professor Chapman of Philadelphia. — *September 27, 1823.*

[Died] — In Lunenburg Co. Mrs. Sally Chappell, 40. — *September 20, 1823.*

[Died] — On Board the Frigate United States, lying at Hampton Roads, Levi Chase, 22. He fell from the mizen mast to the deck, was dreadfully mangled, and died immediately. — *January 10, 1824.*

[Died] — In Charleston, S. C. the 1st inst. where he had gone for the benefit of his health, the Rev. Philander Chase, Jun. of Zanesville, Ohio, son of the Right Rev. Bishop [Philander] Chase. — *March 27, 1824.*

[Died] — In Buckingham Co. the Rev. Rainey Chastein, 85. — *November 22, 1823.*

[Died] — In Washington city, Augusta Alethea Chauncey, eldest daughter of Commodore [Isaac] Chauncey. — *March 20, 1824.*

[Died] — At New-Haven, Con. Hon. Charles Chauncey, LL. D. 76. — *September 27, 1823.*

[Died] — In Prince Edward Co. Mrs. Elizabeth Cheadle, 67. — *December 13, 1823.*

[Died] — In Charlotte Co. Mr. Wm. Chealham, 74. — *October 18, 1823.*

[Died] — In Amherst Co. John Christian, 80. — *October 11, 1823.*

[Died in Frederick Co.] — Mrs. Clare, wife of James Clare. — *September 20, 1823.*

[Died] — At Bridgeport, Shenandoah Co. Elias Clark, Esq. 40. — *November 29, 1823.*

[Died] Near Sumterville, S. C. Mrs. Martha Clark, in the 105th year of her age. . . . She has left a numerous offspring, some of whom are her great-great-grandchildren. — *July 27, 1822.*

Departed, this life, on Sunday, the 9th instant, in the county of Charles City, Miss Elizabeth Clarke, daughter of Mrs. Rebecca E. Clarke, in the 10th year of her age. . . . *November 15, 1823.*

[Died — At Paris, (France,)] Nicholas · Clary, formerly a merchant of Marseilles. — *August 9, 1823.*

[Died] — In Buckingham Co. Capt. Nicholas Cobbs. — *November 1, 1823.*

[Died in Frederick Co.] Robert Coburn, 55. — *September 20, 1823.*

[Died] — In Petersburg, Mr. John Cochran. — *October 4, 1823.*

[Died] — In Philadelphia, Jacob J. Cohen, Esq. formerly of Richmond, a native of Germany, and one of the corps of *Hebrew Volunteers* in S. C. in the Revolutionary War. — *October 18, 1823.*

[Died] — In Prince George Co. Mr. William Cole. — *November 15, 1823.*

[Died] — In this city B. W. Coleman, Esq. Attorney at Law. — *October 18, 1823.*

Died, In Richmond, Mrs. Elizabeth Collier, Æt. 51. — *October 4, 1823.*

. . . The Rev. James Colman, our Missionary at Chittagong, . . . died on the 4th of July, at Cox's Bazar, of a Jungle Fever. Mrs. Colman is at Chittagong, and is very ill of the same fever. . . . — *December 7, 1822.*

[Died] — At Honeywood, Berkley County, Va. Rawleigh Colston, Esq. in the 75th year of his age. — *August 9, 1823.*

[Died] — At Springfield, (Mass.) Mrs. Mercy Colton, aged 96. — *October 11, 1823.*

[Died] — In Augusta, Geo. Mr. Lewis Convert, a native of France, formerly a resident of Richmond. — *August 23, 1823.*

Died, — In Lancaster County, Va. the 21st May, Mrs. Sarah D. Corbin, consort of Mr. George L. Corbin. — She . . . has left a disconsolate husband and two small children. . . . — *June 15, 1822.*

[Died] — At Sand Hills (Ga.) Mrs. Catharine Course, 73. — *August 16, 1823.*

Died, In King William on the 13th of October, Dandridge P. Courtney, a respectable citizen of the county. — *November 1, 1823.*

[Died] — In Louisa County Mr. Albert G. Cowherd, 18. — *August 16, 1823.*

Died, on the 6th inst. after a short illness, Mrs. Euphan N. Cowling, consort of Mr. Willis Cowling of this city. — *December 14, 1822.*

[Died] — In Winchester, Mr. John Coyle, 81. — *November 29, 1823.*

[Died] — In Jefferson Co. Mr. William Coyle. He was thrown from his horse and died the next day. — *November 8, 1823.*

[Died] — In Amherst Co. Mrs. Hannah H. Crawford, wife of Bennet A. Crawford, Esq. — *November 22, 1823.*

William Crawford was executed at Washington, Pa., on the 21st ult. for the murder of his son Henry Crawford. He was an Irishman by birth. . . . — *March 15, 1823.*

[Died] — In Adams Co. Pa. Dr. William Crawford, formerly a Representative in Congress. — *November 8, 1823.*

[Died in Fredericksburg] Mrs. Sophia Crewdson, relict of the late Mr. Henry Crewdson, of Richmond Co., aged 43 years. — *March 27, 1824.*

[Died] — In New-York, Mr. David B. M. Cullogh, 23. — *August 16, 1823.*

[Died] — In Brucetown, Mrs. Maria Cunningham, wife of Mr. Thos. Cunningham, formerly of Charlestown, Jefferson County, 26. — *August 30, 1823.*

[Died] — Near Moorefield, Hardy county, Va. Mrs. Matilda Cunningham, in the 23d year of her age. — *August 9, 1823.*

[Died—In Berkley Co.] Mrs. Curtis, an aged lady. — *September 6, 1823.*

[Died] — At Washington city, Mrs. Ann Cutbush, aged 54 years. — *August 9, 1823.*

[Died] — At West Point, New-York, on the 15th inst. Dr. James Cutbush, Professor of Chemistry in the Military Academy. — *January 3, 1824.*

[Died] — In Hamilton (N. H.) Rev. Manasseh Cutler, LL.D. 81. — *August 16, 1823.*

Died, on the 2d of [September 1821], in St. Bartholomew, the Rev. John Dace, a missionary of the [Wesleyan Missionary] society.... — *June 22, 1822.*

[Died] — At Romney, James Daily, Esq. President of the Branch Bank at that place. — *October 4, 1823.*

[Died] — In Stafford Co. Eliza Travers Daniel, daughter of Mrs. Mildred Daniel. — *November 15, 1823.*

[Died] — At Sierra Leone, Lieut. Dashiell, commander of the United States Vessel, Augusta. — *November 22, 1823.*

[Died] — In Lynchburg, Mr. William Davies, son of the late W. H. Davies, Esq. of Bedford Co. 19. — *November 1, 1823.*

[Died] — In Shepherdstown, Mr. Cornelius Davis. — *August 23, 1823.*

[Died] — In Gloucester Co. Mrs. Lucy Davis, consort of Mr. Arthur L. Davis. — *November 1, 1823.*

[Died] — In Concord, N. H. Lieut. Robert Davis, 89. — *August 23, 1823.*

[Died] At Washington, on the 14th inst. after an illness of two weeks, the Rev. Samuel Davis, Minister of the Methodist Episcopal Church, Æt. about 28. — *September 21, 1822.*

[Died] — In Lynchburg, Mrs. Sarah Davis, consort of Henry Davis, Esq. of that place. — *March 27, 1824.*

[Died] At Winchester, on the 10th inst, Maj. William Davison, postmaster.... — *September 21, 1822.*

[Died] In Georgetown, yesterday morning, of a typhus fever, Charles Dawson, Esq. one of the Clerks in the Office of the Register of the Traesury. — *November 9, 1822.*

[Died] — In Fairfax county, Mr. John Dawson, in the 86th year of his age.... — *January 3, 1824.*

[Died] — In Deerfield, Portage Co. Ohio, Mrs. Day, wife of Col. Day, 69. Her death was occasioned by the sting of a yellow wasp, which she received while engaged in drying apples, and survived but fifteen minutes after the fatal event. — *October 25, 1823.*

[Died] — In Monmouth, Me. 16th ult. Simon Dearborn, Esq. brother of Gen. Henry Dearborn, aged 90. — *March 27, 1824.*

[Died in the City of Washington] Mrs. Catharine Livingston de Bresson, wife of the Secretary of the Legation of France and senior daughter of the Honorable Smith Thompson, of the State of New-York. — *February 7, 1824.*

[Died] — At his residence in Georgetown, D. C. on the 1st inst. Mr. de Greuhm, Minister from the King of Prussia to the United States. — *December 6, 1823.*

[Died] — In Eastville, Northampton county, Va. Dr. Alexander P. L. Denny, Pastor of the Presbyterian Church in Chambersburgh. — *September 27, 1823.*

[Died] In Bartholomew's parish, S. C. Capt. John Herbert Dent, of the U. S. Navy, 42. — *September 6, 1823*

Died, at Murfreesborough, N. C. on the 6th ult., in the 58th year of his age. — Gen. J. F. Dickinson. . . . — *July 13, 1822.*

[Died] — In Caroline Co. Wm. Dickinson, Esq. 62. — *October 11, 1823.*

Died, on the 17th inst. at the residence of her mother in the county of Hanover, Miss Martha C. Diggs, Æt. 18. — *October 26, 1822.*

Died, In Pittsylvania, Mrs. Mildred Dillard, wife of Dr. L. Dillard, 34. — *January 17, 1824.*

Mr. Moses Dixon, a resident of Campbell county, Va. about 14 miles from Lynchburg, committed suicide on the 29th ult. . . . — *February 15, 1823.*

[Died] — At Philadelphia, Judge Walter Dorsey, of Baltimore. — *August 9, 1823.*

[Died] — At Warrenton, N. C. Mr. John D. Drake, 24. — *October 11, 1823.*

[Died] — In York Co. Mr. John Drummond. — *January 17, 1824.*

[Died] — In Petersburg, Miss Ann Dunant. — *March 27, 1824.*

[Died] — In Nottoway County, James Dupuy, Esq. 66. — *August 16, 1823.*

[Died] — In Dinwiddie Co. Mrs. Nancy W. consort of Mr. Matthew Dyer. — *November 8, 1823.*

[Died] — At Lynchburg, Mr. James H. Earle. — *October 25, 1823.*

[Died] — In Fairfax Co. Mr. John Earnshaw, 35. — *October 25, 1823.*

[Died] — In Martinsburg, Mrs. Charlotte Ebberls. — *February 28, 1824.*

[Died] — In South Carolina, Thomas Elliot, Esq. a soldier of the Revolution. — *February 28, 1824.*

Died. At Red Hill, Amherst Co. John Ellis. — *August 30, 1823.*

Died, In Amherst Co. Thos. H. son of Col. J. Ellis. — *January 24, 1824.*

[Died] — On the 15th inst. John W. Eppes, Esq. — *September 20, 1823.*

[Died] — At Savannah, John Eppinger, Esq. late Marshal of the District of Georgia. — *August 9, 1823.*

[Died] — In Washington city, Mr. John Erskine, 40. — *January 24, 1824.*

[Died] — In Berkley Co. Mr. John Evans, Jun. 42. — *September 6, 1823.*

[Died] — At Oakley in the Co. of King William, Captain Thos. R. Evans, in the 52d year of his age. — *March 27, 1824.*

[Died] — At Petersburg, Mr. James R. Farrar, a native of Ireland. — *November 15, 1823.*

[Died] — At Alexandria, Capt. Peter Faulkner. — *October 4, 1823.*

[Died] — Near Millwood, Va. Mrs. Elizabeth Fauntleroy, an aged member of the Baptist Church. — *April 3, 1824.*

[Died in Frederick Co.] Ann Fawcett. — *September 20, 1823.*

[Died in Washington city] Rev. Lewis R. Fechtig, Elder in the Methodist Episcopal Church, and Presiding Elder of the Baltimore District. — *October 4, 1823.*

[Died] — At Arkansas Dr. Richard H. Fenner, formerly of Franklin Co. N. C. 29. — *November 22, 1823.*

[Died] — In King George Co. — Mr. Edward Ferris. — *October 25, 1823.*

[Died] — In Washington Mr. Robert Fisher, a native of Delaware, and a Clerk in the Treasury Department. — *November 22, 1823.*

[Died] — At Sierra Leone, Edward Fitzgerald, Esq. Chief Justice of the Colony. — *November 1, 1823.*

Died, At his residence in Chesterfield Co. William Fleming, presiding Judge of the Court of Appeals, in the 90th year of his age. — *February 21, 1824.*

[Died] — On the 6th, [of May] also at sea, Rev. S. Flood, First Colonial Chaplain at Sierra Leone. — *October 25, 1823.*

[Died in Frederick Co.] Mr. Frederick Flore. — *September 20, 1823.*

[Died] — In Petersburg, Mr. Nelson Flournoy, formerly of Richmond. — *January 31, 1824.*

[Died] — On board the U. States brig Spark, Sailing Master Benj. Follet. — *November 29, 1823.*

Died, In Hanover Co. the Rev. Reuben Ford, one of the oldest Baptist preachers in Virginia, Æt. 82. — *October 18, 1823.*

[Died] — At Philadelphia, Caleb Foulke, Esq. 55. — *October 25, 1823.*

[Died in Hanover County] Mrs. Martha Lavinia Francis, 28, and on the following day, her daughter, Louisa Christian, 7. — *September 27, 1823.*

[Died] — In Surry Co. N. C. Hon. Jesse Franklin, 65. — *October 4, 1823.*

[Died] — At Paris, (France,) William Temple Franklin, grandson of Dr. [Benjamin] Franklin, and editor of his works. — *August 9, 1823.*

[Died] — In Dinwiddie Co. Capt. J. Frazer. — *September 13, 1823.*

[Died] — At Nassau, New-Providence, the Rev. Simon Frazer, D.D. Minister in that town. — *November 15, 1823.*

[Died] — In Washington, Col. Constant Freemason, Auditor of the Treasury for the Navy Department, aged 67. — *March 6, 1824.*

Among the Recent deaths by yellow fever, at New-Orleans our readers may have noticed that of Mrs. Fromentin. We have since learnt that her husband, Hon. Eligius Fromentin, formerly a Senator of the United States, and more recently District Judge in Florida, died [October 6] within twenty-four hours after the death of his lady. — *November 9, 1822.*

[Died] — In Madison Co. Rev. Henry Fry, 85. — *September 6, 1823.*

[Died] — At Staunton, Mr. Bartholomew Fuller, 64. — *August 16, 1823.*

James Fuller, from Alexandria, killed himself with rum [in Monrovia, Liberia]. — *September 13, 1823.*

Died. Yesterday morning at half past 12 o'clock Mr. Alexander Fulton, of Mt. Erin. . . . — *September 6, 1823.*

[Died in this city] Mrs. Alice Gage, widow of the late Arnold Gage. — *March 20, 1824.*

[Died] — In Richmond, Mr. Arnold Gage, a native of Ireland, aged 47. — *August 30, 1823.*

[Died] — In Wenham, Mass. Mrs. Elizabeth Gardner, sister of Hon. Timothy Pickering. — *November 15, 1823.*

[Died in Richmond] Mrs. Martha Geoghegan, Æt. 87. — *December 13, 1823.*

[Died] — In Halifax Co. Doctor John C. Gibbs, 31. — *February 21, 1824.*

[Died] — In Amherst Co. Mr. Wm. H. Gibson, 50. — *September 20, 1823.*

[Died] — In Queen Anne County, Maryland, Mr. William Gibson, one of the Clerks in the Department of the Treasury. — *October 11, 1823.*

[Died] — At Edgefield, C. House, S. C. Gen. John S. Glascock. He died of a gun wound he received in his hand, by his gun accidentally going off, which gave him the lock jaw. — *February 7, 1824.*

[Died] — In Dinwiddie Co. Miss Emily Goodall, 16. — *November 29, 1823.*

[Died in Surry Co.] Mr. Meshach Goodrich, 53. — *December 13, 1823.*

[Died] — In Rockbridge Co. Mrs. Gowel, wife of Mr. Christian Gowel. — *February 14, 1824.*

Died, Yesterday morning, about eight o'clock, Mr. Robert Graham, of Manchester. . . . — *August 16, 1823.*

[Died] — In Dinwiddie Co. Mrs. Julianna S. P. Grammer. — *November 1, 1823.*

[Died] — In N. York, the Hon. Gideon Granger, formerly for several years Postmaster General of the U. S. — *January 18, 1823.*

Died, In Campbell Co. Col. James Grant, a soldier of the Revolution. — *March 6, 1824.*

[Died] — Prince George county, Va. Mr. Uriah Grantham, 43. — *August 23, 1823.*

Died, In this city, John Grantland, Esq. Attorney at Law — *February 14, 1824.*

[Died] — At Malaga, Spain, Mrs. Gravina, widow of the late Henry Gravina, Esq. and sister of the late Mr. Gallego, of Richmond. — *January 3, 1824.*

[Died] — In Boston Mrs. Elizabeth Gray, Consort of Hon. William Gray, 51. — *October 25, 1823.*

[Died] — In Dinwiddie Mrs. Elizabeth Green, 59. — *October 11, 1823.*

[Died in Petersburg] Mr. J. T. Green. — *January 24, 1824.*

[Died in Frederick Co.] Mr. John Green, a native of England. — *October 4, 1823.*

[Died] In Bowdoinham, 28th ult. Mr. Joseph Green, aged 82, formerly of Portsmouth. He was a soldier in the revolutionary war, for several years on board the Ranger, under the command of the intrepid [John] Paul Jones. . . . — *June 22, 1822.*

[Died] Mr. William Green, for some time a resident in Alabama. — *January 31, 1824.*

[Died in Richmond] Mr. James Greig, a native of Scotland, 38. — *September 6, 1823.*

[Died] On Wednesday the 22d ultimo in the 23d year of her age, at her residence in the county of King and Queen, . . . Anne, wife of Mr. William Gresham. . . . leaving a disconsolate husband and two infant children. . . . — *February 1, 1823.*

[Died] — In Richmond, Mr. John S. Gunn, aged 32. — *September 6, 1823.*

[Died] — In this city, Joseph H. youngest son of Mr. Richard Gwathmey, aged one year and eleven months. — *March 6, 1824.*

[Died] – In King William Co. Major Joseph Gwathney, in the 67th year of his age. – *February 21, 1824.*

[Died] In Tyngsboro' M[assachusett]s. Miss Abigail Hadlock, aged 104 years. . . . – *January 18, 1823.*

Died, In this city, Mr. Michael Hagan, Printer, aged 40 years, formerly of Philadelphia. – *March 20, 1824.*

[Died] – At Baltimore, Rev. John Hagerty, 76. He had been a minister in the Methodist Church near half a century. – *September 13, 1823.*

[Died] – In Loudoun Co. a child of Mr. Haines burnt to death by its clothes taking fire. – *November 8, 1823.*

[Died] – In Nelson Co. Mr. Thomas Hales, a native of Ireland. – *October 11, 1823.*

[Died] – In Suffolk Co. Mr. Frederick Hall. – *October 25, 1823.*

[Died] – In Lexington, Va. Miss Grace Hall. – *October 11, 1823.*

[Died] – In Fincastle, Col. Andrew Hamilton. – *November 15, 1823.*

[Died] – In Fredericksburg, Miss Lillias Hamilton, daughter of Capt. George Hamilton, 15. – *January 24, 1824.*

[Died in Richmond] – Mr. John Harban. – *September 27, 1823.*

Died, In Fredericksburg, Mrs. Elizabeth H. Hardia, wife of Mr. William Hardia. – *March 27, 1824.*

[Died] – In Kentucky, Gen. Martin Davis Hardin, formerly a Senator in Congress, 43. – *November 1, 1823.*

[Died] – In Bertie Co. N. C. Mrs. Sarah Hardy, wife of Wm. P. Hardy. – *January 31, 1824.*

[Died] – In the county of Prince George, Col. Wm. H. Harrison. – *March 13, 1824.*

[Died] – In Botetourt Co. Col. Matthew Harvey. – *October 4 and 11, 1823.*

[Died] – In Brunswick Co. Mr. Robert, and Mrs. Susan Haskins. – *September 20, 1823.*

[Died] – At Madisonville, La. Joseph H. Hawkins, a native of Kentucky. He succeeded Mr. [Henry] Clay, as a member of Congress, on his departure for Europe. – *November 15, 1823.*

[Died] – In Georgetown D. C. Mrs. Elizabeth Battaley Haynes, wife of Robert James Haynes, Esq. of Barbadoes, and lately from England. – *October 4, 1823.*

[Died] – At Petersburg, Mr. Lemuel P. Heath. – *August 23, 1823.*

[Died] – In New-Kent Co. Alice Eaton Hendren, daughter of Mr. P. Hendren, Æt. 9. – *November 15, 1823.*

[Died] — In Fairfax Co. Mr. James Herbert of Loudoun. — *September 6, 1823.*

[Died in Monrovia, Liberia] Abel Herd, foolish obstinacy. — *September 13, 1823.*

[Died] — In Hadley, Mass. Mr. George Hibbard, aged 77 — having had 16 children, 109 grand-children and 51 great-grand-children. A few years since Mr. H. his wife and 17 of his descendants made a public profession of religion. — *August 16, 1823.*

[Died] — At Charleston, Jefferson Co. Maj. R. G. Hite, 41. — *September 13, 1823.*

[Died] — In Frederick Co. Mr. Jno. Hodgson. — *September 20, 1823.*

[Died in Frederick Co.] Mrs. Hoff, widow of the late Lewis Hoff. — *September 20, 1823.*

[Died] At City Point, Mr. James Hoffman, of Alexandria, aged 24. — *August 16, 1823.*

[Died in Richmond] — Major David Holloway. — *October 25, 1823.*

[Died] — In Newtown, L. I. Col. Jesse Holly, a hero of the revolution, 70. — *September 27, 1823.*

[Died] — In Georgetown, D. C. Mr. Benjamin Homans, Senr. late Chief Clerk in the Navy Department, Æt. 59. — *December 20, 1823.*

[Died] — In Nottoway Co. Mr. George Hood, a native of Scotland. He was found in the road, beaten and mangled in a shocking manner. One of his neighbours has been arrested and committed to jail. — *January 24, 1824.*

[Died] — At the Bowling Greene, Caroline Co., Major John Hoomes, aged 48 years. — *March 27, 1824.*

[Died] — At Bowling Green, Richard Hoomes, son of Col. John Hoomes, dec. late of that place. — *January 3, 1824.*

[Died] — In Matthews Co. Mrs. Ann Hudgins, consort of Col. J. Hudgins, 28. — *December 13, 1823.*

[Died] — On Wednesday 17th inst. of a pluretic disorder, after the very short illness of about forty hours, Christopher E. Hudson, of Chesterfield county, in the 27th year of his age. . . . — *December 27, 1823.*

[Died in Loudoun Co.] — Mr. Ellis Hughes. — *September 13, 1823.*

[Died] — At Washington City, Mr. Jeremiah Hunt, a Deacon in the 1st Baptist Church. — *November 8, 1823.*

[Died] near the same place [New-Baltimore, Fauquier Co.], James Hunton. — *November 29, 1823.*

[Died] — At Augusta, Ga. Mr. Edward Hurley, formerly of Richmond, 25. — *September 13, 1823*.

[Died] At Washington city, Mrs. Eliza Woodside Hutton, wife of James Hutton, Esq. of the Navy Commissioners Office, 24. — *August 16, 1823*.

Died, On Thursday 30th ult. Hon. Jared Ingersol, President Judge of the District Court for the City and County of Philadelphia. — *November 9, 1822*.

[Died] — In Fairfax Co. Richard Jackson, Esq. 47. — *September 27, 1823*.

[Died] — In Hanover Co. Alfred James, son of Mr. Fleming James of Richmond. — *September 13, 1823*.

[Died] — In Hanover Co. Maria Ferrill, daughter of Fleming James, Esq. of Richmond, aged 6 years. — *September 20, 1823*.

[Died] — In Hanover Co. Rebecca Minor, daughter of Mr. Fleming James of this city [Richmond], 5. — *September 27, 1823*.

[Died] — In Loudo[u]n Co. Mr. Israel Janney. — *August 30, 1823*.

[Died] — In Lunenburg Co. Miss Martha Jefferson. — *October 25, 1823*.

[Died] — In Hampshire Co. Jacob Jenkins, Esq. High Sheriff of the County. — *November 29, 1823*.

[Died] — In Wilmington, Del. Mr. John Jenkins, a celebrated teacher of Penmanship. — *November 15, 1823*.

[Died] — At the residence of Mr. Robt. Booth, in Dinwiddie Co. Rev. Enoch Johnson of the Methodist Church. — *December 6, 1823*.

Died, In Richmond, Mr. John Johnson, formerly of Louisa Co. aged 21. — *September 13, 1823*.

[Died] — In Petersburg, Mr. Nathaniel Johnson, . . . of that place. — *April 3, 1824*.

[Died] — In Shenandoah Co. Mrs. Rachel Johnson, wife of Mr. Charles M. Johnson. — *September 6, 1823*.

Died at Morant Bay, Jamaica, on the 24th of September last [1821], the Rev. George Johnston, one of the missionaries of the Wesleyan Missionary Society. . . . — *June 22, 1822*.

[Died] — At sea, on his passage to England, May 5, Rev. W. Johnston, Missionary in Sierra Leone. — *October 25, 1823*.

[Died] On the 18th instant, at his summer residence, in Orange county, Virginia, Maj. Churchill Jones, aged 74 years. In the death of this aged citizen, we have lost another of the surviving worthies of the Revolutionary War. . . . — *September 26, 1822*.

[Died] At his residence in James City county, on Monday the 16th ult. in the 71st year of his age, Mr. Daniel Jones, sen. . . . — *January 4, 1823.*

[Died] — In Roxborough, Mrs. Deborah Jones, wife of the Rev. Horatio G. Jones, 32. — *October 4, 1823.*

[Died] — In Warwick Co. Mr. John Jones, a distinguished soldier of the Revolution, Æt. 63. — *February 7, 1824.*

[Died] — At St. Louis, in his 65th year, John Rice Jones, Esq. a Judge of the Supreme Court of Missouri. — *April 3, 1824.*

[Died] — In Petersburg, Gen. Joseph Jones, a patriot of the Revolution. — *February 14, 1824.*

Died. In Richmond, Mrs. Lucy Jones, aged 50. — *August 23, 1823.*

Departed this life on Sunday night last [September 22], Mrs. Mary G. Jones, the only surviving daughter of Samuel M'Craw, of this city [Richmond], and relict of the late John R. Jones, in the 29th year of her age. . . . — *September 26, 1822.*

[Died] — In Fredericksburg, Mrs. Rose Jones. — *October 25, 1823.*

[Died] — In Stafford Co. Mr. Thomas L. Jones, 21. — *January 24, 1824.*

[Died] — In St. Mary's Co. Md. Walter Moore Jones, 23. — *August 30, 1823.*

[Died] — In Suffolk, Mr. Robert Jordan, of the Society of Friends, 61. — *January 31, 1824.*

[Died] — In Jefferson county, Mrs. Kabell, on the day following, her husband, Mr. Daniel Kabell. — *August 23, 1823.*

[Died] — In Georgetown, S. C. . . . Maj. John Keith. — *September 27, 1823.*

[Died] — Near Sulphur Spring, Frederick county, Miss Polly Keller, 20. — *August 23, 1823.*

[Died] — At Rapide, Louisiana, George N. Kemper, Esq. son of Col. John Kemper, of Fauquier Co. 28. — *September 6, 1823.*

[Died] — In Poultney, Vt. the Rev. Clark Kendrick, pastor of the Baptist church in that place, aged 48. — *April 3, 1824.*

[Died] — In Richmond, Mr. James Kennedy, Millwright, 35. — *August 16, 1823.*

[Died in Frederick Co.] — Mr. Wm. Kinlin. — *September 20, 1823.*

[Died] — In Georgetown, S. C. Clealand Kinlock, Esq. — *September 27, 1823.*

[Died] — In Cumberland Co. Mrs. Kirkpatrick, consort of the Rev. John Kirkpatrick. — *October 4, 1823.*

[Died] — At Georgetown, Mr. John Knowles. — *August 9, 1823.*

[Died] — In Martinsburg, Mrs. Catharine S. Krauth, wife of the Rev. Charles P. Krauth, 29. — *January 31, 1824.*

[Died] — In Winchester Miss Elizabeth Kring, daughter of Mr. Joshua Kring, of Rockingham Co. — *September 6, 1823.*

[Died] — Mrs. Fanny Lacy, consort of the late Rev. Edmund Lacy, an old and respectable member of the Methodist Church. — *December 6, 1823.*

[Died] — In Bordentown, N. J. Gen. Henry Lallemand. — *September 27, 1823.*

[Died] — At Free town, Sierra Leone, Rev. Geo. Lane, a Wesleyan Missionary, aged 27. — *November 8, 1823.*

[Died] — In Williamsburg, Mr. George Lang, in the 68th year of his age. — *January 3, 1824.*

Died, In Manchester, Mrs. Martha Lang, consort of Mr. William Lang. — *February 7, 1824.*

[Died in Frederick Co.] — Mr. Jabez Larue. — *September 20, 1823.*

Died. — At Harper's Ferry, a few days ago, after a short illness, Colonel Jacint Laval, aged about 60 years. Colonel Laval came to this country during our Revolutionary war, as a coronet of dragoons in the French army under General Rochambeau. . . . — *September 14, 1822.*

[Died] — In Philadelphia, Dr. J. O. B. Lawrence, 32. — *September 6, 1823.*

[Died] In New-Orleans, Mr. John C. Lawrence, Baker, late of Richmond. — *February 1, 1823.*

[Died] — At Dumfries, Va. John Lawson, Esq. a native of Scotland, 69. — *August 23, 1823.*

[Died] — In Richmond, John Lee, Esq. 59. — *September 20, 1823.*

[Died] — In Carlisle, Pa. Mrs. Mary Duncan Lee, wife of Richard H. Lee, Esq. of Leesburg. — *November 1, 1823.*

[Died in Richmond] — Ormond Lee, son of Thomas Lee, 5. — *September 20, 1823.*

[Died] — In Northumberland Co., Mr. Richard Lee, of Cobbs Hall, in the 56th year of his age. — *March 27, 1824.*

Died, in Buckingham, at the seat of Judge [William H.] Cabell, on the 13th inst. Miss Lucy N. Legrand, of Charlotte. . . . — *August 31, 1822.*

[Died] — In Petersburg, Mrs. S. Ann Lemoine. — *January 24, 1824.*

[Died] — At Lynchburg, Mr. James Lewellin. — *August 16, 1823.*

[Died] — Near the Sweet Springs, Mrs. Mary Lewis, consort of the late John Lewis, Esq. — *February 28, 1824.*

[Died] — At Augusta (Ga.) Mrs. Mary Ligon, 46. — *August 16, 1823.*

[Died] — In Norfolk, Mrs. Matty Lindsay, 57. — *August 16, 1823.*

[Died] — In King William Co. Capt. Bernard Lipscombe, a hero of the revolution, 68. — *September 6, 1823.*

Died, At Washington on the 18th inst. in the 66th year of his age, the Hon. Brackholst Livingston, one of the Associate Justices of the Supreme Court of the United States. — *March 22, 1823.*

Died, In Richmond, Mr. John Livingston, Æt. 74. — *October 11, 1823.*

[Died in Frederick Co.] — Mrs. Mary Lockhart, 30. — *October 4, 1823.*

[Died] — In Washington City, Mr. Ira D. Love a member of Columbian College, 26. — *November 8, 1823.*

[Died] On board the ship Moss, on her passage from Philadelphia to London, the Hon. William Lowndes. . . . — *January 18, 1823.*

[Died] — In Richmond, Mrs. Jane Lownes, 37. — *November 1, 1823.*

[Died] — In Barnwell District, S. C. Rev. John Lugg. — *February 28, 1824.*

[Died] — At Belchertown, Mass. Major Elihu Lyman, 81. — *October 11, 1823.*

[Died] — In Chesterfield Co. Mr. J. F. Lynch, son of Mr. Francis Lynch, of Petersburg, 18. — *September 13, 1823.*

[Died] — At Port-au-Prince, W. I. Mr. John Lynch, a native of Caroline Co. Va. — *September 13, 1823.*

[Died] — At Portsmouth, Midshipman James P. M'Call. — *October 25, 1823.*

[Died in Frederick Co.] Mr. Samuel M'Collum, 90. — *October 4, 1823.*

Died, of a Consumption, on Tuesday night the 22d October, at his Father's residence, (in Buckingham County) in the 26th year of his age, Mr. John M'Cormick . . . he left two children. . . . — *November 16, 1822.*

[Died] — In Pendleton County, Mr. John M'Coy, son of Gen. Wm. M'Coy. — *August 16, 1823.*

[Died] — In Winchester, Mr. John M'Coy, son of Gen.. Wm. M'Coy, 20. — *August 30, 1823.*

[Died] — In Ohio, Hon. Jno. A. M'Dowell President Judge of the 6th Circuit of that State. — *October 18, 1823.*

[Died] — In Lunenburg Co. Mrs. Jane MacFarland. — *November 22, 1823.*

We regret to learn of the death of maj. M'Glassin, lately appointed U. States factor in the Arkansas territory, in the place of Matthew Lyon, deceased. — *November 16, 1822.*

[Died in Rockbridge Co.] Mr. Donald M'Kenzie, a native of Scotland. — *February 14, 1824.*

[Died] In the town of Livingston, in the State of New York, on Sunday morning last [June 16], Colonel John M'Kinstry, aged 80. . . . He engaged in [his country's] service; . . . from the memorable battle of Bunker's Hill, . . . to the surrender of Cornwallis at Yorktown. . . . — *June 22, 1822.*

[Died] — In Goochland co. Mrs. Mary M'Lein. — *February 21, 1824.*

[Died] — In Frederick Co. Mrs. Rebecca M'Murry, 27. — *October 4, 1823.*

[Died] — At Petersburg, Hector M'Neill, Esq. — *August 9, 1823.*

[Died] — At City Point, Henry Machen, in the 45th year of his age. — *March 20, 1824.*

[Died in Frederick Co.] Mabra Madden, 54. — *September 20, 1823.*

[Died] — In Montgomery county, Md. Col. Geo. Magruder, 57. — *August 23, 1823.*

[Died] — At New-Orleans, Mr. James Marsh, late of this city. — *December 20, 1823.*

[Died] — At Norfolk, aged only 21 years, Madame Eugenia D'Anfossy Martigny, consort of Buchet Martigny, Esq. Consul of the King of Spain, and daughter of Mr. B. D'Anfossy. — *February 28, 1824.*

[Died] — In Wilkes Co. N. C. Robert Edwin Martin, 17; he was accidentally killed with a gun, on a deer hunt. — *September 6, 1823.*

[Died] — In Sparta, Geo. Robert Gillespie Martin, son of William Martin, Esq. of Granville Co. North Carolina — and grandson of the venerable Nath'l Macon, Esq. of that State, 20. — *November 8, 1823.*

[Died] — In Berkeley county, Va. Mrs. Sarah Martin, 51. — *August 23, 1823.*

[Died] — In Dumfries, Mrs. Elizabeth Mason, relict of Thompson Mason. — *February 28, 1824.*

[Died] At Oakland, Nelson county, on Saturday the 1st inst. Mrs. Lucy Massie, consort of Doctor Thomas Massie, in the 31st year of her age. — *September 14, 1822.*

[Died in this city] Miss Martha Massie, a native of Kentucky. — *February 14, 1824.*

[Died] — In the City of Washington, Mr. Fontaine Maury, Aid to the Marquis La Fayette in the campaign in Virginia, 64. — *February 7, 1824.*

[Died] — In Alabama, Mr. James F. Mayers, formerly of Lynchburg. — *September 13, 1823.*

[Died] — At his residence in Alabama James J. Mayers, Esq. — *October 4, 1823.*

Died. — At Lynchburg, on the 11th inst. Mr. Joseph Mays, merchant of the firm of Kyle and Mays. — *September 21, 1822.*

[Died in Frederick Co.] Miss Lucy F. Meade, 26. — *October 25, 1823.*

[Died] — In Frederick Co. Miss Susan Meade, 34. — *October 25, 1823.*

[Died], At the City of Washington, Mr. Josiah Meigs, Commissioner of the General Land Office. Æt. 70. — *September 14, 1822.*

[Died] At the Cherokee Agency, on the 28th of January, Col. Return Jonathan Meigs. — *March 1, 1823.*

[Died] — In Philadelphia, Mr. John Melish, Geographer, in the 52d year of his age. — *January 18, 1823.*

[Died] — In Prince Edward Co. Mrs. Martha Mettauer, consort of Dr. John P. Mettauer, 26. — *December 13, 1823.*

[Died] On Friday, Nov. 28th, at her residence in Prince Edward Co. Mrs. Mary, wife of Dr. John P. Mettauer, departed this life, aged 25 years and 4 months. She has left . . . a tender husband, three small children and a number of near relatives. . . . — *December 20, 1823.*

Died, In Manchester, Mrs. Mary B. Michaels, aet. 52. — *September 27, 1823.*

[Died] In Washington city, on Saturday last [November 30], Anne Elbertina Middleton, aged 20, consort of Arthur Middleton, Jr., Esq. and only child of Gen. John P. Van Ness. — *December 7, 1822*

[Died in Richmond] Mr. Fleming Miller. — *October 4, 1823.*

[Died] — In Brunswick Co. Dr. John L. Miller. — *September 20, 1823.*

[Died in Fredericksburg] — Mr. Thornton Mills, 23. — *October 25, 1823.*

[Died] — In Tappahannock, of a pulmonary affection, Mrs. Jane Minor, consort of Doctor Minor of that place, 21. — *March 20, 1824.*

[Died at St. Louis] — Mrs. Mitchell, consort of Dr. [Chas. L.] M[itchell]. — *September 13, 1823.*

[Died] — At St. Louis, Dr. Chas. L. Mitchell, formerly of Lynchburg. — *September 13, 1823.*

[Died] — At her residence in the upper part of Middlesex County, on the 6th ult. in the eve of her 66th year, Mrs. Catharine Montague. — *March 6, 1824.*

[Died] — In Augusta Co. Va. Mrs. Agnes Montgomery, wife of the late Rev. John Montgomery. — *February 28, 1824.*

[Died] — At Key West, the Rev. B. R. Montgomery, D. D. 46. — *October 11, 1823.*

[Died] At Beaufort, (S. C.) John H. Montgomery, Esq. late one of the Judges of the Superior Court. — *December 14, 1822.*

[Died] — In Surry Co. Mr. Blank Moody, 47. — *December 13, 1823.*

[Died] — In Powhatan Co. William Moody, 16. — *October 25, 1823.*

Died, At Henry Court-house in the 33d year of his age, Col. Edward Moor, of Germantown, N. C. — *March 13, 1824.*

[Died] — In Fairfax Co. Va. Mrs. Susanna Moore, 34. — *October 11, 1823.*

Died,—At Amherst, (Mass.) the 30th ultimo, Rev. Zephaniah Swift Moore, D. D. President of the Collegiate Institution in that town.... — *July 19, 1823.*

[Died] — In Lynchburg, Mrs. Elizabeth K. Morgan. — *September 13, 1823.*

[Died] — Southern View, Fauquier county, Va. Mrs. Mildred Morgan, in her 42d year. — *August 9, 1823.*

[Died] — In Buckingham Co. Mr. Benjamin Morris, 89. — *November 8, 1823.*

Died, In Prince Edward Co. Doctor John Morton of Cumberland. — *November 22, 1823.*

Died, In Richmond, Mrs. Mary Moseley.... The funeral from the residence of Mr. Povall, this morning at 11 o'clock. — *January 10, 1824.*

[Died] — In Dinwiddie Co. Mrs. Mary Muir, consort of Mr. Gustavus A. Muir, 33. — *February 21, 1824.*

[Died] — At Elizabeth City, N. C. William T. Muse, Esq. aged 52 years. — *August 9, 1823.*

[Died] — At Montreal, S. C. Mrs. Elizabeth, wife of Moses Myers, Esq. of Norfolk, 60. — *November 8, 1823.*

[Died in Frederick Co.] — Mr. John Newman, 39. — *October 4, 1823.*

[Died] — At N. York, Maj. Darby Noon. — *September 20, 1823.*

[Died] — In Alexandria, Mrs. Sarah Fairfax Norris, wife of the Rev. Oliver Norris. — *September 27, 1823.*

Died, In Lynchburg, William Norwell [*sic*, Norvell] Esq. President of the Office of Discount and Deposit of the Bank of Virginia, Æt. 53. — *November 8, 1823.*

[Died] In this city on the 23d ult. William Nott, Jr. aged 32 years. — *March 1, 1823.*

[Died] — At Reading, Penn. Thomas Oakes, Chief Engineer of the Schuylkill Navigation Company. — *August 23, 1823.*

[Died] — In Bath, Mr. Ignatius O'Terrall. — *February 28, 1824.*

[Died] — In Tennessee, Gen. Thos. Overton, in the 72d year of his age. — *March 20, 1824.*

[Died] — In Botetourt, Mrs. Parthena Owens, consort of Wm. Owens. — *January 17, 1824.*

[Died] — At Hudson, N. Y. Capt. John Paddock, 56. — *September 6, 1823.*

[Died] — on the 8th of May, Rev. H. Palmer, Missionary. — *October 25, 1823.*

[Died] — At Regent's Town, Mrs. Palmer, widow of the Episcopal Missionary whose death was lately mentioned. — *November 8, 1823.*

[Died] — In Warren County (N. C.) Mrs. Park, wife of Robert Park, Esq. — *August 16, 1823.*

[Died] — At Coventry, Con. Mrs. Parker, aged 101. — *August 30, 1823.*

[Died] — In Somerset Co. Md. Mrs. Mary Parkes, 115. — *September 27, 1823.*

[Died] — At Pittsfield, Vt. Mrs. Electa wife of the Rev. Justin Parsons. . . . — Mrs. Parsons was the mother of the late lamented Levi Parsons, missionary to Judea. — *April 3, 1824.*

Rev. Levi Parsons, the valuable Missionary . . . died at Alexandria, in Egypt, the 10th of February last. . . . — *June 15, 1822.*

[Died] — In Northumberland Co. Mrs. Elizabeth W. Patterson, wife of the Rev. George Patterson, of the Baptist Church, 34. — *November 8, 1823.*

[Died at Martinsburg] Mr. William Patton. — *October 4, 1823.*

[Died] — At Kennebunk-port, Me. Rev. George Payson, formerly Pastor of the Congregational Church in that Town. — *November 8, 1823.*

[Died] In Wilkinson county, Ga. on the 11th ult. the Rev. Levy Peacock, aged 66. . . . — *January 4, 1823.*

[Died] — In Petersburg, Miss Mary Pearce. — *October 11, 1823.*

[Died] — In this city, Mr. Jesse Pearson, a native of Pennsylvania. — *February 21, 1824.*

[Died] — In Fredericksburg, Mr. William Pearson, a native of Pennsylvania, aged 64. — *April 3, 1824.*

Died, In Chester, Pa. Mr. Benjamin Peck, a revolutionary soldier, aged seventy years. The substance of the following epitaph was prepared some years since by himself, and he had contracted with a stone cutter to place it upon his tomb-stone:

> Here lies poor Peck — who in his day
> Was nothing but a *Peck of clay*;

189

Yet, as his earthly course he ran,
Each measure proved he was a *MAN*,
He long had known life's empty bubbles
And felt himself a *Peck of troubles;*
Now low he lies, as all men must,
And soon will be a *Peck of dust.*
                              — *February 21, 1824.*

[Died] — In Sussex County Miss Ann Peebles, daughter of Mr. Thomas E. Peebles, 19. — *August 16, 1823.*

[Died] — In Westhampton, Mass. Mr. John Petsinger, 72. — *October 11, 1823.*

[Died] — In Charlotte Co. Mrs. Elizabeth Phaup, consort of Mr. Wm. Phaup. — *November 22, 1823.*

[Died] — In Fauquier County, Miss Ann Phillips. — *August 16, 1823.*

[Died] — In Alabama, Mrs. Martha Pickens, wife of the Governor of the State. — *September 20, 1823.*

[Died] In the 24 year of her age, Mrs. Susannah L. Pleasants, consort of Mr. Daniel G. Pleasants. — *March 1', 1823.*

[Died] — In Powhatan Co. Mrs. Mary Poore, 70. — *October 11, 1823.*

[Died] — In Powhatan Co. Mrs. Anne Pope, wife of William Pope, Esq. 48. — *November 15, 1823.*

[Died] — In the County of Prince George, Capt. William Prentis, one of the oldest inhabitants of Petersburg. — *March 6, 1824.*

[Died] In Rangoon, (Burmah,) after a short illness, Mrs. Mary Price, wife of the Rev. J. D. Price, M. D. . . . — *January 18, 1823.*

Died, in this city on Sunday morning the 5th inst. Mrs. Margaret Priddy, relict of the late John Priddy, of Franklin county, N. C. aged 27. . . . — *October 11, 1823.*

[Died — At Petersburg] Mr. Thomas Pride. — *August 9, 1823.*

Died, In Muskingham Co. Ohio, Elder Henry Pringle, of the Baptist church, a native of Va. Æt. 53. — *December 27, 1823.*

[Died] In this city, on Wednesday night [March 19], at an advanced age, Maj. John Pryor, an officer in the Revolution. — *March 22, 1823.*

Died, In this city, Mr. Charles Purcell, late from Ireland, Æt. 34. — *February 28, 1824.*

[Died] — Near Marietta, Ohio, Rufus Putnam, aged about 90, a brigadier-general by brevet at the close of the Revolutionary War, and afterwards a brigadier under Wayne, in the western army formerly of Rutland, Massachusetts. . . . — *November 29, 1823.*

[Died] — At Washington city, Mrs. Elizabeth Queen, aged 22 years.
— *August 9, 1823.*

[Died] — In Sussex Co. Dr. Allen E. Raines, late of Petersburg, 22. —
October 18, 1823.

[Died] — At Paris, Ten. Mr. Charles Ralls, formerly of Fredericksburg,
29. — *January 24, 1824.*

[Died in New York] Mrs. Weathy Randle, 42. — *August 16, 1823.*

Died, in Richmond, suddenly, Mrs. Sarah Raymond, wife of Mr. Henry
Raymond. — *November 15, 1823.*

[Died] — In Wake Co. N. C. Mr. Clement C. Read, of Charlotte Co.
Va. — *September 27, 1823.*

[Died] — In Washington city, Henry H. Redmond, late a Lieut. in the
U. S. Army, 31. — *November 15, 1823.*

[Died] In Hancock Co. Ga. Capt. James Reese, a native of Va. 84. —
September 13, 1823.

[Died at Shepherdstown] Dr. Charles Reetz, by a fall from his horse. —
October 4, 1823.

Died, In Manchester, yesterday morning, Mrs. Alice Reeve, consort of
Mr. Samuel Reeve. Her funeral will be . . . from the house of Mr. George
Hutchison. — *September 20, 1823.*

[Died] — At Litchfield, Conn. the Hon. Tapping Reeve, formerly Chief
Justice of the state. — *December 27, 1823.*

[Died] — At Liberty, on her way to the Springs, Mrs. Sophia Reid of
Lynchburg. — *August 23, 1823.*

[Died] In Philadelphia, on the 14th ult. Mr. Samuel Relf, late Editor
of the Philadelphia Gazette, in the 47th year of his age. — *March 1, 1823.*

[Died in Frederick Co.] Mr. Daniel Rhinehart, 21. — *October 4, 1823.*

[Died] — At Shrewsbury, Col. Asa Rice, 82. — *August 23, 1823.*

[Died] — In Brownfield, Maine, Rev. Jacob Rice, pastor of the congregational church in that place, aged 84. . . . — *March 6, 1824.*

[Died] — In Alexandria, D. C. Miss Anna Maria Riddle. — *August 23,
1823.*

[Died] — At Seaford, in the county of Matthews, John A. Riddle, Esq.
in the 23d year of his age. — *August 9, 1823.*

[Died] — In Anne Arundel Co. in the 69th year of his age, the Hon.
Richard Ridgeley, an Associate Judge of the 3d judicial district of Maryland.
—*March 6, 1824.*

[Died] — At Stephensburg, Mr: Michael Ritenor, 70. — *November 29,
1823.*

[Died] — On board the Fox, Midshipman W. M. Rittenhouse. — *October 25, 1823.*

[Died in Frederick Co.] — Mr. Michael Rittenour. — *September 20, 1823.*

We fully participate in the public sorrow, while we announce the death of Spencer Roane, Esq. one of the Judges of the Court of Appeals. This event by which Virginia feels herself bereaved, took place at the Warm Springs on the 4th day of September. . . . — *September 14, 1822.*

[Died] — In Charlestown, Kanawha Co. Mrs. Ann B. Roberston, 29. — *September 20, 1823.*

Died, In this city, Mr. Francis Robert, of Lexington, Ky. — *December 13, 1823.*

Died, In Richmond, Mrs. Elizabeth M. Robertson, wife of Mr. Archibald Robertson. — *November 29, 1823.*

[Died in Petersburg] Mrs. Jane Robertson, widow of the late David Robertson, Esq. — *January 31, 1824.*

[Died] — In Marietta, Ohio, the Rev. Samuel P. Robins. — *October 11, 1823.*

Died, In this city, Mr. John H. Robinson. — *January 31, 1824.*

[Died] — About the 1st inst in the 24th year of his age, of the prevailing fever at Key West, (Thompson's Island,) Lieut. Stephen M. Rodgers, of the Marine Corps, and only son of the Rev. Dr. Rodgers, of Philadelphia. — *November 8, 1823.*

[Died] — In Gloucester, Thomas R. Rootes, Esq. — *January 17, 1824.*

[Died] — At Huntsville, Alabama, Mrs. F. T. Rose, sister of Mr. [James] Madison, late President of the United States. — *November 15, 1823.*

[Died] — At his residence near Leesburg, Stephen C. Roszell, Esq. formerly a member of the Legislature of Virginia, 48. — *September 6, 1823.*

Died, at his residence in Caswell County, (N. C.) on Wednesday the 17th of April, 1822, Sterling Ruffin, in the 55th year of his age. . . . — *June 1, 1822.*

[Died] — At New-Market, Mrs. Hebner Rupert, 22. — *November 29, 1823.*

[Died] — In Petersburg, Mrs. Andrew Ryan. — *August 30, 1823.*

[Died in Petersburg] Mr. John M. Ryan. — *October 11, 1823.*

[Died] — In New-York city, the Rev. Ezra Sampson, aged 76, the venerable and pious author of the "Brief Remarker," and "Beauties of the Bible." — *January 3, 1824.*

[Died] — In Loudoun Co. Mr. Presley Sanders. — *September 13, 1823.*

[Died] — On the 24th [of April], Rev. W. H. Schemel, Missionary. — *October 25, 1823.*

[Died] — In Salem, Fauquier Co. Mrs. Elizabeth Scott, 84. — *November 29, 1823.*

[Died] — In Fauquier Co. Mrs. Elizabeth Scott, 83. — *December 27, 1823.*

[Died] — In Philadelphia, Mr. Robert Scott, 79. The deceased was appointed by President Washington, engraver to the Mint of the United States in 1794, and faithfully fulfilled the duties of that office to the day of his death. — *December 27, 1823.*

[Died] — In Adams Co. Pa. Hon. William Scott, one of the Associate Judges of that county, 87. — *November 1, 1823.*

[Died] — In Amelia Co. Mr. Efford Booker Seay, 20. — *October 25, 1823.*

[Died] — In Alexandria, Dr. Benjamin Sedwick, 41. — *March 27, 1824.*

Died. — On Wednesday the 22d of May at his father's residence in King and Queen county in the 24th year of his age, after a painful illness of several months, Mr. John W. Semple, son of the Rev. Robert B. Semple.... — *June 1, 1822.*

[Died] — In Washington City, Miss Eliza Carroll Sewell. — *August 30, 1823.*

[Died] — In Norfolk, Col. Wm. Sharp, 48. — *September 20, 1823.*

[Died] — At Norfolk, Col. William Sharpe, 46. — *September 13, 1823.*

[Died] In Philadelphia, Com. John Shaw, of the U. S. Navy, 50. — *September 27, 1823.*

[Died] — In Goochland, Capt. Wm. A. Shelton, formerly of Nelson. — *January 17, 1824.*

[Died] — At Amherst, Mass. Mr. Ralph Shepard, a member of the Senior Class in the Theological Seminary at Andover. — *February 7, 1824.*

Died, Mrs. Sarah, widow of John M. Sheppard, late of Scotchtown, Hanover county. — *January 3, 1824.*

[Died] — In Richmond Mr. Wyatt Shields. His horse ran away with him in a gig and broke his neck. — *November 8, 1823.*

[Died] — In Gosport, Va. Mr. Levi B. Simmons, of the U. S. Ship Peacock. — *September 27, 1823.*

[Died] — In Charleston, S. C. Edward P. Simons, Esq. 29. — *October 25, 1823.*

[Died in Surry Co.] Mr. James Simpson, 53. — *December 13, 1823.*

[Died] — In Richmond, suddenly, Mr. H. Sinton. — *October 18, 1823.*

[Died] — In Fauquier Co. Mr. John M. Skinker, son of Wm. Skinker, Esq. 23. — *February 14, 1824.*

[Died] — In Pittsylvania Co. Mr. Lawrence Slaughter, of Fredericksburg, 35. — *September 27, 1823.*

Mrs. Slaughter, wife of Doctor Wm. Slaughter, of Campbell Co. in a fit of insanity (as is supposed) put a period to her existence by discharging the contents of a loaded gun through her head. — *March 15, 1823.*

[Died] — In Westmoreland Co. Geo. William Smith, Attorney at Law, 28. — *October 18, 1823.*

Died, — On the 10th ult. at his residence in Charles City, Dr. Robert P. Smith, aged 37 years. . . . He administered consolation to his afflicted companion and child, exhorting the latter to remember her Creator. . . . — *May 3, 1823.*

[Died] — In Richmond Co. Ga. Mr. Wm. Smith, a native of Southampton, Va. 58. — *November 22, 1823.*

[Died] — In Fincastle, Miss Jane Snodgrass, 22. — *November 8, 1823.*

[Died] — At Harrisonburg, Penn. Mrs. Mary S. Snyder, consort of the late Governor [Simon] Snyder, 55. — *October 25, 1823.*

[Died in Lunenburg Co.] Mary Frances Somervell, 15. — *September 20, 1823.*

[Died] — At Pleasant Hill, near Port Tobacco, Miss Lucretia Spalding, 26. — *August 30, 1823.*

[Died] — Near Piscataway, Prince George Co. Md. Mr. Michael Spalding, 23. — *September 6, 1823.*

A melancholy event took place on the 8th of January, at Danville, Ky. In firing a salute in honour of the day, the cannon went off prematurely, and Mr. Joseph Sparke was instantaneously killed. . . . — *February 15, 1823.*

[Died] — In Henry Co. Edward C. Staples, 36. — *September 27, 1823.*

[Died] In Manchester, N. H. on Wednesday last, [May 8] Maj. Gen. John Stark, aged 93 years, 8 months and 24 days. . . . — *May 25, 1822.*

[Died] In Philadelphia, on Friday, the 10th ult. Mrs. Maria Staughton, consort of the Rev. William Staughton, D. D. President of the Columbian College, in the District of Columbia. — *February 1, 1823.*

[Died] — At sea, on board the U. S. Ship Peacock, Midshipman Robert Steed, in the 19th year of his age, son of Capt. Robert E. Steed, of Norfolk. — *August 9, 1823.*

[Died in Frederick Co.] Mr. Steel, 83. — *October 4, 1823.*

[Died] — In Norwich, Conn. Rev. John Sterry, pastor of the Baptist church in that city, 57. — *December 27, 1823.*

[Died] — At Norwich, Vermont the Rev. John Sterry, pastor of the Baptist church in that city, aged 57. — *November 29, 1823.*

[Died at Alexandria] William W. Stevens, 18. — *October 4, 1823.*

[Died] — In Baltimore, Dr. William Stewart, late Surgeon in the Army of the United States, 84. — *October 11, 1823.*

[Died] — At Gravesend, N. Y. Mr. Rutgert Stillwell, 78. Though not prevented by indisposition, he had not been off his farm for more than 40 years. — *November 1, 1823.*

[Died] — In Petersburg, Mrs. Frances Stines, consort of Joshua Stines. — *December 6, 1823.*

[Died in Frederick Co.] Mrs. Barbara Stone. — *October 4, 1823.*

[Died] — In New-Orleans, Lieut. Horace C. Story, of the U. S. corps of Engineers. — *September 6, 1823.*

[Died in Frederick Co.] Mr. Francis Stribling. — *September 20, 1823.*

Mrs. Stuart, confined on her passage [to Monrovia, Liberia]; when unloading their goods, worked very hard, went into the water, and died. — *September 13, 1823.*

[Died] — At Milledgeville, Geo., Daniel Sturgis, Esq. — *October 11, 1823.*

[Died] — In Wake Co. N. C. Col. Ransom Sutherland. — *September 6, 1823.*

[Died] In Sanford, Maine, Rev. Moses Sweat, aged 68, pastor of the Congregational Church in that town. . . . — *September 21, 1822.*

[Died] — In Ohio, where he was on a visit to his children, the Hon. Z. Swift, formerly Chief Justice of Con. — *October 18, 1823.*

[Died in Frederick Co.] Mr. George Sypher, late of New-Jersey, 30. — *September 20, 1823.*

Died on the 4th inst. at her maternal residence in the county of Mathews, Mrs. Hester E. H. Tabb, in the 23d year of her age, only daughter of Mrs. S. E. Van Bibber, and consort of Doctor Henry Tabb. . . . — *March 8, 1823.*

[Died in Richmond] — Col. Reuben Tankersley. — *September 27, 1823.*

[Died in Washington City] Mrs. Elizabeth L. Tarboe, aged 23. — *August 30, 1823.*

[Died] — In Cabell Co. Col. Edmund Taylor, of this city, 39. — *October 11, 1823.*

Died, In this city, Mrs. Gabriella Taylor, in the 35th year of her age. — *August 9, 1823.*

Departed this life, after an illness of 7 days, on the 1st inst. at her residence, near Hanover Court-house, Mrs. Alice Temple, relict of John Temple, Esq. — Her bereaved orphans ... cherish the melancholy recollection of her worth. . . . — *May 11, 1822.*

Departed this life, on the 8th ulto. at her Brother, Dr. Thompson's, Martinham, near St. Michaels, Md., Miss Ann M. Thompson, Daughter of Anthony Thompson, of Dorchester County, Md. in the 19th year of her age. . . . — *September 7, 1822.*

Died, In New Orleans on the 29th Feb. of consumption, Mr. Walter Raleigh Thompson, son of Ezra Thomson [*sic*.], Esq. of Poughkeepsie, New-York, and late a resident of this city. — *April 3, 1824.*

[Died] — At Oak Hill, Cumberland county, Va. John T. Thornton eldest son of Capt. Wm. M. Thornton, 16. — *August 23, 1823.*

[Died] — In Amherst Co. Miss Mary Thornton. — *September 27, 1823.*

[Died] — Mary J. B. Thornton and Elizabeth T. Thornton, daughters of Capt. Wm. M. Thornton, of Cumberland Co. — *September 20, 1823.*

[Died] — In Surry Co. Miss Rebecca Thornton. — *October 11, 1823.*

[Died] — In Dumfries, Mrs. Williammina M. consort of Dr. James B. C. Thornton. — *November 1, 1823.*

[Died] — In Circleville, (Ky.) Mrs. Nancy Thrall, 22. — *August 16, 1823.*

Departed this life on the 18th ult. at late her residence in Gloucester, Mrs. Margaret Thrift, aged 78 years, 2 months and 5 days. . . . — *October 18, 1823*

[Died] In Oxford, N. Y. Col. Benjamin Throop, aged 80. The deceased was one of the remaining patriots who gave liberty and independence to his country. . . . — *June 22, 1822.*

[Died in Dinwiddie Co.] — Mr. Burwell Thweatt, 92. — *November 1, 1823.*

[Died] — In Halifax Co. Maj. Giles Thweatt, Æt. 73. — *November 22, 1823.*

[Died in Baltimore] Marmaduke Tilden, Esq. 70. — *February 28, 1824.*

[Died] At his residence in Hanover, on Tuesday the 17th ult. Col. Thomas Tinsley, in the 70th year of his age. — *January 4, 1823.*

[Died in Richmond] — Mr. William D. Tinsley, 23. — *October 25, 1823.*

[Died] — In Woodford county, Ky. the Rev. Henry Toler, pastor of the second Baptist church in Versailles. — *April 3, 1824.*

[Died] — In the County of Gloucester, Mr. William Tomkies. — *March 6, 1824.*

Died, on Monday the 15th of July, at Hamilton-Ville, near Philadelphia,

Manual Torres, Minister of the Columbian Republic near [sic] the U. States: in the 58th year of his age. — *July 27, 1822.*

[Died] — At Washington county, Alabama, Hon. Harry Toulmin, late Judge of the District Court of the United States, for the District of Mississippi. — *January 3, 1824.*

[Died] — In Woodford county, Kentucky, the Rev. Henry Towler, Minister of the Baptist Church at Versailles. — *March 13, 1824.*

[Died] — In Loudo[u]n County, Miss Rebecca A. Townsend, of Georgetown. — *August 16, 1823.*

[Died] — At Farmington, Con. the Hon. John Treadwell, in the 78th year of his age. He was for many years a member of the Council, and afterwards Lieutenant-Governor and Governor of the State. — *August 30, 1823.*

[Died] — In Richmond, Mrs. Ann Trueman, 30. — *September 27, 1823.*

[Died] — At Philadelphia, Mrs. Mary Truxton, relict of the late Com. [Thomas] Truxton, 64. — *September 20, 1823.*

[Died] — At his residence, Jacob G. Tryon, Esq. High Sheriff of the city and county of Philadelphia. — *August 23, 1823.*

[Died] — On the East Rock, in New-Haven, ... Turner, called "The Hermit." . . . — *November 29, 1823.*

[Died] — In Northumberland Co. Mr. Benjamin Turner. — *February 21, 1824.*

[Died] — In Warren Co. N. C. James Turner, Esq. 57. He had been Governor of the state, and Senator in Congress. — *January 31, 1824.*

[Died] — In Washington, Samuel Turner, Esq. chief clerk in the Secretary of the Senate's office. — *February 7, 1824.*

[Died] — In Baltimore, Elisha Tyson, of the Society of Friends, 75. A numerous concourse of relatives and friends attended his obsequies, together, it is supposed, with nearly four thousand *people of colour*, who assembled to pay their last tribute of respect and gratitude to their deceased friend and patron. — *February 28, 1824.*

[Died] — At Martinsburg, Mrs. Underdunk, 51. — *October 4, 1823.*

[Died] — In Pittsylvania Co. Mrs. Sarah Vadin, consort of Mr. Burwell Vadin, in the 82d year of her age; leaving behind to lament her loss, beside a numerous family of descendants, a husband in his 92 year, with whom she had lived 66 years. — *February 28, 1824.*

[Died] — In Jefferson Co. Mrs. Ann Vanhorn, 82. — *October 4, 1823.*

[Died] At Charleston, (S. C.) whither he had gone for the benefit of his health, the Hon. William W. Van Ness, for fifteen years one of the

Judges of the Supreme Court of the state of New-York. — *March 22, 1823.*

[Died] — In Dinwiddie, Mr. William Vaughan, 66. — *January 31, 1824.*

[Died] On Friday the 6th inst. at her father's Robert L. Coleman, in Bedford, Mrs. Elizabeth Venable of Charlotte. — *September 21, 1822.*

[Died] — In Prince George[s] Co. Md. the Rev. Wm. Vergnes, of the Roman Catholic Church. He bequeathed 1000 dollars to the poor of the Country. — *October 18, 1823.*

[Died] — In Prince George Co. Mr. Joseph Voinard, 69. — *November 8, 1823.*

[Died] — In Prince Edward county, Mr. John B. Wade, Æt. 22. — *September 14, 1822.*

[Died] — In Washington city, George Wadsworth, Esq. 45 — *October 4, 1823.*

[Died] — In Chesterfield Co. Mrs. Ester Walden, Æt. 44. — *November 1, 1823.*

[Died, In this city] Miss Mary A. S. Walker, in the 15th year of her age. — *August 9, 1823.*

[Died] — In Charlottesville, Mr. Thomas Walker, 40. — In rolling logs into a saw mill, he was caught by one which passing over him bruised him so that he survived but a few hours. — *December 13, 1823.*

[Died] — In Philadelphia, in the 36th year of his age, Dr. Benj. Walkins, of Virginia. — *March 20, 1824.*

[Died] — In West Hanover, Penn. Gen. James Wallace, formerly a Representative in Congress from that district. — *February 28, 1824.*

[Died] — In Stafford Co. Mr. James Waller, Æt. 35. — *February 14, 1824.*

[Died] — In Prince George Co. Mrs. P. Wamack, 97. — *September 13, 1823.*

[Died] — In Baltimore, Mrs. Elizabeth Ward, 79. — *February 28, 1824.*

[Died in Calcutta, India] the Rev. Wm. Ward of Serampore. . . . March 7, 1823. — *September 6, 1823.*

Died, In Richmond, Mrs. Elizabeth Warden, consort of Mr. James Warden. — *December 6, 1823.*

[Died] In Hardy Co. Mr. William Warden, 74. — *October 4, 1823.*

[Died] — In Foxborough, Mass. Hon. Ebenezer Warren. When the British troops marched from Boston, he quitted home and joined in the battle of Lexington, and was one of three brothers who were in arms that day; the others were General Joseph Warren, afterwards killed at Bunker Hill, and the late Dr. John Warren, of Boston. — *January 24, 1824.*

[Died] — Near Wheeling, Va. Laurence Augustine Washington, Esq. in the 50th year of his age. He was a Nephew and one of the heirs of Gen. George Washington, who educated him, and in whose family he resided for a number of years. — *March 6, 1824.*

[Died] — In Fairfax County, Mr. David Watkins, in the 44th year of his age. — *March 1, 1823.*

[Died] — In Greene Co. Alabama, Henry Y. Webb, one of the Judges of the Circuit Court in that state. — *October 25, 1823.*

[Died] — At Grenada, A. F. Webster, Esq. aged 43. His body weighed 555 lbs. The coffin was so large that it could not be got into the house; the body was therefore put into it in the street, and was carried to the grave by 20 persons. — *August 16, 1823.*

[Died] — At his country residence, near Brooklyn, L. I. John Wells Esq. of New-York, Counsellor at Law. — *September 13, 1823.*

[Died] — In Murfreesboro', N. C. Rev. Samuel Wells, of the Methodist Church, 58. — *September 27, 1823.*

[Died in Richmond] Mrs. Elizabeth Werth, consort of John J. Werth, 44. — *September 6, 1823.*

[Died] — At Westham Locks, Capt. Joshua West, in the 60th year of his age. — *February 21, 1824.*

[Died] — In Brunswick, on the 16th inst. Mrs. Maria Wheelock, widow of the late President Wheelock, of Dartmouth College, aged 68 years. — *March 13, 1824.*

Died, In Richmond, Mrs. Judith White, Æt. 66. — *October 25, 1823.*

[Died in Nelson Co.] — Mr. Lorenzo White, 18. — *October 11, 1823.*

[Died] — In James City Co. Mr. William M. White formerly of Salem. — *October 18, 1823.*

[Died] — At Norfolk, Dr. Alexander Whitehead, a native of Scotland, Æt. 59. — *December 6, 1823.*

[Died] — Mrs. Mary Hartwell Whiting, consort of Francis Whiting, Esq. at Eston Hill, Gloucester county. — *January 3, 1824.*

[Died] — In Worcester, Mass. Mr. Benjamin Whitney, 98. — *August 23, 1823.*

[Died in Botetourt Co.] Mrs. Wiley, consort of Robert Wiley. — *October 4, 1823.*

[Died in Richmond] Mr. Tunby Wilkins, 30. — *September 27, 1823.*

[Died] — In Dublin Co. N. C. the Rev. Jacob Williams, of the Baptist Church, 55. — *November 15, 1823.*

[Died] — In Cumberland Co. Mr. Tarlton Williams. — *September 13, 1823.*

[Died] — In Wrentham, Mass. Rev. William Williams, Pastor of the Baptist Church in that town. — *October 11, 1823.*

[Died in Richmond] — Mr. George Williamson, late of New-York. — *September 13, 1823.*

[Died] — In Petersburg, Capt. William Willis. — *September 6, 1823.*

[Died] — In Annapolis, Md. Mr. Elisha Willson, of Vermont, and an officer in the patriot service of South America, 34. — *September 6, 1823.*

[Died] — In Scitutate, Mrs. Elizabeth Winsor, relict of the late Rev. Joseph Winsor, of Gloucester, aged 105 years and 9 months. . . . — *November 1, 1823.*

[Died] — In Hanover Co. Mrs. Louisa B. Winston, wife of Mr. Peter Winston, 25. — *December 20, 1823.*

[Died] — In the same [Hanover] Co. Sarah Elizabeth, daughter of Peter Winston. — *November 15, 1823.*

Died — on the 27th ult. about half past 9 in the morning, Mr. John Withington, who had for many years magnified his office as a deacon of the Baptist church in Fayette street, New-York. . . . — *April 13, 1822.*

[Died] — In Chesterfield, N. H. Rev. Abraham Wood, senior pastor of the Church and Society in that Town, aged 75, and the 51st year of his ministry. — *November 8, 1823.*

On Tuesday, 4th inst. about 11 o'clock in the evening, Mrs. Jean Wood, in the 68th year of her age, was removed from the present to a better world. . . . — *March 8, 1823.*

[Died] — In Amelia Co. Mrs. Obedience S. Worsham. — *October 25, 1823.*

[Died] — In Essex Co. Mrs. Mary D. Wright, 18. — *October 4, 1823.*

[Died] — In Carolina County Mr. Joseph M. Wyatt, 23. — *August 16, 1823.*

Died. — In Albemarle Co. on the 14th ult. the Rev. Samuel Wydown, of the Episcopal Church. — *March 1, 1823.*

[Died] — In King George Co. Col. Robert L. Yates, from a kick from his horse. — *October 4, 1823.*

[Died] — In Fairfax Co. Mr. John Zimmerman. — *December 6, 1823.*

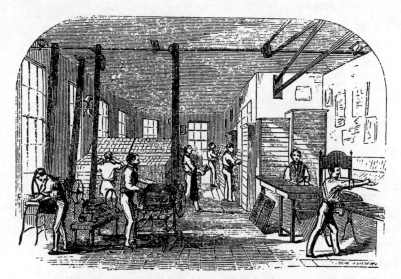

PERSONAL NOTES.

Virginia Independent Chronicle, Richmond Va.

DEC. 6, 1786—

Last Thursday was married Mr. William Waller, merchant, to Miss Sally Macon, of Hanover county.

Yesterday died at Williamsburg, Mrs. Anne Nicholas, relict. of the late Honorable Robert Carter Nicholas, Esquire—November 6.

JAN. 24, 1787—

On the 10th instant died at Norfolk, Mr. James Cross, merchant, a native of Glasgow, and on Thursday, in this city the Reverend William Coutts.

JUNE 13, 1787—

On Friday died after a short indisposition Mr John Hunter Holt, of this city printer.

Tuesday, the 2d instant, died Mr. William Adams, third son of Col. Richard Adams.

Last Wednesday died Mrs. Ann Price, spouse of Mr. John Price, of Henrico.

Oct. 17, 1787—

Early on Wednesday morning departed this life Mr. James Buchanan, the oldest merchant of this city.

Jan. 30, 1788—

Mrs. Susanna Shields, spouse of Major James Shields, near Williamsburg, died, leaving a numerous offspring.

Early on Friday morning at his house in this city, the Hon. Bolling Stark died at an advanced age.

February 20, 1788—

Married Dr. John Cringer, of this city, to Miss Jane Stewart, daughter of Charles Stewart, Esq., of London.

Virginia Gazette.

January 15, 1802 (Friday)—

Married on 17 ult. by Rev. Mr. McRae Aaron Hoskins to Miss Ann Brackett.

Married Mr. William McKenzie, merchant, to Miss Jane Scott.

Jan. 26—

Died at St. Mary's, Georgia, on or about the first of October last, Mr. John Hay, late merchant from Richmond.

Mar. 5—

Married on Saturday evening last, William Munford, Esq., of Mecklenburg county, to Miss Sally Radford, daughter of William Radford, Esq., of this city.

March 26—

Died, Miss Elizabeth Skipwith, eldest daughter of Col. Henry Skipwith, of Cumberland Co.

April 24—

Died Saturday, 17th inst., Mrs. Alice Marshall, wife of William Marshall, Esq., of this city.

May 8—

Died on Tuesday morning Andrew Dunscomb in the 45th year of his age.

Died at his seat near this city on Thursday the 29th of the last month, Capt. James Price.

MAY 12—

Lewis Burwell, executor of the estate of Nathaniel Burwell, deceased, late of King William Co. Advertisements dated at Richmond.

MAY 29—

On Saturday the 22nd of May at 12 o'clock P. M., Mrs. Washington terminated her well spent life.

Died, yesterday morning, suddenly Mr. Zachariah Rowland.

JUNE 5, 1802—

Mr. Archelaus Hughes to Miss Nancy J. Clopton, of this city.

JUNE 9, 1802—

Died Major John Willis, of Spotsylvania county, in this city. Interred in the church yard.

PAGE, ANDERSON, BLAIR, ETC.
(From Richmond Newspapers)

Argus—9 Sept. 1800, p. 3.
Died Sunday morning last (Sep. 7) in 69th year of his age, John Blair.

Examiner—6 Apl. 1803, p. 3.
Mann Page died lately at Mansfield in Spottsylvania County.

Enquirer—24 June, 1828, p. 3.
Died at residence of Mr. Allen S. Fleshman in Halifax, on Apl. 28, 1828, William M. Anderson, aged 19.

Whig—17 Jan. 1832, p. 3.
Died Saturday morning (Jan. 15) about 10 o'clock, Richard H. Anderson of Anderson & Son. He attended William & Mary College and the University of Virginia. Made two trips to Europe and lived for a short time in France.

Whig—20 Mch. 1804, p. 3.
Died on Monday last, March 16, David, son of David and Sarah Anderson, aged eight months.

Enquirer—29 June, 1813, p. 3.
Capt. Robert Anderson either killed or taken prisoner in assault on Hampton. Information by express.
Died, Mrs. Page, wife of John Page, of Rosewell, Gloucester Co., Va.

Whig & Public Advr.—4 Jany. 1833 (from *Norfolk Herald* of Fri.)
Died on Wednesday night, Mrs. Ann, T. Macfarland, wife of Wm. H. Macfarland, in the 28th year of her age.

Enquirer—8 Oct. 1824.
Advertisement of Chiles Terrell's boarding school in Richmond.

Enquirer—Oct. 1808.

Notice—In 1793 a request was made by letter from a gentleman in Virginia (thro Mr. Joseph Johnson, Consul General in London) to Mr. Thomas Digges then in England, to make inquiries for the heirs of the family of Mr. Abraham Milnes who when a youth left Brigghouse near Huddersfield, in Yorkshire for America, and was clerk to a merchant in Virginia, afterward kept a store of his own and did a profitable trade. He died unmarried in 1753 leaving land and property. Unfortunately, by the loss at sea of the ship Jane & Rachel, Capt. Dade, from London to Alexandria, in the year 1798, the letter of request and other papers were lost and even the writers name (which is supposed to be Farly or Farsly) as well as his place of residence has been forgotten but is guessed to be near Petersburg. The subscribers or either of them will be obliged to any informed, etc., etc.

Signed—Geo. Milnes, Merchant, Boston; Thomas Digges, Warburton, Potomac, Md.; Geo. W. Riggs, Georgetown, D. C.

Whig & Public Advertiser—29 Jul. 1834.

Died—July 28, age 58 years, Janet Ralston, who resided in Adams Valley.

July 28th, Mrs. Elizabeth Weisiger, wife of Jacob Weisiger, age 41 years.

Enquirer—Oct. 20, 1827.

Died on the 10th inst., at Warminster, Hon. St. Geo. Tucker, aged 75 years.

Enquirer—Oct. 14, 1808.

Died 1st Oct., aged 36 years, Capt. Leroy Hipkins of the U. S. Navy. (Same paper)—Mrs. Phebe Gray, wife of Henry Gray, of Goochland.

Whig—Friday, Aug. 16, 1834.

Died on 10th inst., Jane Clark, dau. Sampson & Angelica Jones, aged 9 mos. and 15 days.

July 19, 1834—Died—Mrs. Emily Brooke Hill, wife of Nathaniel Hill and only daughter of Owen Gwathmey, of Prince William county, aged 24 years.

Enquirer—12 Oct. 1808.

Died the 5th inst., at her house in Franklin Court, Philadelphia, aged 34 years, Mrs. Sarah Bache, wife of Richard Bache and only daughter of the late venerable father of his country, Dr. Benjamin Franklin.

Married 1829—by Rev. Philip Courtney, M. E. Church, Burwell Gresham & Lucy Taylor.

Enquirer—22 Feb. 1827.

Died at residence of Capt. Wm. Worsham in Prince Edward County on the 1st inst., Mrs. Elizabeth Worsham, in the 99th year of her age.

Enquirer—8 Oct. 1824.

On Friday 1st at residence of Mr. Chiles Terrell in this city John Fergusson, Esq., of Westham Cottage, aged about 53.

On Sept. 28th, 1824—Col. John Carr of Albemarle.

Married 30 Sep. 1824 by Rev. Timothy Swift, Mr. Jno. Sims, Jr., formerly of this city to Elizabeth Ann, dau. Newell Baker of Louisa Co.

Enquirer—7 July 1826.

Married—22nd ulto., at Indian Fields, York County, Va., Mr. Cary Wilkinson and Mary, daughter of Capt. Wm. M. McCandlish.

Married, by Rev. Mr. Keith of Georgetown, D. C., at the residence of Mrs. Anne H. Lee, on the 22nd ulto., Rev. Wm. Louis Marshall of Fauquier and Miss Ann Kinloch Lee, daughter of the late Gen. Henry Lee.

Died—at the residence of her father, Col. James Scott, of Dinwiddie County, Mrs. Mary Macfarland, consort of James Macfarland of Lunenburg County, in the 21st year of her age.

Enquirer—Feb. 24, 1827.

Died—On Sunday 11th inst., in the 56th year of her age, Mrs. Mary Piggott, wife of Francis Piggott of James City.

Small Henrico Book—p. 35, Mch. 1733.

Anderson to Anderson—Deed from Mary Anderson, wife of late Robert Anderson of New Kent to son John, land bought from Geo. Wilkinson, in New Kent (now Hanover) in 1719, etc.

Similar deed to son Charles.

[These deeds, etc., of course, not from newspapers.]

P. 83—Whitley to Richmond Terrell of Blisland Par., New Kent, etc.

P. 87—Richard Brock.

P. 151 (1734)—Will, Thomas Gibson, St. Martins Par., Hanover, etc.

Enquirer—Nov. 20, 1827.

Died—eldest son of Mr. Archibald Blair of this city, at his residence in Hanover County on the 15th inst., Mr. John H. Blair, in the 41st year of his age.

Enquirer—14 Oct. 1808.

Died Oct. 11, 1808, John Page, of Rosewell, in the County of Gloucester, late Governor of this State.

Whig & Public Advertiser—21 May 1833.

Died at 9 o'clock this morning Mrs. Margaret Louther Anderson, consort of Richard Anderson, and her funeral will take place tomorrow from the residence of her *late husband* at 9 o'clock A. M. Should any of the friends and acquaintances of the family not receive a special invitation they will be pleased to attend without further notice.

Whig & Public Advertiser—7 June 1833.

Died this morning a few minutes past one o'clock, after about 10 days of suffering, Richard Louther Anderson, son of Richard Anderson.

Enquirer—Oct. 8, 1824.

Died—On the morning of the 7th inst., Mr. Archibald Blair, Sr., in the 71st year of his age, and one of the oldest and most respected citizens of this city. He was clerk to the Committee of Safety and of the Council of Virginia during the whole period of our Revolutionary struggle.

Enquirer—July 11, 1826 (Tuesday—hence date of death was July 9, 1826).

Died—On Sunday morning last in this city, at the same hour and in the same neighborhood, Mrs. Susan Anderson, wife of David Anderson, Esq., and Mrs. Mary Anderson, the wife of Richard Anderson, Esq. Their interment took place at the same hour. Mrs. Maria Anderson had lingered for seven days on the verge of the grave and her agonized friends scarcely dared hope she would be spared to them. Mrs. Susan Anderson was snatched away by a speedy death. The loss of these ladies will be deeply felt by their weeping families and their sympathizing neighbors and acquaintances.

Marriage Bonds on file in Hustings Court, City of Richmond, Va.

20th Sept. 1808—John H. Blair and Margaret Louther Page, daughter of John Page. Wm. C. Williams security. Accompanied by certificates signed by Archibald Blair, dated 20 Sep. 1808, and John Page dated 19 Sep. 1808.

John G. Blair m. Sarah Heron on 27th April, 1812, she being ward of Chas. J. Macmurdo.

Constitutional Whig—Fri. 7 July, 1831.

Notice—Dissolution of partnership between Beverley Blair and David Anderson.

W. Macfarlane Jones.

OBITUARY OF MRS. MARY PRICE

Richmond Enquirer, March 18, 1806.

"Departed this life suddenly, a few days since, at her seat near Richmond, Mrs. Mary Price, relict of Capt. John Price, dec'd, in the 86th year of her age.

This revered sage, had lived to see the fourth generation descendant from herself, and upon an accurate calculation found to amount to 181 in number.

She possessed in a very eminent degree all the amiable and Christian virtues—as a wife and mother; always tender and affectionate; a friend, most sincere; a mistress, just and kind.

She was a woman of fine understanding, which she retained till within a few hours before she expired; which was a source of many solid enjoyments to her friends.

Christianity which she had for many years been attached to and benevolence, were the leading features in her character. The poor of her neighborhood as well as her friends and relations, will feel sensibly her loss.

> "Oh what a sad delusion here
> So frail, so vain are human things,
> To every bliss succeeds a tear
> Our frailest hopes, but sorrow bring."

(Mrs. Price was a daughter of Col. White, of Hanover County. She lived at "The Grove", Henrico County).

"Obituary

From *The Richmond Enquirer,* August 1, 1826.

(1788-1826)

DIED—Of an hepatic disease, on the 21st ult. in Southampton County, Virginia, *Theophilus Feild, Esq., of Brunswick County,* in the 38th year of his age. He has left a disconsolate wife and three small children. The elegance and refinement of his manners captivated every heart, while his splendid talents, great acquirements and dignified deportment, secured the respect and esteem of his acquaintances: And it may truly be said of him, as he once remarked of a favorite friend, "no sting of conscience ever disturbed the tranquil quiet of his breast." The sphere of his usefulness was not restricted to a neighborhood; but, like the rays of the vernal sun, extended its salutary influence in every direction. It is useless to designate the important services that he has rendered the public; they can not be forgotten by a grateful country. Society will ever cherish his remembrance, as an exemplar of the high-minded Virginia gentleman whose rank and accomplishments could not be surpassed.

"Nullum tetigit, quod non ornavit."

Obituary

"From *The Richmond Whig*, May 27, 1829.

(1767-1829)

DIED, on the 23rd inst. at his residence in Brunswick County, *Dr. Richard Feild,* the senior editor of this paper, in the 62d year of his age. He was a distinguished physician and an accomplished citizen. In the knowledge of the Botanical plants of Virginia, he was only surpassed by Gronovius, while he was fully equal to Greenway. In the other branches of science, particularly Astronomy, he was a great proficient. In his profession, his mind was of a superior order, which enabled him to discard the shackles of the schools, and to devise a new practice, which was not only worthy of the enlightened principles of medicine, but especially adapted to the diseases of this country. Ardent in his desire for information, constant in his investigations, alive to the claims of the community, anxious to relieve the distresses of his fellow-creatures, and perhaps solicitous of fame, he soon attained the first rank as a practitioner of medicine, and, during his usefulness, it was his highest gratification to gain a victory over the arch-enemy Death, in the doubtful conflicts of disease. His medical skill and attainments are recorded in the hearts of many of our citizens, who will never forget the intelligence and benignity which animated his interesting countenance. His chivalry was early tested while a student at Edinburgh, and his patriotism was ever ready in the cause of his country. He was a member of three of the electoral colleges which assisted to elevate Mr. Jefferson and Mr. Madison to the Presidency. As a friend and neighbor, he possessed every quality which could adorn a heart, or dignify a man.   F. H."

OBITUARY OF MRS. JOANNA BOULDIN.

DEPARTED THIS LIFE, on the 15th day of January, 1845, at her residence in the county of Charlotte, Mrs. JOANNA BOULDIN, the widow of Maj. Wood Bouldin, dec., in the 93d year of her age.

A short family history for the present, I presume, will be excusable. Maj. Wood Bouldin, her husband, who died many years since, was an officer in the Virginia line on continental establishment, in the war of the Revolution, and was distinguished for his gallantry and good conduct on the fields of Brandywine, Germantown, and other places. Colonel Thos. Bouldin, the father of the said W. Bouldin, came from the State of Maryland, and settled in Charlotte county, in the year 1774. He held the rank of Colonel under the Colonial Government.

Mrs. Joanna Bouldin was the daughter of John Tyler, Esq., of James City county, State of Va., who was attached to the "Admirality Office," under the Colonial Government, and lived for a while on what is called the "J. P. Estate," about three miles from Williamsburg.

Mrs. Bouldin was the sister of John Tyler, formerly Governor of Virginia, who was the father of His Excellency, John Tyler, now the President of the United States. She was the mother of the Hon. Thomas T. Bouldin, now deceased, a Judge of the General Court of Virginia, and Member of Congress from the Charlotte District; of the Hon. James W. Bouldin, formerly a Member of Congress; and of Louis C. Bouldin, for many years a worthy and distinguished member of the Senate of Virginia. Where is there a mother who has raised such a number of distinguished sons? In short, she was connected with many of the very best families in Virginia, and the U. States.

Mrs. Bouldin had three sons only, who have been named above, and five daughters, two of whom died in early life, and the three remaining were with her to the last, using unremitting exertions for her ease and comfort. For many years before her death, she was confined to her room. Worn down at last by old age and bodily infirmities, she passed off the stage of existence without a struggle. She stood under her afflictions with great patience and Christian fortitude.

Mrs. Bouldin was a member of the Protestant Episcopal Church, and at her burial, the neighbors in general attended, and the last services were performed by the Rev. Mr. Christian, of the Episcopal Church. She lies by the side of her husband, Maj. W. Bouldin, and in the same ground is buried Colonel Thomas Bouldin and his wife and two daughters, and the Hon. Thos. T. Bouldin.

Mrs. Bouldin was well educated for the times in which she lived. None excelled her in the accomplishments of the day. She was taught music by Brammer, and played well on the spinnet, the fashionable instrument of her day; she delighted mostly in Scotch music and songs. In painting and drawing, she was instructed by the celebrated Gilbert Stewart. She was a lady of remarkable intelligence, and fond of cheerful company; beloved by all her friends and acquaintances; affectionate to her children, by whom she was almost adored; a kind, gentle and indulgent mistress. In short, no one perhaps ever lived so long and passed so blameless a life.—*Richmond Enquirer, Feb.* 13, 1845.

WM. H. ROANE.

"Died, at Tree Hill, on Sunday morning, after a very protracted illness, William H. Roane, Esq. His remains will be taken for interment to the family burying ground of the late Judge Lyons in Hanover. His funeral will take place from the residence of James Lyons, Esq., in this city, at half past nine this morning, and his friends, and those of Mr. Lyons, are respectfully invited to attend it at that hour.—*Richmond Enquirer, May* 12, 1845."

211

OBITUARY OF ROBERT BELL.

(Richmond Whig, August 11, 1897.)

Died on Tuesday evening, Mr. Robert Bell, saddler, in the 64th year of his age. Mr. Bell was a native of Scotland, and emigrated to this country about 35 years ago. With the exception of a short residence in Petersburg, he has been an inhabitant of Richmond ever since his arrival in this Country. No man in Richmond was more generally known in Town and Country than Robert Bell, and it can be safely said of him that he never had an enemy; that the man never lived of stricter integrity; or of a more generous heart.

From early habits he was a most industrious man, and being an excellent workman, and universally known as an honest workman, as well as an honest man, he earned by his industry perhaps more money than any other man in Virginia in the same business.

So devoted was he to business from habit that although a believer and professor of the Christian religion, he hardly took time to die—leaving his death-bed often to repair to his work-bench where only he felt at home until the day before his death, when he became too weak to get down stairs. Yet it was not the love of money that urged him to industry. No man was ever more liberal than Mr. Bell.

His heart and hand were ever open to the distressed. Thousands have shared his bounty, and been relieved by his means, while many owe their success in life to his kind offices.

He was a genuine philanthropist, rejoicing in the happiness and prosperity of all around him, and detesting only meanness and cruelty. Had his desire been to secure riches, he might have left a large fortune. As it was, his estate is probably worth $30,000. He lived all his life a bachelor, being, it is said, disappointed in early life, when his heart had formed the tender attachment. He was about making a will, but became delirious before he could sign it. His property will probably therefore go to a brother somewhere in the West and to two sisters in Scotland.

In his death Richmond has lost a useful citizen—his intimate associates a warm-hearted friend—and the needy a liberal benefactor. Peace to his Shade.

His remains were attended to the grave last evening by the R. L. I. Blues, of which he was an honorary, and had been many years an active, member, and by a large concourse of citizens.

RECORDS OF ISLE OF WIGHT COUNTY.

The following is from an old vestry Book of Isle of Wight County, Newport Parish. The leaves, however, containing Births were evidently from an old Register now lost, and were bound up in the vestry Book

The reference to the "Brick Church" brings up the building near Smithfield, which so called "tradition" says was built in 1632. Of course, to any one acquainted with the condition of things in Virginia in 1632 the claim is absurd. Ten years before, the Indian Massacre had done away with nearly everybody in Isle of Wight County. The building of a church of the character of the Brick Church would have taken more money and time than the few inhabitants could afford. There was no brick church begun at Jamestown, the capital, till 1639, and then it was eight years in the building. When Mr. R. S. Thomas produced a brick with the date 1632 upon it, he did not make it clear that it was found in a part where age of the church might be intended. Moreover the appearance of the figures, as seen by the Editor, might very well stand for 1682. The church, it is said, was built by a James Bridger, but the only James Bridger who lived in the colony was Col. James Bridger, whose tombstone, about a mile and a half distant records that he was born in 1631 and died in 1689. He was evidently a native of England, and not of Virginia, and was one of the cavaliers who came to the colony after the death of Charles II. On his tombstone it is stated that Charles' "own express fetched him to attend the King," which implies at least that he was a resident at the time in England.

It was not till November 29, 1683 that the first brick church was built at Williamsburg, then called the Middle Plantation. It appears to have been nearly three years in the building.

At a Vestry held for the Parish of Newport in the County of Isle of Wight 28th September 1771

Present

Robert Tynes	John Day Gent.
Richard Baker	James Bridger
Daniel Herring	John Eley
Nicholas Parker	Richard Hardy

The Parish of Newport	Dr.
	Tob°.
To the Rev^d. Mr. Henry John Burgess	17155
To the Clerk of the Brick Church	1000
To Do Bay Do	1000
To Do Chapel Do	1000
To the Clerk	600
To the Sexton the Brick Church	400
To the Do Bay Do	400
To the Do Chapel Do	400
To the Southwark Parish	120
To John Sym being overlisted one Tithe	12
	22087
To the use of the Parish	25088
To 6 per cent for Collecting	3011
	50186

Cr.

By 2182 Titheables at 23 lb Tob°. per pole	50186

Ord: That the Sheriff do Collect from every Tithable person of This County 23 lb. Tob°. per Tith and on refusal thereof to levy the same by Distress.

214

Ord: that the Church Wardens do pay Robert Tynes, William Blunt & John Day their demands against this Parish and to be paid out of the Depositum

Ord: That Thomas Crocker be Exempted from paying the Parish Levy

Ord: that Robert Tynes & John Day do view the Barn on the Glebe and make Report to the next Vestry

Ord: That John Darden & Abraham Johnston do with the Inhabitants procession all the lands within their Precinct and make return by the same Day of March Next.

Ord: Nicholas Parker & John Eley C. war., for the last year
. . . .

Rich^d. Bidgood son of Wm. Bidgood and Hesther his Wife was born the 13th of Feb^r. 1736/7

Ann Morland the Daughter of Thos. Morland and Mary his wife was born the 11th Day of August at Two O'Clock in the morning 1722

John Morland the son of Thos. Morland and Mary his wife was born the 20th Sep^t. 1716 at 4 O'Clock in the afternoon.

Mary Goodrich the Daughter of Jno. & Mary Goodrich was Born 24th Day of March 1721.

Henry Hayles the son Linton Hayles and Sarah his wife was born ye 10th Day of March 1721

Rebeckah Wiles Woodard the Daughter of Peter Woodard & Margret his wife was born the 29th of Decemb^r 1739/40

James Miller the son of William Miller and Margret his wife was born the 4th day of Decemb^r. 1739

Francis Hayles the son of Linton Hayles and Sarah his wife was born the 10th of May 1740

Joseph Sawyer was born the 20th September 1734 he is the son of Willm Sawyer

Robt. Sweet the son of Corney and Lewcey Sweet was born the 20th July 1740/41

Peiny a Negro belonging to myself was adjudged May the 25th to be twelve years old.

Mary Davis Daughter of Jno. and Mary Davis was born the 23rd of October 1743

Saml. Bourden son of Nic^o. Bourden & Prudence his wife was born Ap^l. 14th 1737

John Bourden son of Nic. and Prudence was born the 10th June 1739

Nic. Bourden son of Do was born the 25th March 1741

Baker Bourden son of Do was born June 10th 1742/3

Jno. Wren son of John Wren & Prudence his wife was ....

Eliz^a. Hodges Daughter of Jno. Hodges and Martha his wife was born the 5th of March 1739

Ann Hodges Daughter of Jno & Martha Hodges was born the 29th of May 1743

Tom a negroe belonging to Jno. Hodges was born the 10th June 1739

Parthenia was born belonging to Jno. Hodges the 26th of March 1741

Pegg a negro belonging to Do Hodges the 20th of June 1743

Melinder a negro girl belonging to Thos. Day was born December the 13th 1744

Frances Portlock Daughter of Charles Portlock and Lydia his wife was born February the 5th 1744/5

Mary Bourden Daughter of Nicholas Bourden & Prudence his wife was born March 30th 1741

Sarah Salter, Daughter of Willm. and Ann Salter his wife was born Dec. 2nd. 1741

Edward Salter son of William Salter and Ann his wife was born Apr. 26th 1743

William Salter Son of William Salter and Ann his wife was born March 19th 1744/5

Mary Salter Daughter of William & Ann his wife was born July 29th 1747

Jesse Barlow, son of Thos. Barlow and Martha his wife was born Sept. 12th 1740

Katherine Baker Daughter of Law. Baker and Ann his wife was born Dec. 3, 1730

Richard Baker, Son of Law. Baker and Ann his wife was born Dec. 23rd 1732

Ann Baker daughter of Law. Baker & Ann his wife was born Sept. 21, 1735

James Baker son of Law. Baker and Ann his wife was born Dec. 2, 1737

Thomas Salter son of Wm. Salter and Ann his Wife was born Dec. 29th 1749

Thos. Wills son of Miles Wills & Mary his wife was born Nov. 10th 1755

Miles Wills son of Miles Wills & Mary his wife was born Nov. 27, 1757

Lawrance Baker son of Richard Baker and Ann his wife was born the 30th day of August 1755

Elizabeth Bell daughter of William Bell and Martha his wife was born April 8th 1736

Nathan Bell son of William Bell and Martha his wife was born July 31st 1738

Martha Bell daughter of Wm. Bell and Martha his wife was born Januay 23rd 1742

William Bell son of William Bell & Martha his wife was born June 8th 1747

John Brantley son of Wm. Brantley and Mary his wife was born 15th of March 1729/30

Wm. Brantley son of Wm. Brantley and Mary his wife was born 20th day of March 1735/6

Joseph Brantley son of Wm. Brantley and Mary his wife was born the 26th day of September 1737

Elias Burt Son of Elias Burt and Rebeckah his wife was born Feb. the 9th 1737/8

Inglish Briggs son of Charles Briggs and Ann his wife was born July 26th, 1733

John Briggs son of Charles Briggs and Ann his wife was born May 28rd, 1735

Charles Briggs son of Charles and Ann was born December 31st, 1737/8

Wm. Inglish son of Wm. Inglish and Dianah his wife was born the 5th November 1735

Jacob Saul Bell son of Saul or Thos. Bell was born the 13th April 1733

John Bidgood the son of Wm. Bidgood and Mary his wife was born the 20th day of August 1737

Benj. Bidgood the son of Wm. Bidgood and Mary his wife was born the 23 day of November 1735

Margrett Woodward daughter of Peter and Margrett his wife was born 15th Jan. 1737/8 being Saturday 3 clock afternoon

William Carey son of Wm. Carey and Martha was born 21st day of July 1735

Joseph Carey son of Wm. Carey and Martha his wife was born the 16th day of Feb. 1737

Frank a negro belonging to George Wiles was born the 11th day July 1730

James Bland son of James Bland & Eliz. his wife was born 26th day July 1738

William Burt the son of Elias Burt and Rebeccah his wife was born March 27th day 1736

John Bidgood son of Wm. Bidgood and Hesther his wife was born 3rd February 1734/5

Peter Woodward son of Peter Woodward and Margret his wife was born the 27th day March at 12 O'Clock at night on Saturday 1736

Mary a negro child belonging unto Mr. Robert Burrel 18th day September 1736

Simon a negro child born belonging unto Mr. Robert Burrel Sept 21st 1736 Witness Elias Burt

Susannah Rosser daughter of Thos. Rosser and Eliz. his wife was born the 20th day October 1736 Witness John Eley.

Joseph Carrol son of Benjamin Carrol and Joyce his wife was born 22nd of Ap. 1736

John Hodges the son of John Hodges and Martha Hodges his wife was born 2nd day of December 1737

Jupiter a negro boy belonging unto Mr. Robert Burrel was born 3rd December 1737 Witness John Clay—

Benj. Carrol son of Jno. Carrol and Eliz. his wife was born the 3rd day of October 1705

Catherine Carrol daughter of Benj. Carrol and Joyce his wife was born the 15th day November 1727

Hannah a negro girl born belonging unto Mr. John Hodges born March 24th 1736

.... a negro girl belonging unto Clay Brantly was born 15th ....

.... a negro girl belonging unto John Clayton was born ....

.... daughter of Benjamin Carrol

VIEW OF BRUTON CHURCHYARD

TOMBSTONE OF MRS. ELIZABETH HILL SKIPWITH.

There was recently removed to Bruton Parish Churchyard in Williamsburg, from the lot whereon stands the house of Dr. T. G. Peachey, honored by the stay of Gen. La Fayette in 1824, a marble slab of beautiful design, bearing the following inscription:

Sacred to the Memory
of Mrs. Elizabeth Hill Skipwith,
Eldest daughter of William Byrd, Esquire.
Born at Westover Nov 26, 1755,
Died at Williamsburg August 6, 1819.

This monument, as the last tribute of duty and filial affection, is erected by her surviving daughters E. C. I., M. C., and R. P. C.

The lady, whose name it was intended to perpetuate, married 1st James Parke Farley, of Antigua; 2d Rev. John Dunbar; and 3rd Col. Henry Skipwith; and died at Williamsburg Aug. 6, 1819. "The three surviving daughters" were probably all by the first marriage with Farley, and were Elizabeth Parke Farley, whose third husband was Gen. George Izard, Maria married Champe Carter, and Rebecca Parke married Major Richard Corbin, of Laneville. Col. Henry Skipwith, the third husband of Elizabeth Hill Byrd, was a son of Sir William Skipwith, of Middlesex Co., and Elizabeth Smith, his wife. (See TYLER'S QUARTERLY, I, p. 70.)

TOMBSTONE OF MRS. ANNABELLA POWELL

A recent contribution to the Preservation of Va. Antiquities made by members of a family has been the removal of the gravestone of Mrs. Annabella Powell to Bruton Churchyard, from Kerr's Hill Farm, near Williamsburg. The ancient stone bears the following inscription—"Here lies in the hope of a joyful resurrection the body of Mrs. Annabella Powell, wife of Benjamin Powell, Esq. of York Co., who departed this life Jan. 7, 1782—in the 50th year of her age." This was published some years ago in the Wm. and Mary Quarterly, and was thus brought to the attention of the members of the Burwell family descended from Annabella Powell. Though residing far from Va., several of these felt sufficient interest in the past to preserve this family relic.

Tomb of Mrs. Ursula (Byrd) Beverley.

Some years prior to the Civil War the tomb of Usurla, daughter of William Byrd (1st) and wife of Robert Beverley, the historian, remained in the churchyard at Jamestown, almost intact. A visitor fortunately copied the epitaph and sent it to a newspaper. It is as follows :

[Arms.]

" Here lyeth the body of
Ursula Beverley late wife of Robert
Beverley, daughter of ye Hon'ble
Col. William Byrd, who departed
this life the last day of October
1698, being much lamented of all
that knew her. Aged 16 years, 11
months and 2 daies."

During the years immediately preceding the war the tomb was mutilated, and about 1861 only a piece containing the arms was left. Dr. Frank Hall, a Confederate soldier, while doing sentry duty in the churchyard, made on July 1, 1861, a sketch of the fragment. We are indebted to Miss Jane Chapman Slaughter for the copy of the drawing published in this number of the Magazine, and for information of its existence.

The arms are Beverley and Byrd empaled. The Beverley arms are not the three bulls' heads and chevron of the book-plates ; but are : *ermine, a rose gules, barbed and seeded ppr.* These are the arms on the seal attached to the will of Major Robert Beverley, the immigrant. And see *William and Mary Quarterly,* III, 234.

Though she died so young Mrs. Beverley left one son, Wm. Beverley, of " Blandfield," who has very many descendants in the families of Beverley, Munford, Kennon, Randolph and others.

It would be eminently appropriate for the descendants of this young wife, who died after such a short life, to replace a stone to her memory at Jamestown, bearing the arms and epitaph as they originally were.

NOTES FROM THE VIRGINIA GAZETTE.

The following notes were made by Fairfax Harrison from a volume containing an incomplete series of the Virginia Gazette from March 21, 1745, to September 25, 1746, in the William L. Clements Library of the University of Michigan:

OBITUARIES.

1745, March 28. Col. Andrew Meade of Nansemond.

" October 10. Mrs. Elizabeth Burwell, widow of the late Col. Lewis Burwell. Thomas Nelson of Yorktown.

" November 21. Col. Theophilus Pugh of Nansemond, "who has been many years a very great trader."

" December 12. "We hear from Richmond County that Mrs. Carter, wife of Col. Landon Carter and daughter of the late Honourable William Byrd, died about a fortnight ago, much lamented."

1746, May 29. "The lady of the Honourable Lewis Burwell, Esq., of Gloucester County, in the 28th year of her age."

SPOTSWOOD-DANDRIDGE.

"We hear from King William County that on Thursday the 24th past Mr. John Spotswood. eldest son of the late Alexander Spotswood, Esq., former Governor of this colony, etc., was married to Miss Mary Dandridge, a daughter of the late Honourable William Dandridge, Esq., who was Commander of one of His Majesty's ships of war and one of the Honourable Council of this colony." (The Va. Gazette, Nov. 7, 1745.)

PERSONAL NOTICES FROM THE VIRGINIA GAZETTE.

DEATHS.

Mrs. Mary Braxton, daughter of the late Col. Carter, President of the Council of this Colony, and wife of Mr. George Braxton, of King and Queen, last Friday. Williamsburg. Sept. 22, 1736.[1]

Capt. Arthur Mosely, of Henrico county, killed by being thrown from his horse. Oct. 13.

Mr. Thomas Booth, in Gloucester county, a justice of the peace for many years and considerable merchant. Nov. 5.

Mrs. Susannah Skaife, wife of Rev. John Skaife,[2] of Stratton Major parish, King and Queen county. Nov. 12.

---

[1] This date and others given, except where expressly stated otherwise, give the date of the paper in which the notice occurs.

[2] From the admission register of St. John's College: "John Scaife, born at Ledburgh, Yorkshire, son of John Scaife, husbandman (*agricolæ*); bred at Ledburgh under Mr. Wharton; admitted sizar for Dr. Berry, tutor and surety Mr. Orchard, 4 April aet. 18." In Bruton Parish Register, among the death notices are: "Nov. 3, 1736, Mrs. Skaife, wife of the Rev. Mr. John Skaife, rector of Stratton Major." "Nov. 6, Mr. John Skaife himself."

Mr. John Skaife, her husband, on Thursday morning, educated at St. John's College, in Cambridge, one of the governors of the college, and for thirty years in the service of his parishioners. Nov. 12.

On Christmas Eve, died in Hanover county, Mr. John Langford, a noted and skillful musician. Leaving behind a poor widow and six or seven small children. Williamsburg. Jan. 7, 1736–'37.

Mr. Francis Eppes, of Prince George, died there lately. Feb. 4.

Miss Betty Washington, daughter of Major John Washington, a young gentlewoman of great merit and beauty, died lately. Feb. 25.

On Wednesday last, died at his home in this city, after a long indisposition, the Hon. Sir John Randolph. March 4.

Capt. Baldwin Matthews, of York county, found dead in his chair with a large wound in his head. A negro suspected. In his 68th year. April 1.

Mr. Charles Chiswell, of Hanover county, aged 46, died last Monday night in this city. Buried in the churchyard. April 8.

Major William Harwood, of Warwick Co., died of a fall from his horse, 2d instant. For many years a justice, member of the House of Burgesses. June 10.

Mr. William Wombwell Clift, of Hanover county, died of a pleurisy; of a good family in Yorkshire, had travelled much, and was a good judge of men and books. June 10.

Thomas Riddle and Richard Land, of Orange county, killed by a negro. June 10.

Capt. Hugh French reported dead at sea. July 25.

Capt. John Tate died at his house near Jamestown, on Wednesday night, Nov. 18, 1737.

This morning, between 5 and 6, at his house, in the 72d year of his age, John Clayton, Esq., his Majesty's Attorney-General and Judge of the Court of Vice Admiralty of the Colony, the first justice in the Commission of the Peace of James City, Recorder of this City. On Wednesday, the funeral solemnized in the church. Nov. 18, 1737.

On Tuesday, died Miss Evelyn Byrd, eldest daughter of Hon. Wm. Byrd, Esq. Dec. 3, 1737.

Lewis Meekum, in Isle of Wight county, thrown from his horse and killed.

Mrs. Cecilia Darracott, wife of Capt. John Darracott, died at his house in Hanover, and interred in New Kent at her father, Mr. William Massey's, plantation. Dec. 9, 1737.

Samuel Moody and another white man, going a ducking in a very small canoe in Moorcock Creek, by Chickahominy Ferry, were upset and drowned the 15th instant.

Capt. Robert Fleming, of Caroline county, one of the representatives in Assembly, died last week. Feb. 10, 1737-'38.

On Tuesday night last, died of a pleurisy, at his house in Charles City, Capt. William Acrill, a popular burgess from that county, a great lawyer. March 24, 1737-'38.

In Goochland, died lately, Mr. Edward Scott, a burgess from there. March 24, 1737-'38.

In Orange county, Col. Goodrich Lightfoot died lately at his house there. July 14.

Died, in Accomac, Mr. Tucker Parker, a burgess for that county. July 14, 1738.

On Sunday last was se'ennight died Charles Brown, M. D.; a man of learning, probity, and honor. June 23, 1738.

Last Monday was se'ennight died, of the gout, at his house in Caroline county, Mr. Benjamin Walker, who had practiced in law several years in the county courts, in which he arrived to a degree of eminence, and at the last general court was admitted to plead there. Sept. 8, 1738.

On Sunday morning last died, after a long and tedious indisposition, Major Abraham Nicholas,[1] some years Adjutant-General of this Colony. Sept. 8, 1738.

n Surry county, Mrs. Allen, wife of Col. John Allen, died last Saturday very suddenly, Oct. 20; 1738.

On Saturday last died, in this city, Mr. Alexander Craig, jeweller and silversmith. Oct. 20, 1738.

Died, at his house in King William, Mr. Humphrey Brooke, a merchant of considerable note and a justice of the peace of said county. Oct. 26, 1738.

In Middlesex county died Capt. William Blackburn, for several

---

[1] In Bruton Parish Register: "Died 5 of March, 1751, Abraham, son of Abraham Nicholas and Ann his wife." "Dec. 18, 1751, Died Mr Abraham Nicholas, Senr, clerk of this church."

years in the commission of the peace, and in 1715 a burgess. Jan. 12, 1738–'39.

In Accomac county died Mr. James Powell, collector of the King's duties in the District of Pocomoker. Jan. 12.

On Wednesday morning last died Mr. Robert Davidson, a practitioner in physick, and Mayor of this city. Feb. 2.

On Tuesday morning last, at Yorktown, Col. Lawrence Smith, for many years a justice of the peace, burgess, of strict honor and probity, &c. March 2.

Eldest son of Col. Edmund Scarburgh drowned in York River. Sept. 21, 1739.

Miss M. Thacker, daughter of Col. Edwin Thacker, of Middlesex, who died at Williamsburg, on Wednesday last. Sept. 21, 1739.

Last Friday, died at his house in James City, Col. John Eaton, one of the representatives in the Assembly and justice of the peace, a tender husband and parent. Oct. 9, 1739.

On Friday night last, died at his house at Jamestown, in the 71st year of his age, Mr. Edward Jaquelin, formerly a representative from Jamestown and for many years justice for James City. Interred in the churchyard at Jamestown. Nov. 16, 1739.

In Gloucester county, this week, died Rev. Mr. Immanuel Jones, minister of Petsworth Parish, many years minister, &c. Feb. 1, 1739–'40.

MARRIAGES.

Mr. Richard Corbin, eldest son of Col. Gawin Corbin, was lately married to Miss Betty Tayloe, dau. of Hon. John Tayloe, one of his Majesty's council of this colony. July 29, 1737.

Philip Ludwell, Esq., only son and heir of Hon. Philip Ludwell, Esq., deceased, late one of his Majesty's council of this colony, was married to Miss Fanny Grymes, eldest dau. of Col. Charles Grymes. July 29, 1737.

Last Sunday Mr. Thomas Hall, of Prince George county, was married to Miss Molly Power, daughter of Major Henry Power, of James City county. Sept. 30, 1737.

Yesterday Mr. John Smith, of Gloucester county, was married to Miss Molly Jaquelin, youngest daughter of Mr. Edward Jaquelin, of Jamestown. Nov. 18, 1737.

Yesterday was sennight Mr. Beverley Randolph, eldest son of the

Honorable William Randolph, Esq., one of his Majesty's council of this colony, was married to Miss Betty Lightfoot, niece of the Hon. Philip Lightfoot, Esq., an agreeable young lady with a fortune of upwards of £ 5000. Dec. 30.

Mr. Carter Burwell was married yesterday to Miss Lucy Grymes, a daughter of the Hon. John Grymes, Esq.. one of his Majesty's council, a very agreeable young lady, of great merit and fortune. January 6, 1737–'38.

Mr. William Nelson, eldest son of Mr. Thomas Nelson, an eminent merchant of York, was married yesterday was sennight at Mrs. Page's, in Gloucester county, to Miss Elizabeth Burwell, a very genteel accomplished young lady, of great merit and considerable fortune. Feb., 1738.

We hear from Henrico county that on Thursday the 13th instant the Rev. Mr. William Stith was married to Miss Judith Randolph, sister of William Randolph, Esq., of Tuckahoe. July 28, 1738.

On Thursday, 20th instant, Mr. Peter Randolph, son of Hon. Wm. Randolph, Esq., was married to Miss Lucy Bolling, daughter of Col. Robert Bolling, of Prince George county, etc. July 28.

In Maryland Mr. William Armistead, son of Col. Henry Armistead, of Gloucester county, was married to Miss —— Bowles, 2d dau. of James Bowles, Esq., deceased, one of the council of that province, and granddaughter of Tobias Bowles, Esq., formerly an eminent merchant of London in Va. trade; a very agreeable young lady, with a fortune upwards of £ 6000 sterl. Feb. 2, 1738–'39.

Last Friday evening Mr. John Lidderdale, a merchant of this city, was married to Miss Elizabeth Robertson, daughter of William Robertson, Esq. March 2, 1738–'39.

Rev. Mr. McCoy, Rector of Hanover Parish in King George county, married to Miss Barbara Fitzhugh, daughter to Major John Fitzhugh, of Stafford county. March 2, 1738–'39.

Col. Edward Digges, eldest son of the Hon. Cole Digges, of the council, married yesterday to Miss Anne Harrison, daughter of Hon. Nathaniel Harrison, Esq., deceased, one of the council, etc. Aug. 10, 1739.

Yesterday Major Benjamin Harrison, son of Hon. Nathaniel Harrison, Esq., formerly of the council, and Auditor General of this colony, married to Miss Susanna Digges, daughter of Hon. Cole Digges, Esq., of the council, etc. Aug. 25, 1739.

PERSONAL NOTICES FROM THE "VIRGINIA GAZETTE."

[PURDIE & DIXON, EDITORS.]

January, 1767, to January, 1769.

Year 1767.

Marriages. Mr. Walter Coles, one of the representatives in Assembly for the county of Halifax, to Miss Mildred Lightfoot, a daughter of the late Colonel William Lightfoot, of Charles City. Mr. William Taylor, one of the representatives in Assembly for the county of Lunenburg, to Miss Patty Waller, eldest daughter of Benjamin Waller, Esq., of this city. March 19.

On Tuesday, the 21st of this instant, died, at his home in Cumberland, Col. John Fleming, member of Assembly for the county, and an eminent practitioner in the law. On the 6th instant, died at Fredericksburg, Mr. William Scott, who for several years acquired great reputation in that neighbourhood through his mercantile connections. * * * The following evening his remains were attended to the place of interment by the right worshipful, the Master and Brethren of the Lodge of Free and Accepted Masons—April 30.

Last Saturday evening, died at his home in this city, Mr. William Waters. Arrivals: In York River, the Lord Baltimore from London, by whom we have advice of the death of the Hon. Philip Ludwell, Esq., one of the members of his Majesty's council in this colony—June 4.

From Northumberland we learn that Mr. Robert Woddrop, merchant of that county, died there about the middle of last month, greatly regretted—June 11.

Last Thursday, died at his home in Prince George Co., universally regretted, Col. Alexander Bolling, one of the representatives for that county—June 18.

On Wednesday, the 1st instant, died at Norfolk, after a lingering illness, Colonel Robert Tucker, who for these many years has carried on a very extensive trade in that place with the greatest credit and honour. On Tuesday, the 30th ultimo, died at his home in Smithfield, Mr. James Eason, merchant there—July 9.

On Wednesday, the 8th instant, died at his seat at Chatsworth, in the county of Henrico, the Hon. Peter Randolph, Esq., surveyor general of his Majesty's customs, and one of the council of this colony. Lately died, Major Harry Gaines, one of the representatives in Assembly for King William county—July 16.

Lately died at his house in Smithfield, after a short illness, Capt. Samuel Wentworth, merchant there for many years—July 23.

Last Friday, died of an apoplectick fit, at Warren's Ordinary, in New Kent county, Capt. George Wilkinson, commander of the ship Madeira Packet, of London—Sept. 10.

On the 10th of July last, died in Halifax county, Mary Hogan, aged 91 years, who for 50 days before her death took no other sustenance than 2 spoonsfull of sour milk—Oct. 22.

Last Monday morning, died at Col. William Allen's, in Surry, where she had been a few days upon a visit, the lady of Benjamin Harrison, Jun., Esq., of Brandon, in the flower of her age, and possessed of every amiable qualification. She has left an inconsolable husband, an afflicted mother, weeping relatives and many sorrowful friends.

Marriages. William Randolph, Esq., to Miss Mary Skipwith, a daughter of the late Sir William Skipwith, Barronet. Edward Lloyd, Esq., of Maryland, to Miss Elizabeth Tayloe, a daughter of the Hon. John Tayloe, Esq.—November 26.

The Year 1768.

On Tuesday evening, died at his house in King and Queen, the Rev. William Robinson, the Lord Bishop of London's commissary for this colony, and rector of Stratton Major. He was a gentleman much esteemed by his parishioners, and all who had the pleasure of knowing him—Jan. 7.

On Saturday, the 2d of this instant, about 9 o'clock at night, died, Col. James Gordon, of Lancaster county, in the 54th year of his age. * * * He spent the last 30 years of his life in said county in trade. * * * The rare assemblage of fine qualities made a very discerning traveller a few years ago remark of the deceased: "That he had not met with any one in the several provinces he had passed through possessing so many real excellencies." [A long obituary.]—Jan. 4.

Yesterday morning, died at her house in this city, after a tedious illness, Mrs. Mary Grymes, relict of Hon. Philip Grymes, deceased. Lately died, in Hanover, Mr. Robin Page, who had for several years labored under the afflicting pain of the gout, and of late was seized with the dead palsy—Jan. 21.

Died of the small-pox, Mr. Dudley Digges, and a mulatto man belonging to the college. Mr. James Marshall quite recovered—Feb. 4.

Early this morning, died at the Palace, after a tedious illness, which he bore with the greatest patience and fortitude, the Hon. Francis Fauquier, Esq., Lieutenant Governor and commander in chief of this colony, over which he has presided near ten years, much to his own honor and the ease and satisfaction of the inhabitants. He was a gentleman of a most amiable disposition; generous, just and wise, and possessed in an eminent degree of all the social virtues. He was Fellow of the Royal Society, and died in his 65th year—March 3.

On Tuesday last, the remains of the Honourable Francis Fauquier, Esq., deceased, were interred in our church. His funeral was attended by the Honourable, the President, and several members of his Majesty's council, the Honourable the Speaker, the Treasurer, his Majesty's Attorney General, all the gentlemen in this city, and its neighbourhood and the militia under arms, to testify the respect due to the memory of so worthy a Governor. After the funeral service the militia made three discharges over the place of interment—March 10.

Last week was married Nathaniel Carpenter, Esq., Collector of his Majesty's customs, to Miss Nancy Fauntleroy—March 17.

Last Saturday morning died, in the 58th year of her age, Mrs. Mary Prentis, relict of the late Mr. William Prentis, of this city—April 14.

On Thursday last, David Meade, Esq., of Nansemond, was married to Miss Sally Waters, of this city—May 19.

Last Thursday the Rev. Mr. Josiah Johnson, one of the masters of this College, was married to Miss Mildred Moody, an agreeable young lady—May 26.

Last Thursday Warner Lewis, Jun., Esq., of Gloucester, was married to Miss Polly Chiswell, of this city, an accomplished young lady—June 2.

On Saturday last was married, at Jordan's, Mr. Robert Goode, of Henrico, to Miss Sally Bland, a daughter of Col. Richard Bland's, an agreeable young lady—June 23.

On Sunday, the 19th instant, after a short illness, departed this life, much lamented, the Honourable Benjamin Tasker, Esq., President of the council in the province of Maryland, &c. —June 30.

On Sunday, the 26 ult., died at his home in Northampton county, Col. Littleton, Esq. * * * He was many years judge of the court and representative of the county in which he lived. On the 21st ult., died, in Gloucester county, much regretted, Mrs. Frances Booth, relict of the late Dr. George Booth—July 7.

On Monday, the 8th instant, died Christopher Robinson, Esq., of Middlesex—July 28.

On Friday, the 14th instant, died, after a short illness, at his seat at Marlborough, in Stafford county, aged 64, John Mercer, Esq., for many years a very eminent lawyer, and remarkable for his assiduity in his profession. He was a gentleman greatly esteemed, and of consequence is much regretted—Oct. 27.

Last Sunday morning died, at the treasurer's, in this city, after a tedious illness, Edward Ambler, Esq., representative in Assembly for Jamestown, a gentleman of most amiable character, which makes his death much lamented by all who had the pleasure of knowing him—Nov. 3.

Anthony Walke, Sen., Esq., who died the 8th ultimo, in the 76th year of his age. "County Lieutenant and Judge of the Court of Princess Anne. . . . From a slender education, such as a little reading and writing as the times could then afford, he made a wonderful proficiency in true and solid knowledge greatly preferable to a knowledge of words and language." [Long obituary.]—Dec. 22.

PERSONAL NOTICES FROM THE VIRGINIA GAZETTE.

Virginia Gazette, edited by William Rind, January, 1769 to January, 1770.

On the 30th of December last died Mr. Dekar Thompson, of Falmouth. January 12.

We are informed that Mr. George Savage, lately of the Secretary's Office, is married to Miss Kendall, a young lady possessed of an independent fortune of at least 6,000£.

We hear from Providence, in New Kent county, that on the 8th instant the Rev. Charles Jeffrey Smith, who proposes to settle and reside on his estate, opened a subscription for erecting a Presbyterian church 70 feet in length and forty in breadth with galleries and a steeple, which was generously encouraged. The building of which will be let to the lowest undertaker on Wednesday, the 22d instant, at said place, by the managers, who will attend there on that day. Feb. 16.

On Thursday last Francis Lightfoot Lee Esq was married to Miss Rebecca Tayloe, a daughter to Hon. John Tayloe. March 16.

This evening Samuel Thompson, Esq., commander of his Majesty's ship *Rippon,* was married to Miss Elizabeth Blair, daughter of the Honourable John Blair Esq. [Poetry.]

On Thursday last was married Capt. Robert Robertson to Miss Susanna Deadman, a very agreeable young lady. March 16.

Died lately, the Rev. Mr. Nevison, rector of Meherrin church, in Brunswick.

Also the lady of Rev. Mr. Warrington, after breakfast, suddenly. April 13, 1769.

On the 5th instant Mr. Charles Digges died suddenly in the prime of life at Dumfries in Prince William county. He was the eldest son of William Digges, Esq., of Maryland. . . His acquaintance was very extensive both in Europe and America. April 13.

On Tuesday last died at Porto Bello after a short illness Mr. Alexander Finnie, for many years adjutant to the middle district of this colony.

On the 25th ulto died in an advanced age at his house in Essex county Col William Daingerfield &c. May 4.

On Thursday the 3d instant Mr. Meriwether Smith of Essex county, and who has obliged the public through the channel of this paper with several spirited pieces relating to the Stamp act and other acts of Parliament, was married to Miss Betsy Daingerfield, of King and Queen Co.

Lately died in Albemarle the Reverend Mr James Maury, Rector of Fredericksville in that county. . . . Let it not therefore be thought impertinent to tell the public that the gentleman here spoken of was born in Virginia and brought up at William and Mary College, and was an honour both to his country and the place of his education. . . . It might have been hard to say whether he was more to be admired as a learned man or reverenced as a good man. [Long obituary]. August 24.

Capt. Henry Talman died a few days ago at his house in New Kent county. Dec. 7.

On Monday the 27th ulto. departed this Life Col Thomas Tabb, long a member for Amelia Co. He had for several years struggled, with uncommon fortitude, with the dropsy, which at last put a period to his days to the great regret of his neighbours and numerous acquaintances, to whom he was ever dear, being their counsellor, friend & benefactor. Few (if any) Virginians traded so extensively as he did; none with better credit, or character; and by his death the Colony has lost one of its most useful members. Dec. 7.

On Friday died at his house in Northumberland county the Hon. Presley Thornton, Esq., one of his Majesty's council in this Colony &c. Dec. 14.

Virginia Gazette, edited by Alexander Purdie and John Dixon.
January, 1771–January, 1772.
1771.

On Monday 3d ult. died at his seat in Southampton county in the 61st year of his age Colonel Jesse Brown, a Gentleman who was thoroughly versed in surgery &c. Jan. 3.

Deaths—Gabriel Cay, Esq., Comptroller of his Majesty's customs for the Port of Hampton. Mr. Thomas Jameson, merchant of Yorktown. George Gurley father of Rev. George Gurley, rector of St. Luke's Parish in this (Southampton) county. Jan. 10.

On Sunday 25th November last William Nelson, junior, and his new married lady made their appearance in Stratton Major church, King and Queen Co., for the first time after marriage, when the Rev. Mr. Dunlap delivered an excellent sermon on the marriage state. Jan 17.

Friday Jan 25 died this morning at his house near this city Mr. Frederick Bryan for many years deputy sheriff of York Co. Jan 24.

On Saturday died, at Mr. Roger Gregory's in King William Co., Capt Charles Seaton, of Bristol, for many years commander of a ship in the Virginia trade. February 14.

Dwelling house of Mrs Langburne in King William Co. burned down. Yesterday was married in Henrico Mr. William Carter, third son of Mr John Carter, aged 23, to Mrs Sarah Ellyson, Relict of Mr. Gerard Ellyson, deced, aged eighty-five, a sprightly old tit with three thousand pounds fortune. Deaths: Mr. George Nicholas, clerk of Dinwiddie, Mrs. Jameson relict of Mr. Thomas Jameson of Yorktown, merchant, lately deced. March 14.

Last week died here (Norfolk) Mr. Richard Knight, merchant, Louisa county, March 12 on Saturday last died Sir William Bickley, Baronet. Richmond, Drowned Mr. Jasper Halket, store-keeper with Mr. Neil Campbell, while crossing a creek on horse-back, his sermon was preached by Rev. William Coutts. March 21.

Married James Parke Farley, Esquire, to Miss Betsey Byrd, eldest daughter of Hon. William Byrd, Esq. March 28.

Death: Mrs. Catherine Davenport, relict of Mr. George Davenport, late of this city. April 18.

On the 14th instant died at Blandford on Appomattox, in the fifty-fifth year of his age, Mr. Samuel Gordon, merchant at that place for many years. He left no children.

Married Hugh Nelson, Esq., second son of his Honor the President [William Nelson], to Miss Judy Page, eldest dau. of Hon. John Page. William Griffin, Esq., to Mrs. Robinson, widow of the late Speaker. May 16.

Married, Doctor James Blair of this city to Miss Kitty Eustace, of New York. Peter Thornton, Esq., of Northumberland to Miss Sally Throckmorton, of Gloucester. May 23.

Robert Burwell's house on Burwell Bay described. June 20.

Marriages: David Kerr, Esq., atty at law in King and Queen, to Miss Fanny Tucker, dau of late Col. Robert Tucker of Norfolk. Death: Mr. Francis Jerdone, of Louisa, an eminent merchant in that county. He acquired a handsome fortune by trade, with the fairest reputation. August 15.

Death: Bowler Cocke, Esq., at his seat at Shirley. Aug. 22.

Yesterday morning died at Westover, in an advanced age, Mrs. Maria Byrd, mother of Hon. William Byrd, Esq. Aug. 29.

On 13th ult. died at his house at Curles in Henrico, aged 75, John Pleasants. Sept. 12.

Death: Armistead Lightfoot, Esq., at his house in Yorktown. Sept. 19.

Death: Mr. Thomas Thompson, of Norfolk, merchant. Mr Robert Crooks, a merchant of that place. Sept. 16.

Married: Sept. 19 John Spotswood, Esquire, of Spotsylvania, to Miss Sally Rowzee, youngest dau. of Mr. John Rowzee, of Essex county.

Last Thursday, Mr. Robert Taylor, of Norfolk, to Miss Sally Barraud, eldest dau. of Mr Daniel Barraud, merchant in that place. John Carter, Esq., of King George, to Miss Philadelphia Claiborne, youngest dau. of Philip Whitehead Claiborne, Esq., of King William county. Deaths: Dr. John Dalgleish of Norfolk, faithful physician. Mr. George Ellis, merchant of Richmond town, at Norfolk; Mr. Thomas Aitchison, of Portsmouth, formerly an eminent merchant in this county. Mr Harry Robinson of King William, atty at law, a fair practitioner &c. Mr. John Kidd, of Philadelphia, merchant at Norfolk. Oct. 3.

Death: Col. Richard Johnson, of Newcastle. Oct. 10.

Death: On 6th of July last in South of France, Captain Byrd, eldest son of Hon. William Byrd, Esq. Mr. John Wilson, shoemaker, and Mr. James Esther, blockmaker, both tradesmen in credit. Oct. 17.

Deaths: Mrs. Catherine Blaikley, of this city, in the 76th year of her age, an eminent midwife, and who in the course of her practice brought upwards of 3,000 children into the world. Mrs. Huldah Read, in the 26th year of her age, wife of Dr. John K. Read, of Hanover Co. Oct. 24.

Death: Richard Baker, Esq., atty at law and clerk of Isle of Wight co. Oct. 31.

On Tuesday last died, in the 85th year of his age, Hon. John

Blair, a gentleman who in the course of a long life discharged the office of Representative, Auditor, Judge, Privy Councillor and President of the Colony. Nov. 7.

On Sunday last, 10th of this month, in King William, died Mrs. Mary Gregory, lady of Roger Gregory, Esq. Marriage: Mr. James Mills, merchant of Urbanna, to Mrs. Boyd, relict of Mr Walter Boyd of Blandford. Nov. 14.

Married: Mr. John Burwell to Miss Nancy Powell, youngest daughter of Mr. Benjamin Powell of this city. Death: Mr Philip Whitehead Claiborne, a few days after being elected one of the representatives for King William, at his house in that county. December 5.

PERSONAL NOTICES FROM THE VIRGINIA GAZETTE.

THE YEAR 1772.

January 2. Thomas Jefferson, Esq., married to Mrs. Martha Skelton, relict of Mr. Bathurst Skelton.

Married Mr. Hugh Innis, one of the representatives for Pittsylvania, to Miss Hannah Eggleston, of James City county.

Died, Mr. Benjamin Howard, clerk of Bedford, and one of the Burgesses for Buckingham.

January 6. Married Capt. Thomas Smith, of Gloucester, to Miss Nancy Plater.

Rev. James Stevenson, rector of Berkeley Parish, in Spotsylvania, to Miss Fanny Littlepage, of Hanover.

January 30. John Hatley Norton to Miss Sally Nicholas, eldest daughter of Robert Carter Nicholas.

Died, Mr. James Mitchell, of Yorktown, in his sixty-eighth year.

March 5. Miss Bridges and Miss Driver, of Isle of Wight, drowned in the Swash near Craney Island in a squall.

Married, Mr. William Taylor, merchant at Holt's, in New Kent, to Miss Nancy Booker, only daughter of Col. Richard Booker, of Amelia.

March 26. Mr. John Brown, of the secretary's office, to Miss Nancy Geddy, daughter of Mr. James Geddy, of this city.

Married, Mr. Edward Travis, of Jamestown, to Miss Betsy Taite.

April 16. Died, Col. John Baylor, at his home in Caroline.

May 28. Died, Mr. Thomas Hornsby, of this city, at an advanced age, who by industry and application acquired a large fortune in trade with the fairest character.

June 11. Died, Mrs. Elizabeth Tarpley, of this city, aged sixty years.

June 25. Married, Mr. William Duval, attorney-at-law, to Miss Nancy Pope, eldest daughter of Capt. Nathaniel Pope.

July 2. Killed by fall from his horse, Cary Goosley, of Yorktown, a promising young gentleman.

July 9. Died, Lunsford Lomax, Esq.

Richmond: Drowned George Donald, aged eleven years.

July 23. Died, Col. Hartwell Cocke, one of the representatives for Surry.

At Oporto: Died, the Rev. and Honorable James Horracks, councillor of state, commissary to the Bishop of London.

July 30. Died, Mr. Richard Starke, attorney-at-law, and clerk to the House of Burgesses.

August 13. Died, Mr. David Kerr, attorney-at-law, and clerk of Middlesex county.

August 20. Died, Mr. Joseph Scrivener, of this city, merchant.

August 27. Mr. William Ballard, Jr., pilot in Hampton, died there of the small-pox.

October 8. Dr. David Black, of Blandford, to Miss Nancy McKenzie, late of this city.

Died, Capt. Theodoric Munford at Col. John Banister's, in Dinwiddie.

October 15. Mr. Charles Duncan, merchant in Blandford, to Miss Jennie Gilliam, of Dinwiddie.

October 22. Mr. Peter Pelham, Jr., clerk of Brunswick, to Miss Bethina Brown, of Southampton county.

Died, Rev. John Thompson, rector of St. Mark's, in Culpeper.

November 5. Mr. Thomas Smith, of Richmond, merchant, to Miss Betsy Warren, of New Kent.

PERSONAL NOTICES FROM "VIRGINIA GAZETTE."
FOR 1776 AND 1777.

Marlbro' Iron Works in Frederick county, 1775. Izaac Zane advertises for 5,000 cords of wood.

The commissioners of the Gun Manufactory advertise for brass for mountings. Fredericksburg, Jan. 24, 1776.*

John Tyler advertises his horse, Romulus, sired by Mark Anthony, whose blood is well known, out of Pompadour, a fine full-blooded mare. "He is a beautiful sorrel, and within half an inch of 15 hands high, well made and five years old this spring."

Died—Col. Richard Hull, of Northumberland, in his 59th year, for many years a representative in Assembly and magistrate for that county. June 7.

Mr. William Gregory, of Charles City county, captain in the 6th Regiment, a very worthy man and much esteemed by all his acquaintances. June 7.

May 31, 1776, died, Mr. James Dillard, Jr., an amiable youth.

Notice given by the commissioners of the convention to lease the lands of Lord Dunmore within the county of York, and sell his slaves and personal estate. June 21, 1776.

---

* The dates represent dates of the newspaper.

Hunter's Iron Works at the Falls of Rappahannock River. June 21, 1776. John Strode, manager of the works.

Advertisement of Nicholas Hobson in regard to two soldiers who "deserted from my company of the 6th Regiment of the Continental Regulars." Aug. 9, 1776.

Rev. William Dunlap, of King and Queen county, to Mrs. Johanna Reeve, of Gloucester county. July 26, 1776.

Died at Hampden-Sidney Academy, in the 22d year of his age, Mr. Samuel Hackley, of Culpeper county (who was studying to prepare for the ministry).

Edmund Randolph, Esq., married to Miss Betsy Nicholas, second daughter of the treasurer.

Col. William Finnie married to Miss Betsy Chamberlayne, of James City Co.

Humphry Gwyn advertises 500 acres on Gwyn's Island. Sept. 6, 1776.

William Roscow Wilson Curle, delegate in convention for Norfolk Borough, to Mrs. Lyon, relict of late Walter Lyon, Esq., of Princess Ann county. Sept. 6, 1776.

Rev. John Bracken, rector of Bruton Parish, to Miss Sally Burwell, daughter of late Carter Burwell, Esq., of Carter's Grove. Sept. 13.

Mrs. Hannah Churchill, of Bushy Park, in Middlesex, relict of Armistead Churchill, Esq., in the 70th year of her age. Sept. 13.

John Whiting, Jr., of Gloucester county, admr. of Francis Whiting, deceased, late of Berkeley county. Sept. 13.

Philip Rootes, William Graham, Benjamin Robinson and Thomas Metcalfe summoned before the committee for King and Queen as "enemies of America." Ordered to be disarmed. September 20.

Died, Mr. Lowdell Blackey Taylor, of New Kent county. September 20.

Died, Mr. William Brown, of James City county. Sept. 20.

Mr. Charles Leonard, a native of Cologne, in Germany, and well known in Virginia for his excellent but capricious performance on the violin. He died in his 76th year, and played his last *solo* in the house of Mr. Blovet Pasteur, of this city. Sept. 20.

Died, Mr. Benjamin Winslow, ensign in the 5th Regiment, and eldest son of Mr. Beverley Winslow. Sept. 27.

Mr. Beverly Dixon, of this city, merchant, married to Miss Polly Saunders. Nov. 1.

Died, Mrs. Lewis, spouse of Warner Lewis, Jr., Esq., of Gloucester; Mr. William Aitcheson, late of Norfolk, merchant; Capt. John Phripp, late of Norfolk, in his 93d year. Nov. 8.

Willis Wills, of King and Queen county, advertises the plantation lately belonging to Mr. Thomas Wills, in Mulberry Island. Nov. 15.

William Drew, Esq., clerk of Berkeley, to Miss Hannah Powell, of this city. Nov. 15.

Died, Dr. Andrew Anderson, of New Kent. Nov. 15.

Virginia Gazette, 1777.

Died, Mr. William Pearson, of this city, tanner. Leaves a widow and children. January 17.

Died, Capt. Thomas Tebbs, of the 2d Regiment. Jan. 17.

Mrs. Anne Peyton, wife of Thomas Peyton, Esq., of Gloucester, died.

"Her father Washington, her mother Thacker,
Death, e'er thou strikest another
Good and lovely fair as she,
Time shall throw a dart at thee."

Jan 17.

Died, Capt. John Fleming, of the 1st Virginia Regiment, fell at Trenton in defence of America. Jan. 24.

Married, Major S. J. Cuthbert, of Georgia, to Mrs. Catharine Blair, of this city. Feb. 4.

The Manufacturing Society in Williamsburg are in want of 5 or 6 likely negro lads from 15 to 20, and as many girls from 12 to 15 years, also one or two weavers, for whom they will give ready money. Those who incline to spin for the Society at their own Houses may be furnished with flax on application to the managers. N. B. Negro girls are received as apprentices. February 14.

John M. Galt and Gabriel Maupin, exors. of Alexander Craig, advertise for sale the lots and houses on Main St. adjoining the Raleigh Tavern, where Mr. Craig formerly lived. Feb. 14.

Roger Blackburn living near Abingdon Church in Gloucester. March 7.

Lewis Hansford, merchant in Smithfield. Mentioned March 7.

Died Mr. Paul Watlington, of Gloucester county, Abingdon Parish, aged 77. March 21.

Extract from the minutes of a convocation of the Visitors of the College of William and Mary begun 31 March. Ordered that the Rector write to the visitors requesting a meeting on May 6. Among other things several articles of accusation have been exhibited against the President of the College, John Dixon, clerk, Professor of Divinity, and Mr. Emanuel Jones, master of Brafferton. Publication ordered also in *Gazette*. Signed, Edmund Randolph, Rector. April 4.

Died, Rev. Patrick Henry, rector of St. Paul's Parish, in Hanover. April 11.

William Plume & Co. advertise to carry on the tannery of Mr. William Pearson. May 9.

Address of the officers in York Garrison, May 10, 1777, to Dr. Corbin Griffin. May 16.

Williamsburg Manufactory. John Crawford, manager. The manufactory is within a few steps of the capitol landing. We propose to procure hemp, flax, cotton and wool for manufacturing. Spinners wanted. May 16.

Hudson Muse, naval officer at Moratico Point. May 16.

Deaths in this city—Cole Digges, Esq., a delegate for the county of Warwick. In Gloucester, James Parke Farley, Esq., of North Carolina. In this city, Mrs. Tazewell, spouse of Henry Tazewell, of Brunswick county. Mr. William Fearson, dancing master. May 23.

Resolutions of the Visitors acquitting Mr. Jones of the accusations against him. June 6.

Died at Alexandria, Capt. Joseph Tate, of the Second Battalion of North Carolina. Interred in the church-yard at Alexandria. June 20.

Mr. John Valentine, of Richmond, to Miss Anne Moore (verses). Married June 27.

Died, Col. John Ruffin, 21st instant. June 27.

Halifax, May 30, 1770. Henry Montfort advertises land. June 27.

Died, Mrs. Elizabeth Bannister, spouse to Col. John Bannister, of Dinwiddie; Capt. Walter Vowles, of the first State Regiment. June 11.

Dr. Justice Livingston, physician, of the privateer brig *Northampton,* to Miss Angelica Laford, of this city. August 1st.

On Friday, 15 Aug., being the day of the foundation of William and Mary College, after prayer and sermon by Mr. Madison, recommending industry in the pursuit of science, two orations were delivered, the first in Latin by Mr. Heath, and the other in English by Mr. William Nelson. Many learned gentlemen were present. Aug. 22.

Ropery now erecting in Richmond by Archibald Cary & Co. Joshua Storrs, manager. Aug. 29.

Rev. James Madison appointed President of William and Mary College. Sept. 5.

John Thornton, Esq., of Stafford county, to Miss Catherine Yates, of Gloucester, fourth daughter of Rev. Robert Yates. Sept. 5.

Died, in North Carolina, Mr. John Pinkney, formerly of this city; printer. September 5.

For sale, the beautiful seat on the Mattapony, where the late Speaker Robinson lived. 1,381 acres of high land, 600 acres of marsh, 120 acres of unused. On the tract is a mill. The plantation is under good fences, with a young orchard of choice fruit. Dwelling house is of brick, two stories high, 4 large rooms and a passage on each floor and good cellars. Brick kitchen, servants' hall, wash house, stables, coach house, granary and a garden walled with brick. Advertised by John Parke Custis. Oct. 10.

Rev. William Coutts having resigned, another minister wanted for Martin Brandon Church. Richard Bland and Pleasants Cocke, church wardens. Oct. 24.

Married Mr. William Howard to Miss Nancy Chisman, both of York county. Dec. 12.

Died, Col. Henry King, of Hampton; Mr. Henry Laughton, of this city. Dec. 12.

Oxford Iron Works, Bedford county. Signed David Ross. Dec. 12.

For sale, 3 plantations in Charles City belonging to the orphans of William Kennon, Esq., deceased, now held by the following gentlemen, William Acrill, John Edloe and David Minge. Dec. 26, 1777.

Died, Mrs. Mary Thornton, spouse of Sterling Thornton, Esq., of Gloucester county. Nov. 22.

John Tyler's advertisement from Indian Fields, Charles City
county, for the sale of 500 acres near the mouth of Queen's Creek
and 526 acres in James City county within 5 miles of the city.
Nov. 22.

Died, Frank Eppes, Esq.; Lt.-Col. of the First Regiment.
Dec. 27.

Died, Mr. Patrick Coutts,[1] of Richmond, merchant. Dec. 27.

---

[1] Mr. Patrick Coutts was a rich Scotchman, who lived at Richmond
and owned a ferry. A story illustrative of his independent character
is preserved. He was a great friend of William Byrd, of Westover,
some twenty miles further down. Both fell sick about the same time.
Finding that he could not live long, William Byrd sent a courier post-
haste to Coutts to tell him to *wait for him.* Coutts, who was also dying,
had strength enough to say, "Tell William Byrd that when Patrick
Coutts makes up his mind to die, he waits for no mon."

PERSONAL NOTICES FROM THE "VIRGINIA GAZETTE."

(*February* 12, 1779—*December* 25, 1779.)

Deaths—Mrs. Rebecca Newton, of Princess Anne, formerly of Norfolk. February 12. (Date of issue.)

Died—Miss Jane Finnie, daughter of Mrs. Joanna Finnie, of Prince George county, in her thirteenth year. February 19.

Marriages—John Banister, Esq., of Dinwiddie, to Miss Nancy Blair, of this city. February 26.

Capt. Edward Travis, of the navy, to Miss Clarissa Waller, of this city. February 26.

Died—Mr. William Salter, of Surry county. March 12.

Marriages—Harrison Randolph, Esq., to Miss Betsey Starke, of this city. March 19.

Death—Lewis Burwell, Esq., of Gloucester county. March 19.

Death—Southy Simpson, of Accomack county, and Senator from that District. March 26.

Death—Mr. John Ware, of King and Queen, in the fifty-second year of his age. April 2.

Robert B. Dudley and Thomas Dudley, executors of Capt. Thomas Dudley, of King and Queen county, mentioned. April 9.

Marriages—Mr. Francis Dandridge, of King William, to Miss Lucy Webb, of New Kent. April 16.

Capt. Addison Lewis, of the Light Horse, to Miss Sukey Fleming. April 16.

Death—At Etham, in New Kent, Mrs. Elizabeth Dawson, relict of the late Rev. and Hon. William Dawson, in the seventieth year of her age. April 16.

Mr. Alexander Purdie, of this city, printer to the commonwealth. Interred in the churchyard of this city. Mr. Archibald Williamson, a native of North Britain. April 16.

Last Wednesday, married, Rev. James Madison, President of William and Mary College, to Miss Sally Taite, of this city. May 1.

Death—John Armistead, Esq., at his seat, in New Kent. May 8.

Deaths—Jasper Clayton, Esq., of Gloucester county; Mrs. Elizabeth Camm, relict of the late Rev. and Hon. John Camm, deceased; Claudius Peter Cary, fencing master; Lemuel Newton, in Princess Anne county. May 22.

Marriage—Dr. James McClurg, of this city, to the amiable Miss Selden, of Hampton. May 22.

Marriage—Samuel Beall, Esq., merchant of this city, to Miss Nancy Booth, of Frederick county. June 12.

Armistead Russell, Esq., of New Kent county, to Miss Elvy Clayton, of same county. June 12.

Death—James Holt, Esq., Senator from the District of Princess Anne, Norfolk and Nansemond. Capt. Edward Dixon, of Port Royal. June 12.

Richard Taliaferro, Sen., of James City county, in the seventy-fourth year of his age, with the gout. July 3.

Mrs. Margaret Burwell, relict of Col. Nathaniel Burwell, at her home in King William county. July 3.

Mrs. Jane Baird, wife of John Baird, Esq., of Greencroft. July 3.

William Wiatt advertises for a large sum of money lost near Charlottesville. July 10.

Death—Bartholomew Thompson, formerly of Norfolk, taken by the British; died of jail fever. July 17.

William Clayton, mentioned as exor. of Capt. Jasper Clayton, late of Gloucester county. July 17.

William Clayton, executor of Capt. Jasper Clayton, of Gloucester county, deceased, advertises sale of deceased's estate. July 17.

Mr. Robert Ayland, door-keeper to the General Assembly. July 31.

Death—Mr. John Briggs, of this city, a native of Liverpool. August 14.

Died—Edward Champion Travis, Esq., in the fifty-ninth year of his age. August 21.

Deaths—Mr. Thomas Eppes, of Prince George county. Hath devised most of his portion to Mr. William Poythress, an officer in the Continental Army. Sept. 25.

Died—Mr. Robert Tucker, of Norfolk county. Sept. 25.

Died—Rev. William Dunlap, rector of St. Paul's, in Hanover. September 25.

On 11th instant, died in child bed, spouse of John Bowdoin, Esq., Northampton county. Sept. 25.

Died—Mrs. Anne Burwell, relict of late James Burwell, Esq., of York county. Mr. Ferdinando Leigh, near Petersburg, in the sixty-fourth year of his age. October 30.

Marriage—Mr. William Starke, of Dinwiddie, to Sukey Edwards, of Brunswick county. November 6.

Marriage—Mr. William Rowsey, of this city, to Miss Fanny Tabb, of Yorktown. November 14.

Death—Anthony Walke, Sen., Esq., of Princess Anne. Nov. 14.

Marriages—Mr. Robert Donald, of Petersburg, to Miss Nancy Osborne, of Chesterfield. Nov. 27.

Capt. William Murray, of Prince George, to Miss Bolling, of Chesterfield. Nov. 27.

Deaths—Mr. James Bray Johnson, of Charles City. Mr. Thurmer Hoggard, of Princess Anne. Sept. 25.

Died—John Wilson, Esq., of Norfolk county. Mr. Richard Charlton, of this city, died at Richmond, on his way from the Springs. Oct. 2.

Capt. William Bibb, of Prince Edward county, to Miss Sally Wiatt, of New Kent. Dec. 4.

Death—Mr. Joshua Storrs, of Hanover. Dec. 11.

Mr. William Turney, late of this city, merchant. Dec. 18

The Year 1780.

Died—Major Thruston James, of James City county, in the sixty-fifth year of his age. Feb. 5, 1780.

Estate of Capt. James Cole, late deceased, of Goochland county, advertised by William Cole and John Cole. Feb. 5.

Died—Matthew Thrift, Esq., of Norfolk. Feb. 26.

Died—Mrs. Sarah Pierce, of Hanover, at an advanced age. March 4.

Marriages—Capt. Nathaniel Burwell, of the artillery, to Miss Patty Digges, daughter of Hon. Dudley Digges, Esq., of this city. March 11.

Died—Mrs. Elizabeth Harris, of Jamestown. March 25.

The Virginia Gazette was in April printed in Richmond.

Married Jacob Rubsamen, of Manchester, to Miss Lucy Bland, daughter of the late Hon. Richard Bland, Esq., of Jordan's, in Prince George county. May 31.

Death—Mrs. Lucy Stith, at Wilton, spouse of Capt. John Stith, of Baylor's Dragoons. May 31.

Died—Mrs. Mary Bentley, wife of Mr. Samuel Bentley, of Amelia county. June 2.

Mr. John Batte, of Prince George county, to Miss Polly Poythress, daughter of Col. Peter Poythress, of same county. June 28.

Died—Mrs. Barbara King, widow of Mr. Miles King, at Hampton.

Lt. Richard Coleman, of Spotsylvania, killed 29 May, at Waxsaw's, in South Carolina. June 28.

Elegy on Capt. Adam Wallace, killed at Waxsaw's, South Carolina. July 12.

Married—Col. Robert Ballard, formerly of the Continental Army, to Miss Plowman, of Baltimore. Aug. 2.

Death—Mr. Edward Parker, of this place, tanner. Aug. 2.

Mr. James Purdie, eldest son of the late Mr. Alexander Purdie, printer. Aug. 2.

Lines to Miss Nancy Finnie, dec'd. Aug. 2.

Died—Mrs. Ann Cocke, spouse of Col. Allen Cocke, of Surry. Aug. 9.

Died—Mrs. Martha Waller, spouse of Hon. Benjamin Waller, Esq. Aug. 9.

Died—John Lewis, Esq., of Spotsylvania, one of the first lawyers in America. Oct. 4.

Lt. Thomas Powell, of the State Artillery, at his father's, in Yorktown. Oct. 4.

John Lennard, of Henrico, died of a fall from his horse.

Capt. William Harwood, of Warwick county. Oct. 4.

Mr. Robert Gates, of Berkeley county, only son of Gen. Gates. Oct. 4.

Died—At Portmouth, Capt. John Willis, late of Bermuda. November 4, 1780.

Deaths—Mrs. Susan Ritcheson, wife of Col. Holt Ritcheson, of King William county. Dec. 16, 1780.

Col. Allen Cocke Whig, for many years a representative from Surry county. Dec. 16, 1780.

Married—Herbert Claiborne, Esq., to Miss Polly Browne, of King William. March 3, 1781.

Died—John Tazewell, Esq., of Williamsburg. April 7, 1781.

Died—Mr. Thomas Archer, Sen., of Yorktown. April 7, 1781.

William Wiatt, of Fredericksburg, mentioned. May 19, 1780.

SOME NOTES FROM THE VIRGINIA GAZETTE FOR 1787.

Thomas Nicholson, Publisher.

Jan. 4, 1787. Mr. Capus, from the Royal Opera in Paris, intends opening a dancing school at his house on Shockhoe hill, lately occupied by Mr. Quesnay, opposite the Capitol. One guinea entrance, and twelve pounds per annum.

Prices Current: Tobacco 23s. to 24s. per 100; ditto, Light, 20s to 21s. 6d; Flour, Augusta, common 32s.; Baltimore superfine 30s. to 40s.; ditto country produce 35s to 42; Beef 4£ to 4£ 5s. per barrell; Pork 4£ ditto; Corn 15s ditto; Oats 3s, 4d per bushel; meal 4s per bushel.

For Sale. The well known seat of Mr. John Hay at Cobham; 4 level lots, a house two stories high, containing 3 commodious rooms, a large well furnished store; a brick cellar underneath the whole length of the house, a stable and kitchen; and about 200 yards from the dwelling a beautiful, strong well built lumber house three stories high and almost forty feet in length. Suitable for a merchant, a gentleman of the medical profession or cattle keeper.

January 11, 1787. Adv. of York Grammar School by Mr. Evans. £10 per annum.

Great fire in Richmond began with the storehouse formerly occupied by John Hartshorn, spread to Mr. Anderson's Tavern. * * Between 40 and 50 storehouses and dwelling houses were consumed, together with Byrd's warehouses and 70 hhds of tobacco.

Rev. Mr. Braeken's Grammar school in Williamsburg. The languages, and writing and arithmetic will be taught. Terms 10£ per annum.

Jan. 25, 1787. Fitzwhylson's English School is removed from Mr. Samuel Couch's to Mrs. Warrick, on the back street nearly opposite the Masons' Hall. Two dollars Entrance and 25 shillings per quarter.

Marriage: Last Thursday sennight at Norfolk Mr. John Boush to Miss Frances Moseley Munford. *Death*: On Wednesday the 10th instant, at Norfolk, James Cross, merchant of Manchester, a native of Glasgow.

Febr. 1, 1787. *Deaths*: Mrs. Page, spouse of John Page, Esq. of Rosewell; Mrs. Tayloe, spouse of Col. John Tayloe of Richmond County; Mr. John Lomax, of Alexandria, noted tavern keeper.

Febr. 8, 1787. James Allen Bradbey advertises his beautiful seat on James River, two miles below Cobham in Surry Co.

Feb 15, 1787. Sunday last was commemorated in this City the birthday of George Washington.

Ben. Powell, marshal of the Court of Admiralty; Will. Russell, Clerk.

February 22. Christian Campbell, of Williamsburg, advertises for public sale his houses and lots in the City, "where I now live".

March 1. Tuesday last at his seat in Chesterfield Hon Archibald Cary, Speaker of the Senate, died.

March 15. Mr. Thomas Dillon, merchant of Cumberland County, married to Miss Betsy Keeling, of said County.

Snuff Mills in Williamsburg, Hunt and Adams.

Stallions advertized: "Medley" lately imported from England at *Mt. Prospect,* seat of William H. Macon, Esq., in New Kent Co.; "Rockingham," at *Hayes,* seat of Mr. John Taliaferro, in King George Co.; "The true Whig," property of William Fitzhugh, Esq., of *Chatham;* "Pantaloon," the beautiful, well bred imported horse of Benjamin Harrison at *Brandon.*

March 22. Died Mrs. Roper, spouse of Mr Jesse Roper, of this City.

Notice of auction at the late residence in Henrico of Sterling Thornton, deced.

Saturday last being the anniversary of St. Patrick, it was celebrated with uncommon elegance. A ball was given in the evening at the Capitol to a very numerous company of ladies and gentlemen.

March 29. Notice of a convention to be held of the Protestant Episcopal Church in Richmond by J. Madison, chairman of the Standing Committee, on May 16.

April 5. Died Rebecca Stith, spouse of Major John Stith of Westbury in Charles City Co.; on Thursday last Mrs. White, spouse of Mr. William White of this City.

April 11. Last Sunday departed this Life Mr. James Honey, a native of Perth in Scotland, but for many years a resident of the City of Williamsburg.

April 26. James Mercer, President of the Fredericksburg Academy, gives a notice of a meeting of of the Trustees 25 May next. The purpose of the meeting is to selict a steward and housekeeper. One guinea a quarter for board and fees, payable in advance for Latin or Mathematics; 20 shilling a quarter, the scholars to furnish their own bed and linen.

May 3d 1787. *To let,* the noted Tavern at the foot of Church Hill, known by the name of "The Bird in the Hand."

June 21. *Deaths:* Gerrard Banks at his seat in Stafford, on Friday evening last; Mrs Formicola, spouse of Seraphino Formicola, publican, in this City on Monday last.

June 28. *Marriage:* Miss Frances Southall, dau. of the late Col. James Southall, of Williamsburg, to Mr. William Daingerfield, of Spotsylvania Co.

July 12. *Marriages* Dr. James Ramsay, of Norfolk, to Mrs. Margaret Boush; Mr. Kincaid, of Manchester, to Miss Betsy Cary, dau. of the late Archibald Cary, Esq, Speaker of the Senate; Mr Adam Craig of this City to Miss Polly Mallory of Warwick Co.

Staunton School, where the Latin and Greek languages, Logic and other branches, are taught in the newest. and best improved method. The teacher, Rev. James Chandler, M. A., had his education in one of the best universities of Europe.

July 19 Just published "The Poor Soldier, A comic opera in two Acts." *Married* Col. William White of Louisa to Mrs. Elizabeth White, of Hanover, 18th instant.

July 26. Thomas Brend, bookbinder and stationer, near the Market House, Richmond.

253

HISTORICAL AND GENEALOGICAL NOTES.

Notes from the Virginia Gazette.

August 23, 1787. On Saturday, the 18th Instant in the 48th year
of her age Mrs. Elizabeth Wythe, spouse of Hon. George
Wythe Esq., of the City of Williamsburg *Died*: On Sunday
Jesse Key of Albemarle Co., but for sometime a merchant
of this city. *Married* Lately at Elizabethtown Mr. Francis
Childs, editor of the *Daily Advertizer,* printed in the City
of New York, to Miss Sarah Blanchard, dau. of Mr. John
Blanchard, merchant, of Elizabeth Town

A few days ago was safely lodged in the public jail of
this city (from the information of William Green) John
Price Posey for being accessory to the firing of the New
Kent prison and clerk's office, which contained all the Records of the County Court. Green being an accomplice.
and the acting person, has turned State's evidence.

Sept 6, 1787. *Deaths* in Williamsburg: Mr. John Greenhow,
merchant; Mrs. Farquharson, spouse of Mr. John Farquharson; Beverley Dickson, Esq., late Naval officer of the
Lower District of James River.

Sept 13: "I hereby give notice that I shall petition the next Assembly to invest me with a fee simple estate in a tract of
land in King William County at present occupied by Col.
Francis West. This land belonged to my brother (by the
Father's side) Roscow Bingham who died at the age of
31. Mrs. West, wife to Col Frances West and mother to my
said brother, had this tract of land given to her by my
father for her life, and after that to my brother Roscow.
Stephen Bingham". *West Point, August 15, 1787."*

October 4, 1787 "Hay Market Inn" to be opened October 1. J.
Pryor.

October 11, 1787 *Died* early this morning James Buchanan, oldest merchant of this city; Mr. George Wright, merchant
of Amelia Co., at Nassau, New Providence.

254

October 18. Resolutions by the people of Williamsburg, Freeholders and other inhabitants at the Court House of said city, October 6, 1787 in favor of a convention, to deliberate on the measures recommended by the Convention lately held at Philadelphia, and for revising the Constitution of the Commonwealth.

November 1 Resolutions introduced by Francis Corbin in the House of Delegates for a convention.

November 15. The James River Company trustees request payment of subscriptions. James Harris manager.

Mr. Henry Heth married to Miss Nancy Blair, both of this city.

November 22, *For Sale*, the plantation of Col Thaddeus McCarty, on the Western Branch of the Corotoman River, Has 280 acres; Brick Dwelling House of two stories, four rooms to the floor, and a large passage below Stairs, with a brick Cellar underneath the whole house. Besides a kitchen, dairy, smokehouse, granary, tobacco houses, corn house &c, and a large and valuable orchard, chiefly of Crab, "which is famous for excellent Cyder," a peach orchard, and sundry other valuable trees. Very conveniently situated for fish, oysters and wild fowl.

Nov: 29, 1787 McGuire's English School in the house adjoining the Masons' Hall. He claims to "have a perfect knowledge of the methods employed in European Schools, acquired by several years experience as a tutor in the City of Dublin and other places."

December 20, 1787. James Innis, Rector of William and Mary College, calls a meeting of the Governors and visitors of the College.

EXTRACTS FROM THE REGISTER OF ST. PAUL'S PARISH, KING GEORGE CO., VA.

Copied, 1929, by John Bailey Calvert Nicklin

Joseph, the son of Thomas and Anne Porter, born August 7th, 1726/7.

Ann, the daughter of Thomas and Ann Porter, was born the 13 day of October and baptized the 17 of November, 1717.

Ann Porter died September 22nd, 1727.

Ann, daughter of Thomas and Ann Porter, born March 15 and bapt. April 30th, 1732.

John, son of Thomas and Ann Porter, born August 4th and baptized 8br 6, 1734. (He died July 14, 1754. Register of Overwharton Parish, Stafford Co., Va.).

__ery the son of Tho: and Ann Porter, was baptized the 1 of May, 1723/4.

Thomas Porter died Feb. 26, 1740 (Register of Overwharton Parish). Joseph Porter and Jemima Smith, married Feb. 24, 1756. Ditto.).

Charles Calvert, son of John and Eleanor Jones, born June 4th and baptized July 6th, 1746.

Behethland, daughter of John and Eleanor Jones, born July 14th and baptized August 14th, 1748.

Sabra, daughter of John and Eleanor Jones, born October 7th and baptized December 9th, 1751.

Nathaniel, son of John and Eleanor Jones, born Feb. 25, 1750/51.

Jane, daughter of John and Eleanor Jones, born March 16, 1762.

John Jones and Eleanor Moss, married August 16th, 1744.

William Strother and Winifred Baker, Westmoreland, married Sept. 26, 1765.

James Scribner and Behethland Beach, married Nov. 7, 1773.

Justinian Birch and Behethland Dade, married June 30, 1777.

Hezekiah Thirk and Behethland Bennet, married Feb. 10, 1778.

Luke Hughes and Behethland Kennedy, married July 10, 1779.

Ambrose Lipscomb and Winifred Mardus, married Dec. 23, 1785.

William Mitchell and Behethland Johnston married Septber 4, 1787.

Dade Massey, Junr., died February 7th, 1735.

Capt. Dade Massey, died April 16th, 1735.

John Storke and Frances Hooe, married March 21, 1750/1.

John Gravat and Behethland Kelly, married Jan. 27, 1751.

Cadwallader Dade and Sarah Berryman, married Aug. 20, 1752.

Thomas Bunbury and Behethland Massey, married Aug. 20, 1752.

John Thornton and Behethland Gilson Berryman, married Dec. 13, 1761.

Robert Kay and Elizabeth Strother were married Dec. 13, 1762.

Enoch Strother and Mary Kay were married Feb. 12, 1763.

John James and Anne Strother were married Sept. 16, 1763.

Behethland Alexander, daughter of Robert and Elizabeth Dade, born December 23d and baptized Febry 10th, 1745.

Andrew Gilson, son of Gilson and Hannah Berryman, born Jan. 3d and baptized June 8th, 1745.

William, son of John and Frances Storke, born Sept. 25 and baptized Nov. 1, 1753.

Thomas, son of Robert and Alice Washington, born Sept. 5, 1758.

William Strother, son of Robert and Alice Washington, born April 20, 1760.

Anne, daughter of Robert and Alice Washington, was born Nov. 10, 1761.

Townshend, son of Robert and Alice Washington, born Feb. 20, 1764.

Lund, son of Robert and Alice Washington, was born Sept. 25, 1767.

John, the son of William and Elizabeth Storke, born July 11th and baptized August 15th, 1725.

Thomas Booth and Behethland Berryman, married Octr. 10th, 1727.

Richard Bernard and Elizabeth Storke married August 29th, 1729.

Margaret, daughter of William and Elizabeth Storke, was born the 18th of Jan. 1720.

Behethland Dade died Jany. 29, 1726.

Mary, the wife of George Stork, died January 10th, 1727.

John, son of Gilson and Hannah Berryman, born June 23d, 1742.

Behethland, daughter of Gilson and Hannah Berryman, born March 23d, 1743/4.

Ann, daughter of Dade and Elizabeth Massey, was born the 19th day of March, 1719.

Behethland Booth died October 9th, 1727. (1728?).

Anthony Strother of St. George's Parish and Behethland Storke of this Parish married August 25th, 1733, by the Rev. David Stuart.

Mention of MAJOR Francis Thornton, Oct. 19, 1716. (Who was he? J. B. C. N.).

Behethland, daughter of John and Mary Polly, born March 30, 1727.

Francis Dade, Jr., died Dec. 4, 1725.

Richard Taliaferro of Essex and Rose Berryman, married June 10, 1726.

Jane, the wife of Francis Dade, died May 23d, 1744.

Sarah, wife of Cadwallader Dade, died Febry. 13th, 1744.

Gilson Berryman, Gentleman, died April 4, 1749.

Henry Dade and Elizabeth Massey, married July 7th, 1726.

Jane, the daughter of Francis and Jane Dade, died the 14 of May, 1718.

Col. Rice Hooe died April 19, 1726.

Frances Hooe died April 26, 1726.

Robert Taliaferro died June 6, 1726.

Robert Crook and Mary Gossling, married April 15, 1745.

Robert Rose and Frances Jones, married June 7, 1752.

Thomas Fletcher and Mary Jones, married Dec. 28, 1753.

David Jones and Mary Boswell, married Feb. 18, 1763.

John Peed and Behethland Jones, married Feb. 14, 1770.

Daniel Hamet and Eleanor Jones, married Dec. 22, 1774.

William Crank and Sabra Jones, married Feb. 8, 1778.

Samuel Marshall and Jane Jones, married June 3, 1782.

Mildred, daughter of John and Behethland Peed, born Sept. 22, 1772.

John, son of Howson and Anne Hooe, born Feb. 23, 1728.

William Toul and Mary Porter were married Oct. 15, 1722.

William Gemison and Elizabeth Dalbin, married December 30th, 1725.

Henry Dade and Elizabeth Massey, married July 7, 1726.

Richard Foote and Katherine Fossaker, married Oct. 6, 1726.

Townshend Washington and Elizabeth Lund, married Dec. 22, 1726.
__*torker and Sarah Stribling, married Aug. 28, 1728.
James Seaton and Grace Dounton, married March 11, 1731.
Chandler, son of Chandler and Mary Fowke, born 7 Nov., 1717.
Jane, the daughter of Francis and Jane Dade, died 14 May, 1718.
Mr. Nathaniel Washington died 15 Sept., 1718.
Ann, the daughter of Dade and Elizabeth Massey, was born ye 19 March, 1720.
Grace, ye daughter of James and Sarah Berry, was born ye 16 of January, 1720.
John Jones died Jan. 19, 1726.
William Buckner died Aug. 3, 1727.
Mrs. M_____* Washington died April 1, 1728.
_____oot died June 7, 1728.
Katherine Hooe died Nov. 8, 1731.
Elizabeth, wife of Henry Dade, died March 18, 1734.
Anthony Buckner died March 21, 1734.
Grace Powell died Oct. 29, 1734.
Anthony Buckner died Sept. 1, 1734.
Mary, wife of Mr. Henry Washington, died Jan. 19, 1735.
Jone Moss died Nov. 1, 1735.
John, son of John and Mary Washington, died Feb. 13, 1736.
Frances Bunbury died April 4, 1737.
James Berry died Jan. 6, 1739.
Capt. John Washington died Feb. 27, 1741.
Mr. Townshend Washington died Dec. 31, 1743.
Nathaniel, son of Capt. John Washington, died Nov. 28, 1745.
Mary Washington, Jr., died May 11, 1746.
Sigismund Massey died June 16, 1746.
Mary, widow of Nathaniel Washington, died Oct. 23, 1747.
Mr. Rice Hooe died Jan. 22, 1748.
Major Jno. Buckner died May 6, 1748.
Jane, daughter of Langhorne Dade, died Sept. 28, 1748.
Capt. Henry Washington died Oct. 22, 1748.
Francis, son of Richard and Catherine Foote, died 8ber 12, 1753.
Massey Thomas and Mary Price, married Nov. 28, 1731.
Robert Clifton and Frances Hill, married July 15, 1733.
Thomas Price and Sarah Buckner, married Sept. 31, 1734.
John Washington and Margaret Stork, married Nov. 23, 1738.
Robert Dade and Elizabeth Harrison, married Jan. 4, 1743.
Samuel Kelly and Behethland White, married Aug. 25, 1741.
Langhorne Dade and Mildred Washington, married Feb. 14, 1743.
Henry Washington, Jr., and Elizabeth Stork, April 18, 1743. Married.
William Jones and Mary Baxter, July 26, 1744. Married.
William Brown and Elizabeth Butler, Aug. 2, 1744. Married.
Townshend Dade and Rose Grigsby, married Dec. 12, 1745.
Howson Hooe, Jr., and Mary Dade, married Sept. 26, 1746.
Francis Thornton and Sarah Fitzhugh, married April 2, 1747.
John Day and Behethland Bowling, married Feb. 23, 1748.
William Lord and Anne Jones, married Oct. 12, 1748.
Bailey Washington and Catherine Storke, Jan. 12, 1749.
Horatio Dade and Frances Richards, married Oct. 5, 1749.
John Washington and Betty Massey, married Nov. 17, 1749.
William Jones and Elizabeth Alsop, married Feb. 9, 1749.

*Illegible.

William Bernard and Winifred Thornton, married Nov. 25, 1750.
Robert Yates and Elizabeth Dade, married Feb. 17, 1750.
Lawrence Washington and Elizabeth Dade, married July 31, 1750.
William Jones and Jane Rainey, married April 20, 1752.
Robert Rose and Frances Jones, married June 7, 1752.
Cadwallader Dade and Sarah Berryman, married Aug. 20, 1752.
Thomas Bunbury and Behethland Massey, married Aug. 30, 1752.
Thomas Fletcher and Mary Jones, married Dec. 28, 1752.
David Parsons and Elizabeth Jones, married Feb. 25, 1759.
John Thornton and Behethland Gilson Berryman, married Dec. 13, 1761.

1724/5.

Richard Foote died 21 of March.
Elizabeth Foote died the 1 of Aprill, 1725.
Benjamin Massey died June 24.
Mr. Daniel McGill died Nov. 5.
William Bunbury died Nov. 16.
William Buckner died Nov. 14.
Rice, son of Rice and Katherine Hooe, was born May 4.
Elizabeth Buckner died Nov. 14.

1716.

Mrs. Frances Lund, daughter of Capt. Samuel _____,* dec'd, died the 19th of October.
Mary Newton died 25 March.
Benjamin Newton and Elizabeth Nicholson were married the 6 May.
John, the son of William and Elizabeth _____,* died the 21 August.

1727.

Mary, —* of Henry and Elizabeth Dade, born June 11.
William, son of Richard and Katherine Foote, born Oct. 31.
Anthony, son of Anthony and Winifred Thornton, born Nov. 15.
Richard, son of Rice and Katherine Hooe, born Oct. 15.

---

*Illegible.

259

DATA FROM THE REGISTER OF ST. PAUL'S PARISH, KING GEORGE (FORMERLY STAFFORD) COUNTY, VIRGINIA, 1716-1793

By Major John Bailey Calvert Nicklin

Behethland

Marriages

Thomas Booth and Behethland Berryman, Oct. 10, 1727.
Anthony Strother and Behethland Storke, Aug. 25, 1733.
Samuel Kelly and Behethland White, Aug. 25, 1741.
John Day and Behethland Bowling, Feb. 23, 1748.
John Gravat and Behethland Kelly, Dec. 27, 1751.
Thomas Bunbury and Behethland Massey, Aug. 30, 1752.
James Cunningham and Behethland Overall, June 21, 1757.
Alexander Jordan and Behethland Gravat, Oct. 30, 1758.
John Thornton and Behethland Gilson Berryman, Dec. 31, 1761.
John Chandler and Behethland Rogers, Sept. 17, 1767.
John Peed and Behethland Jones, Feb. 14, 1770.
James Scribner and Behethland Beach, Nov. 7, 1773.
Justinian Birch and Behethland Dade, June 30, 1777.
Hezekiah Thirk and Behethland Bennett, Feb. 10, 1778.
Luke Hughes and Behethland Kennedy, July 10, 1779.
William Mitchell and Behethland Johnston, Sept. 4, 1787.

Births

Behethland, daughter of John and Mary Polly, March 30, 1728.
Behethland, daughter of Benjamin and Katherine Derrick, Sept. 6, 1739.
Behethland, daughter of James and Elizabeth Bennett, Feb. 15, 1740.
Welford, son of Samuel and Behethland Kelly, July 23, 1742.
Behethland, daughter of Gilson and Hannah Berryman, March 23, 1743-4.
Behethland Alexander, daughter of Robert and Elizabeth Dade, Dec. 23, 1744.
Tabitha, daughter of Samuel and Behethland Kelly, Nov. 7, 1744.
Sarah, daughter of Samuel and Behethland Kelly, Dec. 27, 1746.
Behethland, daughter of John and Eleanor Jones, July 14, 1748.
Behethland, daughter of William and Frances Rogers, March 13, 1748.
Edmond, son of Samuel and Behethland Kelly, Sept. 15, 1748.
Behethland, daughter of Joseph and Sarah Reddish, Aug. 22, 1751.
Ursula, daughter of John and Behethland Gravat, June 10, 1751.
Elizabeth, daughter of Thomas and Behethland Bunbury, Jan. 30, 1756.
Catherine, daughter of George and Behethland Smith, March 24, 1760.
Anne, daughter of Thomas and Behethland Bunbury, July 1, 1764.
Behethland, daughter of William and Frances Johnson, April 19, 1766.
Stephen, son of John and Behethland Chandler, July 6, 1768.
Behethland, daughter of George and Behethland Smith, April 16, 1772.
William Rogers, son of John and Behethland Chandler. Sept. 27, 1773.
Mildred, daughter of John and Behethland Peed, Sept. 22, 1773.

Deaths

Behethland Dade, Jan. 29, 1726.
Behethland Booth, Oct. 9, 1727 (?1728?).

Dade

Marriages

Henry Dade and Elizabeth Massey, July 7, 1726.
Townshend Dade and Parthenia Massey, May 6, 1736.
Baldwin Dade and Sarah Alexander, Aug. 7, 1736.
Robert Dade and Elizabeth Harrison, Jan. 4, 1743.
Langhorne Dade and Mildred Washington, Feb. 14, 1743.
Townshend Dade and Rose Grigsby, Dec. 12, 1745.
Howson Hooe, Jr., and Mary Dade, Sept. 26, 1746.
Horatio Dade and Frances Richards, Oct. 5, 1749.
Robert Yates and Elizabeth Dade, Feb. 17, 1750/1.
Lawrence Washington and Elizabeth Dade, July 31, 1751.
Cadwallader Dade and Sarah Berryman, Aug. 20, 1752.
Horatio Dade and Mary Massey, Jan. 14, 1753.
Charles Stuart and Frances Dade, Aug. 6, 1754.
Walter Williamson and Mildred Dade, March 1, 1755.
Francis Peyton and Frances Dade, April 24, 1755.
Nehemiah Rodham Mason and Sarah Dade, Feb. 12, 1762.
Townshend Dade and Jane Stuart, Dec. 11, 1769.
Buckner Stith and Anne Dade, Feb. 26, 1770.
Lawrence Taliaferro and Sarah Dade, Feb. 3, 1774.
James Gwatkins and Frances Dade, March 25, 1774.
Robert Yates and Jane Dade, April 11, 1777.
Justinian Birch and Behethland Dade, June 30, 1777.
      Blackston and Mary Dade, Oct. 10, 1777.
Lawrence Ashton and Hannah Gibbons Dade, Feb. 1, 1779.
Townshend Dade and Elizabeth Dade, Aug. 5, 1782.
James Park and Sally Dade, March 4, 1796.

Births

Mary, daughter of Henry and Eilzabeth Dade, June 11, 1727.
Robert, son of Henry and Elizabeth Dade, May 14, 1731.
Frances Townshend, daughter of Townshend and Elizabeth Dade, Oct. 7, 1732.
Elizabeth, daughter of Townshend and Elizabeth Dade, Oct. 20, 1734.
Cadwallader, son of Townshend and Elizabeth Dade, Dec. 26, 1736.
Francis, son of Baldwin and Sarah Dade, Dec. 29, 1737.
Anne Fowke, daughter of Townshend and Parthenia Dade, Dec. 13, 1737.
Townshend, son of Langhorne and Mildred Dade, Dec. 25, 1743.
Behethland Alexander, daughter of Robert and Elizabeth Dade, Dec. 23, 1744.
Cadwallader, son of Langhorne and Mildred Dade, Jan. 1, 1746.
Sarah, daughter of Baldwin and Linny Dade, Jan. 20, 1747.
Jane, daughter of Langhorne and Mildred Dade, April 2, 1748.
Franky, daughter of Horatio and Mary Dade, Oct. 10, 1753.
Horatio, son of Horatio and Mary Dade, Aug. 25, 1757.
Hannah Gibbons, daughter of Horatio and Mary Dade, July 1, 1759.
Baldwin, son of Baldwin and Verlinda Dade, Feb. 14, 1760.
Townshend, son of Cadwallader and Sarah Dade, Oct. 28, 1760.
Elizabeth, daughter of Baldwin and Verlinda Dade, June 13, 1764.
Townshend, son of Horatio and Mary Dade, June 3, 1766.
Townshend Stuart, son of Townshend and Jane Dade, Aug. 4, 1774.

Deaths

Jane, daughter of Francis and Jane Dade, May 14, 1718.
Francis Dade, Jr., Dec. 3, 1725.

261

Elizabeth, wife of Henry Dade, March 18, 1733/4.
Elizabeth, wife of Townshend Dade, Dec. 30, 1736.
Sarah, wife of Baldwin Dade, Oct. 30, 1739.
Sarah, wife of Cadwallader Dade, Feb. 13, 1744.
Jane, wife of Francis Dade, May 23, 1744.
Jane, daughter of Langhorne Dade, Sept. 28, 1747.
Jane, wife of Townshend Dade, and daughter of Rev. William Stuart and
    Sarah, his wife, Aug. 10, 1774.

Massey

Marriages

Henry Dade and Elizabeth Massey, July 7, 1726.
James Ralph and Elizabeth Massey, Aug. 19, 1726.
Robert Massey and Winifred McCarty, Dec. 20, 1728.
Dade Massey and Parthenia Alexander, Jan. 17, 1732.
Frances Wright and Anne Massey, Dec. 7, 1737.
John Massey and Elizabeth Powell, June 12, 1736.
Townshend Dade and Parthenia Massey, May 6, 1736 .
Sigismund Massey and Mary Stuart, April 4, 1743.
John Washington and Betty Massey, Nov. 17, 1749.
Thomas Bunbury and Behethland Massey, Aug. 30, 1752.
Horatio Dade and Mary Massey, Jan. 14, 1753.
John Waugh and Jane Massey, April 22, 1761.
Elisha Powell and Winifred Massey, Dec. 20, 1761.
        Coad and Elizabeth Massey, Dec. 6, 1766.
William Alexander and Sigismunda Mary Massey, April 18, 1765.
Sigismund Massey and Sarah Short, July 16, 1770.
William Massey and Hannah Little, Feb. 8, 1784.
Lovell Massey and Sarah Whiting, Dec. 28, 1787.
John Washington and Eleanor Massey, Dec. 24, 1787.
James Grant and Elizabeth Massey, Jan. 10, 1793.

Births

Anne, daughter of Dade and Elizabeth Massey, March 19, 1719.
Betty, daughter of Robert and Winifred Massey, Sept. 8, 1731.
Lee, son of Dade and Parthenia Massey, Sept. 19, 1732.
Robert, son of Robert and Winifred Massey, Sept. 10, 1733.
Dade, son of Dade and Parthenia Massey, Oct. 10, 1734.
Winifred, daughter of Robert and Winifred Massey, Sept. 6, 1735.
Anne, daughter of Robert and Winifred Massey, Aug. 6, 1738.
Frances, daughter of Robert and Winifred Massey, Sept. 22, 1740.
Jane, daughter of Sigismund and Mary Massey, Feb. 8, 1744.
Dade, son of Thomas and Eleanor Massey, March 2, 1746.
Sallie, daughter of Benjamin and Elizabeth Massey, March 8, 1745.
Sigismunda Mary, daughter of Sigismund and Mary Massey, June 29, 1745.
Dade, son of Benjamin and Elizabeth Massey, Jan. 6, 1747.
Taliaferro, son of Benjamin and Elizabeth Massey, April 22, 1749.
Frances, daughter of Benjamin and Elizabeth Massey, July 10, 1751.
Thomas, son of Thomas and Elizabeth Massey, June 1, 1752.
Anne, daughter of Charles and Martha Massey, Jan. 21, 1758.
Mary, daughter of Thomas and Mary Massey, April 15, 1760.
Martha, daughter of Charles and Martha Massey, Sept. 22, 1762.
John, son of Thomas and Eleanor Massey, Sept. 20, 1762.
Winifred, daughter of Charles and Martha Massey, Dec. 4, 1765.
Eleanor, daughter of Thomas and Eleanor Massey, March 24, 1765.

Deaths

Benjamin Massey, June 24, 1723.
Dade Massey, Jr., Feb. 7, 1735.
Capt. Dade Massey, April 16, 1735.
Sigismund Massey, June 16, 1746.

Stribling

Marriages

Joel Stribling and Hester Colclough, Sept. 25, 1723.
Thomas Stribling and Elizabeth Newton, Dec. 7, 1725.
Thomas Stribling and Jane Thomas, Nov. 17, 1729.
Bushrod Doggett and Anne Stribling, Oct. 6, 1737.
Thomas Lewis Parrett and Hester Stribling, April 16, 1744.
Colclough Stribling and Mary Hodge, Oct. 6, 1749.
Thomas Stribling and Elizabeth Peck, March 8, 1751/2.
William Stribling and Elizabeth Derrick, Jan. 7, 1753.
Francis Rose and Hester Stribling, May 31, 1756.
John Curry and Jane Stribling, Sept. 20, 1758.
Reuben Burgess and Martha Stribling, Sept. 1, 1765.
Anthony Price and Elizabeth Stribling, Feb. 17, 1765.
James Rallings and Margaret Stribling, Jan. 5, 1778.
John Knowling and Mildred Stribling, April 11, 1776.
John Smith and Mary Stribling, Jan. 8, 1778.
  Storker and Sarah Stribling, Aug. 23, 1728.

Births

Benjamin and Anne, son and daughter of Joel and Mary Stribling, May 31, 1716.
Thomas, son of Thomas and Elizabeth Stribling, April 25, 1728.
William, son of Thomas and Jane Stribling, Jan. 20, 1731.
Hester, daughter of Joel and Hester Stribling, April 5, 1732.
Frances, daughter of Thomas and Jane Stribling, June 20, 1734.
Bradford, son of Joel and Hester Stribling, Jan. 22, 1736.
Jane, daughter of Thomas and Jane Stribling, Jan. 21, 1737.
Mary, daughter of Joel and Hester Stribling, Nov. 4, 1738.
Elizabeth, daughter of Thomas and Jane Stribling, Sept. 18, 1739.
Anne, daughter of Thomas and Jane Stribling, Jan. 18, 1741.
Margaret, daughter of Thomas and Jane Stribling, March 10, 1743.
Millie, daughter of Thomas and Jane Stribling, Jan. 28, 1748.
Mary, daughter of Moses* and Jane Stribling, Sept. 17, 1750.
Newton, son of Thomas and Elizabeth Stribling, Oct. 10, 1752.
Joel, son of Colclough and Frances Stribling, March 11, 1752.
Jemima, daughter of William and Elizabeth Stribling, March 26, 1752.
Sarah, daughter of Thomas and Jane Stribling, May 17, 1752.
William, son of William and Elizabeth Stribling, March 28, 1755.
Benjamin, son of Colclough and Frances Stribling, June 15, 1756.
Joel, son of Thomas and Jane Stribling, Aug. 17, 1756.
Winifred, daughter of William and Elizabeth Stribling, July 20, 1757.
Joel, son of Colclough and Frances Stribling, March 8, 1758.
William Derrick, son of William and Elizabeth Stribling, June 12, 1759.
John Colclough, son of Colclough and Frances Stribling, Jan. 5, 1760.
Thomas, son of William and Elizabeth Stribling, Feb. 9, 1761.
Jemima, daughter of William and Elizabeth Stribling, Jan. 29, 1764.
Susanna, daughter of Colclough and Frances Stribling, April 27, 1764
Thomas, son of Colclough and Frances Stribling, Oct. 22, 1767.
Mary, daughter of Colclough and Frances Stribling, Feb. 16, 1768.

---

*Evidently an error for Thomas.

263

Deaths

Joel Stribling, Sept. 14, 1718.
Elizabeth Stribling, April 12, 1727.
Joel Stribling, March 19, 1737/8.
Benjamin Stribling, Feb. 10, 1743.
Joel, son of Joel and Hester Stribling, Sept. 27, 1744.

Thornton

Marriages

John Ford and Elizabeth Thornton, Jan. 27, 1730.
Francis Thornton and Sarah Fitzhugh, April 2, 1747.
William Thornton and Elizabeth Fitzhugh, April 26, 1757.
William Bernard and Winifred Thornton, Nov. 25, 1750.
Anthony Thornton and Susanna Fitzhugh, Jan. 5, 1764.
Daniel McCarty and Winifred Thornton, Jan. 15, 1765.
George Thornton and Mary Alexander, Oct. 9, 1773.
William Thornton and Martha Stuart, May 11, 1775.
John Brooke and Lucy Thornton, July 2, 1777.
Presley Thornton and Elizabeth Thornton, March 26, 1784.
Presley Thornton and Alice Thornton, Oct. 19, 1785.

Births

Francis, son of Anthony and Winifred Thornton, July 20, 1725.
Anthony, son of Anthony and Winifred Thornton, Nov. 15, 1727.
Judith Presley, daughter of Anthony and Winifred Thornton, Oct. 3, 1731.
Peter, son of Anthony and Winifred Thornton, March 29, 1734.
Sarah, daughter of Francis and Sarah Thornton, Feb. 10, 1752.
Susanna, daughter of William and Susanna Thornton, March 29, 1758.
William, son of Francis and Sarah Thornton, May 28, 1758.

Deaths

Judith Presley, daughter of Captain Anthony and Winifred Thornton, Oct. 11, 1733.

Washington

Marriages

Townshend Washington and Elizabeth Lund, Dec. 22, 1726.
John Washington and Margaret Storke, Nov. 23, 1738.
Henry Washington, Jr., and Elizabeth Storke, May 18, 1743.
Langhorne Dade and Mildred Washington, Feb. 14, 1743.
Bailey Washington and Catherine Storke, Jan. 12, 1749.
John Washington and Betty Massey, Nov. 17, 1749.
Lawrence Washington and Elizabeth Dade, July 31, 1751.
Charles Stuart and Frances Washington, Feb. 23, 1751/2.
Thomas Berry and Elizabeth Washington, Nov. 19, 1758.
John Washington and Catherine Washington, Dec. 23, 1759.
Andrew Monroe and Margaret Washington, Dec. 21, 1761.
John Buckner and Elizabeth Washington, Dec. 11, 1760.
Nathaniel Washington and Sarah Hooe, Dec. 17, 1767.
Lawrence Washington and Catherine Foote, Oct. 5, 1774.
Robert Smith and Mary T(ownshend?) Washington, July 29, 1773.
Henry Washington and Mildred Pratt, March 12, 1779.

Thomas Hungerford and Anne Washington, June 22, 1780.
John Stith and Anne Washington, Dec. 11, 1783.
William Thompson and Anne Washington, Aug. 3, 1785.
Thornton Washington and Frances Washington, April 2, 1786.
John Washington and Eleanor Massey, Dec. 24, 1787.
Griffin Stith and Frances Townshend Washington, June 14, 1788.
Nathan Smith and Betsy Washington, April 4, 1790.

Births

Mary, daughter of John and Mary Washington, Feb. 28, 1726.
Nathaniel, son of Henry and Mary Washington, Jan. 16, 1726.
Susanna, daughter of Townshend and Elizabeth Washington, Nov. 3, 1727.
Lawrence, son of John and Mary Washington, March 31, 1728.
Anne, daughter of John and Mary Washington, 1723.*
Thomas, son of Townshend and Elizabeth Washington, March 24, 1731.
Bailey, son of Henry and Mary Washington, Sept. 10, 1731.
Frances, daughter of John and Mary Washington, Oct. 20, 1731.
Townshend, son of Townshend and Elizabeth Washington, Sept. 21, 1733.
John, son of John and Mary Washington, Aug. 10, 1734.
Townshend, son of Townshend and Elizabeth Washington, Feb. 25, 1736.
Lund, son of Townshend and Elizabeth Washington, Oct. 21, 1737.
Elizabeth, daughter of Capt. John and Mary Washington, Dec. 21, 1737.
John and Lawrence, sons of Townshend and Elizabeth Washington, March
    14, 1740.
Katherine, daughter of Capt. John and Mary Washington, Jan. 13, 1740/1.
Henry, son of Townshend and Elizabeth Washington, Aug. 29, 1742.
Sarah, daughter of Capt. John and Mary Washington, Oct. 28, 1742.
Lawrence, son of Henry and Elizabeth Washington, Feb. 10, 1744.
William, son of John and Margaret Washington, Dec. 9, 1748.
Henry, son of Bailey and Catherine Washington, Dec. 5, 1749.
George, son of Lawrence and Elizabeth Washington, Jan. 4, 1758.
Thomas, son of Robert and Alice Washington, Sept. 5, 1758.
William Strother, son of Robert and Alice Washington, April 20, 1760.
Henry, son of John and Catherine Washington, Oct. 26, 1760.
Anne, daughter of Robert and Alice Washington, Nov. 10, 1761.
Nathaniel, son of John and Catherine Washington, Oct. 1, 1762.
Mary, daughter of John and Catherine Washington, June 17, 1764.
Townshend, son of Robert and Alice Washington, Feb. 20, 1764.
Ferdinand, son of Samuel and Anne Washington, July 16, 1776.
Frances Townshend, daughter of Lawrence and Elizabeth Washington, Aug.
    18, 1767.
Lund, son of Robert and Alice Washington, Sept. 25, 1767.

Deaths

Mr. Nathaniel Washington, Sept. 15, 1718.
Mrs. M(ary) Washington, April 21, 1728.
Mary, wife of Mr. Henry Washington, Jan. 19, 1735.
John, son of John and Mary Washington, Feb. 13, 1735/6.
Capt. John Washington, Feb. 27, 1742.
Mr. Townshend Washington, Dec. 31, 1743.
Nathaniel, son of Capt. Henry Washington, Nov. 28, 1745.
Mary Washington, Jr., May 11, 1746.
Mary, widow of Nathaniel Washington, Oct. 23, 1747.
Capt. Henry Washington, Oct. 22, 1748.

---

*No date given, but 1723 precedes this entry.

EXTRACTS FROM ST. PAUL'S REGISTER, STAFFORD (NOW KING GEORGE) CO., VA.

Copied by JOHN BAILEY CALVERT NICKLIN.

Hooe.

Births.

Rice, son of Rice and Katherine Hooe, March 14, 1725.
Richard, son of Rice and Katherine Hooe, Oct., 15, 1727.
John, son of Howson and Anne Hooe, Feb., 23, 1727/8.
Gerard, son of John and Anne Hooe, Sept., 14, 1733.
Seymour, son of John and Anne Hooe, June 13, 1735.
Harris, son of Howson and Anne Hooe, Jan., 1, 1736.
John, son of John and Anne Hooe, Dec., 26, 1737.
Verlinda Harrison, daughter of Rice and Tabitha Hooe, Feb., 28, 1739.
Anne, daughter of John and Anne Hooe, Dec., 7, 1739.
Bernard, son of Howson and Anne Hooe, Oct., 30, 1739.
Joseph Harrison, son of Rice and Tabitha Hooe, Jan., 22, 1740/1.
Mary Townshend, daughter of Rice and Tabitha Hooe, Feb., 27, 1741/2.

Sarah, daughter of John and Anne Hooe, March 7, 1742.
Robert Townshend, son of Rice and Tabitha Hooe, Oct., 3, 1743.
William, son of Howson and Anne Hooe, Sept., 9, 1743.
Sarah, daughter of Rice and Tabitha Hooe, May 14, 1745.
Henry Dade, son of Howson and Mary Hooe, June 9, 1747.
Robert Howson, son of Howson and Elizabeth Hooe, Nov., 22, 1748.
Mary Anne, daughter of John Hooe, Jr., and Anne, his wife, Nov.,
7, 1756.
Rice Wingfield, son of Richard and Anne Hooe, June 25, 1764.
Sarah Barnes, daughter of Gerard and Sarah Hooe, June 5, 1769.
Hannah Fitzhugh, daughter of Rice W. Hooe and Sukey, his wife,
March 25, 1791.
Nathaniel Harris, son of William and Anne Hooe, Oct., 15, 1777.
Alexander Seymour, son of Seymour Hooe, April 11, 1781.

Deaths.

Colonel Rice Hooe, April 19, 1726.
Frances Hooe, April 26, 1726.
Katherine Hooe, Nov., 8, 1731.
Parthenia, daughter of John and Anne Hooe, Aug., 26, 1742.
Mr. Rice Hooe, Jan., 22, 1748.

Marriages.

Philip Alexander and Sarah Hooe, Nov., 11, 1726.
John Hooe and Anne Alexander, Nov., 23, 1726.
Howson Hooe, Jr., and Mary Dade, Sept., 26, 1746.
John Storke and Frances Hooe, March 21, 1750/1.
John Hooe and Anne Fowke, March 14, 1755.
Nathaniel Washington and Sarah Hooe, Dec., 17, 1767.
Bernard Hooe and Margaret Pratt, Nov., 2, 1771.
William Allison and Anne Hooe, June 26, 1770.
Oliver Moxley and Anne Hooe, Nov., 5, 1772.
Seymour Hooe and Sarah Alexander, March 9, 1776.
Thomas Roy and Susannah Hooe, Sept., 17, 1777.
William Winters and Caty Hooe, Nov., 1, 1781.
William Hooe and Susanna Pratt, Nov., 13, 1782.
George Mason and Elizabeth Hooe, April 22, 1784.
Rice Wingfield Hooe and Susannah Fitzhugh, May 13, 1790.
Henry Dade Hooe and Jane Fitzhugh, June 17, 1790.

Fitzhugh.

Births.

William, son of John and Barbara Fitzhugh, April 13, 1725.
Thomas, son of Henry and Susanna Fitzhugh, July 16, 1725.
Sarah, daughter of Major John and Anne Barbara Fitzhugh, April 30, 1727.
John, son of Henry and Susanna Fitzhugh, June 14, 1727.
Betty, daughter of Col. Henry and Lucy Fitzhugh, April 20, 1731.
Susannah, daughter of Capt. Henry and Susanna Fitzhugh, Sept., 19, 1732.
Daniel, son of Major John and Anna Barbara Fitzhugh, June 27, 1733.
Anne, daughter of Col. Henry and Lucy Fitzhugh, March 26, 1734.
Elizabeth, daughter of Capt. Henry and Susanna Fitzhugh, Aug., 23, 1736.
Lucy, daughter of Col. Henry and Lucy Fitzhugh, Oct., 26, 1736.
William, son of Col. Henry and Lucy Fitzhugh, Aug., 24, 1741.
George, son of Col. Henry and Sarah Fitzhugh, Jan., 15, 1756.
William Beverley, son of William and Ursula Fitzhugh, March 27, 1756.
Daniel, son of William and Ursula Fitzhugh, March 15, 1758.
Thomas, son of Henry and Sarah Fitzhugh, March 1, 1762.
Nicholas Battaile, son of Henry and Sarah Fitzhugh, May 10, 1764.
Theodorick, son of William and Ursula Fitzhugh, July 20, 1760.
Philip, son of William and Ursula Fitzhugh, May 4, 1766.

Deaths.

Major John Fitzhugh, Jan., 21, 1733.
Anne, daughter of Col. Henry Fitzhugh, Oct., 7, 1739.
Col. Henry Fitzhugh, Dec., 6, 1743.

Marriages.

Nathaniel Gray and Elizabeth Fitzhugh, Aug., 12, 1734.
Edward Barradoll and Sarah Fitzhugh, Jan., 5, 1735/6.
Rev. William McKay, Rector of Hanover Parish, and Barbara Fitzhugh, Feb., 6, 1739.
The Rev. Mr. Robert Rose of St. Anne's Parish and Anne Fitzhugh, Nov., 6, 1740.
William Allison and Anne Fitzhugh, Nov., 21, 1740.
Francis Thornton and Sarah Fitzhugh, April 2, 1747.
Benjamin Grymes and Betty Fitzhugh, Feb. 12., 1747.
Thomas Fitzhugh and Sarah Stuart, June 19, 1749.

William Thornton and Elizabeth Fitzhugh, April, 26, 1757.
John Fitzhugh and Elizabeth Harrison, Jan., 31, 1760.
Anthony Thornton and Susanna Fitzhugh, Jan., 5, 1764.
Henry Fitzhugh and Elizabeth Stith, Oct., 28, 1770.
Daniel Fitzhugh and Susanna Potter, Oct., 24, 1770.
Theodorick Bland and Sarah Fitzhugh, Dec., 5, 1772.
Henry Fitzhugh and Elizabeth Fitzhugh, Nov., 24, 1777.
Alexander Campbell and Lucy Fitzhugh, Dec., 3, 1788.
Rice Wingfield Hooe and Susannah Fitzhugh, May 13, 1790.
Henry Dade Hooe and Jane Fitzhugh, June 17, 1790.

Washington.

Births.

Mary, daughter of John and Mary Washington, Feb., 28, 1726.
Nathaniel, son of Henry and Mary Washington, Jan., 16, 1726.
Susanna, daughter of Townshend and Elizabeth Washington, Nov., 3, 1727.
Lawrence, son of John and Mary Washington, March 31, 1728.
Anne, daughter of John Washington and Mary, 1723.
Thomas, son of Townshend and Elizabeth Washington, March 24, 1731.
Bailey, son of Henry and Mary Washington, Sept., 10, 1731.
Frances, daughter of John and Mary Washington, Oct., 20, 1731.
Townshend, son of Townshend and Elizabeth Washington, Sept., 21, 1733.
John, son of John and Mary Washington, Aug., 10, 1734.
Townshend, son of Townshend and Elizabeth Washington, Feb., 25, 1736.
Lund, son of Townshend and Elizabeth Washington, Oct., 21, 1737.
Elizabeth, daughter of Capt. John and Mary Washington, Dec., 21, 1737.
John and Lawrence, sons of Townshend and Elizabeth Washington, March 14, 1740.
Katherine, daughter of Capt. John and Mary Washington, Jan., 13, 1741.
Henry, son of Townshend and Elizabeth Washington, Aug., 29, 1742.
Sarah, daughter of Capt. John and Mary Washington, Oct., 28, 1742.
Lawrence, son of Henry and Elizabeth Washington, Feb., 10, 1744.
William, son of John and Margaret Washington, Dec., 9, 1748.
Henry, son of Bailey and Catherine Washington, Dec., 5, 1749.
George, son of Lawrence and Elizabeth Washington, Jan., 4, 1758.
Thomas, son of Robert and Alice Washington, Sept., 5, 1758.

William Strother, son of Robert and Alice Washington, April 20, 1760.

Henry, son of John and Catherine Washington, Oct., 26, 1760.

Anne, daughter of Robert and Alice Washington, Nov., 10, 1761.

Nathaniel, son of John and Catherine Washington, Oct., 1, 1762.

Mary, daughter of John and Catherine Washington, June 17, 1764.

Townshend, son of Robert and Alice Washington, Feb., 20, 1764.

Ferdinand, son of Samuel and Anne Washington, July 16, 1767.

Frances Townshend, daughter of Lawrence and Elizabeth Washington, Aug., 18, 1767.

Lund, son of Robert and Alice Washington, Sept., 25, 1767.

Deaths.

Mr. Nathaniel Washington, Sept., 15, 1718.

Mrs. Mary Washington, April 21, 1728.

Mary, wife of Mr. Henry Washington, Jan., 19, 1735.

John, son of John and Mary Washington, Feb., 13, 1735/6.

Capt. John Washington, Feb. 27, 1742.

Mr. Townshend Washington, Dec., 31, 1743.

Nathaniel, son of Capt. Henry Washington, Nov., 28, 1745.

Mary Washington, Jr., May 11, 1746.

Mary, widow of Nathaniel Washington, Oct., 23, 1747.

Capt. Henry Washington, Oct., 22, 1748.

Marriages.

Townshend Washington and Elizabeth Lund., Dec., 22, 1726.

John Washington and Margaret Storke, Nov., 23, 1738.

Henry Washington, Jr., and Elizabeth Storke, May 18, 1743.

Langhorne Dade and Mildred Washington, Feb., 14, 1743.

Bailey Washington and Catherine Storke, Jan., 12, 1749.

John Washington and Betty Massey, Nov., 17, 1749.

Lawrence Washington and Elizabeth Dade, July 31, 1751.

Charles Stuart and Frances Washington, Feb., 23, 1751/2.

Thomas Berry and Elizabeth Washington, Nov., 19, 1758.

John Washington and Catherine Washington, Dec., 23, 1759.

Andrew Monroe and Margaret Washington, Dec., 21, 1761.

John Buckner and Elizabeth Washington, Dec., 11, 1760.

Nathaniel Washington and Sarah Hooe, Dec., 17, 1767.

Lawrence Washington and Catherine Foote, Oct., 5, 1774.

Robert Smith and Mary T. Washington, July 29, 1773.

Henry Washington and Mildred Pratt, March 12, 1779.

Thomas Hungerford and Anne Washington, June 22, 1780.

John Stith and Anne Washington, Dec., 11, 1783.

William Thompson and Anne Washington, Aug., 3, 1785.

Thornton Washington and Frances Washington, April 2, 1786.
John Washington and Eleanor Massey, Dec., 24, 1787.
Griffin Stith and Frances Townshend Washington, June 14, 1788.
Nathan Smith and Betsy Washington, April 4, 1790.

Dade.

Births.

Mary, daughter of Henry and Elizabeth Dade, June 11, 1727.
Robert, son of Henry and Elizabeth Dade, May 14, 1731.
Frances Townshend, daughter of Townshend and Elizabeth Dade, Oct., 7, 1732.
Elizabeth, daughter of Townshend and Elizabeth Dade., Oct., 20, 1734.
Cadwallader, son of Townshend and Elizabeth Dade, Dec., 26, 1736.
Francis, son of Baldwin and Sarah Dade, Dec., 29, 1737.
Anne Fowke, daughter of Townshend and Parthenia Dade, Dec., 13, 1737.
Townshend, son of Langhorne and Mildred Dade, Dec., 25, 1743.
Behethland Alexander, daughter of Robert and Elizabeth Dade, Dec., 23, 1745.
Cadwallader, son of Langhorne and Mildred Dade, Jan., 1, 1746.
Sarah, daughter of Baldwin and Linny Dade, Jan., 20, 1747.
Jane, daughter of Langhorne and Mildred Dade, April 2, 1748.
Franky, daughter of Horatio and Mary Dade, Oct., 10, 1753.
Horatio, son of Horatio and Mary Dade, Aug., 25, 1757.
Hannah Gibbons, daughter of Horatio and Mary Dade, July 1, 1759.
Baldwin, son of Baldwin and Verlinda Dade, Feb., 14, 1760.
Townshend, son of Cadwallader and Sarah Dade, Oct., 28, 1760.
Elizabeth, daughter of Baldwin and Verlinda Dade, June 13, 1764.
Townshend, son of Horatio and Mary Dade, June 3, 1766.
Townshend Stuart, son of Townsend and Jane Dade, Aug., 4, 1774.

Deaths.

Jane, daughter of Francis and Jane Dade, May 14, 1718.
Francis Dade, Jr., Dec., 3, 1725.
Behethland Dade, Jan., 29, 1726.
Elizabeth, wife of Henry Dade, March 18, 1733/4.
Elizabeth wife of Townshend Dade, Dec., 30, 1736.
Cadwallader, son of Townshend and Elizabeth Dade, Dec., 30, 1736.
Sarah, wife of Baldwin Dade, Oct., 30, 1739.
Sarah, wife of Cadwallader Dade, Feb., 13, 1744.
Jane, wife of Francis Dade, May 23, 1744.
Jane, daughter of Langhorne Dade, Sept., 28, 1748.

Jane, wife of Townshend Dade and daughter of Rev. William Stuart, and Sarah, his wife, Aug., 10, 1774.

Marriages.

Henry Dade and Elizabeth Massey, July 7, 1726.
Townshend Dade and Parthenia Massey, May 6, 1736.
Baldwin Dade and Sarah Alexander, Aug., 7, 1736.
Robert Dade and Elizabeth Harrison, Jan., 4, 1743.
Langhorne Dade and Mildred Washington, Feb., 14, 1743.
Townshend Dade and Rose Grigsby, Dec., 12, 1745.
Howson Hooe, Jr., and Mary Dade, Sept., 26, 1746.
Horatio Dade and Frances Richards, Oct., 5, 1749.
Robert Yates and Elizabeth Dade, Feb., 17, 1750/1.
Lawrence Washington and Elizabeth Dade, July 31, 1751.
Cadwallader Dade and Sarah Berryman, Aug., 20, 1752.
Horatio Date and Mary Massey, Jan., 14, 1753.
Charles Stuart and Frances Dade, Aug., 6, 1754.
Walter Williamson and Mildred Dade, March 1, 1755.
Francis Peyton and Frances Dade, April 24, 1755.
Nehemiah Rodham Blaxton Mason and Sarah Dade, Feb., 12, 1762.
Townshend Dade and Jane Stuart, Dec., 11, 1769.
Buckner Stith and Anne Dade, Feb., 26, 1770.
Lawrence Taliaferro and Sarah Dade, Feb., 3, 1774.
James Gwatkins and Frances Dade, March 25, 1774.
Robert Yates and Jane Dade, April 11, 1777.
Justinian Birch and Behethland Dade, June 30, 1777.
John Blackston* and Mary Dade., Oct., 10, 1777.
Lawrence Ashton and Hannah Gibbons Dade, Feb., 1, 1779.
Townshend Dade and Elizabeth Dade., Aug., 5, 1782.
James Park and Sarah Dade, March 4, 1796.

---

*Or Blaxton.

EXTRACTS FROM THE REGISTER OF ST. PAUL'S PARISH, FORMERLY IN STAFFORD, BUT NOW IN KING GEORGE COUNTY

By John Bailey Calvert Nicklin

B. Susanna, daughter of Robert and Esther Nash, Aug., 2, 1746.

M. George Nash and Anne White, Jan., 20, 1769.

B. Katherine Naughton, Sept., 3, 1743.

M. Elizabeth Naylor and John Simpson, Aug., 6, 1735.

M. Mary Neale and Benjamin Derrick, Sept., 30, 1729.

M. Sarah Neale and Joshua Sawyer, June 24, 1732.

M. Anne Neaps and William Skinner, Aug., 20, 1767.

M. William Neselton and Hannah Leonard, July 7, 1765.

M. Elizabeth Netherington and William Walker, Nov., 23, 1731.

M. David Nevins and Janet Patterson, June 6, 1759.

B. Mary, daughter of David and Janet Nevins, June 3, 1764.

B. Janet, daughter of David and Janet Nevins, Aug., 27, 1765.

M. David Nevins and Mary Clark, June 28, 1767.

M. James Newman and Sarah Griffith, Dec., 25, 1759.

M. Zachariah Newble and Anne Hammit, Nov., 6, 1779.

M. Elizabeth Newport and Simon Bowling, June 5, 1728.

M. Benjamin Newton and Elizabeth Nicholson, May 6, 1716.

D. Mary Newton, March 25, 1716.

M. Anne Newton and Simon Bowling, Dec., 5, 1722.

M. Elizabeth Newton and Thomas Stribling, Dec., 7, 1725.

M. Sarah Newton and William Higgins, Dec., 9, 1732.

M. Benjamin Newton and Jane Colclough, Oct., 22, 1740.

M. Elizabeth Nicholson and Benjamin Newton, May 6, 1716.

D. Mary Nicholson, May 13, 1722.

B. Lilly, daughter of James and Mary Noldan, March 8, 1759.

M. Margaret Noling and Benjamin Mehorner, April 5, 1778.

M. Thomas Norfolk and Mary Burkett, Sept., 6, 1737.

B. John, son of Thomas and Mary Norfolk, Jan., 4, 1740/1.
M. Thomas Norman and Elizabeth Duncomb, Feb. 21, 1736/7.
M. Anne Norman and Jesse Briant, Jan., 1, 1790.
M. John Norris and Sarah Turner, Aug., 29, 1751.
M. William Norton and Margaret Hamilton, Feb. 26, 1724/5.
D. Margaret Norton, Jan., 29, 1725/6.
B. William, son of Peter and Anne Noshard, May 15, 1758.
M. Peter Nugent and Martha Sill, Feb., 15, 1731/2.
M. John Oakley and Anne Gordon, Feb., 14, 1744/5.
M. William Oakley and Mildred Sullivan, Feb., 4, 1781.
D. John Oliver, March 5, 1715/6.
B. John, son of John and Margaret Oliver, Feb., 15, 1720/1.
B. Elias, son of John and Margaret Oliver, Feb., 19, 1723/4.
D. Nathaniel and John Oliver, children, Nov., 20, 1725.
B. George, son of John and Margaret Oliver, Jan. 29, 1726/7.
D. Sarah Oliver, Jan. 30, 1725/6.
B. George, son of John and Elizabeth Oliver, Jan., 15, 1727/8.
B. Margaret, daughter of John and Margaret Oliver, Jan., 3, 1732/3.
B. John, son of John and Margaret Oliver, Oct., 18, 1735.
B. Mary, daughter of John and Margaret Oliver, April 7, 1738.
D. Mary, daughter of John and Margaret Oliver, May 28, 1741.
B. Rebecca, daughter of John and Margaret Oliver, Sept., 29, 1741.
M. George Oliver and Jemima Regan, Aug., 1, 1745.
M. Margaret Oliver and Nathaniel Hogdon, March 2, 1746/7.
M. Rebecca Oliver and William Mehony, Sept., 15, 1759.
B. John, son of John and Mildred Oliver, July 14, 1760.
B. Elisha, son of John and Mildred Oliver, April 26, 1768.
B. Sarah, daughter of John and Mildred Oliver, Oct., 1, 1772.
M. Nancy Oliver and James Giles, March 24, 1788.
M. Mary Oneal and John Ellis, Sept., 17, 1722.
D. Mary Oneal, Nov., 12, 1730.
B. William, son of Mary Ore, Sept., 2, 1760.
M. Elinor Ormond and John Conali, June 13, 1725.
M. Mary Orr and David Cable, Sept., 7, 1766.
D. Thomas Osburn, Oct., 18, 1728.
B. Frances, daughter of William and Mary Overall, Aug., 22, 1716.
D. Jane, mother of William Overall, April 5, 1718.
M. John Overall and Mary Ellis, Oct., 8, 1722.
D. William Overall, Jan. 17, 1725/6.
B. Sarah, daughter of John and Mary Overall, Feb., 7, 1725/6.
M. Mary Overall and Anthony Kitchen, Aug., 31, 1727.
M. Sarah Overall and John Dagg, Nov., 14, 1729.
B. Mary, daughter of John and Mary Overall, March 19, 1730/1.
M. Elizabeth Overall and John Whitledge, Sept., 15, 1733.
M. Frances Overall and Nathaniel Whitledge, Oct., 27, 1733.

M. Sarah Overall and Joseph Powell, Sept., 21, 1750.
M. Mary Overall and James Bowling, Feb., 11, 1750/1.
M. Behethland Overall and James Cunningham, June 21, 1757.
B. John, son of Susanna Owens, Feb., 13, 1745/6.
M. Susanna Owens and Thomas Timmons, May 14, 1749.
M. Leah Owens and James Monteith, Aug., 3, 1763.
B. Essena, daughter of Aaron Owens, Nov., 30, 1767.
B. William, son of John and Dulcibella Owens, Sept., 21, 1768.
M. Lucinda Owens and Thomas Jett, Jan., 12, 1775.
M. Jane Owens and James Staples, Feb., 12, 1778.
M. Aaron Owens and Catherine Wilson, March 26, 1785.
M. Aaron Owens and Amie Mannard, May 13, 1791.
M. Letty Owens and Eli Mehorner, June 23, 1792.
M. Elizabeth Oxford and Richard Thomison, June 3, 1724.
M. Elizabeth Oxford and Samuel Bowling, Oct., 8, 1731.
B. John, son of Samuel and Mary Oxford, Nov., 3, 1731.
B. Anne, daughter of Samuel and Mary Oxford, Dec., 28, 1733.
B. Elizabeth, daughter of Samuel and Mary Oxford, Aug., 7, 1736.
M. Edward Oxives and Eleanor Dunfee, Nov., 27, 1724.
B. Isabel, daughter of John and Mary Palmer, Sept., 12, 1740.
M. Thomas Parcmane and Mary Lacy, Aug., 28, 1751.
M. James Park and Sally Dade, March 4, 1796.
D. John Parsons, Dec., 9, 1732.
M. David Parsons and Elizabeth Jones, Feb., 25, 1759.
M. Janet Patterson and David Nevins, June 6, 1759.
M. John Patton and Martha Payne, April 3, 1746.

Explanation of Abbreviations:

B. Born.
M. Married.
D. Died.

DEATHS IN STAFFORD COUNTY, 1715-1730.

(From the Register of St. Paul's Parish.)

Contributed by John Bailey Calvert Micklin.

Elizabeth Adrington,	1725.
Francis Adrington,	1725.
Helen Aison,	1726.
James Allen,	1720.
Sarah (wife of Archibald) Allen,	1721.
John Allen,	1725.
John Baker,	1728.
William Balltrop,	1719/20.
Thomas Baxter,	1722.
Frances Baxter,	1725/6.
Elizabeth Bennett,	1718.
Sarah Berry,	1729.
John Bingham,	1717.
Behethland (wife of Thomas) Booth,	1728.
Frances Bourn,	1723/4.
John Branson,	1716.
Robert Buckner,	1718.
Elizabeth Buckner,	1725.
William Buckner,	1725.
Martha Bussey,	1725.
Elizabeth (wife of Thomas) Butler,	1727.
Thomas Butler,	1728.
John Calico,	1717.
James (?) Campbell,	1725.

Joseph Carver,	1727.
William Cash,	1720.
John Cash,	1729.
Virgin Cheesman,	1720/1.
Grace Clement,	1727.
Hannah Clift,	1725.
John Coggins,	1717.
Elinor Connor,	1718.
Pelatiah Crafford,	1716.
Mary Crannidge,	1716.
Francis Dade, Jr.,	1725.
Behethland Dade,	1725/6.
Elizabeth Dalby,	1727/8.
Abraham Delander,	1715.
Henry Dennis,	1725.
Frances (wife of Matthew) Derrick,	1725/6.
John Dunkirk,	1726.
Anne Elliott,	1725.
Sarah Ellis,	1725/6.
William Flagg,	1720/1.
Elizabeth Foote,	1725.
William (?) Foote,	1729.
Henry Francomb,	1716.
Elizabeth Francomb,	1727/8.
Anne Garrett,	1722.
James Ginnis,	1718.
Mary Grant,	1728.
Elizabeth Gurley,	1726.
Joseph Hampton,	1725/6.
Rebecca Hannidge,	1720.
John Hawkins,	1717.
Christopher Hawkins,	1721.
Elizabeth Hawkins,	1726.
Col. Rice Hooe,	1726.
Frances (widow of Col. Rice) Hooe,	1726.
Timothy Hughes,	1717.
Catherine (wife of Timothy) Hughes,	1717.
Joseph Humphries,	1725/6.
Katherine Humphries,	1725/6.
William Humston,	1728.
Susanna Hurdly,	1725/6.
Sarah Jameson,	1716.
Robert Johnson,	1718.
Rachel Johnson,	1720.
Margaret Johnson,	1720.
Daniel Johnson,	1720/1.

Mary Johnson,	1725/6.
George Johnson,	1726.
Thomas Johnson,	1727.
John Jones,	1725/6.
William Joy,	1718.
Lionel Kelly,	1717.
Sarah Kelly,	1718.
Wilford Kelly,	1728.
John Kidwell,	1725.
William King,	1726.
Thomas Kitchen,	1715/6.
William Knight,	1716.
Lucia (Judith?) Lacy,	1725.
Henry Lavine,	1725.
John Lenpy,	1717.
Mary Leonard,	1717.
William Lowell,	1725.
Frances Lund,	1716.
Robert McCarty,	1725/6.
Daniel McGill,	1725.
Sarah McKay,	1720.
Sarah Mealy,	1718.
Elizabeth Mealy,	1725.
Catherine Moss,	1716.
Robert Moss,	1720.

(To Be Continued)

DEATHS IN STAFFORD COUNTY, 1715-1730.
(From the Register of St. Paul's Parish.)
Contributed by John Bailey Calvert Nicklin.

Frances Moss,	1729.
Mary Newton,	1716.
Mary Nicholson,	1722.
Mary Norton,	1725/6.
John Oliver,	1715/6.
Sarah Oliver,	1725/6.
Jane Overall,	1718.
Richard Payne,	1721.
Anne Porter,	1727.
Richard Powell,	1725/6.
Elizabeth Power,	1725.
Thomasin Prestridge,	1725.
Pemberton Proudlove,	1725.
James Ranton,	1717.
Mathew Regan,	1716.
John Robinson,	1725.
Elizabeth Ross,	1718.
Hugh Ross,	1720.
Alexander Ross,	1728.
Isaac Seaton,	1725.
Thomas Sharpe,	1726.
Sarah Smith,	1720.
Mathew Smith,	1725.
Margaret Smith,	1728.
George Spiller,	1718.
Catherine Stone,	1725/6.
Mary (wife of George) Stone,	1726/7.
Elizabeth Stribling,	1728.
Joel Stripling,	1718.
Martha Sutton,	1725.
Robert Taliaferro,	1726.
Mary Taylor,	1726.
Susanna (wife of Henry) Tennyson,	1720.
William Thompson,	1725.
Edward Thompson,	1728.
Richard Thornberry,	1716.
Ralph Walker,	1716.
Alexander Ware,	1716.
Nathaniel Washington,	1718.
Mary Washington,	1721.

Mary Washington,	1729.
Samuel Wells,	1716.
Joseph Wells,	1716.
Elinor Wells,	1729.
Sarah Whiting,	1723/4.
Isaac Whiting,	1725.
Henry Widgeon,	1725/6.
William Wilford,	1726.
Sarah (wife of Thomas) Williams,	1718.
Jacob Williams,	1723.
Helen (wife of Thomas?) Williams,	1725.
Richard Wood,	1729.
Margaret Wooten,	1725/6.
Mottram Wright,	1729.

Extracts from the Register of St. Paul's Parish, Stafford (now King George) County, Virginia.

[The old register of St. Paul's parish is now in the possession of Mrs. Stuart of "Cedar Grove," King George county, an inheritance from her two ancestors Reverends David and William Stuart, who were ministers of the parish. Thanks are due to her for permission to copy.

By an act passed October, 1776, the boundaries of King George and Stafford were altered and a line run from Muddy Creek on the Rappahannock to the mouth of Potomac Creek was made the division. Prior to this act the portion of the present counties lying on the Potomac formed Stafford county, and that on the Rappahannock formed King George.

In the extracts here given B = born; M = married; D = died.]

B. Rice, son Rice and Frances Hooe,	March 14, 1725
B. William, son John and Barbara Fitzhugh,	April 13, 1725
B. Thomas, son Henry and Susanna Fitzhugh,	July 6, 1725
B. Nathaniel, son Henry and Mary Washington,	Jan. 16, 1726
B. Mary, dau. Rev. David and Jane Stuart,	Feb. 24, 1726
B. Mary, dau. John and Mary Washington,	Feb. 28, 1726
B. Sarah, dau. Major John and Anna Barbara Fitzhugh,	April 30, 1727
B. Susanna, dau. Townesend and Elizabeth Washington,	Nov. 3d, 1727
B. Richard, son Rice and Katherine Hooe,	Oct. 15, 1727
B. Anthony, son Anthony and Winifred Thornton,	Nov. 15, 1727
B. Lawrence, son John and Mary Washington,	March 31, 1727–8
B. John, son David and Jane Stuart,	May 10, 1728
D. Richard Foote,	March 21, 1729
D. Elizabeth Foote,	April 1, 1729
D. Elizabeth Buckner,	Nov. 14, 1729
D. Francis Dade, Jr.,	Dec. 3, 1729
D. Wm. Buckner,	Nov. 14, 1729
M. Richd. Taliaferro, of Essex, and Rose Berryman, of King George,	June 10, 1726

M. Henry Dade and Elizabeth Massey, July 7, 1726
M. Richard Foote and Katherine Tasker [? word
uncertain in copy], Oct. 6, 1726
M. John Hooe and Ann Alexander, Nov. 3d, 1726
M. Philip Alexander and Sarah Hooe, Nov. 11, 1726
M. Richard Bernard and Elizabeth Storke, Aug. 29, 1729
M. Townsend Washington and Elizabeth Lun, Dec. 22, 1726
B. Jane, dau. Francis and Jane Dade, May 14, 1718
D. Frances Hooe, April 26, 1726
D. Behethlen Dade, Jan. 17, 1726
B. Sarah, dau. Rev. David and Jane Stuart, Jan. 6, 1731
B. Thomas, son Townsend and Elizabeth Wash-
ington, March 24, 1731
B. Judith Presley, dau. Anthony and Winifred
Thornton, Oct. 3, 1731
B. Frances, dau. John and Mary Washington, Oct. 20, 1731
B. Elizabeth, dau. Philip and Sarah Alexander, Dec. 24, 1731
B. Susanna, dau. Captain Henry and Susanna
Fitzhugh, Sept. 19, 1732
B. Frances Townsend, dau. Townsend and Eliz-
abeth Dade, Oct. 7, 1732
B. Sarah, dau. Richard and Katherine Foote, Jan. 29, 1732
B. Daniel, son Major John and Ann Barbara Fitz-
hugh, June 27, 1733
B. Townsend, son Townsend and Elizabeth Wash-
ington, Sept. 21, 1733
B. Sarah, dau. Philip and Sarah Alexander, Sept. 30, 1733
B. Gerrard, son John and Anne Hooe, Sept. 14, 1733
B. Frances, dau. Henry Dade, March 12, 1734
B. Anne, dau. Col. Henry and Lucy Fitzhugh, March 26, 1734
B. Peter, son Anthony and Winifred Thornton, March 29, 1734
B. John, son John and Mary Washington, Aug. 10, 1734
B. Richard, son Richard and Elizabeth Bernard, Sept. 20, 1734
B. Elizabeth, dau. Townshend and Elizabeth Dade, Oct. 20, 1734
B. George, son George and Frances Foote, Jan. 20, 1734
B. Seymour, son John and Anne Hooe, June 13, 1735
B. John, son Philip and Sarah Alexander, Nov. 13, 1735
B. George, son Peter and Margaret Hedgman, Dec. 11, 1735
B. John, son Richard and Katherine Foote, Nov. 30, 1735

B. John, son Richard and Elizabeth Bernard,   Dec. 29, 1736

B. Burdet and Baldwine, twin sons of Burdet and
Frances Clifton,   Feb. 3d, 1736

B. Townshend, son Townshend and Elizabeth Washington,   Feb. 25, 1736

B. Elizabeth, dau. Capt. Henry and Susanna Fitzhugh,   Aug. 23, 1736

B. Lucy, dau. Col. Henry and Lucy Fitzhugh,   Oct. 26, 1736

B. Gilson, son George and Frances Foot,   Dec. 3rd, 1736

B. Charles, son John and Susanna Alexander,   July 20, 1737

B. Anne, dau. Burdet and Frances Clifton,   Aug. 24, 1737

B. Lun, son Townshend and Elizabeth Washington,   Oct. 21, 1737

B. John, son John and Anne Hooe,   Dec. 26, 1737

B. Francis, son Baldwin and Sarah Dade,   Dec. 29, 1737

B. Anne Fowke, dau. Townshend and Parthenia
Dade,   Dec. 13, 1737

B. Elizabeth, dau. Capt. John and Mary Washington,   Dec. 21, 1737

B. Henry, son Richard and Katherine Foote,   April 11, 1738

B. Verlinda Howson, dau. Rice and Tobitha
Hooe,   Feb. 28, 1739

B. Anne, dau. John and Anne Hooe,   Dec. 7, 1739

B. John, son John and Susanna Alexander,   Jan. 15, 1739

B. John and Lawrence, twin sons of Townshend
and Elizabeth Washington,   March 14, 1740

B. Sarah, dau. Burdett and Frances Clifton,   April 10, 1740

B. Katherine, dau. Richard and Katherine
Foote,   Nov. 24, 1740

B. Katherine, dau. Capt. John and Mary Washington,   Jan. 30, 1740–41

B. Philip, son Philip and Sarah Alexander,   March 31, 1741

B. William, son Col. Henry and Lucy Fitzhugh,   Aug. 24, 1741

B. Mary Townshend, dau. Rice and Tobitha
Hooe,   Feb. 27, 1741

B. Anne, dau. John and Susanna Alexander,   Feb. 9, 1741–42

B. Sarah, dau. John and Anne Hooe,   March 7, 1742

B. Henry, son Townshend and Elizabeth Washington,   Aug. 27, 1742

B. Sarah, dau. Capt. John and Mary Washington, Oct. 26, 1742

B. Jane and Elizabeth, twin daughters of Burdett
and Frances Clifton,   May 14, 1743

B. —— [illegible], son Richard and Katherine
Foote,   Oct. 3rd, 1743

B. William, son Howson and Anne Hooe,   Sept. 9, 1743

B. Townshend, son Langhorn and Mildred Dade, Dec. 25, 1743

B. Lawrence, son Henry and Elizabeth Washing-
ton,   Feb. 10, 1744

B. Susanna, dau. John and Susanna Alexander, April 12, 1744

B. Cadwallader, son Langhorn and Mildred
Dade,   Jan. 1st, 1746

B. Henry, son Burdett and Grace Clifton,   March 7, 1746

B. Gerrard, son John and Susanna Alexander,   June 13, 1746

B. Sarah, dau. Rice and Tobitha Hooe,   Jan. 20, 1746

B. Robert, son Philip and Sarah Alexander,   Aug. 2, 1746

B. Sarah, dau. Baldwin and Lucy Dade,   Jan. 20, 1747

B. Henry Dade, son Howson and Mary Hooe,   —— 9th, 1747

B. Charles, son Burdet and Grace Clifton,   Dec. 12, 1747

B. Winifred, dau. Anthony and Sarah Thornton, Jan. 14, 1748

B. Jane, dau. Langhorn and Mildred Dade,   April 2, 1748

B. Robert Howson, son Howson and Elizabeth
Hooe,   Nov. 22, 1748

B. William, son John and Margaret Washing-
ton,   Dec. 9, 1748

B. Henry, son Bailey and Catherine Washing-
ton,   Dec. 5, 1749

B. Lucy, dau. Hayward and Sarah Todd,   March 22, 1751

B. Philip, son John and Frances Stuart,   Feb. 18, 1752

B. David, son William and Sarah Stuart,   Aug. 3, 1753

B. John, son Charles and Frances Stuart,   Sept. 22, 1753

B. Franky, dau. Horatio and Mary Dade,   Oct. 15, 1753

B. Benjamin, son Benjamin and Betty Grymes,   Jan. 2, 1756

B. George, son Col. Henry and Sarah Fitzhugh, Jan. 15, 1756

B. William Beverly, son William and Ursula
Fitzhugh,   March 27, 1756

B. Mary Anne, dau. John Hooe, Jr., and Anne
his wife,   Nov. 7, 1756

B. Mary, dau. John and Lucy Alexander,   Nov. 26, 1756

B. John, son John and Frances Stuart,   March 1, 1757

B. George, son Lawrence and Elizabeth Washington,   Jan. 4, 1758

B. Daniel, son Wm. and Ursula Fitzhugh,   March 15, 1758

B. Susanna, dau. Wm. and Susanna Thornton, March 29, 1758

B. Rayley [Raleigh], son Rayley and Susan Chinn,   Jan. 22, 1758

B. John, son Thomas and Ann Clifton,   Feb. 3, 1758

B. John Alexander, son John and Frances Stuart,   April 20, 1758

B. William, son Francis and Sarah Thornton,   May 28, 1758

B. Thomas, son Robert and Alice Washington,   Sept. 5, 1758

B. Parthenia, dau. Anthony and Amy Buckner,   Oct. 14, 1758

B. Elizabeth, dau. Charles and Frances Stuart,   Nov. 15, 1758

B. Sarah, dau. John and Lucy Alexander,   Nov. 17, 1758

B. Hannah Gibbons, dau. Horatio and Mary Dade, July 1, 1759

B. Wm. Strother, son Robert and Alice Washington,   April 20, 1760

B. Theoderick, son William and Ursula Fitzhugh,   July 20, 1760

B. Philip Thornton, son John and Lucy Alexander,   Oct. 14, 1760

B. Townshend, son Cadwallader and Sarah Dade, Oct. 28, 1760

B. Henry, son John and Catherine Washington,   Oct. 26, 1760

B. Mary, dau. Charles and Frances Stuart,   Dec. 22, 1760

B. Philip, son John and Frances Stuart,   Feb. 22, 1761

B. Ann, dau. Robert and Alice Washington,   Nov. 10, 1768

B. Thomas, son Henry and Sarah Fitzhugh,   March, 1762

B. Frances, dau. John and Lucy Alexander,   Aug. 24, 1762

B. Charles, son John and Frances Stuart,   Aug. 23, 1763

B. Elizabeth, dau. Baldwin and Verlinda Dade,   June 13, 1764

B. Nicholas Battaile, son Henry and Sarah Fitzhugh,   May 10, 1764

B. Alice, dau. John and Lucy Alexander,   June 10, 1764

B. Nathaniel, son John and Catherine Washington,   Oct., 1762

B. Mary, dau. John and Catherine Washington, June 17, 1764

B. Rice, son Richard and Ann Hooe,   June 25, 1764

B. Townshend, son Robert and Alice Washington,   Feb. 20, 1764

B. Townshend, son Horatio and Mary Dade,   Dec. 3, 1766
B. Frances Townshend, dau. Lawrence and Mary
   Washington,   Aug. 18, 1767
B. Lund, son Richard and Alice Washington,   Sept. 25, 1767
B. Wm. Thornton, son John and Lucy Alex-
   ander,   June 21, 1768
B. Sarah Barnes, dau. Gerrard and Sarah Hooe,   June 5, 1769
M. George Foote, of this parish, and Frances
   Berryman, of Washington parish,   Dec. 3, 1731
M. Burdet Clifton and Francis Hill,   July 15, 1732
M. Charles Ashton, of Washington parish, and
   Sarah Butler, of this parish,   Sept. 22, 1733
M. Edward Barradall and Sarah Fitzhugh,   Jan. 5, 1735-6
M. John Washington and Margaret Storke,   Nov. 23, 1738
M. Benj. Newton, of Hamilton parish, and Jane
   Colclough,   Oct. 22, 1740
M. Robert Dade and Elizabeth Harrison,   Jan. 4, 1743
M. Henry Washington, Jr., and Elizabeth Storke, May 18, 1743
M. Langhorn Dade and Mildred Washington,   Feb. 14, 1743
M. Burdet Clifton and Grace Seaton,   May 18, 1745
M. Benjamin Grymes and Betty Fitzhugh,   Feb. 12, 1747
M. Francis Thornton and Sarah Fitzhugh,   April 2, 1747
M. Henry Ashton and Jane Alexander,   Feb. 1, 1748
M. Bailey Washington and Catherine Storke,   Jan. 12, 1749
M. Horatio Dade and Frances Richards,   Oct. 5, 1749
M. John Washington and Betty Massey,   Nov. 17. 1749
M. John Stuart and Frances Alexander,   Feb. 16, 1749
M. Thomas Fitzhugh and Sarah Stuart,   June 19, 1749
M. William Stuart and Sarah Foote,   Nov. 26, 1750
M. Lawrence Washington and Elizabeth Dade,   July 31, 1751
M. Charles Stuart and Frances Washington,   Feb. 23, 1752
M. Charles Stuart, of King George county, and
   Susanna Grigsby,   1752 or 1753
M. Horatio Dade and Mary Massey,   Jan. 14, 1753
M. Charles Stuart and Frances Dade,   Aug. 6, 1754
M. John Hooe and Ann Fowke,   March 14, 1755
M. William Thornton and Elizabeth Fitzhugh,   April 26, 1757
M. John Washington and Catherine Washington, Dec. 23, 1759
M. John Fitzhugh and Elizabeth Harrison,   Jan. 3, 1760

M. Daniel McCarty and Mary [Mercer, Monroe or Muse—copy illegible],	April 3, 1764
M. Daniel McCarty and Winifred Thornton,	Jan. 15, 1765
M. John Ashton and Elizabeth Jones [?],	May 16, 1766
M. Nathaniel Washington and Sarah Hooe,	Dec. 17, 1767
M. Henry Fitzhugh and Elizabeth Stith,	Oct. 28, 1770
M. George Thornton and Mary Alexander,	Oct. 9, 1773

EPITAPHS AT "SALISBURY," KING GEORGE COUNTY.

Near the entrance gate of " Cedar Grove," the well known estate of the Stuart family in King George county, lie several heavy but broken slabs, marking the family burying ground of the Alexanders, of "Salisbury," an estate now included in " Cedar Grove." The former site of the house can still be seen at a point not far from the graveyard, and from it a beautiful view of the Potomac is visible.

The epitaphs are as follows:

In Memory ot
Philip Alexander
Who departed this life August
the 10, 1733 in the 13 Year of his Age.
He was Son of
Philip Alexander, Gent.
& Mrs. Sarah Alexander.

Here lies the Body of
Philip Alexander, Gent.
of Stafford County who departed
this Life on Friday the 19th
of July 1753 and in the 49th
Year of his Age.

Here lies the Body of
Sarah Alexander
Wife of
Philip Alexander
Daughter of Rice Hooe &
Frances his Wife
She departed this Life on
the 14 day of August 1758
In the 50th Year of her Age.

EPITAPH OF GEORGE.BRAXTON, at Mattapony Church, King and Queen county:

"Here lies the Body
of George Braxton Esq.
who Departed this Life
the first Day of July 1748
in the 71st Year of his Age
leaving Issue a Son & two Daughters.
He died much lamented
being a good Christian, tender Parent
a kind Master and [illegible] Charitable
Neighbor."

[This, the first of his name in Virginia, first appears among the fragments of the records of King William county in 1703, when he signed a power of attorney as "George Braxton, of Virginia, merchant." Later he is styled Colonel George Braxton. He was a member of the House of Burgesses for King and Queen 1718, 1723 and probably other years. One of his daughters was Elizabeth, who married —— Brooke, and was mother of George Brooke, of "Mantapike," King William county, colonel in the Revolution and Treasurer of Virginia. The son was George Braxton, Jr., who was a member of the House of Burgesses for King William in 1748, and for King and Queen in 1758 and 1761, in which latter year the House ordered a new election to fill the vacancy caused by his death. He married Mary (daughter of Robert Carter, of "Corotoman"), whose tomb is also at Mattapony Church, and was the father of George Braxton and Carter Braxton, the signer of the Declaration of Independence.

Mattapony Church, an old Colonial parish church, is a large cruciform building, and is in perfect preservation.]

TOMBSTONE OF PHILIP ROOTES OF ROSEWALL.

By Rev. Arthur Gray, *West Point, Va.*

Malcolm Harris, M. D., and the writer, have made many interesting discoveries in the course of their studies in the territory originally comprising the "Old *New Kent*". The most valuable finds have been numbers of old papers dating from Colonial times, and many old tombstones, the location of which has not been known to historians.

Among the latter is the tombstone of Philip Rootes of "Rosewall". It reads as follows:

> Underneath this stone
> Lies the Body of
> Philip Rootes
> obiit August the 17, 1757
> Aged 63

Rosewall was situated about two miles above West Point on the Mattaponi river in King and Queen County. It was one of the many fine old mansions existing in this territory. Both Bishop Meade and Charles Campbell, the historian, said that this section was not excelled in Virginia for its wealth and culture, and the magnificence of the homes of many distinguished people.

Of the Rootes family, it is recorded that a dancing master was employed for the daughters. There are traces today of the private race track on the plantation. The Rootes's were known to have kept a fine string of race horses. Such homes as those of the Corbins, the Merediths, the Thorpes, the Robinsons, the Dudleys, the Taliaferro's, the Moores, the Sutherlands, the Fox's, and the Ruffins were a short distance up and down the river.

Today the neck of land between the two creeks where Rosewall was situated is entirely deserted. For many years the only activity in this neck has been the cutting of timber. During the last four or five years even that has not been done, and the roads into the place have so grown up that it is almost impossible to reach the site of the old home except by water. A hole in the ground represents the old cellar, and a few bricks of the foundations may still be seen.

About a hundred yards up the river from the site of the Mansion are traces of an old cemetery. By prodding here, in April of this year (1933), we came upon the above tombstone, broken in two pieces. These were dug from underneath the surface of the ground. No inscription at all was visible at first, but on turning over one fragment there was found to be a very clear inscription, as recorded above. The date "1757" and the age "63" are unmistakable. We made a second visit to this tomb to verify the figures. The date upon the stone is slightly at variance with records that have come down to us from that period.

EPITAPH OF COL. JOHN CARTER, CHRIST CHURCH, LANCASTER CO., VA.

"Here lyeth buried y'e body of John
Carter Esq'r who died y'e 10'th Day of Jan.
Anno Domini 1669 & also Jane y'e
Daughter of Mr Morgan Glyn & George
her son & Eleanor Carter
& Ann y'e daughter of Mr Cleve
Carter & Sarah y'e Daughter of Mr
Gabriel Ludlowe & Sarah her Daughter
which ware all his wives suc-
sively & dyed before him.
Blessed are y'e dead, which die in y'e Lord"

HEALE EPITAPHS AT "PEACH HILL", LANCASTER CO., VA.

Here lyes intered the body of
Joseph Heale Gent.
He was 3d Son of George Heale,
Dec. and Ellen, his wife.
He departed this life ye 6 day
of August 1741.
Left a wife, but no children.
Born ye 8th day of
February 1681.

Here lyes intered the body of
John Heale Gent.
Who departed this life ye 20
day of December 1737.
In ye 59 year of his age.
He was the 2nd Son of
George Heale Gen. Decd
and Ellen his wife.
He died a Bachelor.
Observe the patient man, and see
The end of such, as upright be,
Because on God they will depend
Their troubled days in Peace shall end.

TOMBSTONE INSCRIPTIONS FROM THE FAMILY CEMETERY AT "JERDONE CASTLE," LOUISA COUNTY, VIRGINIA

Copied by GEORGE H. S. KING

Here lies the body of Francis Jerdone who was born in the Town of Jedbury in County of Tiviotdale in Scotland, Jan. 30, 1720. Died August 5, 1771.

Sarah Jerdone wife of Francis Jerdone, born March 10, 1731[1] Died October 23, 1818.

Here lies the body of Francis Jerdone Born in County of Louisa February 9, A.D. 1756 Died April 29, 1841.

Here lies the body of[2] Mary Jerdone wife of Francis Jerdone Born December 2, 1771 in the County of Louisa Died March 12, 1821.

Here lies the body of Jemima Byars who was born Sept. 12, 1767 in the County of Louisa Died August 16, 1824.

Here lies the body of James Jerdone son of Francis Jerdone and grandson of Francis Jerdone Born Feb. 19, 1812 in County of Louisa Died July 25, 1827.

Virginia Infant daughter of Garland & Sarah Jerdone Thompson Born February 29, 1820 Died July 17, 1826.

John Jerdone son of John & Barbara Jerdone Born Jan. 15, 1835 Died July 29, 1839.

Isabella Mitchell Born Sept. 30, 1761 Died April 8, 1825.

Sacred to the Memory of Maria Ann Glanville[3] wife of William Jerdone Born in County of Spotsylvania December 20, A.D. 1812 Died Dec. 25, A.D. 1833.

---

[1]The Jerdone Bible cited in *William and Mary Quarterly*, 1st ser., VI, 35, 37 says Sarah (Macon) Jerdone was born February 21, 1731/32 and married February 10, 1753 (new style), Francis Jerdone. *

[2]Mary, wife of Francis Jerdone (Junior), was nee Byars (*W.&M. Quart.*, 1st ser., VI, 38). Jemima Byars (1767-1824) was doubtless her sister. *

[3]Maria Ann Glanville (Coleman) Jerdone was the daughter of William Baptist Burwell Coleman,, Sr. (1776-1827), of Spotsylvania County and his wife Matilda Baptist (1780-1825). Their handsome tombstones are in a Coleman family cemetery in Spotsylvania County, Virginia.

*For pp. 35, 37 & 38 see *Genealogies of Virginia Families: From the William and Mary College Quarterly Historical Magazine* (Baltimore: Genealogical Publishing Co., Inc., 1982), Vol. III, pp. 163-164.

My Mother Sarah Jerdone wife of General C. G. Coleman Born Feb. 10, 1808 Died Feb. 15, 1863.

Sacred to the Memory of Mary Baptist second daughter of William Burwell and Matilda Coleman and consort of John N. Moss of Louisa County. She was born in Spotsylvania County on October 21, 1809 and Died October 22, 1842.

Sarah J. Thompson Born Sept. 23, 1785 Died Nov. 15, 1831.

Here lies the body of Garland Thompson[4] Born in County of Hanover, Feb. 22, 1787 Died in City of Richmond, May 10, 1835 Aged 48 years, 2 months and 16 days. This stone is erected to his memory by his surviving children. He had many virtues, few faults & No Enemy.

Francis William Thompson Born Feb. 25, 1819 and Died 13 August following. Of Such is the Kingdom of God.

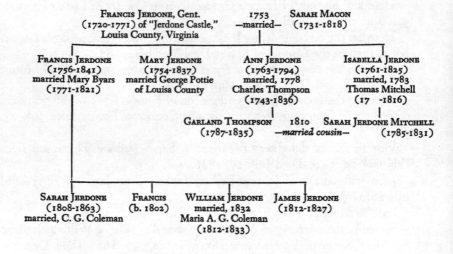

FRANCIS JERDONE, Gent.   1753   SARAH MACON
(1720-1771) of "Jerdone Castle,"   —married—   (1731-1818)
Louisa County, Virginia

FRANCIS JERDONE   MARY JERDONE   ANN JERDONE   ISABELLA JERDONE
(1756-1841)   (1754-1837)   (1763-1794)   (1761-1825)
married Mary Byars   married George Pottie   married, 1778   married, 1783
(1771-1821)   of Louisa County   Charles Thompson   Thomas Mitchell
   (1743-1836)   (17 -1816)

GARLAND THOMPSON   1810   SARAH JERDONE MITCHELL
(1787-1835)   —married cousin—   (1785-1831)

SARAH JERDONE   FRANCIS   WILLIAM JERDONE   JAMES JERDONE
(1808-1863)   (b. 1802)   married, 1832   (1812-1827)
married, C. G. Coleman   Maria A. G. Coleman
   (1812-1833)

[4]Garland Thompson (1787-1835) married November 7, 1810, in Louisa County, Sarah Jerdone Mitchell (1785-1831), who was his first cousin. He was the son of Charles Thompson, Esq. (1743-1836) who married November 19, 1778, in Louisa County, Ann Jerdone (1763-1794). For further account of this Thompson family see: William Ronald Cocke, *Hanover County Chancery Wills and Notes* (Columbia, Va., 1940), p. 140.

TOMBSTONE INSCRIPTIONS FROM THE FAMILY CEMETERY OF THE POTTIE FAMILY IN LOUISA COUNTY, VIRGINIA

Copied by GEORGE H. S. KING

Sacred to the Memory of George Pottie who departed this life March 22, 1815 Aged 40 years.

Sacred to the Memory of William Pottie who died June 11, 1820 aged 19 years.

In Memory of George Pottie Born March 7, 1811 Died Jany. 3, 1849.

In Memory of Mary daughter of George & Edith Pottie Born April 2, 1845 Died August 6, 1846.

In Memory of Fannie daughter of George & Edith Pottie Died Nov. 13, 1855 Aged 8 yrs., 1 mo., & 20 days.

In Memory of Isabella Pottie Daughter of George and Edith Pottie 1838-1846.

In Memory of Dr. Charles Pottie who died November 14, 1859 in 54th year of his age.

Sacred to Memory of Sallie Jordan Pottie daughter of George & Edith Pottie Born Feb. 23, 1810 Died March 15, 1858.

Mrs. E. J. Pottie 1817-1890.

Sacred to Memory of Sarah A. Thompson wife to Captain Charles Thompson of Hanover County who died April 5, 1848 Aged 59 yrs., 3 mos., 3 days. Erected by her husband and children.

Sacred to Memory of Mrs. Sarah J. Thompson who died Dec. 31, 1855 in 75th year of her age.

Inscriptions from graves of Waller Holladay and wife, of Louisa county, Virginia.

In memory of
Sarah Holladay
Born 19th April 1800
Died 3rd April 1840

In memory of
Waller Holladay
Born June 15th 1802
Died Oct. 28th, 1858
Aged 56 years
"Blessed are the dead who die in the Lord"

293

TOMBSTONE INSCRIPTIONS FROM THE FAMILY CEMETERY AT "HILTON," MADISON COUNTY, VIRGINIA

Abstracted by MARTHA W. HIDEN

The following condensed inscriptions are from tombstones in the old plantation cemetery at "Hilton," Madison County, Virginia, a few miles north of the town of Orange. This farm was once the home of George Scott.

George Scott born November 30, 1755, died May 13, 1826.

Betsy wife of George Scott born October 27, 1768, died June 26, 1849.

Richard Crittenden Booten born February 3, 1785, died May 13, 1842.

Lucy W. C. (?) wife of R. C. Booten born December 20, 1789, died September 20, 1846.

James W. Booten born March 1, 1815, died September 6, 1889.

Nannie A. Booten born November 3, 1819, died 1850.

Lucetta, wife of George Booten and daughter of Martin Nalle and Eleanor Barbour born 1819, died 1893.

Lucy Scott Booten, daughter of George and Lucetta Booten born January 1, 1849, died July 28, 1859.

Frances W. consort of Dr. George N. Thrift died February 12, 1834, aged 23 years, 3 months, 19 days.

Robert son of Dr. George and Frances Thrift died February 11, 1834, aged 9 months and 4 days.

The following identifications are added. Richard Crittenden Booten was son of William Booten, Jr., of Culpeper and Madison counties and Frances Crittenden his wife. William Booten, Jr., was the son of William Booten who died testate in Culpeper County in 1787, mentioning son William in his will (Culpeper County, Will Book C, p. 231). William Booten married in Middlesex County January 22, 1738, Judith Hill born in Middlesex County June 2, 1719, daughter of William and Frances Hill (*The Parish Register of Christ Church, Middlesex County, Va., from 1653 to 1812* (Richmond, 1897), pp. 103, 170). Frances Crittenden was the daughter of John Crittenden and Ann Rogers. Joseph Rogers died testate in Culpeper County in 1762, mentioning in his will his daughter Ann (Culpeper County, Will Book A, p. 275). The division of his estate (*ibid.*, p. 293) showed she was the wife of John Crittenden. John Crittenden died testate in Culpeper County in 1802 (Culpeper County, Will Book E, p. 1), mentioning in his will daughter Frances and naming William Booten an executor. The late Mrs. Lucio Hill, nee Mary Crittenden Cave, of "Locust Dale," Madison County, Virginia, a great granddaughter of this couple listed the children of William and Frances Booten as follows: 1. Richard Crittenden Booten, oldest child married Lucy Ware Scott; issue among others, George, who married Lucetta Nalle. 2. John Booten married Ann Powell Hill. 3. Sinclair Booten married Mary Field. 4. William Booten married Jane Wood. 5. Henry Booten married Barbara Goodwin. 6. Martha Booten married Milton Kirtley. 7. Frances Booten, youngest child, married .... Lipscomb. Corroboration of Mrs. Hill's data is found in Hopewell L. Rogers, *Some of the Descendants of Giles Rogers* (Louisville, 1940), though he mistakenly lists Barbara Goodwin as Goodman. That he is in error is shown in *William and Mary College Quarterly Historical Magazine*, 1st ser., Vol. VI, No. 2, Supplement, p. 41, where the marriage of Barbara Goodwin to Henry Booten is noted.*Barbara was a descendent of Major James Goodwin of York County, the immigrant, a member of the House of Burgesses, 1657-1658. George was the son of Thomas Scott who died testate in Madison County 1796 (*W.&M. Quart.*, 2nd ser., XIX, 490).**

*See *Genealogies of Virginia Families: From the William and Mary College Quarterly Historical Magazine* (Baltimore: Genealogical Publishing Co., Inc., 1982), Vol. II, p. 458.
**Ibid.*, Vol. IV, p. 360.

THE HEBRON CHURCH BIRTH REGISTER

By Arthur L. Keith

First Installment

Inasmuch as 1940 marks the bicentennial of the building of Hebron Lutheran Church it seems appropriate to publish the following account in commemoration of that event. Hebron Church stands about two and a half miles north of Madison, Virginia. It arose to satisfy the spiritual needs of the German colony of 1717 and its later accretions. From 1717 to 1725 these Germans lived near Germanna in present Spotsylvania County. They migrated to the region between the Robinson and Rapidan Rivers, present Madison County, in 1725. From 1725 to 1740 they apparently had some sort of a church organization and a place of worship, probably on the site of the present building. The present structure, or at least the main part, was erected in the year 1740, as the date, carved in large characters on one of the massive beams, attests. From that time to the present the building has been in continuous use as a place of worship. The formal organization, however, of the congregation certainly goes back to Jan. 1, 1733, on which date the treasurer of the German congregation filed his report. But some sort of an informal organization must have existed as far back as May 13, 1727, for a communion set, consisting of three pieces of pewter, the gift of one Thomas Giffin of London, bears that date. It would certainly require some months for Thomas Giffin of London to learn that there was such a congregation in the wilderness of Virginia, so we may conclude that this organization existed as early as 1726. A petition, apparently belonging to 1776, published in the *Virginia Magazine of History and Biography*, Vol. XVIII, 268, of the descendants of these Germans contains these words: "Soon after they (their ancestors) were gathered to the place where we now live they concluded to build a Church and a School House." It would probably be safe to say that the Germans upon coming to this region in 1725 almost as their first act organized themselves into a church body. It is claimed that the Hebron Church is the oldest Lutheran Church in the United States with an unbroken history.

It is a cause of deep regret that the extant records begin as late as 1750. There must have been earlier records but they have not been preserved. The extant records are found in the Birth Register now kept in the fireproof vault of the clerk of Madison County. The first date in this Register is Aug. 8, 1750 and the latest birth recorded is dated June 18, 1825. Aside from the record of births several .lists of communicants are found. Some late hand has recorded the names of those voting for and against the selling of the glebe lands in 1848.

From 1750 to 1775 the births are arranged under family heads. The date of birth only is given and not the date of the baptism, which probably followed soon after the birth. Beginning with Oct. 20, 1775, probably with a change of pastors, the births are recorded not under family heads but as the children are presented for baptism and in addition the dates of baptism are now first regularly found. This method was followed until 1778. Then comes a period in which the records were kept very carelessly, probably due to the fact that the church was for some years without a regular pastor. The fewness of the recordations as compared with those of preceding years suggests that the births were not regularly recorded. But in 1787 the original method was resumed and the births once more recorded under family heads and quite often, though by no means always, the dates of baptism are given also. At this time in the middle of the present volume the pages begin to be numbered 1 and run on consecutively. Evidently a new hand had begun the task of recording or else two volumes at some later time were bound in one. In the first period (1750-1775) in some instances some later hand has placed under the family heads those births occurring after 1775. The present writer will also add some not so transferred by this later hand, in order to secure completeness. With these exceptions this paper is concerned only with the period 1750-1775.

Regularly there are in this period several sponsors, quite often two males and two females. These sponsors seem to be chosen from the near relatives of the parents. As genealogical clues these names are important though of course they can not be regarded as actual proof. In the period following 1787 very often *Die Eltern* (the parents) are the sole sponsors. This article will use the English equivalents for the Latin and German words of the original record. The German names however will be given in the original spelling, excepting that the German umlaut will be omitted. It will be remembered that the German feminine surnames were usually written with the suffix—*in*. (Thus Peter Klor and his wife Barbara Klorin).

Many of these Germans married into the Garr family and will be found in the *Garr Genealogy,* published in 1894 by John C. Garr. Some of the names will be found in my article in the *William and Mary College Quarterly,* Sec. Ser., Vol. 9, pages 186-200 and 275-290, the subject of which is *Nicholas Yager and Descendants.* * The writer is a descendant of several of these

*See *Genealogies of Virginia Families: From the William and Mary College Quarterly Historical Magazine* (Baltimore: Genealogical Publishing Co., Inc., 1982), Vol. V, pp. 613-643.

German families and through long study has become familiar with relations not obvious to the general reader, and he will add his own comments and references, always in parentheses. Likewise after the mother's name he will add in parentheses her family name, if known, though they are not found thus in the Register.

Parents	Children	Date of Birth	Sponsors
NICHOLAS KRICKLER and MARGARETHA [KAIFER, KAFER, CAFER]	Elizabeth	Aug. 8, 1750	Michael Utz Marie Kaferin Dorothea Klorin
	Aron	July 9, 1756	Michael Kafer Michael Utz Dorothea Klorin
	Margaret	March 8, 1759	Michael Kafer Johannes Klor Susanna Utz Barbara Chelf
	Nicolaus	April 14, 1762	Peter Klor Michael Kafer Susanna Utz Dorothea Klorin
	Susanna	Sept. 13, 1764	Johannes Klor and wife Dorothea Barbara Chelf
	Anna	Dec. 16, 1768	Michael Utz Dorothea Klorin Elizabetha Christlerin
	Abraham	June 3, 1771	Mattias Rausch Johannes Klor Elizabeth Christlerin
	Jacob and Ludwig, died (twins apparently died before being christened.)		

[The name Krickler appears also as Grickler, Crigler, Creagler. Nicholas was the son of Jacob Creagler who died about 1734, leaving widow Susanna and sons Nicholas and Christopher. Margaretha, wife of Nicholas, was the daughter of Michael Kaifer (Kaffer, Cafer, etc) of the 1717 colony. Elizabeth Crigler married Adam Crisler, see Garr Gen. 66. Aron Crigler married Catharine Crisler, see Garr Gen., 67. Margaret Crigler married Benjamin Garr, see Garr Gen., 64. Abraham Crigler married Lydia Carpenter, May 21, 1795. Their children appear later in the Register. *Sponsors:* Michael Kafer is the father of Margaretha (Michael Kafer had no sons). Maria Kaferin is Michael's daughter who later married George Utz. Dorothea

Klorin, wife of Johannes Klor, is also a daughter of Michael Kafer, married to John Klor in 1750 or before].

Parents	Children	Date of Birth	Sponsors
JOHN WEBER and BARBARA [KAIFER, KAFER, CAFER]	Margaret	Dec. 19, 1752	Andreas Zimerman Mathias Weber Susanna Utzin
	Maria	May 3, 1755	Michael Utz Elizabetha Weberin Barbara Zimermanin
	Hanna	Aug. 15, 1757	Andreas Zimerman Mathias Weber Elizabetha Weberin Susanna Utzin
	John	Feb. 10, 1761	Peter Weber Michael Utz Barbara Carpenter Elizabetha Weberin
	Aron	March 6, 1763	Andreas Carpenter Mathias Weber Elizabetha Weberin Susana Utzin

[John Weber, later Weaver, was the son of Peter Weber who died 1763. John Weber's wife Barbara was the daughter of Michael Kaifer. *Sponsors:* Andreas Zimerman married Barbara Weber, sister of John Weber. Apparently he changed his name to Carpenter between 1757 and 1763, the English equivalent of Zimerman. He was the son of John Carpenter who joined the colony in 1721, died 1782. Mathias Weber was the brother of John. Elizabeth Weber was probably the wife of Mathias and the daughter of Mark Finks whose will dated Oct. 17, 1763, probated March 16, 1764, mentions among others his daughter Elizabeth Weaver].

Parents	Children	Date of Birth	Sponsors
CHRISTOPH BLANKENBUCHER and CHRISTINA [FINKS]	Maria	Sept. 29, 1754	Adam Barlow Adam Weyland and wife Elizabeth Jacob Blankenbucher and wife Barbara
	Catherine	Sept. 28, 1759	Adam Weyland Adam Barlow and wife Maria [?] Jacob Blankenbucher and wife Barbara

Parents	Children	Date of Birth	Sponsors
CHRISTOPH BLANKENBUCHER and CHRISTINA [FINKS]	Ephriam	June 29, 1762	Adam Weyland and wife Elizabeth Jacob Blankenbucher Adam Barlow
	Ludwig	Jan. 21, 1765	Adam Weyland and wife Elizabeth Jacob Blankenbucher
	Jonas	June 18, 1776	Adam Weyland and wife Elizabeth Jacob Blankenbucher Adam Barlow
	Margaret	Nov. 13, 1769	Adam Weyland and wife Elizabeth Jacob Blankenbucher Martin Christophers wife Elizabeth [or perhaps Martin Christopher and wife Elizabeth]
	Sara	Nov. 7, 1772	Adam Weyland and wife Elizabeth Jacob Blankenbucher Marg. Schwarbeg [?]
	Elizabetha	June 9, 1775	Adam Weyland Hanna Einsten [?] Jemimah Barlow
	Hanna	May 25, 1778 (christened June 8, 1778)	Jacob Blankenbucher Maria Wayl. ndin Maria Utzin

[Christopher Blankenbaker was the son of Matthias Blankenbaker of the 1717 colony. His wife Christina was the daughter of Mark Finks. See under John Weber. Ludwig (Lewis) Blankenbaker, born 1765, is probably identical with the one of the same name who married Susanna, about 1784, whose twelve children are recorded later in the Register. Jonas Blankenbaker, born 1767, is undoubtedly identical with the one who married Elizabeth Carpenter, 1790, daughter of William and Mary Wilhoit Carpenter. Margaret or Peggy Blankenbaker, born 1769, married Samuel Carpenter. *Sponsors:* Adam Wayland married Elizabeth, daughter of Balthasar Blankenbaker. She died before Apr. 7, 1776, on which date Adam Wayland had wife Maria ———, who is probably the Maria Wayland acting as sponsor in 1778. Jacob Blankenbaker was the son of John Nicolaus Blankenbaker, who died 1743. Jacob Blankenbaker married 1. Thomas, daughter of John Thomas, who on Nov. 20, 1760, made deed of gift to Jacob Blankenbaker, without mention of any daughter's name. She must have died before June 23, 1753, date of will of George Utz, who mentions daughter Barbara Blankenbaker. Jacob probably had issue by his first wife which would furnish the justification for the deed of gift of John Thomas to him. Garr says that Jacob Blankenbaker also married a Weaver but I fail to find the contemporary record to prove this. Martin Christopher married Elizabeth, daughter of Adam Wayland. The frequent appearance of the Barlow name among the sponsors suggests a relationship which has not yet been discovered].

Parents	Children	Date of Birth	Sponsors
GEORGE MILLER and MARY MARGARETHA	Anna Barbara	March 11, 1754	The parents
	Johannes	June 25, 1758	The parents
	Maria Salome	1761	The parents

Parents	Children	Date of Birth	Sponsors
JOHN ZIMMERMAN and SUSANNA	Joshua	Sept. 12, 1771	Wilhelm Zimmerman Daniel Dulp Magdalina Dulphin Barbara Olerin [later, Ayler]
	Ana Madelena	June 12, 1772 [probably error for 1773]	Adam Dulp David Dulp Maria Schneiderin Elizabeth Breilin
	Rebecca	Nov. 7, 1775	Daniel Dulp Rebecca Dulpin Barbara Zimerman
	Simeon	June 10, 1779	Not given.
	Johannes	June 14, 1782	Not given
	Nancy	Feb. 28, 1788	Not given
	Georg	May 9, 1789	Not given
	Hanna	Apr. 14, 1790	Not given

[The last five names are added later probably by someone who wished to make the family record complete. John Zimerman was very probably the son of John Carpenter, son of John Carpenter of 1721. If this ascription is correct John Zimerman was a brother of Michael Zimerman who married Rebecca Delp (Dulp) about 1776 and had nine children whose births are recorded later in the Register. One of these children is Lydia Carpenter, born Sept. 29, 1777, who married Abraham Crigler, 1795. See above under Nicolaus Krickler. There was another John Zimerman who had wife Katharine before Dec. 23, 1771. He was the son of another John Zimerman who married Ursula Blankenbaker before 1743. Joshua Carpenter, probably identical with the Joshua, born 1771, married Sarah Smith in 1790 and appears later in the Register. *Sponsors:* Wilhelm Zimmerman was almost certainly the brother of John, and not his first cousin of the same name. Since this Wilhelm married a Delp later, probably the very Rebecca Dulpin who served as sponsor in 1775, perhaps John's wife Susanna whose family name we do not have was also a Delp. Elizabeth Breilin could have been the wife of Jacob, Peter, or Michael Broyles, who were born Yowell, Blankenbaker, and Klug, respectively, but her sponsorship was due to no relationship that I am aware of. Barbara Zimerman could have been the wife Barbara [nee Weber] of John Carpenter, uncle of this John, or could have been the wife Barbara [nee Kerker] of the John of 1721. She was still living in 1782. If it was the latter Barbara she was acting as sponsor for her great-grandchild].

Parents	Children	Date of Birth	Sponsors
MATHEUS WEBER and ELIZABETHA [FINKS]	Daniel	March 3, 1757	Andreas Zimerman William Zimerman Barbara Weberin Elisabetha Christlerin
	Maria	Nov. 2, 1760	Johannes Weber Michael Zimerman Maria Zimermanin Elizabetha Christlerin
	Ambes	Nov. 2, 1762	Andreas Zimerman Barbara Zimermanin Heinrich Christler Barbara Weberin
	Elizabetha	Nov. 3, 1763	Johannes Weber Wilhelm Zimerman Barbara Zimermanin Elizabeth Christler
	Sara	July 9, 1769	Andreas Zimerman Heinrich Christler Barbara Weberin Maria Zimermanin

Parents	Children	Date of Birth	Sponsors
MATHEUS WEBER and ELIZABETHA [FINKS]	Matheus	Oct. 23, 1772	Johannes Weber William Zimerman Barbara Zimermanin Elisabetha Christlerin
	Margaretha	Dec. 7, 1775	Andreas Zimerman Heinerich Christler Barbara Weberin Maria Zimermanin
	Veronica	Feb. 12, 1780	Johannes Weber Barbara Carpenterin Elizabetha Christlerin William Carpenter

[Matheus Weber was the son of Peter Weaver whose will made about 1760, probated Aug. 18, 1763, mentions sons John Weaver, Matthias Weaver, Peter Weaver, and daughters Barbary Carpenter, Elizabeth Christler, Catharine Weaver, Margaret Weaver, and Hannah Weaver. Lloyd in her *Clasping Hands with Generations Past,* page 46, says that Matthias Weber married Elizabeth, daughter of Christopher Zimmerman. Christopher Zimmerman who made will Nov. 30, 1748, mentions daughter Elizabeth Zimmerman, apparently still unmarried and perhaps eligible to have married Mattheus Weber in 1756 or before. But Mark Finks in his will dated Oct. 17, 1763, mentions daughter Elizabeth Weaver. There appear to have been only two other Weavers at that time, namely, John and Peter Weaver, and neither had wife Elizabeth. So it must have been Matheus Weaver who married Elizabeth Finks. No Finks appears among the sponsors but the name Finks scarcely ever appears in the Register. The name Zimmerman occurs frequently among the above sponsors but not one of them belongs to Christopher Zimmerman's line. Christopher Zimmerman belonged to the 1717 colony. William Carpenter and his younger brother John joined the colony in 1721. William died in 1745 without issue. John is described in the records pertaining to the settlement of his estate as William's only heir. So Christopher could not have been another brother. There probably was, however, some more remote relationship but it has not been discovered. *Sponsors:* Andreas Zimerman had married Barbara, sister of Matheus Weber. John Weber was of course Matheus's brother. Heinrich Christler had married Elizabeth, sister of Matheus Weber. So far as we know, William Zimerman and wife Maria [nee Wilhoit] were not related to either the father or mother. William Zimerman is identical with William Carpenter. Barbara Carpenter's name though anglicized retains the Ger-

303

man suffix—*in*. The many inconsistencies in the writing of these names may be due to the fact that they were written by different hands. The present writer has not tried to remove them].

Parents	Children	Date of Birth	Sponsors
NICOLAUS BROIL and DOROTHEA [CHRISTLER]	Daniel	Aug. 18, 1757	Heinrich Christler Johannes Weyland Maria Zimermanin Magdalina Fischerin
	Elisabetha	May 15, 1760	Heinrich Christler Johannes Weyland Maria Zimermanin Magdalina Fischerin
	Abraham	Sept. 24, 1762	Wilhelm Zimerman Stephan Fischer Elisabetha Christerlin Catharina Weylandin
	Sara	July 21, 1764	Heinrich Christler Johannes Weyland Elisabetha Gaar Elisabetha Wilheitin
	Maria	July 17, 1766	Johannes Weyland Stephan Fischer Maria Zimermanin Elisabetha Christlerin
	Rosina	Oct. 23, 1770	Michael Gaar Catherina Weylandin Maria Zimermanin
	Phebe	July 30, 1773	Heinrich Christler Johannes Weyland Maria Zimermanin Elisabetha Blankenbucherin
	Lea	May 20, 1775	Johannes Weyland Maria Zimermanin Elisabetha Christlerin

[Nicholas Broil, also Breils, Broyles, etc. was the son of Jacob Broyles who came to Virginia with his father John Broil, 1717. A full account of him is found in the writer's unpublished *Broyles Family History*. Nicholas Broyles married Dorothea, daughter of Theobolt or Deobold Christler, who made will Feb. 20, 1776, probated Nov. 18, 1776. Garr in the *Garr Genealogy, 62*, gives his name as Fawatt Crisler and assigns to him children as they appear in the will with the exception that he gives an Andrew Christler, not found in the will or elsewhere so far as I can discover, and strangely omits daughter Dorothy Broyles who is clearly named in the will. Deobold Christler married Rosina Gaar and their descendants appear in the *Garr Genealogy*, excepting the many who descend from Nicholas Broyles and wife Dorothy. Nicholas Broyles certainly had a son Reuben Broyles whose name does not appear in the Register. A series of deeds in Washington Co., Tenn., to which place Nicholas emigrated about 1782, clearly indicates that Reuben Broyles, son of Nicholas, had married Rosina Broyles, born Nov. 19, 1769, daughter of Cyrus Broyles, and said Reuben died before Sept. 19, 1797, leaving widow Rosina and four small daughters. *Sponsors:* Heinrich Christler was brother of Dorothy Broil. Elizabeth Christler was wife of Heinrich. Johannes Weyland had married Catharina Broyles, sister of Nicholas. Wilhelm Zimmerman had married Maria, daughter of Adam Wilhoit by his wife Catharine Broyles, Nicholas's aunt. So Maria Wilhoit Zimmerman was first cousin of Nicholas Broil. Elizabeth, wife of Michael Gaar, stood in the same relationship, for she was also the daughter of Adam Wilhoit. The relation of the Fischers and of Elizabeth Blankenbucherin to the parents, if any, has not been discovered].

Parents	Children	Date of Birth	Sponsors
HEINERICH MILLER and SUSANNA [SIBLER]	Maria	Feb. 7, 1756	The parents
	Sara	Nov. 7, 1757	The parents
	Heinerich	Jan. 4, 1759	The parents
	Johannes	Feb. 5, 1762	Jacob Mayer and wife Mary
	Susanna Catharina	Dec. 4, 1763	Jacob ———?
	George and Mary [twins]	Feb. 6, 1766 [christened] Jan. 17, 1772	Johannes Schwarbach and wife Margaretha George Utz and wife Mary ? or Margaret ? Adam Weyland
	Elisabetha	Dec. 8, 1768	Adam Weyland and wife Elisabetha
	Adam	Feb. 5, 1769	Adam Weyland and wife Elisabetha
	Sophia	Oct. 23, 1771 [christened in Lancaster]	John Aple and his mother Sophia
	Anna	Jan. 27, 1772	Christoph Blanckenbucher and wife Christina Adam Weylandt

[Upon the authority of the Miller family genealogist, Heinerich Miller lived first at Germantown, Penna., then went to Virginia, apparently before 1756, then back to Penna., and later still
to Virginia. The Lancaster at which Sophia was christened probably means Lancaster, Penna. Sophia Miller married Burgess
Rogers, 1792, Culpeper Co., Va. Adam Miller married Mary
Wilhoit, daughter of John Wilhoit, about 1791. See the *Garr
Gen.*, 90. *Sponsors:* No apparent relationships. This is probably
an indication the Millers were late arrivals and came to the
Hebron community already married].

Parents	Children	Date of Birth	Sponsors
MICHAEL YEAGER and ELIZABETHA [MANKSPEIL, MANSPEIL, [ETC.]	Johannes	Nov. 28, 1750	Johannes Weber Peter Klor Dorothea Carpenter
	Samuel	Dec. 28, 1752	Johanes Zimerman Johannes Weber Barbara Chelf
	Barbara	Aug. 13, 1755 [died soon after]	
	Susanna	Jan. 5, 1759	Nicolaus Yeager Susanna Yagerin Susanna Utz
	Eva	March 11, 1760	Nicolaus Yeagei Susanna Utz Barbara Weberin
	Elisabetha	July 15, 1762	Nicolaus Yeager Susanna Yeager Barbara Weberin
	Jemima	Dec. 13, 1765 [?]	Gotfried Yeager Nancy Graves Elis. Bederin
	Michael	Jan. 13, 1768	Philipp Chelf Barbara Chelf Johannes Yeager
	Hanna	Dec. 1, 1770	Philipp Chelf Barbara Weberin
	Rahel	March 10, 1773	Johannes Yeager Maria Yagerin Susanna Yagerin

|Michael Yager was the son of Adam Yager, son of Nicholas Yager, of the 1717 colony. Very little is known of the Manspeil family. They were in the Hebron community as early as 1734. *Sponsors:* Nicholas, Gotfried, and John Yager were brothers of the father, Michael Yager. Susanna Yager, wife of Nicholas, and Maria Yager, wife of John, were the daughters of John Wilhoit. Peter Klor had married Barbara Yager, sister of Michael, about 1747. Peter Clore died 1763 and his widow Barbara married Philip Chelf about a year later. This accounts for the appearance of Philip and Barbara Chelf as sponsors in 1768. But it does not account for the appearance of Barbara Chelf as sponsor in 1752. This fact suggests that the Register as we now have it was not the original form, that at some later date some scribe grouped the various names under family heads, and gave Barbara the name he knew her by at the time of making this arrangement. In other words, Barbara in 1752 was Barbara Klor and not Chelf until some years later. Johannes Weber is the one who married Barbara Kaifer in 1752 or earlier. No relation of either with either of the parents is known. John Carpenter, the second, son of the John Carpenter of 1721, married Dorothea Koch (Cook) before Aug. 15, 1751, on which date Michael Cook sold to "sons-in-law John Carpenter, Jr., and Philip Snyder". This John Carpenter is probably the Johannes Zimerman, sponsor in 1752, while Dorothea Carpenter, sponsor in 1750, is probably his wife, in spite of the inconsistency in the manner of giving the name. Again we know of no relationship with either of the parents. Nancy Graves may have been the German wife of someone of English descent. The name Bederin does not seem to appear again. Since George Utz, the second, had wife Mary, Susanna Utzin should be the wife of his only brother, Michael Utz].

Parents	Children	Date of Birth	Sponsors
CHRISTOPH KRICKLER and CATHERINE [HINKS]	Maria	Sept. 9, 1751	Andreas Carpenter Johannes Weber Dorothea Klor Catharina Weyland
	Ruben	Jan. 28, 1753	Andreas Carpenter Johannes Weber Dorothea Klor
	Jacob	June 27, 1756	Andreas Carpenter Johannes Klor Barbara Weberin
	Elisabetha	July 7, 1759	Johannes Klor Barbara Carpenter Barbara Weberin

Parents	Children	Date of Birth	Sponsors
CHRISTOPH KRICKLER and CATHERINE [FINKS]	Susanna	Jan. 3, 1762	Andreas Carpenter Barbara Weberin Dorothea Klorin
	Ludwig	Oct. 1, 1764	Paul Lether Johannes Klor Dorothea Klorin
	Johannes	June 10, 1767	Andreas Carpenter Johannes Weber Dorothea Klor
	Christoph	Nov. 28, 1769	Johannes Klor Johannes Weber Barbara Carpenter
	Anna	July 6, 1771	Johannes Klor Barbara Carpenter Barbara Weberin
	James	March 23, 1775	Andreas Carpenter Johannes Klor Catharina Klorin
	William	June 28, 1778 [christened July 6, 1778]	Nicolaus Grickler Michael Utz, Jr. Elizabetha Christopherin

[Christopher Krickler was the brother of Nicholas Frickler whose record is the first in the Register, see above. Not even his wife's first name is given in the Register but we know that she was Catharine, daughter of Mark Finks, whose will, 1763-64, mentioned above, names daughter Catharine Crigler. Ludwig (Lewis) Crigler married Ann Carpenter, daughter of Andreas Carpenter. Johannes (John) Crigler married Sallie Hume, 1789. Christopher Crigler married Frances Botts, 1793. Anna Crigler married John Hume, 1792. William Crigler married Kitty Brown, 1803. *Sponsors:* No Finks appears and only one Grickler, namely, Nicolaus, who may have been either the brother of Christopher or Nicolaus's son of the same name. The Klor name predominates, including Paul Lether whose wife was Margaret, sister of John Klor, but whether this was based upon more than a close intimacy is not known. The Crigler and Clore farms were adjacent. Catharina Weyland, nee Broyles, the Carpenters and Weavers were of no known relation to either of the parents].

308

Parents	Children	Date of Birth	Sponsors
PETER KLOR and MARIA [FREY, FRAY]	Hanna	Apr. 17, 1775	Johannes Weber Johannes Becker Hanna Weberin Mary Freyin
	Elizabetha	Dec. 5, 1776 [christened Jan. 12, 1777]	Johannes Becker Rebecca Frehin Hanna Weberin
	Mary	Aug. 24, 1782	John Wever Rebecka Frey Hanna Swindel
	John	Sept. 18, 1784	John Fray John Weeber Hanna Swindel
	Moses	Nov. 11, 1787 [christened Feb. 10, 1788]	Johannes Weber Hanna Schwindel
	Margaret	Oct. 11, 1789 [christened Jan. 3, 1790]	The parents
	Aron	May 17, 1792 [christened May 24, 1792]	The parents

[Peter Clore was the son of George Clore who died before Sept. 19, 1751, son of the emigrant Michael Clore. A straight tradition in the family gives his wife's name as Mary Fray. The same tradition gives the names of two other children whose names do not appear in the Register, probably because their births belong to the period 1776-1782, in which the records were not well kept. These two names were Peter Clore and Ephraim Clore. Peter Clore was born about 1782, [his age given as 68 in the 1850 census]. He never married. Ephraim Clore married Annie [?] Weaver, Dec. 28, 1801 [license], Madison Co., Va. His name appears later in the Register with wife Amy which is probably correct. Hanna Clore, born 1775, married Elias Weaver, Dec. 27, 1793 [license], Madison Co., Va. They appear later in the Register. Moses Clore, born 1787, married Judith Yager, Jan. 19, 1813 [license]. Aaron Clore, born 1792, married Rosannah Crisler, for whom see the *Garr Gen.*, 77, though Garr errs in making Aaron the son of Peter, son of Peter. The second Peter should be George. Margaret (Peggy) Clore married Carder, and not John Deer as the writer erroneously gave it in the *William and Mary College Quar-*

terly, Vol. XXVI, 181. The Margaret Clore who married John Deer was the daughter of Michael Clore. *Sponsors:* John Becker almost certainly married Elizabeth Clore, sister of Peter. [See below under John Becker. Relationship of the others, if any, not known].

Parents	Children	Date of Birth	Sponsors
GEORGE UTZ, JR. and MARGARETHA	Rahel	Aug. 16, 1763	Peter Weber Barbara Carpenter Elisabetha Schwindel
	Johannes	Apr. 14, 1766	Peter Weber Michael Schwindel Barbara Carpenter
	Absalom	May 5, 1768	Peter Weber Andreas Carpenter Catharine Gaarin
	Georg	Nov. 8, 1770	Peter Weber Michael Utz Elizabetha Weberin Elizabetha Schwindel
	Hanna	Apr. 20, 1773	Andreas Carpenter Hanna Schwindelin Elisabetha Schwindel
	Salomon	June 19, 1775	Peter Weber Adam Utz Hanna Schwindel
	Moses	Oct. 17, 1777 [christened Nov. 2, 1777]	Andreas Carpenter Adam Utz Maria Weberin
	Maria Barbara.	Nov. 22, 1782	Adam Utz Barbara Carpenter Maria Weberin
	Maria and Susanna [twins]	June 19, 1790 [christened June 23, 1790]	None given

[Maria Barbara and the twins are found in later pages of the Register but they are described as the children of George Utz and wife Margaret. *Sponsors:* Catharine Gaar, the wife of Louis Garr, see *Garr Gen.,* 64, was the daughter of Peter Weaver who died 1763. Barbara Carpenter, wife of Andreas Carpenter, was also a daughter of the same Peter Weaver. Since the Webers predominate among the sponsors, we may suggest that Margaretha,

310

wife of George Utz, Jr., was the daughter Margaret named in
Peter Weaver's will, 1763. She is eligible as to her age and no
other Margaret Weaver has been found who is eligible].

Parents	Children	Date of Birth	Sponsors
PETER WEBER and MARIA	Elisabetha	Sept. 28, 1762	Georg Utz and wife • Margaret
	Helena	Nov. 4, 1766	Johannes Weber Anna Hoffmanin, Georg Koch's wife Margaret Utzin
	Diana	Nov. 27, 1768	Georg Utz Anna Hoffmanin Catharina Gaarin
	Maria Barbara	Feb. 4, 1770	Andreas Zimerman Maria Barb. Weberin Augnes Hoffmanin
	Elias	Apr. 16, 1773	Johannes Weber Dieterich Hofman Barbara Carpenter
	Moses and Peter [twins]	Dec. 20, 1774	Peter Klor Johannes Schwindel Augnes Hofmanin Margaretha Utzin
	Rosina	Jan. 24, 1777 [christened March 9, 1777]	John Weber Barbara Carpenter Augnes Hoffmanin

---

[The last name is from a later page and there Maria, wife of
Peter Weber, is called a Calvinist. Peter Weber was the son of
the Peter who died 1763. Maria, being a Calvinist, probably belonged to the Calvinistic family of Hoffmans. Moses Weber,
born 1774, married Rosanna Crisler. See *Garr Gen., 77.* Diana
or Dinah, born 1768, married Abraham Gaar. See *Garr Gen., 84.*
Sponsors: The explanation for the Hoffman sponsors has already
been given. The Weber connections are obvious. The appearance of George and Margaret Utz strengthens the conjecture, given
above, that she was the daughter of Peter Weaver. No explanation is known for the appearance of Peter Klor or Johannes
Schwindel. Peter Weaver's will, Mar. 3, 1816, names the above
children with the exception of Helena, and names two others, Amy,
wife of Ephraim Clore, and Anna, wife of ———— Rouse].

Parents	Children	Date of Birth	Sponsors
ZACHARIAS BREIL and DELILA [CLORE]	Benjamin	Apr. 7, 1768	Michael Yager Ziriakus Breil Elisabetha Breilin
	Nimrod	Dec. 19, 1771	Ziriakus Breil Solomon Klor Marg. Schwarbachin Mary Schmidtin
	Zacharias	March 1, 1774	Ziriakus Breil Salomon Clore Marg. Schwarbachin Elisabetha Bohmin
	Elisabetha	Apr. 6, 1776	Adam Clore and wife Ziriakus Breil
	Solomon	June 1, 1778 [christened July 12, 1778]	Herman Wehman Ziriakus Breils Eva Bohmin
	Susanna	May 30, 1783 [christened Aug. 3, 1783]	Herman Waman Susana Yager Margretha Yagerin

[There were at least five other children whose names do not appear in the Register, namely, Barbara, or Barbara Catherine, Anna, Thomas, Judith, and Rhoda Broyles. Since their mother Delila remained for many years a faithful communicant of Hebron Church, the omission of these names seems to be due to some accident. Zacharias Breil (Broyles) was the son of Jacob Broyles, son of John Broyles of the 1717 colony. His wife Delila was the daughter of Peter Clore who died 1763, son of Michael Clore of the 1717 colony. Peter Clore's wife was Barbara Yager, daughter of Adam Yager, son of Nicholas Yager of the 1717 colony. Zacharias Breil had eight brothers all of whom married and left issue. The children of Nicholas and of Peter Breil are found in the Register, and six of Zacharias's children. The other six brothers were Adam, Ziriakus (Cyrus), Michael, Jacob, John, and Matthias Breil, all of whom had families born in this period, most of them large families, but no child of Ziriakus appears in the record, and of Michael, Matthias, John, and Jacob only one each appears. This is the more remarkable for the reason that Adam Breil was a trustee of the church in 1776, and Michael and Matthias Breil had married daughters of the pastor, the Rev. George Samuel Klug. These facts along with many others suggest strongly that the Register as we now have it is incomplete. The writer believes that the losses occurred before 1775. *Sponsors:* Michael Yager was the uncle of Delila. Ziriakuš was the brother of Zacharias. Elisabetha Breilin could have been the wife of Jacob, Peter, or Michael Breil, each of whom had wife Elizabeth. Solomon Clore and Adam Clore were brothers of Delila. Herman Wayman's first wife was Elizabeth Clore, sister of Delila. Susana Yager was the wife of Nicholas Yager, Delila's uncle. Margaretha Yagerin is probably the daughter of Nicholas and Susanna. Marg. Schwarbachin was probably the wife of the new pastor and of no relation to either Zacharias or Delila. The others can not be placed].

(To be Concluded)

THE HEBRON CHURCH BIRTH REGISTER

By ARTHUR L. KEITH

Second and Concluding Installment

Parents	Children	Date of Birth	Sponsors
WILHELM ZIMERMAN and MARIA [WILHOIT]	Barbara	Feb. 25, 1757	Mathias Weber Michl Zimerman Maria Fischerin Dorothea Breilin
	Samuel	March 15, 1759	Stephan Fischer Michl Zimerman Dorothea Breilin Elisabetha Weberin
	Wilhelm	May 20, 1762	Mathias Weber Nicolaus Breil Maria Fischerin Maria Carpenter
	Elisabetha	Oct. 28, 1765	Nicolaus Breil Michael Zimerman Elisabetha Weberin Elisabetha Gaarin
	Maria	Aug. 26, 1768	Michael Gaar Mathias Weber Dorothea Breilin Maria Carpenter
	Anna	Aug. 2, 1771	Mathias Weber Michl Zimerman Dorothea Breilin Elisabetha Gaarin

[Wilhelm Zimerman or William Carpenter was the son of John Carpenter who joined the colony in 1721, died 1782. His wife Mary Wilhite (Wilhoit) was the daughter of Adam Wilhite, died 1763, son of Michael Wilhite. Barbara Carpenter married Moses Broyles, son of Adam. Samuel Carpenter married Dinah Crisler, see *Garr Gen.*, 76. William Carpenter married Mary Aylor and was pastor of Hebron Church from 1789 to 1812. His family record appears later in the Register. Elizabeth Carpenter married Jonas Blankenbaker, son of Christopher Blankenbaker, see above. A partial account of their children appears later in the Register. Mary Carpenter married Lewis Utz and died about 1800. Anna Carpenter married John Adam Yager, son of Adam. *Sponsors:* Michael Zimerman was brother of William. Maria Carpenter, nee Crisler, was wife of Michael, for whom see below.

Nicolaus Breil was first cousin of Mary Wilhite whose mother was
Catharine Broyles. Dorothea Breilin was the wife of Nicolaus.
Michael Gaar married Elizabeth Wilhite, sister of Mary. No rela-
tion is known for Mathias Weber and the Fischers].

Parents	Children	Date of Birth	Sponsors
CHRISTOPH ZIMERMAN and MARIA [GERBER, TANNER]	Susana	May 7, 1769	Jacob Gerber Elisabetha Holtzklauin Mary Bohannon
	Josua	Aug. 22, 1771	Joseph Holtzklau Jacob Holtzclau Mary Bohannon
	Elisabetha	Nov. 1, 1773	Jacob Gerber Dorothea Gerberin Elisab. Holtzklauin
	Friederich	Nov. 30, 1775 (christened Jan. 6, 1776)	Jacob Gerber Friederich Gerber Elisabetha Holtzklauin
	Maria	Apr. 4, 1778 (christened May 10, 1778)	Friederich Tanner Delila Tanner Elisabetha Holtzklauin
	Nancy	Jan. 14, 1780	Friederich Tana Dorothea Tana
	Margaretha	Aug. 1, 1782	Friederich Tana Dorothea Borderin Elizabeth Holzclau
	Lea	Apr. 16, 1786	Friederich Gerber and his wife Maria Lipin
	Milly	June 14, 1788	Friederich Gerber and his wife Elizabeth Holtzclau

[Christopher Zimmerman was not the brother of Wilhelm
Zimerman though his name follows Wilhelm's in the Register.
There was no known relation between them. Christopher was the
son of John, son of Christopher Zimmerman of the 1717 colony.
Christopher Zimerman's line did not change the name to Carpen-
ter, so far as known. John Zimerman, son of the emigrant
Christopher, married Ursula, daughter of John Nicolaus Blank-
enbaker, before 1743. Mary Gerber (Tanner is the English for
Gerber) was the daughter of Christopher Gerber and wife Eliza-

beth Ayler (Ohler in the German with the umlaut O). Frederick Zimerman, born 1775, married Rosannah Crigler. See *Garr Gen.*, 81. Mary Zimmerman, born 1778, married Lewis Crisler (as his second wife). See *Garr Gen.*, 79. Lea (Leana) Zimerman, born 1786, married John Crisler. See *Garr Gen.*, 80. *Sponsors:* Jacob Gerber was the brother of Maria Zimerman. Dorothy Gerberin was probably the wife of Jacob and sister of Christopher Zimerman. Dorothea Borderin, nee Gerber, was sister of Maria Zimerman, and the wife of Richard Burdine. Friederich Gerber (Tanner, Tana) was brother of Maria. Jacob Holtzklau's wife Elizabeth was a sister of Christopher Zimerman. Mary Bohannon with a non-German name may have been of no relationship].

Parents	Children	Date of Birth	Sponsors
JOHANNES BECKER and ELISABETHA	Jesse	June 6, 1769	Peter Klor Fried. Baumgartner Maria Weberin
	Elisabetha	Sept. 20, 1771	Peter Klor Elisabetha Kassel Maria Kasselin
	Aron	Feb. 5, 1774	Peter Klor Michael Klor Maria Weberin
	Abraham	July 21, 1776 (christened Aug. 25, 1776)	Samuel Rausch Maria Klorin Margaretha Klorin

[Elizabeth, wife of John Becker, was probably the daughter of George Clore, who died 1751, leaving three small children, namely, Michael, Peter, and Elizabeth. Elizabeth would be eligible to marry John Becker about 1768. On this basis we have a plausible explanation for the Clores who serve as sponsors. John Becker was sponsor for two of the children of Peter Clore, and John Becker and wife Elizabeth were sponsors several times for the children of Michael Clore, see below. *Sponsors:* Peter Klor was probably the brother of Elizabeth. Maria Clore was wife of the same Peter. Michael Clore was either brother or first cousin of Elizabeth Becker. Margaretha Clore was wife either of John Clore or Michael Clore, sons of John Clore, Sr., both of whom married women named Margaret].

Parents	Children	Date of Birth	Sponsors
CONRAD KUNZLE and RAHEL	Elisabetha	Nov. 2, 1773	Johannes Schmidt Elisabetha Schmidtin Heinrich Berler Jemimy Berlerin
	Nimrod	Dec. 18, 1775	Georg Christler Anna Christlerin Heinrich Berler Jemimy Berlerin
	Ambrosius	Feb. 13, 1778 (christened Apr. 5, 1778)	Georg Christler Dieterich Hoffman Lea Berlerin Susanna Ohlerin
	Josua	Oct. 18, 1780	None given
	Adam	Feb. 2, 1783	None given
	Nancy	Nov. 22, 1785	None given
	Ruben	March 4, 1789	None given
	Aaron	Jan. 4, 1792	None given
	Peggy	Dec. 20, 1794	None given

[The name Kunzle (with the German umlaut) appears also as Kuntzler and Genszle. *Sponsors:* Johannes Schmidt, who married Elizabeth ————, was the son of John Michael Schmidt and wife Anna Magdaline Tommas (Thomas), son of Michael Schmidt of the 1717 colony. George (John George) Christler had married Anna (Anna Magdalene) Schmidt, daughter of John Michael Schmidt. The record of John Georg Christler and wife Anna Magdalene will be given below where Rahel Kuntzler will appear once as sponsor. John Michael Schmidt also had a daughter Elizabeth who married Adam Berler (Barlow) but this will not explain the appearance of Heinrich Berler, Jemimy and Lea Berlerin as sponsors. John Michael Schmidt apparently had no daughter Rachel (Rahel). John Michael Schmidt was the only child of his father].

Parents	Children	Date of Birth	Sponsors
GEORG KOCH and MARIA SARA REINER	Maria Barbara	Sept. 24, 1751	Christian Reiner Philipp Schneider Magdalina Schmidtin Maria Kochin

Parents	Children	Date of Birth	Sponsors
GEORG KOCH and MARIA SARA REINER	Margaretha	Dec. 14, 1753	Nicolaus Schmid Matheus Schmid Margaretha Schneiderin Elisabeth Reinerin
	Magdalina	March 20, 1756	Matheus Schmid Magdalina Schmidtin Margaretha Schneiderin
	Elisabeth	March 7, 1758	Nicolaus Schmid Christian Reiner Marg. Schneiderin Maria Schmidtin
	Dorothea	Aug. 30, 1762	Christian Reiner Maria Kochin Margaretha Schneiderin Elisabetha Reinerin
	Dina, died		
GEORG KOCH and ANNA MARIA born HOFFMAN of the Reformed Religion	Ludwig	Nov. 7, 1772 (?)	Christian Reiner Nicolaus Schmidt Marg. Schneiderin Elisabetha Reinerin
	Ambrosius	Oct. 14, 1775 (christened Nov. 12, 1775)	Philipp Schneider Magdalina Schmidtin Maria Weberin (Peter Weber's wife)
	Aron	Sept. 11, 1776 (christened Oct. 20, 1776)	Nicolaus Schmid, Sr. Phillip Schneider Maria Weberin
	Sara	Sept. 19, 1777 (christened Nov. 2, 1777)	Peter Weber Magdalina Schmidtin Margaretha Schneiderin
	Cornelius	1782	Peter Weber Barbara Smith

[George Koch (Cook) should be the son of Michael Cook of the 1717 colony. This Michael Cook on Aug. 15, 1751 sold land to "sons-in-law John Carpenter, Jr., and Philip Snyder". Ludwig Koch, born 1772 (?) is probably identical with the Lewis Cooke who married Mary Yager, daughter of Godfrey Yager, Apr. 14, 1793 (license). The *Garr Gen.*, 85, gives an Aaron Cook, born May 20, 1775, who married Leanna Gaar. In spite of the difference in date I regard him as identical with the Aron given above. *Sponsors:* Peter Weber and wife Maria do not appear as sponsors until George Koch had married the second time (to Anna Maria Hoffman). This strengthens my conjecture given above under Peter Weber that his wife was a Hoffman. Phillip Schneider married a daughter of Michael Cook, probably the Margaretha Schneiderin among the sponsors. Maria Koch may have been the wife of some unknown brother of George. The connection of the Reiners is not known. Nicolaus Schmid and Matheus Schmid were the sons of Mathias Smith who does not appear among the 1717 settlers but patented land (jointly with Matthias Beller, Berler, Barlow), June 24, 1726, adjacent to patent of Nicholaus Yager of the same date. The relation of this Matthias to Michael Smith of the 1717 colony has not been learned. Matthias was certainly not the son of Michael who in his will mentions son John Michael as his only heir. The Nicolaus Schmid, Sr., among the sponsors suggests the Nicholas Smith, Jr., who married Susanna Yager, daughter of Godfrey Yager. The relationship of these Schmidts to George Koch, if any, has not been learned].

Parents	Children	Date of Birth	Sponsors
FRIEDERICH GERBER and MARIA	Elisabetha	July 20, 1774	Samuel Rausch Christoph Gerber Maria Zimermanin Marg. Kochin
	Maria	Dec. 28, 1775 (christened Jan. 13, 1776)	Samuel Rausch Christoph Gerber Maria Zimermanin Marg. Kochin
	Margaretha	March 31, 1777 (christened Apr. 20, 1777)	Christoph Tanner and wife Margaretha Michael Rausch Dorothea Tanner
	Jemima	Apr. 23, 1787 (christened June 17, 1787)	Christoph Zimerman Maria Zimermanin
	Nelly	Oct. 8, 1788 (christened Nov. 23, 1788)	Christoph Zimmerman Maria Zimmermanin Anna Rausch
	Moses	Apr. 29, 1790	Christoph Zimmerman Johannes Tanner Maria Zimmermanin Anna Rausch
	William	Jan. 19, 1794 (christened March 16, 1794)	Johann Tanner Jacob Rausch Maria Zimmermanin

[The names Gerber and Tanner appear without distinction. Probably the descendants used the name Tanner, since no later Gerbers are found. Friederich Gerber was the son of Christopher Gerber and his wife Elizabeth Ohler (Ayler), daughter of Henry Aylor. Christopher Gerber was undoubtedly the son of Robert Turner (thus in the original record but certainly meant for Tanner) who on Nov. 8, 1727 proved his importation, claiming that he came to this country in 1720 and brought with him wife Mary and children Christopher, Christiana, Kathrina, Mary and Parva. The wide gap shown in the births of their children, 1777-1787, belongs to the period when the records were poorly kept. There may have been other children born in this period. *Sponsors:* Christoph Gerber and John Tanner were brothers of Friederich. Christoph Zimmerman had married Maria, sister of Friederich Gerber. Dorothea Tanner was the wife of Jacob Gerber and a sister of Christopher Zimmerman. The Rausch relationship is not known but Magdalen Gerber, sister of Friederich had married John Rouse (Rausch). The relation of Marg. Kochin is not known].

Parents	Children	Date of Birth	Sponsors
MICHAEL ZIMMERMAN and MARIA [CHRISTLER]	Solomon	Nov. 20, 1761	Johannes Gaar Heinerich Christler Maria Carpenter Elisabetha Fischerin
	Dina	June 15, 1764	John Gaar Adam Fischer Mary Carpenter
	Rebecca	June 14, 1767	Wilhelm Carpenter Heinerich Christler Margaretha Gaarin Elisabetha Fischerin
	Andreas	July 19, 1770	Adam Fischer John Gaar Maria Carpenter Elisabetha Christler
	Aron	Oct. 18, 1773	Wilhelm Carpenter Heinerich Christler Margaretha Gaarin Elisabetha Fischerin
	Mose (sic)	(christened Nov. 5, 1775)	Willm Carpenter John Gaar Elisabetha Fischerin Elisabetha Christlerin
	Ephraim	Aug. 26, 1781	None given

[Michael Zimerman was the son of John Carpenter who died 1782. His wife Maria was the daughter of Deobold Christler, so mentioned in his will, 1776-1776. The *Garr Gen.,* 67, notes this marriage but strangely fails to give names of their children. There was one other child, not given to the Register, namely, Margaret (Peggy) Carpenter, who died single. The other children married as follows: Solomon Carpenter to Hannah Carpenter, daughter of Andrew Carpenter. Dina Carpenter to George Utz. Rebecca Carpenter to Michael Miller. Andreas (Andrew) Carpenter to Elizabeth Konslar (see above under Conrad Kunzle). Aaron Carpenter to Elizabeth Aylor. Moses Carpenter to Anna Souther. And Ephraim Carpenter to Nancy Crigler. *Sponsors:* Wilhelm Carpenter was brother of Michael. Maria Carpenter was wife of William, nee Wilhoit. Heinerich Christler was brother of Maria, and Elizabeth Christler was either this Heinerich's wife or wife of his brother Adam Christler. Deobold Christler, father of these Christlers, had married Rosina Gaar and this fact will account for the Garrs among the sponsors, including Adam Fischer whose wife was Elizabeth Gaar].

Parents	Children	Date of Birth	Sponsors
JOHN GEORG CHRISTLER and ANNA MAGDA DALENA [SCHMIDT]	Julius	Nov. 12, 1767	Zacharias Schmid Adam Christler Anna Schmidtin Marga. Klorin
	Elisabetha	Aug. 30, 1769	Zacharias Schmidt Adam Christler Elisabetha Christlerin Marg. Klorin
	Abraham	Aug. 25, 1771	Adam Christler Zacharias Schmidt Catha. Marberin [?] Rahel Kuntzler
	Benjamin	May 24, 1773 (died July 26 [?], 1780)	Zacharias Schmidt Heinerich Christler Margaretha Klor
	Absalom	Sept. 24, 1775	Zacharia Schmidt Ludwig Gaar and wife Catha
	Rosina	Jan. 3, 1778	None given
	Joel	Jan. 9, 1780	Adam Christler Michael Gaar Elisabetha Christlerin

Parents	Children	Date of Birth	Sponsors
JOHN GEORG CHRISTLER and ANNA MAGDA DALENA [SCHMIDT]	Juliana	Nov. 16, 1781 (christened Nov. 29, 1781)	Michael Gahr Elisabetha Christlerin Elisabetha Christlerin
	Susana	Nov. 17, 1783	Adam Christler Susana Smithin
	Jonas	Sept. 18, 1785	Michael Gaar Adam Christler Elizabeth Christler
	Loocy (sic)	Sept. 14, 1787 (christened Oct. 28, 1787)	Adam Christler Elisabetha Christlerin Maria Carpenterin
	Anna	June 19, 1790 (christened July 25, 1790)	The parents Elisabetha Christlerin
	Maria	Dec. 1, 1792 (christened Dec. 20, 1792)	The parents

[John George Christler was the son of Deobold Christler and wife Rosina Gaar. His wife was Anna Magdalena Schmidt. Their record appears in the *Garr Gen.*, 66. Anna Magdalena Schmidt was the daughter of John Michael Schmidt, son of Michael Smith of the 1717 colony. Michael (John Michael) Smith of Culpeper Co., Va., made deed of gift to "loveing Son in Law George Christler", Dec. 31, 1771. *Sponsors:* Zacharias Schmidt was brother of Anna Magdalene. The sponsor Anna Schmidt, 1767, was probably the first wife of Zacharias. She died soon after 1767. She was the daughter of John Frederick Fishback and wife Ann Elizabeth Holtzclaw, descendants of the 1714 colony. Susana Smithin has not been placed. She could not have been the Susan, daughter of John Michael Smith, for she is described in 1762 as the wife of John Berry. John Michael Smith had a daughter who married John Narbes (sic) to whom he made deed of gift, Dec. 31, 1771. The name Narbes is not found again and the writer suggests that it is a misreading for Marber and that the Catha. Marberin among the sponsors may have been the daughter of John Michael Smith. The Gaar relations are obvious since John George Christler's mother was a Gaar. Margaret Klor was the wife of John Klor. She was born Nov. 28, 1749, and was the daughter of Michael Blankenbaker and wife Elizabeth Barbara Gaar. She was a first cousin of John George

Christler. The two Elizabeth Christlers were the wives of Heinerich and Adam Christler. The latter's wife was Elizabeth Crigler,
the first name recorded in the Register. Maria Carpenter is evidently the wife of Michael Carpenter (Zimerman). She was a
sister of John George Christler].

Parents	Children	Date of Birth	Sponsors
ADAM CHRISTLER and ELISABETHA [GRICKLER, CRIGLER]	Ambrosius	May 18, 1769	Nicolaus Grickler Heinerich Christler Dorothea Breilin Maria Utzin
	Margaretha	March 15, 1771	Nicolaus Grickler Heinerich Christler Dorothea Breilin Maria Utzin
	Eleonora	Oct. 18, 1774	Nicolaus Grickler Heinerich Christler Dorothea Breilin Maria Utzin
	Aron	Dec. 23, 1775	Benjamin Gaar Elisabetha Christerlin
	Hanna	Sept. 10, 1778 (christened Jan. 18, ——)	Aron Grickler Elisabeth Christerlin Dorothea Breilin
	Catharine	Oct. 19, 1780 (christened Nov. 26, 1780)	None given
	Susanna	Feb. 3, 1783 (christened March 16, 1783)	None given
	Elisabeth	Aug. 7, 1785 (christened Sept. 18, 1785)	Aron Grickler Margaret Gaarin Catharina Sandman?
	William	Feb. 28, 1787 (christened Apr. 1, 1787)	Aron Grickler Benjamin Gaar Elisabeth Christlerin

[Adam Christler was a brother of John George Christler.
He appears in the *Garr Gen.*, 66. His wife was Elizabeth Grickler
(Crigler), daughter of Nicholas Krickler. *Sponsors:* The relations
of the Christlers are obvious from those given under John George
Christler. The Gaar-relations are obvious for the same reason.
Benjamin Gaar had married Margaret Grickler, sister of Eliza-
beth. Dorothea Breilin was the wife of Nicholas Breil and the

sister of Adam Christler. Maria Utzin had married George Utz and was the daughter of Michael Kafer whose daughter Margaret was the wife of Nicolaus Grickler. She was therefore the aunt of Elizabeth. Catharina Sandman's relation is not known. The name is not found again].

Parents	Children	Date of Birth	Sponsors
MICHAEL SCHNEIDER and MARIA	Adam	Aug. 28, 1774	Adam Delp Freiderich Gerber Eliza. Schneiderin Rebecca Delpin
	Anna Magdalena	Jan. 21, 1776	Joseph Schneider Daniel Delp Rebecca Delpin
	Elizabeth	Jan. 28, 1790	None given
	Josua	May 12, 1793 (christened June 16, 1793)	The parents.

[Probably there were other children in the wide gap of 1776-1790. Michael Schneider was undoubtedly a descendant of Henry Schneider of the 1717 colony. Michael Schneider was probably the Michael, son of John Sneider whose will (undated) was probated Apr. 17, 1760, in which the testator mentions wife Mary and his three sons, John, Adam, and Michael Sneider. The will was evidently written in German for the Rev. George Saml Klug (pastor of the Hebron Church) was called upon to translate it. Henry Schneider, the emigrant, made will, Nov. 30, 1742, probated Mar. 26, 1747, in which he describes himself as old and infirm. He mentions wife Dorothea; daughter Ana Magdalena Aler (widow) ; and his grandchildren Henry Sneider, Elizabeth Tanner, and Henry Aler. The name of the father of his grandson Henry Sneider is not given. John Sneider who died 1760, and Philip Snyder who married a daughter of Michael Cook before Aug. 15, 1751 were probably sons of Henry Schneider. *Sponsors:* Friederich Gerber (Tanner) was related to Michael Schneider probably through the Elizabeth Tanner mentioned as granddaughter in Henry Sneider's will, see above. Joseph Schneider was also related but he is not named in the will of John Sneider, 1760. The relation of the Delps is not known. Rebecca Delp, sponsor in 1774 and 1776, is probably identical with the Rebecca Delp who married

Michael Carpenter (son of John Carpenter, son of John Carpenter who died 1782). The children of this Michael Carpenter and wife Rebecca Delp appear later in the Register, their first child being born Sept. 29, 1777].

Parents	Children	Date of Birth	Sponsors
HEINERICH CHRISTLER and ELISABETHA [WEBER]	Dinah	Feb. 8, 1762	Georg Christler Peter Weber Maria Fischerin Elisabetha Weberin
	Joseph	Nov. 13, 1763	Stephan Fischer Matheus Weber Elisabetha Wilhoit
	Elias	Feb. 8, 1766	Georg Christler Matheus Weber Maria Fischerin
	Jemima	Apr. 6, 1768	Stephan Fischer Anna Christlerin Elisabetha Weberin
	Anna	Oct. 27, 1771	Matheus Weber Georg Christler Barb. Carpenter
	Elisabetha	July 28, 1774	Andreas Carpenter Anna Christlerin Elisabetha Weberin
	Heinerich	Apr. 3, 1776	Matheus Weber Georg Christler Barb. Carpenter, Andrew Carp. wife.
	Rosina	July 10, 1787 (christened Aug. 19, 1787)	Georg Christler Barbara Carpenter Elisabeth Weberin

[This family appears in the *Garr Gen.*, 66. Garr gives a Benjamin and Mary Christler, not found in the above record. They probably belong to the period 1776-1787. Peter Weaver's will, probated Aug. 18, 1763, mentions daughter Elizabeth Christler. *Sponsors:* The relations of most of the sponsors are obvious after comparing what has already been given on the Christlers and Webers. Stephan Fischer had married Mary Magdalene Gaar, first cousin of Heinerich Christler. Elisabetha Wilhoit was probably the wife of Michael Wilhoit and sister of Heinerich Christler, for whom see the *Garr Gen.*, 67].

Parents	Children	Date of Birth	Sponsors
ZACHARIAS BLANCKENBUCHER and ELS [ELSA]	Johannes	Aug. 29, 1750	Michael Blanckenbucher Jacob Blanckenbucher Catharina Breilin
	Zacharias	March 25, 1752	Jacob Breil Jacob Blanckenbucher Elis. Blanckenbucherin
	Maria	July 6, 1755	Michael Blanckenbucher and wife Elisabetha Elisabetha Gaarin
	Jacob	Jan. 18, 1758	Michael Blanckenbucher Jacob Blanckenbucher Elisabetha Blanckenbucherin
	Michael	Sept. 11, 1761	Michael Blanckenbucher Jacob Blanckenbucher Catharina Breilin
	Samuel	Oct. 31, 1767	Michael Blanckenbucher Jacob Blanckenbucher Catharina Breilin

---

[The Register adds that there were four others who died, no names or dates given. We also know that Zacharias had at least one other child, namely, Elizabeth Blankenbaker, who married Peter Breil before 1768, and mentioned as Zacharias's daughter in his will, dated 1792. She was probably born before 1750, the date at which the Register begins. Zacharias Blankenbucher was the son of John Nicolaus Blankenbaker, one of the 1717 colony, whose will was probated 1743, with Jacob Broil as one of the executors. John Nicolaus Blankenbaker named one of his daughters, Ursula. John Broyles of the 1717 colony, father of Jacob, had wife Ursula. These are the only use of that name found among these Germans. This fact along with the fact that Jacob Breil and wife Catharina Breilin serve several times as sponsors suggests some relationship which has not yet been discovered. *Sponsors:* Michael and Jacob Blankenbucher were brothers of Zacharias. Elisabetha Gaarin, sponsor in 1755, was of no known relationship to either Zacharias Blankenbucher or his wife].

Parents	Children	Date of Birth	Sponsors
MICHAEL KLOR and MARGARET [WEBER]	Aron	July 28, 1770	Johannes Klor, Jr. Peter Klor Elisabetha Beckerin Marg. Klorin
	Michael	Feb. 10, 1772	Adam Klor Peter Klor Elisabetha Beckerin Marg. Klorin, John Clore, Jr. wife
	Johannes	Sept. 22, 1773	Johannes Klor, Jr. Peter Klor Margaretha Klorin Elisabetha Beckerin
	Levi	March 13, 1775	Salomon Klor Johannes Becker Hanna Weberin Marg. Klorin

---

[Michael Clore was the son of John Clore, son of Michael Clore of the 1717 colony. His wife was Margaret Weaver, born Dec. 19, 1752 (according to the Hebron Register, but Dec. 21, 1752, by the family Bible), died Nov. 24, 1842. Michael Clore was born Dec. 1, 1746, died Dec. 7, 1817. Margaret Weaver was the daughter of John Weber whose record is the second in the Register. See above. Michael Clore and wife Margaret had 12 other children who do not appear in the Register. The writer atempted once to distribute these children whose names he had between this Michael and the Michael, son of George, but he has since learned that the entire 16 belonged to Michael, son of John. There is no certain mention of Michael, son of George, after his will, probated Sept. 19, 1751. *Sponsors:* Johannes Klor was Michael's brother. Peter Klor was his first cousin, son of George. His record has already appeared. Adam Klor and Salomon Klor were also his first cousins, son of his uncle Peter Clore, who died 1763. I regard Elisabetha Becker, wife of John Becker (their record has already been given) as the Elizabeth, daughter of the Peter Clore who died 1751. Hanna Weberin, sponsor in 1775, is the daughter of John Weber, whose daughter Hanna was born Aug. 15, 1757, see above].

327

Parents	Children	Date of Birth	Sponsors
PETER BREIL and ELISABETHA [BLANKENBUCHER]	Zacharias	Sept. 19, 1768	Jacob Breil Johannes Blanckenbucher Elisabetha Wilheitin Margaretha Klorin
	Margaretha	Nov. 25, 1769	Johannes Blanckenbucher Elisabetha Wilheitin Margaretha Breilin
	Jacob	Feb. 17, 1771	Johannes Blanckenbucher Jacob Breil Maria Blanckenbucherin Maria Breilin
	Salomon	July 7, 1772	Adam Breil Johanes Blanckenbucher Maria Blanckenbucherin
	Johann	Nov. 27, 1773	Ziriakus Breil Joh's Blanckenbucher and wife Maria
	Aron	Oct. 26, 1775	Ziriakus Breil Joh's Blanckenbucher and wife Maria
	Maria	1778 (christened March 15, 1778)	Johannes Blanckenbucher Michael Fleischman and wife Delila Breilin
	Daniel	Nov. 27, 1790 (christened Jan. 12, 1791)	Michael Fleischmann Barbara Blanckenbucherin

[Peter Breil and wife Elisabetha also had children Absalom, Ephraim, and Betsy Broyles, no doubt born in the period 1778-1790. Peter Breil was one of the nine sons of Jacob Broyles. His wife Elisabetha was the daughter of Zacharias Blankenbaker who was evidently born before the beginning of the Register. *Sponsors:* Jacob, Adam, and Ziriakus Breil were brothers of Peter. Delila Breilin was the wife of his brother Zacharias Broyles. Maria Breilin could have been the wife either of Adam or of Ziriakus. Margaretha Breilin was the wife of his brother John Broyles. Johannes Blankenbaker was probably Elizabeth's brother who was born 1750, or else the John, son of George, son of Matthias Blankenbaker. Margaretha Klorin was the wife of John Clore and the daughter of Michael Blankenbaker, uncle of Elisabetha. Elisabetha Wilheitin was the wife of John Wilhoit and the daughter of the same Michael Blankenbaker. Barbara Blankenbaker was probably the wife of Jacob, brother of Elizabeth's father Zacharias. Michael Fleischman (which name has not yet appeared in the Register) was related to Peter Breil on his mother's side, Mary Catharine Fleischman, wife of the Jacob Broyles who died 1763].

Parents	Children	Date of Birth	Sponsors
JOHN GAAR and MARGARETHA [WILHOIT]	Lorenz	Nov. 16, 1767	Michael Gaar Georg Christler Eva Fischerin Maria Carpenter
	Abraham	Feb. 28, 1769	Michael Carpenter Eva Fischerin
	Johannes	March 16, 1771	Nicolaus Yager Georg Christler Eva Fischerin Maria Carpenter
	Aron	Jan. 20, 1773	Michael Carpenter Georg Christler Susanna Yagerin Eva Fischerin
	Elisabetha	Jan. 25, 1775	Nicolaus Yager Bernhard Fischer Magd. Fischerin Maria Carpenter
	(name not given)	Nov. 8, 1776	Georg Christler Michael Carpenter Susanna Yagerin Eva Fischerin

[The *Garr Gen.*, 68, shows that the name omitted above was Leanna Gaar. Besides Garr gives six other names not given here, namely, Rosanna, Diana, Margaret, Susanna, Felix, and Benjamin Gaar, born between 1776 and 1788. John Gaar was the son of Lorenz Gaar by his wife Dorothea, daughter of John Nicolaus Blankenbaker. John Gaar's wife was Margaretha Wilhoit, daughter of John Wilhoit. *Sponsors:* Michael Gaar was John's first cousin, son of John Adam Gaar by his wife Elizabeth Kafer, daughter of Michael Kafer. George Christler, as shown above, was also his first cousin. Nicolaus Yager had married Susanna Wilhoit, the sister of Margaretha. Michael Carpenter had married Maria Christler, sister of George Christler. Eva Fischerin was the sister of Margaretha Wilhoit and the wife of Bernhard Fischer.

Magd. Fischerin was the wife of Stephan Fischer and the daughter of John Adam Gaar. Every sponsor was related to either the father or mother].

Parents	Children	Date of Birth	Sponsors
HEINERICH OHLER [AYLOR] and BARBARA	Michael	Oct. 11, 1772	Andreas Carpenter Friederich Tanner Marg. Ohlerin Barbara Carpenter
	Molly	May 10, 1774	Friederich Tanner Barbara Carpenter Barbara Carpenter (twice)
	Susanna	Sept. 23, 1792 (christened Nov. 2, 1792)	The father Andreas Carpenter Lips daughter

---

[The Tanners had an early connection with the Aylors. Aside from this no relationship is apparent].

This concludes the first part of the Register. It is obvious that in almost all cases the sponsors were chosen on the basis of some relationship. In this religious ceremony they were family-conscious. Often the responsibility was claimed by the parents. In later times this practice became much more common. There may have been a relationship in those cases where the writer has been unable to find any. One coming into the family by marriage was quite promptly placed on the same basis as those related by blood. This valuation of relationship, whether by blood or marriage, need not have been a conscious tenet of their faith but it is natural to the German habit of thought.

The nucleus from which the Hebron congregation grew was the *1717* colony. This colony consisted of the following names: Amberger (Auberge), Ballenger, Blankenbucher, Broyles, Clore, Cook, Fleischman, Holt, Kaifer (Cafer), Kerker (Kercher), Moyer, Parlur (Barler, Berler, Barlow), Paulitz (Politsch), Sheible (Shively), Smith, Snyder, Utz, Yager, Zimmerman, and perhaps also Harrensberger, Motz (Mauck), and Lang. The Carpenters (William and John) arrived in 1721. Jacob Crigler and Matthias Smith were in the colony as early as 1726. Of these names the Amburger, Ballenger, Harrensberger, Holt, Kerker, Paulitz, Sheible, Motz, and Lang names do not appear in the Register. Some of them may be found in land and court records. Some of them may have died before 1750 without children or without male heirs. Such was the case of Andrew Kerker who died 1738 leaving an only child, a daughter, the wife of John Carpenter. Michael Kaifer had daughters only so his name vanishes soon after 1750. But the proportion of these early names still found in the Register beginning with 1750 indicates considerable stability of the congregation. In the period following 1775 this condition is altered. Then or a little later the Baptists and Methodists make inroads on the Hebron Church which draw many over to the new faiths. Also about this time many begin to seek other lands. About 1780 six of the Broyles brothers migrated to east Tennessee. About the same time Broyleses, Blankenbakers, Yagers, and others sought new homes in Kentucky. The work of disintegration left its mark upon Hebron and when it revived the constituency was quite altered. But it began once more to prosper and is today a thriving congregation.

We give next the communion roll of the seventeenth Sunday after Trinity, 1776. There are earlier rolls back to 1775, but this roll is here given for the reason that it is much longer than those that precede and probably comes very nearly representing the entire Hebron congregation.

Adam Yager, Senr [?]
Johannes Carpenter Sr. and wife Barbara
Nicolaus Smith and wife Magdalena
Andreas Carpenter and wife Barbara
Johannes Yager and wife Maria
Adam Gaar and wife Elisabetha
Nicolaus Grickler and wife Margaretha
Heinerich Christler and wife Elisabetha
Stephan Fischer and wife Magdalina
Michael Schmidt
Michael Carpenter and wife Maria
Martin Rausch
Philipp Schneider
Jacob Breil and wife Elisabetha
Michael Gaar and wife Elisabetha
Christoph Grickler and wife (name not given)
Conrad Delp and wife Magd.
Matheus Weber and wife Elisabetha.
William Carpenter and wife Maria
Matheus Rausch and wife Elisabetha
Friederich Tanner and wife Maria
Georg Wilhoit and wife Maria
Peter Breil and wife Elisabetha
Nicolaus Yager and wife Susanna
Michael Fleischman and wife Maria
Michael Delp and wife Margaretha
Velentin Banger
Matheus Haus
Johannes Gaar and wife Margaretha

Bernhardt Fischer and wife Eva
Aron Yager
Michael Cook
Christoph Tanner
Philipp Schneider (second time)
Eberhardt Reiner
Daniel Delp
Ephraim Fleischman
Adam Koch, Jr.
Georg Utz, Jr.
Johs. Schmidt. Taylor (Schmidt has a period after it and Taylor
    is elevated in the line. The Taylor may have nothing to do
    with his name but its addition may be intended to represent
    his occupation)
Peter Koch
Adam Utz (on his sick bed)
Johs. Klor and Catharina, John Clore's wife.
Burgunda Wilheitin
Rosina Christlerin
Catharina Bohmin (with umlaut *o*)
Anna Barbara Fischerin
Catharina Breilin
Elisabetha Fincksin
Rebecca Schwendel
Maria Fleischmanin
Maria Milbanks
Barbara Carpenter
Elisabetha Breilin
Hanna Weberin
Elisabetha Fleischmanin
Elisabetha Fischerin
Elisabetha Kochin
Christina Blanckenbucherin
Barbara Kochin
Margaretha Zimermanin
Rosina Blanckenbucherin
Maria Kochin
Elis. Bohmin
Elisabetha Gricklerin
Pheben Yagerin
Maria Schmidtin, Matheus Smith's wife
Rebecca Delpin
Maria Breilin
Maria Mayerin
Susana Mayerin
Maria Utz
Elisab. Holzklauin
Marg. Lederin

Vermillion, South Dakota.

OLD TOMBSTONES IN MATHEWS COUNTY.

COLLECTED BY THE EDITOR.

I.

"YEATMANS."[1]

Sacred to the memory of
Mary Yeatman
Wife of Thomas M. Yeatman
& daughter of John Tompkins
She died in October 1796.
Aged 31 years.

Sacred
to the Memory of
Thomas Robinson
Eldest son of
Thomas Muse Yeatman & Mary Tompkins.
Born Jan'y 5, 1789,
Died Aug. 25, 1832.

II.

OAK GROVE.[2]

Here lyeth Interred
the — of William Armistead,
who departed this life the 13 day,
of June 1711, aged 40 years.

III.

TRINITY CHURCH.[3]

In Memory of
Mr. John Nason
who Died May y[e] 18th 1772
Aged 52.

Here is deposited the Mortal Part of
Lucy Dixon, wife of the Rev. John Dixon.[4]
Her
Exemplary Piety, Domestic Virtues, Liberal Charity
Deservedly Caused her to be
Highly esteemed, cordially beloved, sincerely lamented
By
The Public, Her Family, the Poor.
Obiit Nov[r], 1769, Aetat: 41.

NOTES.

[1] "Yeatman's plantation" lies opposite to "Toddbury" on North River. There are two other headstones, but the briars were so dense as to render approach impossible.

[2] This place lies on East River, and the tomb must be that of William Armistead, eldest son of Col. John Armistead of Hesse. (See Keith's "Ancestry of Benjamin Harrison").

[5] Trinity church is a wooden structure 40 feet long by 27 feet. Kingston church, which stands at the other end of. the county, was rebuilt just before the war, chiefly through the exertions of Miss Elizabeth Tompkins.

[4] Lucy Dixon's husband was Rev. John Dixon, minister of Kingston parish in 1754, and Professor of Divinity, in William and Mary College, from 1770 till his death in 1777. Sons John and Thomas; Anne infant daughter of Thomas; and nephew Roger Dixon. (Chancery papers in Williamsburg.)

SKIPWITH GRAVE STONES

Copied from the Grave-stones at "Prestwould,"
Mecklenburg County, Va.

(Communicated by Mrs. Wirt Johnson Carrington)

"Sir. Peyton Skipwith, Bart: Born Dec. 11, 1740—
Died at "Prestwould," Virginia, Oct. 9, 1805,"
On this slab the Coat-of-arms of the Skipwiths was clearly
and beautifully impanneled, carved in the stone, but not in
bas-relief, rather set in; Motto: "Sans Dieu Je ne Puis."

"To the memory of Mrs. Sarah S. Skipwith, Born the 20
of August, 1793, and departed this life the 27 of September, 1823,
Aged 29 years, I Month & Seven days."

"In memory of Lady Jean Skipwith, Departed this life
19 day of May, 1826."

"To the memory of Evelina Skipwith, Daughter of
Humbertson & Lelia Skipwith. Born March the 8th, and died
21st of July, 1832."

"Fulwer, Son of Humbert—& Lelia Skipwith, March 3,
1836—March 6th-1900."

"Annie Ledyard, Wife of Fulwar Skipwith, Oct. 18th,
1838—April 28, 1905."

"Helen Skipwith, Daughter of S. W. & S. N. Gannell,
Born in Philalephia, Pa., May 4th, 1847, Died at Prestwould,
May 28, 1848."

"Our Darling Annie Ledyard, Daughter of Austin & Mary
E. Skipwith, Feb. 19, 1902—Nov. 20, 1903"

WEEKES

OF CHRIST CHURCH, MIDDLESEX COUNTY, VIRGINIA, AND ASHLEY, HANTS, ENGLAND.

J. B. WHITMORE, F. S. A.

Francis Weekes, son of Abraham Weekes, of Christ Church (see *Virginia Magazine of History and Biography,* Vol. V., 169), mar. Elizabeth, probably sister of Thomas Hobbs, of Lincoln's Inn Fields, London, and Ashley, Hants, "Medicus et Proto-Chirurgus" to Charles II, James II, and William; both living 1716, when "Elizabeth, wife of Francis Weekes of Virginia, merchant, now lodging at the house of ——— Wilcocks, of Harrow" was a deponent in a Chancery suit of Wilcocks v. Page; perhaps she was buried as "Mrs. Francis Weekes" at Ashley, 4 Nov. 1745; they had issue

1. Abraham; said to have been born at St. Clement Danes, London, but baptism not recorded there; called nephew by Thomas Hobbs; adm. a scholar of Winchester College 1692, aged 13; Magd. Coll. Oxford, matric. 4 July, 1696, aged 17; M. A. 1706; probably dead 1723 (see Oxford Historical Society, Hearne's Collections, viii. 112); mar. ——— widow of ——— Walker, who kept the King's Head Tavern, Oxford; they had issue

   1. Elizabeth: died 30 Aug. 1723, aged 14; administration of her estate, as a minor, granted to her grandmother, Elizabeth Weekes, in P. C. C. 11 Aug. 1724.
   2. Francis; called nephew by Thomas Hobbs; d. unm. 1714/5; of St. Martin in the Fields, London; will dated 29 Nov. 1714, proved in P. C. C. 7 Feb. 1714/5; mentions Ashley Farm, Ashley, Hants, and lands at "Rappa Hanock River", Va.
   3. Thomas; called nephew by Thomas Hobbs; bapt. Christ Church 5 Aug. 1683; probably dead 1714; not mentioned in will of brother Francis.
   4. Hobbs; see below:

Hobbs Weekes; bapt. Christ Church 21 Jan. 1686; called nephew by Thomas Hobbs; of Christ Church, Va., and Ashley, Hants; administration of his estate granted in P. C. C. 30 June, 1722; mar. Mary, daughter of Robert Prescott, of Virginia; she buried Ashley 10 Sept. 1733; they had issue:

1. Elizabeth bapt. Christ Church 2 Oct. 1709; probably dead 1756; living unm. 1740.
2. Millecent; b. 2 May, 1713; mar. (license 5 April, 1740) Leonard Cropp, of Holy Rood, Southampton, England, merchant; she living 1756.

3. Thomas Hobbs; b. 11 June, 1715; bapt. Christ Church 30 July, 1715; admitted to Westminster School Jan. 1727/8; New College, Oxford, matric. 12 July, 1731; of Southampton, England, 1738; buried at Ashley, 29 April, 1742; will dated 9 Jan. 1740, proved in P. C. C. 13 May, 1742.

4. Abraham, b. 22 Sept. 1717; bapt. Christ Church 27 Oct. 1717; admitted to Westminster School Jan. 1727/8; of Rookley, Crawley, Hants; d. at Boulogne, France, 8 June, 1755; buried Ashley Hants; M. I.; mar. at Ashley 14 Sept. 1743, Frances, daughter of Sir John Astley, of Pateshull, Salop, Bart.; she remarried in or before 1756 James O'Donnell, Esq., and died Dec. 1764; they had issue

1. Abraham; buried at Ashley 18 April 1745, aged 14 days.

5. Francis; bapt. Sparsholt, Hants, England, 18 March 1719/20; admitted to Westminster School Jan. 1727/8; left 1729; re-admitted Jan. 1730/1; admitted a scholar of Winchester College 1732; left 1737; Queen's College, Oxford, matric., as son of "Thomas" Weekes of Mere Court (now a farm on the edge of Sparsholt village) Hants, 2 Dec. 1737; B. A. 1741; apparently dead 1756.

6. Catherine; living unmarried 1740; apparently dead 1756.

7. Mary; living unmarried 1740; married, before 1756, Henry Hammond, of Southampton, England; d. 2 Nov. 1768, aged 46; buried Barton Stacey, Hants, England; M. I.

NOTE.—The arms on the monument of Abraham Weekes in Ashley church are practically illegible, but sufficient remains to suggest that the family used the arms of Weekes of Honichurch, Devon, viz. ermine, three battle-axes, sable.

TOMBSTONES IN MIDDLESEX COUNTY.

Urbanna.

Here lies CATHERINE, late wife of John
Walker, of Urbanna. She departed this life
the 5th day of October, 1730, in the 33d year
of her age.

Christ Church.

Here lies Interred
the Body of the
HON. JOHN GRYMES, ESQ.,
Who many years acted
in the public Affairs of this Dominion
With Honour, Fortitude, Fidelity,

To their Majesties King George I. and II.
Of the Council of State,
Of the Royal Prerogative,
The Liberty and Property of the Subject,
A zealous Assertor.
On the seat of judgment
clear, sound, unbiased,
In the Office of Receiver General
Punctual, approved.
Of the College of William and Mary
An Ornament, Visitor, Patron.
Beneficent to all,
A Support to the Distressed,
A Pattern of true Piety,
Respected, loved, revered,
Lamented by his Family, Acquaintance, Country,
He departed this Life the 2d Day of November, 1748,
in the 57th year of His Age.

Beneath this stone are deposited
the remains of
MRS. JANE SAYRE,
Wife of Samuel Wm. Sayre,
and daughter of the late
Philip Ludwell Grymes,
who departed this Life
January 1, 1806,
Aged 24.
Rest here, oppressed by pale disease no more;
Here find that calm thou sought so oft before;
Rest undisturbed within this Humble Shrine,
Till Angels wake thee with a voice like thine.

Beneath this Marble
Lies the Body of
PHILIP GRYMES,
only son of Philip Ludwell and Judith Grymes,
He was born September 19th, 1775,
And died November 9th, 1801.

Underneath this Marble
Lies the Remains of
DOCTOR HENRY POTTER,
who departed this life the 20 day
of December, in the 46th
Year of his Age.
Here also lyes enterred the body of
LUCY POTTER,
the daughter of Dr. Henry Potter and
Hannah, his wife who died
the —— day of October.

Here lyes the Body of
JOHN GRYMES,
Eldest·son of
Philip Grymes, Esq.,
and Mary his wife,
Who departed this Life,
The 2^d day of June, 1746,
Aged 15 months.
Of such is the kingdom of Heaven

Here lies Interred the body of
JOHN WORMELEY,
third son of Ralph
Wormeley & Jane
his wife,
Who was born the 21st
Day of July, 1747,
And died the 29th Day of
April, 1749.

Here lies interred the body of
MRS. SARAH WORMELY,
First wife of Ralph Wormely, of the
County of Middlesex, Esq.,
She was the daughter of Edmund Berkeley, Esq.,
of this county.
She departed this life there ye 2d day Dec., 1741,
Aged 26 years.

Underneath this Marble
is interred the Remains of
MRS. ELEANOR WORMELY,
Wife of
Ralph Wormely, Esq.,
of Rosegill & Sister of Col. John Taylor, of
Mount Airy,
Who Died the 23^d of February, 1815,
in the 60th year of her Age.
(*Verses.*)

This monument was erected
in memory of
RALPH WORMELEY, ESQ., of Rosegill,
Who died on the 19th day of January, 1806,
In the 62nd year of his Age.
The rule of honour guarded the action of
this great man. He was the perfect gentleman
and finished scholar, with many virtues
founded in Christianity.

GEORGE L. NICHOLSON,
son of
George Dudley Nicholson,
and Sarah Tayloe Wormeley,
of Rosegill, Middlesex County.
Born at Deer Chase,
December 27, 1814,
Died March 17, 1883.
Them also which sleep in Jesus,
will God bring with him.

This Monumental Marble,
In Remembrance of all that could endear ye living and make
the dead lamented . . . for Benevolence and Truth,
Is Placed Here,
Over the Remains of an Excellent Person . . . ial is
better and more lastingly recorded . . . sed Tes-
timonials of the Wise and Good.

The Filial Piety of Her earlier years was an earnest of
That Social Excellence which all Her afterlife went
to adorn the wife, the Parent, and the Friend.
.   .   .   .   .   .   Generosity,
. . . s best motive. An unbounded charity . . ts,
Only Guide Virtuous Prudence, gained Her as many
Friends, as she had acquaintance.
Humility
. . . st sense of Her Maker and Herself . . . from
Whence it arose, preserved Her from the Envy usually
attendant
On Her Exalted Station,
And procured Her the undissembled affections of all Ranks,
Who admired in Her Goodness without Ostentation,
Elevation without Pride and without Meanness Conde-
scension even to the lowest of Her Inferiors.
Such was
MRS. LUCY GRYMES,
Relict
Of the Honourable John Grymes, Esqr.,
(Whose body reposes near this of His beloved wife.)
Daughter,
Of the Honourable Philip Ludwell, Esq.,
Parent
Of a numerous and deserving Family.
On the 3d of March, In the Year of our Lord 1749,
And in the 52 Year of Her Age, the Divine command
summoned Her to receive the Rewards of a well spent life.
She obeyed with ready and devout Resignment;
And, having given an Illustrious Pattern
Of Living Well
She taught the next great lesson,
How to Die.
(*To be Continued.*)

TOMBSTONES IN MIDDLESEX COUNTY.

Here lies the remains of the
REV. MR. BARTHOLOMEW YATES.
Who departed this life the 26 day of July, 1734, in the 57
Year of his age.
He was one of the visitors of William and Mary College,
And also
Professor of Divinity in that Royal Foundation.
In the conscientious discharge of his Duty
Few ever Equalled Him,
None ever surpassed Him.
He explained His Doctrine by His practice, and Taught, and
Led the way to Heaven. Chearfulness, the Result of
Innocence, always sparkled in His face; and by
The sweetness of His Temper, He gained Uni-
versal Good will. His Consort enjoyed
in Him a tender Husband; His chil-
dren an indulgent Father; His
Servants a gentle Master;
His Acquaintance a
Faithful Friend.
He was Minister of this Parish upwards of 30 years; and to
Perpetuate His Memory, this Monument is Erected at the charge
of His Friends and Parishoners.

Hs
JOHANNES WORMLEY ARMIGER.
Rem nactus admodum ampliam
A claris Majoribus, antiquis loci incolis,
post gravisima munia dignie administrata,
in hac aede humatis acceptus;
Publicorum Officiorum nunquam appetens:
Quippe tranquillo privatoque Contentus Lare:
Parens numerosae et formosae prolis;
Nullius non bonus praeter valetudinem usus;

343

Utili erga plurimos vita, ac spectata orga Omnes,
Praesertim egenos, hospitalitate exemplari proposito;
VII ld. Feby MDCCXXVI, Ann. Aet. XXXVII.
Decessit immaturus flebilis multis maxime Conjugi
Quae marito bene merenti moestissima posuit
Hoc Moneenentum.

BARN ELMS.

This place has a one-story brick building of three rooms, connected
with a two-story building of four rooms.

(ARMS.)*

Here lyeth the Body of
LUCY BERKELEY, who Departed this
Life ye 16th day of December, 1716, in ye 33rd
Year of her Age, after she had been
Married 12 Years and 15 Days. She left
behind her 5 children, viz., 2 Boys and 3
Girls. I shall not pretend to give her full
Character; it would take two much room
for a Grave stone; shall only say that
She never neglected her duty to her
Creator in Publick or Private. She was
Charitable to the poor; a kind mistress
and indulgent mother & obedient wife.
She never in all the time she lived
with her Husband gave him so much
as once cause to be displeased with Her.

GRIMESBY ON PIANKETANK.

Here lieth Interred
The Body of Mr JOHN
GRYMES, who departed
This Life in the Year
Of our Lord 1709.

---

* A chevron between ten crosses pattée, six in chief and four in base.

Here lieth Interred the
Body of Mrs. ALICE
GRYMES, who Departed
This Life in the Year of
Our Lord, 1710.

Here lies the Body of M^rs
ANNA GRYMES, Daughter of
Mr John & Mrs Alice Grymes,
Who lies near this Place. She
Departed this Life the 17th day
of December Anno Dom. 1735,
In the 16th year of her Age.

THE OLD CABELL GRAVEYARD AT "LIBERTY HALL"

by WILLIAM CABELL MOORE[*]

THE "Liberty Hall" graveyard is located on the "Liberty Hall" farm on the James River at Warminster, in Nelson County, about six miles west of Howardsville. It is on a slight elevation in a field below the site of the house, which burned about 1895, and on part of the land patented by Dr. William Cabell about 1724. Here lived Dr. Cabell, his wife Elizabeth Burks Cabell, founders of the Cabell family in Virginia, and some of their descendants for five generations. The farm now belongs to Mrs. Hartwell Cabell, whose husband acquired it by inheritance, he being of the fifth generation of Cabells in descent from Dr. Cabell to whom it had belonged. Mr. Hartwell Cabell died in December 1955 within a few days of his ninety-second birthday.

The graveyard has around it a stout iron fence which Mr. Cabell had built about 1900. The graves of Dr. and Mrs. Cabell are located in the northeast corner and are marked by a marble monument erected many years ago at the instance of their grandson Joseph Carrington Cabell, who lived nearby at "Edgewood." The monument was placed just east of an old elm tree which, according to Alexander Brown in *The Cabells and Their Kin,* is said to have grown out of their graves. This old tree, which at its base measured about five feet in diameter, was taken down in 1955 in order to prevent further damage to the fence and gravestones. The date of Dr. Cabell's birth and his age as originally inscribed on the monument were erroneous. These errors were corrected in 1955. The monument is inscribed on three sides as follows.

On the east side: "Near this spot / Lie the earthly remains of / DR. WILLIAM CABELL / A native of Wiltshire, England / and the Founder / of the family in Virginia / which bears his name / Those of / ELIZABETH CABELL / his wife / and the Mother of his children / Who died Sep. 21, 1756, / lie by his side."

On the south side: "WILLIAM CABELL / Emigrated / From Warminster, England / to the Colony of Virginia / about 1723-4 / Born March 9, 1699 / Died April 12, 1774 / Aged 75 years."

On the west side: "In honour of their memory / was this stone erected / by the piety of their Grandson / JOSEPH C. CABELL."

---

[*]Dr. Moore is a physician in Washington, D. C.

The north side is bare.

The other marked graves are inscribed as follows.

First row, from north to south:

1. "In memory of / COL. NICHOLAS CABELL / He early took a decided and active part / in behalf of the American Revolution / engaging with zeal / in the Military Service of Virginia: / and afterward sat for 16 years / in the Senate of Virginia / from 1785 to 1801. / Born, Oct. 29, 1750 / Died, Aug. 18, 1803 / Aged 52 years." Colonel Nicholas Cabell was the youngest son of Dr. and Mrs. Cabell.

2. "In memory of / MRS. HANNAH CABELL / Wife of Col. Nicholas Cabell / and daughter of / Col. George Carrington, of Cumberland. / Born, April 16, 1752 / Died, Aug. 7, 1817 / Aged 67 years."

3. "In memory of / MRS. ELIZABETH HARE / Daughter of Col. Nicholas Cabell / and wife of Dr. William B. Hare, / who was some time a member of / the Senate of Virginia, / and one of the Council of State. / She was born May 5, 1776, / and died Nov. 28, 1802: / Aged 26 years."

4. "In memory of / NICHOLAS CABELL, JR., / Youngest son of Col. Nicholas Cabell, / Born Dec. 24, 1780: / Died, June 25, 1809: / Aged 28 years."

5. "In memory of / NICHOLAS C. CABELL / Born / February 9, 1796: / Died / October 13, 1821 / His friends cherish the memory / of his fine intellect, / and of his elevated sense of honor, / and have never ceased to grieve / that their fond hopes were extinguished / in his early grave." Nicholas Carrington Cabell was the son of Judge William H. Cabell, son of Colonel Nicholas Cabell of "Liberty Hall," and Elizabeth Cabell, daughter of Colonel William Cabell, Sr., of "Union Hill."

Second row, from north to south:

6. "In memory of / MRS. MARY ANNE CARRINGTON / Relict of / Capt. Benj. Carrington / of Cumberland / And Daughter of / Col. Nicholas Cabell / of Liberty Hall, Nelson. / Born, 2 Jan., 1783: / Died, 6 Feb., 1850: / Aged 67. / A Christian Lady greatly beloved / of her Family & Friends, and a pat / tern of domestic Virtue."

7. "This stone / covers the remains of/ MRS. MARGARET READ CABELL, / Wife of Nicholas Cabell, Jr. / and daughter of / Col. Samuel W. Venable, of Pr. Edward, / Born, Oct. 20, 1782: / Died, May 31, 1857: / Aged 75 years."

8. "In memory of / NATHANIEL FRANCIS / CABELL / of 'Liberty Hall' / son of / Nicholas Cabell, Jr. / and / Margaret Read / Venable Cabell / Born, July 23, 1807 / Died, Sept. 1, 1891."

9. "In memory of / ANN BLAWS / Daughter of / John H. & Ann B. Cocke, / And first wife of / N. Francis Cabell / Born, Dec. 15, 1811, / at Bremo Recess, Fluvanna Co., Va. / Died, Feb. 20, 1862, / at Liberty Hall, Nelson Co., Va."

10. "This stone / covers the ashes of / FRANCIS HARTWELL CABELL / Eldest son of / N. Francis and Ann B. Cabell. / Born, Jan. 27, 1833: / Died, Oct. 10, 1844: / Aged 11 years."

11. "CARY CHARLES CABELL / youngest son of / N. Francis and Ann B. Cabell / Born, Nov. 20, 1854: / was taken away / May 31, 1856: / Aged 18 months."

12. "FRANCIS BARRAUD / CABELL / Born, July 14, 1866 / Died November 22, 1893." Francis Barraud Cabell was the son of the Reverend Philip Barraud Cabell and Juliet Calvert Bolling Cabell.

13. "JULIET CALVERT BOLLING / CABELL / Wife of / Philip Barraud / Cabell / Born August 3, 1834 / Died January 21, 1923 / Aged 89 years." Mrs. Juliet Calvert Bolling Cabell was the daughter of Thomas Bolling and Mary Louise Morris Bolling, of "Bolling Hall," Goochland County.

14. "PHILIP BARRAUD / CABELL / Born June 16, 1836 / Died March 16, 1904." Philip Barraud Cabell was the son of N. Francis and Anne B. Cocke Cabell, of "Liberty Hall."

Third row:

15. "In memory of / ELIZABETH NICHOLAS / Eldest daughter of / N. Francis & Ann B. Cabell / And first wife of / William D. Cabell / Born, July 16, 1834 / At Warminster, Nelson Co., Va. / Died, April 5, 1863. / SISTER."

The grave of Elizabeth Nicholas Cabell is at the head of her mother's grave. This grave and the graves of her father and mother are the only three graves in the graveyard marked with standing stones. All the stones are clearly marked and well preserved but two were cracked and broken by branches falling from the old elm tree. A number of other members of the family undoubtedly were buried here but none of the other graves is marked.

EPITAPHS COPIED FROM THE FAMILY CEMETERY AT "SOLDIER'S JOY," NELSON COUNTY, VIRGINIA

by Lenora Higginbotham Sweeny[*]

"Soldier's Joy," at Wingina, Nelson County, Virginia, was built in the late eighteenth century after the plans of James Roberts, architect, of Goochland County, Virginia, for Colonel William Cabell, of "Union Hill," and given as a wedding present to his eldest son, Colonel Samuel Jordan Cabell, a brave officer in the Revolution.[1]

Around "Soldier's Joy" many pleasant memories cling. Wreathed about it is "the tender grace of the day that is dead." It was a center of the social life of the period, its owner and his wife distinguished in family, wealth and hospitality. He married Sarah, daughter of Colonel John Syme, Jr., of Hanover County, Virginia, and niece of Patrick Henry. They went there to reside in 1785 and Colonel Cabell called his home "Soldier's Joy." He was an original member of the Society of the Cincinnati in the State of Virginia. He died August 4, 1818, at "Soldier's Joy," and is buried there beside his wife, who died May 15, 1814. There is no monument erected to their memory.

The following epitaphs were copied from the tombstones in the family cemetery near "Soldier's Joy":

In Memory of John Higginbotham who was born in the County of Amherst 12th day of April 1772 and died in the town of Warminister on the 23rd February 1822.

In Memory of Jesse Higginbotham who was born in the County of Amherst on the 23rd day of December 1779 and died at Soldier's Joy on the 8th June 1836.

In Memory of Daniel Higginbotham who was born in the County of Amherst on the 27th day of March 1781 and died at Soldier's Joy on the 10th day of August 1845.

---

[*]Mrs. Sweeny is a frequent contributor on genealogical subjects to this and other magazines.
[1]Alexander Brown, *The Cabells and Their Kin* (Boston and New York, 1895), p. 185.

Jesse A. Higginbotham born Jan⁷ 29th 1822. Died of consumption February 27th 1849. He was the son of Reuben A. Higginbotham and Lucretia his wife formerly Lucretia Vaughan of Nashville, Tenn. The deceased intermarried with Miss Elvira M. Henry in the Month of May 1848 preceeding his death and she survives him. As desired by him before his death his remains are here buried by the side of his uncle Daniel Higginbotham, deceased.

John James London who was born in the County of Amherst 11 February, 1813 and died at Soldier's Joy, Nelson County, Virginia, 10th October, 1856.

Alice Winston, daughter of Charles T. and Alice Cabell Palmer, born 17th November, 1886 and died 25 June, 1903.

Clifford Cabell Russell Palmer, born 26 July, 1890 and died 28 September, 1893.

The first three gentlemen, John, Jesse, and Daniel Higginbotham, were sons of Captain John Higginbotham (1726-1814) and his wife Rachel Banks. John Higginbotham, Jr., married December 7, 1815, Margaret Cabell, daughter of Colonel Samuel Jordan and Sarah (Syme) Cabell.[2]

Jesse Alexander Higginbotham,[3] who was a grandson of Captain John Higginbotham, made his will September 30, 1848, "being about to travel to the Island of Cuba"; probated in Amherst County, Virginia, April 5, 1849. Among other bequests he left money in trust to erect a building in sight of his home at Amherst. The upper part to be used by the Clinton Lodge, of which he was a member, and the lower as an academy. This trust was fulfilled and the large brick building situated in a grove of beautiful old trees in sight of Amherst, known as "The Higginbotham Academy," is now owned by the Harrison family.

---

[2]William Montgomery Sweeny, "Higginbotham Family of Virginia," *William and Mary Quarterly*, 1st Ser., XXVII, 123-125. *

[3]"Jesse Alexander Higginbotham, youngest son of Dr. Reuben Higginbotham a native of Amherst County, Virginia, who settled in Nashville, Tenn. Both parents died early and he was left to the care of his uncle, of Nelson County, Virginia.

"He entered Yale in 1839, after graduation he studied law at the University of Virginia and settled in practice in Amherst, the County Seat of Amherst County. He married, 1848, Elvira McClelland, second daughter of John Henry, and granddaughter of Patrick Henry.

"In the following winter he went to the West Indies for his health and died soon after his return. He left no children.

"His widow next married Alexander L. Taylor, of Richmond, Virginia and died in December, 1874." (Robert W. Wright, comp., *Biographical Record of the Class of 1842 of Yale College* [New Haven, 1878].)

*See *Genealogies of Virginia Families: From the William and Mary College Quarterly Historical Magazine* (Baltimore: Genealogical Publishing Co., Inc., 1982), Vol. III, pp. 55-57.

OUT-OF-THE-WAY TOMBSTONES

By Arthur and Elizabeth Gray.

In our search for historical material, we have traveled through the counties comprising the Tidewater section of the original New Kent County, covering this territory closely.

That area embraces, besides the present New Kent, the counties of King William and King and Queen and parts of Hanover and Caroline.

This section was probably more thickly settled with prominent families in pre-Revolutionary times than any other part of Virginia. But to an unusual degree, the old homes have disappeared, or are falling in ruins, and in many important cases the sites of these homes are difficult to locate.

Many of the old churches have gone too. But when a site, either of a home or of a church is located, it is probable that somewhere near there can be found the remains of an old burying ground with slab tombstones and still legible inscriptions.

These stones may be broken and scattered, or it may be that some excavation is required to discover any portion of them.

It is planned to publish periodically the inscriptions found on some the these old stones.

Together with the inscription will be included a short account of the home and family represented:

No. I.—Richard Corbin:

Richard Corbin was the King's Receiver-General during the stormy years that preceded the outbreak of the Revolution. His home in King and Queen County, on the Mattapony River, was known as "Laneville". There are evidences that this was the longest house ever built in Colonial Virginia.

There is a tradition that Richard and his wife, not being on good terms, lived apart, one in each end of this long house. It is said that occasionally when Richard would want to pay his wife a visit of state, he would order his coach and four and drive the long distance from his quarters to those of his wife.

A proverbial expression today in King and Queen County is "As rich as Dick Corbin."

Richard was the son of Gawin Corbin, who married Catherine, a daughter of Ralph Wormley of "Rosegill," Middlesex County. Gawin's home was known as "Buckingham," (now disappeared) in Middlesex County on the Rappahannock River. It was here that Richard was born in 1715. He married Betty Tayloe of "Mt. Airy" and went from Buckingham over to King and Queen and built "Laneville," (also disappeared). When he died, he was buried near the old home "Buckingham."

A few hundred yards from the site of the main house on the Buckingham estate, in a body of woods, one stumbles on a number of fragments, the remains of three or four slab tombstones. One of these stones bears the following inscription:

(Coat of Arms)
Here lies the Body
of the Hon. Richard Corbin Esq.,
who departed this life on the 20th
of May 1790 aged 76 years.
and alfo of
Mrs. Betty Corbin his Lady
who died on the 13th May 1784
Aged 65 years.

No. 2.—MEREDITH.

A few miles up the Mattapony river above West Point, is "Dixon," a small though lovely example of Colonial architecture, still standing in good condition.

This place was owned by William Meredith whose tombstone can be found about 150 yards from the house.

The inscription was difficult to decipher, but after several attempts by different persons, the following was agreed upon as the correct reading:

To the memory of
Mr. William Meredith, whose
humanity, strict integrity
and honour secured to
him the friendship
of all that knew him
who departed this life
the 10th of
November 1760, in
the 56th year of his
age
Also of his inconsol-
able consort, Mrs.
Lettuce Meredith of
exemplary life and virtue
who departed this life
the 6th of April, 1766
in the 62nd year of
her age.

William Meredith was a vestryman and Church Warden of the "New Church" of Stratton Major, which was built on Richard Corbin's land and was the largest and finest church of the Colonial period in Virginia.

It is thought that this William Meredith was of the same family as Colonel Samuel Meredith of the Hanover Volunteers, who married the sister of Patrick Henry.

The present Baptist Church in West Point is built on the site of an old Church of England building. On these grounds there is a tombstone to George Meredith, who died in 1728. This George was probably a brother of William Meredith.

William's son, Samuel, married Christina Gregory, a descendant of Lord Delaware.

No. 3.—ANDERSON.

In the yard of the White House, on the Pamunkey river, the home of Martha Dandridge Custis at the time that she became

Mrs. George Washington, there is a flat tombstone which reads:

James Anderson
who Died March 12th, 1807
Aged 62 years
and
Helen Anderson
His Wife
Who Died November 30th 1809
aged 62 years
and
James Anderson
their son
who Died May 14, 1815
aged 31 years
This tribute of respect is
erected by their Son and Brother

This tombstone is found about 75 yards from the foundations of the original White House.

In an obituary of Mrs. Margaret Anderson Young of Richmond, which was published in the *Daily Dispatch* of June 2, 1882, the following facts about the Anderson family were given:

James Anderson, with his wife and children, sailed to this country and landed in Norfolk, Va., in 1790. Mr. Anderson was for several years employed at Mount Vernon and was a trusted friend of Washington and was present at his death in 1799.

Mrs. Young remembered seeing Washington riding forth to the fields on a rainy day just preceding the illness which resulted in his death.

In her family Bible, which Mrs. Young cherished as her dearest possession there was an entry showing that her father managed the Custis estate "White House," in 1806. In that same year, Margaret Anderson was united in marriage with Richard Young, Parson Blair officiating. The entry states that the "marriage ceremony was performed in the very room where Washington was married to the charming Widow Custis."

Among the fond recollections of guests at Mount Vernon, after Washington's retirement, was a superbly mellow rye whiskey. "This rye was distilled at Mount Vernon under the skilled hand of James Anderson, the General's chief overseer, who had learned the art in Scotland."

No 4.—MACON.

There is an island in the Pamunkey river in New Kent County, almost three miles above the "White House" which is known as "Macon's Island".

The earliest Macon about whom we have information was Gideon. He lived in New Kent in 1682 and was a member of the House of Burgesses in 1696. He was Commander-in-chief of the military forces in 1702. He married Martha Woodward and they had a son William Macon who married Mary Hartwell.

Several years ago, by prodding into the ground of the old graveyard on Macon's Island, now an overgrown mass of bramble and ruin, we uncovered the tombstone of William and his wife Mary.

It reads as follows:

> Here Lie the Bodies of William Macon and Mary his Wife. He was born 11th November 1694 & departed this life in the 79th year November of his Age 1773.
> She was born 18 June 1703 and departed this Life 19 November 1770. They were married 24th September 1719.
> Had issue Ann, Martha, Mary William Henry Elizabeth Sarah Mary Judy Hartwell & Anna of whom two are interred near this

place viz. Ann who died 9 November 1736 Aged 16 and Mary who died 29th January 1733 Aged 9 year.

Elizabeth Macon, mentioned above married Warner Washington, a member of the illustrious Washington family.

A daughter of Gideon Mason, Martha, married Orlando Jones. Of this marriage was born Frances, the mother of Martha Dandridge Custis Washington.

In a letter written by a daughter of Colonel William Hartwell Macon of New Kent County, a grandson of the William Macon of the tombstone, she says: "The Macon family are French Huguenots. The pioneer to this country was the private secretary to Lord Berkley and came over February 1642. I think he settled in New Kent County on the Pamunkey river and raised his family there just 2½ miles above the White House. . . . . . It was on this island that my father went to live and there entertained General Lafayette while on his way to Yorktown at the time of the siege."

Macon's Island is inaccessible to the ordinary tourist, but can be reached by a small boat, through Macon's Creek.

There is no trace of the old home on the "Island" now, but a later home, "Mount Prospect" was built on an overlooking hill after the Revolution by the Colonel Hartwell Macon referred to in the letter, and stands there now.

OLD TOMBSTONES IN NEW KENT COUNTY.

COLLECTED BY THE EDITOR.

I.

ST. PETER'S CHURCH.[1]

Here Lyeth the Body of
Ann Clopton
the wife of William Clopton[2] of the
County of New Kent.   She departed
this Life y° 4: day of March Anno Domini 1716
In the 70th year of her Age.
She left three Sons & two Daughters
By Her said Husband, viz:
Robert, William, Walter, Ann & Elizabeth.
[*Arms.*]

Here
Lie Interred the Bodies of
Thomas & Robert Sons of the
Revd Mr David Mossom[2] Rector
of this Parish: Thomas Departed
this Life March the 29th 1739
Aged 20 yeares.   Robert Departed
this Life December the 17th 1744
Aged 7 months.

Here Lyeth the
Body of Mr Daniel Farrell[3]
Of this Parish who departed
this Life 8th of May 1736
Aged 42 yeares.

Reverendus David Mossom ‘ prope Jacet,
Collegii St. Joannis Cantabrigiae obiti, Alumnus,
Hujus Parochiæ Rector Annos Quadraginta,
Omnibus Ecclesiæ Anglicanæ Presbyteriis
Inter Americanos Ordine Presbyteratus Primus;
Literatura Paucis secundus,
Qui tandem senis et Moerore coufectus
Ex variis Rebus arduis quas in hac vita perpessus est
Mortisq: in dies memor, ideo virens et valens
Sibi hunc sepulturæ locum posuit et elegit
Uxoribus Elizabetha et Maria quidem juxta sepultis
Ubi requiescat, donec resuscitatus ad vitam Eternam
Per Jesum Christum salvatorem nostrum
Qualis erat, indicant illi quibus benenotus
Superstiles Non hoc sepulchrale saxum
Londini Natus 25 Martii 1690
Obiit 4° Jan¹¹ 1767.

II.

CUMBERLAND.

[Skull and cross bones.]
Here Lyeth Inter'd the Body of
Frances the Daughter of
Mʳ Willᵐ ‘ and Mʳˢ Elizaᵗʰ Chamberlayne
who Departed this Life the 17ᵗʰ day
of November 1722 Aged 30 days
Also the Body of Ann Chamberlayne
who departed this Life the 8ᵗʰ day of
October 1725 Aged one year
6 months and 25 days.

Here lieth the
Body of Sarah yᵉ wife
of Richard Littlepage ‘
who Departed this life
the 21ˢᵗ of January
173⅘ Aged
23 Years.

Here Lies the Body
of John Watkins Esq.
late of New Kent county now deceased
who departed this Life the 10th day
of March 1785. Aged 53 years.
He married Betty Claiborne
the Eldest Daughter of Philip
Whitehead Claiborne Esq.
of the county of King William
By whom he had 3 children
One Son and two Daughters
John Dandridge Watkins
Elizabeth   ?   Watkins
and Ann Dandridge Watkins.

Here Lyeth Interred
the Body of
Mrs Frances Littlepage
Widow of Capt Richard Littlepage
She Departed this Life
The 21st day of February
Anno Domini 1732
In the 55th Year of Her Age.

---

* * * dy of
* * lepage who
* * ober 1732.
* * * years.

Here Lyeth the Body of
Judith Littlepage
Who was born the 2^d of August
1715 and departed this Life
the 17th of June 1723.

---

* * page
169–.

NOTES BY THE EDITOR.

[1] New Kent county was formed out of York county in 1654.   St. Peter's parish originally occupied the territory now known as New Kent.   From this tract Blissland parish was formed about 1684.   There is an old vestry-book

359

and register of St. Peter's, beginning about 1683. The present St. Peter's Church is of brick, and was built in 1703, at a cost of 146,000 weight of tobacco. The steeple was built twelve years later. (See Meade.)

² The Clopton family first settled in Hampton parish, York county. The register of the Vicar-General of the Archbishop of Canterbury shows that a license was issued June 4, 1668, to Isaac Clopton, of St. Giles-in-the-Fields, citizen and haberdasher, bachelor, about 24 [years], to marry Miss Martha Hill, of the same, spinster, about 21 [years]; consent of her guardian, Thomas Hill, of Cambridge University, gent (her parents being dead), to be married at Brantford, Middlesex. Was this Isaac Clopton the one sworn "according to Rᵗ. hon'ble the Governor's order," justice of York county, Va., January 24, 1675–'76? He married in Virginia, Mary ——, who married, first, Thomas Bassett, who died before 1660, leaving a son William (probably by an earlier marriage) under 18 years. This son moved to New Kent. She married, secondly, William Fellgate, skinner of London, brother of Capt. Robert Fellgate, of York county, Va. William Fellgate died on Fellgate's Creek, York county, in 1660, and his widow married, thirdly, Capt. John Underhill, formerly of Worcester, England. His will was proved October 24, 1672, and he had, by his wife Mary, John, Nathaniel, Jane, and Mary. His widow then married Dr. Isaac Clopton, by whom no issue; they were both dead by January 25, 167⅚, when her will was proved.

"Mr. William Clopton" was constable of York-Hampton parish in 1682. January 23, 168⅔, he executed a deed of gift to his daughters Anne and Elizabeth. The following from the records of York shows that he was born in 1655:

The deposition of William Clopton aged about thirty Yeares sayth

That coming to the ffrench Ordinary in the Nynth of March last he happened to meet wᵗʰ Mʳ Thos: Watkinson who asked yoʳ Deponᵗ to give him a morning's draught. I told him if he had no money I would. In drinking of which hee asked yoʳ Deponᵗ why he was so unkinde to attach his wife's silver Cup I answered I had done nothing but what I did by the court's order; then he sᵈ the court had done more then they could answer and that he would Justifie and further yoʳ Deponᵗ sayth not   WM CLOPTON

Aprill yᵉ 24ᵗʰ 1685

Sworne to in York Court and is Recorded
              Test   WM MALTYWARD c ℔ ord. cur.

Mr. Clopton turns up next in New Kent, where he was one of the justices. There is an original deed dated July 22, 1710, from "John Bacon of St. Peter's Parish and New Kent Co yeoman to Wm. Clopton jun of same parish and co. yeoman," with arms of Clopton on a wax seal opposite the name of John Bacon. These arms are the same as on the tomb of Anne Clopton and agree in Burke with arms of Clopton, of co. Suffolk, 1586: Sa. a bend erm. betw. two cotises dancettée or. Crest—A wolf's head per pale or and az. On the tomb the bend has a mullet for difference, indicating a third son. More will be said of the Cloptons in next issue. *

³ Capt. Hubert Farrell married Dorothy, daughter of Col. Thomas Drew, of Charles City. (QUARTERLY, Vol. IV., p. 5.) He was wounded in the defence of Jamestown in 1676, and was killed in the fight at King's Creek shortly

*See *Genealogies of Virginia Families: From the William and Mary College Quarterly Historical Magazine* (Baltimore: Genealogical Publishing Co., Inc., 1982), Vol. I, pp. 850-865.

after.   Daniel Farrell, who was born in 1694, and died May 8, 1736 (*Parish Register*), aged 42, was probably connected.   Issue of the last by Elizabeth his wife: Joseph, born October 8, 1725; Richard, born November 28, 1727.

⁴David Mossom (see QUARTERLY, IV., p. 66) became minister of St. Peter's Church in 1727.* There is proof that he was married three times.   Bishop Meade says he was married four times.   He was the person who officiated at the nuptials of George Washington, and continued in the ministry 40 years. According to his epitaph he was educated at St. John's College, Cambridge, and was the first native American admitted to the office of presbyter in the Church of England.   In his autobiography the Rev. Devereux Jarratt attributes a poor character to morals and religion in New Kent.   But it is so much easier to overdraw than to give an exact representation.   Jarratt says that Mossom was a poor preacher, very near-sighted, and, reading his sermons closely, kept his eyes fixed on the paper, and his remarks "seemed rather addressed to the cushion than to the congregation."   As illustrative of the lifeless condition of religion, he mentions a quarrel between Mr. Mossom and his clerk, in which the former assailed the latter from the pulpit in his sermon, and the latter, to avenge himself, gave out from the desk the psalm in which were these lines:

> "With restless and ungoverned rage,
> Why do the heathen storm?
> Why in such rash attempts engage
> As they can ne'er perform?"

His daughter Elizabeth married Capt. William Reynolds.

⁴ St. Peter's Parish Register has the following:

Ann dau to m' Wm Chamberlayne b. March 14, 172¾, died Oct 8, 1725.

Edward Pey, sone of W^m & Eliz^th Chamberlaine born Jan' 20th 172⅝.

Ann Kidley, dau. of Eliza Chamberlayne, widow, born April 10, 1737.

Wm Chamberlayne died Aug 2, 1736.

Edward Pye son of Richard and Mary Chamberlayne born Jan. 1768.

Wm. Chamberlayne made his will Oct. 1, 1735, and had by Elizabeth, his wife, Edward Pye, Richard, Thomas, Mary, Elizabeth. Frances, Anne, and Anne Kidley. "The widow married William Gray, of New Kent.   (Hening, V., p. 117.)   Of these, Richard had by Mary, his wife, Edward Pye, born January, 1768.   Thomas married Wilhelmina, daughter of William Byrd and Lucy Parke.   (Hening, VI., p. 319.)

⁵For an account of the Littlepage family, see Hayden's *Virginia Genealogies.*

*Ibid., Vol. III, p. 815.

TOMBSTONES IN NEW KENT COUNTY.

Inscriptions on old tombstone slabs in a family graveyard in New Kent County, between Black's Store and Quinton, on the Southern R. R., about 20 miles from Richmond, on land deeded on March 28, 1780, by Major Thomas⁴ Massie to Nathaniel Littleton Savage.

Communicated by EUGENE C. MASSIE.

"M. S.
Here lyeth interred the Body of
Mr. William Massie
Son of Thomas Massie
Of the County of New Kent, Gentn
He married Martha A Daughter
of William Macon *
of the said county Esq.
By whom He had two Sons
William and Thomas
Both surviving him who under
a just & dutiful sence of their Father
and Mother's tender affection
and Regard have caused this
and the adjacent Stone to be laid
over the place of their interment
as grateful memorial of them
He departed this life June the 15th 1751
in the 38th year of His Age"

"M. S.
Here lyeth interred the Body of
Mrs. Martha Bland
Daughter of William Macon
of the County of New Kent, Esq.
She was first wife of
Mr. William Massie to whom

She was married November ye 20th 1740
after whose decease She was married
to Richard Bland *
of the Couty of Prince George, Esq.
January the 1st 1759
She departed this life Aug. ye 8th †
in the 37th year of Her Age."

---

* This furnishes sufficient confirmation of the statement in QUAR-
TERLY, XIII, 197, that William Massie married Martha Macon, daughter of Col. William Macon.

† This tombstone confirms the tradition that Martha Macon, after
the death of William Massie, married a Bland, only it was Richard
Bland and not Theodorick. Col. Richard Bland, b. May 6, 1710—
d. October 28, 1776, married (1) Anne, d. Peter Poythress (2) in 1759,
Martha Macon, widow of William Massie, (3) Elizabeth Blair,
dau. of John Blair, President of the Council.

CEDAR GROVE FARM.*

New Kent County, Virginia.

Epitaphs form the Tombstones.

All that is mortal of
Letitia Tyler wife of John
Tyler, President of the United
States lies underneath this
marble. She departed this life
10th. September 1842 at the
Presidents house in the city
of Washington in the 52nd
year of her age. Her life was
an illustration of the
Christian virtues and her
death the death of the
righteous.

———

In memory of
Mary Tyler
Eldest daughter of
Ex-President John Tyler
and wife of Henry L. Jones
Charles City County Virginia.
Born April 15 1815.
Died June 17 1847.
An exemplary daughter,
wife and mother
a sister's tribute.

———

Mary Faibler
Daughter of
Robert and Priscilla Tyler
Died May 13th. 1845
Aged 4 years and four mos.
Sleep sweetest sleep.

———

Sacred to the memory of
Robert Christian
Born May 1785.
Died Aug. 1822.

Sacred to the memory of
Mary Christian
Born Feb. 1785.
Died Mar. 1818.

———

Martha
Daughter of Judge Semple and
wife of Judge J. B. Christian.
Born March 1801
Died Feb 1838
She sleeps in Jesus

———

In memory of
my Father Judge John B
Christian who
died in Williamsburg
Feb 21—1856.
Aged 63 years

And now Lord what is
my hope
Truly my hope is even
in thee

———

In memory of
Ann. B. Christian
wife of Doct. John F. Christian
Born July 1796
Died Sep. 1844
Thou art gone to the grave
But twere wrong to deplore thee
When God was thy ransom
thy guardian thy guide
He gave thee and took thee
and soon will restore thee
Where death has no sting since
the Saviour has died.

———

*This was the residence of Robert Christian, father of Letitia
Christian, first wife of President John Tyler.

364

Little Henry
youngest child of
J. B. and M. Christian
died in Williamsburg
Aged 8 years.

———

In memory of
Mary William
Daughter of William and
Ann B. Savage
Born Dec 1816
Died Aug 1824
Thou wert a lovely little flower
of tender growth and as
time's hand is rent and
unseen drew aside the
curtain of infancy thy
limbs began to gather
strength and thy cheeks
to gather bloom, But death
came and tore thee from
thy Parents stem. Yet
thou shalt bloom again (for
the wintery blasts of death
kill not the buds of virtue)
and shall rize in full immortal beauty and live to die no
more.

———

Sacred to the memory of
Rev. Henry Mandeville Denison
son of the Hon. George and
Caroline
Bowman Denison. Born in
Wilkes-Barre Pa. July 29th, 1822
His manliness of character and
proficiency in sound learn-
ing were known to all long
before he graduated with dis-
tinguished honor at Dickinson
College Penn'a 1840. He was
ordained Deacon by Bishop
Meade in July 1844. His

first field of labor in the
Ministry were Greenville
and Pendleton So. Ca. His
next charge was of Brandon
Parish, Prince George County
Virginia From whence he
removed to Bruton Parish
Williamsburgh Virginia Where
he was twice Rector. While there
he was elected as assistant to
Rev. Doctor Stone Christs Church
Brooklyn. While in that parish
he married Alice the youngest
daughter of Ex President Tyler.
In the fall of 1853 he accepted
the Rectorship of St. Paul's
Church Louisville Ky. In
1857 he resigned and removed
to Charleston So. Ca. and
accepted the Rectorship of
St. Peter's church where
actively engaged in his
ministerial duties from
which no fear of death could
withdraw him. He died on
the 28th of September 1858 of
the prevailing epedemic.
Faithful in all things while
he lived. In death he is
universally lamented.
Denny.

———

Alice
Daughter of Ex President
John Tyler and wife of
Rev. Henry M. Denison.
Born March 23rd. 1828, at
Greenway in Charles City
County. Died June 8th 1854.
at Louisville Ky.
True to her Father
her husband
her child
and her God.

WEBB TOMBSTONES IN THE FAMILY BURYING GROUND AT HAMPSTEAD, NEW KENT COUNTY, VA.

Contributed by W. Mac. Jones.

(From the south end of lot passing northward.)

Mrs. Mary Ann Webb, Wife of Mr. Henry Webb, married June 16th, 1813 and on the 16th of Sept., 1852 she resigned a life which had been consecrated to the service of God and which was adorned by the grace of the Spirit.

Sacred to the memory of Conrade Webb Esqr. who was born May 3rd, 1778. Intermarried with Lucy Osborne 1803 and again intermarried Georgina Braxton 1823. He survived his wives and all his children and departed this life July 26th, 1842.

Here lies interred in hope of a glorious Resurrection the earthly remains of Mrs. Georgina Webb, consort of Conrade Webb of Hampstead. Departed this life the 28th July, 1831 in the 35th year of her age.

Erected to the memory of Lucius Osborne Webb of Hampstead. Departed this life 24th day of October, 1825, aged 13½ months.

Memory of Osborne Webb, son of Conrade and Mrs. Lucy Webb of Hampstead. Departed this life 4th May, 1820, in the 16th year of his age.

This marble marks the spot where were Deposited the earthly remains of Mrs. Lucy Webb, consort of Conrade Webb of Hampstead. Departed this life 25 January, 1816, in the 29th year of her age.

Births and Baptisms.

Norfolk County, Virginia.

TRANSCRIBED BY EDWARD W. JAMES.

Register of Southern Branch, from Octob^r, 1751 to Octob^r, 1752:

Anne, Daughter of Edwd and Mary Denby, borne y^e December the 19th 1751.

Elisabeth, Daughter of Lem^{ll} and Amey Wiles, borne ye 2^d of October, 1750.

Sarah, Daugh^r of John and Sarah Bass, borne ye 13th of Octob^r 1751.

Sofiah, Daugh^r of Thos and Sofiah Edward: borne ye 17th Octob^r 1751.

Mary, D^r of Mark and Mary Burton, borne ye 7th of November, 1751.

Solomon, Son of Solomon and Abi Butt, borne ye 4th of November, 1751.

Mary, Daught. of James and Sarah Pinkerton, bor ye 20th Septr 1752.

Ann, Daught. of Cartwrite and Eliz^a Butt, borne ye 7th November 1751, and Baptiz^d ye 8th of December, 1751.

Jacob, Son of John and Margret Owins, borne ye 4th of Augt 1751.

Thomas, Son of Thos and Feebey Williams borne ye 10th March, 1747–8.

James, Son of Tho[s] and Febey Williams, borne y[e] 16th January, 1750–1.

Matthew, Son of Jeremiah and Eliz[a] Foreman, borne y[e] 3[d] November, 1751.

Sarah, Dau[r] of Patrick and Mary Kevton, borne y[e] 6th of feb[r] 1752.

Mary, Daught. of Robert and Mary Hodges, borne y[e] 21st of Decemb[r] 1751.

Thomas, Son of Jeremiah and Sarah Etheredge borne y[e] 8th Novemb[r] 1751.

Hiram, Son of Benjamin and Courtne Hodges, borne y[e] 20th Decemb[r] 1751.

Elinor, Daugh[r] of Lovy and Affiah Smith, borne y[e] 2[d] October, 1751.

Abi, Dau[r] of Tho[s] and Lydia Williams, borne y[e] 25th Decembe[r] 1751.

Thomas, of William and Martha Wallis, borne y[e] 7th January, 1752, and Baptiz[d] y[e] 12th of April, 1752.

Pattey, Daugh[r] of Henry and Patiene Smith, borne y[e] 10th Novemb[r] 1751.

Sarah, D[r] of Lem[l] and Ann Miller, borne y[e] 3[d] of Novemb[r] 1751.

Peledge, Son of Lem[ll] and Ruth Hodges, borne y[e] 11th of January, 1752.

John, Son of Abraham and Peggey Mesler, borne y[e] 18th of Octob[r] 1751.

William, Son of Michel and Nanney Maning, borne y[e] 19th Septemb[r] 1751.

Ester, D[r] of Lott and Prudance Maund, borne y[e] 15th Feb[r] 1752.

Maxey, Son of Maxeymillion and Mary Marden, borne y[e] 27th of Decemb[r] 1751.

Tamer, D[r] of Jeremiah and Mary Chervey, borne y[e] 19th January, 1752.

Jesse, Son of Solomon and Martha Hodges, borne ye 8th Decemb^r 1751.

Willis, Son of John and Margaret Fereby, borne ye 20th January, 1752.

Lemuel, Son of Peledge and Jane Miller, borne ye 25th Octob^r 1751.

Martha, D^r of Mallichi and Ann Maning, borne ye 25th Octob^r 1751, and Baptiz^d ye 3^d of May, 1752.

Benjiman, Son of Halsted and Mary Ann Hollowell, borne ye 9th Septr 1751.

John, Son of John and Mary Matthias, borne ye July, 1750.

William, Son of W^m and Courtne Bowin, borne ye 4th July, 1752.

Mary Ann, D^r of Abilon and Mary Serrs, borne ye 21st Septr 1752, and Baptiz^d ye 23^d Septemb^r 1752.

Lydia Solley, D^r of Caleb and Sarah Nash, borne ye 6th of June, 1752.

Willis, Son of Richard and Dinah McCoy, borne ye 2^d of June, 1752.

Jesse, Son of Jehosaphat and Eliz^a Hopkins, borne ye 6th of May, 1752.

Anthony, Son of Joseph and Agness Curlin, borne ye 20th June, 1752, and Baptiz^d ye 8th of October, 1752.

Thos Nash. [1]

---

[1]. Clerk of the precinct, probably.

DEATH NOTICES IN THE
NORFOLK GAZETTE and PUBLIC LEDGER
1804-1816

Compiled by MARY C. BROWN*

THIS list of death notices was originally prepared as an index to the file of the *Norfolk Gazette and Public Ledger* in the Norfolk Public Library. Therefore, the dates given are not the days on which individuals died, but are instead the days on which the death notices were printed. Usually, but by no means always, the person mentioned had died only a few days earlier. Inquiries concerning the death notices should be directed to the Norfolk Public Library, Norfolk, Virginia.

A similar list of death notices found in Richmond newspapers of the period was published forty-three years ago; "List of Obituaries from Richmond, Virginia, Newspapers," *Virginia Magazine of History and Biography*, XX (1912), 282-291, 364-371.**

Abbott, Mrs. Mary, wife of James Abbott	June 24, 1812
Aitcheson, Mrs. Mary, relict of William Aitcheson	Sept. 14, 1814
Aitcheson, William, at his seat near this Borough	Oct. 9, 1804
Allan, Thomas, a native of Scotland	Feb. 4, 1811
Allen, Capt. H. M., of the U. S. Artillery	May 12, 1813
Allen, Nathaniel, at Edenton, N. C., for many years a representative of the General Assembly of North Carolina	Dec. 4, 1805
Allen, William, at his father's house in Suffolk	Dec. 4, 1809
Allen, William Henry, late commander of the U. S. sloop of war *Argus*	Oct. 13, 1813
Allmand, Mrs., wife of Harrison Allmand	Nov. 6, 1811
Amos, James	Feb. 8, 1805
Anderson, John	Oct. 2, 1809
Anderson, Margaret	Dec. 30, 1811
Andrews, Loving, of Charleston	Nov. 1, 1805
Ansell, Capt. John, of Princess Anne County	Dec. 5, 1815
Applewhaite, Miss Polly, daughter of the late John Applewhaite	Feb. 25, 1811

*Miss Brown is in charge of the Sargeant Memorial Room of the Norfolk Public Library.
**Pages 149-166, this volume.

Archer, Edward ....Feb. 27, 1807
Armistead, Miss Julia, sister of the late esteemed
   Theodorick Armistead ....July 2, 1816
Armistead, Mrs. Maria, wife of Thomas Armistead..............................Nov. 8, 1805
Armistead, Mrs. Martha, wife of Theodorick Armistead.....................Aug. 15, 1810
Armistead, Mrs. Priscilla, relict of Thomas Armistead.........................July 27, 1814
Armistead, Theodorick, navy agent at this place, a native
   of Petersburg ....Nov. 23, 1812
Armistead, Thomas ....May 22, 1813
Arthurs, William, Jr., of London...Oct. 24, 1808
Asbury, the Rev. Francis, Bishop of the Methodist Church
   of the U. S., near Fredericksburg...April 11, 1816

Babbington, Mrs. ....Sept. 19, 1808
Bagnall, Joseph ....Dec. 2, 1811
Bagnall, Mrs., consort of Richard Bagnall...July 27, 1810
Baker, Mrs. Rebecca...May 29, 1812
Balfour, Miss Catherine, at "Fighting Creek," Powhatan County..............Aug. 29, 1815
Ball, William, ensign of the Winchester Rifle Company
   of Fort Nelson..May 26, 1813
Ballard, William ....March 20, 1812
Banister, Mrs. Nancy, relict of Col. John Banister,
   of "Battersèa," near Petersburg...Jan. 12, 1814
Banks, John, at Richmond, of that place...Oct. 16, 1809
Banks, Mrs. Martha Koyall, consort of Henry Banks, of Richmond,
   and daughter of Dr. John K. Read of this Borough...........................Dec. 10, 1804
Barret, John C..Oct. 20, 1804
Barrett, Capt. John..Jan. 12, 1810
Barron, Capt. Robert...Jan. 1, 1812
Barron, Commodore Samuel, in Hampton..Oct. 31, 1810
                                                      Nov. 2, 1810
Barrott, Edmund ....Nov. 23, 1814
Bausman, Adeline ....Dec. 30, 1811
Bean, James, of the Island of Jamaica...April 7, 1808
Bedinger, Solomon ....Sept. 19, 1808
Bee, Thomas, Federal Judge of the District of South Carolina..............March 6, 1812
Bell, Mrs., consort of Capt. Henry Bell...Dec. 3, 1814
Bell, Capt. John, at Petersburg..Oct. 2, 1813
Belt, William B., at Barbados, an officer in the bank of George Town............Jan. 2, 1811
Bennett, Mrs. Ann, consort of William Bennett......................................June 9, 1813
Bennett, William ....Nov. 23, 1815
Bessom, Capt. John...March 2, 1809
Biggs, Lt. ....April 17, 1813
Blount, Gen. Thomas, a member of Congress from North Carolina............Feb. 14, 1812
Booker, George, at his farm on Back River...July 13, 1808

Bosher, Mrs. John...Jan. 3, 1812
Botts, Benjamin, and wife..Dec. 30, 1811
Boush, Capt. Nathaniel..Jan. 8, 1813
Boush, Robert, at one time President of the Common Council.............Oct. 16, 1809
Bouvart, Madame Eulalie, widow of Mon. D. Donjeur Bouvart..........Sept. 2, 1811
Bowden, Mrs. Elizabeth, wife of Richard Bowden.............................Oct. 3, 1806
Bowden, Richard ....May 27, 1811
Bowdoin, Mrs., consort of John T. Bowdoin, of Surry......................Dec. 5, 1815
Bragg, Henry ....Nov. 8, 1805
Bramble, Capt. John...Sept. 28, 1814
Braxton, Mrs. Taylor..Dec. 30, 1811
Brent, the Hon. Richard, one of the senators from this state..............Jan. 7, 1815
Briggs, John Howell, at his seat near Petersburg...............................March 7, 1808
Broome, the Hon. John, Lt. Gov. of New York..................................Aug. 15, 1810
Brough, Mrs., wife of Robert Brough..Sept. 18, 1806
Brown, Mrs. Elizabeth, consort of Henry Brown...............................Dec. 12, 1808
Brown, Mrs. Elizabeth, consort of John Brown, at
    Shocco Springs, Warten, N. C...Sept. 24, 1814
Brown, Dr. Gustavus, at his seat near Port Tobacco, Md...................Oct. 4, 1804
Brown, John ....Aug. 10, 1815
Brown, William ....Dec. 30, 1811
Brunet, Henry ....Dec. 14, 1808
Brushwood, Thomas ....Sept. 29, 1806
Burcher, Mrs. Margaret, wife of John Burcher..................................Oct. 2, 1804
Burke, Patrick, a native of Ireland..March 25, 1807
Burns, Mrs. Frances, in King William County....................................Nov. 30, 1814
Burns, James, of Bertie County, N. C..Feb. 18, 1815
Burrows, William, late commander of the U. S. Brig *Enterprise*........Sept. 18, 1813
Burt, John, proprietor of the Wigwam Gardens.................................May 31, 1811
Burton, Robert, of Richmond...Feb. 19, 1806
Butler, Ensign John B...June 29, 1814
Buxton, the Rev. John, minister of the Methodist church...................May 15, 1815
Byrd, Mrs. [Mary], relict of the Hon. William Byrd of "Westover,"
    and sister of Thomas Willing of Philadelphia, Pa..........................March 30, 1814
Byrd, Richard W., at "Westover"...Oct. 21, 1815
Byrd, Mrs., wife of Richard W. Byrd, of Smithfield, at "Westover"......Oct. 14, 1814

Calvert, Mrs. Anne...March 2, 1808
Calvert, Cornelius, for forty years an alderman and
    several times mayor of this Borough...Nov. 6, 1804
Calvert, John ....Jan. 16, 1809
Calvert, John T...Nov. 30, 1814
Calvert, Mrs. Margaret, relict of John Calvert, at Suffolk...................Oct. 8, 1814
Camp, Mrs. Ann, consort of John Camp..June 4, 1816
Campbell, James, at Petersburg...April 6, 1814

Capron, George ....Feb. 7, 1806
Carrick, Capt. Andrew, at Fort Johnson, of the ship
    Minerva, of Greenock..Oct. 13, 1804
Carrington, Col. Edward, in Richmond.....................................Nov. 2, 1810
Carroll, the Most Rev. Dr. John, Arch-Bishop of Baltimore.......Dec. 7, 1815
Carter, Charles, at "Shirley" in Charles City County....................July 7, 1806
Carver, Henry Wells..Nov. 26, 1814
Chaine, Joseph, a native of Ireland...Aug. 15, 1808
Chamberlaine, Mrs. Maria H., consort of
    Captain Edward Chamberlaine...Aug. 1, 1816
Chamberlaine, Mrs. Sarah, wife of Captain Edward Chamberlaine.........Jan. 21, 1811
Chapman, Mrs., consort of Robert Chapman.............................May 2, 1810
Christie, James, near Natchez, Miss., a native of Boston,
    formerly of this Borough..Dec. 14, 1810
Clarke, Thomas, a native of Portsmouth, in New Orleans...........Oct. 30, 1805
Clay, Mary ....Dec. 30, 1811
Clay, Mathew, at Halifax Court House, a member of Congress
    from Campbell District..June 9, 1815
Clynch, Bartholomew, of Portsmouth, at New York....................Nov. 11, 1805
                                                 Jan. 20, 1806
Cocke, Mrs. Elizabeth, widow of James Cocke, at Williamsburg........Nov. 2, 1815
Coleman, Samuel, at his seat in Nansemond, late of this Borough........Sept. 14, 1812
Collins, Capt. Freeman C., late of Liverpool, N. S......................May 3, 1809
Collins, Michael, on board the schooner *Dispatch,* of Petersburg........July 7, 1806
Collins, Philip ....Sept. 30, 1807
Colquohoun, Robert, of Petersburg...Oct. 19, 1814
Colthirst, Mrs., late of the Island of Jamaica.............................March 28, 1806
Convert, Mrs., and child...Dec. 30, 1811
Conyers, Miss ....Dec. 30, 1811
Cook, Mrs. William, and child...Dec. 30, 1811
Cooke, George Frederick, celebrated actor, at New York............Sept. 30, 1812
Copeland, Margaret ....Dec. 30, 1811
Copeland, Miss Nancy, of Isle of Wight County........................March 16, 1814
Corbin, John Taylor, eldest son of Maj. Richard Corbin,
    of Laneville ....Jan. 23, 1816
Corling, Charles, at Petersburg...Jan. 15, 1814
Cornick, William, in Princess Anne...Jan. 27, 1806
Cornwall, John, of the Great Bridge..April 21, 1813
Corran, Mrs. Ann, consort of William Corran............................Oct. 31, 1815
Coutts, Miss Elvira..Dec. 30, 1811
Cowan, William ....Oct. 22, 1814
Cowper, Mrs. Rebecca, wife of William Cowper,
    at Murfreesboro, N. C..Feb. 26, 1808
Cowper, Capt. Robert, at his residence in the county of Nansemond.......March 23, 1812

Cox, Capt. James, at Portsmouth..Aug. 3, 1808
Cox, William ....June 9, 1806
Craig, Ann, daughter of Mrs. Adam Craig.......................................Dec. 30, 1811
Creecy, I.t. William, of Chowan County, N. C.................................Feb. 18, 1815
Crosbie, James B..Nov. 27, 1809
Cross, Westenra, a native of Newry...Nov. 3, 1806
Cunningham, William ....July 31, 1807
Currie, Dr. James, at Richmond...April 27, 1807
Currie, William, at Kempsville...Dec. 24, 1804
Cuthbert, James ....Sept. 15, 1813
Cuthbert, William ....Jan. 17, 1812
Cutler, Miss Catherine, in Portsmouth..Sept. 22, 1813

Dana, Phineas, a native of Boston..April 11, 1808
Davies, William, in Mecklenburg County, late Collector
   of this port...Dec. 23, 1805
Davis, Mrs. Emily, wife of James Davis, buried in Portsmouth........Dec. 7, 1808
Davis, John, eldest son of Augustine Davis, editor of *Virginia Gazette*
   of Richmond, at Old Point Comfort..Sept. 18, 1806
Davis, John, at Portsmouth..June 12, 1811
                                                                                                        June 14, 1811
Davis, Mary ....Dec. 30, 1811
Davis, Mrs. Mildred D., consort of Capt. John P. Davis..................April 4, 1808
Davis, the Rev. Thomas, in Nansemond County, he was
   a native of Norfolk...Dec. 9, 1815
Davis, William, at Gosport...May 23, 1808
Dawley, James, of this place, at Murfreesboro, N. C.......................Dec. 14, 1814
Dawson, John, at Washington..April 6, 1814
Decatur, Capt. Stephen, at Frankford, Pa..Nov. 23, 1808
Decatur, Mrs., in Philadelphia, relict of Capt. Decatur...................April 6, 1812
Dexter, Samuel, at Athens, N. Y..May 14, 1816
Dick, William ....March 31, 1809
Dickenson, James ....Aug. 1, 1806
Dickenson, Mrs. Mary..May 12, 1813
Dickson, Henry, of Portsmouth...Dec. 14, 1810
Dickson, John, editor of the Petersburg *Intelligencer*....................July 20, 1814
Dickson, Mrs. Mary, wife of William Dickson, of Gosport...............March 26, 1810
Dixon, George ....Dec. 30, 1811
Donaghey, Mrs. Elizabeth, wife of John Donaghey..........................Feb. 25, 1815
Donaldson, Robert, in Brunswick County, of Fayetteville, N. C.,
   formerly of the House of Delegates..July 6, 1808
Dorsey, Levin ....Jan. 18, 1813
Dowdall, James, a native of Ireland...Nov. 10, 1813
Doyle, Martin ....April 17, 1813
Drayton, Lt. Glenn, of the frigate *Constellation*............................Sept. 7, 1814

Drummond, Mrs. Ann, relict of William Drummond................................Sept. 9, 1805
Drummond, William, of Fredericksburg...Oct. 4, 1804
Drysdale, Mrs. Hannah, consort of Capt. John Drysdale.......................March 4, 1808
Dunlop, Mrs. Mary R., wife of John Dunlop, of Petersburg....................Jan. 25, 1811

Edmonds, Mrs. Josephine, wife of Robert Edmonds, of Yorktown................Jan. 15, 1813
Elligood, William, in Princess Anne County..Oct. 21, 1815
Elliott, Miss, from New Kent County..Dec. 30, 1811
Eyre, Mrs. Grace, relict of William Eyre, in Northampton County.............April 4, 1809
Eyre, Mrs. Margaret, relict of Severn Eyre, of Northampton County.....March 13, 1812
Eyre, Miss Sarah T., daughter of the late William Eyre
    of Northampton County...July 8, 1815
Eyre, William, at his seat in Northampton County................................Dec. 28, 1808

Farmer, Mrs. Sarah..Sept. 21, 1807
Farrer, Mrs. Mary..June 9, 1815
Farrer, Thomas, near Cape Henry..Oct. 2, 1813
Fenwick, Mrs., wife of William Fenwick, of Manchester.........................Oct. 10, 1808
Ferguson, Walter, second son of Finlay Ferguson..................................Oct. 22, 1810
Ferrill, Robert..Dec. 30, 1811
Ferte, Dr. John George..Dec. 18, 1811
Fields, Robert..March 5, 1806
Fisher, Dr. Robert, at Suffolk..May 29, 1815
Frazier, Thomas..Dec. 30, 1811
Fry, Miss Margaret, daughter of John Fry...Oct. 29, 1810

Gadsden, Gen. Christopher, at Charleston..Sept. 11, 1805
Gallego, Mrs. ....Dec. 30, 1811
Galt, Capt. John M., of the U. S. Army...Feb. 8, 1815
Galt, Dr. John M., in Williamsburg..June 20, 1808
Gamble, Mrs. Charlotte S., wife of John Gamble, of Richmond...............Oct. 30, 1809
Gamble, Robert, in Richmond...April 20, 1810
Gardner, Capt. Freeman, of the British schooner, *Commerce*................May 21, 1808
Gardner, Capt. William, of the ship *Nancy*, of Philadelphia...............Oct. 31, 1815
Gaston, Mrs. Hannah, consort of the Hon. William Gaston,
    of Wilmington, N. C. ....July 24, 1813
Gatewood, Mrs., consort of Philemon Gatewood,
    Naval Officer of this Borough...Aug. 1, 1806
Gatewood, Mrs. Ann, consort of Thomas Gatewood...............................July 2, 1816
Gatewood, Sally..Dec. 30, 1811
Gerard, Mrs. ....Dec. 30, 1811
Gibbon, Lt. James...Dec. 30, 1811
Gibbons, Mrs. Ann, relict of Thomas Gibbons.....................................Dec. 17, 1810
Gibbons, Capt. Thomas, in York Town, of this Borough.........................Sept. 5, 1810
Gibson, Mrs. ....Dec. 30, 1811

Gibson, Robert, at Kingston in Jamaica, a native of Scotland, and a
resident of this Borough more than 30 years..May 7, 1816
Gilbert, Reynear ....June 8, 1810
Gilliat, Thomas, in Richmond...July 11, 1810
Gillies, William, in Petersburg...Dec. 18, 1813
Girardin, Mrs., and child..Dec. 30, 1811
Glenn, Mrs., wife of Thomas Glenn...July 18, 1810
Godwin, Dr. Burgh, at his residence in Nansemond....................................April 9, 1810
Godwin, Mrs. Clotilda, in Nansemond...Jan. 23, 1810
Goff, Fanny ....Dec. 30, 1811
Goodman, Jethro, of Elizabeth City, N. C..April 6, 1814
Goodson, Fielding W...Nov. 28, 1815
Gordon, Miss I. Carr...Sept. 29, 1804
Goulding, Mrs. Ann, wife of Daniel Goulding..Sept. 24, 1814
Granbery, George, son of John Granbery, lost at sea....................................Sept. 5, 1816
Granbery, John, lost at sea...Sept. 5, 1816
Gray, George Lewis, at the Island of St. Helena,
formerly editor of this paper...June 3, 1808
Green, Miss ....Dec. 30, 1811
Greenhow, Robert ....Dec. 30, 1811
Griffin, Lady C.[hristiana], consort of the Hon. Cyrus Griffin....................Oct. 19, 1807
Griffin, Dr. Corbin, at York Town..Oct. 6, 1813
Griffin, the Hon. Cyrus, at York, Judge of the U. S. Court
for the District of Virginia..Dec. 17, 1810
Griffin, Dr. Larkin, of the U. S. Navy.. Nov. 2, 1814
Griffin, Llewellyn, grandson of Dr. Corbin Griffin, and only son
of Maj. Thomas Griffin..Oct. 6, 1813
Griffin, Patsey ....Dec. 30, 1811
Griffin, Col. Samuel, in New York, of Virginia...Dec. 10, 1810
Grigsby, the Rev. Benjamin, minister of the Presbyterian church
of this place..Oct. 8, 1810
Griswold, [Roger,] Governor of Connecticut...Nov. 4, 1812
Gwathmey, Lucy ....Dec. 30, 1811

Habersham, Col. Joseph, in Georgia...Dec. 5, 1815
Haldane, Mrs. Elizabeth, in Petersburg...Nov. 16, 1815
Haldane, John ....March 26, 1816
Hall, Mrs. Martha, relict of Dr. Isaac Hall, of Petersburg..........................July 28, 1813
Halliday, Mrs. Ann, wife of Thomas Halliday...Jan. 30, 1807
Halstead, Lattimer, at his residence in Norfolk County...............................Aug. 4, 1813
Hancock, John, in Princess Anne County, for many years
a magistrate of that County...Feb. 26, 1814
Harper, Andrew, a native of Aberdeen, Scotland..July 29, 1811
Harris, Thomas H., in Camden County, N. C.,
a native of Bristol, England..Jan. 30, 1807

Harrison, Benjamin, at Brandon in the County of Prince George............Aug. 12, 1807
Harvey, Juliana ....Dec. 30, 1811
Harvey, Lewis ....April 15, 1807
Harvie, John, of Richmond..Jan. 3, 1812
Hayes, Mrs. Eliza, consort of Joseph Hayes..March 15, 1811
Hayes, Thomas, son of Joseph Hayes, in Dinwiddie County,
    of this place ....Aug. 17, 1814
Haynes, Mrs. Elizabeth, in Princess Anne County............................Oct. 14, 1808
Haynes, Maj. Erasmus, at Kempsville, Princess Anne County,
    of this place ....Dec. 2, 1811
Haynes, Capt. Thomas J..Jan. 3, 1812
Heerman, Mrs. Charity, at her farm in Princess Anne County,
    of this Borough..June 9, 1813
Heerman, Dr. Frederick, at Balltown Springs, of this Borough........Aug. 10, 1807
Henop, Daniel ....March 30, 1814
Henop, Mrs. Elizabeth, consort of John W. Henop............................July 31, 1811
Henry, John, at York, of Richmond...Aug. 26, 1807
Herbert, Capt. Edward...Nov. 16, 1814
Herbert, James, of Norfolk County...Oct. 1, 1814
Heron, Mrs. ....Dec. 30, 1811
Hewes, Abraham, at Alexandris..Nov. 4, 1805
Hill, William, of Liverpool..May 13, 1808
Hodge, Mrs. Sarah, in Smithfield...Oct. 9, 1813
Hodges, Mrs., consort of John Hodges, of Hodges Ferry...............March 16, 1814
Hodges, Mrs. Maria, consort of William Hodges................................June 5, 1807
Holladay, John, in Nansemond, at "Mt. Pickney".............................April 23, 1814
Holmes, Dr. Robert, of Petersburg, on board the ship *Bordeaux*........June 20, 1810
Holt, Rowland, of Surry...Feb. 11, 1815
Hughes, William ....Jan. 13, 1809
Hunter, Ariana ....Dec. 30, 1811
Hunter, Robert B., surgeon's mate of the Hospital............................April 6, 1814
Hunter, Mrs. Sally, wife of Dr. Edward R. Hunter,
    at "Piney Pleasant," Nansemond County......................................Jan. 28, 1811
Hutchings, Mrs. Ann..Nov. 17, 1813

Jacob, Col. Robert, of Northampton County......................................July 13, 1808
Jacobs, Elizabeth, daughter of Joseph Jacobs....................................Dec. 30, 1811
Jacobs, Joseph ....Dec. 30, 1811
Jennings, Mrs. Sarah...Sept. 16, 1808
Jerrod, Mrs. ....Dec. 30, 1811
Johnson, Betsey ....Dec. 30, 1811
Johnson, Mrs. Jane...Oct. 21, 1815
Johnston, Captain Richard, of the brig *White Haven*........................June 13, 1806
Johnston, Samuel, at his seat "Skewarkey,"
    formerly Governor of North Carolina...Aug. 22, 1816

Johnston, William ....Sept. 12, 1810
Jones, Ebenezer, of Massachusetts, suddenly at Portsmouth, Virginia..........May 17, 1811
Jones, Mrs. Elizabeth, consort of Paul G. G. Jones,
    in Powhatan County, of Cartersville...March 7, 1806
Jones, Thomas, at "Pembroke," near Hampton.......................................March 21, 1810
Jordan, Augustus C...March 23, 1810
Jordan, Robert, in Nansemond...Feb. 26, 1810
Judah, child of Barak Judah...Dec. 30, 1811

Kaltesein, Capt. Michael, at Charleston, Commander
    of Fort Johnson...Nov. 13, 1807
Keele, Capt. Robert..April 6, 1812
Keighly, Frederick ....Sept. 9, 1811
Kelly, Mrs., wife of George Kelly...April 4, 1810
Kemp, Col. Peter, in Richmond...July 27, 1812
Kerr, George, at Charleston, formerly of this place..................................July 27, 1814
Kerrison, William Peter, infant, at Portsmouth.......................................Oct. 2, 1813
Keyser, Lt. Peter, at Craney Island, of the 38th Regt.
    of U. S. Infantry...Oct. 5, 1814
King, Charles, son of Miles King...Aug. 20, 1806
King, Mrs. Frances P., wife of Miles King...Oct. 8, 1806
King, Miles ....June 22, 1814
Knox, Maj. Henry, at Boston, Vice-President of the Cincinnati..................Nov. 14, 1806
Knox, William, in Petersburg...March 30, 1812
Krafts, William, Lt. in the Navy of the Batavian Republic.........................Oct. 2, 1805

Lacy, the Rev. Michael, Pastor of the Roman Catholic Church
    for many years...March 1, 1815
La forest, Mrs., of Wythe County...Dec. 30, 1811
Laird, William ....Oct. 5, 1807
Lambert, Capt. Jonathan, near Tristan d'Acuna, formerly of Salem...........Oct. 1, 1814
Latimer, Capt. James, in Elizabeth City County, at "Mill Creek".................Sept. 2, 1811
Lawrence, Capt. James A..Aug. 28, 1813
                                                                                                July 7, 1813
Lawrence, John ....Dec. 29, 1814
Lawson, Dr. Anthony, in Southampton County.......................................Jan. 18, 1810
Lawson, Col. Thomas, in New Orleans, formerly a resident
    of this place..Nov. 27, 1811
Lecroix, Thomas ....Dec. 30, 1811
Lee, Richard Evers, one of the aldermen of this Borough, and President
    of the Branch Bank of Virginia in this place......................................June 11, 1813
Lee, Mrs., wife of Richard E. Lee...July 18, 1808
Lee, Richard H..Oct. 14, 1815
Leftwich, Lt., of the Bedford Artillery, at Fort Norfolk.............................Sept. 16, 1812
Leigh, Dr. William, of Portsmouth..Dec. 15, 1809

Lennon, Hugh, at Kingsport in Jamaica..Dec. 27, 1806
Leslie, Mrs. ....Dec. 30, 1811
Lewis, Major Thomas, of the Sweet Springs..Oct. 6, 1804
Lewis, Thomas, at his seat "Belle Farm" in Gloucester County,
  Colonel of the 4th Regt. of Virginia Artillery.......................................Nov. 25, 1805
Lightfoot, Henry Beskin, died in Richmond, of the Island of Antigua........Nov. 1, 1805
Lincoln, Maj. Gen. Benjamin, at Boston, late Collector of the
  Port of Boston and Charlestown...May 18, 1810
Lindsay, Adam ....Oct. 17, 1810
Littlepage, Miss ....Jan. 3, 1812
Livingston, Mrs. Anne...Sept. 16, 1808
Livingston, Capt. John, of this Borough, on Board the ship *Portia*........Dec. 2, 1811
Love, Alexander, at Richmond, of Norfolk County..................................June 19, 1813
Lovett, John ....June 8, 1814
Loyall, George, for many years one of the aldermen of this Borough........April 30, 1810
Loyall, Mrs., consort of George Loyall...Nov. 21, 1808
Loyall, Paul ....Feb. 2, 1807
Lucas, Capt. Edmund, in Petersburg, of Greensville; late commander
  of the detachment of Virginia militia, at Norfolk................................Dec. 9, 1812
Ludlow, Lt. Augustus C...Aug. 28, 1813
Lyle, James, of the Town of Manchester..Jan. 31, 1812
Lyles, Mrs. Anne, in Alexandria, wife of William Henry Lyles,
  of that town, daughter of William Lowry, of Baltimore...................Dec. 3, 1804
Lyon, Dr. James, of Northampton County...Dec. 4, 1811
Lyons, the Hon. Peter, in Hanover County, President of the
  Court of Appeals of this Commonwealth...Aug. 7, 1809

M'Causland, Miss Emily Jane, Baltimore, daughter of
  Marcus M'Causland ....March 20, 1811
M'Clurg, Walter, at Fincastle, only son of Dr. James M'Clurg,
  of Richmond ....Aug. 25, 1809
M'Credie, John ....Feb. 23, 1807
McDonald, Robert...June 29, 1807
M'Dougal, Miss Maria..Oct. 19, 1814
MacGill, Nathan ....Aug. 3, 1814
McIntosh, Robert, in Surry...Feb. 25, 1815
M'Kenzie, William, at his seat near Plymouth, N. C....................................Oct. 8, 1810
MacRae, Mrs., consort of Colin MacRae, of Manchester,
  on board the ship *Indian Chief*...Oct. 12, 1815

Macallister, Capt. David, of the Ancient Artillery.....................................Dec. 28, 1810
Madison, the Rt. Rev. James, at Williamsburg, Bishop of the
  Episcopal Church in Virginia..March 13, 1812
Maitland, Mrs. Susan, at Petersburg, wife of Robert Maitland,
  of this place...July 13, 1812

Marchant, Jordan, Justice of the Peace for the County................Nov. 11, 1811
Marks, Mrs. Cyprian, wife of Mordecai Marks................Dec. 30, 1811
Marsden, John G.................April 21, 1809
Marsh, Samuel ....Nov. 30, 1814
Marshall, Almerine, of Wythe County................Dec. 30, 1811
Marshall, William, in Richmond................June 4, 1816
Massey, Lt. of the U. S. Marine Corps................Feb. 10, 1812
Mathews, Gen. Thomas, Member of the Convention of 1788,
    delegate to the Assembly................Feb. 21, 1812
Maund, Robert C., of Westmoreland, funeral from Fort Norfolk................Aug. 1, 1816
Maupin, Mrs. Ann B., wife of Dr. George Washington Maupin
    and daughter of James Young................Aug. 22, 1806
Maxwell, Miss Helen, at the home of Thomas Talbot
    on Tanner's Creek................July 20, 1816
Maxwell, Mrs. Olivia Ann, wife of Capt. John Maxwell................July 14, 1814
Mayo, Louisa ....Dec. 30, 1811
Mazzie, Philip, at Pisa in Tuscany................June 25, 1816
Merritt, the Rev. Levy, in Nansemond, Minister of the
    Methodist Church of Portsmouth................July 31, 1813
Metcalf, Anthony ....Sept. 8, 1813
Milhado, Mrs., wife of David Milhado, in Princess Anne County................Nov. 23, 1814
Milhado, Mrs. Mary................Oct. 23, 1809
Miller, Capt. Willis, of Gosport, at Nova Scotia................June 9, 1815
Mitchell, Sir Andrew, at Bermuda................March 28, 1806
Mitchell, James ....May 23, 1808
Moore, James, a native of the Isle of Man................July 24, 1813
Moore, Robert ....July 1, 1807
Morgan, Mrs. Ann, consort of Jacob Morgan, daughter
    of Jonah Thompson, in Alexandria................July 11, 1816
Morgan, George, at Bermuda, for many years Secretary to the Consulate
    of his Britannick Majesty for the State of Virginia................Jan. 29, 1811
Morris, Robert, at Philadelphia................May 20, 1806
Moseley, Alexander ....April 7, 1806
Moseley, Col. Edward H., at Newtown, Princess Anne County,
    Clerk of that County................Feb. 5, 1814
Moseley, Mrs. Eliza, consort of Burwell B. Moseley................Nov. 9, 1815
Moseley, Capt. Hillary................April 21, 1813
Moseley, Gen. William, at Fincastle, Treasurer of the State................Oct. 8, 1808
Moss, Mrs. ....Dec. 30, 1811
Moultrie, Maj. Gen. William, at Charleston, S. C.................Oct. 9, 1805
Muckelston, John ....Aug. 31, 1807
Mutter, Mrs. [Lucinda], wife of John Mutter, of Richmond................Oct. 26, 1814

Nelson, Miss Maria................Dec. 30, 1811
Nestor, George, in Princess Anne County................March 11, 1811

Newton, Thomas, Sr., Collector of this Port..Sept. 11, 1807
Newton, Mrs. Thomas, wife of the Hon. Thomas Newton, Jr.......................May 15, 1805
Niemeyer, Mrs., consort of John C. Niemeyer...Sept. 28, 1812
Nimmo, John, in Princess Anne County, son of James Nimmo,
   of this Borough..Jan. 15, 1811
Nixon, John, at Philadelphia, President of the
   Bank of North America..Jan. 9, 1809
Noble, James ....June 1, 1810
Noblet, Mrs., consort of John Noblet..March 18, 1812
Norris, John ....Nov. 10, 1813
Nuttal, a carpenter..Dec. 30, 1811

O'Connor, Mrs. Eliza, consort of James O'Connor, editor of this paper......June 14, 1811
Oldner, Capt. Joshua..Nov. 26, 1814
Oliphant, Robert, cashier of the Office of Discounts and Deposit
   of the late Bank of the United States..May 15, 1812
Olonne, Lt. William F., of the Artillery, from King and Queen County.....Dec. 30, 1813
Orne, Joshua, of Marblehead, at Bordeaux..March 17, 1806

Page, Miss Elizabeth...Dec. 30, 1811
Page, Miss Mary..Dec. 30, 1811
Page, Octavius, at Boston, son of the late Governor of Virginia.................June 16, 1813
Parker, Mrs. Eliza, wife of Copeland Parker..Feb. 27, 1807
Parker, Col. Josiah, at his seat in the Isle of Wight, many years a
   representative in Congress from this district...March 19, 1810
Patrick, Mrs. Margaret, relict William Patrick of Smithfield.....................Oct. 12, 1810
Patterson, Mrs. ....Dec. 30, 1811
Patterson, Mrs. Anne, relict David Patterson..Aug. 13, 1810
Patterson, David ....Sept. 21, 1808
Patterson, Mrs. Janet...Feb. 23, 1810
Patterson, John, Jr., at his father's seat in Mathews County.....................Nov. 27, 1811
Patterson, Miss Nancy..Dec. 30, 1811
Pennock, Mrs. Ann, wife of William Pennock...Jan. 14, 1807
Pennock, William ....May 9, 1816
Phillips, Midshipman ....April 17, 1813
Phillips, Thomas F., at his seat near Hampton..Nov. 13, 1807
Pickett, Mrs. ....Jan. 3, 1812
Pigot, Captain Ralph..Sept. 7, 1815
Pitt, Edmond, in Chuckatuck, in the County of Nansemond......................Oct. 12, 1815
Pleasants, Richard S., in Williamsburg..July 18, 1806
Pleasants, Samuel, Jr., editor of the *Virginia Argus*
   and Printer to the Commonwealth...Oct. 8, 1814
Plume, William ....Feb. 23, 1807
Poe, Mrs. [Elizabeth], of the Virginia Theatre...Dec. 16, 1811
Poindexter, Warren Ashley, at Williamsburg...Oct. 7, 1811

Pollard, Benjamin, at Baltimore, for years a representative citizen
of this Borough..Nov. 11, 1807
Pollard, Charles Robert..June 16, 1813
Pollok, Allan, at "Chelsea" near Richmond..Feb. 6, 1816
Pollok, Robert, in Petersburg, of that town..May 22, 1811
Potter, Capt. Charles..Dec. 19, 1806
Precious, Capt. Matthew, of this Port, at St. Domingo...........................Sept. 10, 1810
Price, Mrs. Catherine, consort of the Rev. James Price..........................Nov. 4, 1807
Price, Capt. John W. H., of the Swedish schooner *Robert*.................Feb. 10, 1813
Proby, Minson, at Hampton..Dec. 28, 1807
Proby, Paul ....June 18, 1814
Prosser, John, of Richmond...Nov. 2, 1810
Proudfit, John ....Sept. 23, 1812
Provoost, the Rt. Rev. Samuel, Bishop of the Protestant Episcopal
Church in the State of New York..Sept. 14, 1815

Raincock, Christopher, in Princess Anne County, formerly
of this Borough..July 14, 1809
Raincock, William ....May 1, 1809
Raine, Dr. George, of Prince Edward County, surgeon's mate to
Col. Ready's Artillery Regiment..Oct. 9, 1813
Ramsay, Mrs. Mary...May 9, 1808
Randolph, Edmund, in the county of Frederick...Sept. 22, 1813
Randolph, Francis E..Jan. 12, 1814
Randolph, Ryland ....Oct. 21, 1815
Raphael, Charlotte, daughter of Solomon Raphael....................................Dec. 30, 1811
Read, Dr. John, Sr..Feb. 11, 1805
Reading, Capt. Augustus, on board ship..Oct. 7, 1811
Rease, David ....March 13, 1813
Rhodes, Thomas, a native of Ireland..May 12, 1813
Riddick, Lemuel, at Suffolk, one of the representatives to the
General Assembly for the county of Nansemond....................................Feb. 22, 1811
                                                                                                             March 4, 1811
Robb, William, at Baltimore, a native of Scotland....................................Aug. 14, 1804
Roberts, Edward ....Jan. 27, 1816
Roberts, Mrs. Eliza, consort of Edward Roberts, of Norfolk County............Aug. 12, 1811
Robinson, John, of Philadelphia, in Fredericksburg.................................Jan. 15, 1813
Robinson, Mrs., consort of Merritt M. Robinson of this place,
at John Bowdoin's in Surry...June 19, 1813
Rozier, Jean Baptiste...Jan. 3, 1812
Russell, Alexander, at New York..April 29, 1811
Russell, Capt. George W., late of the U. S. Artillery................................Nov. 6, 1815

Sargeant, William Hill, native of England, at his seat on
James River in Surry County...Nov. 4, 1811

Stark, Dr. Bolling, at the seat of William Newsum,
in Princess Anne County..July 9, 1810
Starke, Ann, daughter of Dr. William Starke......................................April 4, 1808
Stearns, David, of the House of Fisk and Stearns.............................Aug. 9, 1804
Steede, Capt. Solomon...March 30, 1810
Stephen, Dr., Registrar of his Britannick Majesty's Court of Vice Admiralty
in the Bahama Islands, from whence he arrived a few days ago.................Oct. 2, 1807
Stevenson, Elizabeth ....Dec. 30, 1811
Stoddert, Benjamin, at Bladensburg, Md..Dec. 30, 1813
Stone, John Hoskins, at Annapolis...Oct. 20, 1804
Stone, Simon, in Princess Anne County..July 6, 1816
Stowe, Willis R., of Bermuda, only brother of Mrs. Granberry,
lost at sea...Sept. 5, 1816
Stratton, John ....Oct. 29, 1814
Street, Mrs. Margaret, on board Palmer's Packet, on her passage
to Richmond, late of this Borough...Aug. 14, 1813
Stringer, Mrs. Sally, consort of Hillary Stringer, and daughter of
George Parker of Northampton County...April 5, 1815
Sullivan, James, Governor of Massachusetts.......................................Sept. 14, 1808
Sully, Matthew, Jr., at Augusta, Ga., formerly of the
Charleston Theatre ....April 22, 1812

Tabb, Mrs., wife of Philip Tabb, in Gloucester.................................Sept. 28, 1814
Talbot, Mrs., wife of Kedah Talbot, of Norfolk County................Dec. 30, 1813
Talpier, Tager, in Germany, 120 years old..Nov. 4, 1804
Tarbell, Capt. Joseph, at Washington, a post Capt.
in the Navy of the U. S..Dec. 2, 1815
Taylor, Mrs. Ann F., consort of F. S. Taylor, and daughter of the
late Maj. Lindsay, Collector of this port..Aug. 19, 1811
Taylor, Dr. James, Sr..Nov. 16, 1814
Taylor, Miss Jane, daughter of Robert Taylor, Sr..............................Oct. 29, 1814
Taylor, John, aged 10 years, son of Richard Taylor.........................June 26, 1809
Taylor, Maj. Lewis L., of the 20th U. S. Infantry.............................Sept. 24, 1814
Taylor, Mrs. Lucy, consort of Nathaniel Taylor, in York Town,
of that place...July 17, 1809
Tazewell, Lyttleton, at Williamsburg..Nov. 23, 1815
Thomas, Mrs. Frances...June 9, 1809
Thomas, James, in Tatnal County, Ga., aged 134 years....................Dec. 17, 1804
Thomas, John Hanson, at Frederick Town, Md..................................May 15, 1815
Thompson, Mrs. Mary, consort of James Thompson........................Oct. 24, 1808
Thompson, William, at his seat "Little England," near Hampton,
formerly of this place...Feb. 2, 1808
Thomson, James ....Oct. 2, 1812
Thomson, William, at Staunton, Deputy Collector of this port........Oct. 23, 1812
Thomson, Mrs., wife of William Thomson, Deputy Collector..........June 18, 1810

Thorburn, Mrs. Martha, consort of James Thorburn................................Jan. 4, 1808
Tinkham, Capt. Spencer, of Wiscassett...Jan. 4, 1808
Tippling, Capt. Erasmus H...April 14, 1815
Toy, Richard...Nov. 2, 1814
Triste, Hore Browse, at New Orleans, Collector of that port...............Oct. 16, 1804
Trouin, Cecelia...Dec. 30, 1811
Trouin, Sophia...Dec. 30, 1811
Trumbull, [Johathan,] Governor of Connecticut....................................Aug. 19, 1809
Tucker, Mrs. Ann, wife of James Tucker...Feb. 6, 1805
Tucker, Miss Elizabeth..Dec. 10, 1804
Tucker, Henry, lately at Bermuda, President and Treasurer
   of that Colony..March 28, 1808
Tucker, Mrs., in Bermuda, wife of James Tucker of this place............Feb. 11, 1807
Tufts, Capt. Timothy, at St. Jago de Cuba, late commander
   of the ship *Elizabeth*, of Baltimore...July 17, 1809
Tyler, John, at his seat in Charles City County, Judge of the
   Federal Court, Virginia District..Jan. 15, 1813
Tyler, Samuel, Judge of the Chancery Court for the
   Williamsburg District..March 25, 1812

Upshur, Littleton, of Northampton County..Aug. 28, 1811

Vanconcellos, Miss Rita..Sept. 7, 1814
Vaughan, Mrs. Susan B., wife of James Vaughan, in Portsmouth........Nov. 2, 1814
Vaughan, William, many years an alderman of this Borough................Nov. 13, 1811
Vaughan, Mrs., relict of William Vaughan...April 22, 1812
Venable, Abraham, President of the Bank...Dec. 30, 1811
Vickery, Mrs. Catherine, consort of Capt. Samuel Vickery.................April 2, 1814
Vickery, Capt. Eli, at Old Point Comfort...July 21, 1809

Waddey, Daniel R..May 27, 1812
Waddey, John R., of the County of Northampton..................................April 3, 1815
Waddey, Mrs. Margaret, wife of Edward S. Waddey............................Sept. 23, 1812
Waddy, Miss Elizabeth..July 23, 1806
Wade, Jane..Dec. 30, 1811
Waldon, James..Dec. 30, 1811
Walke, Anthony, Sr., of Princess Anne...Aug. 17, 1814
Walker, Bolling, of the County of Dinwiddie..Nov. 19, 1814
Walker, Bolling Minford, of the County of Dinwiddie..........................Nov. 23, 1814
Walker, Jacob, a native of Mass., formerly of this place......................Nov. 17, 1809
Wanton, Edward...Dec. 30, 1811
Warren, James B...Feb. 1, 1815
Waugh, James, a native of Ireland, near Great Bridge..........................April 21, 1813
Webb, Kedar, in Nansemond County..Oct. 8, 1814
Webb, Miss Mary, daughter of Capt. George Webb.............................Sept. 14, 1814
Webb, Mrs. Sarah, relict of James Webb, of Norfolk County..............June 22, 1814

Welch, John, nephew, of Sir A. Pigott, late of England...............................Dec. 30, 1811
West, Delaware, of the house of John and Delaware West of this place......Jan. 18, 1810
West, Mrs. Margaret, formerly of the Virginia Company of Comedians,
    and late proprietor of the Norfolk Theatre...June 6, 1810
Whitehead, the Rev. James, Minister of Christ Church, Baltimore,
    died in Baltimore..Sept. 5, 1808
Whitehurst, Dennis, of Princess Anne County...July 27, 1814
Whitlock, Mary ....Dec. 30, 1811
Whittle, Hanse, a native of Ireland. Died at Alexandria,
    on September 22nd...Sept. 26, 1806
Wigginton, Seth B., at New York..Oct. 4, 1805
Wilkinson, Mrs. Ann, wife of Gen'l. Wilkinson, at New Orleans..................April 1, 1807
Wilkinson, William, at his seat in Nansemond...Oct. 5, 1807
Willett, Charles, one of the late proprietors of the *Norfolk Herald*...............Sept. 4, 1807
Williams, Brig. Gen. Jonathan, at Philadelphia..May 24, 1815
Williamson, Mrs. Sarah, wife of John..March 16, 1814
Williamson, Mrs., wife of Thomas Williamson..April 6, 1807
Willock, Thomas, second son of Thomas Willock, of this place.....................March 13, 1811
Willock, Mrs., wife of Thomas Willock...July 6, 1814
Wilson, Mrs. Alice..Sept. 19, 1808
Wilson, Mrs. Ann Maria, wife of Robert S. Wilson..Sept. 14, 1816
Wilson, Miss Harriet ....Nov. 17, 1813
Wilson, Mrs. Mary B., wife of George Wilson...April 11, 1808
Wilson, Mrs. Thomas..Dec. 30, 1811
Wiseham, Richard ....March 5, 1806
Wiseham, William, in the County of Gloucester..Aug. 5, 1805
Wood, James, a member of the Executive Council, member of the
    Sons of the Cincinnati..June 23, 1813
Wood, William, at Baltimore, late His Britannic Majesty's
    Consul for Maryland...Oct. 16, 1812
Wormley, Ralph, of "Rosegill"...Feb. 5, 1806
Wright, Thomas, at Hilton, near Wilmington, N. C..June 12, 1813
Wright, Mrs. S., wife of Thomas, formerly of this Borough,
    died at Williamsburg..Feb. 23, 1807
Wythe, George, Chancellor of this State..June 6, 1806
                                                June 14, 1806

Yates, Charles, at Fredericksburg...June 23, 1809
Young, Mrs. Eliza, consort of James Young..Aug. 12, 1811

OLD GRAVESTONES IN SAVAGE'S NECK, NORTH-AMPTON COUNTY.

Communicated by T. B. Robertson, Eastville, Va.

The oldest settlement on the Eastern Shore of Virginia is in Savage's Neck, near Eastville. It was here that Thomas Savage located in 1619, and started his plantation on land granted from the Indian chief of the locality, the head of the Accomack Indians. The family at one time owned the whole of Savage's Neck out to the present site of the town of Eastville.[1]

On Cherrygrove farm there are two old graveyards still to be found. In the one which is said to be the oldest, there are now a few tombs observable. This one is near the present Cherrygrove residence, and these have epitaphs as follows:

Here lies the body of
Margaret Savage, wife of Littleton Savage and
Daughter of William Burton Gent., who departed this
life the 6th. day of December, 1772, in the 35th
year of her age.

With unremitting attention She studied to discharge the
duties that every situation brought with it.
Nor could her piety to an aged parent be equalled except by an
affection and tenderness which showed that she was the petted
wife and sister.

If ever marble waked the tender sigh,
If e'er compassion claimed the melting eye,
Due to those in whom the virtues join,
'Tis due lamented shade to worth like thine
More religious, affable, and kind,
She owned each grace that decks the female mind.

---

[1] The Savage family may be styled the oldest in Virginia, as Thomas Savage is probably the earliest immigrant from whom descent has been traced.

Here lies the body of
Mary Savage, wife of Thomas Littleton Savage
and Daughter of Col. Littleton Savage,
Who departed this life the 10th. day of Feb., 1794,
in the 20th year of her age

Here lies the body of Coln. Littleton Savage,
Who departed this life the 9th day of Jany., 1805, in the 65th
year of his age, etc.

Here lies the body of Leah Savage, 2nd. wife of Col. Littleton
Savage, and daughter of
Thomas Teagle, who departed this life the 5th. day of June,
1795.

In another place, where are a few indications of other older
graves, is a stone with the following inscription:

Here lies the body of
Mr. Iames Forse Merch. late of Devon in Great Brittain,
who departed this life the 4th. day of Febry. 1754
in the 48th. year of his age. He married Mary Eldest
Daughter of Geo. Thomas Savage, of this County, the surveyor.

On Pleasant Prospect farm is the oldest one now observable. It reads as follows:

Here lies the body of Maj. John Savage, who departed
this life the 3rd. day of Dec. 1746, aged 36 years.

And on a companion tomb by its side is a slab with the following:

Here lies the body of Mary Savage, who departed this life
the 3rd day of Aug., 1770, aged 61 years.

Farther up the Neck is a graveyard of a later date, the oldest
stone having on it the following inscription:

Sacred to the memory of Ann Jacob, wife of Robert C.
Jacob, aged 55 years. Who departed this life July the 23rd.,
1784. She was an affectionate wife, a tenderly parent, and
charitable to all.

The slab over this one has on it the impression of a man's
foot, seemingly petrified in the stone.

HUNGARS CHURCH, NORTHAMPTON COUNTY, VA.

HUNGARS PARISH RECORDS FOR 1660-1661.

Northampton County, Virginia.

Communicated by THOMAS B. ROBERTSON,

Eastville, Va.

The following list of the births, deaths and marriages in Hungars Parish, for 1660-61, will be of interest to many of the descendants of those mentioned. The items are taken from the Records in the Clerk's office here, Book of Orders, Deeds, &c., for that date. The old Parish Register has been lost many years.

"A true account of such persons as have been baptised, married and burried in Hungars Parish from ye 25th. of March anno. 1660 unto ye 25th. of March 1661.

Persons Baptised—

Ann Whitehead daughter of John & Susanna Whitehead, Apr. ye 1st.

Lettuce Granger daughter of Nicholas & Jane Granger Apr. ye 17th.

Hanna Major daughter of Christopher & Mary Major (age 1 yr. 6mo) May ye 6th.

Eliza Whittington ye daughter of William & Eliza Whittington May ye 16th.

Ann Meridith ye daughter of George & Jane Merideth May 16th.

Samll Jones ye sonne of Samll & Mary Jones Apr. 22nd.

Issabel pettyJohn daughter of Jas & Issabel pettyJohn May 16th.

Robt. Bury ye sonne of Robt. & Lidia Bury May 20th.

Will Robinson ye sonne of John & Joan Robinson June 3d.

Mary Grey ye daughter of James & Katharine Grey June 10th.

Rachel Walley daughter of Thomas & Eliza Walley June 29th.

Richd Hill son of Robt. & Jane Hill Aug. 12th.

Ann Richards ye daughter of Michael & Ann Richards Sept. 16th.

Mary Bell daughter of Thomas & Mary Bell Sept. 16th.

Ann Long, Daughter of Daniel & Eliza Long, Sept. 16th.

Mary Cotton daughter of John & Hanna Cotton 8br 21st.

Ann Ffurs daughter of John & Mary Ffurs 9br. 18th.

Richd Elligood sonne of Thomas & Mary Elligd 9br 25th.

William Wilcocks sonne of John & Ann Willcocks Febr. 17th.

Eliza Barnaby daughtr of James & Mary Barnaby Febr. 18th.

Mary Robins daughter of Saml & Mary Robins Febr. 17th.

Eliza Quellian daugh Daniel & Lidia Quillian Mar. 24th.

Persons Married—

Gilbert Hinders & Mary Major March 25th.

William Marshall & Mary Parker May 12th.

John Evans & Joan Munes May 13th.

John Townsend & Eliza Wheatly May 20th.

Mr. William Spencer & Mrs. Eliza Whittington June 14th.

Daniel Ishan & Margaret Howell July 14th.

John Thergettle & Dorothy Wilkison Aug. 26th.

John Buddan & Barbary Hudson Aug. 29th.

Heinrich Waggaman & Winnefred Schyn Aug. 21st.

Christo^r Stanley & Ann Turner Sept. 4th.
John Nuthall & Jane Johnson Sept. 12th.
William Starling & Margt. Edwards Sept. 20th.
Timothy Coe & Eliza Teague Sept. 29th.
Geo. Smith & Ann Ware Sept 23rd.
Thomas Foakes Stockley & Ann Waddelow Sept. 30th.
John King & Jane Bishop 8br 8th.
Hugh Kunneloe & Marian Hary 8br 14th.
Ralph Doe & Mary Custis 8br 29th.
John Savage Dorothy Jordan 9br 18th.
Robt. Hayes & Ann Draiton 9br 20th.
Richd Buckland & Charity Coulston 9br 26th.
John Goldsmith & Mary Longo 10br 13th.
William Chase Sarah Hewitt 10br 16th.
Simon Foscoat & Ann Cook Jany. 30th.
Will Bosman & Eliza Mallocks Febr. 5th.
Roger Walford & Mary Denwood Mar. 1st.
Mr. Edw. Littleton & Mrs. Francis Robins Mar. 7th.
John Mickall and Helen Cornah Mar. 24th.
    Persons Burried—
Argal Smith June ye 7th.
Thomas Edwards sonne of John & Margaret Edwards June
    ye 23rd.
Mary Sanders daughter of James & Virlinda Sanders July
    15th.
Bridget ye wife of William Bosman July 19th.
Mary daughter of Abram Vansalt July 30th.
Robert ye sonne of Robert & Lidia burry July 30th.
Richard Teague Aug. ye 6th.
Ann daughter of Gabriel & Helen Powel Aug. ye 6th.
John Hinnian Aug. 29th.
John Crew Aug. 29th.
James Boone 7br 8th.
Mary ye wife of Robt. Windey 7br 15th.
Isaac Vansalt servt Edw Smith 8br 7th.
Eliza ye wife of Adolph Johnson 8br 22nd.
Thomas Harrison 8br 28th.

Eliza daughter of Jeff & Fran Manchall Nov. 23rd.
Eliza wife of Simon Foscoat 9br 28th..
Wm. Bowen Decbr 5th.
Ann daughter of Giles & Margaret Copes Decbr 22nd.
Eliza wife of John Townsend Decbr 26th.
Mary Ther servt John Vines Jany 5th.
Francis Harrison servt Henr Armtrading Jany 10th.
Robt. Luddington Feb. 3d.
William Andrews seaman to Henry Voss (drowned) Feb.
   25th.
Ann daughter of John & Barbary Winberry Mar. 24th.
       True Copy,

                  JOHN LAWRENCE,
            Clerk of Hungars Parish."

HUNGARS PARISH RECORDS.

Communicated by THOMAS B. ROBERTSON.

EASTVILLE, VA., Feb. 6, 1913.

In Vol. XVIII, page 178 and *seq.* of the WILLIAM AND MARY QUARTERLY HISTORICAL MAGAZINE,* there was given the report of the clerk of Hungars parish, showing the birtns, deaths and marriages for the year beginning March 25, 1660, and ending March 25, 1661. I now give below the report made to the monthly court for the year following, that is, from March 25, 1661 to March 25, 1662. This interesting item from the old records of this county is found in the Book of Deeds, Wills, &c., for the years 1657 to 1666. John Lawrance seems to have been the only parish clerk who took the trouble to file his returns in the clerk's office. Or it is possible that in moving the office around from house to house in those days the reports were destroyed along with many other original papers.

"A true account of such persons as have bin borne, Baptized, Married and buried in Hungars Parish from ye 25th. of March 1661 to ye 25th. of March Anno 1662."

CHILDREN

Richard Johnson ye sonne of Tho and Ann Johnson—Apr¹ 1st.

Bridgett Robinson ye daughter of Jno. and Mary Robinson—Apr¹ 2d.

John Pace ye sonne of Jno and Mary Pace—Apr¹ 2d.

James Bruce ye sonne of James and Mary Bruce—Apr¹ 2d.

Thomas Martiall ye sonne of Tho and Mary Martiall—Apr¹ 2d.

Mary Obin ye daughter of Robert and Ann Obin—Apr¹ 2d.

Bridgett Henderson ye daughter of Gilbert and Mary Henderson—Apr¹ 2d.

Ann Mapp daughter of Jno & Mary Mapp—May 5th.

*Pages 389-392, this volume.

Bridgett Rattcliffe ye daughter of Charles & Bridgett Rattcliffe—May 5th.

Hellen Upshott ye daughter of Arthur and Mary Upshott—May 5th.

John Crow ye sonne of Jno & Elizabeth Crow—May 5th.

John Henderson ye sonne of James and Mary Henderson—May 12th.

Samuel and Joseph Cobb ye sonnes of Jno & Debora Cobb—May 12th.

Henry Stott ye sonne of Henry and Priscilla Stott—May 29th.

William Harmanson ye sonne of Thos and Joane Harmanson—May 29th.

Edw Pepper ye sonne of Jno & Margaret Pepper—June 2d.

William Webster ye sonne of Will & Mary Webster—June 9th.

William Matthews ye sonne of Morice Matthews & Elise Nebulian—June 9th.

Bridgett Tyrant ye daughter of Tho & Margaret Tyrant—June 9th.

Lucy Spindy ye daughter of Rogers & Helen Spindy—June 9th.

Sara and Kathrine Coventon ye daughters of Nehemiah and Mary Coventon—June 10th.

Nathanile Bradford ye sonne of Nathanl. and Alice Bradford—June 23d.

William Edwards ye sonne of Wm & Elizabeth Edwards—June 23d.

Margaret Copes ye daughter of Giles & Margaret Copes—June 23d.

Thomas Hinman ye sonne of Jane Blague (age four years)—July 7th.

William Blague ye sonne of Wm and Jane Blague—July 7th.

Elizabeth Walthan ye daughter of Jno and Elizabeth Walthan—July 14th.

Mary Selby ye daughter of Tho & Mary Selby—Aug 4th.

Peter Watson ye sonne of Robert & Susannah Watson—Aug. 11th.

Margaret Bery ye daughter of Cornelius & Margaret Bery—
Aug 13th. Y
Margaret Thorne ye daughter of Daniel & Mary Thorne—
Aug 25th.
Winyfred Waggeman daughter of Henrick & Winyfred
Waggeman—Sept —

CHILDREN BAPTIZED

Joseph Reynier (?) ye sonne of Jno & Francis Reynier (?)—
Oct. 6th.
Annie Cattlin daughter of Robt & Ann Cattlin—Oct. 6th.
Elizabeth VanSoles daughter of Al and Eliza VanSoles—
Oct. 13th.
John Granger sonne of Nicholas and Jane Granger—Oct.
9th.
William Tilney sonne of Jno & Ann Tilney—Nov 29th.
John Cotton sonne of John and Hannah Cotton—Dec. 8th.
Richard Jacob sonne of Richard & Mary Jacob—Dec. 16th.
John Walley sonne of Thomas and Ann Walley—May 16th.
Richard Sanders son of James & Virlinda Sanders—July
13th.

PERSONS BURIED

William Russell—May 12th.
ffrances wife of Walter Price—May 15th.
Winyfred wife of Henrick Wagman—June 14th.
John Hinman jnr.—August 20th.
Gabriel Powell—Aug 22d.
Thomas Marchial sonne of Wm Marchial—July 12th.
William Wilbrookes sonne of Jno Wilbrookes—July 21st.
Nathl Spratling sonne to Elias Harter—Nov 4th.
Mathew son of Edw Smith—Jan⁷ 6th.
John Robinson—Jan⁷ 15th.
L——— James—Jan⁷ 15th.
Margaret wife of Daniel Johnson—June 15th.
Elizabeth wife of Timothy Coe—March 7th.
14 Mary Wheatly daughter of Daniel Wheãtly—Jan⁷ 8th.

Thomas Poynter ffrances Jamis	} Apr^l 9th	John Sturgis Dorothy Savage	} Sept^{br} 1st
Thomas Smith Elizabeth Reynolds	} Apr^l 21st	Dorman Swilliwan Anne Mecarrell	} Oct^{br} 20th
Lyt Isaac ffoxcroft Bridgett Charlton	} Apr^l 23^d	Abraham Taylor Debora Kechine	} Nov^{br} 3^d
John Gorthan Bridgett Darcy	} Apr^l 28th	George Brickhouse Hanna Luddington	} Nov^{br} 4th
Robt Hickison Elizabeth Crow	} May 5th	Thomas Dupark Elizabeth Powell	} Nov^{br} 13^{tl}
Lyt Henry Bishop Anne Bowen	} May 12th	Thomas Gilley Mary Manlow	} Nov^{br} 23^t
Edwards Dunstan Elizabeth Lingoe	} May 12th	Andrew ffenn Jane Major	} Dec^{br} 8th
Thomas Goodaker Elizabeth Pitt	} May 18th	William Wilkinson Mary Bucks	} Dec^{br} 15^t
Thomas Davis ——— Ryling	} May 26th	John Rogers Mary Hewes	} Jany rd
——— ——— ——— ———	} May 26th	Thomas Ryding Rose Yardley	} Jany 4th
Thomas Garrell Margaret Knight	} May 29th	Joseph Harrison Anne fflybrass	} Jany 24th
Edward Moore Elizabeth Turnor	} June 2^d	Robert Downes Mary Avory	} Jany 31st
John ffausett Rhoda Lamberton	} June 2^d	John Gray Jane Beman	} Feby 7th
Lyt Nicholas Powel Agnes Stratton	} June 6th	Daniel Ishonn Susanna Thomas	} Feby 9th
Robt Hayes Jane Ecristall	} July 17th	John Townsend Elizabeth Danford	} Feby 9th
Daniel Dye Rosa Erevans	} Aug 4th	William White Mary Moore	} Feby 16th
Donock Dennis Elise Nebulian	} July 31	Nicholas Hudson 34 Elizabeth ffreman	} Feby 16th

Teste   Jno Lawrence
Clerk of Hungars Parish in ye
County of Northampton.

IN LOWER PARISH OF NORTHAMPTON COUNTY,
    Nicholas Ran——
    married Dorothy ————
    Gerard Lilliston

—— —— ——

The foot of the page is torn and undecipherable and is noted by dashes in each case. At this time Rev. Ffrancis Doughty was the minister of Hungars Parish. He was from Long Island and belonged to the Dutch reformed church, which is the same as the Presbyterian. It is likely that he was the first of that denomination to preach in this part of the country. In fact there were a great number of Dutch settlers here at that period, as will be noticed by reference to the old records of that time.

REGISTER OF ST. STEPHEN'S PARISH, NORTHUMBERLAND COUNTY.

(Extracts.)

Ann Bushrod, daughter to Thomas, was born March 6, 1694.
Richd. Bushrod, son to Thomas, was born Febry. 10, 1690.
Thomas Berry, son to Thomas, was born Jany. 9, 1683.
William Berry, son to Thomas, was born May 13, 1691.
Mary Barnes, daughter to Thomas, was born March 29, 1679.
James Barnes, son to Thomas, was born Jany. 19, 1681.

Jean Barnes, daughter to Thomas, was born Sept. 15, 1697.
Eliza Barnes, daughter to Thomas, was born March 25, 1703.
Sarah Barnes, daughter to Thomas, was born Aug. 2, 1706.
Richard Booth, son to Richard, was born Aug. 25, 1706.
Francis Booth, son to John, was born Feby. 12, 1710.
Eliza Booth, daughter to Richard, was born June 15, 1709.
John Booth, son to Richard, was born Aug. 13, 1712.
Samuel Blackwell, son to Samuel, was born Jany. 19, 1710.
William Blackwell, son to Samuel, was born April 25, 1713.
Joseph Blackwell, son to Samuel, was born July 9, 1715.
Eliza Blackwell, daughter to Samuel, was born Jany. 9, 1717.
Hannah Blackwell, daughter to Samuel, was born March 30, 1720.
William Betts, son to Charles, was born Jany. 21, 1687.
Mary Betts, daughter to Charles, was born Sept. 28, 1688.
Charles Betts, son to Charles, was born Feb. 21, 1699.
Eliza Betts, daughter to Charles, was born June 13, 1693.
Jonathan Betts, son to Charles, was born May 3, 1702.
Hannah Betts, daughter to Charles, was born July 7, 1706.
Samuel Blackwell, son to Joseph, was born Sept. 23, 1680.
Spencer Ball, son to Joseph, was born March 14, 1707.
Richard Ball, son to Joseph, was born Oct. 25, 1710.
Joseph Ball, daughter to Joseph, was born March 8, 1712.
Sarah Ball, daughter to Joseph, was born March 10, 1714.
Judith Betts, daughter to Charles, was born August 3, 1732.
Hannah Betts, daughter to Charles, was born Dec. 29, 1728.
Winifred Betts, daughter to Charles, was born May 10, 1730.
Daniel Betts, son to Charles, was born Oct. 7, 1731.
Spencer Betts, son to Charles, was born May 29, 1734.
Judith Ball, daughter to Spencer Ball, was born Jany. 17, 1735.
Mary Betts, daughter to Charles Betts, was born March 31, 1735.
Spencer Mottrom Ball, son to Spencer Ball, was born Sept. 9, 1736.
Samuel Blackwell, Jun., was born Nov. 20, 1731.
John Blackwell, was born Feb. 18, 1732/3.
Wm. Blackwell, was born Aug. 16, 1736.

Eliza Blackwell, was born March 25, 1741.

Astan Betts, son of Charles, was born Aug. 12, 174–.

William Betts, son to Charles, was born Sept. 26, 174–.

Joseph Blackwell, son to Samuel and Eliz., was born April 20, 1738.

Ann Blackwell, daughter to Samuel and Eliz., was born Feb. 2, 1747.

Judith Blackwell, daughter to Samuel and Eliz., was born Jany. 8, 1751.

Joseph Ball, son to Joseph and Hanna, was born Mch. 14, 1752.

John Betts, son to Charles and Judith, was born Jany. 9, 1742.

Chas. Betts, son to Charles, was born March 20, 1750.

James Booth, son to James and Eleanor, was born March 6, 1740.

Richard Booth, son to James and Eleanor, was born March 20, 1742.

Eleanor, daughter to James and Eleanor, was born Dec. 9, 1745.

Judith Betts, daughter to Elisha and Mary Ann, was born Aug. 12, 1755.

Spencer Ball, son to Thomas, was born April 15, 1756.

Winder Ball, son to John, was born July 18, 1756.

John Blackwell, son to John and Hannah, was born March 24, 175–.

David Ball, son to Joseph and Hannah, was born Nov. 23, 1754.

Grace Ball, daughter to Joseph and Hannah, was born June 18, 1757.

Thomas Blackwell, son to Samuel and Eliz. his wife, was born Sept. 15, 1752.

David Blackwell, son to Samuel and Eliz. his wife, was born Nov. 27, 1753.

Elizabeth Blackwell, daughter to Sam. Blackwell, Jun. and Sarah, was born June 10, 1756.

Samuel Blackwell, son to Sam. Blackwell, Jun. and Sarah, was born Mch. 25, 1758.

William Betts, son to Elisha and Mary Ann, was born March 29, 1757.

Elisha, son to Elisha and Mary Ann, was born March 1, 1763.

Hannah Ball, daughter to Joseph and Hannah, was born Nov. 24, 1764.

Spencer Morgan Beckley, son to Joseph and Diana, was born, March 18, 1766.

Thomas Berry, son to John and Judith Berry, was born May 6, 1766.

John, son of Joseph and Hannah Ball, was born March 6, 1767.

Sarah Blackwell, daughter of Samuel and Sarah, was born Jany. 9, 1763.

Eleanor Blackwell, daughter of Capt. Samuel and Sarah, was born Oct. 17, 1766.

John Booth, son of James Booth and Sary, was born Jany. 12, 1771.

Anthony Sidnor Booth, son of John and Winny, was born May 21, 1792.

John Conaway, son to Denis, was born Jany. 15, 1673.

Thos. Conaway, son to Denis, was born Jany. 15, 1680.

Lazarus Conaway, son to Denis, was born July 20, 1682.

Christopher Conaway, son to Denis, was born May 3, 1684.

John Cockrell, son to John, was born Nov. 22, 1669.

Eliza Cockrell, daughter to John, was born Nov. 21, 1671.

Hannah Cockrell, daughter to John, was born Feb. 20, 1680.

Edward Cockrell, son to John, was born Dec. 29, 1674.

Richard Cockrell, son to John, was born Dec. 3, 1683.

Eliza Carr, daughter to Joseph, was born Oct. 2, 1692.

Thos. Carr, son to Joseph, was baptized Jany. 7, 1693.

Wilaby Cockrell, son to Thomas, was baptized 1702.

Presley Cockerell, son to Thomas, was baptized Dec. 19, 1704.

John Carnegie, son to John, was born May 24, 1707.

George Conway, son to Denis, was born Nov. 30, 1706.

Eliza Conway, daughter to Denis, was born March 9, 1709.

Winifred Conway, daughter to Denis, was born Dec. 28, 1711.

Judith, daughter to Denis, was born June 21, 1714.

Denis, son to Denis, was born Feb. 15, 1716.

John Coppedge, son to William, was born Jany. 31, 1710.

John Cockrell, son to Richard, was born Sept. 23, 1715.

Joseph Cooper, son to William, was born Dec. 26, 1713.

William Cooper, son to William, was born Oct. 19, 1717.

John Crump, son to John, was born Aug. 21, 1720.

Susannah Crumb, daughter to John, was born July 11, 1723.

William Cordrey, son to John, was born Feb. 16, 1738.

John Conway, son to John and Susannah, was born Nov. 26, 1702.

Ann Conway, daughter to John and Sussanah, was born Aug. 20, 1732.

Winifred, daughter to John and Susannah, was born Nov. 19, 1734.

John Span Conway, daughter to John and Susannah, was born Jany. 15, 1738.

Samuel Cockrell, son to Timothy, was born May 19, 1747.

Chas. Colston, son to Francis and Alice Colston, was born May 31, 1736.

Eliza Griffin Colston, daughter to Francis and Alice Colston, was born Sept. 23, 1738.

Travers Colston, son to Francis and Alice Colston, was born Nov. 10, 1740.

William Colston, son to Francis and Sussanah, was born Oct. 10, 1744.

Rawleigh Colston, son to Francis and Susannah, was born May 11, 1747.

Samuel Colston, son to Francis and Susannah, was born Nov. 21, 1749.

Robert Conway, son to John and Francina, was born May 10, 1749.

Joseph Conway, son to John and Francina, was born Jany. 9, 1754.

Presley Cockrell, son to Presley and Sarah, was born July 7, 1754.

Richard Conway, son to James and Alice Conway, was born Feb. 18, 1765.

Winifred Corbin, daughter of David and Frances his wife, was born Nov. 10, 1777.

Hannah Kenner Crallé, daughter to John and Sarah his wife, was born July 31, 1778.

William Dameron, son to William and Nancy, was born Feb. 5, 1792.

Elizabeth Downing, daughter to Edward, was born June 20, 1731.

Hannah Downing, daughter to Edward, was born Dec. 9, 1733.

Samuel Downing, son to William, was born July 2, 1728.

Chas. Downing, son to John, was born Feb. 4, 1738.

Eliza Downing, son to John, was born Apr. 19, 1740.

Sarah Ann Dunaway, daughter to Joseph, was born Jany. 12, 1742.

Thomas Downing, son to Samuel and Sarah, was born May 23, 1744.

Samuel and Betty, twins, children to Samuel and Sarah Downing, were born Feb. 21, 1747.

John Downing, son to Samuel and Sarah, was born May 1, 1755.

Hannah Downing, daughter to John, was born April, 19, 1740.

Nancy Downing, daughter to John, was born June 20, 1748.

Edward Downing, son to John, was born April 22, 1750.

Sarah Downing, daughter to John, was born Feb. 18, 1753.

Grace Ball Downman, daughter to Frances, was born Sept. 26, 1756.

Anna Dameron, daughter to Jacob and Mary, was born Dec. 1, 1775.

Mary Dameron, daughter to Joseph, was born Mch. 1, 1714.

Katharine Edwards, daughter to Isaac, was born Oct. 27, 1671.

Jonathan Edwards, son to Isaac, was born Feb. 2, 1673.

Eliza Edwards, daughter to Isaac, was born June 14, 1674.

Mary Edwards, daughter to Isaac, was born Oct. 5, 1678.

Isaac Edwards, son to Isaac, was born July 18, 1682.

Isaac Edwards, son to Jonathan, was born Oct. 13, 1709.

Wm. Edwards, son to Wm. was baptized Apl. 10, 1703.

Nicholas Edwards, son to Nicholas, was baptized Apl. 17, 1698.

Isaac Edwards, son to Isaac, was baptized June 10, 1711.

John Edwards, son to Nicholas, was born Dec. 23, 1700.

Wm. Edwards, son to Nicholas, was born May 17, 1706.

William Edwards, son to William, was born Feb. 26, 1704.

Wm. Edwards, son to John, was born May 6, 1734.

Richard Edwards, son to Charles, was born June 23, 1734.

Ambrose Fielding, son to Edward, was born January 31, 1689.

Sarah Fielding, dau. to Edward, was sborn May 12, 1695.

Rachel Fielding, daughter to Edward, was born Sept. 26, 1697.

Thomas Fielding, son to Edward, was born Sept. 22, 1699.

Catherine Fauntleroy, daughter to Griffin, was born Feb. 16, 1709.

Moore Fauntleroy, son to Griffin, was born July 30, 1711.

Ann Fauntleroy, daughter to Griffin, was born Dec. 29, 1713.

William Fauntleroy, son to Griffin, was born August 17, 1718.

James Fushee, son to John, was born July 27, 1729.

Sopha Fushee, daughter to John, was born Nov. 14, 1731.

Mary Foushee, daughter to John, was born Aug. 19, 1719.

Griffin Fauntleroy, son to Bushrod, was born Sept. 28, 1754.

John Foushee, son to James, was born July 13, 1753.

Fredk. Foushee, son to James, was born Dec. 21, 1754.

Sarah Fauntleroy, daughter to Griffin and Judy, Mch. 17, 1756.

Edward Fielding, son to Edward, was born June 2, 1666.

Ann Fielding, daughter to Edward, was born Jany. 7, 1668.

Ambrose, son to Edward, was born May 17, 1677.

Richard, son to Edward, was born March 5, 1675.

Isaac Gaskins, son to John, was born Apl. 2, 1722.

Elizabeth Frances, daughter to Henry, was born March 15, 1724.

Eliza Gaskins, daughter to John, was born Oct. 1, 1725.

Isaac Gaskins, daughter to Francis, was born Sept. 19, 1730.

Jessie Gaskins, daughter to John, was born Sept. 1, 1737.

Thomas Gaskins, son to John, was born Aug. 12, 1742.

Thomas Harding, son to Thomas, was born Sept. 4, 1664.

William Harding, son to Thomas, was born July 20, 1669.

Thomas Harding, son to Thomas, Jun., was born Feb. 21, 1710.

William Harding, son to Thomas, Jun., was born Feb. 15, 1690.

Charles and Francis Harding, twins to Wm., were born July 2, 1704.

Thomas Hickman, son to Thomas, was born July 19, 1669.

Bridget Haynie, daughter to Richard, was born Dec. 6, 1686.

Maximillian Haynie, son to Richard, was born Oct. 31, 1688.
Eleanor Haynie, daughter to Richard, was born Sept. 2, 1708.
Charles Haynie, son to Richard, was born Jan. 23, 1710.
Mary Haynie, daughter to Richard, was born Nov. 3, 1712.
William Haynie, son to Richard, was born Nov. 5, 1704.
Winifred Haynie, daughter to Richard, was born Apl. 7, 1706.
Sarah, daughter to Richard, was born May 11, 1718.
Sarah Hull, daughter to Richard, was born Dec. 18, 1680.
Mary Hull, daughter to Richard, was born Dec. 12, 1682.
Richard Hull, son to Richard, was born April 14, 1685.
Richard Hull, son to Richard, Jun., was born Aug. 4, 1709.
Sarah Hull, daughter to Richard, Jun., was born Nov. 25, 1706.
William Hull, son to Richard, Jun., was born Aug. 31, 1713.
Nicholas Hack, son to Peter, was born May 28, 1687.
Hannah Hack, daughter to Peter, was born March 27, 1692.
Peter Hack, son to Peter, was born March 26, 1695.
Ann Hack, daughter to Peter, was born July 18, 1696.
Spencer Hack, son to Peter, was born Feb. 11, 1700.
Eliza and Mary Hack, daughters to Peter, were born April 2, 1703.
Thomas Hobson, son to Thomas, was born Aug. 30, 1694.
Sarah Hobson, daughter to Thomas, was born Oct. 13, 1698.
Wm. Hobson, son to Thomas, was born April 28, 1700.

(To be continued.)

The Colston children given on page 241* were children of Travers Colston (not *Francis* Colston which is a misprint).

*Page 401, this volume.

REGISTER OF ST. STEPHEN'S PARISH.
NORTHUMBERLAND COUNTY.

(Extracts)

BIRTHS.

John Hobson, son to Thomas, March 4, 1701.
Eliza Hobson, daughter to Thomas, Oct. 14, 1698.
Lety Sina Hobson, daughter to Thomas, May 22, 1712.
Juda Harding, daughter to William, July 16, 1721.
Eliz: Hickman, daughter to Thomas, Nov. 25, 1719.
Uraga? Hayne, son to Maximillian, Feb. 14, 1721.
Max: Hayne, son to Maximillian, Oct. 21, 1723.
Winifred Hayne, daughter to Thomas, Feb. 21, 1718.
Mary Hayne, daughter to Thomas, Nov. 20, 1720.
Matt^w Haynie, son to Thomas, Nov. 4, 1723.
Spencer Hayne, son to Thomas, March 9, 1728.
Jo^n Haynie, son to William, July 22, 1727.
Max: Haynie, son to Henry, Jany. 9, 1719.
John Haynie, son to Henry, May 26, 1723.

Winifred Haynie, daughter to Henry, March 27, 1725.
Elizabeth Haynie, daughter to Max^m, July 20, 1725.
William Haynie, son to William, Oct. 21, 1729.
Sarah Hobson, daughter to William, May 29, 1725.
Judith Hobson, daughter to William, Dec. 9, 1727.
John Hobson, son to William, April 13, 1730.
Mary Anne Hickman, daughter to William, June 17, 1732.
Thomas Hickman, son to Thomas, April 9, 1732.
Mary Anne Hobson, daughter to William, June 17, 1732.
Jemayma Haynie, daughter to Thomas, Sept. 4, 1730.
Jedayde Haynie, daughter to Thomas, Dec. 10, 1733.
Hannah Haynie, daughter to William, Dec. 25, 1731.
John Haynie, son to John, April 26, 1733.
Peter Haynie, son to Isaac, Dec. 17, 1733.
Henry Haynie, son to Henry, Nov. 21, 1730.
Abner Haynie, son to Henry, Jany. 11, 1730.
Sinna Haynie, daughter to Thomas, Dec. 16, 1734.
Bridger Haynie, daughter to Thomas, Jan. 12, 1734.
John Harding, son to Thomas, April 21, 1734.
Alex^r Haynie, son to Jacob, Dec. 13, 1734.
Francis Haynie, son to Joseph, Jan. 15, 1736.
Bettie Hobson, daughter to William, Feb. 8, 1736.
Thomas & Francis Harding, twins to Thos., Sept. 9, 1737.
Richard Hull, son to Richard, April 13, 1717.
Wm. Haynie, son to Isaac, Sept. 29, 1737.
Jesse Haynie, son to Benjamin, March 2, 1738.
Ann Hull, daughter to Richard, Jany. 14, 1739.
Eliz: Haynie, daughter to Stephen, Dec. 20, 1739.
Grace Haynie, daughter to Isaac, Nov. 4, 1740.
Richard Hull, son to Richard, Dec. 14, 1741.
John Hobson, son to Adcock, Oct. 31, 1742.
William Haynie, son to Stephen, Sept. 14, 1742.
Thomas Hobson, son to Adcock, June 11, 1746.
Elizabeth & Thomas Hull, twins to Richard, May 1, 1745.
William Hobson, son to Adcock, Sept. 7, 1748.
Jamma Harding, daughter to Thomas, May 3, 1739.
Mary Harding, daughter to Thomas, April 6, 1741.

Samuel Harding, son to Thomas, March 6, 1744.
Judith Harding, daughter to Thomas, July 18, 1745.
Hattie Harding, daughter to Thomas, April 5, 1748.
Caleb Hobson, son to Adcock, July 13, 1751.
Sarah, Hull, daughter to Richard, Sept. 7, 1747.
Hannah Hull, daughter to Richard, Dec. 26, 1749.
John Hull, son to Richard, Sept. 2, 1752.
Thomas Hickman, son to Thomas, Dec. 31, 1755.
Brereton Jones, son to Robert, Jany. 4, 1716.
Betty Jones, daughter to Robert, Jany. 9, 1718.
Robert Jones, son to Robert Jany. 26, 1721.
Wm. & Thomas Jones, sons to Robert, Oct. 15, 1723.
Rodham Kenner, son to Richard, Mch. 22, 1671.
Richard Kenner, son to Richard, March 3, 1673.
John Kenner, son to Richard, Dec. 27, 1677.
Francis Kenner, son to Richard, Dec. 18, 1681.
Eliza Kenner, daughter to Richard, Mch. 19, 1682.
Hannah Kenner, daughter to Richard, March 13, 1684.
Wm. Keen, son to William, Sept. 11, 1665.
Eliza Keen, daughter to William, May 16, 1669.
John Keen, son to William, Aug. 12, 1671.
Hannah Keen, daughter to William, Feb. 4, 1676.
Sarah Keen, daughter to William, Oct. 7, 1678.
Rodham Keen, son to Francis, Sept. 28, 1707.
Eliza Kenner, daughter to Francis, Feb. 16, 1709.
Howson Kenner, daughter to Francis, May 10, 1712.
Hannah Kenner, daughter to Rodham, Aug. 31, 1695.
Rodham Kenner, son to Richard, Jany. 2, 1717.
Richard Kenner, son to Richard, April 6, 1722.
Elenor Keene, daughter to John, Sept. 29, 1710.
Eliza Keen, daughter to John, Mch. 26, 1715.
Brereton Kenner, son to Winder, Febry. 8, 1730.
Richard Kenner, son to Winder, Feby. 29, 1733.
Eliza Keene, daughter to Newton & Sarah, Mch. 4, 1750.
Thomas Keen, son to Newton & Sarah, March 5, 1756.
William Keene, son to Newton Keene, Dec. 4, 1753.
Sarah Keen, daughter to Newton Keene, Octob. 28, 1751.

John Keene, son to Newton Keene, gent & Sarah his wife, May 18, 1758.

Betty McAdam Keene, daughter to Thomas Keen & wife, Feb. 2, 1786.

John McAdam Keene, son to Thomas Keene & wife, Aug. 9, 1788.

Ann Keene, daughter to Thomas Keen & wife, Octo. 5, 1789.

Janetta Keen, daughter to Thomas Keen & wife, April 19, 1791.

John Newton Thomas Gaskins Edward Keene, son to Thomas, Sept. 13, 1796.

William Keene, son to Wm. & Anne Keene, Dec. 10, 1695.

Hannah Keen, daughter to Wm. & Anne, June 28, 1699.

Elizabeth Keen, daughter to Wm. & Anne, May 2, 1701.

Elizabeth Keen, son to Wm. & Eliz: Sept. 23, 1722.

Newton Keen, son to William and Eliz: Sept. 6, 1725.

Captain Newton Keene's children's ages:

Elizabeth was born March 4, 1749-50; Sary was born Octo. 28, 1751; William was born, Dec. 4, 1753; Thomas was born March 5, 1756; John was born May 18, 1758; Anne was born June 2, 1760; Mary was born April 30, 1762; John was born Febr. 15, 1764; Hannah was born April 6, 1766; Newton was born Mch. 9, 1768; Catherine was born April 13, 1770.

James Lane, son to James, Jan. 17, 1686.

Alexr Lunsford, son to William, May 23, 1697.

Eliza Lawson, daughter to John Lawson, April 30, 1707.

John Oldham, son to James Lawson, Oct. 17, 1708.

Lindsey Opie, son to Lindsey Opie, Mch. 5, 1714.

Fielding Nash, son to Kerych, May 24, 1706.

John Nelms, son to John, June 20, 1711.

Samuel Nelms, son to Richard, Mch. 9, 1712.

Sarah Nelms, daughter to John, March 4, 1713.

Richd. Nelms, son to Richard, Nov. 4, 1714.

Wm. Nelms, son to Richard, March 12, 1714.

Nane Adams, daughter to Richard, March 23, 1717.

Mary Nelms, daughter to William, Sept. 27, 1710.

Hannah Nelms, daughter to William, Feb. 21, 1712.

Joⁿ Neel, son to Rod^m Neel, Jany. 13, 1716.

Mary Newton, daughter to Christopher, March 3, 1687.

Ann Newton, daughter to Christopher, May 6, 1697.

Richard Nutt, son to Richard, Jany. 17, 1694.

Abner Neel, son to Daniel, May 5, 1696.

Nathan Neel, son to Daniel, Mar. 3, 1699.

Eliz: Nelms, daughter to Charles, Oct. 19, 1692.

Charles Nelms, son to Charles, June 27, 1694.

Ann Nelms, daughter to Charles, Nov. 8, 1696.

Wm. Nelms, son to Charles, April 23, 1699.

Eliz: Nelms, daughter to William, Dec. 22, 1702.

Samuel, son to William, June 19, 1699.

Christopher Neel, son to Chr°., June 23, 1671.

Daniel Neel, son to Chr°., July 26, 1673.

Mathew Neel, son to Chr°., Feb. 6, 1677.

Richard Neel, son to Chr°., Aug. 28, 1682.

Rodham Neel, son to Chr°., Oct. 8, 1685.

Patience Newton, daughter to Chr°., Aug. 6, 1693.

Thos. Newton, son to Chr°., Nov. 17, 1690.

Eliza Newton, daughter to Christopher, April 23, 1699.

Christo Newton, son to Chr°., Oct. 14, 1701.

Daniel, son to Daniel Neale, May 29, 1677.

Lucretia, daughter to Daniel Neale, Sept. 5, 1680.

William, son to Daniel Neale, July 1, 1682.

Hannah, daughter to Daniel Neale, July 12, 1684.

Winifred Nelms, daughter to Wm., Aug. 11, 1705.

Moses Nelms, son to Richard, Mar. 30, 1704.

Wm. Nelms, son to Richard, May 11, 1704.

Lucretia Nelms, daughter to Richard, Feb. 16, 1705.

Winifred Nelms, daughter to Richard, April 5, 1719.

Lucretia Nelms, daughter to Richard, Sept. 15, 1723.

Wm. Neel, son to Abner Neel, Sept. 21, 1724.

Judith Nelms, daughter to Charles, July 24, 1717.

Ann Nelms, daughter to Charles, Oct. 31, 1719.

Alice Nelms, daughter to Charles, June 5, 1726.

Daniel Neel, son to Abner, Jan. 25, 1727.

Abe Nelms, daughter to Charles, May 12, 1728.

Abner Neel, son to Abner, Feb. 2, 1729.

John Nelms, son to Joshua, April 26, 1736.

Presley Nelms, son to Charles, Oct. 5, 1730.

Rodham Neel, son to Peter, March 30, 1727.

Lucke Neel, daughter to Abner, Mar. 3, 1731.

Richard Nutt, son to Farnefold, April 23, 1725.

John Nutt, son to Farnefold, Feb. 12, 1728.

Moulder Nutt, son to Farnefold, Sept. 19, 1729.

Farnefold Nutt, son to Farnefold, Sept. 14, 1731.

William Nutt, son to Farnefold, Dec. 6, 1733.

Elizabeth Nelms, daughter to Joshua, July 16, 1734.

Joshua Nelms, son to Joshua, March 24, 1732.

Sarah Nelms, daughter to Joshua, Aug. 27, 1736.

Chr°. Neale, son to Abner, April 8, 1737.

Farnefold Nutt, son to Farnefold, Sept. 28, 1736.

John Neel, son to Abner, Feb. 28, 1739.

Peter Neel, son to Abner, Dec. 5, 1740.

Nine Nutt, daughter to Farnefold, Aug. 20, 1740.

Lettie Nelms, daughter to Joshua, Nov. 14, 1738.

Edw. Northern Nelms, daughter to Joshua, March 6, 1741.

Rodham Neel, son to Abner Neel, Feb. 24, 1743.

Sarah Ann Nutt, daughter to Farnefold, May 1, 1743.

Mary Neele, daughter to Abner, May 27, 1745.

Daniel Neel, son to Daniel, June 3, 1727.

Judith Neel, daughter to Shapleigh Neale, Oct. 4, 1742.

Hannah Neel, daughter to Shapleigh Neale, June 5, 1746.

Jeremiah Nelms, son to Joshua Nelms, Sept. 16, 1743.

Wm. Nelms, son to Joshua Nelms, Oct. 25, 1746.

Nansy Nelms, daughter to William Nelms, Oct. 20, 1748.

Chr° Neel, son to Daniel Neel, Sept. 25, 1749.

Daniel Neel, son to Daniel, Jany. 14, 1751.

John Nutt, son to Farnifold & Mary, Feb. 16, 1749.

Thomas Nutt, son to Farnifold, Jan. 25, 1753.

William Nash, son to John & Mary, May 24, 1758.

Katy Nutt, daughter to Rich'd & Alice Nutt, April 9, 1759.

Winny Nutt, daughter to Richard & Alice Nutt, June 8, 1760.

John Nash, son to John & Mary, May 10, 1761.

Dickey Nutt, son to Rich'd & Alice Nutt, Jany. 9, 1762.

Betty Nash, daughter to John & Mary Nash, June 25, 1764.

James? Nutt, son to Richard & Alice Nutt, May 9, 1773.

Mary Griffin Neale, daughter to Richard & Jeane his wife, Mar. 11, 1776.

William Neale, son to John & Martha his wife, May 10, 1764.

Sally Kenner Neale, daughter to John and Martha, Nov. 29, 1772.

John Neale, son to John and Martha, April 1, 1777.

James Neale, son to John and Martha, Sept. 24, 1778.

Winifred Nash, daughter to George & Lucy, Oct. 27, 1779.

Thomas Neale, son to John & Martha, April 9, 1780.

Mary Satchell Neale, daughter to Presley Neale & Susan, July 26, 1781.

Matthew Neale, son to Presley Keene & Susan, Jany. 13, 1783.

Sarah Presley Neale, daughter to William, Aug. 1, 1784.

Elizabeth Neale, daughter to John & Amey, March 8, 1786.

Tho. Opie, son to Lindsey, March 25, 1716.

Lindsey Opie, son to John, March 5, 1714.

Thos. Opie, son to John, Feb. 25, 1716.

Susanna Opie, daughter to John, Feb. 5, 1719.

John Oldham, son to John, Feb. 28, 1664.

Abig'l Oldham, daughter to John, March 27, 1666.

Rich'd Oldham, son to John, May 27, 1671.

James Oldham, son to John, Aug. 11, 1669.

Spencer Mottrom Pickerell, son to Spencer & Judith, April 17, 1763.

Mary Ann McCormick, daughter to Francis, Sept. 10, 1711.

Eliza McCormick, daughter to Francis, Oct. 31, 1713.

George, son to Adam & Phebe Menzies, Sept. 16, 1755.

Samuel Peachy, son to Phebe Menzies, Sept. 23, 1759.

Wm. Pickrell, son to Wm., Mch. 6, 1694.

George Valandingham, son to Henry & Eliz: Febr. 11, 1770.

Lucy Valandingham, daughter to Francis & Sarah, Aug. 3, 1798.

John Pickrell, son to Spencer & Judith, Nov. 28, 1753.

Charles Pickrell, son to Spencer & Judith, Dec. 23, 1755.

Jane Rodgers, daughter to Richard, Apl. 12, 1686.

John Rodgers, son to Richard, Dec. 18, 1676.

William Rodgers, son to Richard, Feb. 12, 1679.
Ann Rice, daughter to Richard, Jany. 9, 1686.
Sarah, daughter to Richard, Dec. 22, 1739.
Charles Rice, son to Richard, Jan. 4, 1742.
Isaac Rice, son to Johh, Apl. 21, 1734.
William Rice, son to John, July 31, 1736.
John Rice, son to John, March 23, 1741.
Winy Rice, daughter to John, Feb. 9, 1739.
Betty Rice, daughter to John, July 4, 1748.
Sarah Ann Rice, daughter to John, Aug. 1, 1743.
John Rice, son to John, March 23, 1741.
Judith Rice, daughter to Isaac & Sarah, Sept. 26, 1763.
Winny Rice, daughter to Isaac & Sarah Rice, Apl. 21, 1766.
Joseph Rice, son to Isaac & Sarah, July 22, 1768.
Molly Rice, son to Isaac & Sarah, Nov. 5, 1771.
Richard Rice, son to Richard & Judith, April 28, 1777.
Samuel Rice, son to William Pendly Rice & Hannah, Mch. 6, 1778.
William Rice, son to Isaac & Sarah, Sept. 19, 1778.
Betty Rice, daughter to Richard & Judith, Nov. 28, 1778.
John Rice, son to Charles & Sarah, May 11, 1780.
Judith Rice, daughter to Richard & Judith, Sept. 16, 1780.
William Rice, son to Wm. P. Rice & Hannah, June 16, 1781.
Sally Rice, daughter to Richard & Judith, April 25, 1782.
Caty Rice, daughter to Charles & Sarah, Nov. 5, 1791.
John Span, son to Cuthbert, Feb. 26, 1686.
Richard Spann, son to Cuthbert, June 15, 1684.
Samuel Smith, son to Samuel Smith, June 12, 1692.
John Shapleigh, son to Philip, Jany. 23, 1687.
Hannah, daughter to Philip, Oct. 2, 1690.
Judith, daughter to Philip, Sept. 13, 1692.
Sarah, daughter to Philip, July 14, 1695.
Richard Spann, son to Cuthbert, Jany. 19, 1741.
Sarah Thornton, daughter to Thomas, May 23, 1699.
Francis Valendingham, son to Mich'l, Dec. 13, 1666.
Richard Valendingham, son to Michael, Aug. 6, 1672.
Ann Valendingham, son to Michael, Dec. 3, 1668.
Benjamin Valendingham, son to Michael, June 31, 1672.

George Valendingham, son to Francis, Oct. 1, 1718.
Elizabeth Valendingham, daughter to George Valendingham, Sept. 30, 1786.
Benjamin, son to Benjamin Valendingham, Nov. 23, 1756.
George Valendingham, son to Benjamin & Susannah, Aug. 6, 1758.
Thomas Valendingham, son to George & Mary, Jany. 18, 1759.
Ezekiel, son to George & Mary Valendingham, June 1, 1762.
Francis Valendingham, son to Benj. & Susan, Nov. 4, 1763.
Richard L. Valendingham, son to Benj. & Mary, Aug. 6, 1767.
William Wyatt, son to James Wyatt, Sept. 26, 1746.
John Wyatt, son to James Wyatt, Febry. 24, 1749.
Jas. Wyatt, son to James Wyatt, Jany. 10, 1752.
Presley Neale, son to Matthew & Rebecca, Oct. 22, 1802.
Matthew Neale, son to Matthew & Rebecca, Feb. 4, 1805.

DEATHS.

William Keene, son to Wm. & Eliz: Oct. 4, 1700.
Farnifold Nutt, the elder, died May 4, 1762.
Mary Hickman, March 8, 1757.
Capt. Griffin Fauntleroy, Oct. 28, 1755.
John? Fauntleroy, Sept. 24, 1756.
Capt. Ellis Gill, Oct. 27, 1760.
Thomas Gill (Potomack river), Oct. 12, 1765.
Jesse Gaskins, June 27, 1757.
Hannah Eskridge, daughter to Samuel, Oct. 6, 1754.
George Eskridge, son to Samuel, Nov. 1, 1754.
Charlotte Foushee Eskridge, daughter to Samuel, May, 1756.
John Conway, Sept. 27, 1755.
Capt. Edward Coles, Nov. 21, 1764.
George Berry, Jan. 3, 1756.
Charles Betts, the elder, March 14, 1756.
William Berry, July 25, 1761.
Samuel Blackwell, gent, Oct. 17, 1761.
John Rice, June 6, 1762.

EARLY TOMBSTONES IN NORTHUMBERLAND COUNTY.[2]

In an abandoned grave-yard on the eastern edge of the village of Heathsville lies a heavy slab inscribed as follows:

HERE LYETH THE BODY OF
ELIZABETH HAYNIE DAUGHTER
OF RICHARD & JANE BRIDGAR
WAS BORN JULY 16th 1665
MARRIED TO RICHARD HAYNIE [3]
OCTOBER 10th 1681 BY WHOM SHE
HAD 8 CHILDREN & DIED HIS
WIFE APRIL 2   1697.

---

[2] In these inscriptions the lettering on the tombstones is literally followed.

[3] Richard Haynie married a second time, and died about 1724. In his will of Oct. 31, 1734, he names six sons—Bridgar, Richard, McMillon,

414

On the margin of Cod's creek, near the seat of "Northumberland House," where the Preslys and Thorntons long resided, the handsome tomb of Hon. Presly Thornton[1] lies in broken pieces, and only a fragment of the inscription is to be found. The following words are all that appear on the pieces of stone remaining:

With

Sea   in the

County of

his merit

ntil he was in

One of the Council of State

for this Colony

These important stations he filled

to the Publick emolu(ment)

And his own reputa(tion)

Having thus enjoyed the Chief Honors

of his Country

He departed this Life

The 8th Day of December (1769)

in the 48th Year of his (Age).

Near to the above mutilated tomb are two headpieces marking the graves of a Revolutionary patriot[2] and his faithful wife, who came to Northumberland from Philadelphia. The inscriptions are as follows:

In Memory of

Col. James Moore,

an officer of

the revolutionary army,

Who departed this

life May 20th 1813

Aged 56 years.

Ormsby, Charles and Samuel; also four daughters—Katharine, Elinor, Winifred and Anna. His wife "Elinor" survived him.

[1] The will of the Hon. Presly Thornton (prob. May 14, 1770) names his sons Peter Presly and Presly; also three daughters—Elizabeth, Winifred and Charlotte. A full inventory of his personal estate is preserved among the Northumberland records.

[2] Col. Moore was survived by a large family of children, but his daughters only left descendants. They intermarried with the Towleses, Bateses, Hudnalls, Shepherds, Tapscotts and Hulls.

In Memory of
Sarah Moore,
relict of
Col. James Moore,
Who departed this
life Dec. 1st, 1814
Aged 47 years.

On the margin of Hull's creek, near the old Chicacohan residence, the aforetime clerk of Northumberland, who married the daughter of the above Col. Moore, lies buried in a grave marked by a vertical slab, on which is this inscription:

SACRED
to the memory of
FLEMING BATES [1]
Who departed this life
Dec. 26, 1830,
in the 52nd year of his age.
He needs no epitaph whose
life was a constant blessing
to all within his sphere of
action.

Near Burgess' Store, on the margin of a field opposite the residence of Dr. Sydnor, a massive slab appears partly imbedded in the earth. The inscription reads:

Here lies the body
of THOMAS GILL[2] who
departed this life the 12th
day of November, 1739,
in the 60th year of his
Age.

---

[1] Fleming Bates was son to Thomas Fleming Bates and Caroline Matilda Woodson, of Fluvanna, and brother of the Hon. Edward Bates, of Missouri, Attorney-General under President Lincoln.

[2] A Thomas Gill's will is on record in Northumberland, probated Feb. 10, 1707-8. In it he names his sons William and *Thomas,* and daughters Dinah, Susanna Robinson and Frances Waddington.

In the rear of the spot on which the Upper St. Stephens church stood in Colonial days, and not far from the Glebe mansion, which is still standing, an upright slab commemorates one of the last century clergymen, as follows:

IN
Memory of the late Rev'd
Duncan McNaughton, a native
of Perthshire, Scotland,
Who departed this life May 16th, 1809,
in the   year of his age.
The stranger's friend lies here at rest
In this cold silent grave,
We trust that with the rising just
He'll resurrection have.

On "Cypress Farm" at the head of Garner's creek, near the site of the early Keene residence, two heavy slabs are to be seen, one of them partly overgrown by a large persimmon tree. One of them has this inscription:

Here lyeth the body of
William Keene, the Eldest Son
of Thomas and Mary Keene
Born in Kent in Maryland
the 10th day of March anno
Dom. 1642, Who marryed
Eliz[a], the Daughter of John
Rogers Gent. and Ellin his
Wife of Northumberland Co.
in Virginia by Whome he had
two Sons and Four daughters
And dyed y[e] 8 day of Feb.
1684 in y[e] two and Fortieth
year of his Age.

The other tomb, lying near by the above, shows lettering remarkably clear and distinct, as follows:

WAS BORNE AT WOODSTOCK

OF THOMAS BANKS GENT. THE ONLY SON OF THOMAS BANKS,

HERE LYETH THE BODY

DAY. ANNO DOM. 1642
AND SERVED Seven Years an
Apprentice to M[r]. Wallistone Merch[t]
in Southampton. And after came into
Verginia, where he married three
Wives the last of which he tooke
to Wife Eliz[a] [1] the Relict of William
Keene, dec'd, daughter of
John Rogers Gent. and Ellin his
Wife of Northumberland County in
Verginia. Was marryed the 8 day
of december 1687 and dyed the
20 of September. Anno Dom.
1697 In the 56 Year of his age.
as also these two Versers. As I in
Sorrow for thee have been distrest.
If God Permit Me Lye by thee to rest.

GENT AND DORATHY HIS WIFE

[1] Mrs. Elizabeth Banks, after enduring two widowhoods, died in 1722 (will probated March 15, 1722). Her sons by Wm. Keene were William and John. Her daughter Hannah married Col. John Bushrod, of Bushfield, in Westmoreland. Elizabeth married —— Lee. Another daughter married Samuel Samford, and the fourth daughter married John Woodbridge. Her father, Major John Rogers, was an early settler in Northumberland, and long served as one of the justices. A small creek tributary to Hull's creek is still known by the name of Rogers, the plantation and home of the early justice having been on its banks. It seems very probable that Elizabeth Keene was the wife of Charles Lee, youngest son of the immigrant Richard Lee.

On the margin of an arm of the Yeocomico in Cherry Point, near the old Cox homestead, a broken horizontal slab bears the following words:

Here Lieth the Body of
PETER COX (Son of
PETER COX) who was Born
July 10th in the Year of our Lord
1744
And departed this Life May 6th
1792
In the 48th year of His Age.
He was in Principle Moderate
Calvinist, By Profession a Baptist, And
In Life and Conversation a Real
Christian.
In solemn silence let him lie
Nor dare disturb his Dust
Till the Archangel rend the sky
And wakes the sleeping Dust.
This monument in memory of the
Dec'd was Reared by his Widow
JANE COX, Daughter of
WILLIAM HARDING, who was
Born September 22nd, 1746.

THE GRAVE OF RICHARD LEE, THE EMIGRANT – In March 1664 Colonel Richard Lee, then of London and Stratford Langton in Essex, died at his plantation on Dividing Creek in Northumberland County, Virginia, and was buried in the garden of his home there. As late as 1798 his tombstone was still to be seen at the site.

Pursuant to Richard Lee's will, his widow (nee Anne Constable) and younger children returned from England to live at the Dividing Creek plantation, which was eventually inherited by his youngest son, Charles (1656-1701). In the course of time, Anne Constable, Charles Lee, and Charles's wife, Elizabeth Medstand, were in their turn buried near the grave of Richard Lee.

About 1720 Charles Lee II (1684-1734) abandoned the original Lee home on Dividing Creek and built "Cobbs Hall" at a site about half a mile to the east. However, the "Cobbs Hall" family continued to use the burying ground at the original site. Thus Charles Lee II (but not his widow, Elizabeth Pinckard, who remarried and lived and died elsewhere), Charles Lee III (1722-1747), and the latter's two wives, Mary Lee of "Ditchley" and Leeanna Jones of "Hickory Neck," were also buried there. This Leeanna Jones was herself a great-granddaughter of Richard Lee and granddaughter of Charles Lee I. In her will, probated in 1761, she ordered the erection of "a proper brick wall round the Burying place of myself. and ancestors on this plantation."

In 1923 Cazenove Lee undertook to find the grave of the emigrant Richard Lee. At the "Cobbs Hall" burying ground the only evidence above ground was the tombstone of Susan Lee (1802-1852), the wife of William Harvey. Probing in the vicinity, however, Cazenove Lee discovered the foundations of the wall erected pursuant to the will of Leeanna Lee. (Cazenove Lee, "Locating the Grave of Colonel Richard Lee," *Magazine of the Society of the Lees of Virginia,* V, 43-49.) The grave of the emigrant Richard Lee was certainly within that enclosure.

In 1956 E. Walter Harvey, Sr., the present master of "Cobbs Hall," presented the old family burying ground to the Society of the Lees of Virginia, which undertook to clear the site, to restore Leeanna Lee's wall, and to erect a suitable marker. This work has now been accomplished. On May 3, 1958, with appropriate ceremony, the site was rededicated to the memory of the first Richard Lee, of Anne Constable, his wife, and of their "Cobbs Hall" descendants buried there. – *Ludwell Lee Montague.*

SOME ORANGE COUNTY VIRGINIA BIRTH RECORDS*

Contributed by GEO. H. S. KING, *Fredericksburg, Virginia.*

YEAR	NAME	BORN	BAPTIZED
1770	Charles son to James & Ann Beazley	Apr. 16	
1772	Catey daughter to Jas. & Ann Beazley	Feb. 13	
	Patrick son of Joseph & Sarah Bell	Oct. 17	
1771	John son of Isaac Crosthwait	Mar. 29	
1773	Elizabeth daughter of Isaac Crosthwait	Aug. 13	
1772	Frances daughter of Harry & Sarah Gaines	Oct. 6	Nov. 22
	William son to Robert & Sarah Golding	Dec. 11	Dec. 13
1773	Ellis son to Matthew & Mary Hambleton	Apr. 10	May 30
	Henry son to Benj. & Martha Head	Apr. 12	May 30
1775	Mary daughter to Matthew & Mary Hambleton	Oct. 19	
1776	Tavener son to Benj. & Martha Head	June 2	July 28
1772	William son to William & Sarah Leigh	Nov. 1	Nov. 29
1767	George son of Benj. & Mary Porter	Feb. 1	
1777	Benjamin son of Benjamin & Mary Porter	Dec. 1	
1772	Stanley son to Caleb & Nelly Sisson	Nov. 15	Nov. 29
1769	Jacob son to Ambrose & Sarah Stodghill	Apr. 1	
1771	Dorshee daughter Ambrose & Sarah Stodghill	Nov. 15	
1770	James son to William & Elizabeth Smith	June 3	
1773	Paton & Selah children to Wm. & Elizabeth Smith	Apr. 10	
1766	George son Andrew & Elizabeth Shepherd	Oct. 25	
1768	William son Andrew & Elizabeth Shepherd	May 14	
1770	Alexander son Andrew & Elizabeth Shepherd	Jan. 4	
1771	Helen daughter Andrew & Elizabeth Shepherd	Dec. 27	
1773	Mary daughter Andrew & Elizabeth Shepherd	Nov. 12	
1775	Andrew son to Andrew & Elizabeth Shepherd	Oct. 8	
1777	Elizabeth daughter to Andrew & Elizabeth Shepherd	Sept. 11	
1751	Milly daughter to Erasmus & Jane Taylor	Dec. 18	Jan. 9, 1752
1753	Frances daughter to Erasmus & Jane Taylor	Dec. 16	Jan. 8, 1754
1755	Elizabeth daughter to Erasmus & Jane Taylor	Sept. 22	Oct. 3
1757	Lucy daughter to Erasmus & Jane Taylor	Dec. 13	Dec. 25
1760	John son of Erasmus & Jane Taylor	Oct. 26	Nov. 13
1763	Robert son of Erasmus & Jane Taylor	Apr. 29	May 15
1766	Jane daughter of Erasmus & Jane Taylor	Mar. 2	Apr. 24
1767	James son to William & Margaret Turner	Sept. 21	June 12, 1773
1775	Ann daughter to Jonathan Taylor	Dec. 9	

*These births and baptisms are recorded in the back of Orange County, Va. Deed Book No. 17 in Clerk's Office of Orange County. These are all that are entered of white children.

MARRIAGE BONDS OF PITTSYLVANIA CO., VA.
Communicated.

Merlin Young b. Nov. 7, 1767 d. Sept. 15, 1841 son of William Young and Elizabeth married May 12, 1792 Tabitha Witcher b. Oct. 14, 1772 d. Aug. 1, 1840 daughter of Daniel Witcher (son of Col. William Witcher)

Milton Young (brother of Merlin Young, named above) married September 13, 1790 *Nancy Witcher* (sister of Tabitha)—

TANDY Key Young, son of Merlin and Tabitha Young, was born June 26, 1794—died Jan. 7, 1861—married, in Smith Co., Tennessee, on Nov. 18, 1813 to Rachel Semms *Meroney*—a daughter of Captain Philip de Lancey Meroney (1st Maryland Battalion of the Flying Camp) by his second wife Martha Semms Massy whom he married in Franklin Co., North Carolina January 3, 1785.

Rachèl Meroney was visiting her half brother Philip de Lancey Meroney in Tennessee—Her father, Captain Philip de Lancey Meroney, had settled in South Carolina, and died there December 3, 1830.

Rachel Meroney (widow of *Tandy* Key Young), and mother of Congressman Hiram Casey Young from Tennessee) Died on her estate (The Young estate), and was buried on it (in the family burying ground) in Marshall Co., near Byhalia, Mississippi—The widow of Captain Philip de Lancey Meroney also died there in 1858.

As the estate finally passed into strange hands the graves were removed to a neighboring graveyard.

The Young records record interesting "bits" about "Nancy Witcher" Young—some of her outstanding characteristics—

I have always been struck by the perpetuation of the name "Nancy Witcher" in various branches of the Witcher descendants—i. e. Lady Astor—"Nancy Witcher" Langhorne—and I knew intimately a cousin of hers "Nancy Witcher" Keen—now dead—

I have wondered if there was some outstanding reason for this repetition—

One of the gentlemen associated with the British Consulate in Philadelphia is named *Tandy*—

In a conversation he told me he was from Ireland—which "fits in" with the supposition in the "Tandy" article of Tyler's Quarterly that the family was from Ireland.

Epitaphs at Brandon, Prince George County, Va.

I.

Sacred
to the Memory of
NATHANIEL HARRISON
of Brandon, Eldest Son of Nathaniel & Mary
Harrison, of Wakefield. He died
October 1st, 1781, at the age
of 78 years.

II.

Sacred
ᴐ the Memory of
Benjamin Harrison,
of Brandon, only son of Nathaniel Harrison
and his wife Mary Digges. Born on the 13th of
February, 1743. Died on the
7th of August, 1807.

III.

Mrs. Elizabeth Page Powell, relict of Alfred
Powell, & 4ᵗʰ daughter of Benjamin Harrison and his
3d wife, Evelyn Taylor Byrd. Born October 2d,
1804. Died Nov. 27, 1836.

IV.

George E. Harrison, son of Benjamin Harrison and
his 3d wife Evelyn Taylor Byrd. Born 1st
September, 1797, died Jan. 19, 1839.

V.

William B. Harrison, 2d son of Benjamin Harrison
and Evelyn Byrd. Born Nov. 31, 1800.
Died Sept. 22d, 1870.

VI.

George E. Harrison
Born June 20, 1837. Died April
18, 1880.

NOTE.

Nathaniel Harrison, the elder, of Brandon, married 1st, Mary, daughter of Hon. Cole Digges, of "Belfield," York county. She was buried

424

at Denbigh Church, Warwick county, where her tomb, bearing Harrison and Digges arms empaled, remains with the following inscription :

Here lieth
The body of Mary Harrison
Daughter of the Hon'ble Cole Digges, Esq.
President of his Maj'ty's Council for the Colony
and
Late Wife of Colonel Nathaniel Harrison
of Prince George County
By whom she had four children viz :
Nathaniel who was born May 27th, 1739,
and died June 13d, 1740,
Digges who was born October 22d, and died Nov'r 12th, 1741.
(both interred near this place)
Also Elizabeth born July 30th 1737
Benjamin born February 13th 1742.
She so discharged the Several Duties
of Wife, Mother, Daughter, Neighbor
that her Relations & Acquaintance
might justly esteem their affliction insupportable
Was it not chastened with the Remembrance
That every Virtue which adds weight to their loss
Augments her Reward.
Obiit Nov'r 1744 Æt. 27.

Col. Nathaniel Harrison, married secondly before February 15, 1748, Lucy, daughter of Robt. Carter, of "Corotoman," and widow of Henry Fitzhugh, of "Eagles Nest"; but had no issue by this marriage. Col. Harrison appears to have held no office during the colonial period except the rank in the militia indicated by his title; but was an active supporter of American independence, from the beginning of the Revolution, when he was a member of the Prince George county Committee of Safety, as was his son Benjamin Harrison. The son Benjamin was elected a member of the first State Executive Council ; but resigned in a short time, when his father was elected to fill his place. It is believed that Col. Nathaniel Harrison was also the person of the name who was president of the State senate in October, 1779.

Benjamin Harrison of Brandon, the son, married Evelyn Taylor, daughter of Col. Wm. Byrd (3d) of Westover. George Evelyn Harrison of Brandon, married Isabella Harmanson Ritchie, daughter of Thos. Ritchie of Richmond, a lady, who was the honored mistress of Brandon for so many years, and died a short time ago, universally regretted. Wm. Byrd Harrison, whose epitaph is also given, was the owner of Upper Brandon, and the builder of the fine mansion house there.

Brandon, a fortunate exception to the fate of most old estates in Virginia, still remains the property of the Harrisons—the family of the late George E. Harrison, whose epitaph is the last given above. Nathaniel Harrison of "Wakefield," Surry co., named in the first epitaph was member of the Council and Auditor General of the colony. As his epitaph from his tomb at "Wakefield" has only been printed in a newspaper, it may be preserved here: "Here lieth the body of the Honorable Nathaniel Harrison Esq., Son of the Honorable Benjamin Harrison, Esq. He was born in this parish the 8 day April, 1677. Departed this life the 30 day of November, 1727."

The epitaphs of his brother Henry, and his father Benjamin, both councillors, from the tombs formerly at Cabin Point, but now at Brandon, and that of his brother, Benjamin, of "Berkeley," speaker of the House of Burgesses; at Westover, have been several times in print.

HEATH-PRINCE GEORGE COUNTY.

There is in Prince George County several miles from the Courthouse, and just across Blackwater Swamp, an old family burying ground of the Heaths. The property is now owned by a family of Bohemians, and the old stones are fast crumbling away. Through the courtesy of Mr. Wm. David Temple, the courteous veteran Clerk of Prince George County Court, who conducted us to this spot, we were able to make memoranda of such of the stones as it was possible to decipher.

Sacred to the memory of
MAJ. W. B. HEATH
Born 16 Feby. 1792
Died 19 July 1831.

EMILY JANE HEATH
Born Apl. 15, 1830
Died May 17, 1832

—red to the memory —
ELVERTON T. HEATH
born 1824

WIRT R. HEATH
Born 1834
Died 1934

JAMES W. HEATH
*   *   *   *
    *   *

LEMUEL R. HEATH
Born 22 June 1796
Died 18 August 183-

JAMES E. HEATH
Born 1823
Died 1824

MRS. LUCY G., consort of
MR. JESSE HEATH
Died 26 April 1847
aged 63 years.

AGNESS HEATH
born 15 March 1772
died 17 July, 1816.

JUNIUS HEATH
Born 28 Feby. 1822
Died July 24 1822

WM. F. HEATH
Born Aug. 1, 1822
Died Aug. 11, 1822

Deposited here
The remains of
HARTWELL PEEBLES HEATH
In early life he was a poor
industrious and saving. Success
attended his efforts as a merchant
in the town of Petersburg * * * *
he was one of the most zealous
& efficient supporters of all
schemes connected with the improvement
of the town. As a husband he was affectionate,
as a father tender and generous, as a master humane
and indulgent. He was born on this spot on the 21 day of Mch. 1794
and died at his residence on * * * St. in the town of Petersburg.

W. Macfarlane Jones.

30th Jany. 1837.

427

BIRTHS FROM TRURO PARISH VESTRY BOOK

Page 10. George Horyford, son of John and Jane Horyford was born the 19 day of February 1733 and was baptized the one and 20th day of March following.

Anna Barry, the daughter of Edward and Mary Barry was born on Saturday the 8th of August 1730 and was baptized the 27th day of September following.

Mary Barry, the daughter of Edward and Mary Barry was born the 18th day of January 1732 and was baptized the 23rd day of March following.

Humphrey Poake, the Son of William and Sarah Poake was born the 1 and 30th day of January 1732 and was baptized the 23rd day of March following.

Sarah Poake, the daughter of William and Sarah Poake was born the 19th day of November 1734 and was baptized the 19th day of December following.

Page 20. Elizabeth Barry, the daughter of Edward and Mary Barry, was born the 28th day of September 1735 and was baptized by the Rev. Mr. James Keith the 2nd day of February following. John Baxter Godfather, Mary Payne and Anne Ashford, Godmothers.

Frances Haryford, the daughter of John Haryford and Jane his wife was born the 1 and 20th day of May 1737 and was baptized by the Rev. Mr. Joseph Blumfield the 29th day of Same month.

Stacey Ellzoy the daughter of Lewis Ellzoy and Mary his wife was born the 3rd day of May 1734 and was baptized the 7th day of June following.

Sarah Ellzoy, the daughter of Lewis and Mary Ellzoy was born the 24th day of April 1736 and was baptized the 12th Day of May following.

Patience Ellzoy, the daughter of Lewis Ellzoy and Mary his wife was born the 16th day of September 1737 and was baptized the 19th day of April following.

(In the Manuscript Department, Congressional Library, Washington, D. C.)

Ida J. Lee

428

THE OLDEST TOMBSTONE.

"Error wounded writhes in pain, and dies among its worshippers," But error takes sometimes a long time to die. One Thomas Hurd "correctly copied," in October, 1837, an inscription (purporting to be two hundred and twenty-nine years old), on a tombstone of usual size, standing on the banks of the Neabsco Creek, in Prince William county, Va. Mr. Charles Campbell gave

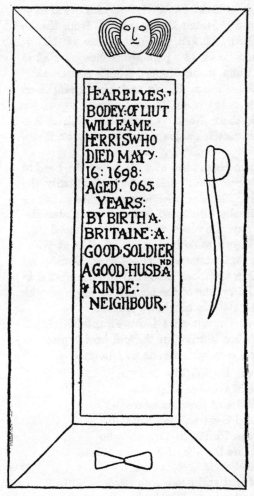

currency to his statement by publishing it in the *Southern Literary Messenger*, for October, 1843, p. 591. In 1890, Mr. Alexander Brown repeated Mr. Campbell's language in his great work, the *Genesis of the United States*. He numbered it Document XLV., but said, "I give this without comment, as I find it." (See Brown, Vol. I., page 150.) It is true that the authenticity of the date claimed, 1608, had been denied in the newspapers.

Determined to get at the truth of the matter, the Editor, in company with Mr. R. L. Traylor, of Richmond, went up to Freestone depot, on the Baltimore & Potomac Railroad, and walked over to the tombstone, near Neabsco Mills, some three miles distant. We found it without difficulty, and took a full-size tracing. The stone was doubtless covered with moss when Thomas Hurd visited it, and the letters were probably obscured. But the proprietor of the land had considerately in late years provided the tomb with a shelter from the weather, and the inscription was deciphered without difficulty. There is no doubt that what was taken for 1608 was 1698! The accompanying illustration is nearly a *fac simile*.

An examination of the Patent Books in Richmond shows a grant to William Harris, 30th May, 1679, of 1,600 acres in Stafford county, "beginning at a white oak standing by an Indian Path which divides this land & y² Land of M² Nathaniel Barton at y² head of Niapsco Creek and y² Maine Runn thereof, from thence along y² Ridge Path S. E. by E. 278 perches, thence N. NE. y² Maine Runn of the Niapsco Creek 140 perches, thence parallel to y² said Ridge & Maine Runn to M² Robert King's corner oak," etc. On Feb. 26, 1690–'91, William Harris and Lewis Markham got a confirmation of this grant from Philip Ludwell, agent for the proprietors of the Northern Neck. On the the 29th of August, 1691, William Harris received a grant for 383 acres on Chappawansic Creek.

The tombstone of William Herris lies at a place " at the head of Niapsco Creek and the Maine Run," and he is undoubtedly the William Harris of the Land Patents, who was probably an officer in the regiment of Col. Herbert Jeffryes, sent over to subdue Bacon's rebellion. In those days the vowel " e " was pronounced " a."

The oldest tombstone known to be in existence is that at Westover, lying between the tombstones of Theodorick Bland and Lt. Col. Walter Aston. Mr. Campbell made out the inscription to be that of Capt. William Perry, one of the council of Virginia, who died August 6, 1637. The stone is now worn smooth.

The oldest tombstone in Virginia that bears an intelligible inscription is that of Mrs. Alice Jordan, in the old burial place at "Four Mile Tree," in Surry county. It runs as follows:

Here Lyeth Buried The Body of
Alice Myles daughter of
John Myles of Branton neare
Herreford Gent and late wife
of Mr. George Jordan in Virginia who
Departed this Life the 7th of January 1650.
Reader, her dust is here Inclosed
who was of witt and grace composed
Her life was Vertuous during breath
But highly Glorious in her death.

The next oldest tombstone is that of Major William Gooch at
"Temple Farm," where Lord Cornwallis surrendered, 1781:

[*Arms.*]
Major William Gooch of T(his)
[Parish]
Dyed Oct. 29 1655
Within this tomb there doth enterred
Lie
No shape but substance true [nobility]
Itself though young in years just t [wenty]
[nine]
Yet graced with vertues morall and [divine]
The church from him did good partici[pate]
In counsell rare fitt to adorn a S[tate]

TOMBSTONES OF THE SCARLETT FAMILY.

These stones were found by Mr. Henry I. Hutton, of Warrenton, at the mouth of Occoquan Creek. They are partially concealed by the water, so that Mr. Hutton found himself unable to
decipher all the lettering.

One of these stones reads as follows:

M.   S.
DIED
1 6 9 5
HEARE LYES MARTIN
SCARLETT GENT.

Two lines in small type could not be made out. Martin Scarlett was a justice of Stafford county in 1680.

The second tombstone reads, as far as deciphered:

(*Skull and cross-bones.*)
HERE LYES YE BODY
OF
. . . . . SCARLETT GENT
. . . .
. . . .

SCARLETT GENT.
MARRIED FEBR^Y . . . . .
DIED 1698

431

Extracts from the Register of Farnham Parish, Richmond county, Virginia.

[The book from which the following entries were taken is now in the county clerk's office at Warsaw, Va. It is evidently a copy from an older record (as there is no sort of chronological order), from a register which had become so dilapidated as to be merely loose pages, which the copyist did not take time to arrange in order. From the small number of marriages and deaths recorded in the copy, it is probable that part of the original was lost. B = born; M = married; D = died.]

B. Elizabeth, dau. Francis and Sarah Armistead, July 12, 1716.
B. John, son of Francis and Sarah Armistead, Feb. 26, 1718.
D. Francis Armistead, April 4, 1719.
B. Wm. Burgess, son Henry and Winifred
    Armistead, Nov. 10, 1775.
B. Ann, dau. Thomas and Ann Beale, Aug. 10, 1672.
B. Thomas, son Thomas and Ann Beale, Jan. 29, 1675.
B. Charles, son Thomas and Ann Beale, Oct. 20, 1678.
B. Ann, dau. Thomas and Elizabeth Beale, Sept. 3d, 1711.
B. Thomas, son Charles and Frances Barber, March 16, 1701.
B. Charles, son Charles and Frances Barber, Aug. 11, 1704.
B. Mary, dau. Charles and Frances Barber, Dec. 26, 1706.
B. Anne, dau. Charles and Frances Barber, Aug. 16, 1709.
B. Elizabeth, dau. Charles and Frances Bar-
    ber, March 4, 1711.
B. William, son Charles and Frances Barber, Nov. 17, 1714.
D. Mary Ball, Jan., 1718.
B. Katharine, dau. John and Mary Benger, Oct. 10, 1723.
D. Katharine Benger, Feb. 5, 1723-4.
D. John Benger, Oct. 31st, 1725.
D. Charles Barber, Nov. 27, 1726.
D. Charles Barber, Jr., Nov. 24, 1726.
D. Betty Beckwith, Ap'l 7, 1726.
D. Elizabeth Beale, March 21st, 1727-8.
D. Thomas Beale, Jr., Oct. 9, 1732.

B. Walter, son Giles and Elizabeth Cole, March 5, 1677.
B. Reuben, son Christopher and Anne Calvert, Nov. 5, 1682.
B. Susanna, dau. Wm. and Anne Colston, Dec. 8, 1686.
B. William, son Wm. and Anne Colston, Aug. 1st, 1713.
B. Traverse, son Charles and Rebecca Colston, Aug. 4, 1714.
B. Winifred, dau. Newman and Katharine
     Brockenbrough, March 21st, 1726.
D. Rebecca Colston, Dec. 29, 1726.
D. Elizabeth Colston, Jan. 18, 1726.
D. Charles Colston, Jan. 25, 1726.
D. Winifred Colston, Jan. 29, 1726.
B. Rawleigh, son Wm. and Million Downman, Apl. 24, 1680.
B. Wilmott, dau. Wm. and Million Downman, Dec. 14, 1681.
B. Million, dau. Wm. and Million Downman, Nov. 21st. 1683.
B. William, son Wm. and Million Downman, Oct. 19, 1685.
B. Robert, son Wm. and Million Downman, Jan. 2d, 1686.
B. Elizabeth, dau. Wm. and Million Downman, Jan. 26, 1688.
B. Traverse, son Wm. and Million Downman, Nov. 15, 1696.
B. Robert, son Wm. and Anne Downman, May 21st, 1720.
B. James, son Wm. and Anne Downman, July 29, 1722.
B. William, son Wm. and Anne Downman, Feb. 4, 1724-5.
D. Jabez Downman, Ap'l 23d, 1730.
D. Travers Downman, Ap'l 25, 1730.
B. William, son Wm. and Anne Downman, Feb. 14, 1724.
B. Travers, son Wm. and Anne Downman, March 16, 1726.
B. Elizabeth, dau. Wm. and Anne Downman, Aug. 20, 1728.
B. Jabez, son Wm. and Anne Downman, Sept. 30, 1730.
M. Mr. Wm. Davenport and Elizabeth Heale, Nov. 26, 1728.
B. William, son Wm. and Elizabeth Davenport, Feb. 6, 1735.
B. Fortunatus, son Wm. and Elizabeth Dav-
     enport, June 12, 1738.
M. Mr. John Eustace and Alice Corbin Peachey, Oct. 6, 1743.
B. John, son Alexander and Sarah Fleming, March 23d, 1690.
B. Charlotte, dau. James and Mary Foushee, June 5, 1692.
B. Susanna, dau. James and Mary Foushee, Dec. 12, 1695.
B. John, son John and Mary Foushee, Sept. 6, 1697.
B. Alexander, son Alexander and Sarah Flem-
     ing, Ap'l 17, 1696.
B. Sarah, dau. Alexander and Sarah Fleming, Ap'l 31st, 1698.

B. William, son Alexander and Sarah Fleming, Dec. 2d, 1706.
B. Charles, son Alexander and Sarah Fleming, Aug. 20, 1708.
B. Elizabeth, dau. Alexander and Sarah Fleming,
    ing,   Feb. 18, 1710.
D. Alexander Fleming,   May 5, 1720.
B. Elizabeth, dau. John and Elizabeth Foushee, Oct. 1st, 1723.
B. Mary, dau. Moore and Margaret Fauntleroy, Feb. 28, 1725.
B. Moore, son Moore and Margaret Fauntleroy, Oct. 1st, 1728.
D. Mary Foushee,   Oct. 3d, 1724.
B. Jean, dau. Thomas and Anne Glascock,   July 10, 1673.
B. Mary and Anne, daus. Gregory and Mary
    Glascock,   Nov. 10, 1673.
B. Mary, dau. Thomas and Anne Glascock.   Jan. 22d, 1690.
B. Frances, dau. Thomas and Anne Glascock,   July 14, 1680.
B. Corbin, son of Leroy and Winifred Griffin,   April 12, 1679.
B. Winifred, dau. of LeRoy and Winifred Griffin, October, 1682.
B. Thomas, son of LeRoy and Winifred Griffin, Sept. 20, 1684.
B. Standley, son of Francis and Ann Gower,   Nov. 17, 1679.
B. Francis, son of Francis and Ann Gower,   April 15, 1682.
B. Elizabeth, dau. David and Catharine Gwin, Dec. 31st, 1692.
B. John, son Thomas and Sarah Glascock,   Jan. 14, 1699.
B. Gregory, son Thomas and Sarah Glascock, March 10, 1700.
B. Elizabeth, dau. Thomas and Sarah Glascock,   April 20, 1703.
B. Thomas, son Thomas and Sarah Glascock,   April 12, 1705.
B. Francis, son Francis and Easter Gower,   Feb. 2d, 1706.
B. LeRoy, son Thomas and Elizabeth Griffin,   Jan. 9, 1711.
B. Elizabeth, dau. Thomas and Elizabeth Griffin, Oct. 13, 1714.
B. Frances, dau. Charles and Frances Grimes,   Nov. 19, 1717.
B. Alice, dau. Charles and Frances Grimes, March 24, 1718-9.
B. Katharine, dau. Standley and Sarah Gower, Sept. 24, 1720.
B. Peter, son Thomas and Sarah Glascock,   March 13, 1714.
B. Sarah, dau. Thomas and Elizabeth Griffin,   Nov. 7, 1716.
B. Ann, dau. Thomas and Elizabeth Griffin,   Jan. 16, 1718.
B. William, son Gregory and Alice Glascock,   May 28, 1730.
B. Jesse, son Gregory and Elizabeth Glascock,   May 10, 1730.
B. William, son George and Judith Glascock, Sept. 1st, 1734.
B. William, son William and Esther Glascock,   July 4, 1733.
D. John Gower,   Sept. 26, 1726.

D.	Frances Gower,	Jan. 7, 1726.
D.	Susanna Gower,	Dec. 11, 1726.
D.	Winifred Gower,	May 20, 1727.
D.	Thomas Glascock,	Jan. 8, 1724.
D.	Frances Gower,	Sept. 10, 1729.
D.	Alice Glascock,	June 25, 1730.
D.	Thomas Griffin,	Sept. 9, 1732.
B.	Francis, son Francis and Rachel Gower,	Dec. 15, 1726.
B.	Sarah, dau. Gregory and Alice Glascock,	Nov. 5, 1727.
B.	William, son William and Esther Glascock,	Feb. 20, 1728–9.
B.	George, son George and Judith Glascock,	Jan. 14, 1728.
B.	Ann, dau. William and Esther Glascock,	Feb. 29, 1730.
B.	Gregory, son Gregory and Elizabeth Glas-cock,	Jan. 21st, 1721–2.
B.	Traverse son Gregory and Elizabeth Glas-cock,	Oct. 1st, 1734.
B.	William, son George and Judith Glascock,	Sept. 1st, 1734.
B.	Thos. B., son LeRoy and Maryan Griffin,	Oct. 17, 1735.
M.	Gregory Glascock and Elizabeth Elder,	Jan. 29, 1730–1.
B.	Betty, dau. LeRoy and Maryan Griffin,	March 17, 1736,
B.	LeRoy, son LeRoy and Maryan Griffin,	Dec. 30, 1738.
B.	Corbin, son LeRoy and Maryan Griffin,	Nov. 2d, 1741.
B.	William, son LeRoy and Maryan Griffin,	Jan. 29, 1742.
B.	Samuel, son LeRoy and Maryan Griffin,	April 20, 1746.
B.	Cyrus, son LeRoy and Maryan Griffin,	July 16, 1748.
B.	George, son William and Esther Glascock,	Dec. 20, 1743.
B.	Mildred, dau. George and Judith Glascock,	Nov. 4, 1749.
B.	Betty, dau. William and Esther Glascock,	Dec. 9, 1749.
D.	Col. LeRoy Griffin,	July 9, 1750.
B.	John Tayloe, son LeRoy and Maryan Griffin,	Aug. 24, 1750.
D.	Million Glascock,	Oct. 25, 1750.
B.	John, son Wm. and Esther Glascock,	Dec. 24, 1751.
B.	Susannah, dau. George and Judith Glascock,	Nov. 28, 1751.
D.	Major George Glascock,	Feb. 27, 1753.
B.	Milly, dau. William and Esther Glascock,	Nov. 24, 1753.
B.	Wm. Chichester, son William and Eliza-beth Glascock,	July 4, 1754.
B.	Judith, dau. George and Judith Glascock,	1776.
B.	George, son George and Judith Glascock,	Jan. 10, 1756.

D. John Glascock,   May 7, 1756.

D. Wm. Chichester, son Wm. and Elizabeth
Glascock,   Aug. 8, 1756.

B. Thomas, son Thomas and Ann Glascock,   Sept. 21st, 1756.

D. Jesse Glascock,   Ap'l 1st, 1757.

B. William, son John and Ann Gaskins,   June 18, 1758.

B. Sarah, dau. George and Judith Glascock,   Oct. 4, 1761.

B. Elizabeth Chichester, dau. Richard and
Hannah Glascock,   April 27, 1762.

B. Richard, son George and Judith Glascock, Aug. 23d, 1764.

B. George, son Peter and Elizabeth Glascock,   Jan. 26, 1771.

B. Ann Corbin, dau. LeRoy and Alice Griffin, Sept. 1st, 1765.

B. Elizabeth, dau. LeRoy and Judith Griffin,   Aug. 18, 1773.

B. Washington, son John and Susannah Glascock,   Aug. 6, 1775.

B. Eleanor, dau. George and Catherine Heal, Nov. 19, 1705.

B. George, son George and Catherine Heal,   Jan. 4, 1707.

B. Elizabeth, dau. George and Catherine Heal, March 8, 1710.

B. Catherine, dau. Dennis and Elizabeth
McCarty,   Ap'l 16, 1678.

B. Daniel, son of Dennis and Elizabeth McCarty, March 19, 1684.

M. Alvin Mountjoy and Ellen Thornton,   May 3, 1728.

M. Billington McCarty and Ann Barber,   June 16, 1732.

B. Daniel, son of Bullington and Ann McCarty, Oct. 22, 1733.

D. Daniel, son of Bullington and Ann McCarty, Aug. 6, 1739.

B. Bullington, son of Bullington and Ann Mc-
Carty,   Oct. 3, 1736.

B. Thaddeus, son of Bullington and Ann Mc-
Carty,   Ap'l 1, 1739.

B. Chas. Barber, son of Billington and Ann
McCarty,   Aug. 23, 1741.

B. John, son of Rev'd Wm. and Barbara Mc-
Kay,   Feb. 13, 1744–5.

B. Fitzhugh, son of Rev'd Wm. and Barbara
McKay,   Aug. 24, 1753.

D. Ann McCarty,   Jan. 7, 1753.

B. Daniel, son of Bullington and Ann Mc-
Carty,   Aug. 24, 1757.

B. Thomas, son of Willoughby and Sarah
Newton, Dec. 20, 1723–4.
B. Rebecca, dau. of Willoughby and Sarah
Newton, Oct. 6, 1726.
B. Elizabeth, dau. of Henry and Elizabeth
Newton, Sept. 30, 1726.
B. Winney, dau. of Charles and Winney Mc-
Carty, Sept. 4, 1775.
B. Mildred Smith, dau. of Thaddeus and
Mary McCarty, Nov. 21, 1780.
M. Thomas Osborne and Frances Smith, Feb. 11, 1726–7.
B. Robert, son of Samuel and Elizabeth
Peachey, March 21, 1673.
B. Samuel, son of William and Phoebe Peachey, Sep. 4, 1699.
B. Alice Corbin, dau. of Samuel and Wini-
fred Peachey, May 16, 1726.
B. Elizabeth, dau. of Samuel and Katherine
Peachey, Nov. 18, 1721.
B. Ann, dau. of Samuel and Winifred Peachey, Aug. 24, 1738.
B. Phoebe, dau. of Samuel and Winifred
Peachey, Dec. 18, 1727.
B. William, son of Samuel and Winifred
Peachey, Ap'l 14, 1729.
B. Winny Griffin, dau. of Samuel and Wini-
fred Peachey, Feb. 26, 1730.
B. Samuel, son of Samuel and Winifred Peachey, Feb. 6, 1732.
B. Thos. Griffin, son of Samuel and Winifred
Peachey, Dec. 3, 1734.
B. LeRoy, son of Samuel and Winifred Peachey, June 19, 1736.
B. Samuel, son of William and Million Peachey, Dec. 16, 1749.
B. Winifred, dau. of Samuel Peachey, deceased, Sept. 3d, 1750.
D. Captain Samuel Peachey, Oct. 2d, 1750.
B. Elizabeth Griffin, dau. of LeRoy and Betty
Peachey, Oct. 20, 1761.
B. Alice, dau. of William and Elizabeth Peachey, July 2, 1752.
B. Susanna, dau. of William and Elizabeth
Peachey, Sept. 14, 1764.
B. Ann, dau. of William and Elizabeth Peachey, Oct. 15, 1766.

B. Thos. Griffin, son of William and Elizabeth Peachey,   Nov. 10, 1770.

B. Elizabeth, dau. of William and Eliz. Griffin Peachey,   Dec. 3, 1775.

B. Samuel, son of LeRoy and Betty Peachey,   Oct. 12, 1767.

B. LeRoy, son of LeRoy and Betty Peachey,   Aug. 21, 1770.

B. Ann, dau. of William and Ann Robinson,   Aug. 25, 1679.

B. Elizabeth, dau. of William and Ann Robinson,   Dec. 4, 1681.

B. Bathana, dau. of William and Ann Robinson,   Dec. 4, 1683.

B. Frances, dau. of William and Ann Robinson,   Nov. 10, 1684.

B. Margaret, dau. of Alexander and Judith Swan,   1680.

M. Alexander Swan and Judith Hinds,   Nov. 15, 1678.

B. John, son of William and Ann Tayloe,   Feb. 15, 1687.

B. John, son of John and Elizabeth Taverner, March 7, 1682–3.

B. Richard, son of John and Elizabeth Taverner, July 30, 1685.

B. John, son of James and Mary Tarpley,   Feb. 21, 1690.

B. James, son of James and Mary Tarpley,   May 8, 1692.

B. Rebecca, dau. of Samuel and Frances Traverse,   Oct. 15, 1692.

B. Sarah, dau. of John and Elizabeth Taverner,   Jan. 7, 1679.

B. Elizabeth, dau. of John and Elizabeth Taverner,   March 25, 1681.

B. Elizabeth, dau. of William and Ann Tayloe,   July 26, 1686.

B. William, son of William and Ann Tayloe,   July 30, 1694.

B. William, son of James and Mary Tarpley,   March 16, 1695.

B. John, son of John and Elizabeth Tarpley,   July 16, 1695.

B. Frances, dau. of Samuel and Frances Traverse,   Aug. 20, 1691.

B. Thomas, son of James and Mary Tarpley,   Feb. 28, 1697.

B. Mary, dau. of James and Mary Tarpley,   Feb. 1, 1691.

B. Elizabeth, dau. of James and Mary Tarpley,   Feb. 1, 1701.

B. John and Betty, children of John and Elizabeth Tarpley,   May 28, 1720.

B. Mary, dau. of William and Mary Tarpley,   Dec. 7, 1723.

B. Edwd. Ripping, son of John and Elizabeth
   Tarpley,   Apl. 19, 1727.
B. Elizabeth, dau. of John and Elizabeth Tar-
   ley,   March 4, 1728–9.
B. John, son of William and Mary Tarpley,   Sept. 29, 1729.
B. James, son of William and Mary Tarpley,   Dec. 8, 1731.
B. Thomas, son of James and Mary Tarpley,   Oct. 28, 1734.
D. William Thornton,   Nov. 14, 1726.
B. Hannah, dau. of William and Mary Tarpley,   Jan. 6, 1735.
B. Lucy, dau. of James and Mary Tarpley,   Aug. 17, 1736.
B. Betty, dau. of Traverse and Betty Tarpley,   July 28, 1738.
B. Sarah, dau. of James and Mary Tarpley,   Sept. 13, 1738.
B. John, son of John and Ann Tarpley,   Dec. 13, 1738.
B. Mary, dau. of James and Mary Tarpley,   Oct. 30, 1740.
B. Winifred, dau. of Traverse and Betty Tar-
   ley,   Nov. 1, 1740.
B. Alice, dau. John and Ann Tarpley,   Nov. 24, 1742.
B. James, son of James and Mary Tarpley,   July 21, 1743.
B. Fanny, dau. of Travers and Betty Tarpley,   July 2, 1743.
B. Lucy, dau. of Traverse and Betty Tarpley,   Jan. 7, 1745.
B. Betty, dau. of James and Mary Tarpley,   Aug. 6, 1746.
B. Saml. Traverse, son of Traverse and Betty
   Tarpley,   Dec. 15, 1748.
B. Milly, dau. of Traverse and Betty Tarpley,   Sept. 28, 1756,
B. Winny, dau. of John and Ann Tarpley,   Sept. 16, 1744.
B. Francis, son of John and Ann Tarpley,   Aug. 12, 1746.
B. Thomas, son of John and Ann Tarpley,   June 3, 1748.
B. Caty, dau. of John and Ann Tarpley,   April 3, 1750.
M. Henry Threllkeld and Eleanor Short,   July 15, 1728.
B. Mary, dau. of Thomas and Sarah Under-
   wood,   Oct. 20, 1687.
B. Seth, son of Mooto [?] and Ann Underwood,   May 1, 1729.
B. William, son of Mooto and Ann Underwood,   Jan. 6, 1726.
M. John Webb and Mary Sanford,   July 14, 1673.
M. Thos. Warring and Alice Underwood,   Oct. 5, 1673.
B. James, son of John and Mary Webb,   Aug. 9, 1673.
B. Giles, son of John and Mary Webb,   Ap'l 15, 1677.
M. Isaac Webb and Mary Bedwell,   Ap'l 16, 1678.
B. Isaac, son of John and Mary Webb,   Dec. 18, 1681.

B. William, son of Paul and Bridget Wood-
bridge, July 14, 1668.
B. John, son of William and Sarah Wood-
bridge, Nov. 24, 1706.
B. Elizabeth, dau. of William and Sarah Wood-
bridge, July 6, 1709.
B. Sarah, dau. of William and Sarah Wood-
bridge, Nov. 18, 1714.
B. Giles, son of Giles and Elizabeth Webb, Aug. 4, 1714.
B. John Span, son of Giles and Elizabeth Webb, Oct. 9, 1705.
B. Isaac, son of Giles and Elizabeth Webb, Sept. 25, 1705.
B. Betty, dau. of Giles and Elizabeth Webb, Feb. 1, 1711.
B. Mary, dau. of Giles and Elizabeth Webb, Nov. 11, 1717.
B. Cuthberth, son of Giles and Elizabeth
Webb, March 3d, 1718-19.
B. William, son of James and Barbara Webb, May 10, 1720.
B. Tabitha, dau. of Giles and Elizabeth Webb, Oct. 9, 1722.
B. Winifred, dau. of Newman and Katherine
Brockenbrough, March 21, 1726.
D. Tabitha Webb, Feb. 9, 1722.
D. William Woodbridge, Nov. 14, 1727.
B. John, son of Isaac and Frances Webb, Feb. 1, 1737.
M. John Wilcox and Ann Jenings, March 2, 1729-30.
B. Isaac, son of Isaac and Frances Webb, Oct. 30, 1739.
B. William, son of John Span and Sarah Webb, May 25, 1742.
D. James Webb, May 10, 1750.
B. Charles, son of Thomas and Ann Barber, Oct. 27, 1731.
B. Tarpley, son of Marmaduke and Elizabeth
Beckwith, Oct. 2, 1718.
B. Betty, dau. of Marmaduke and Elizabeth
Beckwith, Oct. 15, 1723.
B. Margaret, dau. of Marmaduke and Elizabeth
Beckwith, July 27, 1725.
B. Mary, dau. of Marmaduke and Elizabeth
Beckwith, June 12, 1727.
B. Richard, son of Thomas and Elizabeth Beale, Dec. 19, 1723.
B. Reuben, son of Thomas and Elizabeth Beale, Dec. 19, 1725.
B. William, son of Samuel and Ann Barber, Aug. 27, 1728.
B. Thomas, son of Thomas and Sarah Beale, May 17, 1729.

B. Benjamin, son of John and Rachel Branham, Dec. 1, 1728.
B. Spencer Thaddeus, son of John and Rachel
    Branham, Ap'l 22, 1729.
B. John, son of Edward and Elizabeth Barrow, Feb. 20, 1729.
B. Joseph, son of Caron and Margaret Branham, Ap'l 27, 1729.
B. Betty, dau. of John and Rachel Branham, Dec. 21, 1730.
B. Thomas, son of Thomas and Ann Barber, Feb. 28, 1729.
B. Samuel, son of Samuel and Ann Barber, Jan. 16, 1730-1.
M. John Branham and Rachel Gower, March 16, 1726-7.
M. James Booth and Frances Dale, Nov. 5, 1727.
M. Samuel Barber and Ann Foster, Nov. 30, 1727.
M. Thomas Beale and Sarah McCarty, Ap'l 27, 1728.
M. William Beale and Harwar Harwar, Ap'l 29, 1729.
D. Newman Brockenbrough, May 5, 1742.
B. Barbara, dau. of Karan and Susan Branham, Ap'l 16, 1753.
B. Charles, son of Samuel and Winifred Barns, Jan. 16, 1739.
B. Merryman, son of Samuel and Winifred Barns, Sept. 17, 1741.
B. Winny, dau. of Samuel and Winifred Barns, Ap'l 11, 1743.
B. Annot, son of Samuel and Winifred Barns, June 24, 1745.
B. Million, dau. of Samuel and Winifred Barns, Dec. 30, 1747.
B. Samuel, son of Samuel and Winifred Barns, Dec. 6, 1748.
B. Francis Kenyon, son of Charles and Mary
    Barber, July 12, 1768.
B. Samuel, son of Charles and Ann Barns, March 10, 1764.
B. Traverse, son of Charles and Ann Barns, Feb. 15, 1760.
B. Caty, dau. of Charles and Ann Barns, July 25, 1768.
B. Thaddeus, son of George and Betty Barns, July 27, 1768.
B. Newman, son of Newman B. and Lucy Butler
    Barns, Ap'l 14, 1769.
B. Morton, son of Newman B. and Lucy Butler Barns, 1771.
B. Edward, son of Samuel and Betty Butler, Aug. 27, 1770.
B. Frances, dau. of Charles and Mary Barber, Aug. 6, 1774.
B. John, son of William and Elizabeth Barber, Dec. 11, 1776.
B. Luce, dau. of William and Betty Barber, Ap'l 14, 1780.
B. Nancy, dau. of Samuel and Elizabeth Barns, Oct. 28, 1781.
B. Milly, dau. of Charles and Ellison Barns, Dec. 24, 1781.
B. Newman, son of Samuel and Betty Barns, Jan. 14, 1729.
B. Rauleigh, son of William and Elizabeth
    Davenport, Sept. 28, 1741.

B. Lindsay, son of William and Elizabeth
Davenport, Ap'l 22, 1744.

B. Robert Porteus, son of Robert and Elizabeth Downman, May 6, 1744.

B. Elizabeth, dau. of William and Elizabeth
Davenport, Dec. 27, 1749.

B. Mildred, dau. of Robert and Elizabeth
Downman, March 4, 1749.

B. Ann, dau. of Traverse and Grace Downman, Sept. 21, 1748.

B. Grace, dau. of Traverse and Grace Downman, Oct. 4, 1750, and died Oct. 11, 1750.

B. Betty, dau. of James and Lucy Downman, Jan. 10, 1750.

B. Elizabeth, dau. of Robert and Elizabeth
Downman, Feb. 21, 1752.

B. Rauleigh, son of Robert and Elizabeth
Downman, March 26, 1752.

B. Opie, son of William and Elizabeth Davenport, Ap'l 29, 1752.

B. Lucy, dau. of James and Lucy Downman, Aug. 30, 1752.

B. Rauleigh, son of Robert and Elizabeth
Downman, Sept. 5, 1752.

B. Winny, dau. of James and Lucy Downman, Dec. 26, 1753.

B. Ann, dau. of James and Lucy Downman, Dec. 9, 1755.

D. Elizabeth, wife of Robert Downman, 1756.

B. Fanny, dau. of James and Lucy Downman, Ap'l 18, 1757.

D. Margaret Downman, Sept. 20, 1758.

B. Rauleigh, son of James and Lucy Downman, Sept. 20, 1758.

B. George, son of Fortunatus and Elizabeth
Davenport, Dec. 7, 1760.

B. William, son of Robert and Elizabeth
Downman, Ap'l 15, 1741.

B. Traverse, son of James and Lucy Downman, Jan. 20, 1760.

B. Priscilla, dau. of James and Lucy Downman, March 5, 1762.

B. Winifred, dau. of Rauleigh and Elizabeth
Downman, Aug. 11, 1767.

B. William, son of Rauleigh and Elizabeth Downman, Ap'l 26, 1769.

B. Joseph, son of Fortunatus and Elizabeth Davenport, Sept. 7, 1759.

B. Betty Heale, dau. of Fortunatus and Elizabeth Davenport, May 19, 1765.

B. Rachel, dau. of Fortunatus and Elizabeth Davenport, Feb. 27, 1767.

B. John, son of Fortunatus and Elizabeth Davenport, Ap'l 23, 1769.

D. William Davenport, Aug. 7, 1771.

B. Frances Porteus, dau. of Robt. and Elizabeth Downman, Jan. 10, 1772.

B. Richard, son of Rawleigh and Elizabeth Downman, May 28, 1776.

M. Gilbert Hamilton and Ann Beale, Nov. 4, 1732.

B. William, son of Revd. William and Barbara McKay, June 16, 1745.

B. Katherine, dau. of Rev. William and Barbara McKay, Dec. 13, 1757.

B. Billington, son of Bullington and Eliza McCarty, March 18, 1759.

B. Thaddeus, son of Bullington and Eliza McCarty, Sept. 1, 1763.

B. Fanny, dau. of Charles and Winny McCarty, Aug. 3, 1765.

B. Elizabeth Downman, dau. of Billington and Elizabeth McCarty, Nov. 30, 1768.

B. James Hawks, son of James and Ann Webb, Nov. 20, 1750.

B. Amy, dau. of Isaac and Frances Webb, Nov. 20, 1750.

B. Ann, dau. of Isaac and Frances Webb, Jan. 22, 1753.

B. Priscilla, dau. of Isaac and Frances Webb, June 6, 1754.

B. Giles, son of Isaac and Frances Webb, Jan. 25, 1756.

B. Frances, dau. of Isaac and Frances Webb, Feb. 6, 1755.

B. Isaac, son of Isaac and Frances Webb, Nov. 15, 1740.

D. Sarah Webb, Aug. 25, 1754.

D. John Webb, May 3, 1756.

B. Isaac, son of Isaac and Frances Webb, Nov. 19, 1758.

B. Giles, son of Isaac and Frances Webb, Nov. 9, 1741.

B. James, son of Isaac and Frances Webb, Sept. 11, 1743.

B. Cuthbert, son of Isaac and Frances Webb, June 1, 1745.
B. Sarah, dau. of John and Clare Webb, Oct. 20, 1761.
B. William Traverse, son of William and Eliz-
 abeth Peachey, Jan. 7, 1773.

MARRIAGES, BIRTHS AND DEATHS IN RICHMOND COUNTY.

EXTRACTS FROM NORTH FARNHAM PARISH REGISTER KEPT IN THE CLERK'S OFFICE AT WARSAW.

Born, Elizabeth, daughter of Francis & Sarah Armistead, March 28, 1716.

Born, John, son of Francis & Sarah Armistead, Feb. 26, 1716.

Francis Armistead departed this life April 4, 1719.

Born, William Burgess, son of Henry & Winefred Armistead, Nov. 1, 1775.

Born, William, son of John & Jane Barber, Jan. 6, 1698.

Born, William, son of William and Mary Brockenbrough, Nov. 10, 1687.

Born, Elizabeth, daughter of William and Mary Barber, Jan. 11, 1685.

Born, Charles, son of William and Mary Barber, June 19, 1676.

Born, Thomas, son of William and Mary Barber, Jan. 19, 1678.

Born, William, son of William and Mary Barber, Aug. 7, 1679.

Born, Anne, daughter of Thomas & Anne Beale, Aug. 10, 1672.

Born, Thomas, son of Thomas & Anne Beale, Jan. 29, 1675.

Born, Charles, son of Thomas & Anne Beale, Oct. 20, 1678.

Born, Anne, daughter of Thomas & Elizabeth Beale, Sept. 3, 1711.

Born, Winefred, daughter of Newman & Catherine Brockenbrough, March 21, 1723-'4.

Born, Winefred, daughter of Newman & Catherine Brockenbrough, March 4, 1726.

John Booth, departed this life June 15, 1722.

John Booth, Jr., departed this life June 9, 1722.

Katherine Benger departed this life, Feb. 5, 1723-'4.

Mary Benger departed this life May 6, 1724.

John Benger departed this life Oct. 31, 1725.

Charles Barber departed this life Nov. 27, 1726.

Charles Barber, Jr., departed this life November 24, 1726.

Betty Beckwith departed this life April 7, 1726.

Born, Joyce, daughter of William & Joyce Barber, June 9, 1712.

Born, Thomas, son of Charles & Frances Barber, Mch 6, 1701.

Born, Charles, son of Charles & Frances Barber, Aug. 11, 1704.

Born, Mary, son of Charles & Frances Barber, Dec. 26, 1706.

Born, Anne, dau. of Charles & Frances Barber, Aug. 16, 1709.

Born, Elizabeth, dau. of Charles & Frances Barber, March 4, 1711.

Born, William, son of Charles & Frances Barber, Nov. 17, 1714.

Born, Adam, son of John & Phoebe Booth, October 23, 1711.

Born, William, son of John & Phoebe Booth, June 22, 1715.

Born, Richard, son of John & Phoebe Booth, March 28, 1720.

Born, Katherine, daughter of John & Mary Benger, Oct. 10, 1723.

William Brockenbrough departed this life, Jan. 25, 1733.

Sarah Booth departed this life Jan. 25, 1735.

Born, Sarah, daughter of James & Frances Booth, May 8, 1731.

Born, Charles, son of Thomas & Anne Barber, Oct. 27, 1731.

Born, Tarpley, son of Marmaduke & Eliza Beckwith, Oct. 2, 1718.

Born, Jonathan, son of Marmaduke & Eliza Beckwith, Nov. 14, 1720.

Born, Betty, dau. of Marmaduke & Eliza Beckwith, Aug. 15, 1723.

Born, Margaret, dau. of Marmaduke & Eliza Beckwith, July 29, 1725.

Born, Mary, dau. of Marmaduke & Eliza Beckwith, June 12, 1727.

Born, Richard, son of Thomas & Eliza Beale, Dec. 19, 1723.

Born, Reuben, son of Thomas & Eliza Beale, Dec. 19, 1725

Born, William, son of Samuel & Anne Barber, Aug. 27, 1728.

Born, Eliza, son of James & Frances Booth, Aug. 31, 1728.

Born, Thomas, son of Thomas & Sarah Beale, May 17, 1729.

Born, Thomas, son of Thomas & Anne Barber, Feb. 28, 1729.

Born, Samuel, son of Samuel & Anne Barber, Jan. 16, 1730-'1.

Married, Thomas Beale & Sarah McCarty, April 27, 1728.

Married, James Booth & Anne Foster, Nov. 30, 1727.

Married, Philemon Bird to Mary MacGyar, Feb. 25, 1727-'8.

Married, William Beale & (Harnear Harnear?), April 29, 1729.

Married, Thomas Barber & Anne Nash, Jan. 28, 1729–'30.

Born, James, son of James & Frances Booth, June 25, 1734.

Born, John & Jane Bates, son & daughter of Edward & Jane Bates, April 15, 1735.

Born, Abner, son of Philemon & Mary Bird, July 5, 1735.

Born, James, son of James & Frances Booth, Feb. 28, 1736.

Born, Edward, son of Edward & Jane Bates, June 20, 1737.

Born, Damarias, daughter of Philemon & Mary Bird, Nov. 20, 1737.

Born, Joseph, son of James & Frances Booth, Sept. 8, 1740.

Born, Sarah, dau. of Edward & Jane Bates, May 26, 1741.

Newman Brockenbrough departed this life May 15, 1742.

Born, John, son of Philemon & Mary Bird, Feb. 4, 1739.

Born, Frances, daughter of Edward & Jane Bates, Jan. 24, 1742.

Born, Joanna, daughter of Philemon & Mary Bird, July 21, 1743.

Born, Philemon, son of Philemon & Mary Bird, Dec. 19, 1745.

Born, Thomas, son of Edward & Jane Bates, Sept. 12, 1748.

Damarias Bird departed this life Dec. 15, 1743.

Philemon Bird departed this life Jan'y 7, 1752.

Abner, son of Philemon Bird, departed this life March 21, 1750.

Born, Anne Oldham, daughter of John & Sarah Booth, Dec. 13, 1760.

Born, Frances Kenyon, daughter of Charles & Mary Barber, Jan. 12, 1768.

Born, Frances, daughter of Charles & Mary Barber, Aug. 6, 1774.

Born, Luci, daughter of William & Betty Barber, April 14, 1780.

Born, Thadeus Booth, son of John & Winefred Booth, June 21, 1783.

Born, Charles, son of William & Anne Colston, April 17, 1691.

Rebecca Colston departed this life Dec. 29, 1726.

Charles Colston departed this life Jan. 25, 1726.

Winefred Colston departed this life Jan. 29, 1726.

Born, Ralph, son of Ralph & Honor Downing, April 15, 1688.

Born, James, son of Ralph & Honor Downing, Jan. 25, 1690.

Born, Ruth, dau. of Ralph & Honor Downing, Sept. 5, 1686.

Born, Raleigh, son of William & Million Downman, April 24, 1680.

Born, Wilmoth, daughter of William and Million Downman, Dec. 14, 1681.

Born, Million, daughter of William & Million Downman, Nov. 21, 1683.

Born, William, son of William & Million Downman, Oct. 19, 1685.

Born, Robert, son of William & Million Downman, Jan. 2, 1686.

Born, Elizabeth, daughter of William & Million Downman, Jan. 26, 1688.

Born, Traverse, son of William & Million Downman, Nov. 15, 1696.

Born, Traverse, son of William & Million Downman, March 19, 1700.

Born, Robert, son of William & Anne Downing, May 21, 1720.

Born, James, son of William & Anne Downing, July 29, 1722.

Jabez Downman departed this life, Sept. 26, 1730.

Traverse Downman departed this life, April 25, 1730.

Born, William, son of William & Anne Downman, Feb. 14, 1724.

Born, Francis, son of William & Ann Downman, March 16, 1726.

Born, Elizabeth, daughter of William & Ann Downman, Aug. 20, 1728.

Born, Jabez, son of William & Ann Downman, Sept. 12, 1730.

Born, Jean Glasscock, daughter of Thomas & Anne Glasscock, July 10, 1673.

Born, Mary & Anne, daughters of Gregory & Mary Glasscock, Nov. 10, 1673.

Born, Mary, daughter of Thomas & Ann Glasscock, Jan. 22, 1690.

Born, Frances, daughter of Thomas & Anne Glasscock, July 14, 1680.

Born, Alexander, son of Alexander & Sarah Fleming, April 17, 1696.

Born, Sarah, daughter of Alexander & Sarah Fleming, April 31, 1698.

(*To be Continued.*)

MARRIAGES, BIRTHS AND DEATHS IN RICHMOND COUNTY.

(Extracts from North Farnham Register, kept in the Clerk's Office at Warsaw.

Born, William, son of Alexander & Sarah Fleming, Dec. 2, 1706.

Born, Charles, son of Alexander & Sarah Fleming, Aug. 20, 1708.

Born, Elizabeth, daughter of Alexander & Sarah Fleming, Feb. 18, 1710.

Born, Moore, son of Moore & Margaret Fauntleroy, Oct. 1, 1728.

Born, Corbin, son of Leroy & Winnefred Griffin, April 12, 1679.

Born, Winnefred, daughter of Leroy & Winnefred Griffin, Oct. 4, 1682.

Born, Thomas, son of Leroy & Winnefred Griffin, Sept. 20, 1684.

Born, John, son of Thomas & Sarah Glasscock, Jan. 4, 1699.

Born, Gregory, son of Thomas & Sarah Glasscock, March 10, 1700.

Born, Elizabeth, dau. of Thomas & Sarah Glasscock, April 19, 1705.

Born, Francis, son of Francis & Anne Gower, April 15, 1682.

Born, Stanley, son of Francis & Ann Gower, Nov. 17, 1679.

Born, Francis, son of John & Esther Gower, Feb. 2, 1706.

Born, Leroy, son of Thomas & Eliza Griffin, Jan. 19, 1711.

Born, Elizabeth, dau. of Thomas & Eliza Griffin, Oct. 13, 1714.

Born, Katherine, daughter of Stanley & Sarah Gower, Sept. 24, 1720.

Born, Peter, son of Thomas & Sarah Glasscock, March 13, 1714.

Born, Sarah, daughter of Thomas & Elizabeth Griffin, Nov. 27, 1716.

Born, Amy(?), daughter of Thomas & Elizabeth Griffin, Jan. 16, 1718.

Born, William, son of Gregory & Alice Glasscock, May 28, 1730.

Born, Jesse, son of Gregory & Eliza Glasscock, May 10, 1733.

Born, William, son of George & Judith Glasscock, Sept. 1, 1734.

Born, William, son of William & Esther Glasscock, July 4, 1733.

John Gower departed this life Sept. 26, 1726.

Susannah Gower departed this life Dec. 11, 1726.

Francis Gower departed this life Sept. 7, 1726.

Winnefred Gower departed this life May 20, 1727.

Frances Gower departed this life Sept. 10, 1729.

Born, Francis, son of Francis & Rachel Gower, Dec. 15, 1726.

Alice Glasscock departed this life June 25, 1730.

Thomas Glasscock departed this life Jan. 8, 1726.

Born, William, son of William & Esther Glasscock, Feb. 20, 1728–'9.

Born, Sarah, dau. of Gregory & Alice Glasscock, Nov. 5, 1727.

Born, George, son of George & Judith Glasscock, Jan. 14, 1728.

Born, Anne, daughter of William & Esther Glasscock, Feb. 29, 1730.

Born, Gregory, son of Gregory & Eliza Glasscock, Jan. 21, 1731–'2.

Born, Traverse, son of Gregory & Eliza Glasscock, Oct. 1, 1734.

Born, William, son of George & Judith Glasscock, Sept. 1, 1734.

Married, Gregory Glasscock & Elizabeth Elder, Jan. 29, 1730–'31.

Born, Betty, dau. of Leroy & Mary Ann Griffin, Mch. 17, 1736.

Born, Leroy, son of Leroy & Mary Ann Griffin, Dec. 30, 1738.

Born, Corbin, son of Leroy & Mary Ann Griffin, March 2, 1741.

Born, William, son of Leroy & Mary Ann Griffin, Jan. 29, 1742.

Born, George, son of William & Esther Glasscock, Dec. 20, 1743.

Born, Samuel, son of Leroy & Mary Ann Griffin, April 21, 1746.

Born, Cyrus, son of Leroy & Mary Ann Griffin, July 16, 1748.

Born, Mildred, daughter of George & Judith Glasscock, Nov. 4, 1749.

Col. Leroy Griffin departed this life July 9, 1750.

Born, John Tayloe, son of Leroy & Mary Ann Griffin, Aug. 24, 1750.

Million Glasscock departed this life, Oct. 25, 1750.

Born, John, son of William & Esther Glasscock, Dec. 24, 1751.

Born, Susannah, daughter of George & Judith Glasscock, Nov. 28, 1751.

Major George Glasscock departed this life, Feb. 27, 1752.

Born, Milly, daughter of William and Esther Glasscock, Nov. 24, 1753.

Born, William Chichester, son of William & Elizabeth Glasscock, July 4, 1754.

William Chichester, son of William & Elizabeth Glasscock, died Aug. 8, 1756.

Born, Thomas, son of William & Ann Glasscock, Sept. 21, 1756.

Born, Judith, daughter of George & Judith Glasscock, July 10, 1756.

Born, George, son of George & Judith Glasscock, Oct. 4, 1758.

John Glasscock departed this life, May 7, 1756.

Jesse Glasscock departed this life, April 1, 1757.

Born, Sarah, daughter of George & Judith Glasscock, Oct. 4, 1761.

Born, Eliza Chichester, daughter of Richard & Hannah Glasscock, April 27, 1762.

Born, Richard, son of George & Judith Glasscock, Aug. 23, 1764.

Born, George, son of Peter & Eliza Glasscock, Jan. 26, 1771.

Born, Nancy, daughter of John & Susannah Glasscock, June 15, 1771.

Born, Anne Corbin, daughter of Leroy Griffin & Alice his wife, Sept. 19, 1768.

Born, Elizabeth Corbin, daughter of Leroy Griffin & Judith his wife, Aug. 18, 1773.

Born, Washington, son of John Glasscock & Susannah his wife, Aug. 6, 1775.

Born, John Glasscock, son of John Glasscock & Susannah his wife, Dec. 24, 1782.

Born, Elizabeth, daughter of John & Mary Lawson, Feb. 17, 1719.

Born, Joanna & Catherine, daughters of John & Mary Lawson, March 17, 1721.

Born, Sarah, daughter of Richard & Mary Lawson, Feb. 21, 1727.

Born, Thomas, son of Richard & Mary Lawson, Dec. 24, 1730.

Born, Lucy, daughter of John & Mary Lawson, March 3, 1731–'2.

Thomas Lawson departed this life Feb. 4, 1729.

Born, Betty, daughter of Christopher & Sarah Lawson, March 9, 1743–'44.

Born, Joanna, daughter of Christopher & Sarah Lawson, April 17, 1746.

Born, Epaphroditus, son of Christopher & Sarah Lawson, Feb. 23, 1747–'48.

Married, Richard Lawson & Mary Harris, Sept. 22, 1727.

Died, Mary, the wife of John Lawson, July 16, 1740.

Born Caty, daughter of Christopher & Sarah Lawson, April 11, 1751.

Born, Lucy, daughter of Christopher & Sarah Lawson, Jan. 29, 1756.

Born, Catherine, daughter of Dennis & Elizabeth McCarty, 'April 16, 1678.

Born, Luke, son of John & Elizabeth Milner, Sept. 5, 1708.

Born, Benjamin, son of John & Elizabeth Milner, Jan. 27, 1710.

Born, John, son of John & Elizabeth Milner, March 25, 1718.

Born, Winnefred, daughter of William & Judith Milner, Jan. 28, 1724–'5.

Born, Benjamin, son of Benjamin & Frances Milner, Dec. 25, 1730.

Born, Luke, son of Luke & Mary Milner, Dec. 31, 1734.

Born, Dorothy, daughter of Luke & Mary Milner, Feb. 16, 1736.

Married, Chrain(?) McCarty & Mary Mozinger(?), Dec. 30, 1729.

Born, Elizabeth, daughter of Luke & Mary Milner, Nov. 16, 1742.

Born, Daniel, son of Billington & Ann McCarty, Oct. 22, 1733.

Born, Billington, son of Billington & Ann McCarty, Oct. 3, 1736.

Died, Daniel, son of Billington & Ann McCarty, Aug. 6, 1739.

Born, Thaddeus, son of Billington & Ann McCarty, April 1, 1739.

Born, Charles Barber, son of Billington & Ann McCarty, Aug. 23, 1741.

Born, Luke, son of John & Margaret Milner, Sept. 17, 1750.

Born, John, son of John & Margaret Milner, Feb. 16, 1754.

Born, David, son of Billington & Elizabeth McCarty, Aug. 24, 1737.

Born, John, son of Charles & Ann McCarty, July 14, 1749.

Born, Winney, daughter of Charles McCarty & Winney his wife, Sept. 4, 1775.

Born, Rebecca, daughter of Willoughby & Sarah Newton, Oct. 6, 1726.

Born, Solomon, son of William & Ann Nash, April 8, 1726.

Born, John, son of William & Ann Nash, April 20, 1730.

Born, John, son of Thomas & Agathy Nash, Dec. 2, 1729.

Eliza Nash departed this life Nov. 3, 1726.

Anne Nash departed this life Nov. 12, 1726.

John Nash departed this life Nov. 15, 1726.

William Nash departed this life Oct. 15, 1732.

Married, William Nash & Margaret Brian, May 30, 1729.

Married, Richard Nash & Hanna Nash, Oct. 30, 1743.

Thomas Nash departed this life Nov. 29, 1748.

Born, Elizabeth, daughter of William & Judith Nash, Oct. 20, 1751.

Born, Pitman & Hannah, twins of Richard & Hannah Nash, March 11, 1752.

Born, Agatha, daughter of William & Judith Nash, Jan. 7, 1754.

Born, Thaddeus, son of George Nash & Sarah his wife, Nov. 29, 1775.

Born, Sally, daughter of Pitman & Betty Nash, Jan. 15, 1783.

Born, Hannah, daughter of George & Lucy Nash, Oct. 2, 1781.

Born, Jeremiah, son of John & Mary Nash, Aug. 22, 1781.

Born, Sally, daughter of George & Lucy Nash, June 15, 1787.

Born, Sarah, daughter of John Oldham, Jan. 24, 1718.

Born, John, son of James & Winnefred Oldham, June 30, 1715.

Born, Betty, daughter of James & Winnefred Oldham, March 29, 1718.

Born, Nannie, daughter of James & Winnefred Oldham, July 1, 1720.

Born, James, son of James & Winnefred Oldham, Nov. 13, 1722.

Born, Margaret, daughter of John & Sarah Oldham, Jan. 6, 1709.

Born, Mary, daughter of John & Sarah Oldham, June 25, 1712.

Born, Elizabeth, daughter of John & Sarah Oldham, May 12, 1715.

Born, Sarah, daughter of John & Sarah Oldham, Dec. 4, 1718.

Born, Jane, daughter of John & Sarah Oldham, Oct. 6, 1721.

William Oldham departed this life March 21, 1726–'7.

Rebecca Oldham departed this life Sept. 19, 1732.

Married, Peter Oldham & Rebecca Alverson, Feb. 17, 1727–'8.

Born, William, son of William & Mary Oldham, Sept. 4, 1770.

Born, Robert Peachey, son of Samuel & Elizabeth Peachey, March 21, 1673.

Born, Samuel, son of William & Phoebe Peachey, Sep. 4, 1699.

Born, Alice Corbin, daughter of Samuel & Winnefred Peachey, May 16, 1726.

Born, Ann, daughter of Samuel & Winnefred Peachey, Aug. 24, 1738.

Born, Phoebe, daughter of Samuel & Winnefred Peachey, Dec. 18, 1727.

Born, William, son of Samuel & Winnefred Peachey, April 14, 1729.

Born, Winney Griffin, daughter of Samuel & Winnefred Peachey, Feb. 26, 1730.

Born, Samuel, son of Samuel & Winnefred Peachey, Feb. 6, 1732.

Born, Thomas Griffin, son of Samuel & Winnefred Peachey, Dec. 23, 1734.

Born, Leroy, son of Samuel & Winnefred Peachey, June 9, 1736.

Captain Samuel Peachey departed this life Oct. 2, 1750.

Born, Samuel, son of William & Million Peachey, Dec. 16, 1749.

Winnefred, daughter of Samuel Peachey, died Sept. 3, 1750.

Born, Winnefred, daughter of William & Million Peachey, Jan. 8, 1752.

Born, Eliza Griffin, daughter of Leroy & Betty Peachey, Oct. 20, 1761.

Born, Alice, daughter of William & Elizabeth Peachey, July 21, 1762.

Born, Susannah, daughter of William & Eliza Peachey, Sept. 14, 1764.

Born, Ann, daughter of William & Eliza Peachey, Oct. 15, 1766.

Born, Samuel, son of Leroy and Betty Peachey, Oct. 12, 1767.

Born, Leroy, son of Leroy & Betty Peachey, Aug. 21, 1770.

Born, Thomas Griffin, son of William & Eliza Peachey, Nov. 10, 1770.

Born, Elizabeth, daughter of William & Eliza Peachey, Dec. 3, 1775.

Born, John, son of Benjamin & Sarah Rust, Nov. 2, 1725.

Born, Ann, daughter of Benjamin & Sarah Rust, Oct. 4, 1727.

Born, Metcalfe, son of Benjamin & Sarah Rust, Sept. 12, 1729.

Born, Sarah, daughter of Benjamin & Sarah Rust, Sept. 22, 1731.

Eleanor Rust departed this life, Nov. 10, 1722.

Born, James Rust, son of Samuel Rust & Nancy his wife, Dec. 14, 1798.

Born, John, son of Alexander & Judith Swann, July 22, 1691.

Born, Margaret, daughter of Alexander & Judith Swann, 1680.

Born, Edward, son of Edward & Winnefred Spencer, Nov. 20, 1710.

Born, Winnefred, daughter of Anthony of Elizabeth Sydnor, Feb. 6, 1713–'14.

Born, Epaproditus, son of Anthony & Elizabeth Sydnor, May 12, 1715.

Born, Betty, daughter of Anthony & Eliza Sydnor, Feb. 23, 1716–'17.

Born, Duanna, dau. of Anthony & Eliza Sydnor, Jan. 9, 1719.

Born, Lucy, daughter of Anthony & Eliza Sydnor, Feb. 3, 1722.

Born, Ann, daughter of Anthony and Eliza Sydnor, June 24, 1729.

Born, Ruth, daughter of John & Elizabeth Sydnor, May 4, 1729.

Born, John, son of Epaproditus & Mary Sydnor, Feb. 20, 1736.

Born, Robert, son of Anthony & Frances Sydnor, Jan. 23, 1750.

Born, Elizabeth, daughter of Anthony & Frances Sydnor, Nov. 25, 1752.

Born, Anthony, son of Epaphroditus & Mary Sydnor, March 12, 1752.

Born, Giles, son of Epaphroditus & Mary Sydnor, Aug. 8, 1753.

Born, Susanna, daughter of Anthony & Frances Sydnor, April 28, 1754.

Epaphroditus Sydnor departed this life March 15, 1756.

Born, Nancy, daughter of William & Judith Sydnor, Sept. 25, 1766.

Born, John, son of William & Ann Tayloe, Feb. 15, 1687.

Born, Thomas, son of Luke & Ann Thornton, April 5, 1688.

Born, John, son of James & Mary Tarpley, Feb. 21, 1690.

Born, Mark, son of Luke & Anne Thornton, Sept. 23, 1686.

Born, Richard, son of John & Elizabeth Tavernor, July 30, 1685.

Born, James, son of James & Mary Tarpley, May 8, 1692.

Born, Sarah, daughter of John & Eliza Taverner, Jan. 7, 1679.

Born, Elizabeth, daughter of John & Eliza Taverner, March 25, 1681.

Roger, son of Henry and Ann Thornton, June 17, 1686.

Born Eliza, daughter of William & Eliza Tayloe, July 26, 1686.

Born, William, son of James & Mary Tarpley, March 16, 1695.

Born, John, son of John & Elizabeth Tarpley, July 16, 1695.

Born, Frances, dau. of Samuel & Frances Traverse, Aug. 20, 1697.

Born, Thomas, son of James & Mary Tarpley, Feb. 28, 1697.

Born, Mary, daughter of James & Mary Tarpley, Feb. 1, 1691.

Born, Elizabeth, daughter of James & Mary Tarpley, Feb. 2, 1701.

Born, Robert, son of Robert & Mary Thornton, Oct. 20,.1722.

Born, Bridget, daughter of Robert & Mary Thornton, May 25, 1724.

Born, John & Betty, son & daughter of John & Eliza Tarpley, May 28, 1720.

Born, Henry, son of Roger & Isabel Thornton, Nov. 12, 1709.

Born, May, daughter of Roger & Isabel Thornton, Jan. 5, 1712.

Born, John, son of Roger & Isabel Thornton, June 25, 1718.

Born, Anne, daughter of Roger & Isabel Thornton, Feb. 9, 1720.

Born, Mary, daughter of William & Mary Tarpley, Dec. 7, 1723.

Born, William, son of Roger & Isabel Thornton, March 14, 1722–'23.

Born, Mary, daughter of James & Ann Thornton, March 13, 1725.

Born, Roger, son of Robert & Mary Thornton, June 14, 1725.

Born, John, son of Robert & Mary Thornton, April 9, 1727.

Born, Edward Ripping, son of John & Elizabeth Tarpley, April 19, 1727.

Born, Elizabeth, daughter of John & Eliza Tarpley, March 4, 1728–'9.

Born William, son of James & Ann Thornton, Aug. 2, 1728.

Born, William, son of Roger & Eliza Thornton, June 17, 1728.

Born, John, son of William & Mary Tarpley, Sept. 29, 1729.

Born, James, son of William & Mary Tarpley, Dec. 8, 1731.

Born, Thomas, son of James & Mary Tarpley, Oct. 28, 1734.

Bridget Thornton departed this life Jan. 15, 1726.

William Thornton departed this life Nov. 14, 1726.

Matthew Thornton departed this life, Feb. 10, 1730.

Born, James, son of James & Ann Thornton, Aug. 8, 1731.

Born Hannah, daughter of William & Mary Tarpley, Jan. 6, 1735.

Born, Lucy, daughter of James & Mary Tarpley, Aug. 17, 1736.

Born, Betty, daughter of Traverse & Betty Tarpley, July 28, 1738.

Born, Sarah, daughter of James & Mary Tarpley, Sept. 13, 1738.

Married, Luke Thornton & Millisent Longworth, Jan. 2, 1727–'8.

Born, John, son of John & Ann Tarpley, Dec. 13, 1738.

Married, Cornelius Todd to Mary Jones, Dec. 17, 1739.

Born, Mary, daughter of James and Mary Tarpley, Oct. 30, 1740.

Born, Winifred, daughter of Traverse & Betty Tarpley, Nov. 1, 1740.

Born Eliza, daughter of John & Ann Tarpley, April 5, 1740.

Born Alice, daughter of John & Ann Tarpley, Nov. 24, 1742.

Born, James, son of James & Mary Tarpley, July 21, 1743.

Born, Lucy, daughter of Traverse & Betty Tarpley, Jan. 7, 1745.

Born, Betty, daughter of James & Mary Tarpley, Aug. 6, 1746.

Born, Samuel Traverse, son of Thomas & Betty Tarpley, Dec. 15, 1748.

Born, Winney, daughter of John & Ann Tarpley, Sept. 16, 1744.

Born, Traverse, son of John & Ann Tarpley, Aug. 12, 1746.

Born, Thomas, son of John & Ann Tarpley, June 3, 1748.

Born, Caty, daughter of John & Ann Tarpley, April 13, 1750.

Born, David, son of Robert & Frances Thornton, March 24, 1788.

Born, Mary, daughter of Thomas & Sarah Underwood, Oct. 22, 1687.

Born, William, son of Mooto & Ann Underwood, Jan. 6, 1726.

Born, Judith, daughter of John & Sarah Ann Valendingham, Aug. 24, 1760.

Born, Winifred, daughter of Newman & Katherine Brockenbrough, March 21, 1726.

Born, Seth, son of Mooto & Ann Underwood, March 1, 1729.

Married, John Webb to Mary Sanford, July 14, 1673.

Born, James, son of John & Mary Webb, Aug. 9, 1673.

Married, Thomas Waring to Alice Underwood, Oct. 5, 1673.

Born, James, son of John & Mary Webb, Aug. 9, 1673.

Born, Giles, son of John & Mary Webb, April 15, 1677.

Married, Isaac Webb to Mary Bedwell, April 6, 1678.

Born, Giles, son of Giles & Elizabeth Webb, Aug. 4, 1714.

Born, John Span, son of Giles & Elizabeth Webb, Oct. 9, 1705.

Born, Isaac, son of Giles & Elizabeth Webb, Sept. 25, 1729.

Born, Betty, daughter of Giles & Elizabeth Webb, Feb. 1, 1711.

Born, Mary, daughter of Giles & Elizabeth Webb, Nov. 11, 1717.

Born, Cuthbert, son of Giles & Elizabeth Webb, March 3, 1718–'19.

Born, William, son of James & Barbara Webb, May 10, 1720.

Born, James, son of James & Barbara Webb, June 12, 1729.

Born, Thomas Webb, son of Ann Webb, March 28, 1738.

Born, Isaac, son of Isaac & Thomas(?) Webb, Oct. 30, 1739.

Born, John, son of Isaac & Frances Webb, Feb. 1, 1737.

Born, William, son of John Spann Webb & Sarah Webb, May 25, 1742.

James Webb departed this life, May 10, 1750.

Tabitha Webb departed this life Feb. 9, 1722.

Married, John Wilcox & Ann Jennings, March 2, 1729–'30.

Born, John, son of Godfrey & Eliza Wilcox, April 29, 1742.

Born, Winefred, daughter of Godfrey & Eliza Wilcox, Jan. 9, 1741.

LIST OF TOMBSTONES IN OLD CEMETERY AT OLD PROVIDENCE CHURCH*

CONTRIBUTED BY MRS. W. W. KING

Beginning at Southeast Corner, reading from left to right, or east to west:

No. 1. William Moore, d. June 11 1858, aged 74 years.

No. 2. unmarked stone.

No. 3. Margaret Moore, d. Feb. 27 1842, aged 21 yrs, 4 mos. 22 days.

No. 4. Mary Moore, d. March 26 1882, aged 84 yrs, 1 mo. 6 days.

No. 5. John M Wilson, b. April 20 1782, d. Nov. 1 1851.

No. 6. Sally Wilson, wife of John M Wilson, d. July 19, 1848, 59th year

No. 7. Edwin L. Wilson, b. Nov. 28 1852, d. Aug 11 1853.

No. 8. Ina Wilson, b. June 25 1858, d. July 5 1858.

No. 9. Samuel Wilson, d. Feb 20 1874, aged 55.

No. 10. Drusilla F Wilson, wife of Samuel Wilson, b. Mar. 2 1821, d. Feb 2 1903

No. 11. POAGUE, John, d. Feb 6 1867. Martha, d. Feb 9 1831. James E., d. Dec 31 1862. Sabella M. d. Jan. 28 1881. Maria E., d. Sept. 26 1893. Eliza M., d. Jan 1900. Sarah S., d. Feb. 24 1903. William L. b. Feb 28 1825, d. March 12 1919.

No. 12. Hanna R H Gibbs, b, March 27 1820, d. June 29 1900. (Wife of William Allen Gibbs.)

No. 13. A. Richard Gibbs, b. March 23 1788. d. May 10 1858. B. Isabella Gibbs, b. April 17 1792, d. Sept. 25 1855.

No. 14. James Poague, d. Sept 9 1811, aged 64.

Second Row, beginning at east side and reading to the west.

No. 15. James M C Moore, d. Jan 6 1852, aged 73 years, 3 mos,—ds.

No. 16. Martha V Lusk, d. Nov 8 1861, aged 1 yr, 9 mos. 16 das.

No. 17. unmarked stone.

No. 18. Elizabeth Fulton, relic of James Fulton, d. Sept 11 1850, aged 84 years and 5 months.

No. 19. Andrew Moore, d. Aug 10 1791, aged 41 yrs.

No. 20. his wife, Martha Moore, d. July 30 1838, aged 72.

*In Rockbridge County, 2 miles east of Berry's Filling Station, R. 11.

No. 20. Samuel Moore, d Sept 3 1807, aged 33 yrs.
William Moore, d July 31, 1839, aged 59 .yrs.
No. 21. Mary Lusk, d. August 19 1823, aged 1 yr, 8 mos. 19 das.
No. 22. William Lusk, d. Dec 4 1837, aged 3 yrs, 8 mos.
No. 23. Patsy Lusk, b. June 26 1791, d. April 21, 1851.
No. 24. same grave, Sallie Lusk, b. Sept 8 1823, d. Sept 2 1885.
No. 24. William Lusk, b June 4 1788, d. Dec 28 1861.
No. 25. unmarked stone.

Third Row, beginning at east side.

No. 26. Samuel A McNutt, b. May 6 1817, d. Feb. 15 1839.
No. 27. James McNutt, d. Sept 1811, aged 71.
No. 28. Margaret McNutt, d Sept 22 1820.
Robert McNutt, his name only on stone.

Fourth Row, beginning at east side (very irregular row).

No. 29. Margaret, wife of Christian Echard, d. Jan. 4 1842, aged 45 yr 10 mos. 25 das.
No. 30. unmarked stone.
No. 31. stone with M P, only legible writing on it.
Nos. 32-37. unmarked stones.
No. 38. John Tate, d. Dec. 13 1802, aged 63 yrs
No. 39. unmarked stone. Nos. 40-42. unmarked wooden head-pieces.
No. 43. K Thompson, d. —— 18 1819, aged 68 yrs.
No. 44. Eleanor Nelson, consort of James S Nelson, d. July 22 1800, aged 26 yrs.
their son, Samuel D. July 29 1800, aged 5 mos.
No. 45. unmarked stone. No. 46. unmarked wood.

Fifth Row, east to west.

No. 47. unmarked stone. Samuel Steele jr.
No. 48. N. S. d. May 30 1796, aged 74. (Nathaniel Steel.)
No. 49. Elizabeth Steele, wife of Rob't Steele, aged 25.
No. 50. Margaret Steele, wife of Rob't Steele.
No. 51. Wm Steele, aged 48, d. July 9 1818. War of 1812.
No. 52. Thomas Steele, d. July 3 1799, aged 54.
No. 53. James Steele, d. January 10 1823, aged 70.
No. 54. Susan A H Cooper, wife of Joseph Cooper, d. Nov 2 1838, aged 60 yrs.
No. 55. Robert Cooper, d. Aug   1845, aged 40 yrs.

No. 56. William Hall, son of Patrick & Susanna Hall, d. Nov 1814.

No. 57. Patrick Hall, d. Nov 23 1814, aged 63.

No. 58. Susanna McChesney Hall, wife of Patrick Hall, d. Nov 19 1814, aged 65.

No. 59. Robert Hall, son of P & S McCh. Hall, b 1784, d. 1824.

No. 60. Dr. John McChesney, b. Sept 3 1786, d. May 19, 1877.

No. 61. Jane E S Steele, wife of Dr J McCh., b. Apr 11 1798, d. Sept 9 1875.

Sixth Row, east to west.

No. 62. William McCormick, b. April 12 1776, d. April 12 1837 (son of Rob't & Martha Sanderson McCormick). Married Mary Steele. Their children: Rob't & Wm Steele. Second marriage to Sallie McClelland. Their Children: Polly S., Jas. S., Geo, B., Joseph J.

No. 63. Martha Sanderson, b. 1747, d. 1804.

No. 64. Samuel Wilson, d. April 1826, aged 76.
Mary Wilson, d. Aug 1819, aged 60.

No. 65. Robert Cooper, d. Sept 20 1816, age 78 yrs.

No. 66. Susanna H Cooper, d. Nov 5 1817, 75th yr.

No. 67. John Cooper, d. March 1 1828, 57th yr.

No. 68. Margaret Cooper, b. Sept 10 1774, d. June 10 1847.

No. 69. unmarked wood.

No. 70. Jane J McChesney.

No. 71. Susan J Hogshead, d. April 1 1847, b. Apr 6 1821.

No. 72. James A R Blair, b. Oct 8 1818, d. Feb 28 1854.

No. 73. John T Blair, d. June 18 1860, aged 17 yrs (plus).

No. 74. William Steele, b. Nov 24 1791, d. March 18 1855.

No. 75. Diana Steele, b. March 17 1808, d. May 11 1847.

Seventh Row, east to west.

No. 76. Large shaft to Robert McCormick. Robert McCormick, youngest son of Robert McCormick and Martha Sanderson McCormick b. June 8, 1780, Rockbridge Co., Va. Married Mary A. Hall Feb. 8, 1808. Died July 4, 1846. The following children buried in Graceland Cemetery, Chicago, Ill.:
Cyrus Hall, Born Feb. 16, 1809, died May 13, 1884
William Sanderson, Born Nov. 2, 1815, Died Sept 27, 1865
Mary Caroline Shields, Born April 18, 1817, Died March 8, 1888

Amanda Joanna McCormick Adams, Born Feb 8, 1819, Died, Feby 20, 1900.

No. 77. Dr. Wm Marcellus Gold. 1767-1857.

No. 78. Mrs. Mary L Gold (wife of Dr Gold), daughter of Wm Steele, esq d. April 14 1837, aged 27.

No. 79. Nancy Steele, d. July 10 1822, aged 27.

No. 80. Susan C Steele, d. March 23 1821.

No. 81. Thomas Jackson, d. 1821, aged 32.

No. 82. John Wesley, son of JW & N H Houser, d. Aug 18 1861, aged 4 mos.

No. 83. Caroline W Houser, Sept. 16 1868, aged 20yrs(plus).

Eighth Row, east to west.

No. 84. John P. McCormick, b. Nov 8 1820, d. Sept 4 1849.

No. 85. Mary Ann, wife of Rob't McCormick, b. June 24 1780, d. June 1 1853.

No. 86. Robert McCormick, b. June 8 1780, d. July 4 1846.   stones

No. 87. Robert H. McCormick, b. May 24, 1810, d. June 28 1826.   lately

No. 88. Susan J. McCormick, b. Aug 1 1813, d. June 27 1826.   erected

No. 89. William McChesney, d. Sept 1 1860, aged 90.

No. 90. wood, unmarked.

No. 91. William, son of N & M Steele, d. Jan 30 1828, aged 2yrs(plus)

No. 92. wood, unmarked.

Ninth Row, east to west.

No. 93. Sarah Carson, d. March 3 1832, in 89th yr.

No. 94. Samuel Carson, d. March 25 1824, aged 80.

No. 95. Margaret Carson, d. June 1 1879, aged 85.

No. 96. Elijah Carson, b. Jan 12 1789, d. March 26 1860.
W. L. Carson, b. Aug 10 1833, d. Nov 22 1834.

No. 97. Polly Carson, d. Sept 1 1839, aged 40 yrs.

No. 98. Mary A Carson, (daughter of J H & S E Carson), d. Aug 21 1857, aged 1 yr, 19 das.

No. 99. E A Carson, son of J H & S E Carson, d. Oct 31 1859, aged 5 yrs, 5 mos, 11 days.

No. 100. Franklin D Carson, son, of J H & S e Carson, d March 18 1862, aged 9 mos 14 days.

No. 101. Nancy Harris, b Jan 28 1808, d. April 10 1854.

No. 102. Sally Carson, wife of Samuel Carson, d. June 18 1862, aged 61 yrs, 2 mos, 24 days.

No. 103. Samuel Carson, d Dec 19 1863, aged 64 yrs.
No. 104. wood, unmarked.

Tenth Row, east to west.

No. 105. David Carson, d. Nov 7 1836, age 50.
No. 106. Samuel Carson, Senior, d. March 20 1830, age 67.
No. 107. unmarked stone.
No. 108. John Carson, b. Dec 6 1794, d. Oct 24 1852.
No. 109. Christiana Carson, d. Feb 8 1851, age 80 yrs, 7 mos, 7 days.
No. 110. Isabella Withrow, wife of Samuel Withrow, d Oct 17 1858 age 44 yrs. 11 mos. 26 days.
No. 111. My daughter, Mary Withrow, d. June 3 1839, age 17yrs(plus).

Northwest Corner.

No. 112. Nancy Margaret, wife of Robert E Brown, b. Oct 3 1828. d. May 31 1854.
No. 113. Rebecca S Smiley, d. July 19 1840, aged 28 yrs, 1 mo. 12 days.
No. 114. David Steele, erected by D. A. R. in August 1935.
No. 115. Samuel Steele, erected by D. A. R. in Oct. 1935.

RECORD OF THE PEAKED MOUNTAIN CHURCH,

ROCKINGHAM COUNTY, VA.

EDITED BY PROF. WM. J. HINKE AND CHARLES E. KEMPER.

This record is one of the oldest and most important German record-books to be found in the upper part of the Shenandoah Valley. It contains much historical and genealogical information about the early German Reformed and Lutheran settlers in Rockingham county, which cannot be found anywhere else. It gives us for the first time the name of the earliest Reformed minister who preached in that region, the Rev. I. C. van Gemuenden. He ministered to the congregation from February, 1762, to December, 1763. His name shows that he was either born in Holland or of Dutch descent. Unfortunately nothing else is known of him at present.

The Reformed elders in 1762 were Jacob Perschinger (baptism No. 37), John Hetterich (No. 44), and George Zimmermann (No. 45). One of the Lutheran elders was Charles Risch (No. 44).

The first church, mentioned in April, 1762, was located near the mill-race of Mr. Herrmann (Nos. 40 and 64). The congregation also had a school in 1762, because the Lutheran schoolmaster, Gottfried Christian Leuthmanns Leonhardt, is mentioned (No. 43) in that year.

The second church was dedicated on October 23, 1768, by the Lutheran pastor, the Rev. John Schwarbach. On October 31, 1769, an agreement was signed by forty-five persons, according to which the church was to be a union church of Reformed and Lutheran people. The second church was located near the Stony creek.

The third church was dedicated, according to a later record, on May 27, 1804. This building was occupied jointly by the Reformed and Lutherans till recently, when the Reformed people separated and erected a new church, known as "Brown Memorial Reformed Church," in honor of one of their former pastors. It is located at McGaheysville, Va.

The record now published belongs to the Reformed congregation, although it contains many Lutheran entries. Is a folio volume of 156 pages, many of which have remained blank. It contains mostly baptismal entries, 316 in all, together with some communicant lists, extending from 1792–1797, and a few marriage and burial records. The original copy of the agreement of 1769 is still in existence. It is prefaced to the record as a fitting introduction.

In translating the record the English form was substituted for the German in the case of the baptismal or Christian names, but the various spellings of the surnames or family names have been carefully retained. All the baptismal entries were copied at a later time into the second record-book. The spellings of this second record are occasionally added in square brackets, while the present form of the family names is added in round brackets by Mr. Chas. E. Kemper, of Washington, D. C.

Agreement between the Reformed and Lutheran Congregations Worshipping in the Peaked Mountain Church, Rockingham Co., Va., October 31, 1769.

In the name of the Triune God and with the consent of the whole congregation, we have commenced to build a new house of God, and it is, by the help of God, so far finished that all the world may see it.

We have established it as a union church, in the use of which the Lutherans and their descendants as well as the Reformed and their descendants shall have equal share. But since it is necessary to keep in repair the church and the schoolhouse and support the minister and schoolmaster, therefore we have drawn up this writing that each member sign his name to the same and thereby certify that he will support the minister and schoolmaster and help to keep in repair the church and the school as far as lies in his ability. Should, however, one or another withdraw himself from such Christian work (which we would not suppose a Christian would do) we have unitedly concluded that such a one shall not be looked upon as a member of our congregation, but he shall pay for the baptism of a child 2 s. 6 d., which shall go into the treasury of the church; for the confirmation of a child 5 s., which shall be paid to the minister as his fee; and further should such a one come to the table of the Lord and partake of the Holy Communion, he shall pay 5 s., which shall go into the treasury of the church; and finally if such a one desires burial in our graveyard he shall pay 5 s., which shall also be paid into the treasury of the church.

In confirmation of which we have drawn up this document, and signed it with our several signatures.

Done in Augusta county, at the Peaked Mountain and the Stony Creek, on October 31st, Anno Domini 1769.

The present elders:

George Mallo, Sr.
his
John X Heterich (Hedrich).
mark.

Nicholas Mildeberger (Miltenberger).
Frederick Ermentraut (Armentrout).

Philip Ermentraut.
Henry Ermentraut.
Daniel Kropf.
Peter Mueller, Sr.
his
Adam O Hetrich.
mark.
Augustin Preisch (Price).
Jacob Traut (Trout).
George Schillinger.
Anthony Oehler (Eiler).

John Mann.

Alwinus Boyer.
Charles Risch (Rush).
Henry Kohler.
William Long.
Jacob Bercke (Pirkey).
his
Jacob I. E. Ergebrecht.
mark.
John Risch.

Jacob Ergebrecht (Argenbright).
John Mildeberger.
John Hausman (Houseman).
George Mallo, Jr.
Jacob Lingel.
Peter Niclas (Nicholas).
Martin Schneider (Snyder).
Jacob Pens (Pence).

Jacob Kropf (Cropp).
Jacob Niclas (Nicholas).
George Zimmermann.
Christian Geiger.
Augustin Preisch, Jr.

Conrad Preisch.
Jacob Kissling (Kisling).
Matthew Kirsch.
John Bens (Pence).
Adam Herman (Harman).
Michael Mallo.
his
Christopher X Hau.
mark.
Peter Euler (Eiler).
William Michel (Michael).
Jacob Risch.
John Ermentraut.
Conrad Loevenstein.

John Schaefer (Shaver).

Christopher Ermentraut (Armentrout).

BAPTISMAL RECORDS.

PARENTS.	CHILDREN.	SPONSORS.
Henry Wilhelm (1), and wife Anna Elisabeth.	Michael William,[1] born June 25, 1745; bapt. December 20.	Michael Bauer (Bowers) and wife Catharine.
" " (2),	George Henry William, born April 8, 1747; bapt. July 21.	John George Scherp (Shepp?) and wife Marie.
Augustin Preiss (Price) and wife Anna Elisabeth *nee* Scherp (3),	Susanna, born May 9, 1750; bapt. Aug. 15, 1753.	John Ernst Scherp and wife Anna Margaret.
" " (4),	Conrad, born December 24, 1752; bapt. Aug. 15, 1753.	Conrad Wahl and Christina Herman.

PARENTS.	CHILDREN.	SPONSORS.
Augustin Preiss (Price) and wife Anna Elisabeth *nee* Scherp (5),	Augustin, born December 24, 1754; bapt. October 1, 1756.	Matthew Kirsch (Kersh) and wife Anna Margaret.
" " (6),	Elisabeth, born Sept. 8, 1757; bapt. Oct. 15.	Parents.
" " (7),	John Frederick, born Sept. 24, 1759; bapt. October 16.	Frederick Ermentraut & wife Catharine.
" " (8),	Anna Catharine, born May 4, 1763; bapt. June 19, 1763.	Daniel Preiss and wife Anna Catharine.
" " (9),	Maria Catharine, born May 12, 1765; bapt. June 18.	Frederick Ermentraut & wife Catharine.
Valentine Metzger (10), and wife Anna Elisabeth.	George Valentin, born Jan. 21, 1762; bapt. March 2.	Charles Risch (Rush) and wife Maria Elisabeth.
Christopher Ermentraut (Armentrout) (11), and wife Susanna.	Elisabeth, born Feb. 20, 1761; bapt. March 4.	Elisabeth Ermentraut.
" " (12),	Anna Maria, born Feb. 16, 1762; bapt. March 7.	Anna Maria Gallet.
George Ermentraut (13), and wife Barbara.	John Frederick, born December —, 1764; bapt. February 10.	John Frederick Ermentraut.
" " (14),	Catharine Barbara, born July 24, 1769; bapt. August 13.	John Ermentraut and Barbara Miller.
Henry Preiss (Price) & wife Magdalene (15),	Henry David, born March 14, 1759; bapt. June 5.	Henry Ermentraut and wife Magdalene.
" " (16),	Adam, born July 10, 1760; bapt. July 16.	George Adam Mann and Elisabeth Herrmann.
John Nicolaus (17), and wife Margaret, *nee* Lorentz.	Jacob, born July 15, 1724.	Jacob Betsch.

Jacob Nicolaus (Nicholas) married Barbara Zeller, daughter of Henry Zeller (Sellers), on December 7, 1752. They had the following children:

PARENTS.	CHILDREN.	SPONSORS.
Jacob Nicolaus (18), (Nicholas), and wife Barbara.	A son, born July 20, 1753; died without baptism for want of a minister, on July 29.	
" " (19),	Anna Maria, born September 8, 1754.	Henry Zeller and wife Anna Maria.
" " (20),	John, born February 6, 1756.	John Zeller, son of Henry Zeller.
" " (21),	John Henry, born December 6, 1757.	John Henry Zeller and wife Anna Maria.
" " (22),	Anna Catharine, born February 29, 1760.	Anna Catharine Preiss, wife of Daniel Preiss.

PARENTS.	CHILDREN.	SPONSORS.
Jacob Nicolaus (23), (Nicholas), and wife Barbara.	Peter, born April 5, 1762.	Peter Mueller (Miller) and wife Anna Maria.
" " (24),	Susanna, born Jan. 25, 1764.	Jacob Argebrecht (Argenbright) & his wife.
" " (25),	Anna Barbara, born April 22, 1766.	Henry Zeller & his wife.
" " (26),	Elisabeth, born February 9, 1768.	John Zeller & his wife.
" " (27),	Jacob, born December 1, 1769.	Peter Mueller & his wife.
" " (28),	Margaret, born January 1, 1772.	Peter Mueller & his wife.
" " (29),	Anna Elisabeth, born January 4, 1774.	Anna Elisabeth R(isch).
John Caspar Vogt (30), and wife Elisabeth.	Sarah, born Nov. 28, 1761; bapt. March 7.	Peter Funck (Funk) and wife Catharine and daughter Margaret.
Peter Hermann (Harman) & wife Margaret nee Choulyn?(31),	Elisabeth, born May 6, 1763.	George Adam Mann and wife Maria Elisabeth.
" " (32),	Philippina, born ——.	Theobald Hermann and wife Sarah.
" " (33),	George Charles, born Dec. 11, 1761; bapt. March 6, 1762.	George Bernhard Mann & wife Anna Margaret.
" " (34),	Maria Elisabeth, born May 6, 1763; bapt. June 17, 1763.	George Adam Mann and wife Elisabeth.

A° 1762. At the "Pinquit" (Peaked) Mountain and the South "Chanithor" (Shenandoah), in Virginia, the following children were baptized on Saturday, February 27th: [2]

PARENTS.	CHILDREN.	SPONSORS.
Christian Kropf(Cropp), and wife Rosina, nee Kipp. (35),	Jacob, age 26 years.	John Jacob Nicolaus & wife Anna Barbara.
" " (36),	Daniel, age 24 years.	Jacob Arkebrecht (Argenbright) and wife Susanna.
" " (37),	Margaret, age 18 years.	I. C. Van Gemuenden, the Reformed minister at this place, and wife M. A. Van Gemuenden, also Jacob Perschinger, Reformed elder, and wife Maria Catharine.
Ludwig Friedel (Friddle) (38), and wife Margaret.	John Jacob, bapt. April 24 (1762).	John Jacob Mann and wife Barbara.
John Jacob Nicolaus and wife Barbara (39), nee Zeller.	Peter, born April 5, 1762; bapt. April 25, 1762.	Peter Mueller (Miller) and wife Maria Margaret.

The following children were baptized in "Agoste" (Augusta)
County at the "Pinquit Moundyn" (Peaked Mountain), towards the
South "Chanithor" (Shenandoah), in this church at the Mill Creek,
or in their homes:

PARENTS.	CHILDREN.	SPONSORS.
Henry Lang(Long)(40), and wife Anna Catharine, nee Wentz.	Anna Catharine; bapt. April 25 (1762).	Anna Catharine Wentz, widow of Valentine Wentz.
Conrad Biedefisch (Peterfish) (41), and wife Catharine nee Roth.	John Cristian, bapt. July 2.	Parents.
Christian Eberhardt and wife Maria (42), Sophia, nee Carl.	Catharine, bapt. July 2.	Widow Catharine Wentz.
Jacob Hammer (43), and wife Fredericka Rosina, nee Leuthmanns Leonhard.	Anna Maria, bapt. July 2.	Gottfried Christian Leuthmanns Leonhardt, the Lutheran schoolmaster and wife Anna Maria.
John Hetterich (Hedrick), Reformed (44), elder and wife Susanna, nee Hornung.	John William, bapt. August 29.	Carl Risch (Rush), Lutheran elder and wife Maria Elisabeth.
George Zimmermann, Reformed elder (45), and wife Anna, nee, Schulteli.	Barbara, bapt. August 29.	Parents.
Jacob Mueller (46), and wife Maria Barbara, nee Chrombohr.	Anna Maria, bapt. Aug. 29.	Charles Mann and wife Anna Maria.
Frederick Stoll (Stull), and wife Charlotte, nee Ritter. (47),	Esther, bapt. August 29.	Parents.
William Manger (Munger) and wife (48), Susanna, nee Brodbeck.	Henry William, bapt. December 5.	Nicholas Mildenberger & wife Barbara.

A° 1763, the following children were baptized in this church at the
"Pinquit Moundyn," in Virginia, on Wednesday, August 3rd, after
the sermon:

PARENTS.	CHILDREN.	SPONSORS.
Charles Risch (49), and wife Maria Elisabeth, nee Suess.	John Peter.	Peter Mueller and wife Maria Margaret.
Jacob Bentz (Pence) and wife Catherine, nee Perschinger. (50),	Anna Maria.	Anna Maria Nicolaus, single.
Peter Mueller (Miller) & wife Margaret. (51),	Jacob, born April 17, 1765; bapt. June 18.	Jacob Cropp and wife Barbara.

PARENTS.	CHILDREN.	SPONSORS.
Frederick Ermentraut & wife Catharine. (52),	Augustin, born January 22, 1765; bapt. May 18.	Augustin Preisch & wife Elisabeth.
" " (53),	John Henry, born May 8; bapt. June 19, 1763.	Charles Hetterich, single.
Jacob Argebrecht (54), and wife Susanna.	Jacob, born Aug. 26, 1762; bapt. February 14, 1763.	Jacob Nicolaus and wife Barbara.
" " (55),	John George, born Jan. 13, 1765; bapt. Jan. 18.	George Mallo and wife Barbara.
William Manger (56), and wife Susanna.	John Charles, born Nov. —, 1764; bapt. Feb. 10, 1765.	Charles Roesch and wife Elisabeth.
Henry Ermentraut (57), and wife Magdalene.	. . . .	Frederick Ermentraut & wife Catharine.
" " (58),	. . . . born Sept. 1, 1769; bapt. Oct. 7, 1769.	Elisabeth Ermentraut.
Valentine Metzger (59), and wife Mary Elisabeth.	Jacob, born April 16, 1764; bapt. May 20.	Jacob Argebrecht & wife Susanna.
——— Witmann (60),	Elisabeth.	Caspar Vogt and wife Elizabeth.
Charles Hederich (61), and wife Barbara.	John Jacob, born April 11, 1765; bapt. June 18.	Jacob Conrad.
George Adam Mann (62), and wife Maria Elisabeth.	Magdalene, born March 11, 1765; bapt. June 18.	Philip Willems and Gertrude Schell, both single.
Jacob Cropp (63), and wife Anna Barbara.	John, born March 9, 1765; bapt. June 18.	John Argebrecht and Catharine Vogt.

A° 1763, the following children were baptized in the province of Virginia, at the "Pinquit Moundyn," in the church near Mr. Hermann's mill:

PARENTS.	CHILDREN.	SPONSORS.
Matthew Deiss (Dice) and wife Eva Catharine nee Herrber (64),	Anna Elisabeth, bapt. August 28, 1763.	Philip Herrber (Harper), senior elder of the Upper tract, & wife Anna Elisabeth.
Martin Herrloss (65), and wife Catharine, nee Lingel.	Anna Maria Christina, bapt. Oct. 10.	Christopher Kisseling (Kisling) and wife Christina.
Peter Mueller (66), and wife, Maria Margaret, nee Pick.	Anna Barbara, born Sept. 23; bapt. Dec. 5.	Jacob Nicolaus and wife Barbara.
George Mann (67), and wife Elisabeth, nee Hermann.	George, born Oct. 9; bapt. Dec. 5.	Jacob Mann and wife Barbara.
John Caspar Vogt (68), and wife Elisabeth, nee, Wilkiss.	John Caspar, bapt. Dec. 5.	Jacob Arkebrecht, Peter Mueller, Catharine Margaret Vogt.

471

PARENTS.	CHILDREN.	SPONSORS.
George Ermentraudt & wife Barbara, (69), nee Friedtel (Friddle),	Mary Margaret, bapt. December 5.	Anna Elisabeth Ermentraudt, her grandmother.
Jacob Bentz (70), and wife Catharine.	Anna Maria, born Feb. 28, 1763; bapt. Aug. 29.	Jacob Nicolaus and wife Barbara and daughter Anna Maria.
" " (71),	George, born August 18, 1764; bapt. Oct. 15.	George Bentz and Sarah Bentz.
Jacob Mueller (72), and wife Elisabeth.	Catharine Barbara, born Dec. 28, 1764; bapt. Feb. 10, 1765.	John Votsch and wife Catharine.
George Mallo (73), & wife Anna Barbara.	Anna Elisabeth, born Jan. 12, 1765; bapt. Feb. 10.	Charles Roesch (Rush) and wife Elisabeth.
" " (74),	Michael, born Jan. 29, 1757.	Michael Mallo and Barbara Ebermann.
" " (75),	Catharine, born August 12, 1758.	George Foltz (Fultz) and wife Catharine.
" " (76),	Anna Maria, born Feb. 19, 1763.	Daniel Krob and Anna Mary Ergenbrecht.
" " (77),	John, born 1768; bapt. on the 23d of the month.	John Risch and Catharine Miller.
Jacob Herrmann (Harman) and wife Anna Christina. (78),	John Adam Herrmann, born March 4, 1755.	George Mann and Anna Maria Herrmann.
" " (79),	Anna Maria, born May 3, 1757.	George Adam Mann and Anna Maria Herrmann.
" " (80),	Henry, born August 4, 1759.	Theobald Hermann and wife Sarah.
" " (81),	Elisabeth, born Oct. 4, 1761.	Augustin Breiss (Price) and wife Elisabeth.
" " (82),	Anna Catharine, born March, 1763.	Anna Catharine Hermann.
" " (83),	Jacob, born March 9, 1766.	George Mallo and wife Barbara.

On October 23, 1768, the Lutheran and Reformed Union church at the "Bicket Maundy," in Augusta County, was dedicated by the Rev. Mr. Schwarbach,[3] Evangelical Lutheran pastor at the present time.

PARENTS.	CHILDREN.	SPONSORS.
Frederick Stoll (Stull) and wife. (84),	Daughter, bapt. Feb. 14, 1770.	John Clemens and Christina Pesor.
George Adam Mann(85), and wife Elisabeth.	John, bapt. July 20, 1771.	John Mann and wife Susanna.

On October 8, 1776, Rev. Jacob Frank [4] baptized:

PARENTS.	CHILDREN.	SPONSORS.
David Magert (86), and wife Susanna.	Anna Catharine, born April 16.	Paul Lingel and Anna Catherine.
John Hartman (87), and Christina.	John George, born Aug. 1.	Paul Lingel and Anna Catherine.

472

On October 9th (1776):

PARENTS.	CHILDREN.	SPONSORS.
Daniel Grub (88), and Elisabeth.	Mary Catharine, born December 15, 1775.	Peter Miller and wife Anna Maria.
George Schaeffer (89), (Shaver) and Maria Elisabeth.	John Philip, born Dec. 29, 1775.	Charles Risch and Maria Elisabeth.
Henry Moll (90), and Margaret.	Adam, born Dec. 22, 1775.	Adam Herman and Catharine Malvina.
Martin Finder (91), and Barbara.	Barbara, born Feb. 24, 1776.	Jacob Grub and Barbara.
Daniel Preiss (92), and Catharine.	Sarah, born August 20, 1776.	Matthias Schuler (Shuler) and Elisabeth.
Philip Lingel (93), and Barbara.	John, born February 10, 1776.	John Hartman and Christina.
John Manger (Munger) and Anna. (94),	John, born June 2, 1776.	John Heller and Elisabeth.
George Conrad (95), and Catharine.	Philip, born March 8, 1776.	Peter Brummer & Catharine.
John Heller (96), and Elisabeth.	Anna Maria, born Sept. 7, 1776.	John Adam Heller and Barbara.
Peter Ermentraut (97), and Catharine.	Jacob, born August 12, 1776.	Jacob Argebrecht (Argenbright) and Susanna.
Philip Ermentraut (98), and Eva.	Catherine, born August 23, 1776.	Frederick Ermentraut & Catharine.
Adam Heller (97), and Anna Barbara.	Elisabeth, born March 15, 1776.	John Heller and Elizabeth.
Theobald S c h r a m m and Anna. (100),	Catherine, born March 5, 1776.	Michael Traut (Trout) and Catherine Kohler.
George Lehmann (101), and Elisabeth.	Jonathan, born March 2, 1776.	Leonard Miller and Catharine.
Christian Geiger (102), and Margaret.	Adam, born July 30, 1776.	Adam Argebrecht and Elisabeth.
Lewis [Ludwig] Reinhardt (103), and Elisabeth.	John Michael, born Sept. 18, 1776.	Charles Fey and Dorothy.
Michael Koehler (104), (Kaylor), and Elisabeth.	John, born Feb. 2, 1776.	John Beyer and Eva.

NOTES.

[1] The record was not begun in 1745, as might appear at first sight, but in the spring of 1760. At that time all the earlier baptisms were made, Nos. 1–7 on page 1 of the record and Nos. 17–22 on page 3. All these entries are written by the same hand and with the same ink. The next baptism (No. 16) is written by the same hand, but with different ink. The first entries were, therefore, made before July, 1760. Moreover, from the fact that a whole page is devoted to the family of Jacob Nicalaus, and his own date of birth is added, which is done in no other case, it may be concluded with some degree of probability that Jacob Nicalaus opened the record. Who else would be interested enough in his date of birth to prefix it to those of his children? Baptisms Nos. 1–7, 17–23, 30–33 are made by his hand. Of later

baptisms he entered 51, 52, 54–57, 59–63, 70–76. He continued to enter baptisms, therefore, till June, 1765.

[2] Baptisms Nos. 8, 34–50, 53, 64–69 were entered by the Rev. I. C. van Gemuenden, of whose life nothing is known at present, except that he entered these twenty-five baptisms from February, 1762, to December, 1763.

[3] Rev. John Schwarbach was a Lutheran minister, pastor of the Hebron Church, in the present Madison county, from at least 1766–1772. Both dates are uncertain. See *Hallesche Nachrichten*, new ed., Vol. I., p. 581.

[4] Rev. Jacob Frank was pastor of the Hebron Church from the fall of 1775 to November, 1778. See *Hallesche Nachrichten*, Vol. I., p. 581.

(To be Continued.)

PARENTS.	CHILDREN.	SPONSORS.
John Ermentraut (105), and Catherine.	Anna Maria, born April 6, 1776.	Peter Miller and Anna Maria.
Sebastian Nadler (106), and Sophia.	Christian, born Jan. 20, 1776.	Conrad Bietefisch (Peterfish) and Catherine.
Peter Miller (107), and Elisabeth.	Anna Maria, born Feb. 20, 1776.	Anthony Oehler and Catherine.
Heinrich Noll (108), (Null) and Margaret,	Adam.	
John Risch and (109), Anna Maria.	Catherine, born July 17, 1776.	Catherine Winkhaus and Michael Traudt.
Lewis Koeller (110), and Gertrude.	John Philip, born April 8, 1776.	John Tanner and Catherine.
John Tanner (117), and Catherine.	Catherine, born ———	Catherine Miller.
Peter Runckel (112), and Margaret.	Margaret, born April 4, 1776.	Mathias Kersch and Margaret.
Conrad Fotsch (113), and Maria Magdalene.	David, born June 25, 1776.	David Fotsch (Fox).
Henry Demuth (114), and Margaret.	Jacob, born ———.	Jacob Julius and ———.
August Preisch (115), and Mary.	Elisabeth, born July 27, 1776.	Augustin Preisch and Elisabeth.

[This is the last baptism entered by Rev. Jacob Frank.]

PARENTS.	CHILDREN.	SPONSORS.
John Beyer (116), and Eva.	Barbara, born March 17, 1775; bapt. April 18, 1775.	Grandparents.

Anthony Oehler (Eiler) married Anna Catherine Elisa Smith, in the year 1753, on September 4th:[5]

PARENTS.	CHILDREN.	SPONSORS.
(Anton Oehler) (117),	Anna Margaret, born June 12, 1755.	Michael Bitner and Anna Margaret.
" " (118),	John, born March 30, 1757.	John Bretz and Elisa Schmit.
" " (119),	Anna Barbara, born Nov. 15, 1759.	Anna Barbara Smith.
" " (120),	Anna Catherine, born Jan. 25, 1762.	Philip Fischborn (Fishburn) and Anna Catherine.
" " (121),	John George, born June 30, 1764.	John George Schmit, Anna Margaret Ament (?).
" " (122),	Anna Susanna, born Feb. 11, 1766.	Philip Armbrister and Christina.

PARENTS.		CHILDREN.	SPONSORS.
Anton Oehler,	(123),	Anna Maria, born Sept. 20, 1769.	John Peter Mueller and Anna Maria.
" "	(124),	Magdalene, born Sept. 21, 1772; bapt. Oct. 25.	Magdalene Ermentraut.

On June 16, 1783, the following children were baptized in the "Pickit Mountain" church by Rev. Mr. Schmidt.[6]

PARENTS.		CHILDREN.	SPONSORS.
Adam Pence and	(125),	Elisabeth, born April 23.	Elisabeth Ergebrecht.
Margaret.			
Abraham Roo [Ruh] and Margaret.	(126),	Mary Magdalene, born April 3.	Anna Maria Zeller (Sellers).
Martin Schneider and Mary.	(127),	Mary Elisabeth, born April 25.	Jacob Lingel and Catherine.
William Hini (Heine) and Margaret.	(128),	Mary Margaret, born Dec. 24, 1778.	Martin Schneider (Snyder) and Mary.
John Boyer [Beyer] and Eva.	(129),	Mary Margaret, born June 1, 1781; bapt. July 13, 1781.	Matthias Kirsch and Anna Margaret.
George Zimmermann, Sr., and Anna.	(130),	Salome, born Aug. 22, 1771; bapt. July 13, 1783.	
" "	(131),	William, born May 28, 1775; bapt. July 13, 1783.	
" "	(132),	Henry, born May 12, 1778; bapt. July 13, 1783.	
John Risch and Anna Maria.	(133),	Sarah, born March 10; bapt. June 16, 1783.	Peter Nicolas, Jr.

Baptized June 16, 1783, by Rev. Mr. Schmidt.

PARENTS.		CHILDREN.	SPONSORS.
Augustin Prisch and Margaret.	(134),	Barbara, born Dec. 7, 1782.	Barbara Miller.
Frederick Prisch and Catherine.	(135),	Anna Maria, born Feb. 8.	Anna Maria Prisch and Michael Mallo.
Lewis Ronckel and Catherine.	(136),	Frederick, born Feb. 15.	Frederick Hene and wife.
Conrad Brisch and Elisabeth.	(137),	Michael, born Feb. 16.	Michael Mallo.
Lewis Becker (Baker) and Anna Maria.	(138),	George, born Feb. 8.	George Ergebrecht and Elisabeth Herman.
George Weber and Catherine.	(139),	George, born Oct. 23, 1782.	Parents.
Garret Berry and Mary.	(140),	Elisabeth, born April 13.	Augustin Prisch, Jr., and wife.
Jacob Kissling and Barbara.	(141),	Christina, born June 5.	Christine Baer (Bear).
Peter Stein and Elisabeth.	(142),	Catherine, born April 22.	Charles Schmidt and Catherine Ermentraut.

On April 25, 1784, the following children were baptized in this church by Rev. Mr. Schmidt:

PARENTS.	CHILDREN.	SPONSORS.
Charles Schmidt [7] (143), and Anna Maria.	Zachariah, born Feb. 24, 1784.	Frederick Miller and Elisabeth Herman.
Augustin Prisch, (144), Jr., and Margaret.	Margaret, born March 16.	John Risch and Anna Maria.
George Mallo, Jr. (145), and Catherine.	John Peter, born Jan. 30.	Peter Prisch and Elisabeth Mallo.
Henry Venus (146), and Margaret.	Anna Margaret, born Feb. 23.	Jacob Herman and wife.
John Bright (147), [Brett] and Catherine.	Anna Margaret, born Jan. 26.	Augustin Prisch, Jr., and wife.
Christian Geyger (148), and Margaret.	John, born April 10.	Jacob Ergebrigth, Jr., and Elisabeth Ermentraut.
Jacob Hamann (149), and Elisabeth.	Elisabeth, born Oct. 7, 1783.	Widow Reiss.
Henry Pence and (150), Susanna.	Barbara, born Sept. 22, 1783.	Adam Pens and Margaret.

On June 6, 1784, the following children were baptized by Rev. Mr. Schmidt:

PARENTS.	CHILDREN.	SPONSORS.
John Barki (151), [Birke] and Sarah.	Catherine, born May 4.	Her grandmother Catherine Pens.
George Pens (152), and Margaret.	Anna Barbara, born July 29, 1783.	Parents.
George Adam (153), Mann and Elisabeth.	David, born March 10.	John Beyer and Eva.

On June 27, 1784, the following children were baptized by Rev. Mr. Schmidt:

PARENTS.	CHILDREN.	SPONSORS.
John Mildeberger (154), and Anna.	William, born May 25, 1784.	Parents.
Henry Koch (155), (Cook) and Magdalene.	Jacob, born May 25, 1784.	William Trarbach (Trobaugh) and wife.
George Risch (156), and Mary.	Mary Juliana, born Sept. 1, 1784; bapt. Nov. 2.	Grandmother.
Martin Schneider (157), and Mary.	Catherine, born Oct. 5, 1784; bapt. Nov. 2.	Parents.

On April 20, 1785, the following children were baptized in this church by Rev. Mr. Schmidt:

PARENTS.	CHILDREN.	SPONSORS.
Peter Niclas (158), and Anna Marg. Elisabeth.	Anna Barbara, born Feb. 12.	Her grandmother Anna Barbara Niclas.
Conrad Prisch (159), and Elisabeth.	Augustin, born March 5, 1785.	Augustin Prisch and Anna Margaret.

PARENTS.	CHILDREN.	SPONSORS.
Frederick Prisch (160), (Preuss) and Anna Catherine.	Sarah, born March 31, 1785.	George Mallo and Anna Catherine.
Peter Miller (161), and Anna Barbara.	Anna Maria, born June 13, 1785.	Grandmother.

On September 11, 1785, the following children were baptized by Rev. Gottlieb Abraham Deschler: [8]

PARENTS.	CHILDREN.	SPONSORS.
William Michel (162), and Elisabeth.	John Frederick, born Aug. 27, 1785.	John Frederick Michel (Michael) and Elisabeth.
James Frazor (163), and Elisabeth.	Elisabeth, born June 19, 1785.	Margaret Hoffman.
John Boyer (164), and Eva.	John George, born July 18.	John George Koehler and Mary Elisabeth Mallo.

On October 25, 1785, was baptized by Rev. Abraham G. Deschler:

PARENTS.	CHILDREN.	SPONSORS.
Abraham Ruh (165), and Margaret.	Jacob, born August 10.	John Weinberg and Anna Maria.

On December 25, 1785, was baptized by Rev. Abr. G. Deschler:

PARENTS.	CHILDREN.	SPONSORS.
Charles Schmidt (166), and Anna Maria.	John Jacob, born Nov. 14, 1785.	John Jacob Ergebrecht, Jr., Anna Catherine Hermann.

On August 20, 1786, were baptized by the Reformed minister, Frederick Henry Giese: [9]

PARENTS.	CHILDREN.	SPONSORS.
George Mallo (167), and Catherine.	John, born June 4, 1786.	John Pentz and Marie Catherine Preiss.
Peter Miller (168), and Anna Barbara.	John, born August 2.	John Risch and Anna Maria.
George Kugler (169), and Elisabeth.	Barbara, born June 4, 1786.	Jacob Kissling (Kisling) and Anna Barbara.
Jacob Kissling (170), and Barbara.	John Henry, born January 3.	Jacob Baer, Jr.

On September 10, 1786, were baptized by Rev. Mr. Ronckel: [10]

PARENTS.	CHILDREN.	SPONSORS.
Michael Mallo (171), and Christina.	Anna Barbara, born Aug. 25, 1786.	Grandparents.
Augustin Prisch, (172), Jr., and Margaret.	Anna Maria, born July 5.	Anna Maria Prisch.

On November 19, 1786, was baptized by Rev. John Jacob Weymar: [11]

PARENTS.	CHILDREN.	SPONSORS.
Conrad Prisch (173), and Elisabeth.	Elisabeth, born Sept. 11, 1786.	Peter Preisch and Elisabeth Hermann.

On May 4, 1788, were baptized by Rev. Christian Streit: [12]

PARENTS.	CHILDREN.	SPONSORS.
Charles Schmidt (174), and Anna Maria.	Anna Maria, born Sept. 13, 1787.	John Risch (Rush) and Anna Maria.
Henry Miller (175), and Anna Maria.	Elisabeth, born Feb. 22, 1788.	Grandmother Miller.
Peter Nicholas (176), and Juliana.	Jacob, born Sept. 9, 1787.	Jacob Nicholas.
Peter Miller and (177), Barbara.	Elisabeth, born Jan. 30, 1788.	Elisabeth Nicholas.
Henry Nicholas (178), and Magdalene.	Anna Barbara, born Feb. 27, 1788.	Grandmother Nicholas.
William Kaul (179), and Anna Barbara.	Christian, born Dec. 22, 1787.	Parents.
Christopher Hau (180), and Elisabeth.	Anna Catherine, born Oct. 10, 1787.	George Mallo, Jr., and Anna Catherine.
Adam Pens (181), and Margaret.	George, born Jan. 16, 1788.	George Pens, Jr., single.
Augustin Prisch (182), and Margaret.	Juliana, born Dec. 15, 1787.	Peter Nicholas and Juliana.

Baptized on October 19, 1788, by Rev. Jacob Weymar:

PARENTS.	CHILDREN.	SPONSORS.
Peter Nicholas (183), and Juliana.	Anna Maria, born Oct. 9, 1788.	John Risch and Anna Maria.

Baptized on June 7, 1789, by Rev. Jacob Weymar:

PARENTS.	CHILDREN.	SPONSORS.
Wm. Jackson (184), and Margaret.	Sarah, born July 19, 1787.	Christian Geiger and Margaret.
" " (185),	George Charles, born Dec. 28, 1788.	Charles Schmidt and Anna Maria.
Conrad Prisch (186), and Elisabeth.	Frederick, born July 27, 1788.	Frederick Prisch and Catherine.
George Mallo (187), and Anna Catherine.	Elisabeth, born Dec. 30, 1788.	Augustin Prisch and wife.
Martin Schneider (188), and Anna Maria.	Maria Barbara, born Oct. 19, 1788.	George Kirsch and Margaret Lingel.
Jacob Kissling (189), and Barbara.	Anna Maria, born Sept. 6, 1788.	Martin Schneider and wife.
Christian Geiger (190), and Margaret.	Anna Maria, born March 28, 1789.	Henry Pens and Susanna.
Wm. Michael (191), and Elisabeth.	Jacob, born May 23, 1789.	Jacob Mann.
Jonas Hene (192), and Christina.	Elisabeth, born May 18, 1789.	Catherine Hene.

Baptized on Nov. 22, 1789, by Rev. Wm Carpenter: [13]

PARENTS.	CHILDREN.	SPONSORS.
Charles Schmidt (193), and Anna María.	George Michael, born Sept. 29, 1789.	George Mallo, Sr., and Anna Barbara.
John Risch (194), and Anna Maria.	Barbara, born Nov. 12, 1789.	Peter Miller and Barbara.
Peter Miller (195), and wife.	Margaret, born March 18, 1790; bapt. Oct. 1, 1791.	
Christopher Wetzel and wife. (196),	Anna Maria, born April 25, 1791; bapt. July 19.	
John Risch (197), and wife.	Daughter, born Jan. 15, 1791; bapt. Oct. 16, 1791.	

This baptismal register was written by me, Peter Ahl,[14] and begun March 1, 1792.

PARENTS.	CHILDREN.	SPONSORS.
George Mallo (198), and wife.	George, born July 31, 1791; bapt. Feb. 19, 1792.	George Heyne.
Christopher Hau (199),	John George, born Oct. 2, 1791; bapt. April 8, (1792).	John George Ermentraut.
Frederick Preiss (200),	Elisabeth, born March 9, 1791; bapt. April 8.	John Mann and Catherine Koehler.
Francis Reiner (201),	John Matthias, born Jan. 31, 1792; bapt. April 8.	Matthias Kirsch.
Christopher Menner. (202),	Elisabeth, born Dec. 19, 1791; bapt. April 8.	Frederick Preiss.
Adam Schillinger (203),	John George, born Feb. 27, 1791; bapt. April 8.	John George Mann.
Christian Geiger (204),	John Peter, born Nov. 22, 1791; bapt. April 8.	Jacob Argenbrecht.
Peter Preiss (205),	Michael, born May 11, 1792; bapt. June 4.	William Michel.
Conrad Preiss (206),	Anna Maria, born Jan. 5; bapt. June 17, 1792.	Peter Preiss (Price) and wife.
Henry Kissling (207),	Christina, born June 7, 1791; bapt. June 18, 1792.	Christian Hartmann.
Peter Ahl (208),	Catherine, born June 5; bapt. June 24, 1792.	George Mallo and Catherine.
George Wagner (209),	John George, born June 14, 1792; bapt. July 22.	George Mallo and wife.
Peter Preiss (210), (Price),	Henry, born Nov. 29, 1790; bapt. Dec. 12.	Henry Mueller and wife.
John Ermentraut (211), (Armentrout).	Mary Catherine, born July 4; bapt. Aug. 4.	Catherine Ermentraut.
Henry Miller (212),	Sarah, born 1791; bapt. Sept. 21.	George Mallo.

PARENTS.		CHILDREN.	SPONSORS.
Jacob Kissling	(213),	Anna, born 1792; bapt. Feb. 26.	Jacob Miller.
Jacob Hellendahl [Helmenthal].	(214),	Catherine, born 1792; bapt. July 20.	Catherine Herman.
Christian Luecke	(215),	John Henry, born May 26, 1792; bapt. Dec. 2.	William Hettrich.
John Ruesch	(216),	Anna Elisabeth, born Oct. 11, 1792; bapt. Jan. 26, 1793.	Anna Elisabeth Niclas.
Martin Schneyder (Snyder).	(217),	John Matthias, born Jan. 4; bapt. Jan. 26, 1793.	Matthias Kirsch.
Peter Mueller	(218),	Catherine, born Dec. 26, 1792; bapt. Feb. 24, (1793).	John Ermentraut and wife.
Augustin Ermentraut.	(219),	John George, born April 26, 1793; bapt. May 12 (1793).	John George Ermentraut.
John Fey and Susanna.	(220),	Abraham, born Oct. 29, 1792; bapt. June 23, 1793.	Parents.
Peter Neu and Juliana.	(221),	Eva, born Oct. 30, 1792; bapt. June 23, 1793.	Maria Kissling.
John Hardman and Anna Maria.	(222),	Sarah, born June 2, 1793; bapt. June 23, 1793.	Peter Neu and Juliana.
Jonas Hoehn	(223),	John Jacob, born July 1, 1793; bapt. July 22, 1793.	John Jacob Kirsch.
John Beyer	(224),	John, born May 2; bapt. Aug. 18, 1793.	Martin Schneider and wife.
Frederick Preuss	(225),	John George, born Dec. 13, 1792; bapt. Feb. 3, 1794.	George Mallo.
Conrad Preuss	(226),	John Peter, born Dec. 5, 1792; bapt. Feb. 3, 1794.	Peter Preuss.
Francis Reinert	(227),	Eva Catherine, born Sept. 20, 1793; bapt. March 2, 1794.	Eva Catherine Hauel.
Peter Preuss	(228),	Peter, born April 2, 1794; bapt. June 24, 1794.	Frederick Preuss.
George Wagner	(229),	John, born Feb. 28, 1794; bapt. June 29, 1794.	Peter Preuss.
Augustin Preuss	(230),	Christina, born July 2, 1793; bapt. July 20, 1794.	John Weyberg.
Frederick Geiger	(231),	Anna Elisabeth, born Dec. 1, 1794; bapt. Feb. 19, 1795.	Christian Lucke and wife Elisabeth.
Philip Reyer	(232)	John, born Dec. 8, 1794; bapt. Feb. 19, 1795.	John Reyer (Royer) and wife Elisabeth.
John Ruesch	(233),	John, born Nov. 30, 1794; bapt. March 8, 1795.	Ditto.

481

PARENTS.		CHILDREN.	SPONSORS.
Peter Miller	(234),	John Peter, born Aug. 3, 1794; bapt. Aug. 12, 1794.	Peter Nicholas and wife.

On March 6, 1796, the following children were baptized in this church at the Peaked Mountain by Rev. V. G. C. Stochus: [15]

PARENTS.		CHILDREN.	SPONSORS.
George Wagner	(235),	Elizabeth, born Oct. 22, 1795.	Martin Schneider and wife.
Edward Hatfield	(236),	Isaac, born Oct. 28, 1795.	Martin Schneider and wife.
Francis Reinert	(237),	Sally, born Sept. 8, 1795.	George Mallow.
Frederick Ermentraut.	(238),	Christian, born Jan. 1, 1796.	Frederick Geiger.

On the last of March, 1796:

PARENTS.		CHILDREN.	SPONSORS.
Peter Miller	(239),	Anne Elisabeth, born Feb. 8, 1796.	Anna Elisabeth (?).
Henry Koenig	(240),	Anna Maria, born Feb. 15.	Anna Maria Argebrecht.
Christian Lichy [Luecke].	(241),	Elisabeth, born Feb. 23.	Peter Nicolaus.
Gottfried Spilky	(242),	Mary Elisabeth, born Dec. 28, 1795.	(?).
Christopher Werbel [Wirbel].	(243),	Christopher, born Feb. 28; bapt. March 27.	Christopher Ermentraut and wife.
Jacob Heyl	(244).	Jacob, born April 3; bapt. April 17 (1796).	Christopher Werbel and wife.
Jacob Heyl	(245).	Barbara, born March 8, 1795; bapt. April 17 (1796).	Catherine Sprenckelsen.
John Zeller (Sellers).	(246),	Margaret, born Feb. 12, 1796; bapt. April 17 (1796).	Margaret Manger.
James Smith	(247),	Joseph, born March 12, 1795; bapt. April 17, 1796.	David Manger.
Jacob Kissling	(248),	Elisabeth, born March 4, 1796; bapt. April 17, 1796.	Margaret Ermentraut.
Christopher Wetzel.	(249),	Juliana, born March 30, 1795; bapt. May 5, 1796.	Peter Nicholas.
Adam Andre	(250),	Elisabeth, born April 19, 1795; bapt. May 8, 1796.	Parents.
John Oche	(251),	Hannah, born Jan. 6, 1795; bapt. May 8, 1796.	John Megert.
Daniel Nunnemacher.	(252),	Anna Maria, born June 27, 1796; bapt. July 26.	Philip Reyer.

PARENTS.		CHILDREN.	SPONSORS.
Julius Bertram	(253),	Mary Elisabeth, born June 14, 1794; bapt. Feb. 11, 1796.	Martin Schneider.
Julius Bertram	(254),	John, born July 22, 1796; bapt. Aug. 21.	John Bentz.
John Oche	(255),	Abraham, born July 11, 1796; bapt. Aug. 21.	Henry Manger.
John George Koehler.	(256),	John George, born July 27; bapt. Sept. 18 (1796).	John Jacob Risch.
Peter Risch	(257),	Anna Maria, born Oct. 2; bapt. Oct. 10 (died on same day).	Charles Risch and wife. Her grandparents.
Jacob Algebrecht	(258),	Henry, born Oct. 31, 1796; bapt. March 12, 1797.	Henry Bentz.
Christopher Ermentraut.	(259),	Mary Catherine, born Nov. 12, 1796; bapt. March 12, 1797.	Mary Catherine Ermentraut.
Jacob Schaefer	(260),	John, born Feb. 8, 1797; bapt. April 2, 1797.	Parents.
Jonas Hain	(261),	Eva Elisabeth, born April 12; bapt. May 2, 1797.	John Beyer and wife.
Christopher Kirchhoff.	(262),	John Frederick, born Nov. 20, 1796; bapt. May 14, 1797.	John Busch (Bush) and Cath. Mallow.
Henry Zeller and Magdalene.	(263),	John, born March 11, 1797; bapt. June 24, 1797.	William Hedrich and wife.
John Bens	(264),	John, born May 27; bapt. July 30 (1797).	Henry Bens (Pence)
Philip Ryer (Royer).	(265),	Elisabeth, born July 2; bapt. July 30 (1797).	Peter Ryer.
George Mallo	(266),	Anna Maria, born July 26; bapt. Aug. 6 (1707).	Martin Schneider.
Daniel Nunnemacher.	(267),	Peter John, born Aug. 2; bapt. Sept. 3 (1797).	(?) Elis. Koehler.
Peter Miller and Barbara.	(268),	Jacob, born Sept. 28, 1797; bapt. Oct. 2, 1797.	Jacob Nicklas and wife.
Francis Reiner[t]	(269),	Elisabeth, born Jan. 24, 1798; bapt. March 11.	Philip Lung (Long).
Jacob Schaefer and Mary.	(270),	Jacob, born Jan. 12; bapt. March 11, 1798.	Parents.
George Wagener (Waggoner).	(271),	Jacob, born Dec. 30, 1797; bapt. March 11 (1798).	Jacob Nicklaus.
Jacob Reb	(272),	John, born Oct. 8; bapt. March 11 (1798).	George Mallo.
Jacob Reb	(273),	Anna Margaret, born Feb. 25; bapt. April 8 (1798).	David Manger.
Henry Koenig	(274),	Jacob.	

PARENTS.		CHILDREN.	SPONSORS.
Julius Bertram	(275),	John Henry, born Feb. 19, 1798; bapt. April 8, 1798.	John Michael and Cath. Laugs. John Jacob Risch.
John Hehn	(276),	John Jacob, born Feb. 15, 1798; bapt. April 8 (1798).	Margaret Bens (Pence).
Christian Geiger	(277),	Lydia, born Aug. 29, 1798.	
Gottfried Spilke	(278),	John Frederick, born Sept. 24, 1797; bapt. Nov. 9, 1797.	George Koeler (Kaylor). Jacob Nicklas.
Thomas Brill	(279),	Daughter, born Jan. 11, 1798; bapt. April 29,	
Conrad Becker (Baker).	(280),	William, born March 29, 1798; bapt. May 25.	

(*To be Continued.*)

NOTES.

[5] Baptisms Nos. 117–124 are entered in a wretched script, probably by the father himself. Notice the date of his wedding.

[6] Nothing is known thus far about this Rev. Mr. Schmidt. Neither the Lutheran nor the Reformed records mention his name. He can hardly be identical with the Rev. Mr. Schmidt, who labored in Virginia before 1747. See *Virginia Magazine*, Vol. XII., p. 282. Nor can he be identical with Mr. Charles Schmidt, mentioned in the next note, who signed himself as schoolmaster to the accounts of 1785.

[7] From a later signature, placed under the accounts of October 25, 1785, it appears that Charles Schmidt was the school teacher of the congregation. The chirography of the baptismal entries shows that he made them from 1784–'89.

[8] Rev. Gottlieb Abraham Deshler is mentioned in the record of the Frieden's Church, near Harrisonburg, as the first Lutheran pastor of that congregation in 1786.

[9] Rev. Frederick Henry Giese was settled in Loudon county, Va., 1783–1794. He supplied during that time numerous Reformed congregations in Virginia. See *Fathers of the Reformed Church*, Vol. II., pp. 314–16.

[10] Rev. John. William Runkel was the Reformed pastor at Frederick, Md., 1785–1802. For a sketch of his life see *Fathers of the Reformed Church*, Vol. II., pp. 284–308.

[11] John Jacob Weymer was the Reformed pastor at Hagerstown, Md., 1770–1790. See *Fathers*, Vol. II., pp. 193–6.

[12] Rev. Christian Streit was the Lutheran minister at Winchester, Va., after 1785. See *Hallesche Nachrichten*, Vol. I., p. 31.

[13] Rev. William Carpenter was the pastor of the Hebron Church, in Madison county. See *Hallesche Nachrichten*, new ed., Vol. I., p. 582.

 ¹⁴ Mr. Peter Ahl appeared before the Lutheran Ministerium of Pennsylvania in 1790, asking to be admitted as a member of the Ministerium, but his request was not granted. See *Documentary History of the Evangelical Lutheran Ministerium*, 1898, pp. 231 f., 241. In the record of the Frieden's Church, near Harrisonburg, Peter Ahl is mentioned as the third Lutheran pastor of that congregation. The list of the Lutheran pastors, as given in the Frieden's record, between 1786–1820, is as follows: "Gottlieb Teschler, Johann Georg Bottler, Peter Ahl, Adolph Stindel and Georg Riemenschneider. They served, no doubt, the Peaked Mountain congregation at the same time.

¹⁵ Candidate Carl Stock (Stochus is the Latinized form of the name) presented himself before the Lutheran Ministerium in 1791, asking to be ordained, but he was advised to continue teaching school for a while (*Documentary History*, p. 241). He was licensed by the Ministerium in 1793. In 1796 and 1797 he is reported as serving the Peaked Mountain congregation (*Documentary History*, pp. 283, 290). He entered baptisms Nos. 235–262; hence he was the pastor of the Lutheran congregation from October, 1795 to May, 1797.

Record of the Peaked Mountain Church.

Rockingham Co., Va.

PARENTS.	CHILDREN.	SPONSORS.
Adam Flauers and Maria.	(281), daughter, born April 5, 1798, bapt. Nov. 11, 1798.	Eva Schuh.
Peter Reusch and Barbara.	(282), daughter, born May 29, 1798, bapt. Nov. 11, 1798.	Charles Reusch and wife Mary Elizabeth.
George Koehler and Catherine.	(283), daughter, born April 18, 1798, bapt. ——.	Jacob Reb and wife Catherine.
Frederick Ermentrout and Elizabeth.	(284), Valentin, born Sept. 24, bapt. Nov. 10, 1799.	Augustin Ermentrout and wife Margaret.
Julius Bertram and Eva.	(285), John George, born Oct. 28, bapt. Nov. 10, 1799.	George Melle and wife Catherine.
Daniel Nunnemacher and Mary.	(286), Jacob, born May 17, 1799.	Jacob Argebrecht.
Peter Reur (Royers) and Elizabeth.	(287), Annie Maria, born Feb. 26, 1799.	Catherine Reyer.
Philip Rey(er) and Catherine.	(288), Philip, born July 6, 1799.	John Koeler.

Peter Ayler   (289), John, born Nov. 19, John Resch.
(Eiler) and Eizabeth.   1798.
Jacob Nicklaus   (290), daughter, born May 28, Mary Risch.
and Elizabeth.   1798.
Jacob Nicklaus   (291), Mary, born Sept. 8, Mary Risch.
and Elizabeth.   1799, bapt. Nov. 10,
                           1799.
Francis Reinert   (292), Polly, born Dec. 31, Elizabeth Schneider.
                           1799, bapt. June 2,   (16).
                           1800.
Jacog Eichelbrecht(293), Anna, born Dec. 19, Peter Mueller and
(Elizabeth) and Mary.   1799, bapt. June 2,   Barbara.
                           1800.
Henry Penns   (294), John, born Dec. 13, John Penns.
and Catherine.   1799, bapt. June 2,
                           1800.
Peter Zeller   (295), Anna, born Nov. 2, Thomas Brill and
and Magdalene.   1799, bapt. June 2,   Anna Maria.
                           1800.
John Zeller   (296), Anna Maria, born Jan. Anna Maria Zeller.
and Eva.   1, 1800, bapt. June 2,
                           1800.
Peter Miller   (297), Henry, born Jan. 18, Jacob Ergebrecht
and Barbara.   1800, bapt. June 2,   and wife Mary.
                           1800.
George Koehler   (298), Elizabeth, born Oct. 21, Philip Reyer and
and Catherine.   1799, bapt. June 2,   Catherine.
                           1800.
Fr. Geiger   (299), Catherine, born Feb. Christian Geiger and
and Barbara.   17, 1800, bapt. June 2.   Catherine.
George Mallo   (300), Anna, born March 26, Jacob Kisslnig and
and Catherine.   1800, bapt. June 2,   Barbara.
                           1800.
Jacob Nicklas[16] (301), George, born April 3, John Nicklas.
and Elizabeth.   1801.
August Ermen-   (302), Immanuel, born June Christian Leucke and
traut and Margaret.   15, 1801, bapt. Aug. 9.   Elizabeth.
Julius Bertram   (303), Samuel, born 1801, bapt. Parents.
and Eva.   Aug. 9.
Anthony Saur-   (304), William, born May 9, George Panther
bier and Catherine.   1801, bapt. Sept. 6.   (Painter) and wife
                                                   Sophia.
John Zehrfass   (305), William, born June, William Hederich
and Elizabeth.   1801, bapt. Sept. 6.   and wife Catherine.

486

John Hehn and Dorothy.	(306), Catherine, born Aug. 4, 1801, bapt. Sept. 6.	Fred. Hehn, and wife Catherine.
Peter Eiler and Elizabeth.	(307), Oliver, born July 9, 1801, bapt. Aug. 16.	Peter Eyler and Catherine.
Fred Ermentraut and Barbara.	(308), Matthew, born Sept. 8, 1801, bapt. Nov. 1, 1801.	George Ermentraut.
Henry Christ and Catherine.	(309), Sarah, born June 27, 1801, bapt. Nov. 1, 1801.	Peter Seich and Margaret.
John Koehler and Barbara.	(310), John Frederick, born Oct. 27, 1801, bapt. Nov. 1, 1801.	Fred Hehn and Catherine.
Peter Miller and Barbara.	(311), Nicholast, born Oct. 28, 1801, bapt. Dec. 27, 1801.	Parents.
Christian Becker	(312), John, born. Feb. 22, bapt. April 16, 1802.	Thomas Brill and wife.
George Keller	(313), John, born Jan. 26, bapt. April 16, 1802.	John Keller and wife.
Samuel Geret (Garriott) and Sarah.	(314), Anna Catherine, born April 13, 1802, bapt. June 13, 1802.	George Mueller and wife Catherine.
Christopher Wetzel and Ursula.	(315), John Christopher, born May 19, 1802, bapt. June 13, 1802.	John Beyer, and wife Eva.
Henry Hoerner and Elizabeth.	(316) John, born March 13, 1802, bapt. June 13, 1802.	Henry Penns.

Marriages in 1762:

On March 2. Jacob Kropp (Cropp), son of Christian Kropp and Anna Barbara Metzger, daughter of George Valentine Metzger.

On March 2. Peter Mueller, son of Henry Mueller, and Margaret Kropp, daughter of Christian Kropp.

On October 4, 1762. George Schillinger, widower and Anna Elizabeth Horning, widow of Mr. Conrad Stehlmann.

On Dec. 7, 1762. George Adam Mann, single and Elizabeth Hermann, single.

On Saturday, Feb. 27, 1762 was received as member of this congregation, upon confession of her faith, Margaret Kropp (Cropp).

On Saturday, April 24, 1762 were confirmed and on Sunday, April 25th admitted to the Lord's Supper:

John Henry Ermentraudt. (Armentrout.)

Catherine Gall wife of Jacob Guthmann, and Anna Barbara Diether (Dietrick).

Register of the catechisms, admitted for the first time to the Lord's Supper, on April 22, 1792:

Jacob Geiger,
William Geiger,
Peter Mann,
Philip Schaefer (Shaver),
Michael Schaefer,
Henry Pens (Pence),
—— ——,
Mary Preiss (Price),

Frances Preiss,
Catherine Preiss,
Elizabeth Reyer (Royers),
Christina Baumann
   (Benman),
Mary Ermentraut,
Mary Schneyder (Snyder),
Elizabeth Schneyder,

Elizabeth Reyer, Jr.

The adult communicants were:

ELDERS:

George Mallo,
Peter Mueller (Millers),
John Ruesch,
—— ——,
Charles Ruesch,
Augustin Preiss,
George Schaefer,
Gottfried Spilk(y),
Jacob Argebrecht,
Conrad Schneider,
Christian Geiger,
Frederick Geiger,
Catherine Mallo,
Elizabeth Wagner,
Barbara Mallo,
Catherine Prett (Britt),
Susanna Schaefer,
Mary Mueller,

Martin Schneider,
Peter Preiss (Price),
Julius Bertram,
Jacob Argenbrecht,
George Schaefer, Jr.,
Christopher Wirbel,
Augustin Ermentraut,
John Reyer,
John Jacob Kirch,
Frederick Ermentraut,
Jacob Schaefer,
Martin Kirsch,
Nicholas Beck,
Margaret Ermentraut,
Mary Elizabeth Ruesch,
Catherine Ermentraut,
Barbara Ermentraut,
Anna Kirsch,

Margaret Geiger.

Register of the catechisms, first admitted to the Lord's Supper on October 19, 1794:

Peter Ahl,
George Mallo,
John Ruesch,
Augustin Preuss,
Conrad Biedefisch,
John Weinberg,
John Reyer,
Peter Reyer,
Christopher Wetzel,

Nicholas Neu,
Catherine Mallo,
Mary Elizabeth Reyer,
Catherine Reyer,
Catherine Biedefisch (Peterfish)
Elizabeth Reyer,
Elizabeth Luecke,
Ann Maria Deschler,
Elizabeth Meili,

Irene Preiss.

Register of the members of the Peaked Mountain congregation, who died and were buried in the grave yard of the church:

Elizabeth Schaefer (Shaver), born Nov. 21, 1727, died Nov. 6, 1795; buried on the 8th inst. Her age was 17 yrs. 11 mos. 16 days.

Susanna Schaefer, born Sept. 30, 1770, died Nov. 12, 1795; buried on the 14th inst. Her age was 25 yrs. 1 mo. 11 days.

Sarah Schaefer, born July 12, 1782, died Nov. 23, 1795; buried on the 25th inst. Her age was 13 yrs. 4 mos. 11 days.

John Michael Schaefer, born Febr. 6, 1774, died Nov. 25, 1795; buried on the (27th). His age 21 yrs. 9 mos. 18 days.

William Geiger, born June 30, 1776, died Dec. 20, (1795) buried Dec. 22. His age 19 yrs. 6 mos. 20 days.

Elizabeth Ementraut (Amentraut), born in 1725, died Oct. 7, 1795; buried on the 8th inst. Her age was 70 years.

Conrad Schneider, born Dec. 10, 1715, died October 7; buried Oct. 9th. His age was 79 yrs. 10 mos. 3 days.

Anna Maria Risch, born eight days ago; died Feb. 2, 1796.

George Wagner, born 1792, died Dec. 7, 1796, buried Dec. 8th.

Barbara Mallo, born Sept. 26 1726; died Jan. 17, 1797, buried on the 19th. Her age 70 yrs. 3 mos. 22 days.

Register of the children, who were admitted to the Lord's Supper for the first time in the church at the Peaked Mt. on Easter of 1796:

John Bentz (Pence),
Henry Bentz,
—— ——,
Catherine Risch (Rush),
Polly Risch,
Margaret Hein,
Elizabeth Rusch,
Elizabeth Bredt (Britt),

Eva Bertram,
Elizabeth Risch,
Barbara Ermentraut,
Emilia Schneider,
Susanna Geiger,
Elizabeth Bentz,
Bessy Schmidt (Smith),
Catherine Spreckelsen.

At the same time the following members attended the communion:

George Mallo and wife,
Peter Miller,
Augustin Geruss,
Matthias Kirsch,
Charles Risch and wife,
George Eller,
Peter Reier,
Christopher Werbel,
Frederick Ermentraut,
Philip Schaefer,
Gottfried Spilke,
Christopher Ermentraut and wife,
John Ermentraut,
Catherine Singel,

Frederick Geiger and wife,
Nicholas Becker (Baker),
Julius Bertram,
Jacob Risch,
Catherine Schu(h),
Dorothy Kirsch,
John Risch,
Catherine Herman,
Catherine Bredt,
Barbara Mallo,
Christina Herman,
Catherine Weber,
Martin Schneider,
Christian Geiger.

On October 16th (1799) the following members communed:

Matthias Kirsch and wife,
Charles Risch and wife,
John Risch and three daughters,
John Algebrecht (Argenbright),
Nicholas Peck,
Matthias Schneider,
Julius Bertram and wife,
John Ermentraut,
Philip Reyer and wife,
Daniel Nunnemachr
    (Moneymaker),
George Kochler and wife,
Jacob Fries (Frease),
  Gottfried Spilky,

George Schaefer and wife,
Elizabeth Licky (Luecke),
Margaret Manger,
Juliana Nicolas,
Catherine Lingel,
Elizabeth Wagner,
Elizabeth Meinesten,
Elizabeth Koenig,
Catherine Ermentraut,
Catherine Weber,
George Mallo and wife,
Christina Herman,
Barbara Mallo,
  Peter Miller.

Communicants on April 16, (1797):

Peter Risch and wife,
Charles Risch,
Christopher Kirchloff,
Gottfried Spilky,
John Penter, wife and daughter,
Martin Schneider,
Julius Bertram and wife,
Philip Lange (Long) and wife,
John Rish and two daughters,
Elizabeth Euler (Eiler),
Nicholas Peck,
Jacob Kirsch and wife,
Daniel Nunnemacher and wife,
Peter Ryer,

Philip Schaefer,
Matthias Kirsch,
John Bentz,
Elizabeth Bentz,
Elizabeth Koenig,
Catherine Weber,
Emilie Geiger,
Margaret Heyn,
Catherine Ryer,
Barbara Ermentraut,
George (?) Wagner and wife,
George Mallo and wife,
Peter Miller,
Christina Herman,

Catherine Speeckelsen.

Register of the couples married in the congregation at the Peaked Mountain, from Nov. 15, 1795-Nov 15, 1796:

D. C. Stock, Minister.

Jacob Schaefer & the daughter of Peter Bietefisch, (Peterfish) on June 27.

On Sept. 6th were married: The widower Christian Geiger, Sr., and widow Dindore. (Dundore).

On September 30: George Schaefer and Elizabeth Vogt, daughter of Martin Vogt, elder at Peter Ermentraut's church.

On September 25th: Christian Geiger & Emilia Schmidt.

Rockingham County, Peaked Mountain Church, October 25, 1785. The two deacons, Augustine Prisch (Price) and John Risch (Rush) rendered to-day in the presence of the undersigned an account of the money belonging to church and school and there remains in the treasury £2 8s. —p.

This we testify by our signatures:

Charles Schmidt, Schoolmaster.
Peter Nicklas,
Adam Herrmann.

This certifies that on January 2, 1802 an account was rendered by the deacons, Christian Geiger, Martin Schneider,

491

John Seitz and Jacob Nicolaus, and there remain in the hands of George Mallo five pounds, which his mother presented for the use of the church.

GEORGE MALLO,
JACOB ENGENBRECHT,
PETER NICHOLAS.

[16]"The baptisms after June, 1800, were most probably entered by the Rev. John Brown, who was licensed by the Reformed Synod at York, Pa., on May 12, 1800, on application from the congregations in Rockingham, county. He served the congregation from 1800 to 1850. The Reformed pastors before Rev. Mr. Brown were no doubt the same as those of the neighboring Frieden's Church, in whose record, begun in July, 1786, we find the following names: 'Andrew Loretz, Bernhard Willy, Daniel Hoffmann and Johannes Brauns.' Rev. Andrew Loretz, Jr., was pastor in Lincoln county, N. C., from 1786 to 1812. From there he visited Virginia. The ministry of Mr. Bernard Willy began in 1791. He resided in Woodstock, Va. Rev. Daniel Hoffmann began in 1797, and continued to serve the congregation for two years."

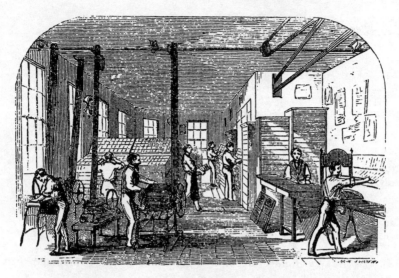

MEMORANDA FROM THE FREDERICKSBURG, VA., GAZETTE, 1787–1803.

[The notes here printed were compiled from the file of the newspaper now in the Library of Congress, Washington, D. C. The notices of schools are of especial interest at this time. The *Gazette* was Federalist in politics.]

1788.

June 5.   Two advertisements of the Fredericksburg Academy.
               Letter from Richmond in regard to the Convention.
               Advertisement of school for French and dancing by Mr. Cenley.
               Advertisement of "The Olio of Theatrical Entertainments."

June 12.   Meeting of the trustees of Fredericksburg Academy. Rules adopted for the school.
               Letter from Richmond in regard to the Convention.

June 19.   Duel between Col. Wm. Fountain and Mr. Macon in regard to an election in Hanover.

July 9.   Report of meeting of trustees of the Fredericksburg Academy.

Aug. 7.   Advertisement of public examinations at the Academy.

Sept. 4.   Advertisement by Berry and Cartes of their school for teaching French (in Fredericksburg.)

Sept. 25.   Advertisement by Francis Conway of sale of 700 acres of land on the Rappahannock River, nine miles below Fredericksburg, known as Conway's Warehouse.

Oct. 2.   Lottery for the Fredericksburg Academy.

Oct. 23.   Died on Friday night last, Mr. John Hall, merchant, in his
           40th year.

           Died in Norfolk on the 11th inst., in his 36th year, Rev.
           Walker Maury, minister of Elizabeth River parish, and
           Master of the Norfolk Academy, &c.

           Advertisement of a teacher of French and another of singing.

Nov. 6.   Died on the 25th ult., Gabriel Galt, at Richmond.

           Died, Captain Archibald Greig, the eldest Commander in
           the Virginia and Maryland trade, and a near relation of
           Admiral Greig of the Russian service.

Nov. 20.   Died at Richmond, on Friday last, Dr. Alexander Skinner.

Nov. 27.   Meeting of the trustees of the Fredericksburg Academy.

1789.

Jan. 1.   Account of celebration of St. John's Day in Fredericksburg.

Jan. 15.   Address to the Freeholders of Spotsylvania Co., in behalf
           of Madison.

Jan. 27.   Extract from a "Letter from James Madison, Jr., to his friend
           in the Country."

           Advertisement of sale of Popcastle and Lambs Creek,. King
           George Co., on the river 15 miles below Fredericksburg.
           Popcastle, containing 1288 acres, was occupied by the late
           Col. Wm. Champ. Lambs Creek, 667 acres, buildings
           greatly out of repair.   It is now in the possession of Col.
           Lewis Willis. Advertisement signed by Francis Willis,
           Georgia.

Feb. 5.   Election in Spotsylvania, &c.

April 9.   Died at his seat on Bull Run, John Carter, Esq.

           Died in this town yesterday, John Taliaferro, Esq., of
           Hayes, aged 44.

April 16. Letter, dated Orange, Jan. 29, 1789, from James Madison,
           Jr., to ———.

April 30. Died at Hill Park, Essex, his seat, on the 19th inst., Bennett
           Browne, Esq.

May 14.   Married on Sunday the 26th ult., Mr. John Mitchell, mer-
           chant, of Baltimore, and Mary, daughter of Col. William
           Peachey, of Mildenhall, Richmond Co.

Aug. 30.   Advertisement of the Port Conway races—to be run under
           the rules of the Bowling Green Jockey Club.

Sept. 10. Died, Thursday last, age 61, Jacob Whitely, for many years
           innholder.

Sept. 17. Prices of tobacco in London.

Oct. 15.   Died, Saturday last, Captain Alexander Kennedy, a native
           of Scotland, aged about 60.

	Died, Monday last, Mr. Wm. Wright, aged 89.
Oct. 22.	Died, Friday last, Mr. Walter Davids, comedian.
	Advertisement of play, " The Suspicious Husband "
Nov. 5.	Died, Monday last, Mr. Lacklan Campbell, merchant, aged, 43.
	Advertisement of play.
Nov. 12.	Died, Thursday last, Mrs. Peggy, wife of Mr. Peter Gast, merchant of this place.
Dec. 24.	Complaint in regard to the action of the House of Delegates as to a chaplain.

1790,

Jan. 7.	Reply to above in regard to a chaplain of the House of Delegates.
Jan. 14.	Address of the Committee of the United Baptist Church in Virginia to the President of the U. S. and his reply.
	Died, Mr. Thos. Brown, innkeeper, aged 61.
Jan. 28.	Married : Wm. Minor and Mildred, daughter of John Lewis.
	Died in Richmond, Lucy, wife of Joseph Latie, of that place.
	Also, in Richmond, died Hugh Patton, merchant.
	Died at his seat in Essex, Robert Brooke Esq.
	Died on the 22d ult. at the island of Barbadoes, Mrs. Frances Thornton of Orange Co.
Feb. 17.	Celebration of Washington's birthday in Fredericksburg— " this morning."
	Article on free schools in New England.
March 11.	Died in Caroline Co., Dr. George Tod, aged 80.
	Died, on Friday last, Mrs. Elizabeth, wife of John Fitzhugh of Stafford Co. in her 61st year.
March 25.	Died, Hon. Wm. Grayson.
April 5.	Died on the 5th inst. Rosanna, wife of Col. John Dixon, printer, Richmond.
May 6.	Died in Orange, Mr. John Bell.
June 24.	Died on Monday last, Francis Dade Jr., aged 14.
Oct. 7	Notice that the Richmond Academy had been turned into a theatre.
Oct. 14.	Died in Culpeper Co., in her 41st year, Molly, wife of Col. James Duncanson, of Fredericksburg.
Dec. 16.	Notice of the consecration of Bishop Madison and of his arrival in Va.

1791.

Jan. 6.	Died Friday last, John Sunderland, merchant, of this place.
	Died at Orange C. H., Joseph Wood, aged 36.
Jan. 13.	Died, Jan. 5, at Salisbury, Loudoun Co., Mrs. Jane Love, in her 45th year.
Jan. 27.	Died at Jacksonborough, S. C., Dr. James Wallace, late surgeon in Bayler's regiment, in 35th year.

Feb. 10.	Died, in this County, Tuesday night, Mrs. Elizabeth, wife of Col. Charles McGill of Winchester.
	Advertisement of the Fredericksburg Assembly (dancing.)
Feb. 17.	Died at Port Royal, Mr. John Tankersley, aged 42.
March 10.	Died last week, Nathaniel Burwell, of Kings Creek, York.
	Died, Sir Thomas Grey Skipwith, of Newbold Hall, England, who has left to the eldest son of Sir Peyton Skipwith, of Prestwould, Va., a landed estate of £4,900 sterling per annum.
April 7.	Died in Richmond, on the 29th ult. Mrs. Sarah, wife of Mr. Gordon, comedian.
April 14.	Visit of Washington to Fredericksburg.
	Price current.
April 21.	Visit of Washington to Alexandria and Richmond.
May 5.	Died on the 27th ult. in his 52nd year, Neill McCoull, a native of Scotland.
Aug. 4.	Died on the 16th inst., General Adam Stephen. He was a native of Scotland.
Aug. 11.	Died, Mrs. Margaret, wife of James Pottinger of this place.
Aug. 25.	Notice of visitation by Bishop Madison.
Sept. 8.	Died in Middlesex, on the 28th inst., Wm. Mullin, of Stafford, aged 57.
Sept. 20.	Notice of meeting of the Grand Lodge of Masons.
Nov. 10.	Notice of meeting of the Grand Lodge at Richmond; Thomas Mathews re-elected Grand Master.

1799.

Jan. 11.	Died, lately, at Boyds Hole, Mr. John Dalrymple, formerly merchant of this town.
	Died in this county, Mr. James Frazier
	Died at Port Royal, Mr. Wm. Gray, merchant.
	Cold weather in Fredericksburg.
Jan. 22.	Died in this county, on Sunday, Frances, wife of Major Benj. Alsop.
	Appointments to U. S. Army from Va.
Jan. 25.	Appointments to U. S. Army from Va.
	Married, on the 17th inst., Foushee Tebbs, of Richmond County, and Ann, daughter of Captain Henry Quarles, of Paradise, Essex Co.
	Advertisement by the trustees of St. George's parish.
Jan. 29.	Advertisement of school by John Gayle.
Feb. 1.	Died, Hon. Henry Tazewell, in Philadelphia.
Feb. 5.	Advertisement offering reward for discovery of persons who damaged the Fredericksburg theatre.
Feb. 8.	Notice of Fredericksburg Charity School.

Advertisement announcing the publication of "The Genius of Freedom," (newspaper in Fredericksburg.)

Feb. 12. Died, Feb. 5th, at Stoney Hill, his seat in Stafford, John R. Peyton.

Feb. 15. Died on Tuesday, the wife of Richard Johnston, merchant of this place.

Letter signed "A Christian," in regard to John Taylor's resolutions on the Alien and Sedition laws.

Advertisement by trustees of St. George's Parish.

Feb. 19. Address of John Nicholas, member of Congress.

Feb. 22. Letter in regard to printing the minority address (in the Va. Legislature) on the Alien and Sedition laws.

Feb. 26. Celebration of Washington's birthday in Fredericksburg.

March 5. Died in Culpeper, Mr. John Williams, Sr.

Letter from Judge Bushrod Washington, dated Feb. 10, 1799.

March 8. Died on Monday in this town, Lachlan McIntosh, aged 52.

Died Tuesday, John Day, tayler.

Died in the County, Ann, wife of Major John Willis.

Advertisement of theatre.

March 15. Advertisement of Tappahannock races.

March 19. Resolutions of Prince Wm. County Court refusing to have the Alien and Sedition resolutions (of the Va. Legislature) read.

March 29. Advertisement of the Fredericksburg Fire Company.

April 2. Meeting of the Subscribers to St. George's Church.

April 9. Great fire in Fredericksburg.

Died in this town on Friday, Mr. George Hazleton, of Norfolk.

Died same day, Ann, wife of John Lewis.

Died on Saturday morning the wife of Captain James Allan.

April 12. Died Thursday, Captain John Legg, of this town.

Died at Fauquier C. H., Septimus Norris, merchant.

April 23. Died in this town on Saturday last, Lucy, (aged 19) daughter of the late Thos. Walker.

Died in Stafford yesterday morning, Mrs. Mary Brown, relict of the late Raleigh Brown.

April 26. Election returns.

April 30. Tuesday—Died Sunday, Mr. James Allen, Sr., aged 84 years and 12 days. Was a native of Scotland and came to Fredericksburg in 1739.

Election returns.

May 3. Died in this county on Monday, Edward Herndon, Sr., in

497

	his 67th year, was the senior magistrate of Spotsylvania Co.
	Election returns.
May 7.	Died in Caroline, Richard Laughlin.
	Letter in regard to a political publication by the President of the Court of Appeals of Va.
	Letter from Patrick Henry to Henry Lee.
May 10.	Advertisement of the theatre.
	Letter in regard to politics in the theatre.
May 24.	Article in regard to the number of Federalists in Fredericksburg.
June 18.	Died, Patrick Henry.
July 5.	Died lately in Middlesex, Hudson Muse.
July 26.	Advertisement of the sale of a large collection of books and music, the property of the late Col. John Gaspar Stadler.
	Notice of the Charity School.
Aug. 6.	Died on the 28th ult., Thos. Wade West, manager of the Alexandria Theatre.
	Discussion in regard to articles in the Republican paper "The Genius of Liberty."
Aug. 27.	Resolutions of Pittsylvania County Court refusing to have the Alien and Sedition Resolutions read.
Sept. 3.	Article in regard to a sermon of Bishop Madison's.
Sept. 10.	Advertisement of match race, five miles, for 200 guineas on Tappahannock course, between Col. Tayloe's Leviathan, 180 lbs., and Col. Tomlin's Wildair, 110 lbs.
Sept. 17.	Account of action between American Ship Planter from Hampton Roads, and a French privateer.
Sept. 24.	Account of the race between Leviathan and Wildair, won by the former by 4 inches.
Oct. 22.	Died in Richmond Co., Thomas Beale, aged 63 years.
Oct. 29.	Advertisement of the Marine Insurance Company of Alexandria.
	[It appears by a reference at this time that Robert Mercer was editor of the "Genius of Liberty."]
Nov. 22.	Married on the 17th inst. at Chestnut Hill, Richmond Co., Lieutenant Jesse Ewell and Mildred Beale.
Dec. 3.	Died on the 18th [ult.] in Lancaster, Col. Henry Towles in his 53d year.
Dec. 6.	Married last evening Willis Lee, of Fauquier, and Polly, daughter of John Richards, of this place.
Jan. 24.	Notice of Alexandria Marine Insurance Company.
Jan. 28.	Notice of Fredericksburg Charity School.
Feb. 18.	Resolutions in Fredericksburg on the death of Washington.

Feb. 28.	Died in this town yesterday, Robert Brooke, late Governor of Virginia.
	Advertisement of Fredericksburg Dancing Assemblies.
March 7.	Advertisement of lease of the houses of the Academy, now the property of the Charity School.
March 11.	Died last week in Caroline, Major John Thornton, of King George.
March 14.	Letter against act passed by the last Assembly for choosing Presidential electors.
March 21.	Letter signed "Freeholders," King George Co., criticising Madison's Report.
April 18.	Died at Blandfield, Robert Beverley, in his 60th year.
June 3.	Married on Wednesday last in Caroline county, Philip Thornton, Esquire, to Miss Sally Conway, daughter of the late Francis Conway, Esquire.
June 6.	An address to the voters for electors in Va. for President and Vice-President, in behalf of the American Republican ticket [Federalist].
July 1.	Letter on the partisan methods of the Republican State Administration (in Va.)
July 4.	Died yesterday, French Strother, of Culpeper, State Senator.
July 8.	Celebration of the 4th of July in Fredericksburg.
	Married in Stafford on Thursday last, Alexander Morson and Anne Casson Alexander, daughter of Wm. Alexander, of Snowden.
July 11.	Mail routes in Va.
July 22.	Letter in reply to one charging the Republican State administration with unfairness.
Aug. 19.	Another letter on same subject.
Sept. 9.	Died, John Blair, Esq., of Williamsburg.
Sept. 12.	Died yesterday morning, Robert Mercer, editor of The Genius of Liberty.
Sept. 16.	Gabriel's Insurrection.
Sept. 19.	Gabriel's Insurrection.
Sept. 23.	Gabriel's Insurrection.
	Died in Northumberland, Catesby Jones, in 45th year.
Oct. 3.	Gabriel's Insurrection.

1802.

Feb. 26.	Died at his seat in Richmond Co. on the 20th inst., Mr. John Fawcett.
March 4.	Account of great religious revival in Kentucky.
March 16.	Teacher for Fredericksburg Female Charity School.
April 27.	Died yesterday Mr. Samuel Stevens, ropemaker.

May 4.	Died yesterday, Alfred, youngest son of Thomas Daniell of this town.
May 18.	Advertisement of Orange Springs.
June 14.	Died on the 7th inst., Col. Wm. Peachey, of Milden Hall, Richmond Co., in 74th year.
June 18.	Preparations for celebrating the 4th of July.
June 29.	Advertisement by Philip Temple, King William Co., of the press &c., in the late office of the Fredericksburg News Letter.
	Advertisement of sale of personal property at Mount Vernon.
July 6.	Celebration of the 4th of July at Spotsylvania C. H.
July 9.	Oration of Garrett Minor, Esq., on the 4th of July at Spotsylvania C. H.
	Died, on the 2nd inst., Mrs. Mary, wife of Col. David Jameson of Culpeper, in 30th year.
	Advertisement of Caroline Springs.
July. 13.	Fourth of July oration by Thomas Ritchie on the Academy Green, Fredericksburg.
July 16.	Died, Gilbert Harrow.
July 20.	General Lewis Littlepage died yesterday.
July 27.	Advertisement of Wax-works exhibition.
July 30.	Died in Culpeper, the wife of Major Churchill Jones. of The Wilderness.
Aug. 24.	Letter from Patrick Henry against slavery, copied from the Philadelphia Magazine.
Oct. 5.	Judge Tucker's charge to the District Court grand jury, Fredericksburg.
Dec. 14.	Article on electing a chaplain for the House of Delegates.
Dec. 17.	Election of John Page, Governor &c.
	Resolution denouncing the abuse of the President by the Federal press.
Dec. 21.	Advertisement, sale by Catlett Conway, executor of the land where Francis Conway, deceased, lived for several years before his death, being 1040 acres (700 of which first class meadow, so that 10,000 lbs. of actual grass or hay, may be made from it,) lying immediately on the Rappahannock, seven or eight miles below Fredericksburg.

1803.

Jan. 21.	Notice of the Alexandria Marine Insurance Company.
	Gift to Washington Academy by the Cincinnati.

Feb. 18.	Letter on candidacy of Col. New for Congress.
March 4.	Letters on same subject and on the candidacy of John Taylor of Caroline.
March 11.	Letter on same snbject.
April 1.	Proposals for the publication of a Republican paper in Fredericksburg to be called The Apollo.
July 22.	Death of John Thompson Callender.
	Married on Thursday, the 14th inst., William Brooke of Fredericksburg, and Mary Eleanor, daughter of Col. Larkin Smith, of King & Queen.
Aug. 16.	Advertisement by Charles B. Carter, of "Richmond Hill," of sale of his entire estate, 1895 acres on Totuskey Creek, about four miles from the Rappahannock river. Large two story frame dwelling, five rooms on a floor and closets, all the houses built within the last ten years.
Sept. 13.	Advertisement of Middleburg Academy in Loudoun Co.
Sept. 16.	Yellow fever in Fredericksburg.
Nov. 22.	Advertisement of sale of personal property of Mann Page, deceased, of Mannsfield.
Nov. 27.	Advertisement by Cottom and Stewart, Fredericksburg, of a circulating library.

1804.

Jan. 13.	Advertisement of sale of personal property and lease of Salisbury, King Ceorge Co., 1700 acres, property of the late John L. Alexander.
Feb. 7.	Meeting of members of the Legislature and others to nominate a Republican electoral ticket.
Feb. 17.	Died on Monday last, Benjamin Grymes, of Eagles Nest, Stafford Co. [King George ?]
March 2.	Great fire at Norfolk.
	Meeting in regard to the Female Institution of Fredericksburg.
March 6.	Meeting in regard to same.
March 30.	Notice of Stevensburg [Culpeper] Academy.
April 13.	Letter in regard to banks.
April 20.	Died on Saturday, in Fauquier, Martin Pickett.
May 4.	Norfolk prices, in rhyme.
	Charity School.
May 11.	Subscription for the Bank of Va. in Fredericksburg.
May 18.	Marine Insurance Co. of Alexandria.
May 22.	Married on the 19th inst., Thos. Pope Bayse, merchant of Fredericksburg, to Miss Hannah Lee Turberville, of Westmoreland.
June 5.	Married in Prince William on the 17th ult., Robert Hooe, of

Stafford and Margaret, daughter of the late Landon Carter, of Prince William.

Married on the 24th of May at the home of L. W. Tazewell, Norfolk, Col. Larkin Smith, of King and Queen and Miss Taliaferro.

Meeting of the Republican stockholders of the Bank of Virginia in Petersbury.

June 15.   Notice of barbacue at Spotsylvania C. H.

Letter from Stith Mead, June 5, 1804, describing revival of religion in Bedford Co.

William and Mary College lottery.

June 29.   Meeting of Fredericksburg Sockholders of the Bank of Virginia.

July 6.   Celebration of the 4th of July.

July 10.   Camp meeting in Powhatan Co.

July 17.   Celebration of the 4th of July at Germanna.

Aug. 7.   Resolutions of Va. Society of Cincinnati on the death of Alexander Hamilton.

Sept. 11.   Notice of the Bank of Potomac, Alexandria.

Oct. 12.   Friday—Died at his seat in Stafford on Monday last, Wm. Alexander, Esq.

Nov. 23.   Died on the 21st inst., Mrs. Sarah Griffin Mortimer, relect of Dr. Charles Mortimer.

Dec. 21.   Died in Georgia in November last, Philip B. Rootes, formerly of Fredericksburg.

(The dates given are those of the papers.)

THE TOMBSTONE OF DR. EDMOND HELDER OF STAFFORD.

(Communicated.)

In 1865 while the late Moncure D. Conway was living in London, be published in *Fraser's Magazine* a pleasant rehearsal of Virginia's links with the mother country, in the course of which he said that in the churchyard of St. George's Church at Fredericksburg there was a tombstone bearing an inscription to the effect that it covered the grave of one who had been a pallbearer for William Shakespeare. Literary London at once challenged this statement, whereupon Dr. Conway, admitting that his authority was merely a recent letter from home, began an investigation. He found at once that there was no such tombstone in St. George's churchyard and that the statement on which he had relied was derived from a newspaper story. Finally he traced it to its origin. Mr. C. J. Brown, of Byfield, Massachusetts, sent him a copy of an inscription taken from an old tombstone on Potomac Creek, upon which Mr. Brown had stumbled in 1862, while serving in the Sixth New Hampshire Volunteers. Mr. Jones testified that it was a crude carving, difficult of decipherment, but that he had, to his own somewhat doubtful satisfaction,[1] made it out to read as follows:

"Here lies intered the body of Edmond Helder, Prectitioner in physick and chyrurgery. Born in Bedfordshire, Obiitt March 11, 1618, Atatis Sua Y 6."

There was thus no mention of Shakespeare on the stone, that being altogether imaginative newspaper embroidery upon the reported date, 1618. Loyally recanting the statement he had made in *Fraser's Magazine*, but stimmulated by the belief that in any event he had come upon "the oldest English epitaph in the new world," Dr. Conway persistently pursued the search during the ensuing twenty years. In September, 1884, he combed the banks

---

[1] The words were spaced with inebriated "S's" which complicated Mr. Jones' interpretation.

of Potomac Creek and was rewarded by coming on a characteristic Virginia phenomenon.[2] Built into the chimney of a modern kitchen he found the stone Mr. Jones had read, but, alas, all the inscription had been defaced except the two first letters, "HE." Local discussion then developed that several residents in the neighbourhood remembered to have read the inscription and felt able generally to confirm Mr. Jones' copy. And so the old stone was removed to Fredericksurg, where it is still exhibited as the original of "the oldest English epitaph in the new world." Dr. Conway finally recorded the story in an entertaining magazine article[3] which he entitled "Hunting a Mythical Pall Bearer."

There is more than a memory of Mr. Pickwick's studies in epigraphy to make one skeptical of this date, 1618. While not impossible, it is not probable. In 1618 ships from Jamestown were trading for corn with the Indians resident on Potomac Creek, but it was thirty years before there was any English plantation there. Moreover, the name Helder does not appear, among the chirurgeons or otherwise, on any of the lists of the earliest adventurers to Virginia. When to these facts is added Dr. Tyler's conclusive demonstration of the misreading of the date of William Harris' nearby tombstone on Neapsco,[4] as 1608, when, in fact, it was 1698, the candid mind is persuaded that Dr. Helder's date was more likely to have been 1678 than 1618. It would be as natural for an amateur antequarian on the lookout for marvels to decipher a "1" out of the "7" of a weathered carving as it was in the similar case of the Harris stone to make an "0" out of a "9."

But it is not necessary to rely altogether on negative evidence

---

[2]In 1677 the Bishop of London protested (*Cal. State Papers*, Am. & W. I., 1677-80, p. 117) in vain against the continuance of what he was pleased to call Virginia's "profane custom of burying in their gardens and orchards."

[3]*Harper's Magazine* (lxxii, 21) for January, 1886. Hence the inscription was reproduced in Neill, *Virginia Carolorum* (1886), p. 91.

[4]*W. & M. Quar.*, iv, 195.* The occasion for this enquiry was that Charles Campbell and Alexander Brown, the latter cautiously, had both given currency to the Harris inscription with the 1608 date. See *Genesis of the U. S.*, i, 150. It may be noted that the Stafford records contain many testimonies sustaining Dr. Tyler's identification of Harris.

*Page 429, this volume.

to justify such philosophic doubt. In the earliest surviving court order book of Stafford County it appears that on June 12, 1690, Matthew Keene sued William Downing in trespass, alleging that he, the plaintiff, *"together with Edmond Helder late of this County decd."* had taken title as joint tenants, by deed of John Peake, dated November 14, 1672, to a certain dividend of land patented by said John Peake,[5] lying near the head of Potomac Creek on the northwest side thereof; that the said Edmond Helder having died without any partition, he, the said Keene, was entitled to the whole dividend by right of survivorship; but that William Downing was in possession of a part of the land and refused to attorn.

At another term of Stafford Court later in the same year (September 10, 1690) William Downing was sued again, this time by one Mary, daughter of William Russell,[6] and wife of James Gallohough, who alleged "that *Docter Edmond Helder* by his last will and testament in writing" did bequeath to her certain cattle with their increase, and did appoint that she "should live with William Downing and Mary his wife till the time of her marriage;" that the said William Downing "being named sole executor in the said will did prove the same," but refuses to give Mary her cattle although she had complied with Dr. Helder's stipulation, had lived with Downing and his wife and had married with their consent.[7]

---

[5]Peake's patent was dated September 26, 1668, *Va. Land Register*, v. 179.

[6]This Mary was perhaps a sister of that William Russell, aged 56 in 1736 when he was well known as a Rappahannock frontiersman, who testified for Col. Byrd as to his hunting expeditions into the back woods as early as 1701. See *Westover MSS.*, ed. Wynne vi, 100.

[7]The William Downing who thus administered on the estate of Dr. Edmond Helder and was doubtless responsible for the latin of his tombstone, appears frequently in the surviving Stafford records, of the end of the seventeenth century, serving on juries and as "coronet," later captain, of militia. When the Northern Neck grant books were opened by Philip Ludwell in 1690, he began to take out, by way of confirmation of previous Virginia patents which he had acquired, a series of proprietary grants dated from 1690 to 1711, all relating to lands on Potomac Creek.

While the Stafford will and deed books of this time are missing and so we cannot invoke Dr. Helder to speak for himself, this evidence is nevertheless sufficient to justify any court in finding as a fact that there was living in Stafford as late as 1672 an Edmund Helder who would answer the description of a "prectitioner in physick and chyrurgery." To complete the identification it remains then necessary only to find such an one who would also answer to the description of having been "born in Bedfordshire."

In the seventeenth century the Apothecaries Company of London was authorized by its royal charter, to license "practitioners in physic." The records of that Society, at Apothecaries Hall, supply the testimony we need, in two pertinent entries in its minute books,[8] as follows:

1657, June 11, "Edmund Helder, son of Richard Helder of Stoughton, co. Hunts, gent., examined, approved and bound to William Royston for 8 years. Fee 4s 8d."

1662, Sept. 3, "Edmund Helder the late apprentice of William Royston, having sued out his Indentures, is turned over to Mr. Skelton for the remainder of his time."

It happens that the reference to the residence of Richard Helder in this record of the Apothecaries Company is an error. At the time that record was made there were, as there still are, two parishes of Staughton. One, the better known, is Great Staughton, which lies on the southwest border of the county of Huntingdon, where it adjoins the parish of Little Staughton, in the county of Bedford. It was in the last named parish where a kinsman purchased the manor in 1650[1] that Richard Helder lived, for in his will, dated February 24, 1668,[2] he describes himself as "of Little Staughton in the Countie of Bedford, Gentleman." That will testifies also that Richard Helder had raised so large a family

---

[8] *Minutes of the Apothecaries Company*, vol. ii, folios 38, 65.

[1] *Victoria County History*, Bedfordshire, III, 165. The family of Helder, *alias* Spicer, were originally of Hertfordshire, where they were seated *temp.* Philip and Mary.

[2] The will was proved, in the local Archdeaconry Court, May 15, 1669.

of sons and daughters that he had found it expedient to bind out several of them as apprentices.

On this evidence we may accept, as correct, the statement on the Virginia tombstone of Richard Helder's son Edmund that the latter was "born in Bedfordshire," but there can no longer be any doubt that that tombstone commemorated one who not only died, but was born, many years after 1618.

The Oldest Epitaph in Virginia.

The stone which bears the following epitaph, the oldest legible one remaining in Virginia, is now in the graveyard at "Four Mile Tree," the old Browne estate on James river in Surry county. It was formerly in the garden there:

> " Here lyeth buried the body of
>   Alice Miles daughter of John
> Miles of Brandon in Hertford
>   Gent. and late wife of Mr. Geo.
> Jordan in Virginia who departed this
>   life the 7th of Jan., 1650.
> Reader her dust is here inclosed
>   who was of art & grace composed
> Her life was virtuous, glorious during breath
>   but highly glorious in her death."

TOMBSTONES AT CLAREMONT, SURRY COUNTY.

THIS MONUMENT
is erected in commemoration
COLONEL WILLIAM ALLEN
OF CLAREMONT
Whose remains are here intered.
He was born
on the 7th day of March 1768
and died
on the 29th day of November 1831.
Aged 63 Years 8 Months and 22 Days.

(*Allen and Bassett Arms.*)

To the Memory of
ELIZABETH
(Daughter of William Bassett Efq:
One of the Council in Virginia;)
A sincere Chriftian, a constant communicant
An affectionate Consort, an Indulgent Parent,
A Tender Mistrefs, a. Friendly Neighbor.
Pious, without Superstition:
Regular, without Ill-humour.
Charitable without Oftentation
Beloved in her Life time
Bewailed at her Death.
Especialy by her Husband, John Allen.
She died on the 14th day of Oct. 1738.
In the 42[d] Year of her Age.

Sacred
To the memory of
ANN ARMISTEAD EDLOE
Consort of
JOHN EDLOE
Who died April 27. 1833.
Aged 56 YEARS & 32 Days.

◦◉◦◉◦◉◦

And I heard a voice from Heaven
Saying unto me; Write. blessed
are the dead which die in the
Lord from henceforth: Yea Saith
the Spirit. That they may rest
From their Labours; and their
works do follow them.   Rev. xiv, 13.

◦◉◦◉◦◉◦

In respectful remembrance of
Their Mother
This monument is erected and
Inscribed by her
Affectionate children.

509

MARTHA ARMISTEAD ORGAIN
BORN
March 31th 1803
DIED
February 12th 1857.

IN MEMORY OF
MRS MARY ALLEN OSBORNE
Oldest daughter of John & Ann A. Edloe.
born Septr 9th 1800. was married
March 20th 1820 to Dr. N. M. OSBORNE
Died Septr 16th 1855 of apoplexy
at the Salt Sulphur Springs Va.

MEMENTO MORI
In remembrance of
JOHN EDLOE
Who died August, 1816,
Aged 51 Years,   Days.
This stone
is erected as a tribute of respect by his children.

IN
memory of
CARTER H. EDLOE
Who was born August 28th 1798
and died August 26th 1843
of apoplexy
This stone is erected by his nieces E. C. & M. M. Orgain.

IN
memory of
R. GRIFFIN ORGAIN
Who was born Septr 25th 1787
and died July 17th 1830.

510

SACRED
to the memory of
MONTGOMERY MACKENZIE
Son of
Griffin & Martha Armistead Orgain
Born the 12th of February 1824
and departed this life
the 15th day of July
of the same year
Aged 5 months and 3 Days.

•◉•◉•◉•

Death may the bands of life unloose
But can't disolve our love
Millions of infant souls compose
The family above.

———————

NOTES FROM ALBEMARLE PARISH REGISTER, SUSSEX COUNTY, VA.

Amy, daughter of Robert Hicks and Mary his wife, born 7 April, 1742.

Absalom, son of Joseph Harwood and Sarah his wife, born 2 August, 1743.

Benjamin, son of Willet Robards and Faith his wife, born October 8, 1749.

Edward, son of Hartwell Marable, christened October 2, 1774.

Elizabeth, daughter of Charles Collier and Lucretia his wife, born August 23, 1734.

George, son of Benjamin Wyche and Elizabeth his wife, born March 7, 1759.

Hannah, daughter Clement Hancock and Anthony his wife, born February 14, 1741.

Goodwynn, son of John Woodward, Jr., and Susanna his wife, born November 25, 1766.

Herbert, son of Augustine Claiborne and Mary his wife, born April 7, 1746. Godfathers: Leonard Claiborne, Wm. Willis. Godmothers: Susanna Stith and Elizabeth Willis.

James, son of William Hicks and Mary his wife, born September 3, 1735.

John, son of Thomas Eldridge and Martha his wife, born April 22, 1741. Godfathers: Wm. Eppes, Wm. Willis. Godmothers: Ann Bolling, Ann Elldridge.

James, son of Edward Ruffin and Anne his wife, born July 23, 1741.

Kinchin, son of Joseph Stacy and Faith his wife, born January 18, 1763.

Nathan, son of Robert Hicks and Mary his wife, born November 6, 1743.

Nathan, son of Samuel Harwood and Agnes his wife, born November 14, 1752.

Philip, son of Philip Harwood and Rebecca his wife, born August 13, 1742.

Robert, son of Robert Tucker and Dinah his wife, born August 22, 1727.

Robert, son of John Goodwin and Winnifred his wife, born March 15, 1739.

Rolfe, son of Thomas Eldridge and Martha his wife, born December 29, 1744–'45.

Susanna, daughter of Augustine Claiborne and Mary his wife, born November 29, 1752.

Charles Augustine, son of Wm. Claiborne and Mary his wife, born February, 1777. Godfathers: Augustine Claiborne and William Leigh. Godmother: Hannah Claiborn.

William, son of Goodrich Hatton, born April 23, 1753.

William, son of Thomas Pennington and Rebecca his wife, born July 11, 1753.

William, son of William Shands, Jr., and Priscilla his wife, born September 22, 1755.

William, son of William Shands, Jr., and Priscilla his wife, born September 5, 1757.

William, son of Henry Faison and Lucy his wife, christened November 2, 1760.

Benjamin, son of Wm. Brodnax and Mary his wife, born August 28, 1772.

Bathurst, son of Augustine Claiborne and Mary his wife, christened April 6, 1774.

Eliza Power, daughter Henry Brodnax and Anne his wife, born March 2, 1765.

Elizabeth, daughter of Benjamin Walker and Lucy his wife, born May 9, 1766. Godfather: David Walker. Godmothers: Eleanor Nobbs, Ann Wilson.

Robert, son of John Walker and Hannah his wife, born October, 1771.

Richard Bland, son of Henry Faison and Lucy his wife, born January 30, 1772.

William, son of Benjamin Wyche and Elizabeth his wife, christened February 28, 1762.

William Smith, son of Charles Collier and Susanna his wife, born May 26, 1762.

William, son of Henry Brodnax and Anne his wife, born March 3, 1762.

Augustine Claiborne, son of Richard Cocke and Ann his wife, born November 20, 1771. Godfather: Augustine Claiborne. Godmothers: Betty Claiborne and Susanna Claiborne.

Christopher Tatum, who had been forty years clerk at Nottoway Church, died January 16, 1750. Certified by John Tatum.

John Stokes died of the small-pox, February 23, 1750-'51. Certified by John Knight.

George Pasmore, aged 100, died July 15, 1751. Certified by Matthew Gibbs. This old man came into ye country a soldier in the time of brave Mr. Bacon being in arms for his country.

Ann Clack died August 21, 1752.

Benjamin Hyde and Mary his wife and three children, all murdered by their own negro man, January 14, 1754.

Daniel Eppes, aged eighty-one, died June 6, 1753. Certified by Edward Eppes.

James Wyche, a child, died September 2, 1753.

Thomas Eldridge died December 4, 1754.

Mary Brown died February 15, 1755. Abraham Brown's second wife.

Capt. John Mason died September 3, 1755. Certified by Capt. John Mason.

Clement Hancock died November 16, 1758. Certified by Clement Hancock.

Judith Eldridge, aged sixty-seven, died October 14, 1759. Certified by William Eldridge.

Capt. James Gee, aged sxty-five, died October 28, 1759. Certified by Henry Gee.

George Booth, aged eighty-four, died August 14, 1763. Certified by George Booth, his grandson.

Elizabeth Mason, wife of John, died August 21, 1763. Certified by Major John Mason.

Edward, son of Henry Faison and Lucy his wife, born May 10, 1767.

Elizabeth Mason, wife of John, died August 21, 1763. Certified by Major John Mason.

Eliza Green, daughter of William Hancock and Rebecca his wife, born October 27, 1766. Godfather: David Jones. Godmothers: Mary and Sarah Jones.

Sarah Capel, aged 102, died September 19, 1763. Certified by Moses Johnson.

John, son of John Hancock and Mary his wife, born August 6, 1751.

Jonathan, son of Jonathan Ellis and Hannah his wife, born January 22, 1752. Godfathers: William Ellis, Thomas Poem.

Jemima, daughter of Robert Hancock and Elizabeth his wife, born December 9, 1753.

Mary, daughter Richard Hill and Margery his wife, born April 15, 1760.

Mary, daughter of John Power and Elizabeth his wife, born March 27, 1759.

Susanna, daughter Charles Collier and Susanna his wife, born February 27, 1761.

Sara, daughter Benjamin Hancock and Jane his wife, born April 6, 1747.

Robert Jones, son of Robert Jones of this parish, Attorney-General of North Carolina, in the forty-ninth year of his age, died October 2, 1766.

Jean Wyllie,* my niece, in her twentieth year, died September 16, 1767. She came into the country at the beginning of June last.

Mary, wife of Hartwell Marable, died December 26, 1770.

Mr. George Nicholas, clerk of Dinwiddie county. "I preached his funeral sermon, 20 March, 1771; d. March 9, 1771." Certified by Mr. John Ruffin, Jr.

Henry Tyler, aged seventy-three, died January 2, 1774. Certified by John Tyler.

Capt. Henry Harrison died January 28, 1772. This gent. was taken ill on Saturday, the 25th of this month.

George Randall, clerk of St. Mark's Parish Church, died February 8, 1772. Certified by Nathaniel Dunn.

* Rev. William Willie was minister of this parish during the period of this Register, 1738–1776.

Capt. William Eldridge died April 7, 1772.

Major Edward Pettway died February 13, 1773.

Mary, wife of Charles Harrison, died July 25, 1775. Certified by Cole Claiborne.

Richard Jones, in his seventy-second year, died February 18, 1774.

Ann, his wife, in her sixty-sixth year, died February 21, 1774. Certified by Hamilton Jones.

Hannah, wife of Capt. James Jones, died January 25, 1774. Certified by Thomas Jones, her son.

James Brown—this young man was married to Mary, daughter of Capt. James Jones, 12 April last—died February 18, 1774.

Col. Richard Blunt died April 13, 1774. He was in his thirty-sixth year, born January 4, 1739.

Henry Hartwell Marable died September 17, 1774.

Robert Jones, in his eighty-first year, died February 14, 1775. Mr. Jones was born in November, 1694.

William Brodnax died March 13, 1775. Certified by William W. Wyche.

Samuel, son of William Brodnax and Mary his wife, born March 24, 1774.

William Cole, son of William Claiborne and Mary his wife, born August 13, 1773. Godfathers: Ferdinand Leigh, Thos. Moore. Godmother: Eliza West.

Capt. Wm. Parham died of the flux May 16, 1775. Certified by Peter Randall.

Henry Briggs, died October 25, 1739.

Sarah Wyche, died December 29, 1739. Certified by George Wyche.

Thomas Eldridge, died November 4, 1740. Certified by Thomas Eldridge.

Elizabeth Eldridge, died September 15, 1745. Certified by Thomas Eldridge.

Capt. Richard Hill, died July 9, 1775.

Martha Eldridge, born October 23, 1749. Certified by Thomas Eldridge.

Ann Ruffin, died October 26, 1749. Certified by Edmund Ruffin.

Ann Ruffin, a child, died November 3, 1749. Certified by Edmond Ruffin.

Col. Thomas Cocke, of Southwark Parish, died December 2, 1750. Certified by Capt. Lemuel Cocke.

Capt. Howell Briggs, in his sixty-sixth year, died April 21, 1775. Certified by Gray Briggs.

Capt. Matthew Parham, in his eighty-first year, died April 18, 1772. Certified by Gray Briggs.

Rev. Alex. Finnie, M. A., rector of Brandon Parish, in Prince George, forty-six years, in the seventieth year of his age, died November 17, 1770. Certified by John Austin Finnie, his son.

Sylvanus Stokes died February 6, 1748–'9. Certified by Jones Stokes.

MARRIAGES IN SUSSEX COUNTY.

From Albemarle Parish Register, kept by Rev. William Willie.

Henry Briggs, died Aug. 25, 1739.

John Gee, died Oct. 5, 1739. Certified by James Gee.

Thomas Eldridge, died Nov. 4, 1740. Certified by Thomas Eldridge.

Martha Cobb, dau. of Allen Jones and Mary, his wife, born Sept. 12, christened Oct. 26, 1764. Godfathers, William Jones, William Willie. Godmothers, Eliza Willie, Jacobina Willie.

Benj. Henry and Betty, son and dau. of Charles Harrison and his wife, born June 30, 1775.

Mary, wife of Charles Harrison, died July 25, 1775. She was safely delivered of two children, and seemed to be in a fair way, but by a mortification was cut off in a few days' illness.

Lucy Binns, daughter of John Cargill and Lucy, his wife, born January 29, 1769. Godfather, Nicholas Massenburg. Godmothers, Lucy Massenberg, Martha Belsches.

Capt. Richard Hill, died July 19, 1775. Mrs. Brooking. This man had joined the Methodist Association, and had frequent meetings at his home, but a few hours before his death gave charge that no Methodist should ever preach under his roof.

Anne Carter, dau. of Henry Harrison & Elizabeth, his wife, born Jan'y 12, 1764. Godfather, John Cargill. Grandmothers, Martha and Judith Avery.

Sylvanus Stokes, died Feb. 6, 1748-9. Jones Stokes.

Dr. John Hay, died April 27, 1760.

Rev. Mr. Henry Elbeck, of Southwarke Parish, died Nov'r 2, 1751.

Major Robert Wynne, died July 23, 1754.

Elizabeth Harrison, Sarah Cargill, sisters, died Aug. 31, 1766.

Jeane Wylie, my niece, died in her 20th year Sept. 16, 1767. She came into this country the beginning of June last.

Rev. Alexander Finnie, rector of Brandon Parish in Prince George for 46 years, in the 70th year of his age, died Nov. 17, 1770.

Major Edward Pettway, died Feb. 13, 1773.

Charles de la Hay, born Sept. 20, 1773.

Lucy Cargill, wife of John Cargill, died Dec. 13, 1773.

Henry Tyler, aged 73, died Jan. 2, 1774. Certified by John Tyler.

Elizabeth, dau. of John Jones and Judith, his wife, born March 5, 1753. Godfather, Robert Jones, Jr. Godmother, Rebecca and Susanna Jones.

Aristotle Eldridge, son of Thomas Eldridge and Eliza, his wife, born Oct. 30, 1752.

Allen, son of Robert Jones, Jr., & Sarah, his wife, born Dec. 26, 1739.

Martha, daughter of Robert Jones, Jr., & Sarah, his wife, born Nov. 1, 1743. Peter Rives, Mary Rives and Sarah Gee.

Here Lyes ye body of Jane
Wife of Augustine Washington
Born at Popes Creek Virginia
Westmoreland ye 24th of Xber
1699 & died ye 24th of 9ber 1729
She left behind her two Sons
& one daughter.

Here Lyeth The Body Of
John Washington Eldest
Son To Cap Lawrence
Washington Who Departed
This Life Ye 10th Of January 169—
Aged 10 Years & 6 Months
Also Mildred Washington
Eldest Daughter Of Said
Washington Who Died
Ye 1st of August 1696
Aged 5 Months.

———

GOODRICH EPITAPH.

"In the Vault under the Family Seat
opposite this Monument are deposited
the Remains of John Goodrich Esqr.
a Native of Virginia in North America
who departed this life in November
1785 aged 63 years
And of Margaret his Wife who
died 12th April 1810 aged 78 years
Also of two of their Sons
James Goodrich who died 26th
May 1787 aged 23 years
And Samuel Goodrich who died
26th October 1807 aged 41 years
Also James Goodrich son of
Samuel Goodrich who died
8th November 1836 aged 47 years
And Sarah Goodrich his wife
who died 20th April 1854
Aged 65 years."

Inscription on a mural monument of white marble and slate just
inside the tower entrance to Topsham church, Devon, England. The
monument is on the left wall of the tower near the entrance. It is minus

some top ornamentation which possibly contained a shield of arms and may have been moved from its original position in the church during alterations.

W. U. Reynell-Upham,
Ringwood, Upham Ph. Rd.,
Cheswick, London, Eng.

[John Goodrich was the well known Isle of Wight county, Va. Tory, who after acting for a term with Lord Dunmore, removed to England.]

OLD TOMBSTONES IN WESTMORELAND COUNTY.[1]

Copied from a slab in the burial ground on Bridges' Creek, near Wakefield, the family seat of the Washingtons.

Here lyeth the body of John Washington, eldest son to Captain Lawrence Washington, who departed this life yᵉ 10ᵗʰ of January, 1690, aged 10 years and six months. Also, Mildred Washington,

---

[1] In order to save space, the length of the lines on the tomb is not preserved. These inscriptions were furnished mainly by Rev. G. W. Beale, of Westmoreland county. Those tombstones visited and verified by the editor are marked (T).

eldest daughter to said Washington, who died on yᵉ 1ˢᵗ of August, 1696, aged 5 months.

From a slab at Stratford, the ancient seat of the Lees.

In memory of the Hon. Thomas Lee, whose body was buried at Pope's Creek Church, five miles above his country-seat, Stratford Hall, in 1756.

Copied from a massive tomb,[1] on the plantation called "Booth's," near Nominy Creek. (T).

Here lies yᵉ body of Col. Henry Ashton, Born in Westmoreland Co., son of Jno. Ashton Gent. by Grace his wife, the 30ᵗʰ day of July, Anno 1671. He married, first, Elizabeth, yᵉ Daughter of Wm. Hardidge, Gent., by Frances his Wife, by whome he had four daughters, Frances, Elizabeth, Ann & Grace. The last only Survived him. Yᵉ other three are Buryed near him. His second wife was Mary, Daughter of Richard Watts Gent., by Mary his wife, by whom he had one Daughter and two Sons, Elizabeth, Henry and John. He was a Good husband, a tender Father, a kind Neighbour, a most Compassionate Master, and an honest man. The manner of his Death was Lingering, Occasioned by a Cancer in his Chest. He died a penitent & a Sincere member of the Church of England yᵉ 3ᵈ day of November, 1731, in the 61ˢᵗ Year of his Age.

From a tomb[2] on "Booth's" plantation, at the mouth of Nominy Creek. (T).

Beneath this Stone is Laid the Body of Elizabeth, the Wife of Col. Henry Ashton, and Daughter of Capt. William Hardidge, by Frances, his Wife, who for Piety to God, Faithfulness, Love and Obedience to her Husband, tenderness to her Children, Carefulness of her family, Charity to the Poor, was Equalled by Few, Excelled by none. She had by her said Husband four Children, Frances, Elizabeth, Anne and Grace. The two Latter only Survived her. After finishing her most Neighborly and Christian life, with joy She Resigned her Soul to God in Faith on Monday, the 25ᵗʰ of February, in the Year of our Lord 1722 and in the 45ᵗʰ Year of her Age, whose Death was Lamented by all who Knew her.

---

[1] This tomb has upon it for arms a mullet within a circle.

[2] This tombstone bears a mullet on a bend for Ashton.

521

*Copied from a tomb[1] near the Potomac, on the "Booth" planta-
tion. (T).*

Underneath this Stone is Layed in Hopes of A Joyful Resurrection the Body of Frances Turberville, first child of Mr. Henry
Ashton, by Elizabeth his wife. She was Married to George Turberville, Gentleman, the 24th of April, 1718, by whom she had one
Child, a Daughter (Elizabeth), on the 12th of January, 1719. She
was a Dutiful Daughter, a Faithful wife, a tender Mother, and
with a Christian Good will to all, she resigned Her Soul to God in
Faith the 24th day of April, 1720, in the 21st year of Her Age.

*From a tombstone[2] in Hickory Hill graveyard, Westmoreland
county, Va., the original seat of the Turbervilles.*

TURBERVILLE

COAT OF ARMS.

CORBIN COAT

OF ARMS.

To the Memory of Lettice TURBERVILE Who Was Born the
15th day of July, 1707, Daughter of Hon. William Fitzhugh Esq., by
Ann his Wife Who Was the Daughter of the Honr Richd Lee.
Those Excellent Natural Endowments Which very Early Discov-
ered themSelves Were Carefully Cherished and Improved by her
Wise and Virtuous Parents. From A Child She Knew the Scrip-
tures Which Made Her Wise unto Salvation : From Her Infancy
She Learned Walh (*sic*) In the Paths of Virtue. She Was Beau-
tifull But Not Vain : Witty But Not Talkativ : Her Religion was
Pure Fervent Cheerful and of the Church of England : Her Vir-
tue Steadfast Easey Natural : Her Mind had that Mixture of
Nobleness and Gentleness As Made Her Lovely in the Eyes of all
People. She Was Marryed to Capt GEORGE TERBERVILLE
May the 16th 1727. the best of Wives Made him the Happiest of

---

[1] This tomb bears a lion rampant for Turberville, but not crowned as on
the next stone.

[2] This stone bears the arms of Turberville (erm. a lion ramp. gu. ducally
crowned or) impaling corbin (erm. on a chief or three ravens sa).

Husbands. She died the 10th of Feb. 1732 Great with Child in 25th Year of Her Age and 6th of her Marryage. Who Can Express the Greif. Soon Did She Compleat Her Perfection, Soon Did She finish Course of Life. Early Was She Exempted From the Miseries of Human Life By God's particuler Grace. Thus Doth He Deal With his Perticuler Favorites.

> All that was good in Woman Kind
> A Beauteous Form More Lovely Mind
> Lies Buryed underNeath this Stone
> Who Living Was Excelled by None.

From a tomb in the graveyard at "Hickory Hill,"[1] the seat of the Turberville family.

This silent stone Is Erected to the Memory of REBECCA LEE TURBERVILLE, fifth daughter of JOHN and MARTHA TURBERVILLE, Who departed this life On Friday, the First day of April, 1785, Aged 12 years, 6 months and Eleven Days.

Reader:

Be attentive and sympathize whilst You survey this last frail tribute of paternal affection.

From a tomb[2] at "Bushfield," near the mouth of Nominy Creek. (T).

Here lies ye Body of John Bushrod, son of Richard Bushrod, Gent., by Apphia, his wife. He was born in Gloucester county, in Virginia, ye 30th of January, 1663. He took to wife Hannah, the daughter of Wm. Keene, of Northumberland county, Gent., and Elizabeth, his wife, and by her left two sons & four daughters, & died the 26th of February, 1719, in the 56th year of his age.

From a tomb at " Mt. Pleasant," on Lee's Creek, an arm of Lower Machodoc.

Hic conditur corpus Richardi Lee, Armigeri, nati in Virginia, filii Richardi Lee, generosi, et antiqua familia, in Merton-Regis, in

---

[1] Hickory Hill, Westmoreland county, was settled by the Turbervilles about 1700, became the residence of Major Robert Beale in 1815, inherited by his wife, Martha Felicia Turberville, daughter of George Lee Turberville, now the residence of John W. C. Davis, grandson of Major Robert Beale.

[2] Besides this tomb there are stones to the memory of Thomas Bushrod (born May 25, 1702, died in February, 1719), son of John Bushrod and Hannah his wife, two infant children of the same, and an infant of William Fantleroy, gent., and Apphia, his wife, grandchild to John Bushrod, and Hannah, his wife.

comitatu Salopiensi, oriundi. In magistratum obeundo boni publici studiosissimi, in literis Graecis et Latinis et aliis humanioris literaturae disciplinis versatissimi.

Deo, quem, summa observantia semper coluit, animam tranquilus reddidit xii. mo. die Martii anno MDCCXIV., ætat LXVIII.

Hic juxta situs est corpus Laetitiæ ejusdem uxoris fidæ, filiæ Henrici Corbyn, generosi, liberorum matris amantissimæ, pietate erga deum, charitate erga egenos, benignitate erga omnes insignis. Obiit Octob. die vi. MDCCVI. ætatis XLIX.

The above epitaphs translated.

Here lieth the body of Richard Lee, Esquire, born in Virginia, son of Richard Lee, Gentleman, descended from an ancient family of Merton-Regis, in Shropshire.

While he exercised the office of a magistrate he was a zealous promoter of the public good. He was very skillful in the Greek and Latin languages and other parts of polite learning. He quietly resigned his soul to God, whom he always devoutly worshipped, on the 12th day of March, in the year 1714, in the 68th year of his age.

Near by is interred the body of Lettice, his faithful wife, daughter of Henry Corbin, Gentleman, a most affectionate mother. She was also distinguished by piety towards God, charity to the poor, and kindness to all. She died on the 6th day of October, 1706, in the 49th year of her age.

From a tomb in Yeocomico churchyard.

Here lyeth the body of Daniel McCarthy, who departed this life the 4th of May, 1724, in the forty-fifth year of his age. He was endowed with many virtues and good qualifications, but the actions proceeding from them bespeak their praise.

Here also lyeth the body of Thaddeus McCarthy, youngest son of Daniel McCarthy, Esq., who departed this life the 7th of February, 1731, in the 19th year of his age.

Near this place likewise is the body of Penelope, wife to Daniel McCarthy, second son of Daniel McCarthy, Esq., and daughter to Christine Higgins, Gent., who departed this life the 26th of March, 1732, in the 19th year of her age, with one child.

From a tomb at Wilmington, near "The Oaks," the early seat of the Newton family.

Beneath this stone are deposited the remains of Mrs. Sarah

Newton, daughter of George Eskridge, and late wife of Capt. Willowby Newton, of Westmoreland county, who after having justly established the character of a dutiful child, a faithful friend, an affectionate mother, and sincere Christian, departed this life on the 2nd of December, 1753, in the 46th year of her age.

———————————

APPENDIX A: Multiple-County Records

WINSTON DALTON'S REGISTER

Contributed by A. M. Prichard, Staunton, Virginia

Dr. Reuben W. Bennett, of Gretna, Virginia, has in his possession an old register of births, deaths and marriages which seem to have occurred, for the most part at least, in the northern portion of Pittsylvania and the southern part of Bedford counties, Virginia. The register appears to have been kept by Winston Dalton, a school teacher; and the following extracts have been copied and arranged in alphabetical order by A. M. Prichard, of Staunton, Va.

Adams, James, hung himself, 24 Mar. 1843.
Adams, Capt. Joel's wife died—9 Oct. 1816.
Achols, Dr. Joel, stabbed by William Bennett—9 Aug. 1837.
Adkins, Henry, died—2 July 1826.
Allen, Hardwell, & Rebecca Madkiff, married—6 May 1837.
Allen, Welcome, (lived in Bannister), died—1 Sept. 1832.
Anthony, Thomas, son of Mark & Milly, died—17 Jan. 1822.
Arthur, William, son of James & Ann, born—23 Mar. 1783.
Arthur, Dinna, dau. of William, died—22 July 1828.
Arthur, William, son of Jacob & Milly, born—21 Feb. 1822.
Arthur, Joab, & Milly Goad, married—16 May 1822.
Arthur, Joab, oldest son of William & Milly, born—21 Feb. 1823.
Arthur, John, & Mary Bennett, married _____.
Arthur, Elizabeth, dau. of John, born 21 Nov. 1823.

Arthur, Mary & Martha (twins), daus. of John & Nancy, born—23 May 1827.

Barber, Caleb, & Matilda Robertson, married 21 Sept. 1843.
Barber, Coalmond, died 10 May 1843.
Barber, Nancy, wife of William, died 27 Apr. 1837.
Barber, Hezekiah, died 26 Feb. 1844.
Bennett, Richard, son of Peter & Frances, born 23 Apr. 1769; died 16 Oct. 1811.
Bennett, Asenath, wife of Richard, died 24 June 1821.
Bennett, Abner, son of Richard & Sena, born 6 May 1796.
Bennett, Abner, & Nancy Edwards, married 13 May 1819.
Bennett, Sena, dau. of Richard & Nancy, born 8 Jan. 1805.
Bennett, McCajah, son of Richard & Nancy, born 4 Jan. 1807.
Bennett, Sally, dau. of Richard & Nancy, born 4 Jan. 1809.
Bennett, William, son of Peter, died 11 Sept. 1837, aged 83 years.
Bennett, James, son of William & Hannah, died 21 May 1826.
Bennett, Micijah, died 24 May 1810.
Bennett, Elizabeth, dau. of William & Sally, born 25 Feb. 1798.
Bennett, Zachariah, son of William & Sally, born 25 Apr. 1800.
Bennett, Bacster, son of William & Sally, born 1 Dec. 1803.
Bennett, Calvin, son of William & Sally, born 29 July 1810.
Bennett, Reuben, & Polly Tosh, married 28 Feb. 1822.
Bennett, Winston, & Elizabeth Berger, married 19 Dec. 1826.
Bennett, James' wife died _ Aug. 1830.
Bennett, Thomas F., son of James Anthony, born 20 Jan. 1828.
Bennett, Mary, & Willis Yates, married 21 Dec. 1836.
Bennett, William, son of James, died 19 Jan. 1838.
Bennett, Letty, wife of James, died 25 Aug. 1830.

Berger, John (Wade), son of Jacob (Junr), died 18 June 1825.
Berger, Jacob, Jr., died 13 Mar. 1833.
Berger, Caty, wife of Jacob, died 23 Dec. 1830, aged 50 yrs. 11 mos.
   27 days.
Berger, Caty's funeral preached by James Kelly & Joel L. Adams 28
   May 1831.
Berger, Daniel, & Eliza Jones, married 26 Feb. 1829.
Berger, George, & Frances Berger, married 29 Feb. 1844.
Bobbett, William, & Nancy Rice, married 8 Feb. 1827.
Bowers, Joanna, drowned at Luse Island 26 Sept. found 6 Oct. 1836.
Bowles, Lucy, wife of John, died 8 May 1819.
Boyce, Arthur, born 8 Oct. 1740; died _____ 1817.
Branson, Westley, died 30 Mar. 1833.
Brown, Nancy, wife of David Rover, born 14 Aug. 1793.
Bruce, Dolly, dau. of John & Nancy, born 7 Nov. 1806.
Bruice, Hensley & Coley, married 11 Sept. 1834.
Burnes, Timothy, & Mourning Barber, married 30 Jan. 1844.

Calloway, Charles, died __ July 1827.
Cammell, John, died 7 Feb. 1827.
Carter, Charles, died 8 May 1827; funeral preached by Rev. John Early,
   27 May 1827.
Carter, Capt. Edward's wife died 24 Mar. 1832.
Carter, Capt. Edward, died 9 Sept. 1843.
Clark, Peter H., started for the western country, 24 Mar. 1827.
Clark, Peter H., Peter Erby, and John M. Townley, started for the
   western country, 17 Nov. 1830.
Clark, Capt. William, of Pitts., died 3 Apr. 1827.
Cleaver, Granny, died 25 Jan. 1812.
Clop, Molly, died 9 Jan. 1833.
Cook, Sally, wife of John, died 14 Apr. 1835.
Cox, John, died 18 July 1841.
Craft, Emily, dau. of George, died 11 Sept. 1841.
Craft, George, son of Philip, murdered by his brother, Armstead, 11
   July 1833.
Crayne, Jacob, started for the western country, 28 Oct. 1830.
Crayne, David S., born 31 Mar. 1821.
Crayne, Ellina Ellender, born 26 Nov. 1822.
Crayne, Jacob, born 6 July 1825.
Crayne, Jacob (Jourdan), born 13 May 1827.
Crayne, Peggy Ann, born 10 Nov. 1829.
Crayne, Jacon & Nancy Debbo, married 1820.
Creamer, Old Miss, died 14 Apr. 1823.
Crickett, Robert, & Elizabeth Tosh, married 11 Oct. 1833.
Crider, Jacob, & Nancy Rover, married 19 Dec. 1832.
Crider, Henry, & Matilda Bennett, married Dec. _____.
Crider, Jacob's son born 22 Sept. 1833.
Crider, Daniel, (Sergn), son of Wae, born _____ 1744.
Crider, Elizabeth, & Wyatt Wallis, married 29 Dec. 1823.
Crider, Melissa, dau. of William & Ceilia, born 28 Feb. 1826.
Crider, Samuel, son of Andrew & Tena, died 22 Oct. 1826.
Crider, Henry, son of John, died __ Aug. 1834.
Crider, John, son of Daniel, died _____ 1834.
Crider, Caty, wife of Daniel, died 1 Feb. 1839.
Custard, John, & Catherine Rover, married 31 July 1817.
Custard, Eliza Ann, dau. of John & Catherine, born 23 _____ 1818.

Custard, James, died 16 May 1827.
Custard, Daniel, & Susannah Berger, married 26 Oct. 1826.
Custard, John (James), son of Daniel & Susannah, born 27 July 1827.

Dalton, John, son of Martin & Caty, born 22 Jan. 1804.
Dalton, Daniel, son of Martin & Caty, born 23 Feb. 1805.
Dalton, Willis, son of Aggy, born 14 Mar. 1811.
Dalton, Frances, died 15 Apr. 1800.
Dalton, David, son of William & Rachel, born 9 Aug. 1808.
Dalton, Cintha, dau. of William & Rachel, born 29 June 1811.
Dalton, Henry, son of William & Rachel, born 5 Nov. 1813.
Dalton, Churchel, son of William & Rachel, born 10 Mar. 1819.
Dalton, _____, 2nd child of Aggy, born 28 Apr. 1816.
Dalton, Solomon, son of Robert & Mary, born 14 June 1760; moved
    to South Carolina from Pittsylvania, 1793.
Dalton, (Aunt) Mary, wife of Solomon, born 10 May 1765.
Dalton, (Uncle) James, died __ May, 1811.
Dalton, _____, wife of Randolph, died 1 Feb. 1812.
Dalton, Martin, started to Tennessee 6 Oct. 1813.
Dalton, Samuel, died 10 July 1814.
Dalton, Molly (blind), died 30 Sept. 1814.
Dalton, Caleb, died 3 Oct. 1814.
Dalton, Sally, & John Toler, married __ Jan. 1807.
Dalton, Winston, commenced teaching school 8 May 1820.
Dalton, Larkin, son of James S. & Sally, born 5 Jan. 1804.
Dalton, Matthew, son of James S. & Sally, born 5 June 1806.
Dalton, Greenville, son of James S. & Sally, born 7 June 1809.
Dalton, John H., son of Robert & Tabitha, born 26 Feb. 1807.
Dalton, Elzy, son of Robert & Tabitha, born 11 Jan. 1809.
Dalton, Shelton, son of Robert & Tabitha, born 20 Feb. 1811.
Dalton, James, son of Robert & Tabitha, born 7 Feb. 1813.
Dalton, Bowker, son of Robert & Tabitha, born 19 Mar. 1815.
Dalton, Robert, son of Robert & Tabitha, born 26 May 1817.
Dalton, Locke, son of Robert & Tabitha, born 6 Nov. 1819.
Dalton, Robert, & Tabitha, married 24 Apr. 1806.
Dalton, Wyatt, started for Tennessee 4 Nov., 1822.
Dalton, Joseph, died 3 Oct. 1825.
Dalton, David, son of Lewis, married Polly Walden, daughter of Henry
    who shot himself, 4 June 1826.
Dalton, Samuel, & Caty Pickral, dau. of Thomas, married 4 June 1826.
Dalton, Lasy, son of James & Polly, married Juney Pickral, 15 June
    1826.
Dalton, Jonathan, son of Tim, & Elizabeth, dau. of Benjamin Dalton,
    married 17 Sept. 1826.
Dalton, John, & Coley Mattocks, married 12 Dec. 1826.
Dalton, John S., died 2 Mar. 1827.
Dalton, Jubal S., & Peggy Wright, married 21 Feb. 1832.
Dalton, David, & Sally Bennett, married 29 Dec. 1834.
Dalton, Peggy, Polly & Siner had measles 22 Apr. 1832.
Dalton, John F., died 3 Apr. 1833.
Dalton, Wyatt, 2nd son born 15 Oct. 1829.
Dalton, John, started for Tennessee 3 Nov. 1812.
Davis, Rev. William, died 13 Aug. 1836.
Debboe, Sena, died 18 Jan. 1826.
Debboe, Old Miss, died 24 Sept. 1822.
Debboe, Joseph, & Polly Dalton, married __ Nov. 1835.

Debboe, Joseph & Caswell Dalton went South 26 Jan. 1837.
Debboe, James, son of Abraham, died 10 Oct. 1830.
Debboe, Phillip, started for the western country 28 Oct. 1830.
Debboe, Phillip, & Peggy Dalton, married 17 Dec. 1834.
Debboe, Benjamin, & Locky Dalton, married 10 Mar. 1830.
Debboe, Eliza, dau. of Benjamin & Locky, died 21 Dec. 1839.
Debboe, Mary Ann, dau. of Benjamin & Locky, born 12 Mar. 1831.
Debboe, Wyatt, son of Benjamin & Locky, born 4 July 1833; and died 17 Dec. 1839.
Debboe, Peggy, dau. of Benjamin & Locky, born 11 Aug. 1835.
Debboe, Mellissa, dau. of Benjamin & Locky, born 3 Mar. 1838.
Debboe, America, dau. of Benjamin & Locky, born 10 Jan. 1840.
Dickerson, Crispin, died 27 Oct. 1832.
Dickerson, Crispin, son of Crispin, born 5 Dec. 1832.
Dillard, Lynch's wife, Milly Ward, died 5 Jan. 1824.
Dixson, Berry, son of Little Berry, died 29 June, 1815, funeral preached at Joseph Toler's by Rev. Shadrach Mussteen, 12 July 1817.
Dixson, Bluford, son of Little Berry, born 27 Aug. 1816.
Dixson, Teny, dau. of Little Berry, born 1 Dec. 1818.
Dixson, Joel, son of Little Berry, born 26 Nov. 1820; and died 7 Feb. 1821.
Dixson, James, son of William & Frances, born 22 May 1779.
Dixson, Ginsey, dau. of James & Susannah, born 20 Aug. 1808.
Dixson, Benjamin, son of James & Susannah, born _____.
Dixson, Hezekiah, son of James & Susannah, born _____.
Dixson, Jeremiah, son of James & Susannah, born 5 Jan. 1814.
Dixson, George, son of James & Susannah, born _____.
Dixson, Jack, son of James & Susannah, born _____.
Dixson, Nancy, dau. of James & Susannah, born 17 July 1821.
Dixson, Mely, dau. of James & Susannah, born _____.
Dixson, James (Solomon) son of James & Susannah, born 7 Feb. 1824.
Dove, Welthy's child, born 3 May 1816.
Dove, Welthy, born 15 Apr. 1797.
Dove, Reuben, born 7 Feb. 1801.
Dove, David, son of Sanford & Nancy, born 13 July 1809.
Dove, Jonathan, son of Sanford & Nancy, born 11 July 1811.
Dove, Bowker, son of Sanford & Nancy, born 28 Jan. 1814.
Dove, Johnson, son of Sanford & Nancy, born 5 Mar. 1816.
Dove, Elizabeth, dau. of Sanford & Nancy, born 13 July 1818.
Dove, Nancy, dau. of Sanford & Nancy, born 13 Nov. 1820.
Dove, Sandford, born 20 Apr. 1785.

Edwards, Daniel E., died 23 Nov. 1832.
Edwards, Harden, & Dolly Graves, married 9 Dec. 1841.

Flanagan, Annis, died 4 May 1817.
Flanagan, James, born _____ 1730.
Flanagan, Mary Ann, dau. of James, born 11 Nov. 1753.

George, Hugh, died 27 June 1819.
George, John, & Sally Hatchet, married 30 Dec. 1823.
George, Cornelius M., son of Hugh & Ceilie, born 19 Aug. 1795.
George, Mildred, dau. of Hugh & Ceilie, born 13 Aug. 1797.
George, James H., son of Hugh & Ceilie, born 18 May 1799.
George, Mary, dau. of Hugh & Ceilie, born 13 Sept. 1801.
George, John, son of Hugh & Ceilie, born 13 _____ 1804.
George, Ceilie, dau. of Hugh & Ceilie, born 13 Sept. 1806.

George, Elizabeth, dau. of Hugh & Ceilie, born 25 Mar. 1809.
George, Ellis, born 22 July 1811.
George, Martha W., born 27 June 181___.
George, Sally, dau. of Cornelius & Ceilie, born 3 Mar. 1816.
George, Ceilie, dau. of Cornelius & Ceilie, born 4 Dec. 1817.
George, Mary, dau. of Cornelius & Ceilie, born 2 Mar. 1819.
George, Edney, dau. of Cornelius & Ceilie, born 1 Dec. 1820.
George, Nolen, son of Cornelius & Ceilie, born 5 Apr. 1822.
George, William, son of Cornelius & Ceilie, born 27 Sep. 1824.
George, Hugh, son of Cornelius & Ceilie, born 27 Sep. 1824.
George, Cornelius, son of Cornelius & Annie, born 25 Feb. 1827.
George, Ceilie, died 10 Dec. 1820. (?)
Goad, Andrew, son of William & Tabitha, born 19 Oct. 1778.
Goad, Polly Jacobs, wife of Andrew, born 16 Oct. 1791.
Goad, Benjamin (Hollins), son of Andrew, born 16 Apr. 1809.
Goad, Nancy, dau. of Andrew & Polly, born 21 Mar. 1816.
Goad, William, son of Andrew & Polly, born 29 Jan. 1818.
Goad, Fanny Lowry, dau. of Andrew & Polly, born 8 Jan. 1820.
Goad, Anna, dau. of Andrew & Polly, born 17 Dec. 1821.
Goad, Mary Melvina, dau. of Andrew & Polly, born 25 Jan. 1823.
Goad, Robert, son of Richard, born 16 Jan. 1822.
Goad, Sally's Jack died 11 Apr. 1821.
Goad, William, & Merilla Snow, married 28 Aug. 1832.
Graves, John, & Mildred George, married 9 May 1817.
Graves, Peyton, & Nancy Hurt, married 20 May 1824.
Graves, Thomas, (son of Peyton), & Joanna Witcher, married 21 Aug. 1828.
Graves, Washington, & Mildred Berger, married 31 Jan. 1832.
Graves, Peyton, died 9 July 1836.
Graves, William, started for Missouri, 10 Nov. 1837.

Hackworth, Jesse, died 29 May 1830, in his 47th year.
Haley, Charles L., & Elizabeth McClanahan, married 9 Jan. 1823.
Hatchett, Harrison, & Widow Smith, married 22 Dec. 1836.
Hedrick, George, died 26 Mar. 1832.
Henderson, Polly, born 7 Jan. 1779.
Hanson, William, was 77 years old, 23 May 1810.
Hollogan, Patrick, born 1 July 1769; died 6 Oct. 1837.
Hollogan, William, son of Patrick, born 19 June 1818; died 17 June 1824.
Hollogan, Love, dau. of Patrick, born 16 Jan. 1809.
Hollogan, Bashaba, dau. of Patrick, born 31 Jan. 1821.
Hollogan, Nicholas, son of Patrick, born 18 Feb. 1823.
Hundley, Nancy, dau. of John & Dorcus, born 8 Aug. 1802.
Hundley, Wyett, son of John & Dorcus, born 7 Nov. 1804.
Hundley, Berry R., son of John & Dorcus, born 7 Jan. 1806.
Hundley, Joseph, son of John & Dorcus, born 7 Nov. 1808.
Hundley, Mary, dau. of John & Dorcus, born 24 Apr. 1811.
Hundley, John B., son of John & Dorcus, born 18 Mar. 1813.
Hundley, Jesse S., son of John & Dorcus, born 5 Dec. 1814.
Hundley, Susannah, dau. of John & Dorcus, born 8 Dec. 1817.
Hundley, William W., son of John & Dorcus, born 2 Oct. 1818.
Hundley, Eliza Jane, dau. of John & Dorcus, born 10 Apr. 1820.
Hundley, Christopher (Francis), son of John & Dorcus, born 20 Aug. 1823.
Hutchison, George, & Susan Dalton, married 2 May 1835.

Jacobs, Claborn, died 20 Jan. 1814.
Jacobs, Elisha, died 16 Jan. 1814.
Jacobs, Allen, & Matilda White, married 9 Feb. (March) 1826.
Jacobs, Hollens, & Patsy Crayne, married 26 Jan. 1832.
Jacobs, Henry, & Nancy Barber, married 20 May 1824.
Jacobs, Mrs. Henry, died 23 Mar. 1831.
Jefferson, Capt. Samuel's wife died 8 May 1843.
Johnson, Major Richard, died 28 Aug. 1826.
Jones, Elizabeth, (dau. of Samuel Smith), died 16 Mar. 1820.
Jones, George, drowned at Samuel Lovel's mill pond 25 Dec. 1832.
Jones, Thomas, father of Richard, died 31 Jan. 1839.

Keen, Ford, & _____ Edwards, married 22 Aug. 1817.
Keen, David's wife, Gilly Edwards, died 9 Apr. 1825; funeral preached
    16 Apr. 1826.
Keen, Nancy, wife of John, died 15 July 1835.
Keesee, John's Sale, 21 Nov. 1823.
Keesee, Ginny, wife of Richard, died 5 Jan. 1826.
Keesee, Richard, & Susanna Cleaver, married 1 Mar. 1827.
Keesee, William, & Anna Pickrall, married 28 Dec. 1826.
Keesee, Jesse, died __ Feb. 1829.

Lawhorn, Mourning's daughter born 6 Oct. 1814.
Lawhorn, Eli Vaughan, son of Mourning, born 1 Dec. 1825.
Lawhorn, Jabez, son of Mourning, born 14 Mar. 1813.
Lee, Major Burwell, died 15 Nov. 1825.
Leftwich, Col. Thomas, died 3 May 1816.
Leftwich, James, son of Thomas, died 4 Aug. 1825.
Leftwich, Augustin, & Mildred Ward, married __ June 1823.
Leftwich, Augustin, & Elizabeth W. Clark, married 13 June 1830.
Leftwich, Sandy, & Sally Smith, married 1 Jan. 1818.
Lewis, _____, & Martha Lilly, married 20 Dec. 1832.
Linticum, Henry, & Nancy Bowcock, married 24 Nov. 1827.
Linticum, William, & Mildred Robertson, married 11 Apr. 1833.
Linticum, Edward, & Mary Wallen, married 4 Jan. 1844.
Lovell, Samuel's funeral preached 20 Nov. 1837.

Mahan, William, & Peggy Wright, married 18 Jan. 1814.
Mahan, Namon, & Elizabeth Smith, married 21 Dec. 1837.
Mahan, Samuel, & Elizabeth Jefferson, married 28 Dec. 1837.
Mahan, George, & Fanny Jefferson married 28 Dec. 1837.
Mahan, Alexander, & Cintha Jefferson, married 25 May 1837.
Mahan, Alexander's daughter born 12 Jan. 1838.
Martin, Robert, died 15 May 1827.
May, Tillitha, dau. of Elizabeth, born 5 May 1810.
May, Benjamin, son of Elizabeth, born 26 Oct. 1815.
May, John (Fullington), son of Elizabeth, born 5 Aug. 1816.
May, Anna Bowker, dau. of Elizabeth, born 19 Aug. 1820.
McClanahan, Winny, dau. of John & Sally, born 30 Dec. 1825.
McClanahan, Francis, died 18 Oct. 1825.
McClanahan, Francis' wife died 16 Apr. 1832.
McCrickard, Samuel, & Jane Keesee, married 15 Aug. 1844.
McDowell, William, died 28 Nov. 1816.
McNeeley, Avery, died 17 Feb. 1833.
McNeeley, George, son of George, born 18 Feb. 1808.
McNeeley, George, died 16 Feb. 1837.
Mease, Mrs. died 10 May 1843, aged 102 years.

Mitchell, John, son of Samuel & Siner, died 1818.
Minter, Augustin, son of Jesse & Elvy, born 13 Aug. 1826.
More, David, died __ Mar. 1831.
Muse, John, son of John, died 24 Jan. 1832.
Muse, John, died 6 Sept. 1843.

Newman, Elizabeth, dau. of Polly, born 19 Apr. 1819.
Nichols, Old Mrs., died 15 Feb. 1833.
Norcutt, Joseph, died 20 June 1841.

Oakes, Robert, died __ Apr. 1827.
Owen, Pleasant, died 30 June 1841.

Pane, Henry, & Caty Tosh, married 29 Nov. 1827.
Parker, John, died 23 Mar. 1811.
Parker, Joseph, married 15 Apr. 1813; "stabbed" 21 Sept. 1828.
Parker, Pleasant, died 12 Nov. 1814.
Parker, Lucky, died 16 Jan. 1816.
Parker, Elizabeth, died 15 June 1820.
Parker, James, died, 1827.
Parker, Wyett, son of William, died 19 Sept. 1827.
Parker, George, & Susannah Keesee, married 11 Jan. 1827.
Parker, Willia, (Pig River), died 21 Dec. 1828.
Parker, Richard, & Elizabeth Linticum, married 1 July 1841.
Parker, Meeking Mulsted, son of Joseph & Nancy, born 29 Mar. 1814.
Parker, Elizabeth, dau. of Joseph & Nancy, born 18 Sept. 1815.
Parker, Isaac Burdit, son of Joseph & Nancy, born 31 Oct. 1819.
Parker, Luida Jane, dau. of Joseph & Nancy, born 26 Aug. 1820.
Parker, Charles Henry, son of Joseph & Nancy, born 14 Apr. 1822.
Parker, Mary Ann, dau. of Joseph & Nancy, born 29 Apr. 1825.
Parsons, Vincent, son of John Henry, born 11 Aug. 1826.
Parsons, John, died 23 Mar. 1831.
Pemberton, Joseph, died 10 Apr. 1823.
Pickral, Solomon's daughter killed by a tree 20 Jan. 1816.
Pickral, Henry, died 2 July 1814.
Pullen, Peggy, died 12 Nov. 1809.
Pullen, Thomas, died 14 Oct. 1811.
Pullen, Thomas, & Fanny Chelei, married 17 Dec. 1832.

Ramsey, Henry, & Polly Robbins, married 27 Nov. 1828.
Ramsey, Isaiah, & Matilda Crider, married 7 Dec. 1841.
Rice, Benjamin, & Matilda Goad, married 14 Oct. 1826.
Robbins, George's wife died 24 Feb. 1824.
Robertson, Joseph, died 15 Sept. 1825.
Rover, Abraham, died 20 June 1830; funeral preached by Blair and Adams, 25 Aug. 1830.
Rover, Henry, son of Abraham, died 7 Apr. 1817.
Rover, John, & Sally Bennett, married 13 Jan. 1814.
Rover, David, & Nancy Brown, married 3 Mar. 1814.
Rover, John, son of David & Nancy, born 12 Jan. 1815.
Rover, Mary Elizabeth, dau. of David, born 3 Aug. 1817.
Rover, Nancy, dau. of John & Sally, born 14 Dec. 1814.
Rover, Abram, son of John & Sally, born 14 Oct. 1816.
Rover, Richard, son of John & Sally, born 14 Sep. 1818.
Rover, Asenath, dau. of John & Sally, born 14 Feb. 1823.
Rover, Purmely, dau. of John & Sally, born 5 Nov. 1820.
Rover, John C., son of John & Sally, born 9 Dec. 1824.

Rover, Abram's little daughter died 22 Apr. 1832.
Runnels, Dabney, & Sally Mahan, married 25 Jan. 1828.

Sanders, Doctor, & Martha Berger, married 11 July 1838.
Shelton, Richard, killed by a horse 1831.
Shelton, Meeking, & Anna Berger, married 3 June 1838.
Shockley, Elizabeth, dau. of Joseph & Frances Toler, born 19 July 1778.
Shockley, Elizabeth, wife of John, died 7 May 1836.
Shockley, Shadrack, son of John & Elizabeth, born 3 Nov. 1808.
Shockley, Frances, dau. of John & Elizabeth, born 27 Apr. 1810.
Shockley, Polly, dau. of John & Elizabeth, born 25 Nov. 1818.
Shockley, Absalom, son of John & Elizabeth, born 31 May 1822.
Shockley, Shadrach, & Elizabeth Toler, married 18 Dec. 1828.
Smith, Capt. Ralph, died in Mar. 1827.
Smith, Major John's mother died 17 Nov. 1807.
Smith, Anna Bowker, died 7 Nov. 1823.
Smith, Bowker, died 22 Sept. 1841.
Smith, Ralph, & Ardine Wright, married 7 Dec. 1843.
Smith, Bowker, & Priscilla Northcutt, married 19 Dec. 1843.
Smith, Jabez's wife died 1 Mar. 1844.
Smith, Col. John, died 13 Aug. 1836.
Smith, Bowker & Jabez, started for the west 18 Dec. 1836.
Snow, Thomas, born 29 Nov. 1757; died 17 Mar. 1830.
Snow, Abner, died 16 May 1835.
Snow, Richard, & Polly Parker, married 31 Jan. 1828.
Snow, Rachel, wife of Thomas, died 3 Sept. 1838.
Stone, Edmund, & Nancy Dickerson, married 5 Feb. 1827.
Stone, Edmund, died 16 May 1835.
Sutherlen, Philip, & Polly Berger, married 25 Apr. 1815.
Swanson, William, died 25 May 1827.

Talor, Obediah, was 70 years old, 22 Aug. 1844.
Thompson, Thomas, & Ginny Toler, married 27 Apr. 1815.
Thompson, Nathan, & Milly Martin, married 7 Sept. 1826.
Toler, Joseph, b. 15 Sept. 1743; d. 10 Nov. 1819.
Toler, Frances, wife of Joseph, d. 30 June 1833.
Toler, Benjamin, son of Joseph, died 3 Apr. 1813.
Toler, Jenny, dau. of Joseph, married Thomas Thompson 15 Apr. 1815.
Toler, Elizabeth, dau. of Joseph, (married John Shockley), born 19
    July 1778.
Toler, John, & Sally Dalton, married __ Jan. 1807.
Toler, Judith, mother of John, died 17 Nov. 1807.
Toler, Elizabeth, dau. of John & Sally, born 12 Dec. 1808.
Toler, Christopher, son of John & Sally, born 29 July 1810.
Toler, Joshua, son of John & Sally, born 1 Apr. 1812.
Toler, Anna, dau. of John & Sally, born 29 Oct. 1815.
Toler, Absalom, son of John & Sally, born 3 Jan. 1817.
Toler, Jonathan, son of John & Sally, born 19 Aug. 1821.
Toler, Sally, dau. of John & Sally, born 29 Apr. 1824.
Toler, Elizabeth, dau. of Elijah & Polly, born 19 Sept. 1808.
Toler, Frances, dau. of Elijah & Polly, born 7 June 1811.
Toler, Benjamin, son of Elijah & Polly, born 16 Mar. 1814.
Toler, Catherine, dau. of Elijah & Polly, born 19 Sept. 1825.
Toler, Nancy, dau. of Joshua, born 20 Apr. 1785; married Sanford
    Dove, 29 Jan. 1807.
Toler, James, & Sally Hurt, married 25 Dec. 1817.
Toler, Henry, son of Polly, born 6 Dec. 1801.

Toler, Robert, son of Sally, born 22 June 1791.
Toler, Berry, died __ July 1824.
Toler, Absalom, & Elizabeth Linticum, married 18 Jan. 1825.
Toler, Mary Ann, dau. of Absalom & Elizabeth, born 6 May 1828.
Toler, Peyton, & Elizabeth Toler, married 6 Aug. 1825.
Toler, Hannah, died 5 Mar. 1827.
Toler, William, started for the western country 2 Aug. 1829.
Toler, Elijah, son of William, & Lucy Hutson, married 9 Nov. 1832.
Toler, William, & Fanny Barker, married 9 Jan. 1833.
Tosh, Elizabeth, dau. of George & Caty, born 24 Apr. 1809.
Tosh, George, died 17 Nov. 1837.
Turk, Caty, wife of Christian, died 11 July 1827.

Waggoner, Christopher, died 5 Feb. 1840.
Waggoner, Miss, died 25 Oct. 1833.
Walden, Charles, died 25 May 1830.
Walden, Mary Ann, wife of Henry, & dau. of Jessee Keesee, died 23 Apr. 1826.
Walden, Henry, shot himself, 11 May 1820.
Wallis, David, & Nancy Goad, married 9 Apr. 1825.
Wallis, Wyatt, & Elizabeth Crider, married 29 Dec. 1823.
Wallis, James, started to Ohio, 4 Oct. 1828.
Ward, Henry, died (at the Bridge), 23 Apr. 1823.
Ward, John, died 11 Oct. 1826.
Ward, Robert A., died 8 Oct. 1828.
Ward, Robert, son of John, died 5 May 1837.
Ward, John, killed by a tree, 2 Aug. 1838.
Watson, Abijah, died __ June 1827.
Weeks, William's wife hanged herself 11 Nov. 1811.
Weeks, William, & Siner Adams, married 18 Apr. 1816.
Wheeler, Charity, dau. of Micajah & Patsy, born 16 June 1800; died 15 June 1810.
Wheeler, Preston, son of Micajah & Patsy, born 24 Feb. 1804.
Wheeler, Willis, son of Micajah & Patsy, born 12 Sept. 1807.
Wheeler, Matilda, dau. of Micajah & Patsy, born 15 May 1810.
Witcher, Daniel, died 10 Jan. 1815.
Witcher, John, son of William & Polly, died 22 Apr. 1825.
Witcher, William, died 9 Oct. 1822.
Witcher, Caleb, died 18 July 1835.
Wright, Hulldy, died 1 Dec. 1825.
Wright, Lewis, son of Thomas, died 28 July 1827.
Wright, Joseph, & Susan Dickerson, married 1 Dec. 1836.
Wright, William's wife died 17 Feb. 1837.
Wright, Cintha, dau. of John P., had a child and put it in a hollow log 8 May 1837.
Wright, John P. & Christopher started south 20 Nov. 1837.
Wright, Christopher, born 30 Dec. 1795.
Wright, Elizabeth, wife of Christopher, born 6 May 1802.
Wright, Allen T., son of Christopher & Elizabeth, born 1 Sept. 1823.
Wright, John P., son of Christopher & Elizabeth, born 15 Jan. 1825.
Wright, Ardinna, dau. of Christopher & Elizabeth, born 14 Jan. 1827.
Wright, Sarah Ann, dau. of Christopher & Elizabeth, born 25 Oct. 1828.
Wright, Joseph J., son of Christopher & Elizabeth, born 29 Oct. 1830.
Wright, Polly, dau. of Christopher & Elizabeth, born 13 Sep. 1832.
Wright, Elizabeth, dau. of Christopher & Elizabeth, born 27 Oct. 1834.
Wright, Christopher, son of Christopher & Elizabeth, born 25 June 1836.

Wright, William, & Nancy Witcher, married 11 Jan. 1838.
Wright, Christopher, started for Charleston, S. C., 11 Mar. 1838.
Wright, John P., & Rebecca Jones, married 8 July 1841.
Wright, Royal, cut his throat, 14 Dec. 1838.
Wright, Sally, died 1 Dec. 1838.
Wright, John P.'s wife died 13 Apr. 1843.
Wright, Joseph's wife died 6 Sept. 1843.

Yates, Washington, & Milly Roach, married 2 Feb. 1832.
Yates, Serepta, dau. of Elizabeth, born 10 June 1824.
Young, William (Hatchett), & Lucinda Man, dau. of Harrison, married 11 Dec. 1828.
Young, Peyton, son of Peyton, died 24 Jan. 1832.

OLD TOMBSTONES IN NORTHAMPTON AND ACCOMAC COUNTIES, VA.[1]

I.

WARWICK, OR "QUINBY'S FARM",

In Northampton County.

In memory of Arthur Upshur[e]
born in y[e] County of Essex in y[e]
Kingdom of England who died
January 26, 1709 in y[e] 85th Year
of his Age.

In memory of Mary y[e]
Wife of Arthur Upshur
born in y[e] County of Warwick
in y[e] Kingdom of England
who died July y[e] 3d 1703
in y[e] 85th year of her Age.

535

APLINGTON.

[*Arms.*²]

Here lies the Body of
John Custis, Esq., one of the
Councill and Major Generall of
Virginia who departed this life ye
29th of January 1696 aged 66 years
And by his side a son and daughter
Of his Grandson John Custis whom
He had by the daughter of
Daniel Parke Esq. Capt. Generall
And Chief Governor of the Leeward
Islands.
Virtus Post Funera.

[*Arms.*]

Beneath this Marble Tomb lies yᵉ body
of the Honorable John Custis,⁴ Esq.,
of the City of Williamsburg and Parish of Bruton
Formerly of Hungars Parish on the Eastern Shore of
Virginia and the County of Northampton the
place of his nativity.
Aged 71 years and yet lived but seven years
Which was the space of time he kept
A Bachelor's House at Arlington
On the Eastern Shore of Virginia.
This information put on this tomb was by his
own positive order.

—Wm. Colley, Mason, in Fenchurch Street, London, Fecit.

III.

WILSONIA NECK.

Here lyeth yᵉ body of John Custis, Esq., one of the council of
Virginia colonel, and commander in Chief of the Militia on the
Eastern Shore of this coloney. He was the son of the Hon. John
Custis, of Arlington, and departed this life 26th of January, 1713,
and in the sixtieth year of his age. His first wife was Margerett,

Here lies the Body of
JOHN CUSTIS Esq one of the
Councill and Major Genam ll of
Virginia who departed this life ye
of January 1696 aged 66 years
on this side a son and daughter
his Grandson John Custis whom
he had by the daughter of
Daniel Parke Esq Capt General
and Chief Governor of the Leeward
Islands
Virtus Post Funera

ye daughter of Mr. John Michaell, by whome he had seven sons and two daughters, who with three of their sons lies near him. His second wife was Sarah, the daughter of Colonel Southy Littleton, and widow of Mr. Adam Michaell, who survived him, but hopes to be buried by him when she dies, as was his desire. Which accordingly now she is, and departed this life the 18th day of April, Anno Domini, 1720, and in the fifty first year of her age.

IV.

"POULSON PLACE," AT ONANCOCK.

Coll Tully Robinson[5]
late of Accomack Co., Va., who was
born August 31st 1658, and
departed November 12, 1723,
aged 65 years and twenty
— days.
A gentleman honourable, an
Ornament to all places. He
was loyall to his prince,
Unshaken to his friend, and
a true believer in the Church
of England.

V.

ONANCOCK.

[*Arms.*[6]]

Here lies the body of
Major Charles West[7]
who departed this life
Februry the 28th 1757
in the — year of his age.

VI.

DEEP CREEK.

Anthony West
Son of Anthony West and Eleanor his wife
Born August 24, 1760
Died February 2^d 1795

538

Revell West
Son of Anthony West and Eleanor his wife
Born March 15ᵗʰ, 1755.
Died December 26, 1802.

NOTES.

1. The editor received these inscriptions at second hand, and cannot vouch for the *order* of the lines, which is, doubtless, in some cases, not exact.

2. Arthur Upshur was the ancestor of Abel P. Upshur, Secretary of State during Tyler's administration, and one of the ablest men Virginia ever produced. Arthur Upshur (or Upshott, as his name is spelt in the earliest records) is said to have come from England as an apprentice of Colonel William Kendall. He appears to have taken a leading place on the Eastern Shore, though, as was the case with many country gentlemen in England about that time, he made his mark, being unable to write. The following patents appear in his name: 300 acres at head of Occahannock Creek—head-rights, Mary Risden, James Risden, Landilla Risden, Arthur Carpenter, Philip Sonshack, John Albert, March 11, 1655; 700 acres in same locality, October 20, 1661; on Matchepungo Creek, 2,000 acres, September 29, 1664; 2,000 acres formerly granted to Lieut.-Coll. Kendall, and assigned to Upshur September 29, 1665; 350 acres at the head of Broad Creek, a branch of Nassawaddox Creek. About 1655 "Arthur Upshott of Occahannock" married Mary, widow of James Risden; and about 1663 he married Mary, sister of George Clarke, philomedicus, and widow of Richard Jacob. Upshur may have had an earlier wife still. He had issue: 2, *Arthur;* 3, John; 4, Helen, who married ——— Stott; and 5, Ann, who married Benjamin Dolby. 2. ARTHUR married Sarah, co-heir with Anne, her sister (who married Andrew Hamilton, of Pennsylvania), of her father, a Quaker of great influence, Thomas Browne, inheriting 631 acres called "Brownsville," and on which resides Thomas T. Upshur, one of her descendants. The old dwelling-house is still standing, now converted into servants' quarters. The descent of Mr. Thomas[7] T. Upshur is: Arthur[1] (died in 1703), Arthur[2], Thomas[3], Thomas[4], John[5], Thomas[6], Thomas[7] T. Upshur. Abel P. Upshur was descended as follows: Arthur[1], married, 1st, Mary Risden; 2d, Mary Jacob; had Arthur[2], who married Sarah Browne; they had Abel[3], who married Rachel Revell, daughter of John Revell; they had Arthur,[4] who married Leah Custis, daughter of Henry Custis; they had Littleton,[5] who married Ann Parker, daughter of George Parker and his wife Ada Bagwell; they had ABEL[6] PARKER UPSHUR, who married, 1st, Elizabeth Dennis, who died s. p.; he married, 2d, Elizabeth Upshur, daughter of John and Ann Brown Upshur, and she had Susan Upshur, who married Lieutenant Ringold of the navy; issue, an only child, James T. Ringold, an attorney at law in Baltimore, Md.

3. These arms are described in John Custis's will as "three parrots," but I have seen no copy of the arms on the tombstones.

4. John Custis married, about 1706, Frances, daughter of Daniel Parke, Jr. A letter of Philip Ludwell, Sr., in 1707, refers to the marriage as if of recent occurrence. She died March 13, 1714–'15. (*Bruton Parish Register.*)

539

John Custis died November —, 1749 (*Ibid.*), and his will was dated November 14, 1749, and was proved at London, November 19, 1753. In it he directs his body to be carried from Williamsburg, where he resided, to Arlington, to be interred by the side of his grandfather, Honble John Custis, Esq., under a handsome white marble tombstone engraved with his arms, "three parrots." (*New Eng. Hist. and Gen. Register.*) As he was seventy-one years of age in 1749, he was born in 1678, and was twenty-eight or twenty-nine years old when he married Frances Parke. He probably reckoned his bachelorhood from his majority. The inscription eulogizing this period of "seven years" is found in his will. In the old family burying-ground, now owned by Major Mercer Waller, near Williamsburg, are tombstones of Frances Custis, his wife, and of two children whom her only son, Daniel Parke Custis, had by Martha Dandridge, afterwards George Washington's wife. (See Inscriptions, *Va. Hist. Soc. Collections*, Vol. XI.) Meade mentions as in the burying-ground the tombstone of Daniel Parke Custis, but it has been carried off. It appears from the inscriptions now published that John Custis had two other children besides Daniel Parke Custis. The emigrant Custis ancestor was John Custis, of Rotterdam, who was in Virginia in 1640. He had six sons: Thomas, of Baltimore, in Ireland; Edward, of London; Robert, of Rotterdam (a tavern-keeper there, whose daughter married Argall Yardley, son of the Governor, about 1649), and John, William, and Joseph, of Virginia. John, the son, was sheriff of Northampton county in 1664, and in 1676 was major-general during Bacon's Rising; and his estate of Arlington gave its name to the well-known Custis estate near Washington. The family was evidently originally from county Gloucester, England. The will of John Smithier, of *Arlington*, in the parish of Buybury and county of Gloucester, dated February 16, 1618, proved October 31, 1626, mentions his cousins, Henry Custis, *alias* Cliffe; "my son-in-law Edward Custis, *alias* Cliffe; and his son John Custis," as also William Custis, Nicholas Custis, etc. (*New Engl. Hist. and Gen. Register*, 195, 201.) See, for further information regarding the Custis family, Meade, I., 263; Geo. W. P. Custis's *Reminiscences; The Marshall Family; Standard*, III., 150; *Potter's American Monthly*, VI., 85; and other references in Goode's *Virginia Cousins.*

5. Colonel Tully Robinson was son of Captain William Robinson, a magistrate of lower Norfolk county. His daughter Scarborough married John Wise, ancestor of General Henry A. Wise. For an account of the Wise family, see *Richmond Standard*, IV., 3; Hambleton's *Life of Henry A. Wise.*

6. This tomb bears the West arms: on a fesse dancettee three leopards' faces jessant-de-lis. Anthony West came to Virginia in the James in 1622. (Hotten's *Immigrants.*) His will is dated October 12, 1651, proved May 5, 1652. His issue by Ann —— were: John and Katharine, the latter of whom married, 1st, Ralph Barlow, and 2dly, Sir Charles, eldest son of Lieut.- Colonel Edmund Scarburgh. John West became lieutenant-colonel, and was a contemporary of Colonel John West, of West Point. In Bacon's Rebellion he took sides with Bacon, and he and his kinsman, William Scarburgh, had to beg Sir William Berkeley's pardon on their bended knees. He married Matilda Scarburgh, and had Anthony, Alexander, John the Eldest, Benony, Jonathan, John the Younger, and several daughters. Major Charles West, of the text, was a son of either John the eldest or of Jonathan, as each of them had a son Charles; probably, however, of John "the eldest," who married Fran-

ces Yardley. Anne, the widow of Anthony West the immigrant, married, 2dly, Captain Stephen Charleton, who is pleasantly described by Colonel Norwood, in the account of his voyage in 1649, as living in Northampton in much comfort and hospitality. By a former wife, Bridget, Charleton had two daughters, Bridget and Elizabeth, between whom he divided his estate, with the proviso, however, that should the elder, Bridget, die without issue, her share should go to the support of a minister in the parish. Bridget married Isaac Foxcraft, but died without issue, and for many years the church in Nohrthampton had the property; but many years later the overseers of the poor brought suit for the same, and, after much litigation, the courts decided against the church. (See Meade, I., 256.) Elizabeth, the other daughter, was persuaded to elope with one John Gittings, at the age of twelve years, but died soon after; and there is on record in Northampton a singularly able paper by Surveyor-General Edmund Scarburgh, the second of the name, and brother of Sir Charles Scarburgh, protesting against the conduct of John Gittings. (See, also, Meade.)

INSCRIPTIONS FROM VARIOUS TOMBSTONES IN DINWIDDIE, CHESTERFIELD, HENRICO AND NEW KENT COUNTIES, VIRGINIA.

TRANSCRIBED

BY

CHURCHILL GIBSON CHAMBERLAYNE.

(From the family burying ground at "Porter Hill," corner of Harrison and Early streets, Petersburg, Va.)

IN
Memory of
MRS. LUCY ANN FANNY
wife of
John C. Armistead,
who departed this life
September 3rd 1824,
Aged 26 Years.
and 21 days.
Also her infant Son
GEORGE R. ARMISTEAD,
Aged 6 Days.

Sacred
TO THE MEMORY OF
JOHN C. ARMISTEAD,
WHO DEPARTED THIS LIFE
April 11, 1832,
Aged 50 Years.
In tender regard
Of his many virtues
As HUSBAND AND PARENT,
This monument is erected by his
Widow and Orphans
As the memento
Of their devoted affections.

IN
Memory of
WM. A. SYME,
Son of
Marcus A. & Mary
Ann Armistead,
Born Oct[r] 8, 1830,
Died Oct[r] 4, 1832.

Sacred
to the memory
of the
REV'D WILLIAM HARRISON [1]
who departed this life
20th of November 1814
Aged 84 Years.
In tender regard of whom
His Widow
hath caused this monument to be erected.
Here let him rest in peace
And let us try to live like him
That we like him may die.

SACRED
to the memory
of
MRS. ANN HARRISON.
who departed this life
July the 2nd 1829
Aged 60 Years.
Her Children
from a sense of duty & affection
have caused this monument
to be erected
in memory of
their tender Parent.
If worth departed claims the heartfelt tear,
Then stop—and let it stream profusely here.

543

SACRED
To the memory of
MARTHA M.
Wife of
THOMAS J. PERKINSON;
OF AMELIA;
Departed this life
DECEMBER, 29. 1836,
AGED 27 YEARS.
Blessed are the dead who
die in the Lord.

_(From the family burying ground at Matoax, the home of John
Randolph, Sr., father of John Randolph of Roanoke. This
place is about two miles west of Petersburg on the Appomattox river, in Chesterfield county, Va. The graveyard is on
a hill almost immediately overhanging the river.)_

MARTHA HALL
OB: IV: NON: MART:
M,DCC,LXXXIV.
Æ: XXXVIII.
Quam Sprevit Hymen Pollux
PHŒBUS que colere.

JOHANNES RANDOLP[H]
ob XXVIII OCTO:
MDCCLXXV.
Æ: XXXIV.
Non Ossibus Urna, nec Mens
Virtutibus absit.

I H S
FRANCESCÆ TUCKER.[2]
Blandæ Conjugis
Sti: GEORGII TUCKER.
Quis Desiderio sit Modus.
Obiit XVIII: Januarii,
MDCCLXXXVIII,
Æt: XXXVI.

544

SACRED
To the memory of
SYLVESTER J. PIERCE
Who departed this life
Dec. 25th 1865,
Aged 54 years.

(*From the family burying ground at "Oak Hill," Chesterfield
county, Va. "Oak Hill" is on the north bank of the Appomattox river, between Fleet's Hill and the Richmond Turnpike, opposite Petersburg.*)

JOHN RONEY
Died Feby 17th 1855
Aged 34 years.

In memory of my dog
CARL,
The faithful friend of
FANNY RICE.[3]
Died April 13, 1893.

(*From the family burying ground at "Violet Bank," on the Richmond Turnpike, in Chesterfield county, about half a mile
north of Petersburg, Va.*)

SACRED
To the memory of
MRS. ELIZABETH S. GILLIAM,
Relict of
JOHN GILLIAM, M. D.
And daughter of
THOMAS SHORE Esq.
of Violet Bank Chesterfield County.
Born January 26, A. D. 1797.
Departed this life March 20, A. D. 1858

545

HERE
ARE DEPOSITED THE REMAINS
OF
JOHN GILLIAM M. D.
OF PETERSBURG VA.
BORN APRIL 9TH. A. D. 1790
DEPARTED THIS LIFE AUGUST 15TH. A. D. 1843
IN MEMORY OF THE DECEASED
THIS TOMB
IS ERECTED BY HIS AFFLICTED WIFE.

WILLIAM McILVAINE WALLACE
Eldest son of
Dʳ J. M. Wallace of Philadelphia.
Born August 28, 1848.
Died February 20 1854.
Of such is the kingdom of Heaven.

(From a tablet in St. Peter's Church, New Kent county, Va.)

M S
Near this place lyes interred yᵉ
Body of Mʳ William Chamberlayne
Late of this Parish Merchᵗ.
Descended of an ancient & Worthy Family
in the County of Hereford.
He married Elizabeth yᵉ eldest Daughter
of Richard Littlepage of this County,
by whom he has left issue three Sons,
Edward Pye, Thomas,⁴ & Richard,
& two Daughters, Mary & Elizabeth
Ob: 2° Augᵗ 1736 Ætat 36.
Hoc Marmor exiguum summi amoris
Monumentum posuit Conjux mœstissima.
1737
Also Ann Kidly ⁵ Born Sence
Her *Father's Decease,*
M. Sidnell Briftol. fecit.

546

BENEATH REPOSE THE REMAINS

OF

WILLIAM JENNINGS

Born Oct'r 8th A. D. 1813.

Died Oct'r 29th A. D. 1851.

ALSO

His Infant Son

OSCAR JENNINGS

Born Jan'y 25th A. D. 1849.

Died Feb'y 10th A. D. 1849.

NOTES.

(1) Rev Wm Harrison was Minister of Bristol Parish Va from Nov-22nd 1762 to Feby 4th 1780. For references to him, see Slaughter's "A History of Bristol Parish," also "The Vestry Book and Register of Bristol Parish, Virginia 1720-1789"

(2) Mother of John Randolph of Roanoke. On page 292 of "The Vestry Book and Register of Bristol Parish, Virginia 1720-1789" there is this entry: "Frances Daughter of Theod Bland born 24th Sept 1752."

(3) While filling an engagement at the theatre in Petersburg in April 1893 Miss Fanny Rice, the actress, had the misfortune to lose her pet dog by sickness. It was attended by Dr. Potts a local veterinary surgeon, and at its death was buried by him at "Oak Hill" where he was then living.

(4) Thomas Chamberlayne married Wilhelmina Byrd, daughter of Col. William Byrd 2nd. See Hening's Statutes at Large, Vol. 6. Page 319.

(5) In Hening's Statutes at Large, Vol 5 Page 117 there is given an Act of the House of Burgesses making provision for this child.

INSCRIPTIONS ON OLD TOMBSTONES IN WESTMORE-LAND AND NORTHUMBERLAND COUNTIES.

(Copied from the tombstones by Rev. Dr. G. W. Beale, of Heathsville, Northumberland county, with the exception of the inscription on the tomb of Mrs. Ann Lee, which is taken from Dr. Lee's "Lee of Virginia," and of that on the tombstone of Izatis Anderson, near Cherry Point, which was copied by Mr. I. Basye Marsh.)

At Nominy Church, on the creek of the same name, there was at the time of the destruction of the building by the British in 1814, a tomb commemorative of the first wife of Hon. Richard Henry Lee, the inscription on which, as found among Mr. Lee's papers, and published by Dr. E. Jennings Lee, is as follows:

Sacred to the Memory
of Mrs. Ann Lee,* wife of R. H. Lee
This monument was erected by her
Afflicted husband in the year 1768.
Reflect, dear reader, on the great
Uncertainty of human life, since neither
esteem, temperament nor the most amiable
goodness could save this excellent lady from death.
In the bloom of life. She left behind her four children,
two sons and two daughters.
Obiit 12th December 1768, æt 30.

Was there so precious a flower
But given us to behold it waste,
The short-lived blossom of an hour
Too nice, too fair, too sweet to last.

---

* Mrs. Lee was the younger of the two daughters of Capt. William Aylett's second marriage with Elizabeth Eskridge, daughter of Major George Eskridge, of Sandy Point. Her sister Mary married Mr. Lee's brother, Thomas Ludwell. Her half-sisters by her father's previous marriage with Anne Ashton, were Elizabeth and Ann, who respectively married William Booth and W. Augustine Washington. Mrs. Lee's mother, after Captain Aylett's death, about 1744, married again, Col. James Steptoe, a widower with two daughters, Elizabeth and Ann, who married Philip Ludwell Lee, and Willoughby Allerton, and after their deaths P. R. Fendall and Samuel Washington. The four children referred to as surviving Mrs. Lee were Thomas, who afterwards settled in Prince William county, Ludwell, who went to Loudoun; Hannah, who married Corbin Washington, and Mary, who married William Augustine Washington. Mrs. Lee was buried in the old burial ground under the hills at Mount Pleasant.

At the bottom of the garden at Nominy Hall, the last century residence of Councillor Carter and his father, an upright slab has on it these words:

Here to the right of the late
J. J. Maund,* Esq., is
deposited the body of his dutiful
Daughter,
Mʳˢ Ann Arnest,
Who departed this life
On the 23ᵈ day of May,
1818, in her 28ᵗʰ
Year.

Such consummate goodness and worth combined
Are rarely met with in the human mind.
Go, sweet Anna, such excellence by thy Maker given
Will find acceptance in the court of Heaven.

———

Here lieth
The Body of the once very useful
Magistrate and Deacon,
JOSEPH PIERCE, *
A lover of Truth, Justice and the
RELIGION OF JESUS CHRIST.
Who departed this Life June 5th,
1798, about the 70th year of his Age.

The serpent need not gape for prey,
  Nor Death his victory boast,
For Jesus takes the Sting away
  And all their power is lost.
Then let the Just with Jesus sleep,
  In undisturbed repose,
And only lie thus buried deep
  To rise as once He rose.

---

* J. J. Maund emigrated from Wales (Pembrokeshire) and married August 1, 1789, Harriet Lucy, one of the daughters of Hon. Robert Carter and Francis Tasker. Their eldest daughter—Anna Martin Maund—married Dr. John Arnest, and died (as above) May 23, 1818, leaving three sons and a daughter—George (of Texas), John (of California), Thomas M. (of Nominy Hall, Westmoreland), and Sophia (Mrs. Dozier).

Here lies the remains
of the late SARAH E. PIERCE,
late wife to Joseph Pierce.*
She had 5 daughters and 4
sons. She departed this life
the 20th day of Septembr in the
Year of our Lord 1783 in the
49th year of her Age.

In Memory of
MARGARET G. HERNDON,
Born June 17th 1808.
Died Decembr 26th, 1841.
The memory of the just is blessed.
Erected by Elder R. H. Herndon.

The three inscriptions given above were copied from three
upright slabs in the grave yard at Level Green, the old Pierce
homestead, one mile from Templeman's, Westmoreland county.
The slabs were found beneath a cluster of graceful and majestic
cedars beside a woods, and not many rods distant from where the
old mansion stood, not a vestige of which is now visible.

At Wilmington the early seat of the Newtons, near the head
of Bonum's Creek, in Westmoreland, two horizontal slabs sup-
ported each by six carved stones, may be seen near the road. The
inscription from one of these, placed over Mrs. Sarah Newton,
was published in a previous issue of the QUARTERLY (Vol. VII.,**
No. 2, October, 1898). The other tomb appears to have been
erected at the same time that its companion was, and chiselled by

---

* Capt. Joseph Pierce was the second son of William Pierce of Westmoreland, whose will of August, 1733, mentions him, and was grandson
of William and Sarah Pierce, early settlers in the county. The elder
William made his will March 25, 1702. His name is perpetuated in
Pierce's Creek, an arm of Nominy. Capt. Joseph Pierce married Sarah
Ransdell, and among his children were son Ransdell, and daughters
Martha, Sally Ransdell, Margaret (married elder R. H. Herndon), Fannie, and Sibella (married Samuel Templeman). Captain Pierce, in his
will, dated January 1, 1796, liberated a large number of slaves. He is
honorably mentioned in Semple's *History of Virginia Baptists*.

**Pages 524-525, this volume.

the same hand—the two stones being in size, general design and style of lettering precisely alike. Owing, however, to flaws in the stone the inscription on one tomb is nearly obliterated. The following words are indistinctly legible.

Beneath this stone are deposited
The Remains of
M^{rs} E L I Z A B E T H O L D H A M *

* * * * * *

* * * * * *

Samuel Oldham,† of Westmorel^d County

* * * * * *

* * * * * *

* * * Faithful Friend

* * * * * *

Departed this Life
On the   Day of April, 1759,
In the 72^d year of her Age.

In the graveyard at Mantua, on Coan River, in Northumberland, formerly the residence of Col. James M. Smith, are to be seen, within a brick enclosure, a number of tombs. One of them is thus inscribed:

Sacred
To the Memory of
JAMES SMITH
born in the township of Cahery
County of Derry, Ireland.
He departed this life
on the 8th of February, 1832
in the 64th year of his Age.

---

* The above mentioned tombs at Wilmington were, doubtless, loving tributes paid by the first Willoughby Newton, of Westmoreland, to his wife and his mother. Mrs. Elizabeth Oldham was the daughter of Nehemiah Starke, of Washington Parish, and stepdaughter of Major Andrew Gilson, who married Behethland Dade. She married, first, Capt. Thomas Newton (son of the emigrant John, "master mariner"), and after his death, in 1728, she married again, Col. Samuel Oldham. In a deed (September 28, 1728) conveying her part of land granted by patent to her mother Gilson, she styles Willoughby Newton "my son and heire."

† A diligent search for the parentage and children (if any) of Col. Samuel Oldham has failed of success.

Two slabs here bear pathetic testimony to the similar bereavement of their young wives by father and son.

To the Memory of
Ann, the wife of
James Smith
and daughter of
Daniel Muse,
who closed an humble
and useful life
On the 16th October, 1799,
in the 21st year of her Age.

Sacred
to the memory of
ELIZABETH, consort of
James M. Smith,
And only daughter of
Eli Hewitt, Esq.
of Baltimore,
who departed this life
on the 16th of September, 1827,
In the twentieth year of her Age.

Other slabs at Mantua read as follows:

Sacred
to the memory of
AGNES A.,*
wife of
JAMES M. SMITH,
And Daughter of
Willoughby and Sally Newton,
of Westmoreland Cot^y,
who departed this life
May 8th, 1849, in
the 42d year of her age.
Blessed are the dead who die in the Lorwd.

* Mrs. Agnes A. Smith was a daughter of Willoughby Newton and
Sally (Poythress) Newton, of Lee Hall, in Westmoreland, her mother

Sacred
To the Memory of
CHARLES HOWARD,
Son of
Thomas and Catharine Howard,
of Richmond, Va.
who departed this life
October 3ᵈ, 1854,
In the 41ˢᵗ year of
his age.
"He fell asleep."

Sacred to
the memory of
HUGH B. HILL,
son of Robert and Temperance Hill
of Buckingham County,
Virginia, who departed
this life on the
20ᵗʰ December, 1849,
in the 25th year
of his age.

Near Cherry Point, in Northumberland county, lies a tombstone which bears an inscription conveying a moral just the reverse of that of Col. John Custis' tombstone at Arlington, in the county of Northampton, which latter states that, "though Col. Custis died at the age of 71, he lived but seven years, which was the space of time he kept a bachelor's house at Arlington on the Eastern Shore of Virginia."

---

having been, previous to her marriage to Mr. Newton, the wife of "squire" Richard Lee. Mrs. Elizabeth Oldham, the relict of Captain Thomas Newton, previously mentioned, was her great-great-grandmother.

Here lies the body of
IZATIS ANDERSON,
late of this county, who was born
on the 7th day of February, 1779, and died
the 11th day of August, 1823,
Aged 44 years 6 months and 7 days.
He was a worthy and estimable man
A kind neighbor, a faithful friend
and good citizen.
In other relations of life he might have been
equally praiseworthy, but he died a bachelor,
having never experienced the comfort of being
a husband or father. This situation he found
so comfortless that in his last will he
directed this stone to be placed over his
remains, with an inscription
warning all young men from imitating an
example of celibacy,
which had yielded to himself
no other eventual fruits
but disappointment and remorse.
Inscribed at his request by his friends,
Hierom L. Opie
and
Fleming Bates.

EARLY TOMBS IN WESTMORELAND, RICHMOND AND NORTHUMBERLAND COUNTIES.

By Dr. G. W. Beale.

In the yard of the Episcopal Chapel, at Port Conway, is a slab which has been removed from Smith's Mount, in the vicinity of Leedstown, in Westmoreland, where, in a neglected condition, it was likely to suffer mutilation. It bears the following inscription:

Beneath this marble

Are deposited

the remains of

MAJOR HARRY TURNER *

1751,

And

ELIZABETH his wife

1752

Who with Credit and Esteem

Poſſeſſed and enjoyed

An Ample Fortune

From which Unerring Wisdom

Thought fit to snatch them

In their Bloom

Together with three Sons

Who all dyed

In their infancy.

At Chestnut Hill, in Richmond county, a massive slab, which has sunk to the level of the earth, is marked as follows:

---

* Major Harry Turner was the only son to reach manhood of Dr. Thomas Turner, the immigrant. He married Elizabeth, the only surviving daughter of Col. Nicholas Smith, of "Smith's Mount," in Westmoreland. Major Turner left one son, Thomas, who married Jane Fauntleroy, daughter of Col. William Fauntleroy, of "Naylor's Hole." Thomas Turner had by his wife Jane four sons and four daughters.

(*Arms.*)

Here lies the body of
CAPT. THOMAS BEALE, JUN[r] †
Who tooke to wife ANN,‡ the daughter
Of Col. William Gouge, and had
By her two sons and two daughters.
He departed this life on the
Sixteenth day of October, Anno
dom. 1679.
Ætatis suæ 30

In midst of tempests when the torrents raved
Deeply for mercy to the Lord I craved,
Whose goodness then so pitied me distrest
His mercies wrought my soul's eternal rest.
Miserecordia vicina est miserae.

At Doctor's Hall, in Richmond county, near where Rappahannock Creek empties into the river of that name, among horizontal slabs and headpieces, that lie for the most part broken and in disorder, the following fragmentary inscriptions appear:

---

† Capt. Thomas Beale was the only son of Col. Thomas Beale, of York county, who was a member of the council under Governor Berkeley. He is named in *Hening*, Vol. II., p. 421.

‡ Mrs. Ann Beale was daughter of Major William Gooch, of Temple Farm, near Yorktown. Her children by Capt. Beale were sons Thomas and Charles, and daughters Anne and Hannah(?). After Capt. Beale's death she was married to William Colston, clerk of Rappahannock county, and had by him sons William and Charles and daughter Susanna.

William Colston directed in his will (October 7, 1701) that a gravestone should "be sent for out of England for the grave of my deare wife Anne," but no sign of it has been visible for many years. The arms on the tombstone of Capt. Thomas Beale, at Chestnut Hill, corresponds to the arms in Burke's *Heraldry of Beale of London:* Sa. on a chev between three griffins' heads erased ar. three estoiles gu. Crest: A unicorn's head erased or, semce d'estoiles gu.

John Brockenbrough *
Ob. 20 Nov. 1801 Æt. 60
[Sa]rah Brockenbrough *
1810. Æt. 60.
John Harvie Brockenbrough †

.   .   .   .   .   .

.   .   .   .   .   .

[Departed this life] on the 20ᵗʰ day
of October, 1810.

Here repose the remains of
Henrietta A. Nelson,
daughter of
Dʳ. Wᵐ A. Brockenbrough ‡
Who died Feb'y 4, 1854
Aged 4 years and 4 mos.
The Spirit hast led this Angel
child from earth to Heaven.

In the grave-yard at Sabine Hall, in Richmond county, the
residence of Mr. R. Carter Wellford are several tombs, from
which the subjoined epitaphs are taken. One, surmounted by
the Carter coat-of-arms, is as follows:

---

* John Brockenbrough, M. D., was son of Col. William Brockenbrough
and Margaret Fauntleroy. He was one of the signers of the Westmoreland Protest of 1764 against the Stamp Act. He married Sarah Roane,
who bore him five gifted sons and a daughter, Lucy. Of his sons, William was judge of the Virginia Court of Appeals; John, president of
Bank of Virginia, and intimate friend of John Randolph of Roanoke;
Arthur, proctor of University of Virginia; Austin, M. D., of Tappahannock, and Thomas.

† John Harvie Brockenbrough was presumably a son of Dr. John
Brockenbrough, of Richmond, and Gabriella (Harvie) Randolph, and
died in infancy.

‡ Dr. William A. Brockenbrough married Miss Mary Carter Gray,
daughter of Dr. T. B. W. Gray. They had ten children, a number of
whom still survive.

Epitaphs in these days savoring
More of Flattery than Truth
'Tis confessedly difficult to credit
Much the Elegies on the
Dead
But that merit may not fail of meeting with it deserts
From those whose duty it is
To acknowledge it
This tomb is erected to the memory of
ELIZABETH CARTER *
Eldest daughter of John Wormley, late
of Middlesex county, Esqr.
By her grateful husband Landon Carter, Esqr. of this
Parish and County. She departed
this life ye 31st day of January in
the year of our Lord, 1740, and in the
27th year of her age, leaving
Four children to lament their
Loss sustained in her Death with
That of their Father

If true Piety, Perfect Friendship
Parental Tenderness and Conjugal
Affection are deserving of esteem
She must be truly admired whose Life was
One continued
Proof of her being of the number of the
Sincerest Christians,
Best of Friends,
Best of Mothers
And best of Wives
As these virtues do necessarily produce
An easy department
Her rare Beauty
And Comeliness of Body
Were greatly advantaged by them
And as Prudently Protected by a decent
Reservedness in Behaviour.

---

* Elizabeth (Wormley) Carter is named in *Hen. Statutes*, Vol. V.,
p. 86, as having received of her father a legacy of £800. She had a

The inscriptions on the tombs of Landon Carter and his wife, Catharine Tayloe, are as follows:

LANDON CARTER *
Born June 16th, 1757,
Died Aug. 30th, 1820.
CATHARINE CARTER †
‗ Wife of Landon Carter
Born October 10th, 1761.
Died December 22^d, 1798.

Midway between Warsaw and Mount Airy, in Richmond county, in a field on the north side of the main road, stands a solitary headstone inscribed as follows:

This Tomb is
Erected to the Mem-
ory of SIMON SALLARD
only SON of
CHARLES and ANN
SALLARD who
departed this life
the 10th of September, 1760, and in the
seventh year of
his age.

Near the rear wall of North Farnham Church, and broken in two near the ground by the pressure of a locust tree that has been allowed to grow beside it, is an upright slab, the lettering on which reads as follows:

---

brother Ralph, and sisters Judith, Sarah and Agatha, the first named of these sisters having married Col. George Lee, of Mt. Pleasant, in Westmoreland. Mrs. Carter was the first of the three wives of Col. Landon Carter, and bore him two daughters and a son—Elizabeth, Lucy and Robert.

* Landon Carter was son of Robert Wormley Carter and Winifred Beale, and was named for his grandfather, the founder of Sabine Hall.

† Catharine Carter was the sixth daughter of Col. John Tayloe and Rebecca Plater, of Mt. Airy. She was mother of four of Mr. Carter's children, viz., Winifred, Lucy, Elizabeth and Robert Wormley. After her death, her husband married Miss Mary B. Armistead, who also bore him four children.

559

Beneath this Stone
Lie the Remains of KATHARINE
The wife of
ARCH'D M^cCALL, Merch^t in Tap^a,
And only Daughter
of
Dr NICHOLAS * & ELIZ^a FLOOD
Who departed this Life
On the 5th January, 1767,
In the 25th year of her Age
Leaving issue
Two daughters ELIZ^a &
KATH. FLOOD.

Near the Yeocomico, in Cherry Point, Northumberland county, on the plantation known as Texas, which was so called by the late Colonel Ferdinand Blackwell after his return from an unsatisfactory residence in the "Lone Star" State, is a neglected grove standing in the midst of one of the large fields, and overshadowing a number of tombs commemorating various families who have lived on the farm. Interesting among these tombs is one of massive form which lies flat upon the ground, and is sunk to its level. It notes probably the earliest death in the Northern Neck represented by a stone. The inscription is as follows:

HERE LYETH THE BODY OF M^r
DAVID LINDSY † DOCTOR OF
DIVINITY WHO DEPARTED THIS LIFE
THE 3^d DAY OF APRIL 1667.

---

* Dr. Nicholas Flood married Elizabeth Jones, sister of Dr. Walter Jones, and lived near Farnham Church. He was a brother of Dr. Wm. Flood, who lived near him. He died in 1778, and his will—an interesting document—is on record at Warsaw. In it he gives minute directions as to his burial beside his daughter "at the east end of North Farnham Parish Church." Mrs. McCall had two daughters, Elizabeth and Catharine, who were educated in England.

† The Rev. David Lindsy's will was probated in Northumberland court. His wife's name was Susanna. His only daughter was married to Capt. Opie, and was named Helen. He also left a son named Robert. The simple and unpretentious inscription on David Lindsy's tomb, as here correctly given, is in singular contrast with the erroneous version of it contained in the book entitled *The Lindsays of America*.

HERE ALSO LYETH THE BODY
OF CAPT. THOMAS OPIE † IUNIOR OF
BRISTOL, GRANDSON OF M^r
DAVID LINDSY WHO DEPARTED
THIS LIFE THE 16th DAY OF
NOVEMBER, 1702.

A solitary slab in the yard of old Wicomico Church, in North-umberland, is to the memory of the wife of John Degge (or Digge), who appears in 1783 to have resided in Christ Church Parish, in Lancaster, and to have wife named Dorothy, pre-sumably by a second marriage. This slab is sunken below the surrounding turf, and the epitaph in verse is illegible. The inscription, as far as it can be now deciphered, is as follows:

Beneath this Marble
Lieth the Body of
SARAH DEGGE wife
of
JOHN DEGGE who departed
this life the 3^d day of February, 1778,
in the 57th year of her age.
Give now my exalted soul
O God . . . . .

Under a little cluster of trees, near the margin of Taskmaker's Creek, in Northumberland, on an upright marble headpiece, with no other tomb or grave visible, appears the following inscrip-tion:

In Memory
of
MITCHELL SCARBURGH
Who was born 1718
and died 1764.

---

† Captain Thomas Opie, Jr., left at least one son, John, who married Ann Metcalf, and died in 1722, leaving two sons, Lindsay and Thomas, and daughter Susanna. From him have sprung a numerous line of de-scendants in Virginia, Maryland and other States.

In the grave-yard at Ditchley, in Wicomico, Northumberland, the inscriptions on the tomb of Hancock Lee, Esq., and his two wives, are as follows:

Here Lyeth the Body of
HANCOCK LEE seventh son of the
Honorable Richard Lee who
Departed this life May the 25th
Anno Dom. 1729 Æta 56 years.
Also Mary * his first wife, only
Daughter of William Kendall, Gent.
Who departed this life December
The 24th Anno Dom. 1694
Æta 33 years,
And Sarah † his last wife
Daughter of Isaac Allerton, Esq.,
Who Departed this life
May the 17th Anno Dom. 1731.
Æta 60 years.

---

* Mrs. Lee appears, from *Hen. Stat.*, Vol. VI., p. 443, and Vol. VIII., p. 278, to have been well endowed with lands by her father, Col. Wm. Kendall, of Newport House, Northampton county. Her children by Hancock Lee appear to have been William, Anna and Richard.

† Col. Isaac Allerton, who died in Westmoreland, in December, 1702, in his will names among his children "my dear daughter Sarah Lee." Her children by Hancock Lee were Hancock, Isaac, John, Ann and Elizabeth.

EARLY TOMBS IN WESTMORELAND, RICHMOND, AND NORTHUMBERLAND COUNTIES.

(*Continued from page* 130.)

By Rev. Dr. G. W. Beale.

Tombs in White Chapel Church Yard, Lancaster Co., Va.

In the yard of White Chapel Church, in Lancaster county, there are a group of heavy horizontal tombs, and several vertical slabs, cŏmmemorative of members of the Ball family and their wives. One of the massive tombs has this inscription:

Here lies Interred the
Body of Mr DAVID BALL *
a twin and seventh son of
Capt WILLIAM BALL Gent.
Dece'd was born ye 26th of
Sep. 1686, and departed
this life ye 14th of December, 1732
in the 47th Year
of his Age.

A tomb near the one above bears these words:

Here lies the Body of
Mr JEDUTHAN BALL † son of Col^o
JAMES BALL of Lancaster county.
Born the 9th Day of July, 1725,
and Died the 5th Day of March,
1749, in the 25th year of his Age.

---

* David Ball was the sixth son of Capt. William Ball, the second of the name in Lancaster. He was brother to Col. James Ball, whose tomb is near his own. He was twice married, but left no issue.

† Jeduthan Ball was the fourth son of Col. James Ball and Mary Conway, and was brother to James and Jesse Ball, whose tombs are near his own. He married Elizabeth Fox, and was father of Col. Burges Ball, of the Revolution.

A similar horizontal stone is thus inscribed:

Here lyeth Interred the Body of
JESSE BALL ‡ Gent.
He was born 27th Day of June 1716
and departed this Life
the 11th Day of Aug., 1747,
in the 32nd Year of his Age.

The three inscriptions below are from the tombs of Col. James Ball, of Bewdley, and two of his wives:

Here lieth the Body of
MARY * the Wife of JAMES BALL
Daughter of EDWIN CONWAY Gent.
deceased, who departed this life
the 15th Day of September, 1730
in the 44th year of her Age.
leaving three sons and five Daughters
She was a loving Wife, a tender Mother
a peaceable, good neighbour, and lived
and died a pattern of Piety and Virtue.

Here also lieth interred ye Body of
ye above mentioned JAMES BALL Gent., dec'd,
Who departed this Life the 13th Day
of Oct. 1754, in ye 76th Year of his Age
having lived in the constant
Practice of Temperance and Sobriety
and other moral Virtues & died in
a Steadfast Faith in CHRIST
& full hope of a glorious Resurrection

---

‡ Jesse Ball, an older brother to Jeduthan, married Mary, daughter of J. Philip Smith, who names her in his will of July 11, 1743. She was sister to Baldwin M. Smith, and was married a second time (1749) to Col. John Lee, of Westmoreland. She again married John Smith. Jesse Ball's marriage is usually incorrectly given in the published genealogies of the Balls.

* She married Col. Ball April 18, 1707, he being a widower at the time, and sne a widow. Her previous husband was John Daingerfield, and his previous wife Ann (Elizabeth?) Howson.

Here lyeth the Body of
MARY ANN † Wife of JAMES BALL
Gent. and daughter of the
Reverend JOHN BERTRAND
She departed this life the 12th
of February 17⁴⁹/₅₀ in the 60th
Year of her Age.
She was a dutiful Wife, a Tender
Mother, and very Charitable to the Poor.

The following three commemorate Col. James Ball II., and
two of his wives:

In memory of

Col. JAMES BALL
2nd Son of James &
Mary Ball, his 2nd wife
daughter of
Edwin Conway.
Born Dec. 31st, 1718.
Died Nov'r 24th, 1789.

Here lieth the Body of
MILDRED BALL Wife of JAMES BALL
Jun'r, Gent. who departed this life the
1st day of Dec'r 1751 in the 26th year
of her Age
Leaving one son and three Daughters,
having faithfully discharged
the several Duties incumbent on a wife
and Parent, a Neighbour & a Christian.

---

† She was a widow when she married Col. Ball, having been married
before to William Ballendine.

In memory of

LETTICE *
3^d wife of
Colonel James Ball,
daughter of
Richard Lee of Ditchley
Died Nov'r 17th 1811,
in the 80th year of her age.

In memory of

Col. JAMES BALL †
Son of James & Lettice Ball
Born Feb. 20, 1755,
Died Dec'r 18, 1825.
And FANNY his wife
daughter of Rawleigh
& Frances Downman
Of Morattico.
Born May 4th, 1758.
Died Jan'y 23rd. 1821.

One grave contains the faithful pair.

---

* Lettice (Lee) Ball was daughter of Richard Lee and Judith Steptoe.

† Col. Ball lived at Bewdley, where he died not long after the death of his promising son William Lee Ball, whose end came in 1824, while a member of Congress, and who was buried in the Congressional Cemetery in Washington.

On a dark stone slab sunken to the level of the soil, and placed near one of the doors of the church, is the tomb of one of the early clerks of Lancaster. The inscription is in these words:

Here Lieth interred the Body of
JOHN STRETHLEY ‡ Gent.
who departed this life the
8th Day of December, 1698,
in 50th year of his Age.

INSCRIPTIONS FROM TOMBSTONES
In King and Queen, Westmoreland, Hanover and Albemarle Counties.

I.

From a tombstone lying near the Mattaponi River, in King and Queen county, near Little Plymouth.

Here lies the body of Thomas Thorpe Gent. who died on the 19th day of August, 1759, aged 58 years.

II.

From Smith's Mount in Westmoreland county.

(Arms.)
Beneath this Marble
Are deposited
The Remains of
Major Henry Turner (1)
1751
and
Elizabeth his wife
1752.
Who with Credit and Esteem
Possess'd and enjoy'd
An Ample Fortune
From which unerring wisdom
Thought fit to snatch them
In their Bloom.
Together with three Sons
who All dyed
In their infancy.

---

‡ He was probably related to Capt. William Ball, as one of the latter's sons appears to have been named for him.

III.

From a tombstone near Beaverdam, Hanover county.

I H S
Patrick Belsches
Born 19th September 1733
and
Departed this Life
6 January 1766.

IV.

From the churchyard at Point of Fork, Hanover county.

In memory of My Father
Capt. Thomas Price Senr.
Who died 21st December
1836.
Aged 82 years.
This stone was Erected
By his affectionate son,
P. H. Price.

In memory of My Mother
Barbara Price,
Who died 21st of May 1831
Age —————— yrs.
This stone ————— ected
by her affectionate son.
P. H. Price.

John Samuel Temple
Born Nov. 24th 1800
Married Maria D. Price
Oct. 7th 1824
Died Aug. 2nd 1834.

Maria Doswell Temple
Wife of
John Samuel Temple
Born Feb. 2nd 1807
Died Feb. 21st 1837.

Mrs. Elizabeth T. Price,
who died March 1st 1850.

Thomas Price Jr.
Son of Thomas & Barbara Price
who departed this life the 31st of
October 1838 aged 57 years.

Ann Callis,
Born in Hanover Nov. 4th 1774
died in Louisa county
Sep. 8, 1846.

Judith Carter Nelson,
Daughter of Gov. Jno. Page,
& widow of
Judge Robert Nelson
of Williamsburg,
obt. Augt. 24, 1845.
Æ 62

Hugh Thomas Nelson,
who died at Oakland
in the county of Hanover,
Jan. 10th 1843
in the 36th year of his age.
He was the eldest son of
Thomas & Judith Nelson
and Grandson of
Col. Hugh Nelson &
Genl. Thomas Nelson.

Thomas Nelson
born at Chilton Hanover Co.
Nov. 24th 1780
Died at Oakland, Hanover Co.
June 5th 1859.
Hughella N. Page.
obt. Aug. 15, 1844
Æ 22

Susan, wife of Francis Page
& daughter of
Gen. Thomas Nelson,
Born at York Town, Va.,
Octr. 3ᵈ. 1780
Died at Frederick Town Md.
Jany. 8ᵗʰ 1850
Æt. 70

Francis Page, born at
Rosewell Gloucester Co. Va.
1ˢᵗ April 1780
died at Rugswamp, Hanover Co.
Nov. 4ᵗʰ 1849
Æt. 70

Alice Grymes Digges
daughter of Gov. Jno. Page,
& widow of Dudley Digges,
ob. 10 May 1846.

Lucy, wife of
Hugh N. Pendleton
Granddaughter of
Govʳˢ. Thos. Nelson & John Page,
and only child of
Judge Robert Nelson
On the 20ᵗʰ of May 1837
At the age of 33 years and a
few days, her spirit returned
unto him who gave it.

Dudley Digges, died Apl. 4ᵗʰ 1839
Aged 74.

Edmund Pendleton, born 18 April 1774
died 23 January 1847.

Thomasia Meade, wife of the
Rt. Rev'd William Meade
born May 6th 1796
died July 26th 1836

Mrs. Lucy Nelson,
Relict of
Gov. Thomas Nelson.
she died Sep. 18th 1830
Aged 87 years and 14 days.

Jane Byrd Page, daughter of
John & Jane Page,
of North River, Gloster County
and wife of
Nathaniel Nelson, of York Town,
who died at Offley Hoo, in Hanover
county, Feby. 2nd 1782 in the 19th
year of her age.

V.

From tombstones in Aylett Burying-ground, on "Fairfield" Farm, King William county, Va. (2)

Here lies Interred the Body of
Martha Aylett wife of Philip Aylett
and Daughter of the Honourable
William Dandridge and Unity
Dandridge, who died the 25th of
April 1747 in the 26th year of her
age and left behind her two
Daughters and two sons, Viz:
Unity Williams, Ann and John Aylett.

Here lies the body of
Philip Aylett [1] son of
Col. William Aylett
Who died at "Montville"
11th of Septr 1835 in 65th year
of his age.

[1] He married Elizabeth Henry.

Here lies the Body of
Patrick Henry Aylett
Son of
Philip Aylett
of King William
Who died Whilst a student at
the University of Virginia
on the 28th of January, 1829,
Aged 20 years and
7 months.

Here lies the Body of
William Aylett
Son of
Philip Aylett
Who died at Montville
On the 11th February, 1829
Aged 22 years
and 1 month.

Gen[l] Philip Aylett
of Montville
Born 1787
Died 10 Sept. 1848
This stone is erected to his memory
by his bereaved Widow & Children.

In Memory
of
Judith Page
Wife of
Gen. Philip Aylett
Died
At Selma Alabama
May 7, 1860
aged 56 years.

VI.

Inscriptions copied from tombstones in the "Lewis" Graveyard, near
Charlottesville, March 14, 1892, by Robert W. Lewis.

Here
Lies the Body of
Nicholas Lewis
Born January 19th 1734,
And Departed this
Life December 8th 1808.

In
Sacred
Memory of
Thomas Walker Lewis
Born June The 24th 1763,
And Departed this life
June the 7th 1807.
Aged 44 years.

NOTES.

(1) Major Henry Turner, or Harry Turner, as he was generally called, was son of Thomas Turner, who was son of Thomas Turner (King George County Records). Thomas Turner was sworn clerk of King Geòrge, Sept. 6, 1723. His will was dated 19th of February, 1757, and was proved May 4, 1758; mentions land in King George, Prince William and Westmoreland counties; names his son-in-law, Capt. Edward Dixon, and the latter's sons Harry Dixon and Thomas Dixon, grandsons Thomas Turner and Henry Turner, granddaughter Sally Turner, niece, Ann Wrenn's son, John Wrenn; refers to his son Harry Turner's will; names daughter Mary Turner. His son, Major Harry Turner died before his father in 1751; and in his will mentions his father Thomas Turner, brother Thomas Turner's son Charles, nephews Harry Dixon and Turner Dixon; names son Thomas and wife Elizabeth. Elizabeth Turner, last named, was daughter of Colonel Nicholas Smith, whose epitaph has been already printed. (See QUARTERLY, VI., p. 42.)* Soon after Major Turner's death, she married Bowler Cocke, Jr. She left an only son, Col. Thomas Turner, who married Jane (born August 15, 1749), daughter of Col. William Fauntleroy, of Nayler's Hole, in Richmond county, about the year 1767, and left a family of eight children—four sons and four daughters. The sons were Henry, Thomas, Richard and George. In 1794, Henry Smith Turner advertised "Smith's Mount," consisting of 1700 acres, for sale.

(2) I owe these inscriptions to Miss Alice Page Aylett, daughter of Col. William R. Aylett, and niece of Patrick Henry Aylett. She writes: "By the side of the tombstone of Martha Aylett is another, whose inscription is worn off. I have heard that Unity West lies here. Elizabeth Henry (daughter of Patrick Henry) lies by her husband, Philip Aylett, but has no tombstone. Donald Robertson, who came from Scotland

*See *Genealogies of Virginia Families: From the William and Mary College Quarterly Historical Magazine* (Baltimore: Genealogical Publishing Co., Inc., 1982), Vol. IV, p. 484.

about 1760, had a school near Aylett's Warehouse, on the King and Queen side of the Mattaponi, and worshipped in old Cattail Church. His daughter Lucy Robertson married Mr. Semple, and was the mother of Mrs. Ada Semple Bradford, of Springfield, Illinois, who lately made a handsome gift of silver plate to our church. Mrs. Bradford has a number of the school books of Donald Robertson, with some of his pupils' names in them." (John Walker Semple, son of John Semple, a lawyer of King and Queen county, and Elizabeth Walker, and grandson of Rev. James Semple, pastor of Long Dreghorn, Ayrshire, married, first, Miss Laurie, of Caroline county, and, secondly, Lucy Robertson. Issue, *inter alios* Adaline Matilda, who married John S. Bradford, of Springfield, Illionis.)

INSCRIPTIONS ON SOME OLD TOMBSTONES.

COPIED BY JOSEPH LYON MILLER, M. D.

Tombs at Winchester, Va.

MAJOR GENERAL DANIEL MORGAN
departed this life
On July the 6th, 1802.
. . . . 67th year of his age.
Patriotism and Valor were the
prominent Features of his Character
and
the honorable Services he rendered
his country
During the Revolution . . .
crowned him with Glo . . .
rema . . . in the Heart . . .
Countrymen
. . . petual Monum . . .
to his
Memory.

---

* Look into some modern geography for this lake and its discoverer— I think Schontino.

In Memory of
Mary, the beloved Wife of
M^r. Philip Dalby
late of Winchester.
She departed this Life
In Hope of a joyful Resurrection
Through Christ
The first day of January
1790
Aged 28 years.

This stone is a hard bluish black one, and has an elaborate border traced around the inscription. In one corner is the name of the maker— "Firinadge Leicister, Sculp., England."

———

Here Lieth the Body of
PRISCILLA ROBINSON,
Wife of
Albert Robinson
of Baltimore Towne,
who departed this life
The 7th of July, 1790
aged 30 years.
In her were blended
The affectionate Wife
& Sympathizing Friend
Amiable in her manners
& Sincere in her friendship
She possessed in an eminent degree
The love & esteem
of all who had the pleasure
of her acquaintance.

———

Mural tablet in the vestibule of the Episcopal church.

In Memory of
THOS. LORD FAIRFAX,
who died 1782,
and whose ashes
Repose underneath
this church,
which he endowed.

The Fairfax arms are cut above the inscription. The inscription is not correct, as Lord Fairfax died December 7, 1781.

There are many tombstones at Winchester antedating the civil war, but I did not make copies of them.

INSCRIPTIONS ON TWO OF THE OLD TOMBSTONES IN CHRIST CHURCH-YARD, ALEXANDRIA.

This Monument
Sacred to the once lov'd & esteem'd
CAPT. GEORGE MUNFORD,
late of New London, in the
colony of Conneticut.   He
departed this Transatory
Life at George Town July 17th 1773
in the 28th year of his age.
Behold Fond Man
See here thy Pictured Life
Pass some few years thy flow'ry Sprinᵍ.
Thy sober Autumn fading into age
pale concluding Winter comes at last
& Shutts the scene.

In Memory of
HENRY BOYER, who
departed this life
March 7th, 1799, Aged
43 Years and 4 days
All you that comes my
grave to see
Prepare yourselves to
follow me
Repent and Turn to
God in time
you may be taken in
your prime.

576

Here lyes the Body of
ARCHIBALD McPHERSON,
born in the county of Murray
in North Britain who died
August 17th 1754, aged 49 years.
He was judicious, a Lover of Learning,
Open-hearted, generous and sincere,
devout without Ostentation,
disdaining to cringe to vice in any Station,
Friend to good men an affectionate husband.
Hoap of . . . alone remains to Thee
. . s᾿all Thou art and all th . . shalt be.   Pop
Elizabeth, his disconsolate Widow
as a Testamony of their Mutual affection,
erected this monument to his memory.

_____

. . . .

The Body of JAMES DUNCANSON.
He was born in Scotland
the 11th Feb. 1735,
arrived in Virginia in July 1752
Died the 1st March 1791.
Weed his Grave deare Men of Goodness
For he was your Brother—Stern.

_____

Here lies the body of
WILLIAM LEWIS, who departed
this life january the 28th 1763.
Aged 40 years.
Also Ann his Daughter die^d.
in 1755 aged 13 months
and George his Son died
1763, aged 5 ye . . .

Fragment.

Also CHARLES M ROTHSO . . .
Departed this Life Septem . . .
29th 1084 Aged 3 years.

The second figure of the date is clear-cut as when first done, and there is not the slightest trace of some other figure having been erased. The "O" was probably intended to be a "6."

Fragment. ———————

        . . . Body of CATHARINE,
        . . . Wife of James Maury
        . . . iverpool in the 22ᵈ of May 1791
        . . . living it was her Purpose
        . . . returned & died among
        . . . her own people
    While dying she desired that these remains
            Should rest here.
        She was the best of Women.

        ———————

        IOHN : IONES
            1752.

        ———————

            Sacred
        to the memory of
        GEORGE RICHARDSON,
            Stone cutter
        Who was killed by accident
            May 12, 1807,
            aged 45 years.
    Stay passenger; thy steps; reflect awhile
    Tho' now in health and vigour thou may smile
    Tomorrow's sun thy obsequies may see
    The silent gray may then thy mansion be
    Then seek in life God's favour to possess,
    And to thy soul secure eternal happiness.

        ———————

TOMBSTONES IN WARWICK COUNTY.

Blunt Point.

Tombstone of William Roscow.

(Arms.[1])

Under this stone lyeth the Body of
William Roscow Gentleman who
was born at Charley in the county

---

[1]These arms are different from any in Burke's *General Armory.*

of Lancaster on the 30th. day of November
Anno Dom 1661.
And departed this life at Blunt Point
in ye county of Warwick the X day of
November Anno Dom 1700.
And in the 36th year of his age
Also here lyes the Body of Mary wife
of the above William Roscow
And Daughter of Coll. Wm. Wilson
Of Elizabeth City county who was
Born in October, 1675.
And dyed Jan. the 11, 1741, in the 67th
year of her Age.

Denbigh Church.

Tombstone of Mary Harrison.

(Arms.[1])

Here lieth
The Body of Mary Harrison,
Daughter of the Honble Cole Diggs, Esq.,
President of his Mag^{tys} Council of this Colony,
And
Late Wife of Colonel Nathaniel Harrison
of Prince George County,
By whom she had four children viz:
Nathaniel who was born May 27, 1739
and died June 23, 1740
Digges who was born October 22, and died Novr 12, 1743
(both interred near this place)
also Elizabeth born July 30th., 1737.
Benjamin born February 13, 1742.

---

[1]The shield bears, dexter, annulets 3, 2 and 1 between two bars
ermine; sinister, 5 eagles displayed, for Digges.

She so discharged the Several Duties
of a Wife, Mother, Daughter, Neighbor
that her Relations & Acquaintances
might justly estimate their Affliction unsupported,
was it not chastened with the Remembrance
That every Virtue which adds weight to their loss
Augments her reward.
Obiit Nov. 12, 1714. Aet. 27.

Bolthorpes.

Tombstone of William Cole.

(Arms.[1])

Here lyeth the Body of William Cole
Esqr. of the county of Warwick who
departed this life the 4th. day of March
1693-4 in the 56th, year of his age
There does not need this marble to proclaime
His worth nor to immortalize his name
Firmly Recorded on the book of fate
Devouring time shall not his glories blot
Nor can (this age) his memory be forgot
A virtuous and industrious life he led
To all who would in Hono^{rs} footsteps tread
He was in all his stations just and greate
And stood as firm a pillar of the state
Of him may this be loudly sounded far
He was unspotted on ye bench
untay^{n}ted at ye bar.

---

[1]See QUARTERLY, frontispiece to Vol. V, No. 3, for arms.

Tombstone of Anne (Digges) Cole.

(Digges arms.)

Here lyeth the Body of Ann the
wife of William Cole, of Warwick
county, Esq., one of the Daughters of
Edward Digges, Esq., son of
Sir Dudley Digges, Master of the
Rolls to King Charles
the first. She Departed this life
the 22nd. day of November, 1686,
in the 29th. year of her age
Near also this place lyeth
the Body of Edward Cole
and Digges Cole
Children of said Anne.

———

Tombstone of Martha Cole.

(Cole arms.)

Here lyeth the Body of Martha the
Daughter of William Cole & Martha
his wife (daughter of John Leare, Esq.)
She departed this life the 19th. day of
April, 1698, in ye eighth year of her age.
near also to this place lyeth the body of
John Cole & Mary Cole, two children of
the said William and Martha.

———————

Rich Neck.

Tombstone of Gill A. Cary.

(Arms.[1])

Gill A. Cary,
son of
John & Susannah Cary.

———————————

[1]For description of arms, see Quarterly No. III.

582

Born March 18th, 1783.
Died March 25th. 1843.
Mark the perfections & Behold
the upright; for the end of that
Man is Peace.

Tombstone of John· B. Cary, Jr.
John B. Cary, Junr.,
son of
John B. & Columbia Cary.
Born November 25th. 1846,
Died August 10th. 1860.
"Whosoever thereforeshall confess me
Before Men, him will I confess also
Before my father which is in Heaven."
Jesus.

Tombstone of Mary Cary.
Here lyeth ye Body of MARY the wife
of MILES CARY & Daughter of THOMAS
MILNER and MARY his wife late of
Nanzemond County dec'd. Shee was
Born the 6th of Auguft 1667, and Died
the 27th of October 1700 in the 34th
year of her Age. Ifsuelefs.
Alfo the body of COL°. MILES CARY
Hufband of the said MARY who
died February 17th. 1708 & left 2 sons
WILSON & MILES & 2 Daughters
MARY & ANN by MARY ye Daughter
of Col°. W^m. WILSON of Hampton.

TOMBSTONES IN ELIZABETH CITY COUNTY.

The old Churchyard near Hampton.

Tombstone of John Neville, Esq.
(Arms.[1])
Here lyes the Body of
JOHN NEVILLE, Esqr. VICE ADMIRAL

---

[1]For description of arms see QUARTERLY II., 140.

of his MAJESTYES FLEET and COMMANDER
in chiefe of ye squadron cruising
in the WEST INDIES.
Who dyed on board ye CAMBRIDGE
the 17th, day of August, 1697.
in ye Ninth Yeare of the Reigne of
KING WILLIAM the third
Aged 53 years.

———

Tombstone of Thomas Curle.

(Arms.[1])

In hopes of a Blessed Resurrection
Here lyes the Body of Thomas Curle
gent who was born November 24th 1640
in the Parish of St. Michael in Lewis in the
County of Sussex in England and Dyed
May the 30th 1700
When a few years are come, then I shall
goe the way whence I shall not Return
Job. 16ch. 22v.

———

Tombstone of Peter Heyman.

This Stone was given by His
Excellency Francis Nicholson
Esq Lieutenant and Governor
Generall of Virginia in Memory of
Peter Heyman Esq Grandson
to Sir Peter Heyman of Sumerfield
in ye County of Kent he was
Collector of ye customs in the

---

[1]These arms are: a chevron between 3 fleurdelis. Crest: A hedgehog

Lower District of James River and
went voluntarily on Board ye Kings
shipp Shoreham in Pursuit of a
Pyrate who greatly infested this
coast after he had behaved himself
seven hours wth undaunted courage
was killed wth a small shot ye 29th
Day of April 1700
in ye Engagement he stood Next y^e
Governour upon the Quarter Deck
and was here Honorably interred
by his order

Tombstone of Rev. Mr. Andrew Thompson.

Here lieth the Body of
Reverend M^r. Andrew Thompson
who was born at Stone blue in
Scotland and was Minister of this
Parish seven years and departed
this life the 1st of September 1719
in ye 46th year of his Age leaving
a character of A sober Religious
Man

Hampton Churchyard.

In 1845 the oldest inscription in the churchyard was that of Capt.
Willis Wilson who died Nov. 19, 1701. Among the public men buried
here were Dr. George Balfour who died in 1830, Major James Glassell
who died Nov. 3, 1838 and Lt. James D. Burnham, who died March
6, 1838.—Howe, *Historical Collections of Virginia*, p. 249.

Tombstone of John Jones Spooner.

Sacred
To the memory of the Rev^d.
John Jones Spooner

Rector
of the church
in Elizabeth City County
Who departed this life
Sept 13th 1799
Aged 42 years.

———

Tombstone of Jane Latimer.

In memory of Jane
wife of William Latimer
Junr she was the Daughter
of John Constance Sin(clair?).
who departed this life
April 17th 1803 Aged 21
years 11 months and 13 days
(verses)

———

Tombstone of Rev. Benj. Brown.

Departed this life
January 17th 1806
The Revd Benj. Brown
Rector of this Parish

———

Tombstone of Henry Mowatt.

In memory of
HENRY Mo * * T Esq[1]
Late Captain of
his Brittannick Magistyes
ship the Assistance
who having served his country

---

[1]Henry Mowatt, Esq., who in October, 1775, burned the town of
Portland, Maine, because it refused to give provisions to the British.

forty four years
died on the 11th day of April
1798 Aged 63 years
universally lamented

———

Tombstone of Rev. Henry Skyren.

Sacred to the memory
of
the Revd Henry Skyren
Rector of Elizabeth City Parish
Born in Whitehaven England
A. D. 1729
Died in Hampton Virginia
A. D. 1795
This monument was erected by
his surviving children
Elizabeth Temple
&
John Spotswood Skyren

———

Tombstone of Nancy (French) Strange.

Sacred to the memory of
Nancy (French) Strange
Born 5th January 1780
who died at sea the 5th of October
and was here interred the 8th,
1805
The Christ is ye Christians all

———

Tombstone of Jane Jennings.

In memory of Jane
wife of Charles Jennings
who departed this life
October 15th 1781
Aged 22 years

Tombstone of Charles Jennings.

In memory of Charles Jennings
Aged 67 years
who departed this life
1st January 1816

———

Tombstone of George Massenburg.

Sacred to the memory of
George Massenburg
who was
born on the 15th May 1762
and died the 25th Oct 1823
in the 61st year of his age

———

Tombstone of William Jennings.

William Jennings
who departed this life
Oct the 10, 1791
Aged 41 years

———

Tombstone of William Thompson.

Sacred
To the memory of
William Thompson
who died at Little England
the 18th Janu^{ry} 1808
aged 58 years

———

Tombstone of Anne Day.

In memory
of Ann the wife of John
Day who departed
this life July 13, 1(8)02 in
the seventieth year of her age

(Arms.[1])

Under this stone
lieth Interred the Body of
Capt George Wray
who departed this life
the 9th of April 1758
in his 61st year
Isaiah chap. 55th First
& second verses
Thus saith the Lord
keep ye judgment and
do justice for my salvation is near to
come and my righteousness to be revealed
Blessed is the man that
doth this and the son of the man that layeth
hold on it and keep
either his hands from doing any evil.

---

[1]These arms are the same as those of Sir Christopher Wray, *temp.*
Queen Elizabeth.—Burke, *General Armory.*

DEATHS OF VIRGINIANS

From 1832 to 1844

(From Howe, *Historical Collections of Virginia*)

"Below are obituary notices, drawn from the Obituary in the American Almanac, of public individuals, natives and residents of Virginia and the District of Columbia, who have died within the last ten or twelve years. The perusal will create retrospections, too often lost amid the engrossing scenes of the present, and the demands of the future."

1832

Oct. 13—At Norfolk, John E. Holt, nearly twenty years mayor of that borough.

Nov. 19.—At Washington city, aged 60, Philip Doddridge, a member of Congress, a distinguished lawyer, and one of the ablest men in the body of which he was a member.

1833

Jan. 29—At Warrenton, N. C., in his 64th year, John Hall, recently judge of the Supreme Court of N. Carolina. He was born in Staunton, Va., and when a young man removed to N. C. His life was pure, and his integrity unspotted.

May 24—At Philadelphia, aged 60, John Randolph of Roanoke.

Nov. 17—At Columbus, S. C., aged 90, Colonel Thomas Taylor. He was born in Amelia Co., Va. in 1743. He has been styled "the patriarch of the states-right party of South Carolina."

Dec. 21—At Twiford, in Westmoreland Co., Va., in his 74th year, John P. Hungerford. He was an officer in the Revolutionary War, and afterwards a member of Congress.

1834

Feb. 11—In the Capitol at Washington, Thomas Tyler Bouldin, M. C. Before he was elected a member of Congress, he had been a lawyer of high rank, an able and upright judge; and he was highly respected for his integrity.

Feb. 18—At Washington city, in his 62d year, the Hon. William Wirt, the author of the Life of Patrick Henry, and of the British Spy.

April 13—At Norfolk, Gen. Robert B. Taylor, an eminent lawyer, and a judge of the General or District Court of Va.; a man greatly respected, and much lamented.

Oct. ——At Petersburg, of cholera, aged about 48, Gen. William H. Brodnax of Dinwiddie Co., Va., distinguished as a lawyer and philanthropist, and for several years a very prominent member of the House of Delegates. He signalized himself in the debates on the abolition of slavery of 1831, advocating a gradual and cautious abolition; and also in opposition to the doctrines of President Jackson's Proclamation of Dec.. 1832.

Near Monongahela, Va., aged 97, Col. John Evans; a commander of a regiment of militia in the Revolution, and a member of the convention that formed the first Constitution.

1835

March 2—In Bath Co., Va., aged about 77, Gen. Samuel Blackburn, a soldier of the Revolution, an eminent lawyer, and for many years a conspicuous member of the

591

legislature. At his death he liberated his slaves, forty-six in number, charging his estate with the expense of transporting them to Liberia.

April 7—At Philadelphia, in his 73d year, James Brown, who was born in Virginia in Oct. 1766. In 1812 he was elected a member of the U. S. Senate from Louisiana, and in 1823, appointed minister to France. He was distinguished as a lawyer and a statesman.

April 25—Aged about 40, Jonathan P. Cushing, President of Hampden-Sidney College, which office he had held for fourteen years. He was born in New Hampshire. The institution over which he presided was greatly indebted to his well-directed zeal, talents, and influence, and he was highly esteemed for his virtues. By his will he emancipated his slaves, sixty in number, providing amply for their removal to Liberia; and also gave about $40,000. to establish schools in Albemarle, and the adjoining county.

May 13—In Brunswick county, in his 84th year, Rev. Edward Dromgoole, father of the Hon. George C. Dromgoole; a minister of the gospel sixty-three years, and a magistrate and member of the county court forty-five years.

July 1—At Richmond, in his 77th year, Maj. James Gibbon, collector of customs of the port of Richmond, and a gallant officer of the Revolutionary army, known as "the hero of Stony-Point." Col. Gibbon, on the 16th of July, 1779, then a lieutenant, led one of the two "forlorn hopes," of twenty men, when Gen. Wayne carried the fortress of Stony-Point by storm. Of his twenty men, seventeen were killed or wounded. He was greatly respected and esteemed, and his remains were interred with the highest honors.

July 6—At Philadelphia, in his 80th year, John Marshall, Chief-Justice of the United States.

June 28—At Baltimore, Md., aged about 50, of a fractured skull, from the fall of a chimney, Thomas Marshall, of Fauquier Co., the eldest son of Chief-Justice Marshall, being on a journey to attend the death-bed of his father. He graduated in Princeton in 1803; was distinguished as a scholar, a lawyer, and a member of the legislature; and was highly esteemed for his talents, his many virtues, and his exemplary and useful life.

May 26—At Columbia, S. C., aged 70, Gen. Francis Preston, of Washington Co., Va., a member of Congress from 1793 to 1797, and father of the Hon. William C. Preston.

Nov. ——At Lexington, Va., George Baxter, a distinguished lawyer.

Nov. ——In Caroline Co., aged about 48, John Dickenson, an eminent lawyer.

Oct. 7—In Alabama, Charles Tait, in his 68th year. He was born in Louisa county, but removed at an early age to Georgia, where he was, for several years, a judge of the Superior Court, and a senator in Congress, from 1809 to 1819.

Dec. 3.—At Washington city, aged 47, Richard Wallack, a distinguished lawyer.

1836

March 22—At Washington, D. C., in his 82d year, Gen. Mountjoy Baily, an officer of the Revolution.

Jan. 28.—At Abingdon, John H. Fulton, a respected member of the 23d Congress.

April 29—In Logan Co., Ohio, Gen. Simon Kenton, aged 82, a native of Virginia. He was a companion of Col. Boone, in exploring the West, and in commencing its settlement, and he endured many hardships.

March 25—At Belmont, Loudon Co., Va., aged 76, Ludwell Lee, a second son of Richard Henry Lee, a gentleman highly respected.

Nov. 9—At his residence, in Goochland Co., Va., aged 67, James Pleasants, M. C. from 1811 to 1819; U. S. Senator from 1819 to 1822; governor of Virginia from 1822

to 1825, and a member of the convention from 1829-
30, for amending the state constitution. He was twice
appointed to the bench, but declined, from a distrust
of his own qualifications. He was a man of rare
modesty, greatly respected and esteemed for public and
private virtues.

Oct. 10—In Albemarle Co., Va., aged upwards of 70, Mrs. Martha Randolph widow of Gov. Thomas M. Randolph,
and the last surviving daughter of Thomas Jefferson;
a lady distinguished for her talents and virtues.

1837

Jan. 8.—At his seat in Culpeper Co., aged 63, Dabney Carr, a
judge of the Virginia Court of Appeals; a man
much respected and esteemed for his amiable character, his talents, learning, industry, solidity of mind,
and uncommonly fine colloquial powers.

Aug. 16—At the Sweet Springs, John Floyd, M. C. from 1817
to 1819, and governor of Virginia from 1829 to 1834.

April 12—In Beaver Co., Penn., Gen. Abner Lacock, in his 67th
year. He was born in Virginia, removed early in life
to Pennsylvania, and was, from 1813 to 1819, a member of the U. S. Senate.

March 18, 1836,—In Albemarle, Va., Hugh Nelson, formerly
speaker of the House of Delegates, a judge of the
General Court, a member of Congress from 1811 to
1823, and afterwards U. S. Minister to Spain.

June 28, 1836—At Montpelier, Orange Co., Va., in his 86th year,
James Madison, the 4th President of the United States.

June 3—In Virginia, in his 53d year, Allen Taylor, judge of the
General Court, 17th Circuit.

Jan. 7.—At Needham, in his 70th year, Creed Taylor, late chancellor of the Richmond and Lynchburg District.

Nov. 5—Aged 57, David Briggs, an eminent attorney, formerly
mayor of Fredericksburg, and counsellor of state.

Nov. 20—At his father's residence, in Bedford Co., John Thompson Brown, of Petersburg, Va., aged 36. He was for
several years a very distinguished member of the legis-

lature, was rising rapidly at the bar, and regarded as one of the most eminent men of his age in the state.

Oct. 7—At Yorktown, aged 64, Major Thomas Griffin, second in command at the battle of Hampton, and M. C. in 1803-5.

Nov. 30, 1836.—At Bellegrove, Major Isaac Hite, an officer in the Revolutionary war.

Dec. 15—At Gosport, in his 85th year, Capt. John Cox, who, early in the Revolution was commissioned as a captain in the naval service of Virginia, and was one of the most distinguished and efficient patriots in the contest.

Dec. 2.—In Goochland Co., aged 62, Dr. Andrew Kean, one of the most eminent physicians of Virginia.

Sept. 8—In Albemarle Co. aged 85, Mrs. Lucy Marks, the mother of Meriwether Lewis, who, with William Clarke, explored the Rocky Mountains; a woman of uncommon energy and strength of mind.

Sept. 19—At Clinton, Fauquier Co., aged 83, Capt. William Payne, who commanded the Falmouth Blues for several years in the early part of the Revolution; and a company of volunteers at the siege of Yorktown.

July 22—In Kanawha Co., aged 71, Philip R. Thompson, M. C. from Virginia in 1801-7.

1838

March 26—In Missouri, Gen. William H. Ashley, first lieutenant-governor of that state, and a native of Powhatan Co., Va.

May 7—At Washington, D. C., Abraham Bradley, for many years assistant Postmaster-general.

Feb. 2—In Stafford Co., John Coulter, formerly a judge of the Circuit Court of Appeals.

Jan. 9—At Staunton, aged 36, John J. Craig, a man much respected; distinguished for his talents as a lawyer, and a member of the legislature.

Feb. 6—At Charlotte, C. H., aged 40, Nash Le Grand, for several years a member of the state council.

Jan. 6,—At Richmond, Va., suddenly, aged about 35, Edward V. Sparhawk, editor of the Petersburg Intelligencer; a gentlemen of fine talents, extensive acquirements, and a highly respectable and useful member of society.

Dec. ——At Richmond, aged 60, John Brockenbrough, judge of the Court of Appeals.

Sept. 1—At St. Louis, in his 69th year, William Clarke, a native of Virginia, companion of Meriwether Lewis in the expedition across the Rocky Mountains, and governor of Missouri Territory, from 1813 to 1820.

Sept. 15—At Huntsville, Ala., Col. William Lindsay, a native of Va., and a highly respectable man and officer of the U. S. Army.

Dec. 21—At Alexandria, D. C., Thompson F. Mason, judge of the Criminal Court of the District of Columbia.

1839.

April 8—At Wheeling, Alexander Caldwell, judge of the U. S Court in the Western District of Va.

Nov. 3.—In Hanover Co., in his 72d year, suddenly, while feeling the pulse of a dying patient, Dr. Carter Berkeley, a lineal descendant (?) of Sir William Berkeley, a graduate of the Edinburg Medical School, a distinguished physician and much respected for his upright, benevolent, and religious character.

Nov. 20—At Lynchburg, in his 69th year, William Daniel, a conspicuous member of the legislature in 1798-99; and for the last twenty-three years, a judge of the General and Circuit Courts; a man much respected for his talents and legal knowledge.

Nov. ——At New Orleans, Capt. Gilbert T. Francis, a native of Va., His life was romantic and eventful, and he passed through surprising adventures in foreign countries. Though of defective education, his great energy of character and extensive travels made him the most entertaining of companions.

Oct. 2—In Culpeper Co., in his 88th year, Col. David Jameson, an active militia officer of the Revolution; afterwards a member of the House of Delegates, a respected magistrate, and a member of the county court.

May 20—At Richmond, aged about 75, Daniel Call, brother-in-law to Chief-Justice Marshall, an able and eminent lawyer, author of 6 vols. of law reports, known as "Call's Reports."

Jan. ——At Richmond, aged about 88, Chas. Shirley Carter, an eminent lawyer and advocate, attorney of the state in the Circuit Court of Henrico Co.; formerly a distinguished member of the legislature.

Oct. ——At the University of Virginia, aged about 48, Chas. Bonnycastle, Prof. of Mathematics. He was a native of England, and a son of John Bonnycastle, the author of a celebrated algebra. He was a man of profound and vigorous mind, the author of a valuable work upon Inductive Geometry.

Nov. 14—At the University of Va., (of a pistol-shot discharged by a disguised student,) aged 39, John A. G. Davis, Prof. of Law in the University. He was a man of a high order of intellect, of untiring industry, of amiable and philanthropic character, and he was an exemplary member of the Episcopal Church. He published in 1838, a valuable law-book—"A Treatise on Criminal Law, and a Guide to Justices of the Peace." As a successful instructor, he could hardly be surpassed; and it is thought, since graduates of his law-school have taken their places at the bar, the profession of Virginia has breathed a more enlarged spirit, and displayed a wider and a higher tone.

Dec. ——At Nashville, Tenn., Felix Grundy, a native of Berkeley Co., Va., and a distinguished member of the U. S. Senate from Tennessee.

Nov. ——In Va., aged about 63, Richard E. Parker, a judge of the Supreme Court of Appeals.

Jan. 19—At Morven, Loudon Co., in his 75th year, Thomas Swan, an eminent lawyer, and formerly attorney of the U. S. for the Dist. of Columbia. "He attained the highest rank in his profession, uniting to the most extensive learning the most effective eloquence as a pleader. His influence over juries, arising from this cause, and partly from the universal confidence in the purity of his character, is believed to have been seldom, if ever, surpassed, in the instance of any other American advocate.

1841

Feb. 25—At Washington, D. C., aged about 60, Philip P. Barbour, of Orange Co., an associate judge of the Supreme Court of the U. S.

April 24—In Va., aged 77, George Baxter, D. D., Prof. in the Union Theo. Sem. in Prince Edward Co.; formerly president of Wash. College, at Lexington, and one of the most eminent and respected Presbyterian Clergymen in Virginia.

Oct. 22—At Washington, D. C., (of billious fever), aged 61, John Forsyth, of Georgia, a man of talents and eloquence, and secretary of state in Mr. Van Buren's administration. He was born in Fredericksburg, Va. in 1781.

April 4—At Washington city, in his 69th year, William Henry Harrison, President of the U. States. He was born in Charles City Co., Va., on the 9th of Feb. 1773.

June 10—At Washington city, in his 92d year, Richard Harrison, late auditor of the treasury, and a man highly respected.

April 27—At Washington city, aged about 80, Rev. Andrew T. McCornish, a respected clergyman, for 23 years minister of the first Episcopal church formed in Washington.

June ——At Washington city, George Washington Montgomery, who was born in Valencia, in Spain, of a distinguished Irish family, and a man of superior talents and education. He came in early life to this country, and was long employed in the department of State. He was the author of Bernardo del Carpio, "an exquisite historical novel of the 8th century, and the translation of Irving's Conquest of Granada."

Sept. 1.—Near Georgetown, D. C., in his 88th year, Joseph Nourse, register of the U. S. Treasury from 1789 to 1829, and one of the vice-presidents of the American Bible Society, and a man much respected. He was born in London in 1754; emigrated with his family to Virginia, and entered the revolutionary army in 1776, and served in different departments connected with it till the close of the war.

1842

Feb. 24—In Madison Co., Hon. Linn Banks, from 1818 to 1838 speaker of the House of Delegates.

June 8—In Orange Co., Hon. James Barbour, ex-governor of Virginia, aged 66.

Aug. 13—John P. Emmett, Esq., Prof. of Chem. in the University of Va. He was the son of the late Thomas Addis Emmett, and a man of talents and learning.

Jan. 5—At Savannah, Ga., Col. Thomas Haynes, aged 55, who was born in Va. He was treasurer of Georgia, and commanded respect and great public influence.

1843.

Nov. 23—In Fauquier Co., Thomas Fitzhugh, aged 81. He was a highly respected citizen, and had been for many years presiding judge of the County Court.

Dec. 14—In Washington city, Chas. W. Goldsborough, chief of the bureau of provisions and clothing of the navy department, and author of a naval history of the U. S. He was one of the oldest and most respected inhabitants of the city.

Nov. 30—In Rappahannock Co., Maj. John Roberts, aged 85. He served in the Revolutionary army and negotiated the exchange for the prisoners obtained by the convention at Saratoga in 1777. Afterwards he was a member of the legislature for 13 successive years, and had great influence in its deliberations.

Aug. 27—At the White Sulphur Springs, Hon. Lewis Summers, of Kanawha, aged 65, for 24 years one of the judges of the General Court of Va.

1844

Feb. 10—At Fredericksburg, Carter Beverley, Esq., aged 72.

Feb. 28—By the accident on board the U. S. steamer Princeton, Thomas W. Gilmer, of Charlottesville, secretary of the navy. His various public trusts he discharged with great ability. He was respected in public, and beloved in private life.

March 29—At Norfolk, Com. E. Pendleton Kennedy, of the U. S. N., aged 65. At the time of his death, he was commander of the line-of-battle ship Pennsylvania.

Feb. 28—By the accident on board the steamer Princeton, Com. Beverley Kennon, chief of the bureau of construction, repairs, and equipment, in the navy department. He had long been attached to the naval service, in which he had attained a distinguished reputation.

Feb. 28—By accident on board the Princeton, Hon. A. P. Upshur, secretary of state, aged 54. He was born in Northampton Co., in 1790.

THORNTON FAMILY.

By John Bailey Calvert Nicklin,

Chattanooga, Tenn.

OBITUARY NOTICES.

Thomas Griffin Thornton.

From: "The National Intelligencer," Washington, D. C., June 17, 1830, p. 3, column 3.

"Fredericksburg, Va., June 15, 1830.

MURDER.—On Saturday last, Thomas Griffin Thornton, Sheriff of Caroline county, was murdered. The body was found by Mr. Lawrence of Spring Garden. It seems that he was dispatched by two gun-shot wounds; one in the abdomen and the other in the back. His horse appears to have been led about fifty yards from the scene of the murder and shot. On Sunday afternoon a man was arrested in this town, on suspicion of having participated in this most dreadful transaction. Of the circumstances which fixed the eyes of the peace officers upon him, we know nothing. The matter, however, is in a way to be carefully investigated.— 'The Arena.' "

"Another Most Atrocious Murder.

From: "Richmond Commercial Compiler," June 17, 1830, page 2, column 3.

Fredericksburg, June 16.—On Saturday afternoon last, Griffin Thornton, Esq., Sheriff of Caroline county, was shot, together with his horse, about a mile from his dwelling-house. It is believed there were several concerned in this horrible transaction, as it said the reports of two or three guns were heard at the time of the supposed murder.

The neighborhood was soon in possession of the fact of his death, and the perpetrators were sought after. They (the posse) were first led to the house of Charles Young, being near, and not finding him at home, they took the liberty of searching for his gun, which when found in-

dicated the appearance of having been recently discharged, and some blood
on it; these, with some other circumstances, impressed the belief that he
was one concerned in the murder. Young, it appears, the following night,
directed his course to this place (Fredericksburg) and was seen and known
early the next morning near to town; he was pursued by a party from
Caroline and committed to jail.

Mr. Thornton was a valuable member of society—the chasm occasioned
by his unnatural death cannot be readily filled. The distress in which
it has involved a wife and a large family, with very many connections,
cannot easily be conceived much less described.—'Herald.' "

Communication.

From: "Richmond Enquirer," Dec. 19, 1816, p. 3.

DIED lately at his seat in Orange County, Geo. Washington Thornton, in the prime of his life. This gentleman possessed many of the virtues and some of the frailties incident to human nature. That sentiment
of Terence, which is said to have commanded so much applause, may be
applied to him:—"Homo sum, nihil humania me ahienum est."

Communicated.

From: "Richmond Enquirer," Jan. 29, 1822, p. 3.

Departed this life on Sunday the 20th instant, Mr. JOHN THORN-
TON, sen., of the Forks of Hanover, in the 78th year of his age. Mr.
Thornton, during a long life, sustained the most exemplary character: as
a patriot he was warmly devoted to his country, as a parent affectionate,
as a master kind and indulgent, as a neighbor friendly, and as a companion
the delight of the company. Possessed of a fine fortune, he enjoyed life
without abusing it; no man was ever more completely master of himself;
there was no pleasure he could not taste, and enjoy in reason and modera-
tion; and he had the peculiar felicity of being enemy to no man, and having no man for his enemy.

Communicated.

From: "Richmond Enquirer," Aug. 19, 1823, p. 3.

Departed this life on the 7th instant in the 18th year of his age,
JOHN T. THORNTON, eldest son of Capt. Wm. M. Thornton of Oak
Hill, Cumberland County, Va. He was a youth of an amiable disposition
and manners, and possessed in an eminent degree the love and esteem
of all who knew him.

From: "Richmond Enquirer," Sep. 19, 1823, p. 3.

DIED—on the 3d inst., MARY I. B. THORNTON, and on the 8th
inst., ELIZABETH T. THORNTON, each after a very short illness; the
first in the 9th and the last in the 11th year of her age, daughters of

602

Capt. Wm. M. Thornton, of Oakhill, Cumberland county, and grand-children of Mr. Samuel Anderson. They were two sweet, beautiful and amiable little girls, particularly beloved by all the connexions of the family, and most remarkably attached to each other. "They were lovely and pleasant in their lives, and in their deaths they were not divided."

> Ended are their short-lived hours,
>   Lodged within the mouldering tomb;
> But the fair Elysian flowers
>   Rise to everlasting bloom;
> Youth's engaging beauties now
>   Smile eternal on their brow.

From: "Richmond Enquirer," Sep. 26, 1828, p. 3.

DIED, on the 2nd. instant, Mrs. ELIZABETH THORNTON, consort of Capt. Wm. M. Thornton, near Caira. In all the tender and sacred relations of a daughter, a wife, a mother, a neighbor and a friend; her loss will be affectionately, deeply and long deplored; for in each of those relations, she eminently evinced all those virtues of the heart which give dignity, endearment and worth to the name of Woman.

From: "Richmond Whig," Nov. 2, 1830, page 3.

Commonwealth vs. Charles Young.—On a bill of indictment for the murder of Thomas Griffin Thornton June 12, 1830.

This trial came on last week before the Superior Court of Law for the County of Caroline, Judge Brockenbrough presiding, and occupied the whole session of the Court. In consequence of the inclemency of the weather, the Grand Jury did not convene until Tuesday; a bill of indictment sent up to them was, in a short time, returned a "True Bill." The prisoner was then arraigned upon the indictment, and pleaded "Not guilty." A motion for change of venue was then made by the counsel and resisted by the Commonwealth's Attorney—many witnesses were examined, and after a long argument, the Court rejected the application. A motion was then made, which was acquiesced in by the prosecutor, to set aside the venire summoned, on the ground that the summoning officers were nearly connected by blood or marriage with the deceased. This motion was sustained by the Court—and the Prosecutor having taken the precaution of having two impartial men qualified at the last County Court, as special Deputy Sheriffs, the Court directed them to summon seventy-two men good and true by the next meeting. The whole of Wednesday was occupied in attempting to procure a jury. During the day fifty-three persons were examined, six of whom were selected by the prisoner and seven challenged peremptorily—the balance set aside, having formed and expressed an opinion of the prisoner's guilt or innocence. The greater part of Thursday was occupied in procuring the remaining half of the jury, which was at length empannelled and sworn. The examination of witnesses occupied the remainder of that day, the whole of Friday and part of Saturday. About twelve o'clock the argument of counsel commenced and at 10:00 o'clock P. M. the Jury retired and after an hour had elapsed, returned with a verdict of "Guilty of murder in the first degree."

We have never seen more interest excited by any trial. To this interest the high standing of the deceased and the character of the evidence against the prisoner mainly contributed. The evidence was, throughout, purely and exclusively circumstantial. There was not a single positive proof adduced, and yet we have never seen testimony of any kind, which left upon the minds of all who heard it, a stronger conviction of the guilt of the accused.

The late hour on Saturday night, at which the verdict was rendered, induced his Honor to adjourn the Court until Monday morning; when sentence of death was pronounced in a feeling and impressive manner. (Taken from the "Fredericksburg Arena.").

Died.

From: "Richmond Whig & Public Advertiser," Oct. 11, 1833, page 1.

At his residence in Caroline County, on Sunday the 29th ult., in the 59th year of his age, after a painful protracted decline of several months, PETER THORNTON, beloved and lamented by a numerous family and extensive acquaintances. He was the zealous and patriotic citizen, the hospitable and friendly neighbor, the affectionate and provident husband, and the tender and indulgent parent. Indeed, if the prompt and habitual observance, through life, of the manifold, moral obligations which devolve upon man in the several relations of citizen, neighbor, husband and father, can insure respect, while living and regret at death, such surely have followed him.

Died.

From: "Richmond Whig & Public Advertiser," Oct. 17, 1837, page 4.

On the 4th of August, in the town of Madisonville, Mississippi, in the 24th year of his age, THOMAS C. THORNTON, a native of Virginia, Hanover County. The deceased was a young man of irreproachable character and uncommon talents. For the purpose of bettering his fortune and building up for himself a name notorious at once for moral and intellectual worth, he tore himself from the comforts of home and the endearments of friends, to exert his abilities in a Southern clime; but in vain did he burn the midnight taper; in vain did he turn over and over the legal page, storing his mind with the information necessary to enable him to contend successfully with those around him—though the eye sparkled and the cheek glowed when he contemplated upon the coming harvest of his youthful exertions, disease lurked within; Death threw his cold and icy arms around him, and all, all withered, save the hope of eternal felicity in the eternal World.

Near the same place, on the 15th of August, Mr. JOHN S. THORN-
TON, in the 28th year of his age. His illness was of short duration,
and may be attributed to his attention to his brother, whose decease
occurred two weeks prior. He was a young man of honesty, sobriety and
industry; and obtained, as he deserved, the good wishes and feelings of all
who were acquainted with him.

Died.

From: "Richmond Whig & Public Advertiser," July 31, 1838, page 4.

On the morning of the 14th of July, in the 35th year of her age,
after a lingering illness of some months, Mrs. LAVINNIA THORN-
TON, consort of Francis Thornton of Buckingham, leaving a devoted
husband, four children, and numerous relations and friends to bewail their
irreparable loss.

It seldom falls to the hand of friendship to announce the departure,
or to record the virtues of one so engaging in all the relations of life as
was she to whose memory these lines are but a feeble tribute. Gifted
by nature with an intelligent mind, an amiable disposition, and an affectionate heart, she was eminently fitted to discharge the various duties that
devolved upon her as a wife, a mother, and a member of society. Her
mild and even temperament, and the native benignity of her feelings uni-
formly diffused the smiles of peace and satisfaction throughout her family
circle, and elicited in return the sincerest gratitude and love. But however much may be said of the natural charms which had been so lavishly
bestowed upon her, it was as a christian that she appeared most lovely
and interesting. Her's was not an unmeaning profession, for deception
formed no part of her character. The piety with which Heaven had gifted
her, flowed in a smooth, and clear, and deep stream; and like the sweet
fountains that glide through the lovely meads of nature, reflecting the
rich beauties of the heavens, it bore on its pure and quiet bosom the bright
transcript of the celestial scenery. She was a faithful and devoted member of the Episcopal Church, and her conduct showed that she believed
its doctrines, and loved its pure and elevated worship. Long will her
memory be cherished with fondness by those with whom she went forward
to the sacred altar, and held the sweet communion of christian intercourse.
Her painful and protracted illness she bore with fortitude and patience.
At times, her sufferings were severe, but she murmured not; she meekly
and quietly endured all, assured that her "afflictions would work out for
her a far more exceeding and eternal weight of glory." From the ex-
treme debility of her body, doubts occasionally overshadowed her mind,
but like the clouds that occasionally flit across the disk of the sun, they
served only to add a richer brilliancy to her hopes. She died as she had
lived, with a firm reliance on the merits of the Saviour, "having the testimony of a good conscience;" in communion with the Holy Catholic

Church; in the comfort of a reasonable, religious, and holy hope; and in perfect charity with all mankind. A large concourse of friends and acquaintances gathered around her grave, after the usual religious exercises had closed, to pay the last sad tribute of respect to her mortal remains, and many were the tears of unfeigned sorrow that fell from sympathizing hearts, when her corpse was deposited in its "narrow cell," there, "in solitude and silence to sleep the years away," till the trump of the archangel shall summon it to the bar of the final judgment. But the tears of grief that bedewed her resting place were mingled with those of joyful hope—for the eye of faith beheld her happy spirit united to the blissful throng of the redeemed, chaunting, with heavenly melody, the praises of our Redeemer. May the dear relatives and friends whom she has left behind, and to whom, whilst living, she was so much devoted, follow her holy example of deep and ardent piety, and like her, depart in peace, to enter the bright abodes of everlasting felicity

———————————

A TOMBSTONE IN GREENSBOROUGH, ALABAMA

(The Four sides)

1.
In memory of our
Father and Mother
Archer Hunt Christian
Charles City, Va
Sarah French Christian
neé Pierce
New Kent, Va

2
In memory of our neice
Susan Browne
De Yampest
And Cousin
Henry Christian

3
In memory of our
Sisters
Anne Jordan
Betty Wyatt
Caroline
Mary Warner

4
In memory of our
Brothers
John Fleming
Archer Hunt

607

Epitaphs of Virginians in Georgia.

April 12, 1898.

In going through the cemetery at Greensborough, Ga., on yesterday, I found the following monument inscriptions:

"In memory of Ann Austin Winston, born in Goochland county, Va., April 19, 1788, died in Green county, Ga., January 5. 1820."

"John Coleman, born in Va., Feb. 20, 1784, died Oct. 29, 1841. As a husband, devout and sincere, as a father, kind and affectionate."

"In memory of Mrs. Lucy Willis, who was born in Mecklenburg co., Va., and died in Green county, Ga., on 4th April, 1843, in 82nd year of her age."

"Elizabeth, daughter of Vincent and Priscilla Sanford, born in Va., Aug. 5, 1810, and died Aug. 1830 (or 1880)."

"Vincent Sanford, born in Va., April 17th, 1777, died March 27, 1859."

"Burr Sanford, born in Va., Nov. 18, 1807, and died 1826."

"Jeremiah Sanford, born in Va., Nov. 4, 1739, died Aug. 12, 1825. He was a soldier of the Revolution, a friend of Washington and an honest man."

The Sanfords were from Loudoun county.

JOHN L. HARDEMAN.

———

INSCRIPTIONS ON THE TOMBSTONES IN THE EDWARD TYLER BURYING GROUND, NEAR JEFFERSONTOWN, JEFFERSON COUNTY, KENTUCKY. COPIED THE 7TH DAY OF FEBRUARY, 1931, BY JAMES BLYTHE ANDERSON.

In
memory of
Edward Tyler
who departed this life
May 20, 1802, in the
85 year of his age

In
memory of
Ann Tyler
consort of
Edward Tyler
Departed
this life July 31st
1820, aged 88
years

In
Memory of
Nelly Allison
Consort of Wm.
Allison, who de-
parted this life
Feb. 27th, 1797,
Aged 27 years

This stone is
Erected
In respect and memory
of
Moses Tyler
who was born
January 1st, 1755,
and died
January 27th, 1839,
Aged 84 years
and 27 days

In
memory of
Phebe Tyler
Consort of Moses Tyler
who departed this life
August 31st, 1831,
Aged 73 years
and 7 months

Infant son
of Presley &
Frances J. Tyler
who departed
this life July
26th, 1835

In
memory of
Allen Rose
who departed this life
the 17 day Nov. 1842
Aged 50 years, 10 mos. & 7 days

In
memory of
Mary Rose
consort of Allen Rose
who departed this life
the 20th day of
October, 1841.   Aged
45 years 6 mo. & 21 days

In
memory of
John E. Rose
Son of A. & M. Rose
who departed this life
the 19th of July, 1829,
Aged 10 months & 2 days

In
memory of
Samuel T. Rose
Son of A. & M. Rose
who departed this life
the 8th day of July,
1829.   Aged 3 years, 11 months, 16 days

In
memory of
Elizabeth K. S. Rose
Daughter of A. & M. Rose
who departed this life
the 8th of June, 1824,
Aged 15 months, 13 days

In
memory of
an infant of A.
& M. Rose, who was
Born Sept. the 13th,
1838

In
memory of
Levi T. Rose
son of A. & M. Rose
who departed this life
the 15th day of August,
1837
Aged 19 years & 5 days

In
Memory of
James W. Rose
son of A. & M. Rose
who departed this life
the 25 of August
1838.   Aged 13 *years*,
9 months & 7 days

(On one stone is inscribed)

A. McHatton
J. McHatton
W. McHatton

In
memory of
Leah McKonn
consort of
Robt. McKonn
who departed this
life Apr. 12th 1822
Aged 68 years

In
memory of
Edward Tyler
who departed this life
March 25, 1840,
Aged 73 years and 8
Days

In
memory of
Nancy Tyler
consort of Edward
Tyler, Sen., who
departed this life
March 31st, 1817
Aged 50 years, 4
months & 2 days

In
memory of
Nelly Tyler
who departed
this life
November 20th, 1802
Aged 2 years, 1 month
& 20 days

In
memory of
Edward Tyler
junr., who departed
this life december
14th, 1822.   Aged 28
years, 7 months
& 4 days

In
memory of
Samuel Tyler
who departed this life
September
2nd, 1823.   aged
20 years, 2 months,
27 days

In
memory of
Charles P. Tyler
Born Aug. 10, 1811
Died Oct. 8, 1835
Aged 24, 1 mo.
and 28 days

(On one stone marking two graves is inscribed)
(Front)

In	In
memory of	memory of
Thomas Sturgeon	Elizabeth Sturgeon
Born Sept. 11, 1793	wife of
Died Sept. 5, 1822	Thomas Sturgeon
Aged 28 yrs., 11 mos.	Born Dec. 25, 1791
and 25 days	Died July 13, 1833
	Aged 41 yrs., 6 mo.
	and 18 days

(Back)
Thos. Sturgeon, Jr., married Elizabeth Tyler 28 Aug., 1817.

Near the Edward Tyler Burying Ground is the "Walking Billy" Tyler
Grave Yard, with the following inscriptions copied same date:

William Tyler	Sarah Tyler
Died	Died
Sept. 23, 1836	Sept. 3, 1834
Aged	Aged
80 y., 11 m., 23 d.	About 67 years

Standage	Dr. Joseph Landram
daut. of	consort of
Wm. & L. Tyler	Elizabeth Ann Landram
died	Died
Oct. 16, 1840	Dec. 31, 1853
Aged 1 yr., 4 ms., 16 days	Aged 33 yr's., 8 m's., 12 D's

Nancy, daughter of Edward and Ann (Langley) Tyler, m. 1st Peter A'sturgus,
m. 2nd James Denny, m. 3rd Michael Humble. The children of Nancy
(Tyler) Denny were Edward and Mary (Polly) twins, Cynthia and James W.
Polly m. 1st Andrew S. McCormick, m. 2nd Dr. John Taylor, a nephew of
Chancellor Creed Taylor of Virginia. Cynthia m. Basil Prather.
On a hill in Boyle County, Kentucky, overlooking the Southern Railroad

station of Faulconer are five fast-disappearing tombs but you could yet read in 1930:

Sacred	Sacred	Sacred
To the Memory of	To the Memory of	To the Memory of
Michael Humble	Nancy Humble	James W. Denny
Died July 29th, 1819	Died Nov., 1838	Born January 20th, 1792
	Aged 75 years	Died February 1, 1833

Sacred
To the Memory of
J. E. D. McCormick
Born April 18th, 1815
Died August 4th, 1831

Sacred
To the memory of
Mrs. Cynthia Prather
consort of Basil Prather
Departed this life in
58 year of her age
of faith   August 4th 1847

TOMBSTONE OF LUCY GOODE: "Senator Starling Marshall lives in the country on the old Col. William Marshall place, and I don't often see him, but he came in at the last meeting of our Henderson County Historical Society (Ky.), in which he takes interest, and he tells me the inscription is now illegible and nearly gone. He gave me from his records the following:—Lucy Goode, born 1760, in Powhatan County, Va., married William Marshall March 21, 1782, in the same county, and died in Henderson County, Kentucky, in 1826."—*Susan S. Towles, Henderson, Kentucky.*

TOMB OF CAPTAIN HENRY FAUNTLEROY.

The enclosed photograph may be of interest to some of your readers, showing a memorial stone placed by me, November, 1929, in the graveyard surrounding Old Tennent Church, Monmouth Co., N. J., to Captain Henry Fauntleroy, 5th Va. Continental Line, who was killed in the Battle of Monmouth, which was fought between this old Church and Monmouth Court House (now called Freebold), N. J. This interesting old graveyard was established in 1731 and the present quaint old church was built in 1751 on "White Hill", in a beautiful grove of white oaks. Many quaint old grave stones together with beautiful modern monuments surround this old church.

General Washington commanded 11,00 Americans in this Battle in which 8 officers and 61 non-commissioned officers and privates were killed; 18 officers and 142 non-commissioned officers and privates wounded; 5 sergeants and 126 men missing, some of whom were overcome by fatigue and heat, and subsequently reported for service. It is a curious fact that all the Americans dead are now in unknown graves. About 100 years after the Battle, three skeletons were accidentally unearthed in one place, and their graves were marked by brown head-stones marked "Unknown".

General Washington reported that he had buried on the field 245 British. Lt.-Col. Henry Monkton, Commanding the 2nd Battalion 45th Fort [Foot?] Grenadier Guards, was killed near the Old Parsonage in a desperate struggle between his command and that of General Anthony Wayne, and was buried by the Americans near the southwest corner of Old Tennent Church; and 50 years later his grave was marked by a memorial stone placed there by an American. His is the only known grave of the British dead. General Washington in a letter to his brother, Col. John Augustine Washington, dated "Brunswic, in New Jersey, July 4th, 1778", says, "Among our slain officers is Major Dickinson and Captain Fauntleroy, two very valuable ones". And, in a letter to Governor Patrick Henry, of Virginia, dated July 4th, 1778, says "Capt. Fauntleroy, of the 5th, was unfortunately killed by a random cannot ball".

Captain Henry Fauntleroy was a first cousin of Hannah Bushrod, the wife of Col. John Augustine Washington. His four brothers, John, Griffin Murdock, Joseph, and Robert were officers in the Va. Continental Line Troops. His cousin, Major Griffin Fauntleroy, 1st Va. Light Dragoons Continental Line (son of Capt. Bushrod Fauntleroy), was mortally wounded at the battle of Guilford Court House, N. C., 15th March, 1781. It was in the Battle of Monmouth that Mrs. Mary Ludwig Hays carried water in a cannon bucket from a nearby stream to General Knox's gunners, of whom her husband, John Hays, of Carlisle, Pa., was one, and whose gun she served when he was later over-

ERECTED NOVEMBER, 1929, BY P. C. FAUNTLEROY ON WEST SIDE OF
TREMONT CHURCH NEAR FREEHOLD (MONMOUTH C. H.), N. J.

come by the terrible heat of the day. She was nicknamed by the soldiers, "Molly Pitcher".

P. C. Fauntleroy,
Col. U. S. Army, Retired.

BYRD EPITAPHS IN OHIO.

Contributed by Mrs. L. C. Anderson, Bainbridge, Ohio.

In the old cemetery at Sinking Springs, Highland Co., Ohio, are the following inscriptions on plain marble slabs:

Chas. W. Byrd
Died
Aug. 25, 1828
Aged
58 yrs., 1 mo., 8 days.

Hannah, wife of Chas. W. Byrd
Died
Aug. 14, 1839
Aged
49 yrs., 8 mos., 24 days.

Samuel O. Byrd
Died
April 4, 1869
Aged
45 yrs., 10 mos., 18 days
Son of
C. W. & Hannah Byrd.

Frances E.
consort of
Samuel O. Byrd
Died
May 30, 1851
Aged 26 yrs., 1 mo., 7 days.

Charles Willing
Infant son of Samuel O. and
Frances E. Byrd
Died May 19, 1849
Aged
1 yr., 4 mos. & 13 days.

Highland county joins Ross county. In the latter is located Chillicothe, Ohio's first capital. Highland county was formerly a part of Adams county, West Union being the county seat of Adams county.

Chas. W. Byrd was U. S. Judge in Ohio, and previous to that was Secretary of the Northwest Territory. He is mentioned in will of his mother, Mary Willing Byrd, of Westover, 1813.

WASHINGTON EPITAPHS

In the burying ground of Christ P. E. Church at Brownsville, Fayette Co., Pennsylvania, are two monuments on which are the following inscriptions:

"In Memory of
Archibald Washington
a Native of Virginia
was born in the County
of Southampton, the 25th
day of Febry, A. D. 1785, and
departed this life, the 10th of
April 1818.

In Memory of John H. Washington,
a native of Virginia,
was born in the County
of Southampton, the 8th of
June A. D. 1780, and departed
This Life the 13th of April, 1818."

These two Washingtons were enroute to Kentucky, and were awaiting a boat to go there by way of the Monongahela and Ohio rivers, when they fell victims to smallpox at Brownsville.

Edmund Hayes Bell,
Washington, D. C.

EPITAPH OF MRS. WINSTON.

"Dorothea Spottswood Henry Winston
Daughter of Patrick Henry of Virginia
Born at 'Red Hill' in Virginia on August 2, 1778
Died in Memphis, Tennessee on June 17, 1854
Erected by the Commodore Perry Chapter of Memphis in October, 1907
under the regency of Mrs. Stephen C. Toof."

MRS. BENJAMIN HARRISON'S EPITAPH AT THE WHITE
SULPHUR SPRINGS.

Consecrated by filial duty & affection
to the memory of
MRS. EVELYN TAYLOR HARRISON
a daughter of Col. Byrd of Westover &
the relict of Benj. Harrison Esqr. of Brandon.
She expired at the White Sulphur Springs
on the 12th of Oct'r 1817 aged 51 years.
After a protracted & painful illness
borne with that resignation & fortitude
which a confidence in the truths of
the gospel never fails to inspire.
Religious without bigotry.   Charitable
without ostentation.   Urbane & courteous
without insincerity.
She filled with exact propriety the
relations of social life & died regretted by
all her acquaintance who knew how to
appreciate moral worth in an enlightened
& benevolent female.

GEORGE THORNTON.

We are indebted to Mr. Leo Culleton, of London, for the following copy of the epitaph of a young Virginian who died in England, whither he had probably gone for an education. He was son of William Thornton (born Dec. 14, 1680, died 1742 or 1743), who was a Burgess from King George Co. 1723, and 1726.

Parish of Almondsbury, Co. Gloucester (England).

George Thornton, a native
of Virginia, the beloved Son of
William Thornton, of Rhapahanock River,
in the County of King George,
was born 19th Dec. 1724.

He came to this place November last
and died the 19th day Dec. 1740,
having that Day fully completed
the 16th year of his age

Notice of a tombstone inscription in Bigland's Hist. of Glouc., Vol. I, p. 47, 191, f. 1, 2.

VIRGINIA NOTES FROM ENGLISH RECORDS.

Communicated by Charles E. Banks, Brookline, Mass.

Tobias Smyth, of "Nutmegge Quarter", in Virginia was married to Phebe Fauntleroy, of Crandall, co. Hants 18 Nov. 1641 at S. Christopher-le-Stocks, London.

John Gallow, or Gallon, was apprenticed to Jeffrey Willett, carpenter, now bound for Virginia, 1619. (Parish Mss. S. Dunstan-in-the-East, London).

Christopher Boyes, of Blunt Point, Virginia, gent. deposed 7 April 1636, in London, aged 38 years. (Pub. Rec. Off. H. C. A. Vol. 52.)

William Tucker, of Elizabeth City, Virginia, Esquire, deposed 12 May 1630, no age given, relative to affairs there 1628. (ibid, Vol. 49).

William Tucker, of Rotherhithe, co. Surrey, armiger, deposed 17 Jan. 1633, aged 44 Years relative to a voyage to Virginia, (ibid, Vol. 50).

John, son of John Harris, gent., and Dorothy his wife, of Virginia, was baptized 1 May 1624, at S. Dunstan's, Stepney, London.

Capt. Samuel Matthews of Denby, Virginia, deposed in January, 1637, no age given. (P. R. Office, H. C. A. Vol. 53).

James Knott of Mausanum, "in the lower Countie of Newe Norfolk in Virginia gent," aged 35 yeares or thereabouts, deposed in 1638, as a resident there for twenty years, relative to the Virginia Massacre of 1622. (P. R. O. Register of Affidavits, vol. XI, Trinity Term, 1638, No. 208). This was contributed to, and published in, the Genealogists Magazine, v. ii, no. 2, London, June 1926. by the undersigned.

Charles Edward Banks

Brookline, Mass.

APPENDIX C: Bible Records from
The Virginia Magazine of History and Biography
ANDERSON BIBLE RECORDS

Cousin Celely Anderson's Bible.
Aunt Cecely' daughter—old Family Bible owned by cousin Nancy—
Hanover County, Virginia.

Births

Elizabeth Anderson Jan. 6th, 1786
Robert Anderson August 28, 1788

Children of J. Anderson and Ann Ellett

Agnes Anderson Sep. 21st, 1800
William Matt Anderson Dec. 11 1801
Richard N. Anderson March 25, 1804
Nancy Ellett Anderson 2nd Mar. 1807
Mildred Agnes Anderson 27 Sept. 1809
Patsy Maria Anderson Nov. 20, 1814
Royal G. Shepard Sep. 29th, 1824

Walter Gould Anderson May 13, 1783
Mary Ann Crawford May 13, 1793

Children of John and Nancy Anderson

Mary Catherine Anderson 25 Jan. 1817
John Anderson 1820, April 29
Susana Louisa Anderson 29 April 1820
Cecly V. Martin Mar 28th 1804
John W. Anderson May 16th 1833
Hillary Walter Anderson April 20th 1836
Robert Nelson Anderson Sep 4th 1830

William Anderson April 15th 1744
Cecely Anderson August 2nd 1748

Their children, children of William and Cecely
Mildred Anderson 21st May 1769
Nelson Anderson June 3, 1771
Robert Anderson June 27, 1773
Mary Anderson Oct. 10, 1774
Richard Anderson Oct. 12, 1776
John Anderson Jan. 5, 1779
Elizabeth Anderson 2 August 1782
Eliz. Clough Anderson Sept. 17, 1783
Nancy Ellet Sep. 11, 1779

Marriages

William and Cecely Anderson April 3, 1768
John and Nancy Ellett 11 Dec. 1799
William M. Anderson and Cecely F. Anderson Dec. 1st 1824
Richard N. Anderson
Mildred S. Anderson and Seymore Johnson 17 March 1830
Walter Goldsmith and Mary Ann Crawford May 1st 1810
Stephen O. Duuval and Ann Eliza Anderson Thursday 18 March 1847.

Deaths

Robert Anderson Oct. 17th 1773
Richard Anderson May 10th 1794
Eliza Anderson August 15th 1784
Robert Anderson June 17th 1789
William Anderson July 22nd 1792
Cecly Anderson Sep 30, 1802.

Children of John and Nancy Ellet

Agnes Anderson Sep 22nd 1800
Nancy Anderson. Wife of John Anderson Jan. 31st 1821
Mary Anderson Ellet wife of Ben Ellet March 16th (March) 1830
Eliza C. Anderson Wife of John Martin March 29th 1835
Hilary Watson son of W. M. August 19th 1837
William 'Matt Anderson son of John and Nancy April 19th 1857
John Martin Jan. 9th 1857 aged 82.

S. Duuval married a sister of Robert Anderson living in 1878 in Hanover Co. Mrs. David Anderson was a Miss Moseby

Wm. P. Anderson

COPIED FROM DAVID BALL'S BIBLE, OF KILMARNOCK, LANCASTER CO., VA., PAGE 677

DAVID BALL—HIS BOOK PURCHASED JUNE 1808, PRICE $12

David Ball m. Sarah V. Newton Mar. 20, 1783, and m. Elizabeth Portues Ball his second wife Dec. 6th, 1788.

Albert Ball son of D. Ball & Eliz. was m. Feb. 14, 1828 to Fanny M. Blakey dau. Yelventon C. Blakey & Judith.

David Ball son of Joseph & Hannah was b. Nov. 23, 1754.

Sarah Vaux Ball wife of David b. July 14, 1767.

Eliz. V. Ball dau. of David B. & Sarah was b. Oct. 30, 1784.

Eliz. P. Ball 2nd wife of David b. Feb. 11, 1767.

Mildred Downman B. dau. of D. B. & Eliz. b. Oct. 6, 1789.

Ann P. Ball b. Apr. 26, 1791.

Sarah Ball b. Aug. 6, 1792.

Harriet Ball b. June 13, 1794.

William Ball b. Oct. 21, 1796 & d. Dec. 30. 1796.

Louisa Ball b. Nov. 11, 1797.

Juliet B. b. July 13, 1801.

David B.   June 18, 1804.

Albert B.   June 10, 1807.

Fanny M. Blakey wife of Albert Ball b. Oct. 25, 1811.

David Y. B. son of Albert & Fanny b. Oct. 25, 1828.

Oscar O. Ball son of same b. Mar. 4, 1831.

John May Ball son of same   Feb. 21, 1833.

Sarah V. Ball departed this life the 17th of June 1785.

Mildred D. Ball d. April 24, 1791.

Wm. Ball d. Dec. 30, 1796.

David B. son of Joseph & Hannah d. Dec. 3, 1815 aged 61 years 10 days.

Harriet B. d. of David Ball & Eliz. P. d. Oct. 20, 1818 aged 24 yrs. 4 mo. 13 da.

Sarah Conway d. of David B. & Eliz. P. Jan. 27, 1821.

Dr. David B. d. Mar. 19, 1828 son of David & Eliz. P. aged 23 yrs. 9 mo. 12 da.

Eliz. P. B. d. Dec. 31, 1831 aged 64 yrs. 10 mo. 21 da.

John May B. son of Albert & Fanny d. July 28, 1834, aged 4 years 7 mo. & 8 days. (Copier's note: This does not agree with birth date above.)

Louisa Ann d. of Hilkiah & Harriet his wife b. Oct. 12, 1818.

David Ball, owner of the Bible, was the son of Joseph Ball (designated by Hayden as 56) and Hannah. Joseph Ball (56) was the son of Capt. Geo. Ball (designated by Hayden as 10) and Grace Haynie (incorrectly stated by Hayden as Grace Waddy. She was the daughter of Anthony and Sarah (Harris) Haynie. Sarah married secondly Francis Waddy who died without issue. Hence the error.)

David Ball's will is recorded in Book No. 20, page 427 (year 1815) of the records of Northumberland County, Virginia.

Sarah Vaux Ball, wife of David, born July 14, 1767, was Sarah Vaux Newton prior to her marriage, Mar. 20, 1783, to David Ball. It is thought that she was the sister of Willoughby Newton of Linden, Westmoreland Co., Va., and also was the unborn child mentioned in John Newton's will (proved Feb. 24, 1767—See Selden, p. 495). John Newton died before Jan. 6, 1767. Sarah Vaux Newton was born July 14, 1767. It is also thought that John Newton's wife was Elizabeth Vaulx, born after 1739, daughter of Robert Vaulx who died about 1755, Westmoreland Co., Va.

Charles M. Noble.

WINSTON-BARRETT BIBLE RECORDS.

I enclose a copy of the records contained in the Barrett family Bible in possession of one of my cousins in Tennessee. If you care to publish it, you are at liberty to do so and I should appreciate it if you would at the same time publish a request for any of the descendants of Robert Barrett to send me any data on this family as I have already collected much material and I want to publish my notes as soon as they are complete in the form of a book on the Barrett family. In order to do this, full co-operation of all branches of the family is necessary.

Barrett Bible Records

On a page separate from the Barrett records is the following:
Barbara Overton born Feb. 5, 1690; died October 12, 1766.
John Winston born 1729; died January 23, 1772.
Alice Winston died in 1773 at the age of 43.
William Overton Winston born November 16, 1747.
Mary Todd Winston born March 16, 1748; died February 27, 1751.
Barbara Winston born November 30, 1750; died November 8, 1823.
James Winston born March 12, 1753.
Mollie Winston born March 28, 1755; died Nov. 13, 1761.
John Winston born October 4, 1757.
Elizabeth Winston born January 1, 1760.
Joseph Winston born April 12, 1763.
Martha Winston born June 21, 1765.
Bickerton Winston born January 28, 1768.
Alice Ann Winston born August 8, 1769.
In the regular Barrett records is the following:
Robert Barrett married Barbara Winston 15th of August, 1771.
Robert Barrett died June 9th, 1823.
Barbara Barrett died November 6th, 1823.
John Yates and Nancy Coleman were married May 11, 1785; she died in Dec., 1810, and he died in Dec., 1812.
William Overton Barrett and Mary Yates were married May 16th, 1811.
John Yates Barrett and Sarah A. Winn were married Sept. 8, 1840.
Barbara Winston Barrett and Daniel Pierce were married April 18, 1842.
Nancy Coleman Barrett and William S. Mayfield were married May 19, 1834.
Nancy Coleman Barrett married, second, Joseph Robertson Aug. 7th, 1842.
Mary Overton Barrett and John Patton were married Aug. 20th, 1844.

Births

Robert Barrett born Oct. 26th, 1772.

Robert Barrett born ———— ——, 1773.

John Winston Barrett born December 10th, 1775; died Oct. 3rd, 1821.

Elizabeth Lewis Barrett born May 2nd, 1778; died October 3rd, 1821.

Elizabeth Winston Barrett born August 2nd, 1779.

William Overton Barrett born June 10th, 1783; died May ——, 1866.

Lewis Barrett born April 21st, 1785.

James Winston Barrett born February 16th, 1791.

Nelson Berkeley Barrett born October 3rd, 1793; died April 8th, 1815.

Elizabeth Lewis Barrett ————.

Robert Barrett ————.

The pages are yellow with age and the ink faded so that not all dates can be read.

Geo. W. Chappelear

GEORGE WYTHE BAYLOR'S BIBLE.

Copied by Mrs. J. M. Cunningham-Dale.

MARRIAGES

George W. Baylor, born January 5th, 1785 and married to Betsy D. Timberlake on the 3d day of December 1807.

He was the son of Major Walker Baylor, who was the son of Col. John Baylor of Caroline County, Virginia, who intermarried with Frances Walker. She [Betsy Timberlake] was a Friend-Quaker. They were descendants from England.

George W. Baylor's mother was the daughter of Joseph Bledsoe.

Betsy Davis Timberlake born October 19, 1789 and married George W. Baylor on the 3d day of December, 1807.

Mary Jane Baylor married to Joseph Henry Bledsoe November 18th, 1729.

John P. Allen born March 3d 1810 and was married to George Ann Baylor on the 25th day of September, 1824, who was born August 25, 1818.

(These dates are as given in copy, but are evidently incorrect.—Ed.)

BIRTHS

Richard Walker Baylor born 13th day of December, 1808, first son of George W. and Betsy Davis Baylor.

Mary Jane Baylor born 20th July, 1810, first daughter of George W. and Betsy Davis Baylor.

Courtenay Baylor born 20th May, 1813, second daughter of George W. and Betsy Davis Baylor.

George Ann Baylor born 25th August, 1818, the third daughter of George W. and Betsy Davis Baylor.

Walker Baylor Allen was born 31 of July 1835.

DEATHS

Died on the 9th day of March, 1812 Philpot Curran Baylor an infant son of George W. & Betsy Davis Baylor.

Died on the 16th day of April, 1822 Courtenay Baylor, second daughter of George W. & Betsy Davis Baylor.

Died on the 5th day of March, 1838 Betsy Davis Chinn, consort of Aquilla Chinn. She was Betsy D. Timberlake and consort of George W. Baylor.

Died on the 14th of Sept. in the morn 1822 Major Walker Baylor, father of George W. Baylor.

Mistress Mary Timberlake, 2d wife of Richard Timberlake & formerly the wife of Samuel Smith, dec'd, born in the month of May, 19, 1747, the daughter of Thomas Munden & Rachel Munden, who was the daughter of John Payne and Nancy Page, who was the daughter of Carter, all of whom were originally from Great Britain except Thomas Munden, whose father was from France and married in England, and Mrs. Mary Timberlake is the mother of Betsy D. Timberlake, now the wife of George W. Baylor, her youngest child.

The old Bible is now in possession of Susan Thornton Henning (Merriwether), of Allendale Farm, Shelby County, Kentucky, a granddaughter of George W. Baylor.

A BEVERLEY-RANDOLPH FAMILY BIBLE (RECORD).

In Possession of Mrs. John B. Reid, of Birmingham, Ala.

On title page is written "Maria Carter". Opposite (facing) the title page is written:

"Maria Carter, Her Book, given unto her by me, her grandmother, Maria Byrd, Anno Mundi 5753".

On the fly-leaves:

Page 1.

William Beverley, born Oct. 27th, 1763, at Blandfield, and died in Paris, Sepr., 1823.

Maria Beverley, born Decr. 15th, 1764, at Blandfield and died Octr., 1824, at Williamsburg in her 61st year.

Robert Beverley, born July the 30th, 1766 at Blandfield, who died Jan. 14th, 1767.

Robert Beverley, born at Blandfield 12th March, 1769 and died May, 1823.

Lucy Beverley, born at Blandfield 24 Feb. 1771, and died in 1854.

Burton Beverley, born at Blandfield 24 Nov. 1772, & died July 16, 1781.

Carter Beverley, born at Blandfield 15th April, 1774 and died February 10th, 1844.

Byrd Beverley, born at Blandfield 17th August, 1775.

James Mills Beverley, born at Blandfield 22d Decr. 1776, who died April 8th, 1779.

Anna Munford Beverley, born at Blandfield 6th January, 1778, and died October 7th, 1830.

Munford Beverley, born at Blandfield March 8th, 1779, and died at sea February, 1820.

Peter Randolph Beverley, born Octr. 17, 1780 at Blandfield.

Evelyn Byrd Beverley, born June 6, 1782 at Blandfield and died Sept. 10th, 1836.

McKenzie Beverley, born June 3d, 1783 at Blandfield.

Jane Bradshaw Beverley, born August 27th, 1784 at Blandfield.

Harriet Beverley, born 12th April 1786, and died in May, 1829.

Page 2 (of fly-leaves).

Robert Beverley, son of William & Elizabeth Beverley, born Augt. 21st, 1740, old style, married his wife, Maria Beverley 3d Feb'y 1763, who was born the 22d Nov. 1745, Maria Carter the daughter of Landon Carter Esq., Sabine Hall, by Maria the daughter of Honble William Byrd Esq.

James Mills Beverley died at Blandfield April 8th, 1779. Burton Beverley died at Blandfield July 16th, 1781 of a phrenzy.

Robert Beverley, son of William and Elizabeth [destroyed] died April 12, 1800, aged 60. She was a Bland.

Maria Beverley, daughter of Landon Carter Esqre, of Sabine Hall, by Mary the daughter of Honble William Byrd Esqre of Westover, died August 21st, 1817 at Williamsburg, aged nearly seventy two (72).

Old Aunt Rose, the maid of great-grand-mama, birth not recollected, died in the year 1827, aged one hundred and fifteen (115). Old James Boy—spouse of Rose, birth not recollected, as to the day, died in the year 1825, aged (101).

Culpeper Johnson died April 16, 1834, aged 76 years.

Easter Johnson his wife died Decd. 28th 1841, aged 70 years.

——— ———, a faithful servant died July 23rd, 1842, aged 76.

Page 3 (of fly-leaves).

Brett Randolph, son of Richard Randolph of Curles, married Lucy Beverley, daughter of Robert Beverley of Blandfield, Nov. 21st, 1789.

A son born Novr. 24th, 1790, died Decr. 13, 1790.

Edward Brett Randolph born Jany. 9th, 1792 and died August the 4th, 1898, Columbus, Miss.

Robert Carter Randolph, born July 22nd 1793.

Richard Randolph, born May 20th, 1795.

Victor Moreau Randolph, born July 24, 1797.

John Thomson Randolph, born Jany. 27th, 1800 and died August 23rd 1819, in his 19th year, near Fort Montgomery, Ala.

Benjamin Franklin Randolph the second, born Feb. 2nd, 1803.

Benjamin Franklin Randolph, born July 27th 1801 and died Augt. 8th, 1802.

Ryland Randolph, born July 29th, 1805 and died in Lexington, Kentucky, June 9th, 1833 of the cholera, aged 28.

Theodorick Bland Randolph, born July 1st, 1807.

Ann Maria Randolph, born March 2nd, 1811.

FINIS

William Byrd Beverley born October 4th 1813, died in October, 1846. Page 4. All is 19th century data.

Page 5 (of fly-leaves).

Brett Randolph born at Curles, Henrico County, Virginia, July 20, 1766, died Jan'y 23rd, 1828, at Goshen, Lowndes County, Mississippi, in his 62nd year.

Amaryllies Beverley died Novr. 28, 1835, in Green County, Alabama, of a pulmonary complaint—aged 25 years.

Brett Noel Randolph died Octr. 18th, 1836, aged 14 years 4 months.

———

629

BIBLE RECORDS.

BEVERLEY, MEADE, ETC.

(Contributed by Commander Reginald B. Henry, U. S. N.)

Marriages

Carter Beverley, 3rd son of Robert Beverley, of Blandfield, Essex County, married Jane Wormeley, of Rosegill, Middlesex County, the 25th of June, 1795.

Eleanor Wormeley married Francis Gildart of Mississippi, 1819.

Rebecca Wormeley married John E. Meade of Virginia, 1830.

Elizabeth Bland married her cousin, E. B. Randolph, of Va., 1824.

Ann Tayloe married Benjamin Farrar, of Mississippi, in 1823 & afterwards her cousin, Carter Randolph, of Louisiana, in 1826.

Carter Burwell married Mrs. Lucie of Alabama, 1850.

William Beverley married Harriette Crane June 10th, 1846.

Charlotte S. Meade, second daughter of Jno. E. Meade, married Julian C. Ruffin of Pr. Geo. Va. at Cedar Level May 26th, 1852.

Elizabeth R. Meade was married to David Callender of Petersburg Nov. 8th, 1855, at C. Level.

Eleanor B. Meade was married to Rev. W. H. Platt of Petersburg June 23rd, 1857.

Births

Carter Beverley born 17 of April, 1774.

Jane Wormeley born the 29th of February, 1776.

Lucy Byrd Beverley born 19 of March in 1796.

Robert Lee Beverley born 11th January, 1798.

Byrd Wormeley Beverley born 15th February, 1799.

Eleanor Wormeley Beverley born the 6th of April, 1801.

Rebecca Wormeley Beverley born the 4 of September, 1803.

Elizabeth Bland Beverley born 14 of December, 1804.

Robert Byrd Beverley born the 3rd of April, 1806.

Ann Tayloe Beverley born 31st of March 1808.

Carter Burwell Beverley born 4 of October, 1810.

William Beverley Beverley born 6 of October, 1813.

Jno. E. Meade, Esqr., son of David & Elizabeth Meade of Amelia Co., Virginia, was born July 16th, 1792.

Elizabeth Randolph, daughter of Jno. & Rebecca Meade, was born in Pr. Geo. County 4th Sept., 1831.

Charlotte Stockdell, 2nd daughter of Jno. & Rebecca Meade, was born at Cawsons 23rd May, 1833.

Eleanor Beverley, their 3rd child, was born at Cawsons, Pr. Geo. Co. 18th December, 1834.

Carter Randolph, their 4th child, was born at Cawsons, Prince George Co., Va., 9th Nov., 1836.

Jane Wormeley, their 5th child, was born at Cawsons 15th April, Easter Sunday, 1838.

John Everard Meade, their 6th child, was born at Cedar Level, Prince George Co., Virginia, March 16th, 1841.

Julian C. Ruffin, born in Pr. Geo. Co., Va., July 14th, 1821.

Deaths

Carter Beverley died the 11 of January, 1842.

Jane Beverley died February 23, 1814.

Lucy Byrd died 28 of November 1796.

Robert Lee died 19th of December, 1805.

Byrd Wormeley died 5 of September, 1803.

Eleanor Wormeley died 11 January, 1823.

Robert Byrd died 17 of November, 1849.

William Beverley died 31 of October, 1846.

Departed this life at Cawsons June 24th, 1837, Carter Randolph, son of Jno. & Rebecca Meade.

Died at Strawberry Hill in Petersburg, Jane Wormeley, fourth daughter of Jno. & Rebecca Meade, 24th June, 1839.

Departed this life at Cedar Level in the sixty third year of his age our Father, John Everard Meade, 27th Dec., 1854.

BIBLE RECORDS.

BLUNT, KELLO, NORFLEET, ETC.

(Contributed by Mrs. William S. Manning, Jacksonville, Florida)

Copied from two leaves torn from a Bible in the Douglas Family, given to Mrs. George Lewis, of Tallahassee, Florida, by her half brother, William Cary Douglas, of Saint Louis, Mo.

Page 677, Family Recrod

Marriages

James Kello and Mary W. Blunt were married 23rd March 1809.

Thomas W. Vaughan and Margaret B. Kello were married the 26th of November 1829.

Married on Thursday January 21, 1836, Samuel James Douglas, attorney at law, of Petersburg, Va. to Louisa H. B. Kello, Southampton Co. Va.

Married on the 27th of January 1847, S. James Douglas to Lizzie, daughter of Genl. Thomas Brown of the city of Tallahassee.

Page 678. *Births*

Ann Eliza Kello, daughter of Ja. and Mary W. Kello was born the 22nd day of February 1810.

Margaret B. Kell,o daughter of James and Mary W. Kello was born the 30th day of January 1813.

Mary W. Kello daughter of James and Mary W. Kello born the 17th day of June 1814.

Louisa Henrietta Blunt Kello, daughter of James and Mary W. Kello was born 15th day of October 1816 about 11 o'clock a. m.

William Patrick Kello son of James and Mary W. Kello was born 21st day of April about 11 o'clock a. m.

Born Oct. 19 1812 Samuel James Douglas, son of James and Mary Douglas of Petersburg.

Page 679. *Deaths*

Ann Eliza Kello daughter of James and Mary Kello died the 7th day of October 1812 with Cynanche trachealis in 23 hours after she was taken ill. Age 2 yrs. 7 mo. 15 days.

Mary W. Kello, daughter of James and Mary Kello departed this life the 5th day of October in the year of Our Lord 1817.

Dr. James Kello departed this life the 7th day of Sept in the year of Our Lord 1820, after a long and Painful illness of about ten months.

William Patrick Kello, son of James and Mary W. Kello died the 22nd of February 1830.

Page from a Bible Record. This page is in the possession of Miss Mary Douglas Lewis, 402 East Park Avenue, Tallahassee, Fla.

Joseph Norfleet son of Cordall and Mary Norfleet was born the 13th October 1772.

Elizabeth Norfleet was born 20th August 1774.

John Norfleet was born the 20th Sept. 1776.

Sarah Norfleet was born the 12th Sept. 1778.

James Norfleet was born the 12th Sept. 1780.

Cordall Norfleet died (no date).

James Gee and Mary Norfleet was married 18th Ma (torn edge) 1794.

James Henry Gee son of James and Mary his wife was born the 13th June 1795. Ob. 30th Sept 1795.

William Henry Gee was born 18th April 1797.

Lovinia N. Gee was born 21st August 1798.

Sarah Jones formerly Norfleet died 22nd Sept. 1798.

John Norfleet died the 14th July 1798.

Lovinia N. Gee died 30th Sept. 1798.

Mary Gee wife of James Gee died the 9th November 181 (torn off).

William N. Blunt and Elizabeth Norfleet was married the 24 of November 1790.

Mary Wilkerson Blunt daughter of Wm. and Elizebeth Blunt was born 7th of Sept. 1791.

Ann Gilliam Blunt was born 23rd Jan. 1793.

Sarah Norfleet Blunt was born 19th Jan. 1795.

Louisa Rebecceh Blunt was born 8th July 1796.

Eliza Norfleet Blunt was born 14th April 1798.

John Norfleet was born 24th March 1800.

Martha Priscilla Blunt was born 5th March 1802.

William Cordall Blune was born 22nd July 1804.

Sarah Norfleet Blunt died 30th July 1804.

William Cordall Blunt died 24th Aug. 1807.

William Blunt, Sen., died 27th April 1807.

William Blunt, Jun., died 17th Nov. 1807.

Elizabeth Johnston formerly Blunt died 6th March 1813.

Nathaniel Wilkerson and Ann G. Blunt was married 18th January 1810.

John Wilkerson son of Nathaniel and Ann G. his wife was born 17th January 1811.

Nathaniel Wilkerson was born the 28th July 1813.

Nathaniel Wilkerson, Sen., died 15th May 1813.
Nathaniel Wilkerson, Jun., died 18th Jan. 1814.
John Wilkerson died 13th Sept. 1814.
Thomas Ridley and Ann G. Wilkerson was married 24th July 1816.

BROWN, SAUNDERS, ETC. BIBLE RECORDS.

Certain Bible Records from Family Bibles in the possession of
F. A. Omohundro, Richmond, Va.

William Brown, born March 10, 1740, died Nov. 1832; Sarah Brown, his wife, born January 8, 1741, died 1816.

James Brown, son of above, born April 29, 1764, died 1774; William Brown, son of William Brown and Sarah, his wife, born Sept. 7, 1769, died in infancy.

Ann Brown, daughter of William Brown and Sarah, his wife, born May 15, 1772, died 1812; married James Quesenberry Dec. 1794.

Sarah Brown, daughter of William Brown and Sarah, his wife, born Oct. 6, 1775; married James Bullock.

Ruth Brown, daughter of William Brown and Sarah, his wife, born Nov. 4, 1779; married ——— Kendall.

Solomon James Slauter Brown, son of William Brown and Sarah, his wife, born Nov. 24, 1782, died about ½ after 6 o'clock in the evening of July 29, 1862; married Lucy Waller Saunders July 7, 1818, daughter of Col. William Saunders and Sarah, his wife, born May 2, 1801, died Aug. 28, 1840.

Sarah Ann Brown, daughter of S. J. S. Brown and Lucy, his wife, was born April 18, 1819, died Oct. 6, 1821.

William Saunders Brown, son of S. J. S. Brown and Lucy, his wife, was born Dec. 7, 1820; married to Joshua M. Ijams May 20, 1847.

James Monroe Brown, son of S. J. S. Brown and Lucy, his wife, born June 11, 1822.

Mary Walker Brown, daughter of S. J. S. Brown and Lucy, his wife, was born Aug. 14, 1823, died Aug. 12, 1825.

Virginia Madison. Brown, daughter of S. J. S. Brown and Lucy, his wife, was born Nov. 4, 1824, died March 27, 1827.

Maria Louisa Brown, daughter of S. J. S. Brown and Lucy, his wife, was born July 9, 1826, was married to Doctor F. F. Ninde Dec. 13, 1848.

Lucy Waller Brown, daughter of S. J. S. Brown and Lucy, his wife, was born Dec. 13, 1827, was married to Andrew F. Donnally April 28, 1850.

Martha Ann Brown, daughter of S. J. S. Brown and Lucy, his

wife, was born Sept. 2, 1829; was married to George D. Ashton July 1, 1847.

Edwin Dorsey Brown, son of S. J. S. Brown and Lucy, his wife, was born May 22, 1831; married Lucy Dickerson Quesenberry Aug. 12, 1854.

Sarah Virginia Brown, daughter of S. J. S. Brown and Lucy, his wife, was born Oct. 18, 1832, married Col. James M. Wynn about 4 o'clock in the morning of Feb. 21, 1865.

John Wesley Brown, son of S. J. S. Brown and Lucy, his wife, was born Dec. 26, 1834.

Caroline Letitia Brown, daughter of S. J. S. Brown and Lucy, his wife, was born Jan. 14, 1837; married Capt. Henry W. Wingfield Jan. 28, 1864.

George Buckner Brown, son of S. J. S. Brown and Lucy, his wife, was born June 1, 1838.

Henry Maxfield Brown, son of S. J. S. Brown and Lucy, his wife, was born Aug. 2, 1840.

Col. William Saunders died May 11, 1819.

Mrs. Sarah Saunders, his wife, died Nov. 11, 1827.

Mrs. Ann Jones, mother of Mrs. Sarah Saunders, died May 17, 1819.

Ann Madison Saunders, daughter of Col. William Saunders and Sarah, his wife, was born March 17, 1791; married George Buckner Dec. 1807.

Lucinda Jones Saunders, daughter of Col. William Saunders and Sarah, his wife, was born Nov. 9, 1792.

Mary Walker Saunders, daughter of Col. William Saunders and Sarah, his wife, was born Jan. 4, 1795.

John Jones Saunders, son of Col. William Saunders and Sarah, his wife, was born Nov. 24, 1796.

Emily Jones Saunders, daughter of Col. William Saunders and Sarah, his wife, was born Aug. 1, 1799; married to Col. Thomas B. B. Baber May 21, 1817.

Lucy Waller Saunders, daughter of Col. William Saunders and Sarah, his wife, was born May 2, 1801; married S. J. S. Brown July 7, 1818, died Aug. 28, 1840.

Lavinia Jones Saunders, daughter of Col. William Saunders and Sarah, his wife, was born June 11, 1803; married Reuben Saunders Nov. 22, 1825.

Sarah Saunders, daughter of Col. William Saunders and Sarah, his wife, was born Aug. 27, 1805.

Marie Walker Saunders, daughter of Col. William Saunders and Sarah, his wife, was born Nov. 27, 1807; married Reuben Garnett Nov. 18, 1823.

William Alexander Saunders, son of Col. William Saunders and Sarah, his wife, was born Nov. 17, 1809, married Mary E. Monroe Oct. 1, 1829.

Susan Frances Saunders, daughter of Col. William Saunders and Sarah, his wife, was born May 10, 1812, married Reuben B. Richerson Nov. 4, 1830.

Anna Hill Saunders, daughter of Col. William Saunders and Sarah, his wife, was born July 10, 1814, married William Colton May 17, 1835.

Francis William Buckner, son of George and Ann Buckner, was born July 1, 1810.

Mary Ann Buckner, daughter of George and Ann Buckner, was born Dec. 2, 1812.

George Buckner, son of George and Ann Buckner, was born Aug. 22, 1815.

James I. Garnett, son of Reuben Garnett and Marie, his wife, was born Aug. 6, 1824.

Reuben Garnett, son of Reuben Garnett and Marie, his wife, was born March 6, 1826.

Sarah Ann Elizabeth Saunders was born Aug. 20, 1826, married Dr. R. H. Cox July, 1844.

Reuben Walter Raleigh Saunders was born Dec. 28, 1827.

Mrs. Sarah T. Pitts died Nov. 5, 1828.

Col. Thomas B. B. Baber died April 30, 1871.

William Alexander Saunders died July 3, 1857.

Ann Hill Colton died August 17, 1871.

Polly Louisa Kendall, daughter of Joshua Kendall and Betsy, his wife, was born March the 28th day, in the year of our Lord 1799.

William Washington Kendall, son of Joshua Kendall and Betsy, his wife, was born January the 25th day in the year of our Lord 1801.

Note—The first member of this Brown family in Virginia was William Brown, whose will is recorded in the old Rappahannock Co. Wills Order Book dated March 18, 1676, in which he mentioned his wife, Elizabeth, and his sons William, John and Maxfield.

There is also a deed in Richmond Co. Va. clerk's office from the second William Brown to John Suttle, dated April 3, 1694, conveying certain land located in what is now King George Co., Va., in which he mentions his father, William Brown, and his brothers John and Maxfield. And deeds in King George Co. Court clerk's office from Maxfield Brown to his sons George and Newman dated March 4, 1736.

The late Judge James H. Brown, of Charleston, W. Va. (born Dec. 25, 1818, died Oct. 28, 1900), member of West Virginia Court of Appeals, was of this family.

S. J. S. Brown was clerk of King George County, Va. from 1838 to 1845, and his son, William Saunders Brown, also held this office continuously for 44 years, from 1845 to 1887.

NOTES FROM BIBLE RECORDS.

Old Burnley Bible in the possession of Mrs. W. B. Ardery,
Rocclicgan, Paris, Ky.

Garland Burnley was born January 12th 1753
Elizabeth Swan Jones daughter of John Jones and Mary his wife
was born the 25th day of May 1755
Swan Jones son of do. was born the 1 May 1757
Harden Burnley son of Zach. Burnley and Mary his wife was
born the 19th day of March 1761
Judith Burnley daughter of do. was born December 23 1763
Reubin Burnley son of do. was born May 14 1766
James Burnley son do. was born 26th day March 1769
Mary Burnley daughter of do. was born 11th July 1771
John Burnley son of do. was born July 6th 1774
Sally Jones Burnley was born 16 May 1777
Mary Bell Burnley daughter of Richd Burnley was born on February the 16th 1776

Records copied from the Spencer Bible now in the possession of
Mrs. William B. Ardery, Rocclicgan, Paris, Ky.

First Page—Marriages

George Spencer was married to Elizabeth Hogue the 15th of the
3rd month 1838
Solomon H. Spencer was married to Frances Strickler the 8th of
the 7th month 1878
Sarah J. Spencer was married to Simpson G. Haines the 26th of
the 9th 1867.
Isaac Jesse Spencer to Sarah Louise Pendleton the 19th of the 9th
month 1878.
Martha Louisa Spencer to Joseph Wallace Satterthwait the 30th
of the 10th month 1881.

Deaths

George Spencer deceased the 3rd of the 1st month 1863
William Spencer son of George and Elizabeth Spencer deceased
the 6th of the 11th month 1862

Joseph Spencer son of George and Elizabeth Spencer deceased the 5th of the 3rd month 1863

Second Page—Births

John Spencer was born the 11th of the 3rd month 1763

Lydia Spencer was born the 4th day of the 2nd month 1762

Hannah Spencer their daughter was born the 7th of the 4th month 1783

Margaret Spencer their daughter was born the 29th of the 12th month 1784

Joseph Spencer their son was born the 12th of the 11th month 1786.

Alice Spencer their daughter was born the 18th of the 12th month 1788

Aaron Spencer, their son was born the 17th of the 3rd month 1791

Uphany Spencer their daughter was born the 26th of the 10th month 1793

John Spencer their son was born the 21st of the 8th month 1795

George Spencer their son was born the 8th of the 8th month 1797

Lydia Spencer their daughter was born the 30th of the 9th month 1799

Amy Spencer their daughter was born the 5th of the 7th month 1801

Betsy Spencer their daughter was born the 24th of the 10th month 1805

Sally Spencer their daughter was born the 6th of the 3rd month 1808

Third Page

Joseph Spencer was born the 12th of the 11th month 1786

Sarah his wife was born the 3rd of the 10th month 1793

John their son was born the 10th of the 1st month 1811

William their son was born the 20th of the 3rd month 1812

Elisha their son was born the 3rd of the 6th month 1814

George their son was born the 12th of the 6th month 1816

Amy their daughter was born the 16th of the 1st month 1819

Joseph their son was born the 23rd of the 5th month 1821.

Martha Louisa Spencer daughter of George and Elizabeth was born the 14th of the (?) month 1857

George Spencer was born the 12th of the 6th month 1816

Elizabeth his wife was born the 24th of the 9th month 1815

Joseph Spencer their son was born the 13th of the 5th month 1840

Soloman their son was born the 11th of the 11th month 1841

William Spencer their son was born the 1st of the 3rd month 1844

Sarah Jane Spencer their daughter was born the 12th of the 9th month 1847

Isaac Jesse Spencer was born the 10th of the 11th month 1851

Fourth Page—Deaths

Margaret Spencer deceased the 11th month 1787
John Spencer deceased the 2nd month 1798
John Spencer Senr. deceased the 9th of the 7th month 1816
Lydia Spencer deceased the 10th of the 6th month 1820

John Spencer son of Joseph and Sarah Spencer deceased the 9th of the 1st month 1811

Elisha their son deceased the 3rd month 1818
Joseph Spencer deceased the 15th of the 2nd month 1821
William Spencer deceased the 20th of the 8th month 1832
Sarah S. Vanlaw deceased the 12th of the 4th month 1837

Note: Sarah Spencer, wife of Joseph Spencer, married second, Mr. Vanlaw.

Note: The above John Spencer, born 1763, was the son of Nathan and Hannah (Lofborough) Spencer, who moved to Loudoun county, Virginia, from Pennsylvania in the year 1761. Nathan was born in Upper Dublin Township, then in Philadelphia county, now in Montgomery county, Pennsylvania, in 1734 and married April 19th, 1756, Hannah Lofborough. He died in Loudoun county, Virginia, in 1806, and his will is a matter of record in the clerk's office of that county. Nathan Spencer was the son of Samuel Spencer, Jr., and his wife, Mary (Dawes) Spencer, of Upper Dublin Township, Philadelphia county, Pennsylvania. Samuel Spencer, Jr., was born October 22, 1699, probably in Upper Dublin Township, Philadelphia, now Montgomery county, and was one of two sons born to Samuel Spencer, Sr., and his wife, Elizabeth (Whitten) Spencer. His mother died when he was less than three years of age, his brother, William, being an infant of eighteen months. When Samuel Spencer, Sr., made his will in 1705, Samuel being then six years old and William under four, he requested that his eldest son, Samuel, "be fitted with a good Suit of Cloathes fitt for such a lad and to be forthwith sent to Barbadoes to his Relacons there". No reference is made as to what should be done with the younger son, William, but he, no doubt, was already being cared for by his mother's family. For some reason the executor did not comply with this request, as there is no evidence that Samuel Spencer, the younger, ever was in the West Indies and it was probable that he was prevailed upon by the boy's nearest relations, his grandfather, Robert Whitten and uncle Richard Whitten to allow him to remain in Pennsylvania. At this time too England was at war with France and Spain, and frequent alarms of hostile ships in the Delaware Bay disturbed the movements of vessels sailing from Philadelphia, and this may have deterred the family from sending such a little boy on such a hazardous voyage to the distant island of Barbadoes. Authority: "Descendants of Samuel Spencer, of Pennsylvania", by Howard M. Jenkins.

<hr>

BURWELL.

Entries from Family Bible in the Possession of Mr. George H. Burwell, Clarke Co.

1. Lucy Burwell was born at Brandon* Oct. 3, 1740 at 2 o'clock in the morning.
2. Elizabeth Burwell was born at Carter's Grove 21st February at 12 o'clock in the day 1742.
3. Judith Burwell was born at Brandon ye 11th of April at 3 o'clock at noon 1744.

<hr>

* Brandon in Middlesex Co.

4. Alice Burwell was born at Brandon 4th of May 1745.

.5 Sarah Burwell was born at Williamsburg Sunday 30th of November 1746.

6. Mary Burwell was born at Carter's Grove Thursday 6th of April 1749.

1. Nathaniel Burwell was born at Carter's Grove April 15th 1750, being Easter Sunday.

2. Carter Burwell was born at Carter's Grove January 25th 1754.

3. Lewis Burwell was born at Carter's Grove 5th June 1755.

The above are the names of the children of Carter Burwell and Lucy Grymes, who were married at Brandon 16th January 1738.

Nathaniel Burwell and Susanna Grymes were married at Brandon 28th November 1772.

1. Carter their son was born at Carter's Grove 16th Oct. 1773 and departed this life at Carter's Grove Feb. 9th 1819.

2. Philip, their son, was born at Williamsburg 15th January 1776. Died Feb. 11, 1849, aged 73.

3. Lucy, their daughter, was born at Carter's Grove Nov. 20th 1777 and departed this life at Carter Hall 22nd March 1810.

4. Nathaniel, their son, was born at Carter's Grove 16th Feb. 1779. Died Nov. 1st 1849, aged 70 yrs.

5. Lewis, their son, was born at Carter's Grove 4th January 1781, and died 28th September 1782.

6. William, their son, was born at Carter's Grove 14th July 1782, and died 2nd Oct. 1782.

7. Lewis, their son, was born at Carter's Grove 26th Sept. 1783 and died at Prospect Hill Feb. 24th 1826, aged 43 yrs.

8. Robert, their son, was born at Carter's Grove 24th July 1785, and died at New Market of melariah 22nd Aug. 1813—28.

Susanna Burwell died at Carter's Grove 24th July 1788 in the 37th yr of her age.

Nathaniel Burwell and Lucy Baylor, relict of George Baylor, 2nd daughter of Mann Page, late of Mannsfield were married at Mannsfield 24th of January 1789.

1. Tayloe Page, their son, was born at Carter's Grove 24th November 1789 and departed this life at Carter Hall on Wednesday the 23rd 1811 at 5 minutes past 4 in the morning.

2. William Nelson, their son, was born at Carter's Grove 23rd April 1791, died at Glen Owen the summer of 1822.

3. Susanna Grymes, their daughter was born at Millwood 16th Oct. 1792, and died 19th Oct. 1793.

4. Mann Page, their son, was born at Millwood 19th December 1793 and died 5th Aug. 1794.

5. Elizabeth Gwyn, was born at Carter's Grove 26th June 1795.

6. Mary, their daughter, was born at Millwood 18th January 1798.

641

7. George Harrison, their son, was born at Millwood 6th Oct. 1799, died Oct. 5, 1873, at Carter Hall.

8. Thomas Hugh Nelson, their son, was born at Carter Hall 29th January 1805, died 1841.

The above named Nathaniel Burwell departed this life at Carter Hall on 29th March 1814, about 10 o'clock in the morning, all the family being present.

Philip Burwell died at Chapel Hill February 11th 1849, about 11 o'clock in the morning, buried at Old Chapel.

Nathaniel Burwell died at Saratoga November 1st 1849 at half past one in the morning, buried at Old Chapel.

Thomas H. Burwell died at Old Point Comfort on his way up the country 1840 in the 37th yr of his age, buried in Williamsburg.

Elizabeth Gwyn Hay died at Millwood, Clarke Co., on 13th day of April 1855, buried at Old Chapel.

George H. Burwell died at Carter Hall on a beautiful bright Sabbath day at half past two P. M. Oct. 5th 1873, all but one of his family present.

Mary B. Whiting died at Clay Hill Dec. 15th 1880 aged 82—10 mos & 27 days, the last of her family and this record fills up the page commenced to be written on one hundred yrs ago.

DESCENDANTS OF RICHARD WILLING BYRD

We are indebted to Lieutenant Commander Reginald B. Henry for a copy of the entries in a family Bible, now owned by Mrs. Edmund S. Ruffin, of Norfolk, a daughter of Richard Willing Byrd and Jane B. DeJarnette, his wife, and a great granddaughter of Richard Willing Byrd, of Smithfield, Va. The descendants of the latter, who was a son of William Byrd, 3rd, of "Westover", have not been given fully in any printed pedigree. The entries in the Bible are as follows:

Richard W. Byrd and Emily B. Wilson were married the 27th November A. D. 1806.

———— Ann R (or B) Byrd was born on the 27th day of August A. D. 1807.

Charles Willing Byrd was born on the 19 day of October A. D. 1811.

Robert Fisher Byrd was born on the 14 day of December and died on the 23d A. D. 1813.

One nameless child died on the 6th of October 1814.

Mrs. Emily B. Byrd died on the 8th of October A. D. 1814.

(signed) Richd W. Byrd

May the 14th 1815

Richard W. Byrd (husband of Emily B. Byrd) died on 15th of October 1815.

George James Byrd and Carolina Virginia Taylor second daughter of Arthur Taylor of Norfolk were married on the 14th day of October A. D. 1829.

(signed) G. J. Byrd

Nov 15 1829

On another page are the following entries:

George James Byrd and Caroline Virginia Taylor were married on the 14th October 1829.

George James Byrd our first son by the above union was born on the 22nd October A. D. 1830 at Norfolk Virginia.

Richard Willing Byrd was born on the 3rd of August A. D. 1832.

Arthur Virginius Byrd was born on the 28th of January A. D. 1834. George James Byrd husband of Carolina Virginia Byrd died on the 21st of March 1834.

On another page under marriages is the following entry:

Richd Willing Byrd & Jane B. De Jarnette were married on the 6th of September 1864.

This is followed by records of other marriages of very much later times.

Commander Henry gives the following additional information in regard to the family:

Mary Ann Byrd married Richard Kennon, M. D., and had one child, a daughter, who married E. C. Doran.

Charles Willing and Robert Fisher Byrd were married.

George James Byrd married Carolina Virginia Taylor and had issue: 1. George James, born 1830, died unmarried; 2. Richard Willing (1832-78), married, 1864, Jane B. de Jarnette; 3. Arthur Virginius, born 1834, unmarried.

Richard W. and Jane B. (de Jarnette) Byrd had issue: 1. Virginia Taylor, born 1866, married, 1888, Andrew Dew Hart; 2. Richard Willing, died unmarried; 3. Cordelia Willing, born 1868, married (1st) W. J. C. Waller, M. D., (2nd) 1895, Edmund S. Ruffin; 4. George Virginius, died unmarried; 5. Robert de Jarnette, died unmarried; 5. Jane Evelyn; 6. Ellen de Jarnette, died unmarried.

BYRD BIBLE RECORDS

In going over the article on the descendants of Richard Willing Byrd in the July Magazine I noted some errors which are as follows:

(a) The record of the birth of the first George James Byrd was omitted. He was a son of the first Richard W. Byrd and Emily B. Wilson. The entry should be immediately above that of Charles Willing Byrd and reads:

George James Byrd was born on the 26th day of Sept. A. D. 1809.

(b) The first name of the wife of the above G. J. Byrd was "Carolina", not "Caroline". The former is correct and was so spelled in three of the four places where it is mentioned.

(c) On p. 286[*] it is stated that Charles Willing and Robert Fisher Byrd "were married". This should be "were not married". R. F. Byrd died when he was less than one month old.

(d) The numbers of the two younger children of R. W. and Jane B. (de Jarnette) Byrd should be 6 and 7 instead of 5 and 6.

Except for the above the entries were entirely correct as printed.

Reginald B. Henry.

---

[*]See above, this page.

RECORDS IN CARTER FAMILY BIBLE

John Michel Carter, son of Thomas and Ann Carter (formerly Brodnax), was married to Ann Bowyer, daughter of Elizabeth Whiting and Arthur Landon Davies at the house of her father near Gloucester Court House on Thursday evening the 30th day of December, 1824, by the Rev. Mr. Eastwood.

Births

Marco Bozzaris, son of John M. and Ann Bowyer Davies Carter, was born at Fendall Gregory's house in King William County, on Tuesday, the 11th day of April, 1826, at five minutes past 3 o'clock P. M.

Martha Brodnax, daughter of John M. and Ann Bowyer D. Carter, was born in the city of Richmond on Friday, the 18th day of April, 1828.

Lucy Emily, daughter of John M. and Ann Bowyer D. Carter, was born in the city of Richmond on Saturday, the 16th of January, 1830.

Henry Ann Nelson Cabell, daughter of John M. and Ann Bowyer D. Carter, was born on Saturday, the 26th day of May, 1832, in Richmond, Virginia.

Marriages

Marco Bozzaris Carter, son of John Michel and Ann D. Carter, was married to Harriet Payne, daughter of John S. and Susan Scott Payne at "White Hall", the residence of her father in the county of Campbell, on Wednesday, the 25th day of January, 1860, by the Rev. Mr. Kinckle.

John Cabell Cobbs, son of Edmund and Elizabeth Cobb, was married to Martha Brodnax, daughter of John M. and Ann Bowyer D. Carter, on Thursday morning, the 30th day of August, 1849, at the house of Capt. Robert S. Coleman, in the County of Bedford, by the Rev. Mr. Sale.

Junius H. Elcan, of Memphis, Tenn., and Henry Ann Cabell N. Carter were married on the 7th of March, 1865, by the Rev. Charles Collins at the house of Dr. Augustine Somerville, in Tipton County, Tenn.

Married on the 6th of March, 1872, by the Rev. I. H. Williams at the house of Marco B. Carter, Henry Landon Davies and Henry Ann Carter Elcan, both of Lynchburg.

Deaths

Mrs. Ann Bowyer Davies, wife of John Michel Carter, departed this life in Richmond on the 23rd day of June, 1833, at 5 o'clock P. M.

Marco Bozzaris Carter died in the city of Petersburg, December 10th, 1874, buried in Masonic section of Blandford Cemetery.

Mrs. Lewis L. Chapman

CHAPMAN FAMILY OF ISLE OF WIGHT

Records copied from the old Chapman family Bible, the Geneva translation, known as the Breeches Bible. (Gen. 3-7.)

The oldest records are illegible. A near relationship existed between the Norsworthys and Chapmans, hence the preservation of this Bible by our maternal ancestors.

John Chapman son of Charles Chapman and Ann his wife was married to Frances Ward, Daughter of Thomas Ward Feb. 15th 1704.

Benj'n. Chapman son of sa'd John and Frances Chapman was born Feb. 8th, 1706 and Baptized tenth day following. Jas. Chapman, Wm. Clark and grandmother Mary Clark Witnesses. And departed this life August 23rd, 1723 in the sixteenth year of his age.

Joseph Chapman son of John & Frances Chapman was born Nov. 13th: 1724. • Henry Lightfoot wit. Hugh Giles wit. and Mrs. Sarah Davis Witness.

Rachel Norsworthy daughter of Joseph (John?) Chapman and Frances was born August 6th 1722. Mary Forbes and William Norsworthy Witnesses.

My wife Frances Chapman died on the 22 of July 1727 in the 39th year of her age. I was then married unto Mary Marshall, Widow, and daughter of Thomas Bevan Dec'ed, and the 28th day of December following between nine and Tenn at night was born unto us a son named William and Baptized May following 1730. Tho. Bevan, Ju'r. George Norsworthy and Elizabeth Bevan, witnesses.

My daughter Patience Chapman was married to Moses Wills Feb. 13th. 1723.

On the 3rd of May 1725 was Borne unto Moses Wills and Patience his wife Daught. named Mary.

Ann Wills was born Nov. 29th, Day 1730, daught. of Moses and Patience Wills.

Sabre Chapman Darter of Joseph and Lydia Chapman was born Sept 22nd 1755. Wit. Joseph Haskins and Mrs. Rachel Chapman.

John Chapman son of sa'd Joseph and Lydia Chapman was born Feb. 29th, 1763. John Whitfield wit. Samuel Barnes Wit.

By request of Mr. R. S. Thomns I have copied some of the records from the old " Breeches Bible " in my possession.

I regret very much that some of the records—the oldest—are now illegible, the ink having eaten away the paper. I hope the enclosed may be of service to you.

Yours very truly,

N. W. NORSWORTHY.

CLAYTON-REEVES-SUTHERLAND.

I am taking the liberty of enclosing a compilation of the family records of certain branches of the Clayton, Reeves and Southerland families based on the records contained in two bibles in the possession of my wife's aunt, Mrs. J. C. Southerland of Memphis, Tennessee. One of the bibles, according to family tradition, belonged to Mary Clayton, wife of Willis Reeves, and the other to the Southerland family. I thought that the George Clayton record might be of especial interest to you as I have not seen in any printed record references to this son of Samuel Clayton.

I have assumed that "Samuel and Eliza Clayton" were Samuel Clayton, of Caroline county and Elizabeth Pendleton.

I think it possible that Temperance Hill, wife of John Clayton (4) may have been a daughter of Green Hill of North Carolina, Treasurer of Halifax District, etc. His son, Green Hill, Jr., married in Brunswick county, Jan., 1773, Mary Seawell, and the marriage bond of John Clayton and Temperance Hill was signed by G. Hill.

E. K. VOORHEES

Descendants of GEORGE CLAYTON, compiled by E. K. Voorhees, from Bible records in the possession of Mrs. John Clayton Southerland of Memphis, Tenn.

1. George Clayton, son of Samuel and Eliza Clayton, b. Oct. 5, 1720, d. Dec. 9, 1765; m. (1) Barbara ———— July 12, 1750, who was b. Jan. 28, 1729-30, d. Aug. 14, 1756; m. (2) June 9, 1757, Delphia ————.

(1) CHILDREN OF GEORGE CLAYTON AND BARBARA ——.

2. Richard Gass Clayton, b. May 7, 1751, d. June 13, 1755.
3. George Clayton, b. Dec. 7, 1752, d. April 9, 1753.
4. John Clayton, b. Jan. 20, 1754, d. prior to May 29, 1783; m. Dec. 15, 1776, Temperance ————, who was b. Feb. 10, 1761, d.

July 17, 1799; she m. (2) May 29, 1783, George Hicks. (Marriage bond dated Nov. 26, 1776, Brunswick Co., Va., for John Clayton and Temperance Hill. The order books of the Brunswick Co., Va., Court show that John Clayton was lieutenant, Nov. 24, 1777, and Feb. 22, 1779, captain.) (For children see forward.)

5. Mary Clayton, b. Nov. 11, 1755.

CHILDREN OF GEORGE CLAYTON AND DELPHIA ————.

6. Lucy Clayton, b. Sept. 29, 1758, d. Dec. 29, 1767.

(4) CHILDREN OF JOHN CLAYTON AND TEMPERANCE HILL.

7. Mary Clayton, b. May 15, 1779, d. March 18, 1817, m. Dec. 19, 1805, Willis Reeves. He m. (2) Jan. 10, 1822, Thisbe ————. (Willis Reeves was (probably) a son of John and Mary Reeves. He emigrated from North Carolina to West Tennessee at an early period, probably soon after 1830. Mrs. Imogen Southerland Voorhees has a book containing the following inscription: "Aaron Devany, his book, bought of James Yarborough, merchant at Louisburg, March 11, 1805, price, 1/6. Willis Reeves, his book, July the 8, 1805." The Louisburg mentioned is doubtless Louisburg, Franklin Co., N. C.) (For children see forward.)

8. Sally Clayton, b. March 1782, d. Oct. 1, 1805, m. Dr. John Claiborne. (Dr. John Claiborne was a son of Thomas Claiborne, sheriff of Brunswick county, Va., 1789-1792, and was b. 1777, d. Oct. 9, 1808; he was a member of Congress from 1805 until his death.)

CHILDREN OF GEORGE HICKS AND TEMPERANCE HILL.

9. Martha Hill Hicks, b. Aug. 23, 1785, d. May 2, 1809, m. ———— Avent.

(4) CHILDREN OF GEORGE HICKS AND TEMPERANCE HILL.

10. Hannah Hicks, b. July 19, 1788, d. March 31, 1808, m. Thomas Claiborne. (He was a brother of Dr. John Claiborne and was a member of Congress from Tennessee, 1817-1819.)

11. James Green Hicks, b. June 25, 1790.

12. John Hicks, b. Oct. 20, 1794, d. April 5, 1813.

13. George Hicks, b. June 4, 1797.

(7) CHILDREN OF WILLIS REEVES AND MARY CLAYTON.

14. James O'Kelly Reeves, b. Sept. 9, 1806.

15. Sally Lewis Reeves, b. June 28, 1808, d. April 7, 1827.

16. Martha Eliza Reeves, b. Aug. 16, 1810, d. July 20, 1855, m. Sept. 21, 1833, John Llewellyn Southerland. (He was appointed an

649

Ensign by Gov. William Hawkins of North Carolina, Oct. 1, 1814. At that time he was of Edgecombe county.) (For children see forward.)

17. John Claiborne Reeves, b. May 17, 1812, d. 1905, unmarried. (He was a prominent citizen of Somerville, Fayette Co., Tenn., for a half century; clerk of the county court, editor, etc.)

18. George Washington Reeves, b. April 6, 1814.

19. Willis Pendleton Reeves, b. Feb. 3, 1816, d. Dec. 9, 1816.

20. Son, b. and d. March 7, 1817.

CHILDREN OF WILLIS REEVES AND THISBE ————.

21. Mary Andes Reeves, b. Nov. 22, 1822.

22. Calvin Jones Reeves, b. Oct. 17, 1824.

23. Atlas Jones Reeves, b. Jan. 24, 1827.

24. Willis Gales Reeves, b. March 16, 1829.

25. Benjamin Franklin Reeves, b. Aug. 26, 1831.

26. Thomas Jefferson Wesley Reeves, b. June 12, 1834.

(16) CHILDREN OF JOHN LLEWELLYN SOUTHERLAND AND MARTHA ELIZA, REEVES.

27. James Southerland, b. Dec. 24, 1834, d. Jan. 9, 1875, m. Dec. 24, 1867, Imogen Latham, b. Jan. 26, 1846, d. at Washington, D. C., Jan. 25, 1920, daughter of Francis Stanton Latham and Jane Catherine Smith. (James Southerland enlisted in the Blufl City Grays, Memphis, Tenn., at the outbreak of the war between the states and was paroled at Gainesville, Alabama, May 11, 1865, at which time he was second lieutenant, Company A, Forrest's Old Regiment, and had been in command of the company for some time.) (For children see forward.)

28. John Clayton Southerland, b. Dec. 31, 1836, d. 1915, m. March 4, 1880, Kate Latham, daughter of Francis Stanton Latham and Jane Catherine Smith. (He was a member of the same company as his brother in the Confederate service.) (For children see forward.)

(27) CHILDREN OF JAMES SOUTHERLAND AND IMOGEN LATHAM.

29. Imogen Southerland, m. Edward Kinsey Voorhees, son of Ellison Hoagland Voorhees and Eugenia‑ Boyd.

30. Katherine Southerland.

31. James Southerland, d. 1894.

32. Mary Southerland.

(28) CHILDREN OF JOHN CLAYTON SOUTHERLAND AND KATE LATHAM.

33. Kate Southerland, d. 1881.

34. John Clayton Southerland, d. 1911, m. Frances Mayeant Battaile.

35. Francis Stanton Southerland, m. Sallie Mae Hidiberg.
36. Helen Southerland.
37. James Southerland, m. Julia ————.
38. Martha Eliza Southerland, m. Harry Crump.

COLE BIBLE RECORD

From the Prayer Book of James Cole, who removed from Eastern Virginia to Augusta County, and now owned by Misses Lucy Cole and Mary Turk of that county.

Elizabeth Dancy Cole, daughter of James & Fanny Cole, born 8 Feb. 1778.

Polly Roscow Cole, daughter of James & Fanny Cole, born 25 Dec. 1779.

Lucy Wills Cole, daughter of James & Fanny Cole, born 3 June 1781.

Roscow Cole, son of James & Fanny Cole, born 25 Jan. 1783.

James Cole, son of James & Fanny Cole, born 3 May 1784.

Ann Cole, daughter of James & Fanny Cole, born 9 June 1787.

William John Cole, son of James & Fanny Cole, born 7 Sept. 1789.

Frances Catherine Jane Cole, daughter of James & Fanny Cole, born 5 July 1791.

Jane Robertson Cole, daughter of James & Fanny Cole, born 25 Nov. 1793.

Permelia Cole, daughter of James & Fanny Cole, born 9 June 1797.

Martha Wills Cole, daughter of James & Fanny Cole, born 27 July 1801.

Mathew Cole, son of James & Fanny Cole, born 12 Jan. 1805.

Copied from above by Augusta B. Fothergill, August, 1923.

Mrs. Geradine and Mrs. Greenhow, two of the above daughters, were victims of the Richmond Theatre fire, December, 1811. Roscow Cole lived in Williamsburg; his sister, Lucy Wills Cole, married Isiah Shipman, of Augusta County.

(Contributed by Mrs. Augusta Fothergill, Richmond, Va.)

CORBIN FAMILY OF CULPEPER COUNTY

(Contributed by A. M. Prichard, of Staunton, Va.)

William Corbin, a fac simile of whose family record taken from his family Bible, appears in 34 Virginia Historical Magazine 358. It there appears that he had a son, Mitcham Corbin, who was born January 25, 1789. Sarah Elizabeth Corbin, daughter of Mitcham Corbin, married John Willis Luttrell, and their family record, taken from their Bible, appears in 34 Virginia Historical Magazine 175. The connecting link, viz: the family Bible of Mitcham Corbin has been recently brought to light from the attic of Mrs. Hugh Tucker Chelf, of Culpeper, Virginia, who permitted the family record to be copied therefrom by the contributor of this article who thus offers, through the Virginia Historical Magazine, to the host of William Corbin's descendants, complete data for membership in the National Society of the Daughters fo the American Revolution.

MITCHAM CORBIN'S FAMILY BIBLE

Marriages

Mitcham Corbin and Ann Corbin, his wife, married 12 Aug., 1811.
John R. McCormick & Angelina H. McCormick married 19 Dec., 1836.
John W. Luttrell & Sarah E. Luttrell married 8 July, 1839.
A. G. Corbin & Mary E. Moreland married 3 Dec., 1839.

Charles Short & A. S. Corbin married 22 Sept., 1845.
Jos. N. Armstrong & Mary F. Corbin married 12 Aug., 1851.
John W. Corbin & Martha Nelson married 11 Dec., 1851.
Oswald M. Corbin & Annie R. Bywaters married 25 May, 1858.
Lemuel A. Corbin & Mary D. Coons married 26 May, 1858.
Octavius Jeffries & Annie McCormick married 18 Dec., 1856.
Richard T. Luttrell & Virginia Corbin married 12 Jan., 1864.

Births

Mitcham Corbin born 25 Jan., 1789.
Ann Corbin born 14 Oct., 1795.
Albert G. Corbin born 21 Oct., 1812.
Martha Corbin born 7 Aug., 1814.
Sarah E. Corbin born 21 Apr., 1816.
Secy Ann Susan Corbin born 10 June, 1818.
Angelina H. Corbin born 4 Feb., 1820.
John W. Corbin born 19 Aug., 1822.
Lemuel A. Corbin born 26 Dec., 1824.
Mary F. Corbin born 26 Jan., 1827.
Mitcham O. Corbin born 25 Jan., 1831.

Grandchildren

Ann Mariah McCormick born 13 Oct., 1837.
Cornelia McCormick born 25 Oct., 1839.
Hannah Luttrell born 22 Dec., 1840.
Elbert McCormick born 10 Oct., 1841.
Virginia T. Corbin born 1 June, 1842.
Sylvester W. Corbin born 20 Apr., 1845.
Sarah Ann Luttrell born 5 Dec., 1842.
Mitcham Luttrell born 19 Aug., 1845.
Arthur M. McCormick born 28 June, 1845.
John T. McCormick born 1 Aug., 1847.
Ann M. Short, b 3 Oct., 1851.
Mortimer Luttrell born 15 Nov., 1848.
William D. McCormick born 22 Nov., 1851.
Josephine Armstrong born 26 May, 1852.
John M. Short born 20 May, 1853.
Cynthia Z. Armstrong born 14 July, 1854.
Lucy A. McCormick born 17 July, 1854.
Lemuel O. Short & Fannie Betta Short born 17 May, 1855.
Stephen B. McCormick born 1 Apr., 1861.

Great-Grandchildren

Mary A. Jeffries born 23 Oct. 1857.
William A. Jeffries born 30 Sept., 1859.
Cornelia Jeffries born 14 Jan., 1864.

Deaths

Martha Corbin died 16 Apr., 1815.
Elizabeth Bywaters died 25 Sept., 1834.
John Bywaters died 28 Feb., 1837.
Nancy Corbin died 13 Dec., 1859.
Mitcham Corbin died 11 Oct., 1860.
John R. McCormick died 10 Nov., 1867.
John W. Corbin died — Mar., 1880.
John R. McCormick died 10 Nov., 1867.
Sarah E. Luttrell died 18 Sept., 1882.
John W. Luttrell died 14 Aug., 1894.
Bettie Armstrong died — May, 1860.
Elbert McCormick died — Oct., 1861.
Nanie Jeffries died 6 Jan., 1882.
O. M. Corbin died 30 Mar., 1891.
A. R. Corbin died 8 May, 1893.
Joseph N. Armstrong died 12 Jan., 1881.
Susan A. Short died 17 Oct., 1892.
Charles Short died 31 Mar. —, aged 81 years.
Mary F. Armstrong died 18 Sept., 1898.

ENGLISH RECORDS RELATING TO VIRGINIA.

(From Report of Royal Historical Manuscripts Commission. The Manuscripts of the Earl of Dartmouth, Vol. II.)

JAMES ABERCROMBY TO [LORD DARTMOUTH].

1775, February 13. Oxenden Street.—Recommending Mr. G. Corbin to be of the Council in Virginia.

Autograph letter signed. 1 quarto page. (P. 269)

[Gawin Corbin, son of Richard Corbin, of "Laneville," King and Queen county, Receiver General of Virginia, was, in accordance with this recommendation, appointed to the Council and was the last man added to that body during the colonial period.

He was educated in England and returned to Virginia about 1761, where he resided at "Buckingham House," Middlesex county. He was a burgess for Middlesex at the sessions of November, 1766, March, 1776, March, 1768, May, 1769, November, 1769, May, 1770 and July, 1771. He married Joanna, daughter of Robert Tucker, of Norfolk, Va.

The following family record is taken from a paper once in the possession of a granddaughter of Gawin Corbin:

Gawin Corbin returned from England, Aug. 6th, 1761. Married Joanna Tucker, November 17th. 1762.

[Births]

Bettie Tayloe Corbin daughter of Gawin and Joanna Corbin, born March 28, 1764 at 8 min. past 5 o'Clock in the morning. God-fathers: Col. Robert Tucker and Capt. Constantius John Phipps; God-mothers: Mrs. Bettie Corbin and Mrs. Joanna Tucker.

Ann Corbin, daughter of Gawin and Joanna Corbin born Dec. 17, 1757 [1767] at 40 mim. after 1 o'clock in the morning. God-fathers: Carter Braxton and Tayloe Corbin Esqrs. God-mothers: Mrs. Bettie Corbin and Mrs. Eliza Braxton.

Felicia Corbin daughter of Gawin and Joanna Corbin born Feb. 6th, 1770 at 25 mins. past 5 o'clock in the morning. God-fathers: Richard Corbin Esq. and Dr. Robert Spratt. God-mothers: Miss Alice Corbin and Jane Tucker.

Jane Lane Corbin, daughter of Gawin and Joanna Corbin born Oct. 3d, 1772 at 11 o'clock in the morning. God-fathers: John Tayloe Corbin and Thomas Corbin Esqrs. God-mothers: Mrs. Maria Corbin and Miss Courtney Tucker.

Richard Henry Corbin son of Gawin and Joanna Corbin born Aug. 4th, 1775 at 4 o'clock in the morning. God-fathers: The Hon. Ralph Wormeley and Mann Page of North River Esqrs. God-mothers: Mrs. Sarah Tayloe and Miss Alice Corbin.

Jane Corbin daughter of Gawin and Joanna Corbin born Sept. 8, 1777 at night. God-fathers: George Bird and R. Corbin Tucker Esqrs. God-mothers: Miss Ann Tucker, Bettie Braxton, Jane Wormeley and Eliza Robinson.

Of his daughters: Betty, said to have married George Lee Turberville; Felicia married Orris Chilton, and another married —— Beale.

The following is the inscription on the tomb of Gawin Corbin:

(Corbin arms)

'Till the trump of the Most High shall awaken him

To a glorious immortality
The sole reward
To such exemplory virtue,
Here rests
The body of Col. Gawin Corbin
The eldest son of
Col. Richard Corbin, and
The presumptive heir
Of the family.
He received a liberal education
in England And by his merits was promoted to the
Highest honors of his country
As a Councellor
He was impartial, learned, judicious
As a man
He was generous, open, unaffected.
Whilst he lived
He was admired, loved, respected.
When he died
He was envied,[?] honored, and lamented
His dissolution happened on July 10th
in the 39th year, seventh month
and fourth day of his age.]

[The year of death not given in copy, but is stated to have been July
10, 1779.]

———

CORBIN.—In the Church at Malvern, Worcestershire, Eng., is a
tomb with the following epitaph: "Margaret late wife of William
Lygon esq., and only child of Thomas Corbyn esq. Obit. 21 Oct.
1699, aetat 42. William Lygon, who died in 1720, married Margaret
daughter and heir of Thomas Corbyn de Hallend, Com. Warwick."
She was born April 11, 1658, married Aug 7, 1688, and died Oct. 26,
1699. Nash's *Worcestershire*.

Mrs. Lygon was descended from the elder brother of Henry Corbin, ancestor of the Virginia family.

———

COTTON—TALBOT BIBLE RECORDS

COTTON, TALBOT.—Cotton from old Bible. Ralph Cotton, son of John Ralph Cotton, born January 10th, 1742, married Elizabeth, daughter of William Kitchen, Loudoun county, Va.

Henry, born September 4th, 1763; Susannah, born February 14th, 1765; Peggy, born August 4th, 1767; Jemima, born August 8th, 1769; Mary Jane, born January 27th, 1772; John, born February 12th, 1774; William, born March 13th, 1776; Sarah, born May 10th, 1778; Nathaniel, born April 7th, 1783; Ralph, born January 17th, 1786; Robert, born September 4th, 1788.

TALBOT.

Matthew Talbott, born September, 1699; Charles, his son, born November 6th, 1723; Mary, dau. of Charles, born December 8th, 1755. Mary married Plummer Thurston, 1777. Williston, son of Charles, married Elizabeth Cocke, December, 1769; 1st wife, ——— Talbot, married Ezekiel Thurston.

Allan Talbot, son of Williston, married Martha Ridley Thornton, daughter of Sterling Thornton, 1814. Allan was Elizabeth Cocke's son.

657

EDGAR-ANDERSON BIBLE RECORDS.

(Contributed by W. MacFarlane Jones)

BIRTHS

Robert Edgar, born 17 June, 1793.
James Edgar, born 28 Dec., 1795.
Nancy Edgar, born 28 Jany., 1797.
Margreat Edgar, born 25 June, 1799.
William Edgar, born 5 Sept., 1810.
John Edgar, born 28 Nov., 1804.

Larkin H. Anderson, born 30 June, 1796.
Nancy Anderson, born 28 Jany., 1797.

THE CHILDREN OF L. H. & NANCY ANDERSON

James T. Anderson, born 19 Jany., 1822.
Susan M. Anderson, born 1 Sept., 1824.
Robert Anderson, born 19 Dec., 1826.
(One entry cut out)
Ann E. Anderson, born — July, 1829.
Elizabeth Anderson, born 11 May, 1832.
Mary Anderson, born 8 Nov., 1835.
Sarah Ann Anderson, born Sept. 1st, 1818.
Larkin H. Anderson, born 30 June, 1791.
Nancy Anderson born Jany., 1797.

Robert Edgar died 17 June, 1812.
William Edgar died 28 Nov., 1810.
Margaret Edgar died 20 Jany., 1822.
John Edgar died 28 Sept., 1832.
Letitia Edgar died 16 Sept., 1835.
Anne Anderson died 9 Sept., 1864.
Larkin H. Anderson & Nancy Mills, formerly Nancy Edgar, were married 19 April, 1821.
Nancy E. Anderson born July 11, 18—.
Robert N. Mileston & Sarah Ann Mills married Sept. 8, 1836.
Calvin Green & Margreat Anderson married May 7, 1844.
Ann Anderson & E. Porter married 21 November, 185-.

Robert Edgar died 18 November, 1804.
William Edgar died 28 Nov., 1810.
Margreat Winston died 26 Jan., 1822.
Letitia Edgar died 16 Sept., 1837, aged 65 years.

FITZHUGH FAMILY BIBLE ENTRIES

Copy from Dudley Fitzhugh's Bible in Possession of Mrs. Laura Gray.

Births—William Fitzhugh, son of Col. Henry Fitzhugh and Sarah, his wife, was born on Tuesday the 23d of April, 1754, and was baptized by the Rev. Musgrave Dawson, his sponsors were Mr. Thos. Fitzhugh and wife, Mr. John Fitzhugh and Mrs. Sarah Conway.

Sarah Fitzhugh, consort of William Fitzhugh, was born the 17th of December, 1757.

Dudley Fitzhugh, son of Wm. Fitzhugh and Sarah, his wife, was born the 20th of October, 1789, at 9 o'clock A. M. and was baptized by the Rev. James Thompson, his sponsors were his mother, his sister Anna Harrison Fitzhugh, his uncle, George Fitzhugh, his brother Henry Fitzhugh and Mr. John Matthews.

Lucy Brooke Fitzhugh, consort of Dudley Fitzhugh was born the 4th of August, 1794 and was baptized by the Rev. J. Thompson.

Deaths—Sarah Fitzhugh, consort of William Fitzhugh of Prospect Hill, departed this life the 28th of Sept., 1804.

Wm. Fitzhugh of Prospect Hill, son of Col. Henry Fitzhugh, departed this life the 22nd of April, 1817, in the 63d year of his age.

Dudley Fitzhugh of Llewellyn, son of William and Mary Fitzhugh of Prospect Hill, departed this life on the 1st day of January, 1848, in the 59th year of his age.

Marriages—William Fitzhugh of Prospect Hill was married to Sarah Digges, daughter of Col. Edward Digges of Yorktown, Va., 22nd of February, 1778.

Dudley Fitzhugh, son of William Fitzhugh and Sarah, his wife, was married to Lucy Brooke Digges, daughter of Major Thomas Digges and Elizabeth, his wife, the 7th of June, 1820, by the Rev. William Williamson.

James and John Gordon, immigrants from the North of Ireland Samuel Gordon was the youngest son of John and Lucy Gordon.

Sarah Fitzhugh who was Sarah Digges, wife of William Fitzhugh of Prospect Hill, left the following children, viz: Ann H. who intermarried with Thomas G. Thornton and now a widow;

Elizabeth Cole who intermarried with Samuel Gordon; Sarah B. Fitzhugh who intermarried with Elias Edmonds now a widow; Edward D. Fitzhugh; Cole Fitzhugh; Dudley Fitzhugh; Thomas L. Fitzhugh; and Maria Fitzhugh who intermarried with Thomas Catlett, now a widow.

That Elizabeth C. Gordon, daughter of Sarah Fitzhugh, died leaving the following children, viz:—Thomas G.—Sally who intermarried with Peter Dudley—William F.—Lucy Ann—Maria—and Elizabeth C.

Above is an extract from Minute Book of Fauquier County Court January 28, 1835– 1834-5 Page 209—(I copied this as relating to the Digges connection. A. R. B.)

Copied from my copies for Mrs. Mary M. Wilson, 515 N. Spring Ave., St. Louis, Mo., by A. R. Bartenstein, this 7th April 1906.

A. R. BARTENSTEIN,
Fauquier Co., Warrenton, Va.

Copied from Cousin Griffin Gordon letter as copied from my grandfather Samuel Gordon's Bible in his possession—as to Gordons.

A. R. BARTENSTEIN.

Samuel Gordon was married to Elizabeth Cole Fitzhugh 19 February 1801.

Sarah Digges Gordon daughter of Samuel and Elizabeth Gordon was married to Peter Dudley August, 1821.

Wm. F. Gordon son of Samuel and Elizabeth Gordon was married to Mary Jane McCreary Dec. 22, 1830.

Wm. F. Gordon and Elizabeth Jane Newton were married 16 October, 1843.

Edward H. Fitzhugh and Maria Gordon were married August 23, 1838.

Elizabeth Cole Fitzhugh Gordon married Ferdinand Bartenstein February 1847. (In our Bible married Jany. 12, 1847).

Thomas Griffin Thornton Gordon was born Feby. 18, 1802.

John Gordon was born August 3, 1803.

Sarah Digges Gordon was born May 24, 1805.

Wm. Fitzhugh Gordon was born August 13, 1807.

Samuel Gordon was born November 22, 1809.

James Gordon was born Sept. 1812, died April 16, 1814.

Lucy Ann Harrison Gordon was born Feby. 17, 1815.

Children of Wm. F. and Mary Jane Gordon as follows:

James McCreary Gordon was born Feby. 2, 1833.

Wm. Fitzhugh Gordon was born 28 Sept. 1834.

Thomas Griffin Gordon was born Jany. 21, 1839.

Samuel Douglas Gordon was born Dec. 16, 1840.

James Gordon was born Sept. 12, 1812, died April 16, 1814.

Elizabeth Cole Gordon, consort of Samuel Gordon, died April 5, 1819.

John Gordon, son of Samuel and Elizabeth, died 1821.

Samuel Gordon Senior died April 27, 1823.

Samuel Gordon, son of Samuel and Elizabeth, died June 12, 1828.

Wm. Fitzhugh Gordon, son of Samuel and Elizabeth, died July 24, 1865, aged 58 years.

Sarah D. Price, daughter of Samuel and Elizabeth Gordon, died Dec. 14, 1863.

Elizabeth Cole F. Bartenstein, daughter of Samuel and Elizabeth, died Feby. 27, 1878.

Lucy A. H. Gordon, daughter of Samuel and Elizabeth, died Nov. 11, 1887.

Elizabeth Jane Gordon, wife of Wm. F. Gordon, died Nov. 15, 1891.

Samuel D. Gordon, son of Wm. F. and Mary Jane Gordon, died May 12, 1891.

Wm. F. Gordon, son of Wm. F. and Mary Jane, died Nov. 1893.

Children of Ferdinand and Elizabeth Cole F. Bartenstein:

Andrew Remhardt Bartenstein born Oct. 2, 1847.

Sarah Fitzhugh Bartenstein born Oct. 5, 1849.

William Gordon Bartenstein born July 2, 1851.

Laura Bartenstein born August 13, 1853.

Margaretta Barbara Bartenstein born Oct. 27, 1855.

Edward Henry Bartenstein born Nov. 26, 1857.

Elizabeth Cole Bartenstein born June 18, 1861.

Ann Harrison Fitzhugh, sister of Elizabeth Cole Fitzhugh, married Thomas Griffin Thornton Oct. 29, 1795.

GRAY, WICKHAM, SHORE, &C.

(From Family Bible Records)

Joseph Gray and Sarah Simmons were married the 14th December, 1729.

William Gray was born 12th April 1732—died 2d October 1750.

Mary Gray was born 10th February 173/4.

Elizabeth Gray was born 16th January 1735/6—died 24th September 1761.

Anne Gray born 1st Jan. 1737/8.

Sarah Gray born 7th November 1739.

John Gray born 25th July 1741—died 4th April 1760.

Edwin Gray born 18th July 1743.

Peter Gray born 23d June 1745—died 26th December 1761.

James Gray born 1st March 1746/7.

By a second marriage

Joseph Gray born 10th June 1749—died 23rd January 1754.

Lucy Gray born 11th March 1750/1.

Jane Gray born 26th June 1753—died 27th February 1754.

Mary Gray married Littleton Tazewell 13th Feb. 1753.

Sarah Gray married Major James Wall, of Greensville Co., Va.

Edwin Gray was a member of the U. S. Congress early in the century.

James Gray was dreadfully wounded at the battle of Brandywine.

Lucy Gray married Cod. John Edmunds, of Brunswick Co., Va., 19th October 1769.

Mr. and Mrs. Tazewell had two sons and one daughter, Mary. She married the Rev. Wm. Fanning, an Episcopal clergyman, March 7th, 1782 [1772?]; had one child, Mary Smith Fanning, born September 25th, 1775. She married Mr. John Wickham, Dec. 24th, 1791. She had two sons, William Fanning and Edmund Fanning Wickham. Wm. F. was born 23rd November 1793. Edmund was born 30th July 1796. Mrs. Mary Smith Fanning Wickham died Feb. 1st, 1799.

Mrs. Mary Smith Fanning Wickham died Feb. 1st, 1799.

John Wickham died Jan. 22nd, 1839—aged 76.

Henry, son of Mary Gray and Littleton Tazewell, was born the 27th November, 1753—died January 4th, 1799, in Philadelphia, where he was Senator U. S.

Littleton Waller Tazewell, born 17th December 1774—died 6th May 1860. He was Senator of U. S. and Gov. of Virginia.

Wm. F. Wickham married Anne Carter, daughter of Robert Carter of Shirley, and had an only son, General William Carter Wickham. He married Lucy P. Taylor, a granddaughter of Col. John Taylor of Caroline.

Edmund F. Wickham married Lucy Carter, daughter of Robert Carter of Shirley, had 4 children, 2 sons and 2 daughters. John is now a Judge of one of the highest courts in St. Louis.

W. Leigh Wickham, merchant in St. Louis, unmarried.

John married a daughter of Col. Graham, and has a large family. His daughter, Mary Fanning, married Julius Y. Archer, S. C., who was killed at the battle of Missionary Ridge. His widow died 3 or 4 years ago leaving a son and daughter, Samuel P. E. F. W.; daughter Lucy married George H. Byrd, merchant of N. Y.

Major and Mrs. Wall had 5 daughters and 4 sons. Mary married Mr. Grayson, of England, had a large family.

Jane Gray born ———. Married Thomas Shore of Violet Bank, a merchant shipper, had 3 daughters.

662

Elizabeth Smith Shore born Jan. 26th, 1797—died March 20th, '58. Married Dr. John Gilliam 14th Feb. 1823, had a large family.

Mary Louisa Shore born March, 1898 (1798?), died May, 1878. Married Dr. Wm. Sheppen, of Philadelphia, had a large family.

Jane Gray died in infancy.

Dr. and Mrs. John Gilliams' daughter Jane married her cousin, Thomas Lee Shippen, 11th Jan. 1860, had only one child, a son, William, born May 20th, 1861. Jane Gray Gilliam Shippen died August 3rd, 1875.

James Skelton, son of Elizabeth Smith Shore Gilliam, was Past Assistant Surgeon, U. S. N. Married Georgia Clifford Nicoll, daughter of Judge John C. Nicoll, of Savannah, Georgia. Judge of the Supreme Court of Georgia, 26th November 1857. Lost on board U. S. S. Levant in going from Sandwich Islands to Panama, September, 1860 His widow never recovered from the shock and died August 1st, 1869. Let only one child, a daughter, Lula A. Gilliam Thomas.

Theophilus Field Gilliam married Mary Eppes.

Eliza Shore married Robert Maitland Dunlop, son of James Dunlop. Married at Violet Bank by Rev. W. H. Platt 4th March 1862. Has only one child, a daughter, Lydia Shore Dunlop.

Mrs. Dr. Wm. Shippen's daughter Jane married Edward Wharton, of Philadelphia. Had only one child, a daughter, Mary Louise. She and her father died while on a visit to Mrs. Ellen Wharton in Baltimore.

Thos. Lee Shippen married Jane Gray, daughter of Dr. John and Mrs. Eliza Smith Gilliam, of Violet Bank.

Wm. Shippen married Achsah, daughter of Charles Carroll, of Baltimore. Had only one child, a son, Charles Carroll, a physician.

Alice Lee Shippen married Dr. Joshua M. Wallace, of Philadelphia. Left only one child, a son, Shippen Wallace, a chemist, in Philadelphia.

GRAY, WICKHAM, &C.

Joseph Gray and Sarah Simmons were married Dec. 14, 1729, and had issue.

By a second marriage he had five daughters and one son. Of these,

Mary Gray mar. 1st Littleton Tazewell, and had one son Henry, who died at the early age of thirty-three.

Henry Tazewell became the father of Littleton Waller Tazewell, afterwards Governor of Virginia, and who was named for his maternal grandfather, Col. Littleton.

Mary Gray married 2nd the Rev. William Fanning of Brunswick Co., Virginia.

They had one daughter, Mary Smith Fanning, who, being the half sister of Henry Tazewell, was the half aunt (?) of Littleton Waller Tazewell—later Governor of Virginia. Curiously enough after her death this nephew of hers and her bereaved husband were both aspirants for the hand of the same lady—Miss Elizabeth Maclurg, who married John Wickham.

Mr. John Wickham and his first wife, Mary Fanning, had two sons, William and Edmund Fanning Wickham. Mrs. Wickham died in 1799.

Wm. Fanning and his brother married two sisters, Lucy and Anne Carter, daughters of Robert Carter of Shirley.

Wm. F. Wickham and his wife Anne, lived at Hickory Hill in Hanover county, and were the parents of Williams Carter Wickham, afterwards general in the Confederate Army.

John Wickham, who died young.

Williams Carter Wickham married Lucy Taylor, a grand daughter of Col. John Taylor of Caroline.

Edmund Fanning Wickham married Lucy Carter, and had three sons and two daughters—

John Wickham, judge of one of the highest courts in St. Louis, who married Miss Graham, and brought up a large family of sons and daughters.

Leigh and Alfred Wickham who died unmarried.

Lucy Carter, who married George H. Byrd of Brandon and New York, and has sons and daughters of whom four only are living,

Wickham Byrd who married Miss Burwell and has one daughter.

William Byrd, has several children.

Anne Harrison Byrd, unmarried.

Lucy Byrd, married Dr. Elliot of New York, and has two daughters—

Mary Fanning Wickham, married Julius Porcher of South Carolina, who was killed at the battle of Missionary Ridge. They had two children—

Samuel married and has several children.

Anne Carter married Gen. C. StG. Sinkler, and died, leaving three daughters, all of whom are married.

Mr. John Wickham married for his second wife, Miss Elizabeth Selden Maclurg, daughter of Dr. James M. Maclurg, who was the uncle of the late Dr. McCaw of Richmond, both of them beloved physicians in the old days of long ago.

John Wickham and Elizabeth Maclurg lived in the house now known as the Valentine Museum which he built. Here they brought up a very large family—all of whom are now dead, and their descendants scattered from the East Coast to the West, from the North to the South.

One can hardly think of a part of this country in which there is not a representative of this family. In Richmond there are only four, Mr. and Mrs. T. Ashby Wickham, Mr. Henry T. Wickham, Mrs. R. Emmett Richardson and their families.

GREEN, AMELIA COUNTY, &C.

A descendant of Col. Grief Green has in her possession a Bible containing this brief and much mutilated record: "The Daughter of Marston Green & Eliz^a his wife—the 19 Day of December 1766.
——— Green the Son of Marston & Eliz his wife was bor—   ay the 23 Day of June 1770." In all probability this means the births of Mary and Grief Green.

Thomas Green married Elizabeth Marston, lived and died in Nottoway Parish, Amelia couny. They had at least one son Marston who married Elizabeth ———, and had at least two children, Mary and Grief.

Mary married James Harper of Petersburg, Va., and had issue. Grief served in the war of 1812 as Lieutenant Colonel in 98th (Green's) Regiment of Virginia Militia. He was commissioned Nov. 1st, 1811, and served from July 5th to July 31st, 1813. He also served as Lieutenant Colonel in the 6th (Sharp's) regiment of Va. militia from July 31st, 1813, to January 11th, 1814. He was a man of large frame and is said to have been quite severe toward his men. He was a lawyer of prominence. At one time he lived near Burkeville, Nottoway county, but later moved to Halifax county. His plantation was afterwards owned by the Alexander family.

Col. Grief Green, prior to 1815, married Rebecca Mayo, daughter of Joseph Mayo (of William) and his wife Martha Tabb (of Wm. and Susannah Gould Tabb). By this marriage there were two daughters, Eliza Aperson, who married Stith Bolling Spragins, and Signora, who married James Oliver.

Mrs. Grief Green died in 1816 and the colonel married a widow Knox, by whom he had one son, Henry, who served with distinction in the Mexican and Civil Wars.

The Green burying ground is in Nottoway county, near Burkeville, and was surrounded by a brick wall.

GRIFFIN FAMILY RECORD

(Copied from Mrs. Nancy Chiswell Lewis's Bible.)

Marriages: "Stephen Orren Wright was married to Mary Louisa Griffin, daughter of Dr. Samuel Stuart & Sarah Lewis Griffin, Nov. 23, 1836, in the City of Williamsburg, by Rev. John H. Wingfield, Rector of Trinity Church Portsmouth, Va.

James Lewis Corbin Griffin, married to Jane Hester Denning of St. Johns, New Foundland, 30 June 1842.

J. L. G. married to Fanny Mary Denning of St. Johns New Fd'land, 15 March 1853.

Mottram Dulany Ball, married to Sallie Lewis Wright, daughter of S. O. & M. L. Wright, 17 Oct. 1860.

Samuel Stuart Griffin, married to Sarah Lewis, daughter of Mrs. Sarah Tabb, previously Mrs. Lewis & Mrs. Thruston, at Gloucester Town, Va. Nov. 19, 1808.

John Bartrand & Paul, brothers, left France during the persecution of Lewis XIV., came over to London, & from thence to America. They were both clerks in the Church of England. John Bertrand, the elder, settled in Rappahannock Co. Va., after having married in London on the 29th, Sept., 1686, Charlotte Jolly, a French Nobleman's daughter, with whom he escaped from France. J. B. left two children. William the elder, died in 1760, left an only daughter, Mary Ann. She intermarried with Leroy Griffin, the father of Thomas Bertrand Griffin, Corbin Griffin, Cyrus Griffin, &c. Paul Bertrand, the other brother, settled in Calvert Co., Md., on a farm purchased by him, called Hayes, west of Patuxant river, & died soon after his marriage, leaving a widow & one son, named Paul. The widow went to London, with her son Paul. Paul, married & settled at Bath & died without issue, about the year 1755, leaving a widow—about in 1766. This widow was named Mary, & was the daughter of one Dearling, a very eminent Toyman of London.

J. L. G. was married to G. H. D. in York Co.,Va. by Rev. John Curtis, Pastor of the "Campbellits," otherwise called "Disciples" church [Lower Grafton] in York Co. Va.

Births: Stephen Orren Wright, son of Col. Stephen & Abby Wright, was born in Norfolk, Va., Oct 8, 1814. Tas. Parish, La, by Mr. ——— Rouse J. P. to S. B. S. L. W. were married in the William & Mary Col. Chapel by Rev. R. T. Brown, son-in law of Rev. Dr. W. H. Wilmer, formerly Pres. W. & M.—Dr. S. S. G. was living in York Town, Va., when he married Miss Sallie Lewis.—J. L. C. G. [This entry is copied as it apparently was written.]

Mary Louisa wife of S. O. W., was born in Gloucester Co., Va., March 31, 1817.

Sallie Lewis, daughter of Stephen O. & Mary Louisa Wright, was born in Norfolk, June 2, 1838.

Stephen Griffin, son of S. O. and M. L. Wright was born in Norfolk January 4, 1845 and died in Williamsburg May 29, 1845.

Nancy Chiswell Brown (an orphan child) was born in York Co. Sep 20, 1838.

Mary Louisa Stuart daughter of M. D. & Sally L. Ball was born at "Stony Lonesome," Prince William Co. Va. Aug 9, 1861.

William Dulany Ball, son of M. D. & S. L. Ball was born June 25, 1865 in Williamsburg & died Jan 1866.

Sally Lewis Ball daughter of the same was born Dec. 14, 1866 at Fairfax C. H. Va. Mottram Corbin [Ball] was born at Fairfax C. H. March 11, 1868.

Caroline Linton Ball, daughter of the same, was born in Baltimore Md. Nov. 23, 1869; James Stuart Ball, son of the same was born in Alec andria, Va. Nov. 5, 1872, Annie Addison [Ball] was born in Alexandriax Va. Jan'y 20, 1875.

Cyrus Anstruther son of S. S. & S. Griffin born July 26, 1810, at York-Town, Va.

James Lewis Corbin Griffin, son of S. S. & S. Griffin, born March 17, 1814, at Lewisville, also called "Brew House"on Seven River, Gloucester Co. Va.

Mary Stuart, daughter of S. S. & S. Griffin, born April 31, 1817, at Lewisville, aforesaid.

Thomas Stuart, son of the same, born May 16, 1819 & died Feb. 24, 1822, at Lewisville, Gloucester Co. Va.

John Mercer, son of the same, born at Lewisville, Gloucester Co. Aug. 24, 1822, & died Sept. 3, 1822 at this birth place.

Fayette, son of S. S. & S. Griffin born March 21, 1812 at Williamsburg.

Nancy Chiswell Brown daughter of Mansfield Brown & Sarah his wife, was born Sept. 20, 1838 in York Co., Va.

Mansfield, son of Mansfield & Sarah Brown, was born Dec. 30, 1840.

Julia Ann, daughter of S. S. & S. Griffin born June 3, 1828 and died June 20, of the same year in Williamsburg.

Mary Stuart daughter of the same born June 8, 1830 died June 20, 1830 in Williamsburg.

John Griffin son of Judge Cyrus Griffin and brother of S. S. Griffin, born April 20, 1771 at Traquair, seat of the Earl of Traquair in the County Peebles, Scotland.

His Uncle, Charles, Earl of Traquair died Oct. 17, 1827, leaving his son Charles, Earl after him, & Lady Louisa his issue.

Lady Lucia Stuart, sister of Lady Christina Griffin (the latter the mother of John. Samuel Stuart, Mary and Louisa Griffin) died in London Jany 2, 1829. Charles Stuart, 7th Earl of Traquair, died at Traquair, Dec. 1827, being 83 years old. He was the brother of Lady Christina and Lady Lucia Stuart.

John Lewis, husband of Ann Chiswell Griffin died Nov. 28, 1827, in Gloucester Co., Va.

Ann Chiswell Lewis (wife of the last named) daughter of William Griffin & S. G. died in Gloucester Co., Va., Dec. 27, 1843.

Mary, widow of Thomas Griffin of York (who died in York Town Oct 1836), & eldest daughter of Cyrus & Christina Griffin died at Fauquier Springs, Va. Sept 6, 1851.

Louisa, widow of the late Hugh Mercer, of Fredericksburg, & daughter of Cyrus & Christina Griffin, died at Savannah, Ga, at the residence of her son, Gen. Hugh W. Mercer, Dec 28, 1859.

William Griffin, father of Ann Chiswell Lewis, & uncle of S. S. Griffin, died Feb. 11, 1793 about two o'clock Monday morning.

Mrs. Susanna Griffin, wife of William Griffin, died Feb. 21, 1805, at about ½ after 6 in the evening.

Stephen Griffin, son of Stephen Orren & Mary Louisa Wright died in Williamsburg, May 29, 1845, age 4 months & 24 days.

Lady Christina Griffin, Consort of Cyrus Griffin and mother of Samuel Stuart Griffin died 8th of October, 1807, in Williamsburg, Va., & was intered in the cemetery of the Prot. Episc. Church.

Cyrus Griffin, father of S. S. Griffin died Dec. 10, 1810, in York-town, Va. aged 62.

Sarah Tabb, mother of Sarah Griffin (the latter being Consort of S. S. Griffin) died in Gloucester Town Va, Dec. 8, 1821, in the 68th year of his age.

Cyrus Anstruther, son of S. S. & S. Griffin died in Williamsburg, Va., Oct. 10, 1834.

Fayette, son of S. S. & S. Griffin died Nov 24, 1850, and was buried in the Episc. Church Yard, Bruton Parish of Williamsburg, near his departed mother Sarah Griffin.

Sarah Griffin (nee Lewis) Consort of S. S. Griffin died in Williamsburg Va. Nov 12, 1846, in the 59th year of her age.

Samuel Stuart Griffin died in Williamsburg, Dec. 19, 1864, in the 83rd year of his age (He was born in Philadelphia, Pa., Jan'y 6, 1782).

Jane Hester, Consort of J. L. C. Griffin, died in Williamsburg, on July 28, 1848.

J. L. C. Griffin Jr. infant son of J. L. C. Griffin, & Jane Hester, his wife, was born June 20, & died June 22, 1848, in Williamsburg, Va.

Henry Stuart, infant son of J. L. C. Griffin & Fannie Mary, his wife, was born 1855 at Frankfort, Ky. & died in that city July of the same year.

Charlie Denning, son of J. L. C. G. & F. M. G., was born at Sharon, Madison Co., Miss., Sept. 28, 1856, & died at the residence of their friend, Mr. Thomas Lewis Gilmer & wife, in the same place, Sept. 3, 1857.

Samuel Stuart Griffin, born at Philadelphia, Pa., January 6, 1782, & died at Williamsburg, Va., Dec. 19, 1864.

Sarah Lewis, wife of S. S. Griffin, born at Gloucester Town, Va., June 24, 1787, & died at Williamsburg, Va., Nov. 12, 1846.

From "Register" in Mrs. A. W. C. Waller's Family Bible.

Marriages: James Lewis & Sarah Thruston were married by Rev. Mr. Fontain, Dec. 18, 1784.

Robert Thruston & Sarah Brown were married at Belle Farm, in Gloucester Co., Va., by Rev. Mr. Smith, Dec. 22nd, 1804.

A. W. C. Catlett, daughter of John W. C. Catlett, of Timber Neck, in Gloucester Co., Va., was married at the residence of her father, on Feb. 22, 1849, to C. C. P. Waller, son of Hetty & Benjamin Waller of Williamsburg, Va.

[In my cousin A. W. C. W's Family Bible "Register," the date of my mother's birth, is set down June 24, 1786, but I think 1787 is right.— J. L. C. G.]

Births: Robert Thruston, son of John & Sarah Thruston was born March 30, 1782, & baptized May 7, 1783.

Sarah Lewis, daughter of James & Sarah Lewis, was born June 24, 1786, at Gloucester Town, Va.

Ann Harwood Lewis Thruston, daughter of Robert & Sarah Thruston, was born Oct. 7, 1805.

Agnes Jane Thruston, daughter of Robert & Sarah Thruston, was born at Gloucester Town, Dec. 30, 1806.

John Benjamin, son of A. W. C. & C. C. P. Waller was born in Williamsburg, Va., Feb. 13, 1850 [on Ash Wednesday].

Hetty C. Waller, daughter of the same was born in Williamsburg Dec. 24, 1851.

Mary Louisa, daughter of the same was born in Williamsburg, March 11, 1852. C.C.P., son of the same was born in Williamsburg, April 14, 1853.

Wilmer Nelson, son of the same was born Feb. 13, 1855, in Williamsburg.

Agnes Thruston, daughter of the same was born in Williamsburg, March 31, 1858. C. C. P. [2nd], son of the same was born in Williamsburg, March 2, 1861.

Ann S., daughter of the same was born in Gloucester Co. (at Valley Front), January 24, 1864.

W. Page, son of the same, born in Gloucester Co., April 21, 1865.

Robert Page, son of A. W. C. & C. C. P. Waller, born in Williamsburg, March 6, 1867.

A. W. C. Waller, daughter of John W. C. Catlett & Agnes Jane, his wife, was born at Lansdowne, Gloucester Co., Va., Nov. 9, 1829.

Sally Brown Brunskin Nelson, daughter of the same was born at Lansdowne, Gloucester Co., Va. March 11, 1828.

Sarah Letitia Thruston, daughter of Robert & Sarah Thruston, was born at Gloucester Town, Nov. 2nd, 1808—Eleanor Thruston, daughter of R. & S. Thruston, was born at Gloucester Town, January, 1810.

William Stevenson Thruston, son of Robert & Sarah Thruston, born at Gloucester Town, Feb. 26, 1813.

Edward Taliaferro Thruston, son of the same, born Aug. 27, 1817.

Sarah Tabb, (previously Mrs. Thruston & Mrs. Lewis) departed this life at Gloucester Town, Dec. 8, 1821, aged 70.

Sarah, Consort of Robert Thruston, departed this life at Lansdowne, Gloucester Co., Dec. 8, 1818.

Robert Thruston of Lansdowne died at Lansdowne, Feb. 22, 1857.

William S. Thruston, M. D., died at Matthews C. H. Va., Feb. 14, 1861.

Charles Carter Page Waller, Consort of A. W. C. Waller departed this life in Williamsburg, Feb. 6, 1867. Perfectly well at dinner, cheerful, & enjoying the society of his devoted family, he was in the evening seized with Gout of the stomach, which was transferred to the brain, & of which he died: a corpse at 7 o'clock, P. M. of that day. Regretted & beloved by all; truly may it be said of him HE HAD NO ENEMIES.

[The paragraph relating to C. C. P. W. son., was written by his widow, A. W. C. W. J. L. C. G.]

Miss Mary Lark, for many years, the close friend of the late Mrs. Hetty Waller, mother of C. C. P. W. son., & now & for many years, also the the friend intimate & dear of Mrs. A. W. C. Waller, was born in Oct. 5, 1800.

Benj. Seawell of Gloucester Co., Va., was born Dec. 25, 1800.

The late Rev. Thomas Whittemore, for many years Editor of the "Trumpet & Universalist Magazine—previously, Pastor of the University Society at Cambridge Port, Mass., was born in 1800, & died March 21, 1865.

John W. C. Catlett, father of Mrs. A. W. C. W. & of Mrs. S. B. B. Nelson, was born Dec. 25, 18—.

671

FROM HALL FAMILY BIBLE.

The ages of William Hall & Aney's children:
John Hall was born August 16, 1752

Sarah	do.	May 24, 1754
Betty	do.	May 3, 1757
Mary	do.	Dec. 6, 1758
Ann	do.	September 3, 1760
Judy	do.	March 11, 1764
Patty	do.	December 15, 1764
William	do.	October 15, 1765
Jane	do.	October 7, 1768
Joseph	do.	February 11, 1772
Ambrose	do.	February 4, 1774
Nicholas	do.	June 6, 1777

Hastin Hall took down the ages of his father & his uncles & his aunts 5th day of January, 1847.
Hastin Hall was born July 21, 1806
Hastin H. Hall was married to Lucy Beck September 9, 1830.
The ages of Hastin H. Hall's children:
Joseph Nicholas Hall was born May the 30th, 1831

Mary Ann Hall	do.	July the 26th, 1832
William Scott Hall	do.	July 22, 1834
Lucy Jane Hall	do.	April the 14, 1836
Júlany Ann Hall	do.	October 18, 1838
Sarah Francis Hall	do.	May the 30, 1840.

Sarah Jane Cason was born December the 17, 1857
Joseph Hastin Hall was born April 26, 1859
Hastin William Hering was born May the 10, 1861

Lydia Hall died September the 4, 1848
Mary Ann Hall was married October the 23, 1855
Lucy Jane Hall was married April 23, 1857
Julany Ann Hall was married July the 12, 1860

Melvin Hall died October the 24, 1836
Joseph Hall (Lydia's husband) was born 1772 & died June the 29, 1855
Hastin H. Hall died the 23rd of February, 1884
Lucy Hall was born May 18, (?)2, died May the 6, 1889.

Bolling Hall, 1767-1836, Entries in a copy of *"The Book of Common Prayer.—* New York, Printed by William A. Davis, 1803." Written on title page is "Bolling Hall, August, 1807" [The following are the entries]

"Bolling Hall was born 25th Decr. 1767—and was married on the 25th day of Oct. 1798 to Jane Abercrombie, who was born 25 Decr. 1781.—Polly Wilkie Hall, their first child, was born widnesday the 5th Feby. 1800.—Nancy Hall was born on tuesday 13th May 1801—3 o'clock a. m.—Martha Bryan was born on tuesday the 8th Decr. 1803—8 o'clock a. m.—Elize Dixon Hall was born on monday 7th July 1806—6 o'clock p.m.—Jane Abercrombie Hall was born on sunday night 13th Sptr. 1807.—Emma Bolling Hall was born 8th Decr. 1809.—Bolling Hall was born saturday morning 8th May 1813.—Laura Hall was born on the 26 day of May 1815.—Amanda Hall was born 7 February 1818.—Mary Bibb Hall was born on the 17th August 1821.—Sarah Hall was born the 11th October 1824.—[on next page appears the entry]—Bolling Hall died 25 Feb. 1836."

Of the above entries the first eight are written with a light pen and in one handwriting. The next four entries are in same handwriting but made with a much heavier pen (probably goose quill). The entry of Bolling Hall's death is in different handwriting, and evidently with a steel pen point. In 1944 Mrs. W. M. Marks, 525 S. Perry St., Montgomery, Ala., owned this prayer book.

This is to certify that the handwriting in the Bolling Hall Prayer Book is identical with letters written by him in the collections of the Alabama [SEAL] State Department of Archives and History.—Marie B. Owens, Director, Dept. Archives & History. Voncile B. Sayus, Notary Public.

HARRIS OF LOUISA COUNTY.

(Contributed by Mrs. Wm. B. Ardery, Rocclicgan, Paris, Ky.)

Harris Bible

The following records copied from the Bible of Frederick Harris, of Frederick's Hall, were sent me by his granddaughter, Mrs. Juliana Pendleton, wife of William B. Pendleton, of Louisa county, Virginia.

David Harris married Miss Louisa Knight of London.
Nath'l Harris married Miss Ellen Goodwin.
Catherine Mary Harris married Dr. William J. Pendleton.
Eliza Dorothea Harris married Dabney Carr Overton.
Juliana Harris married Alexander Barret.
Charlotte Rebecca Harris married Joseph K. Pendleton.

Grandfather Frederick Harris died April 9th in the 63rd year of his age.

Frederick Harris and Catherine Snelson Smith were married 28th day of December 1805.

Children of Frederick Harris:

> David Bullock Harris.
> Christopher Smith Harris.
> Frederick Lewis Harris.
> Nath'l William Harris.
> Eliza Dorothea Harris.
> Catherine Mary Harris.
> Charlotte Rebecca Harris.
> Juliana Harris.
> Sarah Lavinia Harris.

..ote: The above Frederick Harris died in Louisa county, where his will was probated in the year 1842. He was the son of Frederick and Eliza (Terrill) Harris of Louisa county.

HARRIS-FLOURNOY BIBLE RECORD.

(Contributed by Mrs. S. E. Lindley, Sullivan, Indiana)

Jordan Harris, born 20th May, 1763. Married 12 April, 1789, Elizabeth Cannon, born 16 May, 1771.

William Jordan Harris, born 7 Aug., 1791.

Maria Turpin Harris, born 14 Feb., 1796.

John Harris, born 1 Oct., 1797; died 6 Oct., 1797.

Horatio Turpin Harris, born 24 Mch., 1799.

Jordan Harris. Married 9 Jan., 1803, Nancy Jude, born 22 Aug., 1763.

Mary Elizabeth Jordena Harris, born 16 Oct., 1803.

John Francis Harris, born 28 January, 1808.

Jordan Harris died Oct. 7, 1826.

Thomas H. Flournoy, born 17 April, 1797. Married Nov. 20th, 1821, Jordena Harris, born 16th Oct., 1803.

Aljernon Flournoy, born 21th April, 1823.

Jordan Harris Flournoy, born 28th Feb., 1826.

Gustavus Adolphus Flournoy, born 2nd Feb., 1828.

Thomas H. Flournoy, born 17 April, 1797. Married Sept. 29th, 1836, Mary A. Roberson, born 7th Feb., 1818.

On another page is the following:

James? (indistinct) Jefferson, son of Nancy and Moses, was born 5th of April, 1821.

Martha, the daughter of Lucy and Benjamin, was born 9th of Jan., 1823.

Rosena, the daughter of Nancy and Moses, was born 13th of Feb., 1823.

James Kirkpatrick, age 89 yrs., 5 mo., 20 days, died Nov. 3, 1873.

Married Maria Harris Kirkpatrick, born in Powhatan Co., Va., Dec. 15, 1793, died in Caldwell Co., Ky., Dec. 6th, 1863.

HAYNIE.

This was taken from my great grandfather, Matthew Thomson's Day
Book, and was all in his handwriting until his death, when his sons continued it. There are also many other dates of the births and marriages

675

of the children of Haynie Thomson, and different members of the Thomson family:

(Memorable Dates)

Wm. Haynie was born November 12, 1739, and died December 7, 1816, married in August 1767 Sarah   , born April 26, 1739, and died November 13, 1809.

Henry Haynie was born December 6, 1768, died May 1837.

Richard Haynie, born April 1, 1771, died in 1779.

Betsy Haynie, born June 17, 1773, died December 1779.

Sally Haynie, born August 14, 1775, and married first George Cleveland April 16, 1792, then Francis Kirtley, died a widow August 8, 1825.

Nancy Haynie, born July 25, 1777, married Edward Whaley April 15, 1794.

Richard Haynie born September 26, 1779.

Betsy Haynie, born December 17, 1781, married Wm. Smith April 16, 1800, died February 5, 1803.

Sibel Haynie, born November 20, 1783, married Matthew Thomson April 16, 1801, died March 20, 1843.

Anna Haynie, born March 19, 1785, married Joseph Thomson August 16, 1808.

The children of Matthew Thomson and Sibel Haynie:

Haynie Thomson born July 16, 1802.

Harrison Thomson, born January 6, 1804, died February 5, 1804.

Kitty Thomson was born April 14, 1805.

Emily Thomson, born July 31, 1809, died January 10, 1816.

Harrison Thomson, born September 8, 1811, married November 27, 1828.

James Lewis Thomson born June 26, 1813, and married July 7, 1836 to Susan Davis.

Sanford Thomson born March 7, 1815, and married Susan Smith June 23, 1841.

Benjamin Franklin Thomson born January 19, 1817, and married September 14, 1837.

Wm. Neill Thomson, born December 27, 1818, married Nancy Quisenberry February 4, 1840.

Eliza Thomson born June 22, 1822, and died December 12, 1832.

Harrison Thomson's Children:

Elizabeth Thomson born March 7, 1831.

Emily Thomson born May 27, 1833.

Albert Whaley Thomson born January 15, 1835.

Matthew Franklin Thomson born December 11, 1837, and died November 21, 1838, 30 minutes after midnight.

Ann Maria Thomson born April 14, 1840.

Sanford Thomson born August 19, 1842.

Harrison Thomson, son of Harrison and Joicy Thomson, born May 8, 1845.

Manlius V. Thomson, born June 19, 1848, died on the night of August 5, 1854, about 11 o'clock, with the dreaded scourge cholera; snatched from us in health with the brief notice of about 6 hours.

Matthew Thomson died February 12, 1839, in the 66th year of his age. Sibel Thomson, wife of Matthew, died March 20, 1843.

Edward Whaley born February 18, 1773.

The ages of Edward Whaley's children:

Betsy Whaley born July 13, 1796.

James Whaley born April 10, 1798.

Wm. Whaley born February 10, 1800.

Sally Whaley born November 20, 1801.

Albert Whaley born March 23, 1804.

Benjamin Whaley born November 28, 1805.

Franklin Whaley born September 27, 1807.

John Whaley born July 13, 1809.

Volney Whaley born March 2, 1811.

Harrison Whaley born November 23, 1813, and died August 11, 1815.

America Whaley born April 26, 1816, and married November 17, 1831.

James Whaley was married to Peggy Strode September 18, 1823.

John Whaley married December 23, 1830, to Nancy H. Forquau (it seems to read).

(Scattered Notes) (Don't know what connection)
Washington and Priestly Wilkerson live in Alabama, Haynie in Lexington, and Moses in Falmouth (Pendleton County).

John Wilkerson, born March 12, 1757, died June 15, 1834.

James Wilkerson, born November 29, 1758, died December 5, 1834.

Wm. Wilkerson born March 3, 1761.

Moses Wilkerson born April 12, 1763.

Priestly Wilkerson born May 26, 1767.

Kitty Thomson married Eli Bigger January 15, 1824.

Mrs. Huls born August 10, 1755, her daughter, Polly born August 19, 1778.

Good many dates about John Patton, James Patton, Daniel Harrison, Patton Harrison, Sibal Peake, etc., as well as the Kirtley and Bigger children.

[A notarys' certificate, as to correctness of copy follows].

677

HAYNIE.

The "WILLIAM HAYNIE, born 12 Nov. 1739", mentioned in Matthew Thomson's "Memorable Dates", was recorded as born, as above stated' on the register (preserved at Heathville C. H.) of Upper St. Stephen's parish, Northumberland Co. Virginia, and as the fifth child of Mr. "Ansby" Haynie, of this parish.

The name "Ansby" was written by the parish clerk, or the parish minister, for "Ormsby", which was the correct name of said William's father, as appears from the Court records of this county.

The children of ORMSBY HAYNIE recorded in this parish register:

Richard, b. 29 Sep. 1729.   Sarah, b. 11 May, 1737.
Charles, b. 21 Oct. 1731.   William, b. 12 Nov. 1739.
George, b. 16 Mar. 1732.   Elizabeth, b. 17 Feb. 1743.

The aforesaid ORMSBY HAYNIE was one of the fourteen children of Captain RICHARD HAYNIE, of St. Stephen's parish. (this before the parish was divided into Upper and Lower.)

This RICHARD HAYNIE, who was sometime a captain of militia of this county, as a Burgess, represented this county, with others, in the Va. House of Burgesses, for seven years, 1695, '96, '97, '98, 1703, '04, '05. He was born about, or in 1660, and died in 1724. He was twice married. He married first, 10 Oct. 1681, Elizabeth Bridgar, of this St. Stephen's parish, (according to her tombstone, in a "farm graveyard, near Heathville C. H.), born 16 July, 1665, died 2 April, 1697. "She had eight children." He married secondly, 1700-1, Elinor————, who survived him, and administered on his estate, (Her will proved in 1754). By her he had six children.

Captain RICHARD HAYNIE had by his wife ELIZABETH BRIDGAR:—

Bridgar (in father's will).   ORMSBY (in father's will).
John, (in bro. Bridgar's will).   Anne, (in father's will).
Elizabeth, b. 6 Dec. 1686.   Katherine, (in father's will).
Maxmilian, b. 31 Oct. 1688.   Samuel, (in father's will).

He had by his second wife, Elinor,

Mary, b. 3 Nov. 1702.   Elinor, b. 2 Sep. 1708.
William, b. 5 Nov. 1704.   Charles, b. 23 Jan. 1710.
Winifred, b. 7 April, 1706.   Sarah, b. 11 May, 1718.

678

Abstract of the will of RICHARD HAYNIE, aforesaid,
Signed by him, 31 Oct. 1724, Proved at Heathville C. H. 18 Mar. 1724-5.
"Deed Book, "1718-1726, fo. 389).

To son Bridgar, land by road, near the Court House, and all of my plantation where I now live.

Shoudl he die, leaving no heir, then the same lands to go to my sons Maxmilian Haynie and ORMSBY HAYNIE, and their heirs, &c.

To my son ORMSBY HAYNIE and my son Charles Haynie, certain other land.

To my son Samuel Haynie 80 acres of land, adjoining the land of Richard Oldham.

The rest of my land to be equally divided between my daughters, Katherine, Elinor, Winifred, and Anna. To them he also gave some negroes.

To my daughter Elizabeth Smit, a gold ring of the price of 25 shill.

My wife Elinor and Major George Eskridge to be executors.

The inventory of the personal estate of Captain RICHARD HAYNIE was filed in Court, in 1725, by his relict, Elinor Haynie. Besides the items of "3 books", "a packet of books", and "3 other books", it was the usual inventory of a farmer of that period, and included a cupboard, two feather, and flock beds, a "truckell bed", handirons, two spits, two tables, three chests, six chairs, bellows, pots, pothooks, chafing dish, four spinning wheels, a brass snuff box, three tobacco boxes, pewter bottles, looking glass, glass bottles, and a silver headed cane, a seal skin trunk, a pair of spectacles, ink-horn, &c.

1713-4, Jan. 21. "Captain Richard Haynie" having "been presented by the Grand Jury for absenting himself from Church, contrary to law," could give no good excuse for this crime, was compelled to pay the customary fine, with the costs. (Court Order Book, 1713-4). However, there seemed to be no hard feeling towards the Captain, for the same day, the Court appointed him overseer of the road from the Court House to his house.

The will of Elinor, the second wife, and relict of Captain RICHARD HAYNIE, was presented in Court for probate by Samuel Haynie, an executor, 10 Sep. 1754. Charles Cuppage was his security.

ORMSBY HAYNIE married in 172-, SARAH————. He died intestate. He died in 1743-4, and on 12 March, 1743-4, SARAH HAYNIE, his widow and administratrix, came into Court, and confessed judgement for the sum of 848 lbs. of tobacco due as a debt to Matthew Zuille, Jr. of this county. Ar the same time, as adm'x, Sarah also confessed judgement for 621 lbs. of tobacco due Wlliam Hughlett.

As to Captain RICHARD HAYNIE'S service as a Burgess, see Stanard's "Colonial Virginia Register", (printed book).

The inventory of "Mr. ORMSBY HAYNIE"'s personal estate was made at his house, 13 Feb. 1743-4. It is a long farm inventory. (Record Book. 1743-1749, Heathville C. H.).

I think these are all the "vital" items I found, but when I write out all the notes I took at Heathville, I may find others.

Charles H. Browning.

Nicholas Morris, died 1660   =
St. Stephen's parish, North'd Co.   (or "Wicomico parish").

  John Haynie.   Jane Morris.
1650 Jan. 20. Grantee for 950 ac.   In father's will, 1660, "Jane
              =   Haynie."
North'd Co. Other patents later.   Married about 1650.
Burgess, Mar. 1657-8. St. Stephen's.

  Captain Richard Haynie.   Elizabeth Bridgar, 1665–
                                1693.
St. Stephen's parish. Land owner.   First wife, married 10 Oct.
                                1681.
Burgess, 1695, &c.   Their son "Ormsby", in
                                father's will.
Will 31 Oct. 1724, pr. 1724-5.   Apparently fifth child, and
                                fourth son, and b. 1689-90.
(Brother to Capt. John Haynie, of St. Ste-
  phen's. Burgess, 1703-4-5. Who died in
  1724).

  Ormsby Haynie.   =   Sarah.
Upper St. Stephen's parish.   Adm. on husband's estate,
                                Mar. 1744.
Dies intestate before Feb. 1743-4.

  William Haynie.   =   Sarah.
b. 12 Nov. 1739, fifth child, recorded in register of Upper St. Stephen's parish,
  North'd Co. at Heathville C. H. Aug. 1911.

JOHNS FAMILY BIBLE RECORD.

We are indebted to Mrs. Willie Johns Parish, of Roanoke, Va., for the following copy of a family Bible record. She states that Col. John Johns lived at New Store, Buckingham county. Edmund Winston Johns became a noted divine of his day.

From another source it is learned that Col. John Johns and Elizabeth Winston were married in 1766; that he died about 1821 and she in 1784 or 1788. Glover Johns, named below, married in 1803, Martha (born in Buckingham, 1780, died 1828) daughter of Joel Jones, and died in 1834 in Miss. Glover and Martha Johns had John Jay Johns, born June 27, 1818, in Buckingham Co., Va.; married Jane Amanda Durfree, and died April 3, 1899, at St. Charles, Mo. Glover and Martha Johns also had a daughter, Mary, who married William Cowan.

It has been stated that Elizabeth, wife of John Johns, was a daughter of Judge Edmund Winston, but this is a mistake. His daughter Elizabeth (1783-1856) married Dr. Bennett W. Moseley.

Col. John Johns b. Oct. 14, 1746; wife Elizabeth Winston, b. Oct. 30, 1749. They married Feb. 28, 1766. Children:

William M. Johns, b. Jan. 10, 1766.

Edmund Winston Johns, May 24, 1767.

Judith Johns, May 2, 1768.

Glover Johns, Dec. 25, 1769.

Anthony Benning Johns, March 11, 1771.

Martha Johns, Oct. 27, 1772.

Mary Johns, Jan. 4, 1775.

Samuel Johns, Sep. 28, 1777.

Elizabeth Johns, March 24, 1779.

Sarah Johns, March 12, 1780.

Ann Johns, March 6, 1781.

John Johns, June 3, 1784.

KENNON RECORD

The family record of the Kennons is as follows:

Lewis Kennon, son of Charles Kennon and his wife, Mary Howell (Lewis), was born in Halifax county, Va., 14th day of June, 1784.

Eliza Wyatt Winslow was born in Orange county, Va., 6th May, 1790.

Married to Lewis Kennon 23d January, 1816. Died 23d September, 1824.

(After her death.)—Dr. Lewis Kennon to Mary Chadwick, 10th of Jan. 1828, by Rev. Sam'l Davis, Burke county, Ga.

Children to Lewis Kennon and his wife, "Eliza":

Charles Henry Kennon, born 8th March, 1817, Saturday, P. M. Dead.

Charles Henry Kennon, born 24th May, 1818, Sunday, 1 o'clock.

(The latter was my father who, to inherit large properties entailed, took and retained the name of Winslow, his mother's maiden name.)

(My father married Maria Louisa Walter, daughter Jeremiah Walter and Elizabeth Wilmot, of Charleston, S. C.)

Children of Dr. Lewis Kennon and wife, Mary: Elizabeth W. Kennon, born September 20, 1778; Mildred L. Kennon, born May 18, 1781; Lewis Kennon, born June 14, 1784; Charles H. Kennon, born August 3, 1786; Nancy Kennon, born December 16, 1790; Mary B. Kennon, born April 3, 1795; Patsy, born Nov. 16, 1796; Lucy Kennon, born May 26, 1798; Richard Kennon, born May 28, 1800; William *Howell* Kennon, born March 14, 1802; Rebekah Kennon, born October 28, 1804; Eliza Kennon, born May 7, 1806; Erasmiss Kennon, born January 31, 1810; Sally Kennon, born November 20, 1811.

Children of Henry Kennon ·Winslow and Maria Louisa Walter: Randolph Bowling Winslow, Elizabeth Winslow.

William Poe Winslow married Annie L. Ludlow, New Orleans, January 31, 1880. Several children. He died New Orleans, May 8, 1899.

Elizabeth W. Kennon Winslow married Henry Darpit, April 25, 1881.

Children of Henry Darpit and E. W. K. Winslow; Bush, born February 4, 1882; Henry, born July 31, 1884; Walter, born July 24, 1886; Myrtle Dorothy, born December 11, 1893.

———, New Orleans, La.

MEMORANDUM OF SOLOMON KING'S PREDECESSORS, ETC.

(Contributed by W. E. McClenny, Suffolk, Va.)

Michael King was born in Old England and Came out of the City of Norwich to Virginia and their Served his time With John Wright in Nansemond County after that he Marred with Elizabeth *Hiry* (indistinct) and Lived in the upper Parrish of Nansemond County on the Southern branch of Nansemond River. &c—and he had by his wife Six Children Viz. -Nathan William Michael Henry John & Elizabeth—and their he bought A plantation with Land in the year 1686 and Bult a Large Dwelling hous with Brick and Bought Several Negro Slaves and also a Larg Copper Still &c. Written by me Solomon King, son of Charles King the Said Charles Was Son of William Which was son of Michael the Older————

Charles King Father of Solomon King Departed this Life January the 15th 1762————

Mary King Mother of Solomon King Departed this Life february the 2 Day 1762————

Henry King Uncell to the Said Solomon King Departed this Life December the 7 Day 1771————

Mary Hare aunt t othe Said Solomon King Departed this Life February the 11 Day 1774————

John Lee Father in Law to the Said Solomon King Departed this Life febuary 9 Day 1770————

Henry King Brother to Solomon King Departed this Life April the 15th Day 1782————

Bathsheba Porter Daughter of Solomon King Departed this life march 10th, 1789.

On another leaf of this Bible the following is found:
Jethro Sumner Son of Jethro Sumner was Born in the year of our Lord 1798 And was Married unto Elizabeth Mary Lawrence the 29th day of June 1820—The said Elizabeth M. Lawrence was born in the year of our Lord 1796.

683

Dempsey L. Sumner son of Jethro Sumner and Elizabeth his wife was born August 1st. 1823.

Elizabeth Mary Sumner Departed this life December 13th 1823.

Jethro Sumner Departed this life March the 10 1836.

Jethro Sumner Son of Jethro Sumner was Married with Ann Norfleet the 11th of June 1824.

Mary Elizer Sumner Daughter of Jethro Sumner and Ann his Wife was born July 11th 1825.

Mariah An Cumner was born January 1st 1827.

Martha Jane Daughter of Jethro Sumner and Ann Sumner was born the 5th of September 1829.

Charles Edward Sumner was born Oct. the 4th, 1831.

(The Bible from which the above has been copied was printed in Edinburg: by Alexander Kincaid, HIS MAJESTY'S PRINTER.

MDCCLXIX.)

(The original spelling and capitalization followed in the above.)

BIBLE RECORDS

Lewis, Cobbs, Waddy, Boyle, Searcy, Etc.

Property of Mr. Ben. C. Lewis, Shelby County, Kentucky

Shelby County Court Records

Elizabeth Lewis m. 10th August, 1814, George Osborn.

Mary Lewis m. 12th February, 1809, William Fenley.

William Lewis m. ———, 1810, who?

Susanna Lewis m. March 26, 1812, Richard Fenely.   Daughter of Isaac.

Ann Lewis m. 11th April, 1820, David Lilly, b. 1798, d. Plattsburg, Mo., 1839.   Had brother, Pleasant Lilly.

Ann Lewis Lilly died Clinton County, Mo., 1882.

The Holy Bible.   Property of Mr. Ben. C. Lewis, Shelby County, Ky. Records as written in Bible:

Isaac Lewis, Sr., was born June 20, 1760.

Nancy Overfield Lewis, his wife, was born Jany. 15th, 1761, and married 3rd of February, 1785.

684

Polly Lewis, now Finley, m. Dec. 24, 1807.
William Lewis married 1810.
Susanna Lewis, now Fenley, married March 1812.
Elizabeth Lewis, now Osborn, married Aug. 11, 1814.
Benjamin O. Lewis married 4th Dec., 1817.
Ann Lewis now Lilly, married 11th April, 1820.
Sally Lewis was born 28th Dec., 1785.
William Lewis was born October 7th, 1787.
Polly Lewis was born August 1st, 1789.
Susanna Lewis was born July 26, 1791.
Elizabeth Lewis was born Sept. 11th, 1793.
Samuel Lewis was born Jan. 25th, 1796.
Benjamin O. Lewis was born June 5, 1799.
Ann Lewis was born May 27, 1800.
Isaac Lewis was born March 13, 1802.
Charles Lewis was born Dec. 2, 1866.
Ada Webber was born Aug. 27, 1868.
Benjamin Glass Lewis was born Aug. 14, 1870.
Joseph Cary Lewis was born July 22, 1884.
Emily Lewis was born Sept. 26, 1818.
Elender Lewis was born Oct. 22, 1821.
Thomas D. Lewis was born Sept. 19, 1828.
Albert B. Lewis was born 27th May, 1830.
William H. Lewis was born Jan. 18, 1832.
Perlina Ann Lewis was born March 6th, 1837.
Isaac Newton Lewis was born Dec. 13, 1840.
Virgil Lewis was born March 31st, 1843.
Samuel Lewis—Deceased March 4th, 1816, age 20 years, one month, 7 days.

Elizabeth Osborn—Deceased April 4th, 1821, age 27 years and 6 months.
Lucinda, wife of B. O. Lewis, died May 20, 1845.
Paulina, wife of B. O. Lewis, died Dec. 1, 1860.
B. O. Lewis died Sept. 23, 1870.
Charles Lewis, son of L. N. Lewis and Mattie Lewis, died Sept. 17, 1867.
Isaac N. Lewis died Nov. 21, 1919.
Ada Lewis died Jan. 16, 1920.
Mattie J. Lewis, wife of L. N. Lewis, died Nov. 5, 1923.
Albert B. Lewis died Feb. 9, 1849.
Paulina Lewis Smith died Aug. 17, 1906.
Thomas D. Lewis died July 13, 1886.

The End

Waddy Bible. Samuel Waddy, 1844. Property of Mrs. Charles Weakley (formerly Cecil Waddy), 1928.

Marriages

Samuel Waddy and Elizabeth Hobbbs, married 9th June, 1804.

Lud Fore and Sarah Adoline Waddy, married 27th July, 1830.

Nicholas Smith and Nancy Jane Waddy, married Jan., 1823.

Daniel E. Wilson and Frances Eliza Waddy, married 22nd Jan., 1835.

M. N. Bogle (Jno.) was married to Frances Eliza Wilson late Waddy) the 30th April, 1839.

Ephraim G. Jessey and Susan M. Waddy, married 19th August, 1841.

Jno. N. Bog(y)le and Amanda Melvina Waddy, married 30th Sept., 1847.

William Lewis Waddy and Maria L. M. Thurston, married 16th Dec., 1847.

Ben F. Danley and Amanda M. Boyle, married 15th March, 1853.

Thomas B. Moon and Helen V. Wilson, married 26th Dec., 1853.

John F. Boyle and Matilda Dorsey, married May 10, 1873.

Births

Jane Cobbs, born 1753, 27th April.

Robert Cobbs, born 23d of Nov., 1754.

Judith Cobbs, born 5th April, 1757.

Samuel Waddy, born 2d May, 1772.

Elizabeth Hobbs, born 25th Dec., 1780.

Nancy Jane Waddy, born 25th Oct., 1804.

Joseph Owen Waddy, born Sept. 24th, 1806.

Mary Lewis Waddy, born 11th Oct., 1808.

Sarah Adoline Waddy, born 28th May, 1811.

Frances Eliza Waddy, born 5th Feb., 1814.

Susan Mildred Waddy, born 28th June, 1816.

William Lewis Waddy, born 30th March, 1819.

Amanda M. Waddy, born 7th June, 1822.

Mary Elizabeth Smith, born 18th Sept., 1825.

Mary Jane Fore, born 10th June, 1831.

Samuel Fore, born 5th July, 1832.

Helen Vaughn Wilson, born 10th Dec., 1836.

Geo. William Waddy, born 26th July, 1852.

Thompson Miller Waddy, born 28th Dec., 1855.

Lucinda Ida Waddy, born 6th July, 1858.

Maria Louise Waddy, daughter of W. L. Waddy and M. L. Waddy, born 23rd July, 1861.

M. F. Jesse son of Ephraim Jesse and Susan M. Jesse, born Nov. 13, 1851.

Hellen G. Jesse d. of Eph. & Susan M. J., born 1st March, 1854.
William G. Jesse, son of Eph. & Susan M., born 14th Oct., 1857.

Deaths

Nancy Jane Smith deprated this life 27th Dec., 1826.
Joseph Owen Waddy departed this life 17th of Sept., 1829.
Mary Lewis Waddy departed this life 26th Jan., 1831.
Mary Jane Fore departed this life 10th August, 1831.
Samuel Fore departed this life 15th Sept., 1832.
Daniel E. Wilson departed this life 22d Jan., 1837.
Mary Elizabeth Smith departed this life 25th July, 1837.
Nicholas Smith departed this life 18th Oct., 183—?
Sarah Adoline Fore departed this life 22d Jan., 1845.
Frances Eliza Boyle departed this life 26th July, 1845.
John W. Boyle departed this life 12th Aug., 1848.
Mary Eliza Boyle departed this life 21st Sept., 1848.
John N. Boyle d. 12th Aug., 1848.
Thomas Barkley Moon d. 11th Oct., 1855.
Samuel Waddy Danley d. 28th Oct., 1855.
Samuel Waddy d. 22d Aug., 1836.
Elizabeth Waddy d. Sept. 20, 1855.

Thurston Bible

Births

Richard Searcy b. 21st Aug., 1738.
Edmund Searcy b. 25 March, 1767.
Hannah Searcy his wife b. 12 Dec., 1777.
Harriett Searcy daut. of Edmund, b. 17 Dec., 1806.
Richard Edmund Plummer son of same, b. 4 Aug., 1817.
Mary Ellenor Sarah daut. of same, b. 19 March, 1820.
Maria Searcy b. 27 May, 1799 wife of Robert Thurston, m. Jan. 2, 1814.

Robert Thurston was born 16th Jan., 1783.

Deaths

Edmund Searcy died 15th Oct., 1825.
Hannah Searcy died 19th Sept., 1834.
Harriett Searcy died 1st Feb., 1810, daughter of above.
Richard Edmund Plummer son of same, died 15th April, 1824.

687

Edmund Searcy m. 6th Sept., 1796 to Hannah Miller.

Robert Thurston m. 2nd Jan., 1814 to Maria Searcy.

Mary Elenor Searcy married 11th April, 1839 to Joseph Welsh Walker.

Births

Mary Plummer Thurston daughter of Robert and Maria, was born Oct. 20, 1814.

Edmund Plummer Thurston son of same, born 22d Nov., 1816.

2nd daughter of same was born April 25, 1818.

Lucinda Elizabeth Thurston daughter of same b. Jan. 23, 1826.

Maria Loucresia Miller Thurston daut. of same, b. May 3, 1832.

Sophia Bailer Walker daut. of Joseph and Mary Ellenor b. Nov. 6, 1840.

Robert Samuel Waddy son of William L. Waddy and Maria b. Feb. 18, 1850.

Deaths

Maria Plummer Thurston died Nov. ——, 1815.

Edmund Plummer Thurston died Dec. 27, 1816.

Babe died May 16, 1818.

Maria Louise Miller Waddy died Dec. 26, 1907, age 75 yrs., 6 mo., 23 days.

William Lewis Waddy died Sept. 11, 1895.

Born

William Lewis Waddy b. March 31, 1819.

Maria Searcy Waddy wife of Dr. Robert Thurston b. May 27, 1799.

Dr. Robert Thurston b. Jan. 16, 1783.

Marriages

Joseph Welsh Walker and Mary Ellenor Searcy, married April 11, 1839.

William L. Waddy and Maria L. Thurston, married Dec. 16, 1827, age 15 yrs. 7 mo. 13 days.

Lucinda E. Thurston and Robert H. Smith married Feb. 23, 1842. Age 16 yrs. 1 mo., when married.

LUTTRELL FAMILY BIBLE RECORDS.

Contributed by A. M. Prichard, Staunton, Va.

State of Virginia, County of Augusta, to-wit:

I, J. W. Robson, a notary public in and for the county and state aforesaid, do certify that I have made a careful examination of an old family Bible which is now in the possession of Mr. A. M. Prichard, at his home, in said county and state; and that the said Prichard, being by me first duly sworn, did depose and say that said Bible had been loaned to him by Mr. Richard Harrison Duncan of Culpeper County, Virginia, who, at the time of said loan, stated that it was his grandfather's family Bible, and that it had come into his possession through his mother; and I further certify that the following is a true copy of the Family Record contained in said Bible, to-wit:

FAMILY RECORD

MARRIAGES

Burrell Luttrell and Hannah his wife was married the 22nd January 1807.

A. G. Stallard & Sarah his wife was married the 28 November 1833.

Richard Luttrell & Mary his wife was married January 15th 1838.

John W. Luttrell and Sarah his wife was married July 8th 1839.

James W. Luttrell and Frances his wife was married, August 27th 1840.

Burrell E. Luttrell and Mary Ritchie his wife were married August 23rd 1859.

William Doyle and Lucie A his wife were married July 7th 1859.

William Duncan and Mary E his wife was married 21 of October 1866.

George R. Doyle and Sallie Elliott were married April 26 1891.

BIRTHS

Burrell Luttrell was born October 25th 1785.

Hannah Luttrell was born August 27th 1787.

Sally Luttrell was born December 23rd 1807.

Richard Luttrell was born January 6th 1809.

Juliett Ann Luttrell was born September 22nd 1810.

James W Luttrell was born Feb 22nd 1813.

John W Luttrell was born March 4th 1816.

Elizabeth Rachel Luttrell was born January 3rd 1822.

Burrell Edmund Luttrell was born Dec 29 1838.

Hannah Button Luttrell was born Dec. 22nd 1840.

Lucy Ann Luttrell was born April 13th 1841.

Mary Elizabeth Luttrell was born March 30 1846.

Julia Francis Luttrell was born October 9th 1857.

Laura Franklin Doyle was born 21st April 1860.

Capitol L. Luttrell was born December 18th 1860.

Mary William Doyle was born October 18th 1861.

George Richard Doyle was born 7th August 1863.

Lucie Marie Luttrell was born December 28th 1863.

Richard Harrison Duncan was born January 5th 1868.

William Edward Duncan was born March 10th 1870.

Cora Virginia, daughter of George R. Doyle and Sallie Elliott, his wife, born Jan. 26, 1892.

George Elliott Doyle, son of G. R. Doyle and Sallie Elliott, was born Oct. 13, 1893.

DEATHS

Burrell Luttrell died November 26th 1831.

Hannah Luttrell wife of Burrell Luttrell died Aug. 1844. Daughter of Harmon Button.

Lucy A Doyle Daughter of Richard & Mary E Luttrell died November 15th 1863. 2nd Timothy 1st ch. 10 verse—Rev. B. Grimsley.

Lucie Mary Luttrell daughter of Burrell E & Mary Ritchie Luttrell died October 2nd 1864.

Mary E Luttrell wife of Richard Luttrell died July 6th 1870.

William D. Duncan husband of Mary B Duncan died March 12th 1871. Son of Harrison Duncan.

Richard Luttrell died February 11th 1874.

Charles Luttrell died Sept 24th 1896. Son of B. E. Luttrell.

Mr. George R Doyle died June 2nd 1897. Son of William Doyle and Lucie A Luttrell his wife.

Sallie Elliott Doyle wife of G. R. Doyle died February 20, 1909.

Mr. William Doyle died Decemb 12th 1894.

Willie Milton the child of William and Mary M Duncan died October 31st 1900.

Mary Ritchie Luttrell wife of Burrell E Luttrell died March 19th 1909.

Burrell Edward Luttrell died June 4 1915.

Mary Elizabeth Luttrell wife of William D Duncan died Sept. 19, 1913.

J. W. Robson,
Notary Public in and for Augusta County, Virginia.

(To be continued)

LUTTRELL FAMILY BIBLE RECORDS
Contributed by A. M. Prichard, Staunton, Va.

State of Virginia, County of Augusta, to-wit:

I, J. W. Robson, a notary public of said county and state do certify that I have examined the Family Record taken from the Family Bible of John W. Luttrell (deceased), late of Culpeper County, Virginia, now in possession of A. M. Prichard, at his home in said Augusta County; and that the said Prichard, being by me first duly sworn, did depose and say that he had borrowed said Record from Mrs. Maude Wayman Riley of Fauquier County, Virginia, who removed it from said Bible which had fallen apart from age and use, she being a granddaughter of said John W. Luttrell, and having come into possession of said Bible through her mother; and that the following is a true and accurate copy of said Family Record, to-wit:

MARRIAGE CERTIFICATE

This is to certify that Mr. John Willis Luttrell and Miss Sarah Elizabeth Corbin were solemnly united by me in the holy bonds of matrimony at Mr. Mitcham Corbin's on the eighth day of July in the year of our Lord, one thousand eight hundred and thirty nine conformably to the ordinance of God and the laws of the State.

In the presence of Few relatives and friends.

Signed, Cumberland George.

FAMILY RECORD

MARRIAGES

John W. Luttrell & Sarah E Corbin were married July 8th 1839.
Hannah B Luttrell & J A Holtzman were married the 19th Dec 1860.
Sallie A Luttrell & J J Wayman were married the 4th of Dec. 1871.
B M Luttrell & Florence I Harris were married 17 of Oct 1877.
L M Luttrell & F W Button were married Dec 5th 1877.
C J Luttrell & W D Robson were married Dec. 19th 1883.
Lizzie T. Holtzman and Will T. Bridgewater Nov 15th 1893.
Miriam W Holtzman & Willie Burnley Nov 15th 1893.
J Maude Wayman and O. K. Riley Dec. 18, 1901.
J. Wyer Robson married to Hazel Thurman Aug. 1910.
Betty D. Robson & A. M. Prichard Oct 10, 1911.
Elston Robson & Louise Abbott Mar. 1913.
Luttrell Robson & Hattie Mason Feb. 1912.
Esther L Burnley and Harry T Allen were married April 3, 1920.

BIRTHS

John W. Luttrell 4th March 1816.
Sarah E. Corbin 21st April 1816.
Hannah B. Luttrell 22nd Dec. 1840.
Sallie A Luttrell Dec. 5th 1842.
Mitcham C. Luttrell Au. 19th, 1845.
Burrell M. Luttrell, Nov. 15th 1848.
Mary L. Luttrell, Sep 3rd 1855.
Cora J Luttrell Apr 28th 1860.

GRANDCHILDREN

Little Lou Holtzman Oct 18th 1861.
Annie C Holtzman Aug 20th 1863.

Lizzie T Holtzman Feb 22nd 1867.
Miriam W Holtzman Jan 27th 1871.
Esther L Holtzman Apr 13th 1875.
Willie M Holtzman Mar 21st 1877.
Maude J Wayman Oct 27th 1875.
Lillian M; Wayman Aug 3rd 1881.
J Mortimer Button Dec 28th 1878.
Jennie E Button June 5th 1880.
Helen R Button Oct 1882.
Douglas W Button Oct 15th 1884.
Bettie Douglas Robson Nov 10th 1884.
John Wyer Robson Apr 22 1886.
Geo Elston Robson Dec 8th 1887.
Luttrell Robson Oct 30th 1889.
Fannie Louise Robson July 15, 1891.
James Earle Robson Apr 30th 1893.
Annie Norris Robson Mar 15, 1895.
Mortimer F. Robson Aug 9, 1896.
Betty Lee Robson July 9, 1911.
William T. Robson Feb. 1913. } Wyer's children
Margaret F Robson Sep. 1914.
Cora Thelma Robson April 28, 1898.
Harmon Robson, Oct'r 21, 1899.
John Oliver Riley at Linwood Monday Nov. 3rd 1902.
Sarah Madeline & Harley Maynard Riley March 27th 1905.
Virginia Ruth Riley Apr 11th 1907.
Eleanor Lillian Riley Feb 13th 1911.
Mary Ashton Robson Mar. 9, 1913—Luttrell's
Geo. H. Robson Feb. 1914—Elston's
Dorothy Jacqueline Robson, Mar. 1916.
Margaret Miriam Allen Jan. 7, 1921.
Frances Jewels Allen.

DEATHS

Little Lou Holtzman died August 1862.
B Mortimer Luttrell died Oct 30th 1878.
Mitcham C. Luttrell, Dec. 21st 1880.
Sarah E Luttrell, Sept. 17th 1882.
John W. Luttrell, Aug. 14th 1894.
Annie N Robson April 20th 1896.
James Earle Robson Jan. 1, 1906.
Hannah B Holtzman Jan 1907.
J. J. Wayman Apr. 24th, 1914.
S. L. Wayman Nov. 25th, 1914.
Lula M. Button, died Oct. 10th 1916.

C. Jacque Robson died Oct. 15th 1916.
Lillian M Wayman O'Brien died Jan 10th 1918.
John A Holtzman died Sept 10, 1915.
Annie C. Holtzman died Aug 21st 1919.
Wm M Burnley died Jan 26, 1919.
Maynard H Riley died March 4, 1925.

J. W. Robson,
Notary Public in and for Augusta County, Virginia.

MADISON FAMILY BIBLE RECORDS

Edited by Patricia P. Clark*

The Sarah Madison [Mrs. Sarah Catlett (Madison) Macon] Family Bible, printed by Thomas Baskett in London in 1759, contains records of the Madison, Conway, and Macon families. Recorded on its pages are the birth and death of James Madison, fourth president of the United States. The Bible (Mss6:4M265:1), which once belonged to his sister, was deposited in the Virginia Historical Society jointly by Mrs. Conway Macon Knox and Mrs. Malcolm Bridges of Richmond, Virginia, March 25, 1954.

Irving Brant in his biography of Madison comments that the Sarah Madison Bible is possibly one of the four Bibles left by James Madison, Senior, the father of the president. The entries are not in chronological order and, with the exception of the last two and the recording of James Madison's death, are all in the same hand, indicating that they were copied from another source. Their authenticity, however, cannot be challenged.[1]

President Madison was born the year England discarded the Julian Calendar and adopted the Gregorian Calendar. By the Julian Calendar the new year began on March 25, and the day after December 31, 1750, was therefore January 1, 1750. The calendar change decreed by Parliament in 1751 was made in two steps. The day after December 31, 1751, became January 1, 1752, and the day after September 2, 1752, became September 14, 1752, eleven days being omitted by the calendar. Madison was born, therefore, on March 5, 1750 (Old Style), but his birthday is now usually given as March 16, 1751 (New Style). To confuse the matter even more, the Old Style day of the month is sometimes combined with the New Style year. This was done in recording the birth of James Madison in the Sarah Madison Bible.

The Sarah Madison Bible records are transcribed here. Some doubtful entries, either illegible or missing, have been supplied in brackets from Brant's life of James Madison or from the Madison Family Bible records at the Princeton University Library. In the case of the marriages of Frances Madison and Elizabeth Madison neither Bible record is complete.

The Bible also contains obituary notices clipped from newspapers with dates and ages supplied by hand. Abstracts of these follow the other records.

---

*Mrs. Clark is a member of the staff at the Virginia Historical Society.
[1]Irving Brant, *James Madison: The Virginia Revolutionist, 1751-1780* (New York, 1941), pp. 30, 407.

Ambrose Madison was Married to Frances Taylor August the 24th 172[1].

James Madison was Born March 27, 1723, and was Baptized April 21 and had [for God]fathers Thomas Madison & James Taylor & for Godmothers Martha Taylor & Eliza[beth] Penn.

Elizabeth Madison was Born June 14th 1725, and was Baptized July 3d & had [for G]odfathers James Taylor & Richard Thomas and for Godmothers Martha Tay[lor] and Elinor Madison.

Frances Madison was Born March 6th 1726, and was Baptized April 9th & had [for] Godfathers James P[en]dleton & for Godmothers Isbell Pendleton & Elizabeth Penn.

Ambrose Madison Departed this Life August 27, 1732, being Sunday Night.

Frances Madison Departed this Life on Wednesday Morning about 2 OClock 25 of November 1761 and was inter'd the Sunday following. Her Funeral Sermon was preached on Wednesday the 30th of Decemr. following by the Revd. Mr. James Mar[ie][2] junior, on Revelations. Ch. 14. v. 13.

Nelly Conway was Born January 9th 1731.

John Willis was Married to Elizabeth Madison the

Taverner Beale was Married to Frances Madison

James Madison was Married to Nelly Conway September 15th 1749.

James Madison junr. was Born on Tuesday night at 12 OClock, being the last of the 5th & begining of the 6th Day of March 1751 and was Baptized by the Revd. Mr Wm Davis Mar. 31 and had for God Fathers Mr John M[oore &] Mr Jonatn. Gibson & for God-Mothers Mrs Rebecca Moore Miss Judith Catlett & Miss Elizabeth Catlett. Died the 28 June 1836. Intered 30 June.

F[ra]nces [sic] Madison was Born on Munday, Morning abt. 7 OClock June 1[8], 17[5]3 & was Baptized by the Revd Mr Mungo Marshall July the 1st & had [for] God-Fathers, Mr Taverner Beale & Mr Erasmus Taylor, & for God-Mothers Miss Milly[3] Taylor & Mrs Frances Beale.

[Am]brose Madison was Born on Munday Night, between 9 & 10 OClock Ja[n]uary 27th 1755 & was Baptized by the Revd Mr Mungo Marshall [March] 2nd [and] had for God-Fathers Mr. James Coleman & Col. George Taylor & for [God]-Mothers Mrs Jane Taylor & Alice Chew.

Catlett Madison was Born on Fryday Morning at 3 OClock Febru[ary 10th] 1758, & was Baptized by the Revd. Mr. James Maury February 22nd

---

[2]Though consistently spelled "Marie" in the Madison Family Bible, the name is usually spelled "Marye."
[3]Spelled "Milley" in the Madison Family Bible records in the Princeton University Library.

& had [for] God-Fathers Col. Wm Taliaferro & Mr Richard Beale & for God-Mothers [Mrs. Eli]zabeth Beale & Miss Milly Chew.

Nelly Madison was Born February 14th, 1760, and was Baptized March 6th [by] the Revd. Mr. Wm. Giberne & had for God-Fathers Mr. Larkin Chew & Mr. Wm Mo[ore &] for God-Mothers Miss Elizabeth Catlett & Miss Catharine Bowie. The said Nelly was born on Thursday morning just after Daybreak.

[Wil]lliam Madison was Born May 1st, 1762, & Baptized May 23d [by the Revd.] James Marie junr. & had for God-Fathers Mr Wm Moore & Mr Jos[eph Chew? and for] God-Mothers Miss Mary Willis & Miss Milly Chew. He was born [Saturd]ay Morning about 25 minutes after 1 o'Clock.

[Sa]rah Madison [bor]n August 17th, 1764, & was Baptized September 15th by [the Re]vd. James Marie junr. & had for God-Fathers Capt. Richard Barbour & [An]drew Shepherd & for God-Mothers Mrs Sarah Taylor & Miss Mary Con[way. Sh]e was born 45 minutes after 5 o'Clock P.M. on Fryday.

[El]izabeth Madison was Born February 19th 1768, half an hour after 12 [OClock &] was Baptized February 22nd, by the Revd. Mr. Thomas Martin & had [for] God-Fathers Majr. Zachariah Burnley & Capt. Ambrose Powell & [for Go]d-Mothers Miss Alice & Miss Milly Chew.

[M]rs Madison Deliver'd of a Still born Child July 1[2]th 1770.

[R]ueben Madison was Born Sepr. 19, 1771, btween 5 & 6 o'Clock in the eve[ning &] was Baptized November 10th, by the Revd. Mr John Barnett and had for [God]-Fathers Mr Thomas Barbour & Mr James Chew & for God-Mothers [M]iss Alice & Milly Chew.

Frances Taylor Madison was Born Octr. 4th 1774, & was Baptized Octr. 30th by the Revd. Mr John Wingate, & had for God-Fathers Mr Thomas Bell & Mr [R]ichard Taylor & for God-Mothers Miss Frances Taylor & Miss Elizabeth Taylor. [She] was born on Tuesday morning abt. a quarter after 3 OClock.

[C]atlett Madison Departed this Life on Saturday 18th of March 1758 at 3 o'Clock [in] the morning. Aged 36 days.

[El]izabeth Madison Departed this Life May 17th 1775, abt. half after 12 OClock [be]ing Wednesday. Aged 7 years & 3 Months lacking 2 Days.

[R]ueben Madison Departed this Life June 5th, 1775, at 11 OClock in the Morn[i]ng being Monday. Aged 3 Years 8 Months & 17 Days.

[A]mbrose Madison Departed this Life October 3d, 1793 between 2 & 3 OC[lock in] the morning, being Thursday. Thirty eight Years eight Months & f[ive Da]ys.

Francis Madison departed this Life April 5th 1800, abt 10 OClock being [Sa]turday. Aged 46 Years 3[4] Months & 17 Days.

[Ja]mes Madison departed this Life February 27th 1801, abt. 10 OClock [in the] morning being Fryday. Aged 77 Years and 11 Months.

[Nel]ly Madison departed this Life February 11th 1829 abt 8 OClock [in the] morning being Wednesday Aged 97 years and one month.

[Lucy] Hartwell Conway daughter of Thomas & Sally Macon departed this life Saturday May 13th 10-4 P.M. 1871 Aged [ ] years [2] months & 20 Days.

OBITUARY NOTICES

June 28 1860[5]

Died. . . . Conway C. Macon . . . suddenly at his residence on 7th street, near Grace, Thursday evening, in the 68th year of his age. Mr. Macon was born in the county of Orange, A.D. 1792, where he spent the larger portion of his life. Of late years he resided in Richmond, and filled with ability the important office of tobacco inspector at Seabrook's warehouse. He was a nephew of President Madison, and a perfect type of an Old Virginia gentleman. He served during the war of 1812, being stationed on the banks of the Potomac. . . .

Novr 1829

[Died,] At Key West, in Florida, on the 11th inst. Col. EDGAR MA-CON, Counsellor and Attorney at Law. — Col. Macon was a native of Virginia, and a near relative of the venerable Ex-President Madison. . . . He sunk to an early grave in the 27th year of his age.

July 1831

[Died,] On the 21st inst. at Mount Erin, SARAH ELIZABETH, eldest daughter of C. C. Macon, Esq. of Orange. . . . *Aged 15*

1853

Died, at his residence in Orange County, on the 1st day of May, REU-BEN MACON. . . . *Aged 45*

---

[4]Correctly given as nine months instead of three in the Princeton University Madison Bible records.

[5]In this and the following obituaries clipped from newspapers, all italicized words and numbers are handwritten; the rest is printed.

1856

Died on, the 3d inst., at the residence of his sister, Mrs. Lucy H. Conway, in the county of Orange, WILLIAM AMBROSE MACON, in the 59th year of his age. . . .

1838

Death — At his residence near Orange Court House, Virginia, on Wednesday, the 3d of January, REUBEN CONWAY. . . .

1838

Died, very suddenly, at his residence, in the county of Orange, on the morning of the 3d inst., REUBEN CONWAY, Esq., in the 50th year of his age. . . .

Reuben Conway was born the 12th of March 1788 and was married to Lucy Hartwell Macon Daughter to Thomas & Sally Macon July 25 1811.

My father Thomas Macon died Feby 26 1838 in the 73rd year of his age; an Obituary appear'd in the Richmond Enquirer of which I never got possession of.

L. H. Conway

1843

Died, in Orange county, at the residence of Mrs. Conway, her daughter, on Tuesday evening, the 17th ult., Mrs. SARAH CATLETT MACON, relict of the late Thomas Macon, and the last surviving sister of the late President Madison, in the 80th year of her age. The immediate cause of her death was a paralysis. . . .

A MARSHALL FAMILY RECORD.

(Contributed by the late Henry Strother)

"An interesting collection of heirlooms, and one probably unparalleled by others in the Valley, is that of Mrs. S. L. Wiley, of 1450 J Street, a gentle lady of that state where family pride is strong—Kentucky. Mrs. Wiley, nee Marshall, is of a family that has given the country soldiers and statesmen, with a place in history for more than 800 years.

One of the oldest relics of this collection is a Bible belonging to ———— Marshall. The old Bible is of a 1591 edition representing the characteristics of the 16th century books. What remains of the binding is leather, and considering the age and the strenuous experiences of the old volume one is lead to the conviction that the leather in its prime was as stanch and unimpressionable to hard usage as was the granite old 'Defender' the Marshall. When the Marshall family moved from Fredericksburg, Va., to Kentucky, this Bible was lost and remained so for years. However, long after, it was found and purchased by D. A. Jennings, and presented by him to Millie Field Marshall upon her wedding day in 1812. A hundred pounds accompanied the gift. In the great overflow of the Ohio and Mississippi rivers this book with all the household effects of Millie Field Marshall was swept away. Twenty years after it again came into her possession, having been sent by a family of creoles who found it in the Bayou Sara drift. Millie Field Marshall bequeathed the historic book to her daughter-in-law, Mrs. Wiley's mother, and in this way it found its way into this Fresno collection, that numbers a score and more of relics of great interest, but of a few only, space permits telling about."

Henry Strother.

Ft. Smith, Ark., April 16, 1911.

(Copy of letter from Mrs. Mary Marshall Wiley
to W. M. Paxton, of Platte City, Mo.)

"1450 J Street, Fresno, Calif., March 8th, 09.)

"My Dear Honored Cousin

I send you a copy of our records from Family bible as you requested—sorry not to be able to send more. Can you tell me any thing about Wm. Marshall of Mecklenburg Co. who married Elizabeth Williams? Why was he called Colonel? He was born 1672 and a brother of 'John of the Forest' who was born 1682. I find that one William Marshall served as a private in Revolution 1777-1778 in Col. Christian Febrigers Command, which I think was the William who married Ann McLeod because he was born in 1730. We have always been severed from our relatives save the Andersons and know so little of the Marshalls except the C. J's family. We are reading your poems aloud.

Sincerely your cousin,

(signed) Mary Marshall Wiley."

(Here follows the family Bible record which accompanied the above.)

"1. John Marshall, at the siege of Calais, demanded the restoration of his title as Earl of Pembroke, Jan. 17th, 1558.

2. William Marshall married ——— ———?

3. John Marshall, Capt. of Cavalry under Charles I, emigrated to Virginia 1650.

[These first three generations are evidently traditional. There is no record evidence for them.]

4. Thomas Marshall, born 1655, mar. Martha Jane Pendleton (died 1704), Westmoreland Co.

Issue 3 sons

5. William, b. 1672   Thomas b. 1678 & John born 1682
   Elizabeth Williams   *Elizabeth Markham*

5. William Marshall eldest son born 1672 married Elizabeth Williams b. 1680, issue 1 son.

6. William Marshall born Aug. 27, 1730 Caroline Co. married Ann McLeod born 1742, daughter Torquil McLeod and Aunt of George Rogers Clark. Issue 9 children.

1. Elizabeth Marshall b. July 14th 1769 m. Hugh Roy, issue John Roy.

2. Anne Clarke Marshall b. Feb. 10th, 1772, m. Wm. Samuels, issue Mrs. Judge James Pryor and Mrs. *Henry* Pryor (error *Samuel* Pryor, H. Strother).

3. Frances Marshall b. 1774 m. Robt. Thompkins, issue 3 sons and 4 daughters.

4. Mary Marshall b. Nov. 10th, 1776 m. Wm. Webb, issue Wm. & Horace Webb.
5. Robert Marshall born 1777 (died young).
6. Sarah Marshall b. Nov. 10th 1779 second wife R. C. Anderson.
7. Lucy Marshall b. 1780 (died unmarried).
8. George Rogers Marshall — 1782 m. Mary Hoskins (no issue).
9. John Marshall b. Sept. 27th 1784 m. Mildred Field in 1812, lived in Jefferson, Henry & Ballard Co's Ky.

Mildred Field Marshall was born 1738 daughter of Lewis Field & Hannah Lewis. The father of each killed at Point Pleasant Oct. 10th 1774: namely Col. *John Field* & Col. *Chas. Lewis.*

John Marshall and Milly Field Marshall had 4 children, when he was drowned in a storm in Ohio River 1830 near old Caledonia, Ills., opposite his home at Marshall's Landing, Ky. where he had moved in 1820 (near Fort Jefferson) in order to bury himself in the wilderness being *completely estranged* from the *Marshalls,* because of his following *Mr. Clay.* 4 children as follows:

1. William Marshall b. 1814 Richmond, Va., died in New Orleans Oct. 10, 1840 unmarried.
2. Anne Logan (Nancy) m. Henry Price.
3. Lewis Marshall (died in infancy).
4. Lewis Field Marshall b. Oct. 29, 1825 died Feb. 19, 1877 married Mary Helen Marshall Fore daughter of Joshua and Narcissa Fore. Issue, 10 children:

1. William P. Marshall born Nov. 11th, 1855, died Jan. 25, 1884.
2. Joseph Marshall, born 1857.
3. Mary Louise Marshall, Oct. 10, 1859, m. Stephen L. Wiley.
4. Lewis Field Marshall, Jr. b. Nov. 17, 1861, died April 5th, 1836.
5. Jennie E. Marshall, b. Aug. 9, 1864, married 1888 Robert B. Seate (issue Eloise M. Seate m. Vernon Story Aug. 25, 1908) m. 2nd Robert B. Seate 1890; m. 3rd Hoggatt Clopton of Long Beach, Calif.
6. Charles Anderson born April 25th 1866.
7. Albert Rust Marshall b. Feb. 10, 1868.
8. Edward C. Marshall b. May 16th 1870.
9. Infant daughter.
10. Josephine Ogden Marshall b. May 25th 1873 married 1st Wm. A. Jackson, issue: Lewis Marshall Jackson born Sept. 3, 1900; married 2nd, Edwin King Fernald, issue Edwin King Fernald Jr. b. Feb. 17th 1909."

(Copied from, and compared with the original letter and paper by me at my home in Ft. Smith, Ark.)

Henry Strother.

MASON-GRAHAM BIBLE RECORDS

MASON-GRAHAM.—Bible Records; from the Bible of Sally Barnes Hooe Mason, Wife of Johr. Stith of King George Co., Virginia, and grand-daughter of George Mason, of Gunston Hall, Fairfax Co., Virginia. Contributed by Dr. G. M. G. Stafford, Baton Rouge, La.

The contributor's maternal aunt, Caroline H. Graham (Mrs. J. B. Cralle) left a paper in her own handwriting containing the data given below. She added the following sentence at the end of the paper:—"Copied from Cousin Sally Stith's Bible at Roanoke." This "Cousin Sally Stith" was her first cousin, being a daughter of Sally Barnes Hooe Mason and John Stith, and the Bible in her possession was her mother's. Caroline H. Graham was a daughter of George Mason Graham, son of George Graham and Elizabeth Mary Ann Barnes Hooe (daughter of Gerard Hooe and Sarah Barnes of "Barnesfield," King George Co., Va.). George Graham's wife was the widow of George Mason of "Lexington," eldest son of George Mason of "Gunston Hall," and Sally Barnes Hooe Mason (Mrs. Stith) was one of her daughters by the first marriage. The items in Mrs. Cralle's paper are as follows:

"George Mason of 'Gunston Hall', Fairfax Co., Va., died 1792, aged 66.— George Mason of 'Gunston Hall',[1] Fairfax Co., Va., was married to Elizabeth Mary Ann Barnes Hooe April 22, 1784.

"Elizabeth Mary Ann Barnes Hooe[2] was born March 28, 1768.—Elizabeth Barnes Mason was born March 9, 1785.—George Mason was born August 11, 1786.— William Eilbeck Mason was born February 18, 1788.—Ann Eilbeck Mason was born April 1, 1791.—Sally Barnes Hooe Mason was born May 27, 1794.—Richard Barnes Mason[3] was born January 16, 1797.—George Mason of 'Lexington,' Fairfax County, Va., died 5th December, 1796, aged 44.—George Graham,[4] aged 33, was married to Elizabeth Mary Ann Barnes Mason, aged 35, widow of George Mason of 'Lexington,' July 16, 1803.—John Graham was born 31 March, 1806.— George Mason Graham[5] was born 21st August, 1807.—Mary Ann Jane Graham was born 13 February, 1811.—Died on 27 May, 1814, aged 46, Mrs. Elizabeth M. A. B. Graham."

---

[1]This should be "George Mason of Lexington." Later when his father died he became the owner of Gunston Hall but his title of "George Mason of Lexington" has always been used to distinguish him from his celebrated father.

[2]Daughter of Gerard Hooe and Sarah Barnes, of "Barnesfield," King George Co., Va. Her grandparents were Capt. John Hooe and Ann Alexander, and her great grandparents were Col. Rice Hooe (the builder of "Barnesfield" in 1715) and his third wife, Frances (Townshend) Dade.

[3]Richard Barnes Mason, brigadier general U. S. A., first military governor of California (1849), died in 1850 at Jefferson Barracks, St. Louis, Missouri. His widow married Major Don Carlos Buel, later brigadier general, U. S. A.

[4]George Graham, born at Dumfries, Prince William Co., Va., in 1770, son of Richard Graham and his wife, Jane Brent, daughter of George Brent of "Woodstock." He was Asst. Secty. of War under Madison and Monroe; First President of the Branch of the U. S. Bank at Washington, Special Envoy of Pres. Monroe to Galveston, Texas, in 1818, to treat with General Charles Lallemand and Jean Lafitte who had occupied Galveston, which trip he made all the way on horseback; Commissioner of the General Land Office until his death in 1830.

[5]George Mason Graham, son of George Graham and Elizabeth Mary Ann Barnes (Hooe) Mason, settled in Louisiana in 1828. Prosperous planter. Captain of volunteer company of infantry to Mexican War. First chairman of Board of Supervisors of the Louisiana State University. Adjutant General of Louisiana after the Civil War. Died at his home, "Tyrone Plantation," in Rapides parish, La., in 1891.

MASSIE BIBLE RECORD

Contributed by Miss Meddie M. Massie, Paducah, Ky.

William, son of Thomas and Mary Massie, born May 28th, 1718.

Martha, daughter of William and Mary Macon, born Aug. 12, 1722.

William Massie married Martha Macon, November 20th, 1740, and departed this life June 15th, 1751.

Martha, daughter of William and Mary[1] Macon, departed this life Aug. 8th, 1759, aged 37 years. She was first married to William Massie as above mentioned and afterwards to Col. Rich'd Bland of Prince George Co. on the 1st day of Jan. 1759.

William Massie, son of William and Martha[2] Massie, was born December the 25th, 1741.

Thomas Massie, son of William and Martha[3] Massie, was born Aug. 11th, 1747.

William Massie was married to Elizabeth Pinchback Nov. 26th, 1768.

William Macon Massie, son of William and Elizabeth Massie, was born December 25th, 1769, and departed this life the 6th day of November, 1771, aged 1 yr. & 10 months.

Martha Massie, daughter of Wm. and Elizabeth Massie, born 6th day of November 1771, being day on which (and about the time) her brother William Macon Massie died. She departed this life on the 11th day of September, 1772, aged 10 months.

Thomas Pinchback Massie, second son, born 9th of August, in the year (A. D.) 1773.

Mary Massie, second daughter, was born the 17th day of June 1776, now well and hearty as is her brother T. P. Massie.

Hugh Massie, 3d son born March 10th, 1778, now very healthy.

Wm. Macon Massie, 4th son and of the same name of my first child, born Jan. 12th, 1780 and departed this life in Staunton, in Augusta Co. July 2nd, 1780 (or 81, date partly destroyed).

Wm. Macon Massie, 5th son and of the name of my first and fourth son, born Nov. 28th, 1781, now a fair and likely child, 2 years and more than 5 months old. Great Creator ————————————— (entry damaged, but seems a prayer for sparing this child).

* * * * (William?) Massie, in March, 1783, when * * * * at the death * * * * for the satisfaction of his children, however * * * * he believes on the best information since that the entry is accurate.

Elizabeth Massie departed this life July 26th, 1782.

William Massie was married to Ann Cobbett the 6th day of August 1786.

William Massie departed this life the first of Feb. 1793, aged 52 years.

Mitchell Royster was born in the year 1791, the first day of December, and in the year 1811, the 25th day of April, moved to Kentucky[4] from Virginia.

(Mary Massie her hand and pen April 3rd, 1792.[5]

Hugh Massie, son of Wm. and Elizabeth Massie, was married to Mary Royster the 5th day of Sept. 1810.[6]

Ann Elizabeth Massie, daughter of Hugh and Mary Massie, first child, born August second, 1812.

William Mitchell Massie, first son, and second child of Hugh and Mary Massie, born the 15th day of January 1814.

Thomas Littleberry Massie, third child and second son of Hugh and Mary Massie Born the 12th day of October 1815.

Hugh Massie, fourth child and third son of Hugh and Mary Massie, born May 8th, 1819.[8]

John Woodson Massie, fourth son and fifth child, born September 18, 1820.

Mary Massie was born on the 7th of May (or March, entry damaged) 1822, when in second ———— ———— ———— departing in body ———— in the year of our Lord 1825, the 18th day of October.[9]

Martha Massie, third daughter, was born 20th of January 1824.

Mary Massie, consort of Hugh Massie, departed this life April 5th, 1838, aged 48 years, 7 months and 15 days.[10]

Hugh Massie departed this life the 12th day of August 1841, aged 63 years and 5 months.[11]

The old Bible containing this record was published in London, Eng., in 1724, and was owned by William Massie, Jr. Brought to Kentucky in 1811 by Hugh Massie, and now in possession of his great grand-daughter, Miss Meddie M. Massie, Paducah, Ky.

---

[1] Mary (*Hartwell*) Macon.

[2] and [3] Martha (*Macon*) Massie.

[4] A brother of Mary Royster, wife of Hugh Massie; this being about the time the Massie family left Virginia for Kentucky, as oldest child born in Shelby Co., Ky., Aug., 1812.

[5] This Mary was the sister of Hugh Massie, not his wife.

[6] Mary Royster was the daughter of Littleberry Royster and wife Anne Farris, dau. of Sherwood Farris and wife Elizabeth Gathright.

[7] The family now moved to Todd Co., near Trenton, and near Christian Co. line, also near Tenn. state line.

[8] This Hugh died in infancy.

[9] Died from effects of burns (fell in fire).

[10] Was buried near Trenton, Ky.

[11] Was buried near Trenton, Ky.

MAURY BIBLE RECORDS.

From the bible of James Maury 1746-1840, 1st American Consul to
Liverpool, England, son of Rev. James Maury, 1717–18–1769, defendent
in the celebrated "Parsons Cause", 1765. The bible is in the possession of
Mrs. John Morris 208 East 34st St., Savannah, Ga., a direct descendant,
the data is of peculiar interest to genealogists many of whom have wished
to know the names of the antecedents of the Rev. James Maury's wife
Mary Walker, 1724-1793.

Joseph Leidy

October 14, 1918.

Transcript from the bible of James Maury, 1746-1840, 1st American Consul to Liverpool, England.
James Walker, born March 7, 1692.
Ann Hill, born 1708 (month not named).

These were the parents of my honored mother, (Mary Walker).
James Maury,
Liverpool, 1 August, 1817.

James Maury, son of Matthew Maury and Mary Anne Fontaine, his wife, born April 8th, 1718, departed this life June 9, 1769.
Mary Walker, daughter of James Walker, and Anne (Hill) was born Nov. 22, 1724, departed this life March 20, 1798. They were married Nov. 11, 1743.

The above copied from the bible of my beloved parents. I think my father was born in 1717.
For the above named Matthew (Maury) and Mary Ann (Fontaine) who were the parents of my father see head of the 5th of the annals of our ancestor, James Fontaine.
The above named James Walker was a physician in King and Queen County, Va.; he married Ann Hill the daughter (I think his name was Leonard Hill), a merchant who lived at or near Bowler's on the Rappahannock River. This venerable lady when between 70 and 80 years of age, had the smallpox in the natural way, of which she recovered with the loss of her sight, died about 1787-88.
(Signed) James Maury,
Liverpool 1, August, 1817.

The sons and daughters of the Rev. James Maury 1717-1769 and his wife Mary Walker, of King William County afterwards of Albemarle, County.

1. Matthew Maury born Sept. 10, 1744, died May 6, 1808.
2. James Maury born Feb. 3, 1746, died March 23, 1840.
3. Leonard Hill Maury born _____, died in infancy.
4. Ann Maury born Nov. 16, 1748, died Jan. 8, 1816.
5. Mary Maury born Sept. 17, 1750, died April 5, 1822.
6. Walker Maury born July 21, 1752, died Oct. 11, 1788.
7. Catherine Maury, born July 15, 1754, died July 26, 1786.
8. Elizabeth Maury born Apr. 1, 1756, died April 1, 1833.
9. Abraham Maury born Apr. 28, 1758, died _____, 1834.
10. Fontaine Maury born Feb. 3, 1761, died Jan. 1, 1824.
11. Banjamin Maury born Jan. 16, 1763 died about Feb. 25, 1811.
12. Richard Maury born May 19, 1766, died April __, 1840.
13. Matilda Hill Maury, born Oct. 28, 1769, died about Nov. 7, 1821.

N. B. The first named 5 of us born in King William Co; My brother Walker born in Louisa Co.; the remaining 7 born in Albemarle Co.

FAMILY RECORDS AS CONTAINED IN BIBLE ORIGINALLY OWNED BY ANNA THOMPSON McDONALD, NOW IN POSSESSION OF E. L. McDONALD, LEXINGTON, KENTUCKY

(Contributed by Mr. McDonald through Judge Lyman Chalkley)

I.

Angus McDonald (immigrant) married Anna Thompson, June 20, 1766, and their children were:
Mary, born May 9, 1767.
John, born August 19, 1768.
Angus, born December 30, 1769.
Eleanor, born September 5, 1771.
Anna, born June 25, 1773.
Thompson, born March 29, 1776.
Charles, born April 8, 1778.

Angus McDonald (immigrant) died August 19, 1778, and his wife, Anna, died January 2, 1832, aged 86. (The following note is in the family Bible: "This Anna McDonald was Miss Thompson and the wife of Col. Angus McDonald and was married to him June 20, 1766, and raised Angus W. McDonald, who was her grandson, and gave this bible to him (signed) E. H. McDonald").

II.

The above Angus McDonald (son of Angus and Anna) married Mary McGuire, January 11, 1798, and died October 14, 1814. Their son, Angus W. McDonald, was born February 14, 1799. A daughter, Millicent, was born ——————— ——, ——, and a third child, Edward Charles, was born July 26, 1803.

III.

Angus W. McDonald married Leacy Ann Naylor, January 11, 1827, and they had the following children, viz:
1. Mary Naylor, born December 27, 1827.
2. Angus William, Jr., born May 16, 1829.
3. Ann Sanford, born October 30, 1830.
4. Edward Allen Hitchcock, born October 26, 1832.
5 William Naylor, born February 4, 1834.
6. Marshall, born October 18, 1835.
7. Craig Woodrow, born May 28, 1837.
8. Susan Leacy, born December 10, 1839.
9. Flora, born June 7, 1842.

Said Angus W. McDonald was married to his second wife, Cornelia Peake, May 27, 1847, and their children were:
1. Harry Peake, born April 14, 1848.
2. Allen Lane, born October 7, 1849.
3. Humphrey Peake, born December 31, 1850.
4. Kenneth, born July 18, 1852.
5. Ellen, born September 30, 1854.
6. Roy, born August 25, 1856.
7. Donald, born September 5, 1858.
8. Hunter, born June 12, 1860.
9. Elizabeth, born October 29, 1861.

Angus W. McDonald died December 1, 1864. The record of marriages of his children follows:

Mary N. McDonald and Thomas C. Green were married in Romney, Hampshire County, Virginia, April 27, 1851.

Ann Sanford McDonald and James W. Green were married at Wind Lea, Hampshire County, Virginia, December 20, 1855.

Angus W. McDonald, Jr., and Betty Morton Sherrard were married near Romney, Hampshire County, Virginia, February 17, 1857.

William N. McDonald and Katherine S. Gray were married Aug. 13, 1867, at Selma, Loudoun Co., Va.

Marshall McDonald and Mary E. McCormick married Dec. 18, 1867, at Frankford, Clarke Co., Va.

Flora McDonald and Leroy Eustace Williams were married at Cool Springs, Clarke County, Virginia, December 18, 1867.

E. H. McDonald and Julia Yates Leavell were married at Media, Jefferson County, Virginia, October 19, 1869.

Susan Leach McDonald and John B. Stanard were married at Lexington, Virginia, August 6, 1872.

Harry P. McDonald and Alice Keats Speed, were married at Louisville, Kentucky, April 14, 1875.

Allan L. McDonald and Fanny B. Snead were married at Louisville, Kentucky, February 13, 1878.

Kenneth McDonald and America R. Moore were married at Louisville, Kentucky, November 20, 1879.

Roy McDonald and Nelly Cain were married at Louisville, Kentucky, November 23, 1882.

Nelly McDonald and Henry Line married Louisville, Ky., Apr. 28, 1887.

Donald McDonald and Betsy Breckinridge Carr were married at Roancke, Virginia, October 26, 1887.

Hunter McDonald and Eloise Gordon were married at Columbia, Tennessee, February 10, 1893.

Angus W. McDonald and Mary E. Riddell (his second wife) were married at Charles Town, West Virginia, June 5, 1894.

IV.

Edward H. and Julia Y. McDonald had children as follows, viz:
1. Edward Leavell, born September 3, 1870.
2. Anne Yates, born March 4, 1872.
3. Julia Terrill, born October 17, 1873.
4 William Thomas, born August 6, 1875.
5. Angus W., May 2, 1877.
6. Peerce Naylor, born July 5, 1879.
7. Mary Aglionby, born April 4, 1881.
8. Marshall Woodrow, born August 24, 1884.
9. John Yates, born January 10, 1887.
10. Francis Leavell, born May 28, 1891.

Marriages of the above children are as follows, viz:

Julia Terrill McDonald and John W. Davis were married at Media, Jefferson County, West Virginia, June 20, 1899.

Edward Leavell McDonald and Florence Mabel Pinniger were married at Louisville, Kentucky, December 20, 1902.

Peerce Naylor McDonald and Frances Browse were married at Spring Run, West Virginia, June 8, 1910.

Mary A. McDonald and Robert T. Browse were married October 21, 1911, at Media, West Virginia.

Angus W. McDonald and Elizabeth Woodbridge Brown were married at Charleston, West Virginia, June 27, 1912.

John Yates McDonald and Dorothy Bosworth were married at Elgin, Illinois, August ——, 1922.

Marshall Woodrow McDonald and Ernestine Hutter were married at Lynchburg, Virginia, October ——, 1923.

V.

Children of the above were born as follows:

To John W. and Julia Davis—

Julia McDonald Davis, born July 23, 1900.

To Edward L. and Florence McDonald—

1. Edward L., Jr., born October 23, 1905.

2. Harriett Davis, born August 8, 1907.

3. Angus William, born May 29, 1912.

To Robert T. and Mary Browse—

Elizabeth McDonald, born May 17, 1914.

To John Yates and Dorothy McDonald—

1. John Bosworth, born July 29, 1923.

2. Angus.

To Marshall W. and Ernestine McDonald—

William N. and Kate Gray McDonald married August 13, 1867. Had children as follows:

1. William N. McDonald, Jr., married Emma Hicks, had one child, Katherine Gray McDonald, who died in 1928.

2. Ellen Douglas McDonald, married John B. Neill, had three sons:
   a. John Baldwin Neill, Jr., married Jean Harris, had two children:
      John Baldwin Neill, III.
      Jean Harris Neill.
   b. William McDonald Neill, married Hildegard Klamroch.
   c. Lewis Neill.

3. Craig Woodrow McDonald, born 1870, died 1901.

4. Flora McDonald, died in infancy.

5. Fannie McDonald, died in infancy.

6. Nannie Gray McDonald, 1877, married Ellery L. Eustaphieve in 1899, who is now deceased.

7. Hugh Marshall McDonald, married Elizabeth Loadwick, have one child:
   William Naylor McDonald, September, 1914.

8. Katherine Powell McDonald.

9. Leacy Naylor McDonald, married William E. Suddath in June, 1910. Had three sons:
   a. James Walker Suddath, II, November, 1911.
   b. William McDonald Suddath, died at 14 months.
   c. William Edwards Suddath, Jr., March 28, 1917.
10. Mary Green McDonald, married Bayard Stevens in October, 1910. Had three children:
   a. John Stevens, VII.
   b. Bayard McDonald Stevens.
   c. Nancy Gray Stevens.

MOSELEY BIBLE RECORD

Contributed by CARR HENRY

The Bible from which this record was taken was in 1938 in the possession of William Moseley of Decatur, Alabama, son of William Moseley and Martha Adelia Pryor (Kimball) Moseley. It was published by H. C. Carey and I. Lea, Chestnut Street, Philadelphia, 1825. The record was copied by Theo Davis Hill (Mrs. Walton Hill) of Tuscaloosa, Alabama, who is a great-granddaughter of John Patrick Moseley and Frances Ann (Kimball) Moseley. A few minor changes have been made in spelling and punctuation to facilitate printing. Matter shown in parentheses is not in the Bible but was furnished by William Moseley and Miss Druella Moseley, daughter of Drury Vaughan Moseley who married Mary Ann Minor.

(William Moseley,* youngest son of Edward Moseley and Amy [Green] Moseley, was born June 3, 1776, in Charlotte County, Virginia).

Isabella Camp Moseley° was born October 3, 1798 (she married Frederick Hood and moved to Arkansas).

Diana Amy Elizabeth Frances Moseley° was born September 11, 1800 (she married Edmund Patrick and Horace Green; all died in Alabama).

Nancy Moseley° was born January 30, 1803 (she married Robert Moore and moved to Texas).

Martha Cocke Moseley° was born November 12, 1805 (she married Nat. Pride).

William Moseley§ was born August 24, 1810 (in Bedford County, Tennessee).

Edward Moseley§ was born August 19, 1812 (in Bedford County, Tennessee; died young).

Hillery Moseley§ was born February 16, 1815 (in Bedford County, Tennessee).

John Patrick Moseley§ was born October 13, 1816 (in Madison County, Alabama; married Frances Ann Kimball and Marian Hutchins).

Drury Moseley§ was born July 18, 1820 (in Morgan County, Alabama; married Mary Ann Minor).

Eliz. Ann Moseley§ was born December 18, 1822 (married Henry High).

Sally Moseley§ was born August 30, 1825 (married Charles Lane).

Mrs. Temperance Moseley‡ was born August 9, 1783 (in Mecklenburg County, Virginia).

Martha Adelia Pryor Kimbell was born February 9, 1825.

William Moseley# was born September 17, 1856.

Martha Elizabeth Moseley# was born February 25, 1859.

Archie Halsey Moseley◈ was born June 11, 1880.

Wm. Moseley◈ was born October 5, 1881.

Hillery Moseley◈ was born March 8, 1883.

---

* William Moseley who married Ann Williams and Temperance Vaughan.

† Ann Williams, first wife of William Moseley. They were married in Halifax County, Virginia. She was the daughter of John Williams and Diana (Coleman) Williams.

‡ Temperance Vaughan, daughter of Drury Vaughan and second wife of William Moseley. According to the records of Halifax County, Virginia, Wm. Moseley and Tempey Vaughan were married *15 April 1809,* by Leonard Baker.

Martha Pryor Moseley◈ was born December 8, 1885.

Wm. Moseley◈ was born February 17, 1887.

Marriages

Wm. Moseley* and Ann Williams† married August 22, 1797.

Wm. Moseley* and Temperance Vaughan‡ married March 25, 1808.

Wm. Mosley§ & Martha Adelia Pryor Kimball married November 13, 1855.

Wm. Moseley⁕ & Sue Sneed Halsey married September 9, 1879.

Deaths

Ann Moseley† died September 11, 1807.

Wm. Moseley* died September 11, 1807.

Hillery Moseley§ died January 14, 1835.

Sally Moseley§ died March 11, 1851.

Martha Adelia Pryor Moseley died May 1, 1859.

Martha Eliz. Moseley⁕ died February 5, 1860.

Temperance Moseley‡ died June 11, 1864.

Drury Vaughan Moseley§ died September 24, 1868 (in Morgan County, Alabama).

John Patrick Moseley§ died September 16, 1874 (near Decatur, Alabama).

Eliz. Ann High§ died November 14, 1876, in Ellis County, Texas.

(William Moseley§ died February 27, 1899, Decatur, Alabama).

---

* Child of William Moseley and Ann (Williams) Moseley.

§ Child of William Moseley and Temperance (Vaughan) Moseley.

⁕ Child of William Moseley and Martha Adelia Pryor (Kimball) Moseley.

◈ Child of William Moseley and Sue Sneed (Halsey) Moseley.

PAGE FAMILY BIBLE.

Births

Charles Carter Page was born December 18, 1778.

Sarah Cary Nelson was born April 6, 1780.

Elizabeth Burwell Page was born January 3, 1800.

Caroline Nelson Page was born June 20, 1801.

Robert Carter Page was born April 16, 1803.

Lucy Mann Page was born December 18, 1804.
Mary Page was born May 14, 1809.
Norborne Thomas Page was born November 6, 1812.
William Armistead Page was born December 13, 1814.
Caroline Matilda Jones was born February 13, 1819.
Mary Carter Page was born April 29, 1846.

Deaths

Charles Carter Page died October 17, 1822, aetat 43 yrs. 9 mo. 29 da.
Thomas Atkinson died March 20, 1837, aetat 68 yrs.
Elizabeth Burwell Page died August 17, 1819, aetat 19 yrs. 7 mo. 14 da.
John Camm Pollard died August 3, 1835, aetat 42 yrs. 11 mo. 7 da.
Lucy Mann Page died July 25, 1815, aetat 10 yrs. 7 mo. 7 da.
Mary Page died September 13, 1814, aetat 4 yrs. 3 mo. 29 da.
William A. Page died February 26, 1855.
Sallie Cary Atkinson died January 31, 1861, aetat 80 yrs. 9 mo. 24 da.

Marriages

Charles Carter Page and Sarah Cary Nelson were married February 8, 1799.
Thomas Atkinson and Mrs. Sarah Cary Page were married August 20, 1827.
Doct. Beverly R. Welford and Elizabeth Burwell Page were married October 16, 1817.
John Camm Pollard and Caroline Nelson Page were married June 20, 1823.
Robert Carter Page and Martha Ann Temple were married September 22, 1829.
Norborne Thomas Page and Mary Louisa Jones were married November 6, 1833.
Wm. Armistead Page and Caroline Matilda Jones were married March 24, 1841.

Chiswell Bible Records

John Chiswell married ye 19 May 1736.
Elizabeth Chiswell born ye 24 May 1737.
Mary Chiswell born ye 22 February 1739.

[The other records in the old Chiswell Bible are missing.]

COPY OF ENTRIES IN ELIZAH PARTLOW BIBLE, NOW IN POSSESSION OF MRS. JOHN F. ELLISON, RED BLUFF, CAL.

William White was born March 15, 1751.
Catherine, his wife, was born June 9, 1762.

Richard B. White was born July 17, 1784.

Lewis G. White was born Dec. 22, 1785.

William White, Jr. was born Jan. 24, 1787.

Lipscomb White was born Sept. 5, 1788.

Ann Thomas White was born Jan. 17, 1790.

Milicent White was born Oct. 7, 1791.

Elizabeth White was born March 10, 1793.

Alice L. White was born May 16, 1794.

Chilton O. White was born Jan. 18, 1796.

Warner W. White was born Aug. 3, 1798.

Reuben White was born Nov. 17, 1799.

Silas White was born Jan. 2, 1801.

Edmond White was born Jan. 20, 1802.

James Thomas White was born Dec. 27, 1803.

Eliza White was born Oct. 10th, 1805.

Elijah Partlow, son of John and Sarah Partlow his wife, was born in the year of our Lord 28th of Oct. 1775.

Ann T. Partlow, the daughter of Wm. White & Catherine his wife, was born Jan. 17th, 1790.

Elijah J. Partlow was born 7th of Aug. 1813.

Wm. E. J. Partlow was born Feb. 10, 1815.

Catherine Sarah Ann Partlow was born Dec. 30, 1816.

Richard B. Partlow was born 15th of April 1819.

Martha Ann & Mary E. Partlow were born Sept. 23, 1822.

James M. Partlow was born April 11, 1824.

Eliza M. Partlow was born Jan. 4, 1826.

Maria E. Partlow was born Feb. 11th, 1806.

James B. Partlow was born Aug. 23rd, 1808, departed this life Dec. 23rd, 1832.

Maria E. Cason started out for Missouri Monday 5th of Sept. 1831.

William M. Phillips was born Jan. 4th 1814.

Geo. P. Phillips was born Feb. 2nd 1817.

James M. Lewis was born & baptized by the Rev. H. C. Booggs Sept. & June 1814.

Columbia Ann Elizabeth Phillips was born July 31, 1835.

Maria Ann Phillips, Catherine & Ann Phillips went to the West on Thursday 1st of Oct. 1835.

William L. White born Aug. 16, 1819.

Elijah J. Partlow started to Tennessee on Monday 14th 1840.

Eliza I. White was married to Andrew McDowell 21st of Dec. 1831.

Ann T. Anderson was married to Thomas U. Lipscomb on Thursday 15th of Sept 1831.

Elizabeth Smith was married to Samuel Luck on Thursday 25th of Oct. 1830.

Tindale Carpenter was married to Miss Southlin 1831.

Catherine S. Ann Partlow was married to W. M. Phelps on Thurs. Dec. 6th 1831.

Elijah M. Partlow married to Elliner Farrar on Thurs 22nd 1830.

Mary E. Partlow married to William L. White on Thursday 12th Sept 1839.

Benj. C. Cason was married to M. A. Brown on 7th of Dec. 1852.

George B. Cason was born March 2, 1793.

Benj. C. Cason was born 2nd Sept. 1821.

M. A. Brown was born 7th Feb. 1834.

George I. Cason was born 9th Sept. 1853.

James B. Cason was born 21st of Dec. 1854.

Minnie B. Cason was born 4th of May 1859.

Daisy Cason was born 7th Dec. 1860.

Kate Cason was born 7th Aug. 1863.

Daisy Cason died Dec. 21st 1863.

Mary Adaline Robinson born Howard Co. Mo. Feb. 7th 1834. Died at Red Bluff, Cal., March 29, 1912. Maiden name Mary Adaline Brown.

Eliza M. Partlow departed this life Aug. 29 1826.

John B. L. Partlow departed this life Dec. 23 1832.

Ann T. Partlow departed this life on Sat. 20 of Aug. 1840.

Catherine S. Ann Phillips departed this life 2nd of Nov. 1840.

Richard B. L. Partlow was murdered & burned by his fathers 2 negro women Nance & Isabell on Thursday the 20th of Nov. 1840.

Elijah Partlow departed this life on Friday morning seven minutes after two o'clock the 9th day of July in the year of our Lord, 1841 at his son in laws George Cason in the county of Howard Missouri.

William White departed this life 1812.

My father desired for Douglas to preach from the text "Mark the perfect man & behold the upright: For the end of that man is peace."

I, George Cason bought this book at the sale of Elijah Partlow, deceased and gave it to my son Benj. C. Cason in the year of our Lord 1841.

John B. Cason departed this life the 18th day of Feb. 1858.

Benj. C. Cason died Wed. at 3 A. M. at Jacksonville. Ill on the 17th of May 1865.

Minnie B. Cason married John F. Ellison at Lake View, Or. Tues. Aug. 31 1880.

———————

PHILLIPS & ANDERSON FAMILY BIBLE RECORD

Marriages.

Richard Phillips and Katherine Smith were married August 8th, 1727.
William Phillips and Frances Gregory were married March 10th, 1756.
Francis Anderson and Lucy Phillips were married July 12th, 1802.
Josephus W. Anderson and Sarah C. Campbell were married April 27th, 1858.
Richard G. Anderson and Susan Ann Elizabeth Yates were married Oct. 27th, 1836.
C. W. Chamblin and Mary F. Anderson were married 4th Jany., 1865.
R. W. Anderson, State of Colorado, was married to Miss Lenora Knight of Colorado on the 21st Octr., 1876.

Births.

William Phillips was born August 3rd, 1728.
Anna Phillips was born Feby. 5th, 1729.
Richard Phillips was born April 14th, 1732.
Elizabeth Phillips was born June 20th, 1737.
Susanna Phillips was born March 25th, 1742.
Thomas Phillips was born Sept. 10th, 1744.
Francis Anderson was born on the first day of February, 1780.
Richard Gregory Anderson, son of Francis Anderson and Lucy his wife was born on Tuesday night, June 17th, 1806.
Josephus Washington Anderson, son of Francis Anderson and Lucy his wife was born on Sunday night, July 31st, 1809.
Eliza Delaware Anderson, daughter of Francis Anderson and Lucy his wife was born on Sunday the 14th day of June, 1812.
Richard Phillips was born January 12th, 1757.
Elizabeth Phillips was born Feby. 17th, 1758.
Anna W. Phillips was born Sept. 7th, 1761.

Agnes West Phillips was born May 5th, 1765.

William Ballard Phillips was born April 29th, 1768.

Catharine Smith Phillips was born Sept. 15th, 1770.

Susanna Phillips was born April 9th, 1773.

Lucy Phillips was born J 'y 29th, 1776.

Ann Elizabeth Anderson, daughter of Richd. G. and S. A. E. Anderson, was born Nov. 12th, 1837.

Mary Frances Anderson, daughter of Richd. G. and Susan A. E. Anderson, was born Feb. 27th, 1845.

Boswell P. Anderson, son of Richd. G. and Susan A. E. Anderson, was born August 13th, 1847.

Richard T. W. Anderson, son of Richd. G. and Susan A. E. Anderson, was born Sept. 9th, 1853.

Clara G. Anderson, youngest daughter of R. G. & Susan A. E. Anderson, was born 19th November, 1860.

Rich. Wm. Chamblin, son of C. W. & M. F. Chamblin, was born 27th October, 1865.

Sarah C. Campbell, daughter of Edward and Sarah C. Campbell, was born November 28th, 1837.

John Wesley Anderson, son of Josephus W. and Sarah C. Anderson, was born Saturday morning, March 26th, 1859.

Ida Wills Anderson, daughter of Josephus W. and Sarah C. Anderson, was born Wednesday morning, 18th July, 1860.

Ada Littleton Anderson, daughter of Josephus W. and Sarah C. Anderson, was born Thursday morning, October 24th, 1861.

Francis Edward Anderson, son of Josephus W. and Sarah C. Anderson, was born Friday morning, 30th September, 1864.

Charles Carter Anderson, son of Josephus W. and Sarah C. Anderson, was born Friday morning, Sept. 20th, 1867.

The above named persons are children of Josephus W. Anderson and Sarah C., his wife.

Deaths.

Eliza Delaware Anderson departed this life on Thursday night, 12 o'clock, Nov. 12th, 1812.

Josephus W. Anderson departed this life at Gordonsville, Va., on the 30 day of Augt., 1871, 25 minutes after 9 o'clock A. M.

Richard G. Anderson departed this life in North Garden 20th of July, 6 o'clock in the morning, 1887.

John Wesley Anderson departed this life Friday morning, April 15th, 1859.

Ida Wills Anderson departed this life Friday evening 27th July, 1860.

719

Mary Frances Chamblin, daughter of Richd. G. and Susan Anderson his
wife departed this life in Fairfax co., Va., on the 12th day of Augt.,
1884. Aged 39 years, 5 mos. and 16 days.
She lived and died a follower of Jesus Christ.
Clara Gaines Anderson, infant daughter of R. G. and Susan Anderson,
departed this life May 26th, 1862, aged 18 mos., 19 days.
Lucy Anderson, widow of Francis Anderson, departed this life Thursday
evening, Feby. 26th, 1863.

QUARLES—Notes Found in a Copy of "The Book of Common Prayer"

QUARLES.—Notes found in a copy of "The Book of Common Prayer" belonging
to Owen Terry, grandson of Waller Quarles, of King William County, Virginia:
"Bettie, daughter of Solomon and Dorothy Quarles, born Oct. 9, 1760—Solomon
Quarles died Jan. 24th, 1774—Dorothy Quarles born July 1st, 1776—[in different
handwriting] Judith Quarles, daughter of Waller Quarles & his wife Keziah Ellett, born May 31, 1807—Susan A. Quarles, daughter of Waller Quarles & Keziah

Ellett, his wife, born Dec. 27, 1809—Susanna E. Quarles, daughter of Waller Quarles and Keziah Ellett, his wife, born 1812, married Alexander Bond." When these records were copied the Prayer Book then belonged to Waller Quarles Terry, brother of Owen Terry, King William C. H.

The Quarles family descent is as follows: Solomon Quarles, of King William Co., born ....; died Jan. 24, 1774, married *circa* 1750, Dorothy Waller, born *circa* 1725-30; died 1792, issue: (1) Bettie Quarles, born Oct. 9, 1760; died ....; married *circa* 1778, Thomas Mallory (issue: (a) Solomon Waller Mallory, in Prince William, 1812). Thomas Mallory married *second*, Mary Ellett—(2) Mary Quarles, born *circa* 1762; died ....; married *first*, John Terry (issue: (a) Solomon Quarles Terry; (b) Ann Edwards Terry); she married *second*, John Reins (issue: (a) Richard Reins)—(3) Sarah Quarles, born *circa* 1764; died 1823; married *circa* 1782, John Houchens, born *circa* 1760; died 1813 (issue: (a) Ann Catherine Houchens, born King William Co., 1794; died Richmond, Va., 1894; married 1822, Bernard Lambeth Powers, born King William Co., 1790; died there, 1840)—(4) Waller Quarles, born 1773; died ....; married *circa* 1800-10, Keziah Ellett (issue: (a) Judith Quarles; (b) Susan A. Quarles; (c) Susanna E. Quarles, married Alexander Bond.

As the King William County records are so very fragmentary, we offer the following items as proof of the foregoing: (1) The will of John Waller, of Spotsylvania Co., dated August 2, 1753; probated October 1, 1754, devises to granddaughter, Dorothy Quarles, daughter of my son, Thomas Waller, a slave named George, born of Angela, Feb. 22, 1751 (Spotsylvania County records, Will Book B, 1749-59, page 216). (2) Dorothy Quarles, in King William Co. Personal Property Tax List, 1783, is charged with a slave George. (3) Dorothy Quarles, her 200 acres of land, and slaves (with which she had been for some years chargeable) disappeared from the King William Tax Lists in 1792. Then in 1807 the 200 acres of land (formerly Dorothy Quarles') was sold and release deed signed by Thomas Mallory and Mary (his second wife), Waller Quarles and Keziah, his wife; John Reins and Mary, his wife, and John Houchens and Sarah, his wife (King William Co. records, Book 5, page 130). The King William Co. Land Tax List, 1793, shows that Dorothy Quarles' 200 acres of land (as charged in former lists; she having died in 1792) was added to lands of her son in law, Thomas Mallory, and in 1807 (when the above referred to sale was made) the same 200 acres was deducted from Thomas Mallory's lands. This 200 acre tract was sold to Lavinia Allen who held it until 1810 when it passed to Reuben Lipscomb and is described (under his name) as 200 acres, four miles west of King William Court House, adjoining Aquinton Church—(4) The "Dorothy Quarles, born July 1st, 1776" (as recorded in the Prayer Book) we are wholly unable to identify. We particularly call attention to this fact hoping that some reader of this note may be able to offer a suggestion as to her identity. (5) A deed in 1810, by Thomas Mallory to John Houchens and Waller Quarles, conveyed slaves Joe, *George,* Oliver and Amey (King William County records, Book 5, page 459). The slave George was doubtless the same George bequeathed by John Waller, of Spotsylvania County in 1753, to his granddaughter, Dorothy Quarles, daughter of his son, Thomas Waller. There is no reference to Mrs. Mary (Quarles) Terry-Reins, the other heir; but the King William records are very fragmentary and items do not appear consecutively —(6) In Dec. 1793, Mrs. Mary Terry [who was Mary Quarles, married *first* John Terry] being about to marry John Reins, deeded household effects to her children

Solomon Quarles Terry and Ann Edwards Terry (Ibid, Book 3, page 43)—(7) On Feb. 12, 1812, Solomon Waller Mallory witnessed a deed of Warner Wormeley's (Ibid, Book 6, page 154), and in 1812, Solomon W. Mallory, of Prince William County, gave power of attorney to settle the estate of Thomas Mallory, of King William Co. (Ibid. Book 7, page 440). The above items are contributed by Ann Waller Reddy, Richmond, Virginia.

QUARLES AND DOBBS BIBLE RECORD

I send you the two Bible records in my possession and our direct Quarles line, of which I have proof, except Aaron Quarles, of King William Co. He, his sons, Maj. James, who had a son, Col. James Isaac the elder, born 1745 and others, inherited a part (each) of the "Woodberry", which was said to be the home of Capt. John Quarles. Was he the emigrant? Even the publications of the data sent may induce other descendants to send their data and thus form a chain and possibly the missing links. Let us hope so. I have the Quarles coat of arms and motto, also some records from England, a daguerreotype each of my mother and her eldest sister, Lucy Brockenbrough Quarles, in the most beautiful colors and they were lovely girls. I have handsome photos of my father, in the Knight Templar and Shrine uniforms, but you do not publish pictures in the Virginia Magazine of History and Biography I believe. I have my Fauntleroy as well as Daingerfield-Smith, Tayloe, part each of the West and Henry families, but my cousin, Miss Juliet Fauntleroy, Altavista, Va., will publish a book on the Fauntleroy line. If you would like a copy of my direct line of Fauntleroy, Daingerfield, Smith, Meriwether, Bathurst, etc., I will be glad to send to you. It might help in the Quarles solution. I am not making public the Fauntleroy until Miss Juliet publishes her book. I am especially anxious to get the Brockenbrough, Braxton, Jno. White, from King William Co., who m. Judith Braxton, dau. Carter by 1st wife Judith Robinson, dau. Christopher, Jr., Spotswood (Alex., the gov.), etc., in order to get ancestors for signers Cincinnati (John White), Knights of the Golden Horseshoe and others. The will of Capt. Wm. Henry Quarles was prob. in Essex Co., Va., Oct. 15, 1810. The will of his son, Francis West Quarles in Essex Co. (W. B. 18, p. 172), July 17, 1815. Lucy Daingerfield (Smith) Quarles, his wife (will prob.) Feb. 21, 1820, W. B. 19, p. 88.

Capt. Wm. Henry Quarles mentions his two plantations, "Paradise" in King William and "Retreat" in Essex; four children, to-wit: Francis West Quarles, Susannah Littlepage Dabney, wife of Geo. Dabney; Ann Howell Tebbs, wife of Foushee G. Tebbs; Eleanor Williamson Parkhill, wife of Jno. Parkhill; three grandsons, to-wit: Henry Quarles, George Dabney and Henry Tebbs. He appointed his son-in-law, Geo. Dabney, Esq., his son-in-law, Foushee G. Tebbs and his brother, Isaac, and his f'd, Francis Smith, executors of his will. *William and Mary Quarterly,* 2nd series, Vol. 6, No. 1, Jan., 1926, pp. 72 and 73 give proof of the fact that Capt. Wm. Henry Quarles was son of Maj. James Quarles.* Our library (public) is very small and has no genealogy. I shall be eternally grateful for help on the Quarles line and also others should you see fit to publish it. Thanking you most heartily, I am

Miss Nellie West Dobbs

QUARLES

"A memorandum of the children's names and ages. Signed: Francis West Quarles.

1-2. Henry West Quarles and Ann E. Quarles, son and daughter of Frances West Quarles and Lucy D. Quarles, were born the 20th day of November, 1795.

3. Lucy D. Quarles, daughter of Francis West Quarles and Lucy D. Quarles, his wife, was born the 5th day of January, 1798.

4. Francis Edwin Quarles, son of Francis West Quarles and Lucy Daingerfield Quarles, his wife, was born the 25th day of December, 1799.

5. Susannah Fauntleroy Quarles, daughter of Francis West Quarles and Lucy D. Quarles, his wife, was born the 13th day of June, 1804.

6. Sarah Jane Smith Quarles, daughter of Francis West Quarles and Lucy D. Quarles, his wife, was born the —— day of July, 1810.

7. Martha Catherine Quarles, daughter of Francis West Quarles and Lucy D. Quarles, his wife, was born the 27th day of August, 1812.

8. George Bathurst Parkhill Quarles was born the 6th day of December, 1814. No. 8 is in a different hand-writing. This record is in the possession of the great grandchildren of Francis West Quarles and his wife, Lucy Daingerfield Quarles, Nellie West Dobbs and Joseph Henry Dobbs, Va. and High Point, N. C.

Marriages

1. Henry West Quarles m. 1833 Jane McDaniel, Amherst Co.
2. Ann E. Quarles never married.

*See *Genealogies of Virginia Families: From the William and Mary College Quarterly Historical Magazine* (Baltimore: Genealogical Publishing Co., Inc., 1982), Vol. IV, pp. 224-225.

6. Sarah Jane Smith Quarles m. George Washington Marston.

5. Susannah Fauntleroy Quarles m. 1st, ———— Muscarelli; m. 2nd, Jacob Cannon Nicholson, of Baltimore, Md., and had issue.

4. Francis Edwin Quarles m. 1828 Belinda Ann Thornton, great granddaughter of Dr. Wm. Cabell, Esq. ("Cabells and Their Kin", by Alexander Brown.) Issue.

8. George Bathurst Parkhill Quarles married in Rome, Ga., and left issue. Rev. Charles Page officiated at marriage. Family record from Bible of Henry West Quarles, now in possession of his grandchildren, Nellie West Dobbs and Joseph Henry Dobbs, Va. and High Point, N. C.

Henry West Quarles was born in King William Co., Va., 1795; moved to Amherst Co., Va., in April, 1830, to practice law. He married March 12, 1833, Jane McDaniel (1816-1871) and built "White Hall" and "West Dale" on land belonging to the "Sweet Briar" estate, which was then owned by her father, Wm. McDaniel (1774-1857) and his wife, Elizabeth Pendleton (1787-1838), married, 1801. Elizabeth Pendleton was the daughter, only child to live, of Ensign, Lieutenant, Capt. and Major Brevet James Pendleton (1750-1832) and his wife, Sarah Rucker (1750-1825), married 1869. The children of Henry West Quarles and Jane McDaniel, his wife, were:

1. Sarah Elizabeth Quarles (Feb. 9, 1834-Aug. 9, 1840).
2. Lucy Brockenbrough Quarles (Dec. 10, 1835-Feb. 3, 1858).
3. Anne Daingerfield Quarles (Oct. 21, 1837-Oct. 21, 1916).
4. Mary Henry Quarles (Sept. 3, 1839-Dec. 20, 1891).
5. Virginia West Quarles (Sept. 5, 1841-May, 1913).
6. Susan Fauntleroy Quarles (April 24, 1844-Feb. 22, 1861).
7. J. Quarles, a son, born in Baltimore, Md., 1846, Jan., died there 10 hrs. old.

Henry Francis Quarles (April 6, 1847-Dec., 1908).
9. George William Quarles (March 31, 1849-July, 1906).
10. Ella Jane Quarles (Sept. 6, 1852-July 8, 1890).
11. A daughter, born June 10, 1854, died 2 hrs. old.

Marriages

2. Lucy Brockenbrough Quarles married Dec. 20, 1854, Richard G. Davenport; Rev. Jno. B. Hardwick officiating. Issue: two daughters, died before death of the mother.

3. Anne Daingerfield Quarles married Henry James Dobbs and had issue: Nellie West Dobbs and Joseph Henry Dobbs.

Quarles Bible Record—continued

1. Mrs. Sarah Jane Marston, sister of H. W. Quarles, died at "West Dale" Oct., 1844, age 34 years.

2. Mary C. Quarles, sister of H. W. Quarles, died at "White Hall" June, 1835.

3. Susan F. Nicholson, formerly Susan F. Quarles, died near Baltimore on the —— day of ————, 1858.

4. Francis E. Quarles, son of Francis West and Lucy D. Quarles, died in New Kent Co., Va., June 20, 1863.

5. George Bathurst Parkhill Quarles died in Rome, Ga., 1865.

---

1. Record of my grandfather, Henry West Quarles, and his children, brothers and sisters will be found in *William and Mary Quarterly*, January, 1930, pp. 25-42.

DOBBS

Kedar Dobbs (Jan. 10, 1749-1816), Norfolk Co., Va., m. 1780, Miss Willoughby ( ).

Willoughby Dobbs, Norfolk Co., Va. (April 16, 1782-1835), m. Oct. 12, 1805, Rachel Edmonds (1784-1840).

Joseph Edward Dobbs (1806-1850) m. March 12, 1840, Mrs. Leitha Scott (widow) (1808-1852).

Lt. Henry James Dobbs, C. S. A. (1841-1915), Norfolk, Va., m. Anne Daingerfield Quarles (1837-1916), Amherst.

Issue: Nellie West Dobbs and Joseph Henry Dobbs.

We are descended from Sir Richard Dobbs, Lord Mayor London, England, 1551, through grandson, John, who established "Castle Dobbs", Carrickfergus, Ireland.

Rev. Richard Dobbs, born 1690 in Ireland, brother Arthur Dobbs, gover. North Carolina, 1753-1765, in whose will he is mentioned, was rector of a church in Middlesex Co., Va., is our direct ancestor.

References: Wheeler's North Carolina History, Norfolk Co., Va., Deed Book, 47, pp. 92 and 104, Norfolk Co., Va., Marriage Bonds, Appraisement Book, 4, Norfolk Co., Va., Family Records, Middlesex Co., Va., Records, Saffell's Revolutionary Records.

RANDOLPH BIBLE RECORD

The following copies from entries in an old Bible were communicated in 1904 by Mrs. W. E. Reeves, of Newton, Iowa. The names of the parents of the children born 1700 &c, are not given; but the name Osborne would indicate that they were of the family of the name in Stafford and Prince William. The name Isham was probably given as a compliment to to Isham Randolph of "Dungeness", for the persons named in this Bible record were certainly not descended from William of "Turkey Island." By deed in Prince William County, Oct. 20, 1750, John Randolph, of Prince Wm., and his wife Ann, one of the daughters & co-heirs of Thomas Osborne of Prince William, conveyed a tract of land to Cuthbert Harrison, who had married Osborne's widow. The will of John Randolph was dated Sept. 11, 1789, and proved in Prince William, Nov. 5, 1790, legatees, wife Anne, daughter Sarah, daughter Peggy, daughter Betsy, daughter Mary Ann, sons John and Thomas Osborn Randolph, son Wm., daughter Mildred Oliver, daughter Mary Tyler, daughter Frances. The will of Wm. Randolph dated August 2, 1792, was proved in Prince Wm. Sept. 2, 1972, legatees: wife Elinor, and children Robert, William, George and Mildred.

Apphia Randolph, born Mar. 16, 1700.

Josiah Randolph, born Apr. 11, 1703.

John Randolph, born Feb. 9, 1705.

James Randolph, born Feb. 29, 1707.

Jeconias Randolph, born Mar. 1, 1710.

Alice Randolph, born Jan. 15, 1712.

William Randolph, born Sept. 22, 1716.

Mary Randolph, born July 19, 1718.

The third child, of the above family, was deaf and dumb and he was named for an uncle. The following is a list of the children of Josiah Randolph and Jane, his wife.

Tabitha Randolph, born Apr. 13, 1749.

Richard Randolph, born Aug. 21, 1752.

Edmund Randolph, born Jan. 4, 1756.

Isham Randolph, born Mar. 23, 1758.

Apphia Randolph, born Apr. 28, 1761.

Frances Randolph, born June 8, 1764.

Josiah Randolph, born Oct. 1, 1766.

Osborn Randolph, born May 1, 1769.

These are authentic records, taken from family Bibles.

RANDOLPH—CORBIN.

Exact copy of entries made in Bible belonging to Mrs. Maria Beverley Randolph, Corbin.

Richard Randolph of Curles, Jr. Henrico Co. married Maria Beverley "Blandfield" Essex Co., Dec. 1st, 1785.

1. Richard Randolph their son born at "Turkey Island" Sep. 2, 1786 & d. July 13, 1787.
2. Richard Randolph (No 2) born at "Blandfield" Oct. 7th 1788.
3. Robert Beverley Randolph born at "Turkey Island" Nov. 10th 1790.
4. William Byrd Randolph b. at Monte Blanco March 29, 1792.
5. Maria Beverley Randolph born at Blandfield April 4th, 1794.
6. Midgley Randolph born at "Curles" April 29, 1796.
7. Peter Beverley Randolph born in Williamsburg Jan. 22, 1798.
8. Gawin Lane Corbin Randolph, born in Williamsburg Sep. 17, 1799.

Richard, Randolph of "Curles" died in Williamsburg, March 18, 1799 aged 41 years.

Gawin Lane Corbin of "Kings Creek" married Mrs Maria Randolph April 12, 1800.

1. Their son Richard Randolph Corbin was born at "Kings Creek" April 11, 1801.
2. Lucy Beverley Corbin born at "Kings Creek" Sep. 1st, 1804.
3. John Tayloe Corbin born at "Kings Creek" Aug 21, 1806, d. March 1st, 1809.
4. Ann Byrd Corbin born at "Kings Creek" Nov. 26, 1808.

"AN ACCOUNT OF THE TIME OF THE BIRTHS OF THE CHILDREN OF WILLIAM AND ELIZ'A RANDOLPH.

Beverley born the twenty seventh of December 1710 & dyed on the first day of January 1713

William was born the fourteenth day of February 1711. & dyed at sea on his voyage to England 15th day of Sep'r 1722

Beverley was born the twelfth day of November 1713

Elizabeth was born the 24th day of October 1715

Mary was born the twenty second day of July 1719

Peter was born the twentieth day of October 1717

William was born the 22d day of November 1723

Elizabeth Randolph mother of the aforenamed seven children & a dear wife to the unfortunate William Randolph dyed the 26th of December 1723 at twelve a Clocke in the night, and was buryed the 3d of January following. She was born the first day of January 1691."

This account, which may well be of value, has been copied off from the fly leaf of the first volume, small folio, "Works of the Most Reverend Dr. John Tillotson, late Lord Archbishop of Canterbury" &c &c. London. 1712. This excellent edition of Tillotson was presented to the library of Hampden Sidney College, (where the books now are), by the Rev. Dr. Benjamin Mosby Smith (1811-1893), of Powhatan County, for many years Professor in the Theological Seminary at Hampden Sidney.

It had been thought that Dr. Smith secured these books in Germany, where he was a student in his youth. But a closer examination led to the finding of the Record given above which was certainly the work of no German; and besides, written beneath Dr. Smith's bookplate, appear the words "Presented by my aunt Nicholas." And within the same volume are pencilled the names "R. C. Nicholas" and "John Nicholas." Everything proves the descent of this rather extraordinary Tillotson.

The writing of the record, on the fine paper of 1712 and good ink of the period used, is about as clear now as then. In pencil after the account ending in 1723 are the hardly decipherable words: "William Randolph, father of the above seven children and Husband of Elizabeth Randolph died about the 19th——1742 in the sixty-first year of his age."

A. J. Morrison.

ENTRIES IN READ BIBLE

The Revd Thomas Read was born on Gwyns Island in Virginia, 18th March 1748 [he died 1826], and was married to Sarah Magruder Daughter of Zadok and Rachel Magruder 14th October 1779—Sarah his wife was born 23d June 1755; and had Issue as in record of Births—

The Revd Thomas Read, is the son of Gwyn and Dorothy Read, who was the daughter of the Revd Mr. Clack & Jane his wife, born 24 August 1714, they had Issue—

1. Robert Read born 4 April 1734.
2. Lucy Read born 26 Decr. 1735.
3. James Read born 20 Mar. 1737.
4. Gwyn Read born 5 Apl. 1740.
5. Dorothy Read born 11 Nov. 1742.
6. Jane Read born 25 Nov. 1744.
7. Jòhn Read born 12 Mar. 1746.
8. Thomas Read born 18 Mar. 1748.
9. Mary Read born 27 May 1751.
10. Mildred Read born 30 May 1753.
11. William Read born 20 July 1755.
12. Francis Read born 6 Augt. 1756.
13. William Read born 25 Oct. 1758.

The Revd Thomas Read's children—

1. John Magruder Read born July 12th 1780.
2. Ann Read born June 8th 1783.
3. Elizabeth Read born Jany. 12th 1787.
4. Robert Read born Apl. 22nd 1789.
5. Susanna Read born July 4th 1791.
6. Thomas Read born May 7th 1794.
7. James Read born June 4th 1796.

Deaths of the above—
Ann Read died 14 June 1783.

Gwyn Read, Father of the Revd Thomas Read died June 1762—Dorothy his wife May 1797.

Col. Zadok Magruder died 12 April 1811 aged 81. Rachel his wife died 8th Jany 1807—The Father and mother of Sarah Read wife of the Rev. Thomas Read.

Marriages—

John Magruder Read to Mary Ann Clark the 9 November 1802.

Susanna Read to Alexr. Suter April 20, 1815.

Robert Read to Jane Lynn Lackland Oct. 21st 1817.

[Gwyn Reade, who died June 1762, was son of Benjamin Reade and grandson of Col. George Reade. See William and Mary Quarterly, XV, 117–123.] *

———

*See *Genealogies of Virginia Families: From the William and Mary College Quarterly Historical Magazine* (Baltimore: Genealogical Publishing Co., Inc., 1982), Vol. IV, pp. 260-266.

READ-PENN BIBLE RECORDS
Contributed by Mrs. John E. Lane

Records from family Bible printed and published by M. Carey, No. 121 Chestnut Street, Philadelphia, 1814. Owned by Dr. John T. W. Read, of Bedford county, who was named for his three brothers, John, Thomas and Wyatt, who fell fighting under George Washington at

Valley Forge. His home, a large brick house, "Liberty Hall", lies one mile west of New London on the Salem Turnpike. On the fly-leaf of this Bible his signature appears thus,

"John T. W. Read's Book
December 6th, 1815."

This Bible is now owned by his great granddaughter, Miss Daisy I. Read, Evington, Va., Route No. 2.

MARRIAGES

John T. W. Read and Elizabeth Alexander married the 25th of December, 1808.

Ann Isabella Read and Fred'k G. Peters were married on the 6th of Sept., 1827, by the Rev'd Nicholas H. Cobbs.

Nathan Reid, Jr., and Eliza A. Read were married on Wednesday, the 3rd of March, 1830, by the Rev'd N. H. Cobbs.

William A. Read and Mary Jane Hall were married the 11th of Sept., 1834, by the Rev'd W. T. Rice.

Robert A. Read and Frances Ann Pendleton were married on the 5th of Nov., 1834, by the Rev'd Mr. Bowman.

John T. W. Read and Eliza Douthat were married by the Rev'd William S. Read on the 4th of Feb'y, 1835.

Samuel Read and Theresa Samantha Arnold were married by Rev. Cleland Nelson on Wednesday May 3rd, 1843.

John T. W. Read and Rebecca Pryor were married on 15th Jan'y, 1846, by the Rev'd Isaac Cocherin.

John T. W. Read, son of Wm. and Johanna was born the 24th June 1777.

Elizabeth Read, daughter of Robert Alexander and Nancey, was born the 16th Feb'y 1787.

Ann I. A. Read was born (Sunday) Sept. 24, 1809.
Elizabeth A. Read was born (Monday) March 1, 1811.
Robert A. Read was born (Friday) 11th Sept., 1812.

Wm. A. Read was born (Monday) 12th Sept., 1814.

Samuel Read was born (Sunday) 15th Feb., 1817.

John Alexander Read, son of Wm. A. & Mary Jane Read, was born 19th of July, 1835.

William Read, son of Jones Read, was born 27th July, 1777.

Nancy Read, daughter of Jones Read, was born 8th March, 1779.

A list of the names and births of over thirty negroes is next recorded.

DEATHS

Edmund Read departed this life on 27th Feb'y 1826 in the 46th year of age.

Elizabeth Read, wife of Samuel Read, departed this life 27th March, 1829.

Sam'l Read departed this life on Jan. 28, 1831.

William C. Read, son of Sam'l Read, departed this life on the 21st Sept. 1833, at 11 o'clock A. M.

Elizabeth Read, wife of John T. W. Read, died 10th Jan'y, 1833.

Eliza Read, wife of John T. W. Read, departed this life on Thursday the 30th of May, 1844, at 8 P. M.

Dr. John T. W. Read, son of William and Johanna Read, departed this life on the 27th day of August 1852 at about ½ past 9 o'clock P. M.

Records from family Bible printed and published by M. Carey & Son, No. 126, Chestnut Street, Philadelphia, 1819: owned by Robert Cowan Penn, of Bedford county, his home, St. Helena, being located about seven miles south of Liberty (Bedford), Va.

This Bible is now owned by his granddaughter, Mrs. Thomas G. Read, Evington, Va., Route No. 2.

MARRIAGES

Robert C. Penn and Lucinda Steptoe intermarried on the fifteenth day of June 1814.

Julia Penn and Nelson Crawford intermarried on the ———— in the State of Alabama.

Virginia Penn and Dr. Charles Snow intermarried on the ———— day of ———— in the year ———— of ———— in the State of Alabama.

Alfred Penn and Evelyn C. Bradfute intermarried on the 11th of Sept. 1833 in the town of Lynchburg, Va.

Matilda Penn and Isaac Patrick intermarried on the 17th day of May in the year 1815.

Elizabeth Penn and William B. Harris intermarried on the ———— day of ———— in the year 1815.

Margaret Penn and ———— Shortridge intermarried on the ———— day of ———— in the State of Alabama, in the year 1822.

CHILDREN OF R. C. AND LUCY PENN

Frances L. Penn and David Rodes intermarried on the 12th day of May 1846, at St. Helena, in Bedford county, Va.

Bettie Penn and Hezekiah Jordan intermarried on the 7th of Nov. 1850.

BIRTHS

Robert C. Penn born the 19th day of Feb., seventeen hundred and eight nine—1789. At "The Grove" east of New London).

Lucinda Steptoe, born on the 25th day of March seventeen hundred and ninety five—1795. (At "Federal Hall" near New London).

Ada Augusta, the first child of Elizabeth J. and Hezekiah T. Jordan born at "St. Helena" in the county of Bedford, Va., on the eleventh day of Sept. in the year of our Lord eighteen hundred and fifty one—1851.

Imogene, the second child of Elizabeth J. and Hezekiah T. Jordan, born at St. Helena in the county of Bedford, Va., on the 8th day of December in the year of our Lord eighteen hundred and fifty three (1853).

John Y. Jordan July 11th, 1857, died Sept. 26, 1890—aged 33 years.

James Steptoe Penn, the first child of Robert and Lucy Penn, was born on the 20th day of March eighteen hundred and seventeen (1817).

Frances Louise Penn was born the 21st day of January eighteen hundred and eighteen (1818).

LaFayette Penn was born on the 6th day of Aug. eighteen hundred and twenty (1820).

Elizabeth Johnson Penn was born the 9th day of Oct. eighteen hundred and twenty three (1823).

Margaret Penn born on the third day of April, one thousand eight hundred and twenty eight (1828).

DEATHS

Died at St. Helena in the county of Bedford the 9th of November at the residence of his parents, James S. Penn in the 39th year of his age in the year 1854.

Died at St. Helena, Bedford County, Va., Robert C. Penn, on the 2nd day of July 1856, in the 67 year of his age.

Died at her residence in Bedford County on the 10th day of July 1878 in the 84th year of her age, Mrs. Lucinda Penn, widow of Robert C. Penn.

> "Though lost to sight
> To memory dear."

Bettie Johnston Jordan, consort of Thomas Hezekiah Jordan, died in Lynchburg, Va., March 17, 1912 in the 90th year of her age.

James Penn, Senior, died in New Orleans in the month of Feb. 1823, aged 58 years.

James Penn, Junior, killed on the Missouri river by the Ricogee Indians in the spring of 1823, in the 25th year of his age.

William Penn died of yellow fever at St. Stevens in the State of Alabama in the month ———— in 1822 in the 22nd year of his age.

Isaac Patrick died at Tuskaloosa in the State of Alabama in the year 1823.

———

Died at his residence (Federal Hill) near New London in the county of Campbell on the 9th day of Feb. 1826, James Steptoe, Sr., in the 75th year of his age.

Died at our residence (St. Helena) in Bedford County, on the 19th of Aug. 1828, Margaret Penn, third daughter of Robert and Lucy Penn —aged four months and nineteen days.

> "A sweet and lovely child."

Died at his mother's near Tuskaloosa in the State of Alabama, on the 18th of January 1830 Gab'l Penn, in the thirty fifth year of his age.

Died near Winchester in the State of Tenn. in the month of Sept. 1832 Betsy Harris in the ———— year of her age.

Alfred Penn died 1875.

Died at the Glebe in the County of Amherst on the 22nd of January 1826, Mrs. Sarah Penn in the 80th year of her age.

Died—near Tuskaloosa in the State of Alabama on the 15th of December 1832 Margaret Penn in the 62 year of her age. She was the mother of Robert, Gab'l, James, etc., etc.

Died in the town of Tuskaloosa, Ala., Matilda Patrick, daughter of the late James Penn, Esq., and relict of the late Isaac Patrick in the year 1834.

Departed this life, 1840, in Fincastle on the 29th of April after an illness of twelve days LaFayette Penn, son of Robert and Lucy Penn, aged nineteen years.

We have every reason to believe that he died with the full assurance of a blessed immortality, and although our loss is *great indeed*, we humbly hope it is in his everlasting gain. "Let me die the death of the righteous, and let *my last end be like his.*"

READE OF GLOUCESTER

George Reade of Gloucester, who came to Virginia in Harvey's second administration, married Elizabeth, daughter of Nicholas Martian, and died in 1671, a member of the Council under Berkeley, must always be of interest in the Virginia tradition because he was one of the ancestors of George Washington and Robert E. Lee. The meagre vestiges of his family which survive the destruction of the Gloucester records are collected in *Va. Mag.*, iv, 204; vi, 408; *W. & M. Quar.*,

In the family of Tompkins of King William there is a Bible which throws a pale ray of new light on some of these Reades. It contains genealogical entries transcribed by Elizabeth Mildred Gwyn Tompkins (1788-1856), wife of William Temple Fleet, of "Fleet Street" from a similar, but older, record, since destroyed by fire, in the possession of her nephew, Richard Tompkins of "Enfield." Mrs. Fleet was a

*See *Genealogies of Virginia Families: From The Virginia Magazine of History and Biography* (Baltimore: Genealogical Publishing Co., Inc., 1981), Vol. V, pp. 256 & 492.

granddaughter of Christopher Tompkins (1705-1778) and of Joyce (1701-1771), daughter of the Thomas Reade of Gloucester who was son of George, and himself married (Hening, viii, 483) Lucy, daughter of Edmund Gwyn of Gwyn's Island. By tradition the Thomas Reade last mentioned left eleven children. The two sons, Thomas and John are authenticated. Of the daughters, the five following have been taken as proven by the genealogists, viz: Lucy (1701-1731), m. John Dixon of Bristol (M. I. in *W. & M. Quar.*, iii, 29). Joyce (1701/2-1771), m. Christopher Tompkins of Caroline (*Va. Mag.*, xix, 196). Mildred, m. Philip Rootes of "Rosewall" in King & Queen, *Va. Mag.*, iv, 204).* Mary, m. Mordecai Throckmorton (*W. & M. Quar.*, iii, 50; xiv, 117).** Anne, m. Matthew Pate of Gloucester (*W. & M. Quar.*, xiv, 117). **

With this list may now be compared the Tompkins record of the daughters of Thomas Reade, viz:

> Joyce Reade married Tompkins
> Lucy Reade married Rootes
> Dorothy Reade married Throgmorton
> Sarah Reade married Cary
> Mary Reade married Duval [intended for Dixon?]
> Mildred and Catherine.

The confusion in this list as compared with the proofs of the other families into which the daughters married shows that the Tompkins Bible entry was made in a generation later than that recorded, but its value as testimony lies in its substantial accuracy and the addition of the three daughters (Sarah, Dorothy and Catherine), who bring the total number of children up to the traditional eleven.

To the Cary family this record of a wide spread connection has a special significance as it may be a clew to the *provenance* of Sarah (1710?-1783), wife of Wilson Cary (1702-1772) of Ceelys. The long and patient, but fruitless, search by the late Wilson Miles Cary of Baltimore for the family name of this Sarah is rehearsed in *Va. Mag.*,*** ix, 107, and *The Virginia Carys*, p. 105.

What gives colour to this clew is that the marriage of one of the Reades (who on the present hypothesis would have been a sister of Wilson Cary's wife) to Matthew Pate might explain the possession of Pate books and Gloucester lands by the son of Wilson Cary.

F. H.

---

*Ibid., p. 256.
**Genealogies of Virginia Families: From the William and Mary College Quarterly Historical Magazine* (Baltimore: Genealogical Publishing Co., Inc., 1982), Vol. V, p. 88 and Vol. IV, p. 260.
***Genealogies of Virginia Families: From The Virginia Magazine of History and Biography* (Baltimore: Genealogical Publishing Co., Inc., 1981), Vol. I, p. 692.

FROM ROBERTS FAMILY BIBLE.

Richard T. Roberts and Elizabeth W. Walton was joined together in Holy Wedlock the 16th day of December 1829

James M. Butler and Sarah E. Roberts daughter of the above January 19th, 1860

James H. Roberts and Lennie M. Campbell were married Sept. 18th, 1866

Stephen S. Flannagan and Susan M. Roberts were married Jan. 5th 1871

Richard T. Roberts and Louisa E. Donahoe were married Jan. 4th 1872

William C. Roberts and Marcia A. Roberts were married Dec. 24, 1874

Moses H. White & Mattie R. Roberts were married April 30th 1884

W. J. Roberts & Patty Wale were married Oct. 26th 1898

Chas. D. Roberts and Carrie Lee Stewart were married June 17th 1903

Chas. D. Roberts was married the 2nd time to Lucy M. Stewart June 27 1909

Richard T. Roberts was born on the 4th day of January 1808

Elizabeth W. Roberts was born May the 25th 1809

William Claiborne Eldest son of Richd. T. and Elizabeth W. Roberts was born on the 10th of September 1830

James Henry second son of the above R. T. & E. W. Roberts was born on the 3rd of April 1833

Victoria Virginia eldest daughter of R. T. & E. W. Roberts was born on the 12th of March 1836

Richard Thomas Third son of R. T. and E. W. Roberts was born on the 18th day of June 1837

Sarah Elizabeth Roberts daughter of R. T. and E. W. Roberts was born the 19th of March 1840

Adelina Minor Roberts Third daughter of Richard T. & Elizabeth W. Roberts was born the 7th Decr. 1842

Martha Rhoda Roberts fourth daughter of Richard T. & Elizabeth W. Roberts was born the 16th day of November 1843

Susan Mildred Roberts was born October 21st 1847

Melville Erasmus Roberts fourth son of R. T. & E. W. Roberts was born on the 9th day of August 1850

George E. Butler was born March 22nd 1861

Willie J. Butler was born June 12th 1862

Mollie W. Butler was born Nov. 12th 1865

Lena H. Flannagan was born Dec. 25th 1871

Virgilia C. Flannagan was born Oct. 8th 1874
Katherine Stewart Roberts was born May 15th 1904
Grace P. Roberts was born Feb. 23d 1877
Lewis E. Roberts son of R. T. Roberts was born Feb. 14th 1887
Parker A. Roberts was born Dec. 27, 1889
William J. Roberts was born Oct. 3rd 1872
Ann E. Roberts was born March 2d 1874
Lennie C. Roberts was born Aug. 3 1875
Belle M. Roberts was born Jan. 31 1877
Charles D. Roberts was born March 30 1879
Sadie Roberts was born July 20th 1881
T. R. W. Roberts was born July 20th 1884
Victoria Virginia Roberts died on the evening of the day on which
she was born 12th of March 1836
Adelina Minor Roberts died on the morning of 19th day December
1842
Melville E. Roberts died January 11th 1865
James M. Butler died August 30th 1866
James H. Roberts died November 1st 1867
Elizabeth W. Roberts wife of R. T. Roberts died Dec. 31st 1882
Richard T. Roberts died Feb. 10th 1866
Sadie Roberts died July 31st 1883
Parker A. Roberts died July 17th 1890
Belle M. Roberts died Jan. 20th 1897
Sallie E. Butler wife of James M. Butler died Nov. 3rd 1897
William C. Roberts died March 8th 1898
Stephen S. Flannagan died Apr. 10th 1904
Carrie Stewart Roberts died Dec. 18th 1906
Ann Elizabeth Roberts died July 22nd 1908

WILLIAM ROBERTSON

Resident Williamsburg, Virginia, 1700-1739
Sometime Clerk to the Council of Virginia

The following are copies of entries in an old bible in my possession; the bible was published at Cambridge in 1673:

"John Lidderdale born at Melrose in Scotland July 9th, 1713 at Caske Milk on Tuesday 19th August 1777 at 7 a m.

"Elizabeth Robertson born at Williamsburg in Virginia Jany 25th 1721/2 and died at Carlisle on Tuesday 4th March 1777 at 7 a m.

"They were married at Williamsburg on Friday 23rd Feby 1738/9.

"Robert Lidderdale born at Wmsburg Wednesday 25th Feby 1740/1 at 2 a m and died 8th Sept. 1741 Tuesday at 6 p m.

"John Lidderdale born at Wmsburg Friday 9th July 1742 at 11 P M and died 5th Octobr following Tuesday at 10 a m.

"William Robertson Lidderdale born at Wmsburg Monday 3rd June 1745 at 2 a m and died at Gretna in Scotland on the 8th of July 1814.

"John Lidderdale born at Bristol Thursday 29th March 1750 at 4 a m and died Munday 7th May at 7 a m thereafter.

John Lidderdale born at Clifton Sunday 24th Oct 1756 at 10 a m and died at Camberwell in Surrey Wednesday 28th Oct. 1761 at 7 P. M.

"Thomas Lidderdale born at Clifton Thursday 10th May 1759 at 10 p m and died on Thursday 23rd August thereafter at 6 p m.

"Thomas Lidderwell born at Camberwell in Surrey Munday 22nd Decem 1760 at 1 a m and died at Cunbergras Key near the Bay of Honduras 29th December 1799 at 1 P. M."

I have in my possession some seals which belonged to William Robertson Lidderdale No. 3 above, which show the Lidderdale arms quartering those of Robertson of Struan viz. 1st and 4th Azure, a chevron ermine, for Lidderdale of St. Mary's Isle and 2nd and 4th Gales three wolves' heads erazed against armed and langued azure and one of the seals has also a wild man chained lying under the escutcheon which also appertains to Robertson of Struan.

In Vol. IV, History of the Lands and their Owners in Galloway by P. H. M'Kerlie, page 182, it states.

"John (Lidderdale) succeeded his father David in the representation and became the owner of Castle Milk Dumfries-shire. He married in 1738 Elizabeth (who died in 1777) daughter of ——— Robertson of Struan, Perthshire . . . "

W. R. LIDDERDALE FORREST.

SHORE.

Contributed by Margaret Haw Morton, Charlotte C. H., Va.

The following records were copied from leaves cut from the family Bible of John Shore during the war between the States.

Henry Smith, son of John and Elizabeth Shore, was born on Sunday night, 20 minutes past 10 o'clock, the twenty fourth day of January in the year of our Lord one thousand seven hundred and sixty eight, in the Parish of St. Paul's, county of Hanover; married by the Rev. John D. Blair on Saturday evening the 24th day of January 1795 to Martha Bickerton, daughter of Geddes and Mary Winston, who was born the 17th day of February in the year of our Lord one thousand seven hundred and seventy four in the county of Hanover and had issue:

1st. John, son to Henry and Martha Shore was born on Monday the nineteenth day of October in the year of our Lord one thousand seven hundred and ninety-five, at half past eight o'clock in the morning, in the city of Richmond.

2d. Juliet Landon, daughter of Henry and Martha Shore was born on Thursday the sixteenth day of February in the year of our Lord one thousand seven hundred and ninety seven at half-past three o'clock in the morning in the city of Richmond.

3d. Henry Belchier, son of Henry and Martha Shore was born in the city of Richmond on Monday the sixteenth day of January in the year of our Lord one thousand seven hundred and ninety nine at a quarter before 2 o'clock in the afternoon, died the 22d day of July 1800, aged 1 year, 6 months and 6 days.

4th. Martha Smith, daughter of Henry Smith and Martha Shore, was born in the city of Richmond on Thursday the twenty second day of October in the year of our Lord one thousand eight hundred and one, at a quarter before four o'clock in the evening. Died the 16th day of September 1802, aged 10 mos. 25 days.

5th. William, son to Henry and Martha Shore was born in the city of Richmond on Thursday the 25th day of May in the year of our Lord one thousand eight hundred and three, at half past seven o'clock in the morning. Died the 6th day of August 1804. Aged one year, two months and twenty five days.

Henry Smith Shore, married a second time, to wit, on Thursday the 2d day of August 1804, by the Rev. John D. Blair, to Catherine Robinson, daughter of William Overton Winston, of Hanover Co., who was born in Hanover County the 23d day of February 1777. Issue:

1st. Maria Isabella, daughter to Henry Smith and Catherine Robinson Shore was born in the city of Richmond on Monday the 14th day of Octo. 1805, at 20 minutes past three o'clock in the afternoon.

2d. Harriet Winston, daughter of Henry Smith and Catherine Robinson Shore was born in th ecity of Richmond on Saturday the 24th day of June 1809 at a quarter of an hour before one o'clock in the morning.

3d. Catherine Smith, daughter of Henry Smith and Catherine Robinson Shore was born in the city of Richmond on Thursday the 18th day of Feby. 1813 at twelve o'clock at night.

4th. Jane Louisa, daughter to Henry Smith and Catherine Robinson Shore, was born in the city of Richmond on Sunday the 8th day of Feby. 1818 at half past 5 o'clock in the morning.

———

John Moncure, third son of John G. and Harriet Winston Hull, was born on the 13th day of December 1835.

Mrs. Martha Bickerton Shore departed this life in the city of Richmond on Thursday the 19th day of May 1803 at forty minutes past 11 o'clock in the forenoon, aged twenty nine years, three months, and 2 days.

Jane Louisa, daughter to Henry Smith and Catherine Robinson Shore, died in the city of Richmond on 10th day of Octo. 1825 at noon, aged seven years, eight month sand 2 days.

Henry Smith Shore departed this life on Wednesday the 7th of November 1832 at a quarter past 12 o'clock in morning, aged sixty-four years, 9 mos. 13 days.

Harriet Winston, daughter of Henry Smith and Catherine R. Shore (having intermarried with John G. Hull 1st Apl. 1820) departed this life in the city of Richmond on Wednesday Mch. 9, 1836 at 9 o'clock p. m. in the 27th year of her age.

Thomas Gaskins, first son of John G. and Harriet W. Hull died in the city of Richmond January 9, 1832. 7 mos. 22 days.

Henry Shore, second son of John G. and H. W. Hull died at sunset in County of Stafford 26th Mch. 1837, 3 yrs. 7 m. 23d.

John G. Hull departed this life city of Baltimore Apl. 9, 1841, aged 35 years, 5 mos. 26 ds.

Catherine Robinson Shore, wife of Henry S. Shore, departed this life on Thursday morning, Dec. 21st, 1854 in 78th year of her age.

John Shore, son of Henry S. and Martha B. Shore died Sat. Dec. 4th, 1858, 63d year of his age.

Juliet L. Drew, daughter of Henry S. and Martha B. Shore departed this life Feb. 21, 1862. In 66th yr. of her age.

Catherine S. Sheppard, wife of Capt. John M. Sheppard, and daughter of Henry S. Shore died in Richmond Oct. 3d, 1876 at fifteen minutes before 9 o'clock P. M. in the 64th year of her age.

Maria Isabella Lewis, wife of Warner Lewis and daughter of Henry Smith Shore (and Catherine Robinson Winston Shore) died at Lewis Level 5th day of January 1885 at 20 minutes past 4 o'clock P. M. in the 80th year of her age.

SPRAGINS–BOLLING

Thomas Spragins was born in Henrico Co. near the Chickahominy in 1720 and married Maacah Abney of Henrico Co. They moved to Halifax Co. about 1740 and settled on Staunton River near the mouth of the Catawba Creek where Thomas died in 1792.

Their two oldest children were Melchizedek, who married Sarah Lanier of Granville Co., N. C., and Melchijah who married Rebecca B. Bolling.

The two oldest children of Col. Robert Bolling and his wife Anne Stith were Robert who married Anne Cocke, and Stith who married Mrs. Elizabeth Hartwell.

The seventh child of Robert and Anne (Cocke) Bolling was Susannah. The second child of Stith and Elizabeth (Hartwell) Bolling was Alexander. This Susannah Bolling married Alexander Bolling her first cousin. Their third child was Stith Bolling who in 1776 married Charlotte Edmunds and the only daughter of this marriage was Rebecca B. Bolling who married Melchijah Spragins. The two children of this marriage were Stith Bolling Spragins who married Eliza Apperson Green a daughter of Col. Grief Green, and Melchijah Spragins who married Anne B. Carter.

A Bolling Bible Record.

There has been in my wife's family for many years an old Bolling Bible, but only recently has it come into my hands for inspection and investigation.

The volume is 16x11x2¾ inches, bound in "marbled" leather.

On the frontis-page it has "London: Printed by Thomas Baskett, Printer to the King's Most Excellent Majesty and by the assigns of Robert Baskett. M.DCC.LIX. Price One Pound Five Shillings Unbound."

It bears on the front page, written in a beautiful hand: "Samuel Davies to Mrs. Susannah Bolling as a small token of gratitude for her kindness."

The Rev. Samuel Davies was the second Presbyterian minister to preach in Virginia, and afterward became president of Princeton College. Samuel Davies went to Hanover County in 1747.

It was in the old Pole Green Church, December 3, 1755, that the Presbytery of Hanover met for the first time, and Samuel Davies was one of the six ministers present.

This old Bible is particularly interesting for the Bolling family data which it contains, and which I give in full:

Alexander Bolling, born March 12, 1721; old style.

Susanna Bolling, born June 16, 1720; old style.

Alexander and Susanna Bolling were married December 23, 1745.

Elizabeth Bolling, daughter of Alexander and Susanna Bolling, born June 24, 1747.

Robert Bolling, son of Alexander and Susan Bolling, born March 24, 1751; O. S.

Stith Bolling, son of Alexander and Susanna Bolling, born May 11, 1753; N. S.

Ann Bolling, daughter of Alexander and Susanna Bolling, born March 31, 1755.

John Bolling, born October 13, 1756; died November 9, 1759.

Alexander Bolling, Jr., born December 2, 1761.

Susanna Bolling, born December 5, 1764.

Sally Bolling, born March 25, 1766.

Alexander Bolling, Sr., died June 11, 1767.

Elizabeth Bolling, married to Peter Jones, April 6, 1769.

Peter Jones died January 10, 1771.

Elizabeth Jones, daughter of Alexander and Susanna Bolling, married to Christopher Manlove, November 24, 1771.

Jane Manlove, daughter of Christopher and Elizabeth Manlove, born October 8, 1772.

Robert Bolling married to Franky Green, May 10, 1772.

John Bolling, son of Robert and Franky Bolling, born March 10, 1773.

Frances, wife of Robert Bolling, died March 15, 1773.

Sally Bolling, died June 17, 1773.

John Bolling, son of Robert and Franky Bolling, died 1st of May, 1817.

Rebecca Bolling Manlove, born 24th of April, 1774, died July 5, 1817.

Thomas Bolling Manlove, born November 4, 1776.

Elizabeth Manlove, died 2d November, 1776.

Stith Bolling, married to Charlotte Edmunds, October 10, 1776.

Rebecca B. Bolling, daughter of Stith and Charlotte, born February 14, 1778.

Robert Bolling married to Clara Bland, widow, December 18, 1779.

Eliza Yates Bolling, daughter of Robert and Clara Bolling, born————.

Alexander Bolling, son of Stith and Charlotte Bolling, born————.

Several of the above dates are incomplete because the page has been torn.

Rebecca B. Bolling, daughter of Stith and Charlotte Bolling, married Melchijah Spragins. After the early death of her husband, Rebecca Bolling Spragins, with her two sons, Stith Bolling and Melchijah, moved to near Huntsville, Ala.

The undersigned would be very glad to be informed of the date of the marriage of Rebecca Bolling and Melchijah Spragins or any further history of the Spragins family.

Rev. J. Ogle Warfield,
Chestnut Hill,
Philadelphia, Pa.

DIARY OF COL. FRANCIS TAYLOR

In recent correspondence with Mr. Trist Wood, 7338 Irma St., New Orleans, regarding the Diary of Col. Francis Taylor so often referred to, I gathered the following data:

1. James Taylor, of New Kent Co., the Immigrant: had
/2. Col. James Taylor, m. Martha Thompson: had
   a. Frances Taylor, m. Ambrose Madison (gr-parents President M).
   b. Martha Taylor, m. Thos. Chew.
   c. James Taylor, whose 1st w. was Alice Catlett, neé Thornton. (gr-parents Gen. Jas. Taylor, War of 1812).
   d. Zachary Taylor, m. Elizabeth Lee (gr-parents Pres't. Taylor).
   e. COL. GEORGE TAYLOR: 10 sons officers in Rev., among them COL. FRANCIS TAYLOR the DIARIST.
   f. Tabitha Taylor, m. Thos. Wild.
   g. Erasmus Taylor, m. Jane Moore.
   h. Hannah Taylor, m. Nicholas Battaile.
   i. Mildred Taylor, m. Richard Thomas.

The Diary of Col. Francis Taylor, 1786-1799, in 13 vols., one vol. per year (Originally 14, one missing) was found by Dr. A. G. Grinnan in the attic of "Rosebud", Orange County, Va., the home of Robert Taylor and given him by Mary, Robert's wife, (she neé Taylor); sold by Dr. Grinnan to Wm. Kyle Anderson, U. S. Consul at Hanover, Germany(grandson of Commodore Richard Taylor) who at his death left it to his sister with request that ultimately it go to Virginia Historical Society.

Col. Frank Taylor, Diarist, was son of Col. George Taylor, *and never married.* He lived at "Midland" left him by his father's will, dated 5th Sept., 1789. He was Colonel in the "Liberty or Death" Culpeper Minute Men, and their marching to Williamsburg was commissioned Captain 2d Va. Regt. (May 8, 1776) Major 15th Va., 1778. Lieut. Col. Convention Guards, Dec. 24, 1778. Colonel March 5, 1779. I (Mr. Wood) have a very complete account of him.

Col. Francis Taylor's uncle, James T. of "Bloombury" Orange Co., m. Mrs. Catlett, neé Thornton, and had Major Francis Taylor b. 27 March 1751, served in Rev., later of "Locust Grove", Franklin (now Granville) Co., N. C. Major Francis Taylor left a diary but I (Wood) have never been able to find it.

Col. Francis Taylor the Diarist is sometimes confused with his cousin, Major Francis Taylor, b. 1751. Both served in the Rev'n. The Diary so often quoted is certainly that of Col. Francis T., of "Midland", b. 1747, d. 1799, Son of Colonel George.

Col. Francis Taylor, nephew of Maj. Jonathan Taylor (Sent to receive the surrender or transfer of garrisons of La. when the territory was taken over by the U. S.) also left a Diary, in possession of his descendants. Major Jonathan was son of Col. Jonathan of the Rev'n.

Gen. James Taylor, son of Col. James T. of "Midway", Caroline Co., and nephew of Major Francis, whose diary was lost, also left his Reminiscences and Record. The Diary of Col. Francis has never been published; there has been some talk of publishing it in the Records of the Ky. Historical Society.

General James Taylor's Reminiscences begin with the Rev'n., in which he served as a boy with his father, Col. James. Hubbard Taylor, Gen. James' brother, left an autobiography—short.

The sister of Hon. Wm. Kyle Anderson, (to whom he left the Diary of Col. Francis Taylor), was Mrs.·T. S. Venable, of Owensboro, Ky., and it is my (Wood's) understanding that it is now in the possession of her son, Mr. J. A. Venable.

Fall Taylor, was half brother of Gen. Thomas Haynes T., and descendant of Commodore Richard Taylor, brother to the Diarist, Col. Francis Taylor: Gen. Thomas Taylor began a Taylor Family Record, got his bro. Fall interested in it, and Fall devoted the rest of his life to it.

Dr. Grinnan annotated the Diary of Col. Francis Taylor: So did Consul Anderson: So did Fall Taylor. Fall Taylor's sister, of Frankfort Ky., was sometime ago contemplating publishing the diary—probably with Fall's annotations. (This refers probably to proposed publication by Ky. Historical Society).　　　　W. B. McGroarty.

TEACKLE, ETC.

May 28th, 1913

An Old Pocket note book came to me from my uncle, the late Severn Teackle Wallis, which contains a record of the children of my great-great-grand Father, Thomas Teackle, son of John Teackle, who was the son of the Reverend Thomas Teackle.

The old book is seven and one quarter inches long by three and one half wide, is covered with yellow vellum, with a curious brass clasp, having three holes in which to fasten the catch, as the pocket book was full or empty; & is filled with thick paper leaves to receive notes.

The entries made on them is in the hand-writing of my great great, Grand-Father, Thomas Teackle, give the following record of himself and his children.

Thomas Teackle, son of John & Susannah Teackle— Born November 11th 1711 and Marryed to Elizabeth Custis, November 9th 1732.

Elizabeth, daughter of Thomas Custis & Ann born August 27th 1718.

John son of Thomas Teackle & Elizabeth his wife, born February 11th 1733/4

Thomas, son of s'd parties born April 11th 1734

John, son of the s'd parties born October 27th 1736

Susanna, daughter of the s'd parties born May 5th 1738.

Ann, daughter of the s'd parties born January 6th 1739/40 about midnight.

The s'd Ann departed this life the 20th day of the same instant.

Ann, daughter of the s'd parties born January 8th 1740/1

Elizabeth, daughter of sd parties born Dec. 13th 1742.

December 25th 1744,—This day at midnight we had a daughter born, which lived not above a minute.

Caleb, son of the aforesaid Parties born January 14th 1745/6

January 27th 1747/8 Thursday we had a son born which departed this life on February 3rd following.

Margaret, daughter of the afors'd parties born April 9th 1749.

Leah, daughter of the afores'd parties born November 19th near midnight 1751.

Mason, daughter of the aforesaid parties born January 1st 1754 and departed this life on the 25th day of February 1754 aged eight week wanting one day.

Severn Teackle, son of the afores'd parties born October 25th 1756.

Sarah, daughter of the afors'd parties born April 8th 1759

John Teackle son of the s'd parties departed this life April 30th 1734.

John Teackle, the third son of the above s'd parties departed this life February 25th 1751/2 about nine of the clock at night aged 15 years & 4 months wanting a day.

Following this record is entered in a different handwriting:

Thomas Teackle departed this life 28th July 1769.

Severn Teackle the youngest son of Thomas Teackle & Elizabeth, his wife was my great grand father, and married Lucretia Edmondson. Their daughter Elizabeth Custis Teackle married my grandfather Philip Wallis. Their daughter Louise M— James F. Giffen. Their daughter Louise Elizabeth Wallis Giffin.

Severn Teackle' brother, Thomas, my ancestor.

THE THORNTON BIBLE AT ORMSBY,
Caroline County

THE THORNTON BIBLE AT ORMSBY, CAROLINE COUNTY, near Guinea Station, is dated 1769, and has these entries.

Henry Fitzhugh Thornton, son of Anthony and Susannah Thornton, born July 14, 1765, married Ann R. Fitzhugh, Sept. 22, 1785.

Wm. Thornton, born Sept. 20th, 1767, died Oct. 14, 1783.

John Thornton, born March 4, 1771, married Sarah Fitzhugh, Sept. 17, 1795, she born July 22, 1779, died Feb. 25, 1810.

John Thornton married "[2nd]" Jane Laughlin, Oct. 22, 1812, died Dec. 22, 1821 ["3rd wife Miss Dade—First wife only one who had children"].

Thomas Griffin Thornton, born June 11, 1775, married Ann H[arrison] Fitzhugh, Oct. 29th, 1795,

Anthony Thornton son of Henry and Ann Thornton, born 29th July 1786, baptised by Rev. Robert Buchan, had for sureties Mr. John Henry, George and Daniel Fitzhugh, Mrs. Susannah Thornton, Mrs. Alice Fitzhugh, Miss Fanny Richards, Mrs. George Fitzhugh.

Susannah Fitzhugh Thornton, daughter of John and Sarah Thornton, born Oct. 13th 1797, baptised by Rev. Tredale, had as sureties Mr. William, George, Thomas and Henry Fitzhugh, Mrs. Mary, Miss Ann D. and Elizabeth C. Fitzhugh.

George Fitzhugh Thornton, born May 22nd 1799, baptised by Rev. John Wiley, Sureties Mr. Griffin Thornton, Mr. John Baylor, Mr. George Fitzhugh, Jr., Mrs. Lucy Burrell, Mrs. Ann H. Thornton, Mrs. Ann D. Baylor, Miss Mary Fitzhugh.

John Griffin Thornton, born Nov. 13, 1800, baptised by Rev. Thompson. Sureties—Mr. George Fitzhugh, Edward Diggs, Thomas Knox, Mordica, Edward and Henry Fitzhugh, Mrs. Elizabeth Powell, Mrs. Sarah Fitzhugh, Mrs. Elizabeth Diggs, Miss Sarah Fitzhugh, Miss Porcia Diggs.

Mrs. Tompkins the present mistress of Crmsly added the comments in quotation marks.

TOMPKINS' FAMILY BIBLE ENTRIES

(Contributed by Miss LUCIE P. STONE, Hollins, Va.)

The enclosed is a copy (verbatim) from a very old family Bible. I send it to you, thinking that it may be of some value and to know if this Joyce Read was a descendant of George Read?

Christopher Tompkins Born on North River Gloucester County, October 17th 1705—Departed this life in Caroline County where he lived upwards of forty years, Mar. 16, 1779. *Joyce* His wife (who was a Read) born in Gloucester Co on Gwyn's Island was born Mar. 6th 1701— and Departed this life in Caroline County Aug. 8th 1771 leaving six sons and a daughter all she ever had.

(1) *Robert,* Eldest son, died the 7 of June, 1795, in the sixty fifth year of his age. *Wm* Tompkins, 4th son, was born in Gloucester County on North River 1736 and Departed this life in Caroline County february 24th 1772 leaving four children 2 sons and 2 daughters.

Benjamin Tompkins born the nineteenth of September 1732 and was married to Eliz. Goodloe (who was born May the twenty eight 1738) (M.) November 11-1758.

[Different handwriting.]

(1) Catherine, their daughter, born Oct. 11, 1759, died the 25 of April, 1804.

(2) Roberts, a son, b. Jan. 17, 1762.

(3) Daughter jane, b. 12, 1764, died July 3, 1834.

(4) William, a son, Dec. 30, 1765, d. Mar. 1, 1834.

(5) Jno., a son, Oct. 30, 1767.

(6) Francis, a son, Sept. 7, 1769.

(7) Lucy Gwyn, Aug. 17, 1771.

(8) Sarah, Nov. 26, 1773.

(9) Henry, Oct. 2, 1775, drowned Dec. 1798.

(10) Christopher, Jan. 24, 1778.

(11) George, born Mar. 20, 1780.

(12) Eliz. Buafort, b. Sept. 26, 1782.

(13) Mary, b. Aug. 4, 1784.

Eliz. Goodloe m. Benj. Tompkins (son of Christopher & Joyce Read), died on 23 of July, 1811, aged 78 years, 10 mos. & 4 days. His son, Wm. Tompkins, died March 1, 1834, married *Sarah Shores,* daughter of Thomas Shores, and had—

Frances Elliot, Jan. 25, 1796.

Julia, Jan. 3, 1798.

Albert Galatin, b. Aug. 21, 1799.

Catherine Cowper, b. April 16, 1801.
Christopher Delmas, b. July 31, 1802.
Hiram, b. Jan. 2, 1804.
William, b. Nov. 8, 1805.
James Monroe, Oct. 13, 1807.
Sarah Ann, Jan. 9, 1809.
Lancelot Minor, Nov. 30, 1813.
Eliz. Craven, Feb. 28, 1820.

[Joyce Read was probably daughter of Benj. Read. See *William and Mary Quarterly*, xiv, 121.]*

TOMPKINS-CUSTIS FAMILY BIBLE RECORD.

From Family Bible owned by Mrs. King, Staunton, Va.

John Tompkins was born June 19, 1718, died 21st of August, 1757.
John Tompkins and Anne Custis were married by Rev. Mr. Barlow Thursday the 25th of February, 1747.

(a) John Custis Tompkins, son of John Tompkins and Anne was born Nov. 27, 1748.

(b) William Tompkins 2nd son born Sept. 16, 1750.

(c) John Tompkins 3rd son born Nov. 20, 1751.

(d) Bennit Tompkins 4th son born Jan. 22, 1755.

John Custis Tompkins 1st son of John and Anne died Dec. 15, 1748.
William Tompkins 2nd son D Sept. 25, 1750.
John Tompkins 3rd son d
John Custis and Anne Kendall were married by the Rev. Mr. John Holebrook, March 5, 1732.
John Custis son of John and Anne born July 7, 1734.
Henry Brown Custis born Jan. 2, 1736 and died the following March 2.
Peggy Custis was born little before daybreak Sunday ye 16 July 1738.
John Custis departed this life Oct. 7, 1738.
Hannah Custis born Aug. 9 and died Aug. 20.
John Custis born April 10, 1743.
Hancock Custis B. May 19, 1745 was baptized May 31 by Rev. Mr. Jno. Holebrook and died Jan. 27, 1761.
Col. John Custis departed this life 1st day December 1746 aged 40 years 4 months 6 days.
John Custis the second of that name and third son of the above Col. John Custis died Aug. 24, 1747.

---

*See *Genealogies of Virginia Families: From the William and Mary College Quarterly Historical Magazine* (Baltimore: Genealogical Publishing Co., Inc., 1982), Vol. IV, p. 264.

WEBB OF ESSEX.

James Webb, b. 1705, married Mary Edmonson 1731, died in 1771. his father-in-law was a vestryman of South Farnam Parish, Essex Co. Virginia between 1731 and 1750.

Children of James Webb and Mary Edmonson, 1st, William, b. Feb. 10th, 1732, in March 24th 1733; 2nd, James, b. July 2d, 1734, m. Mary Smith, daughter of Captain Francis Smith & Lucy Meriweather of Essex Co. Virginia.

3, Mary, b. October 4th, 1736, died September 6th, 1739.

4th, John, b. April 3d, 1739, died Sept. 20th, 1740.

5th, Mary, b. Oct. 18th, 1740, m. Samuel Smith, May 1761, moved to North Carolina, died Nov. 20th, 1827, she had three sons, Col. Maurice Smith, Col. James Webb Smith of Jackson Co. Tenn. and John Webb Smith of N. C.

6th, John, b. April 2d, 1743, d. Aug. 1745.

7th, William, b. May 1st, 1748, m. Frances Young of Essex Co. Virginia May 1st, 1771, moved to Granville Co. N. C. 1776, he d. 1809, she d. 1810. They had nine children.

8th, John, b. Jan. 18th, 1747.

9th, Thomas, b. Feb. 27th, 1754.

10th, Elizabeth, b. June 20th, 175–.

Record of James Webb, Jr., b. July 2d, 1734, d. Dec. 1773, found in old Bible of Dr. Wm Smith Webb of Clark Co. Ky. (part of leaf torn out or worn out)

"James Webb, jr. was b. Feb. 24th, 1734, m. Mary Smith, 1757., da. of Francis Smith and his wife Lucy. Lucy Smith's maiden name was Meriweather, she was the daughter of Francis Merrweather and wife Lucy."

"James Webb and wife Lucy had four sons and two daughters."

James Webb, son of this James Webb d. 1773.

"Mary Webb daughter of Francis Smith and wife Lucy died Anno. Dom. 1787."

Children of James Webb jr. and wife Mary Smith.

Frances Webb, no records.

James Webb, no records.

†George Webb.

*Dr. William Smith Webb of Clark Co. Ky. was born May 17, 1768, in Essex Co. Virginia, was graduated at the Medical College of Philadelphia, under Dr. Benjamin Rush in 1790, and died June 15, 1845 in Clark Co., Ky.

WILLISON BIBLE RECORDS

This volume of the Bible with the other of the New Testament belonged originally to Sir William Callander of Bancloigh & Dorator, in the Shire of Sterling, North Britain, and is Presented as a memorial of the ancient Family of Callander from John Willison in Port Glasgow, to his son James Willison of Dorator, at Cabin Point, James River in the Province of Virginia North America an Dom 1704. The ible was printed at London, by Christopher Barker, 1585.

Beginning of family record.

(1st) James Willison son of the above John Willison and Margaret Dunbar was born in Port Glasgow, North Britain. February 15th, 1751, N. S., and was married to Mary I'Anson, daughter of John I'Anson, M. D., and Lucy Cocke. Their issue as follows viz.:

(1st) John Willison Born in Prince George County Virginia, October 22d, 1778, baptized 4th January 1779 by the Rev. Mr. Benjamin Blagrove. Godfathers Archibald Dunlop, Thomas I'Anson, Godmothers Mary Mackie and Margaret Ross.

(2) Archibald Dunlop Willison, Born in Prince George, Dec 12th 1779 Baptized March 12th 1780 By the Revd William Harrison, Thomas Peter, and James Tait Godfathers; Mrs. Thomas Peter and Mrs. Tait Godmothers.

(3rd) Lucy Willison Born September 5th 1782, in Surry County at Cabin Point, and baptized Nov. 1st 1782 by the Revd. Mr. Thomas Hopkinson, John Stewart and Robert Peter, Godfathers; Mrs. Fletcher & Miss Nancy Cocke, Godmothers.

Archibald Dunlop Willison departed this life August 20th 1784 and lyes buried at the Family burying ground at Colin Cocks.

(4th) Margret Dunbar Willison was born at Cabin Point, in Surry County September 23rd 1784. Baptized by the Revd. Mr. John Burgess. Archibald Campbell, M. D. & Colin Cocke Godfathers, Miss Polly Allen and Miss Peggy Belsches Godmothers.

(5th) Mary I'Anson Willison was born at Dorator near Cabin Point in Surry County September —th 1787, and baptized by the Revd. Mr.

John H. Burgess at Little Town. Mr. Archibald Campbell and Mr. Chs. Thomas I'Anson Godfathers, Mrs. Mary I'Anson Godmother.

James Willison Died at Dorator on Monday 25th June 1787 and was buried at the family burying ground over the Creek.

Mary Willison wife of James Willison departed this life on —th September 1787, and was buried at the family Burying ground at Colin Cocke's over the Creek on —th 1787.

Lucy Willison departed this life February 23d 1794 and lies buried at the Family burying ground at Colin Cockes.

Mary I'Anson Willison departed this life on Saturday February 6th 1796 and buried at the family burying ground over the Creek.

Margret Dunbar Willison was married to Colin Campbell of Surry County the 7th October 1801 and died on Saturday evening the 24th April 1802 and buried at the burial ground.

John Willison son of the above James Willison, was married by the Revd. Mr. Chapin to Miss Mary Burbidge Dandridge of New Kent County on Monday 26th August 1805. (Daughter of Bartholomew Dandridge). Issue:

(1st) Frances LucyWillison born in Charles City County at Mr. George Minges (Rowe) June 14th 1806 baptized by Revd. Mr. James Madison Godfathers George Minge, Braxton Harrison, Godmothers Martha Halyburton and Miss Susanna Armestead.

(2) Martha Dandridge Willison Born in Charles City County at Mr. George Minges (Rowe) November 18th 1808.

(3) John Willison born in Charles City County at Mr. George Minges (Rowe) November 17th 1810.

(4th) James Dandridge Willison was born in Charles City County at Mr. George Minges (Rowe) February 22, 1813.

Martha Dandridge Willison departed this life on Wednesday night 3 o'clock the 25th October 1814 and buried in Mr. George Minges Family burial ground in Charles City (Rowe) on Friday the 28th Instant by the Rev. Mr. Bowrey.

(5th) Mary Elizabeth Willison born Charles City Co. at Mr. George Minges (Rowe) June 1st 1815.

(6) Martha Dandridge Willison born in Surry County August the 9th 1817.

John Willison departed this life on Tuesday night 12 o'clock the 29 of December 1817, and was buried at the (Rowe) in Charles City County.

Martha Dandridge Willison departed this life on Monday night 10 o'clock 28th August 1820 and was buried at the (Rowe) Charles City County.

John Willison departed this life at Manchester, Mississippi, Dec. 1837 and was buried in the burying ground of that town with Masonic honors.

Mary B. Willison departed this life in Petersburg on Friday night November 16th 1839 and was buried at Blandford Church burying ground.

James Dandridge Willison was married by the Rev. Mr. Burtolk on

Thursday June 1839 to Miss Cathrine H. McIntosh daughter of Gen. Wm. McIntosh, Fort Gibson, Ind. Ter. Issue:

(1st) Kiamesha Dandridge Willison was born June 11th 1840 near Fort Gibson, I. T.

(2nd) William Dandridge Willison was born June 16th, 1842, near Fort Gibson, Ind. Ter.

William Dandridge Willison departed this life 1843.

(3rd) Mary Burbidge Willison was born Nov. 25th, 1844, near Fort Gibson, I. T.

(4th) Sallie McIntosh Willison was born Nov. 16th, 1846, Fort Gibson, I. T.

(5th) Rubie Dandridge Willison was born Feb. 5th, 1848, Fort Gibson, I. T.

(6th) Sue Dandridge Willison was born Dec. 13th, 1850 near Jefferson, Texas.

Sue Dandridge Willison, died 1851 and was buried in the family cemetery.

(7th) James Dandridge Willison was born Dec. 31st, 1852, near Jefferson, Texas.

Kiamesha Dandridge Willison was married to Thomas Harding Scott, Jefferson, Texas.

(8th) Lucy Bowers Willison was born April 1861, Jefferson, Texas.

Rubie Dandridge Willison was married Feb. 5th, 1856, to Walter R. West Red River Co., Texas.

James Dandridge Willison departed this life near Jefferson, Texas, in the 58th year of his age on the 14th of May 1870 and was buried at the family burying ground.

Sallie McIntosh Willison was married Aug. 1871 to Wm. L. Hailey by Rev. E. G. Benners, Jefferson, Texas.

Mary Burbidge Willison was married in 1872 to Geo. Shannon near Muscogee, I. T.

Lucy Bowers Willison was married 1882 to Henry C. Fisher at Fisher Town, Creek Nation, I. T.

James D. Willison was married to Miss Mary Mackey, Jan. 9th, 1879 by the Rev. H. F. Buckner at Texana, Cherokee Nation, I. T. Issue:

(1st) Howard Dandridge Willison was born Oct. 19th, 1879 near Eufaula, I. T.

(2nd) Irine Bowers Willison was born June 27th, 1881, near Eufaula, I. T.

(3rd) James Mackey Willison was born April 27th, 1885, at Gibson Sta., I. T.

(4th) May Cathrine Willison was born April 27th, 1885, at Gibson Sta., I. T.

May Cathrine Willison died Sept. 2nd, 1887 and was buried at family burying ground near Gibson Sta., I. T.

(5th) Hellen Willison was born Aug. 18th, 1891, Gibson Sta., I. T.

THE WILSON FAMILY
Of Princess Anne, Norfolk, Etc.

Thomas Wilson, the Emigrant from the Island of Great Britain, intermarried with a Miss Willis [There is no record evidence for Thos. Wilson or his wife] and settled in Princess Ann Co., at or near the Poplar Grove, where he raised a numerous family of sons and daughters. John the elder is understood to have early moved up the Chesapeake bay and most likely, settled on the waters of the Potomac. Solomon and Willis intermarried in the Neighbourhood of their birth and raised large families of children. Samuel the third son, intermarried with a Miss Mason and died in Norfolk, about the year 1710, leaving his wife pregnant, who bore him a son named Willis, who came into the care of his Uncle Solomon Wilson. He was a clerk to one of the County Courts of that Section of the Country.

Willis having been instructed in the art of navigation which was a favorite pursuit of the family made himself what was at that day termed a sea captain. In his voyage up James River he became acquainted with a Miss Goodrich, with whom he intermarried about the year 1732, and had or left an only son by the name of Benjamin, born 26th Dec. 1733 at or near the mouth of the Chickahominy River, the patrimonial estate of his grandfather Benjamin Goodrich who left two daughters Elizabeth the wife of Willis Wilson and the wife of Samuel Boush of Norfolk. Willis Wilson died in the year 1740, a member of the House of Burgesses, his son Benjamin being disappointed in the enjoyment of his patrimonial estate from his father and mother, she having married a second husband transferred his interest, with her own to him, and his great uncle Solomon Wilson, who raised his father, had dissipated what belonged to him, so that Benjamin had very slender means with which he moved at an early age and settled on the Willis River in the County of Cumberland, about the year 1750.

He intermarried with Anne Seay daughter of James Seay a Hugeunot family from the waters of York River and had issue seven sons and six daughters, Mary, Elizabeth, Willis, Benjamin, Anne, James, Mason, Samuel, Mathew, Alexander, Goodrich, Mantua and Unity.

Benjamin Wilson died the 27th Oct. 1814, and Anne his wife on the 26th of April 1814, having lived together man and wife sixty years, the wife being one year the youngest.

This record was made by Willis Wilson in his family Bible. He died at Bonbrook, his residence in Cumberland Co. Feb. 10th 1822.

Mary, oldest daughter of Benjamin Wilson and Anne Seay married Thomas Munford of Cumberland Co., their only child Mary Thomas Munford married Joseph Hobson of Cumberland and they lived at the Blenheim Estate in Powhatan Co. and had the following children: Phoebe Anne, Joseph Virginius, Thomas Ludwell, Maria, Mary, John Caleb, Lavinia, Sarah Booker, and Willis Wilson.

Phoebe Anne married Hilary Harris of Buck Hill, Louisa County. They lived at Mill Quarter, Powhatan Co. and had the following children: Mary Maria, Joseph, Anne Lavinia, John Wilson, Hilary Valentine, Christiana, Abner, Sarah Octavia, Willis Overton, Martha Pryor and Fanny Morton.

FROM YATES FAMILY BIBLE.

James Yates was born May 3rd, 1763.
Lucy Yates was born Augt. 25th, 1759.

Betsey Yates was born 28th Oct., 1782.
Sarah Yates was born 11th Sept., 1784.
B. P. Yates was born 2nd Oct., 1786.
Lucy P. Yates was born Novr. 4th, 1789.
Gerrard Yates was born 29th April, 1792.
Benjamin Yates was born 4th Augt., 1794.
Frances Yates was born Nov. 1st, 1797.
Aylett R. Yates was born ———— 1800.

Clarissa Ann Yates was born June 13th, 1791.

James Harrison Yates the eldest son of B. P. Yates & Clarissa Ann, his wife, was born Feby. 11th, 1814.

Wm. Mortimer Yates was born 31st May, 1815.

Susan Ann Elizabeth Yates was born 20th Feby., 1817.

Mary Frances Yates was born April 24th, 1819.

Lucy Ann Yates was born 4th Feby. 1827.

Thomas Aylett Yates was born 12th Jany. 1831.

James Yates departed this life in 1828.

Boswell P. Yates departed this life 12 Day Jany. 1857 in North Garden, Albemarle.

Aylett R. Yates departed this life in April, 1815.

Wm. Mortimer Yates departed this life 27th of October, 1840.

Mary Frances Yates departed this life November 18th, 1840.

Lucy Ann Yates departed this life 22d of Augt., 1829.

Susan A. E. Yates was married to R. G. Anderson October 27th, 1836.

Ann Elizabeth Anderson, eldest daughter R. G. Anderson & Susan his wife was born November 12th, 1837 (at Stony Pt., Albemarle).

Mary F. Anderson was born 27th Feby. 1845 at North Garden, Albemarle, Second daughter of R. G. & S. A. E. Anderson.

Boswell Anderson, Son of R. G. Anderson & Susan A. E. Anderson was born 13th Augt. 1847, 7 o'clock in morning.

R. T. W. Anderson was born Sept. 9th 1853.

Clarissa Gaines Anderson daughter of R. G. & S. A. E. Anderson was born 19 Nov. 1860.

Charles W. Chamblin (of Loudoun co.) was married to Mary F. Anderson daughter of R. G. & S. A. Anderson Jany 4th 1865 by Rev. Wm. F. Broadus of Charlottesville Va.

Clara Anderson infant daughter of R. G. & Susan Anderson departed this life on 26th May 1862, 15 minutes after 7 A. M.

James H. Yates was married to Juliett E. Hunter February 28th, 1839.

Juliett E. Yates was born 25th March 1817.

Saml. Boswell Yates was born 15th June 1840—First son of James H. Yates & Juliett E. Yates his wife.

Sarah Frances Yates was born 11th January 1843.

Mary Cathrin Yates was born 28th Augt. 1846.

James Mortimer Yates was born 4th Decmr, 1852.

Becker (cont.)
Nicholas 490
Peter 316
William 484
Beckerin, Elisabetha 327
Beckley, Diana (Mrs.)
400
John 157
Joseph 400
Spencer Morgan 400
Beckman, Jeremiah 169
Beckwith, Betty 432, 440,
445, 446
Eliza (Mrs.) 446
Elizabeth (Mrs.) 440
Jonathan 446
Margaret 440, 446
Marmaduke 446
Mary 440, 446
Tarpley 440, 446
Beddingfield, Mary 10
Theophilus 10
Beddo, Geo. 169
Bedell, Dorothy 71
Edward 71
Elizabeth 71
George 71
Lewis 71
William 71
Bederin, (?) 307
Elis. 306
Bedinger, Solomon 371
Bedwell, Mary 439, 459
Bee, Thomas (Jdg.) 371
Beeson, Jacob 169
Bell, (?) (Mrs.) 371
David 159
Edmund Hayes 616
Elizabeth 217
Graham 43
Henry (Cpt.) 371
Jacob Saul 217
John 495
John (Cpt.) 371
Joseph 421
Martha 217
Martha (Mrs.) 217
Mary 390
Nathan 160, 217
Patrick 421
Robert 212
Sarah (Mrs.) 421
Saul 217
Thomas 151, 390, 697
Thos. 217
William 217
Wm. 217
Beller, Matthias 319
Belsches, Martha 517
Patrick 568
Peggy 751
Belt, William B. 371
Beman, Jane 396
Benger, John 432, 446
Katharine 432
Katherine 445, 446
Mary 445
Mary (Mrs.) 432, 446
Benjamin, Nathan Curtis
169
Benman, Christina 488
Benners, E. G. (Rev.)
753
Bennet, Charles (Rev.)
169
James 169
Bennett, (?) 20
Abner 526

Bennett (cont.)
Ann (Mrs.) 371
Asenath (Mrs.) 526
Bacster 526
Behethland 260
Calvin 526
Elizabeth 276, 526
Elizabeth (Mrs.) 260
Fisher Rice 113
Frances (Mrs.) 526
Hannah (Mrs.) 526
James 260, 526
James Anthony 526
Letty (Mrs.) 526
Mary 526
Matilda 527
McCajah 526
Micijah 526
Nancy (Mrs.) 526
Peter 526
Reuben 526
Reuben W. (Dr.) 526
Richard 15, 20, 526
Sally 526, 528, 532
Sally (Mrs.) 526
Sena 526
Sena (Mrs.) 526
Thomas F. 526
William 371, 526
Winston 526
Zachariah 526
Bens, Henry 483
John 467, 483
Margaret 484
Bentley, Mary (Mrs.) 250
Samuel 250
Bentz, Anna Maria 470,
472
Catharine (Mrs.) 472
Elizabeth 490, 491
George 472
Henry 483, 490
Jacob 470, 472
John 483, 490, 491
Sarah 472
Berecke, Jacob 467
Berger, Anna 533
Caty (Mrs.) 527
Daniel 527
Elizabeth 526
Frances 527
George 527
Jacob (Jr.) 527
John 445
John (Wade) 527
Martha 533
Mildred 530
Polly 533
Susannah 528
Berkeley, (?) 734
(?) (Gov.) 556
Carter (Dr.) 596
Edmund 91, 92, 340
Lucy (Mrs.) 344
Nelson 169
Sarah 340
Thomas Nelson 169
William (Sir) 540, 596
Berkley, (?) (Lord) 356
Berler, (?) 330
Adam 317
Heinrich 317
Matthias 319
Berlerin, Jemimy 317
Lea 317
Bernard, (?) 90
Ann 90
Anna (Mrs.) 76, 90

Bernard (cont.)
Cordery 90
Elizabeth (Mrs.) 169,
282, 283
George 90
Henry 53
James 53
John 90, 169, 283
Lucy (Mrs.) 90
Margaret 90
Mary (Mrs.) 53
Peter 56
Peter (Cpt.) 90
Philip 90
Richard 90, 257, 282,
283
Robert 90
Thomas (Cpt.) 90
William 76, 90, 259,
264
William (Col.) 71, 90
Berry, (?) 493
(?) (Dr.) 223
Elisabeth 476
Garret 476
George 413
Grace 258
James 258
John 322, 400
Judith (Mrs.) 400
Mary (Mrs.) 476
Sarah 276
Sarah (Mrs.) 258
Thomas 264, 270, 397,
400
William 397, 413
Berryman, Andrew Gilson
256
Behethland 257, 260
Behethland, Gilson
256, 259, 260
Frances 286
Gilson 256, 257, 260
Hannah (Mrs.) 256,
257, 260
John 257
Rose 257, 281
Sarah 256, 259, 261,
272
Bertram, Eva 490
Eva (Mrs.) 485, 486
John 483
John George 485
John Henry 484
Julius 483, 484, 485,
486, 488, 490, 491
Mary Elisabeth 483
Samuel 486
Bertrand, John 667
John (Rev.) 565
Mary (Mrs.) 668
Mary Ann 667
Paul 668
William 667
Bery, Cornelius 395
Margaret 395
Margaret (Mrs.) 395
Bessom, John (Cpt.) 371
Best, Mawdestly G. (Maj.)
85
Betsch, Jacob 468
Betts, Astan 399
Charles 398, 399, 413
Chas. 399
Daniel 398
Elisha 399
Eliza 398
Hannah 398

Burwell (cont.)
George 70
George H. 640, 642
George Harrison 642
James 22, 70, 71, 72,
73, 249
James Bacon 72
Jane 62, 71, 72
Joanna 71
John 238
Judith 640
Lewis 22, 61, 62, 70,
71, 72, 73, 90, 203,
228, 247, 641
Lewis (Col.) 18, 228
Lewis (Maj.) 6, 60,
61, 62, 71, 72, 73
Lucy 71, 72, 640, 641
Lucy (Mrs.) 60, 61, 90
Mann Page 641
Margaret (Mrs.) 248
Martha 6, 71, 72
Martha (Jr.) 6, 71, 72
Martha (Mrs.) 61, 62
Mary 62, 72, 641, 642
Mary Baptist 292
Matthew 71
Nathaniel 71, 73, 203,
496, 641, 642
Nathaniel (Col.) 248
Nathaniel (Cpt.) 72,
249
Nathaniel (Maj.) 62
Nathaniel Bacon 72
Nathaniel Bacon (Col.)
73
Nathaniel Bacon (Cpt.)
72
Nathaniel Bacon (Jr.)
72
Philip 641, 642
Rachel 72
Robert 236, 641
Sally 242
Sarah 641
Susanna 641
Susanna Grymes 641
Tayloe Page 641
Thomas H. 642
Thomas Hugh Nelson 642
William 70, 71, 292,
641
William Nelson 641
Bury, Lidia (Mrs.) 390
Robt. 390
Busch, John 483
Bush, John 483
Bushrod, Ann 397
Apphia (Mrs.) 523
Hannah 613
Hannah (Mrs.) 523
John 523
John (Col.) 418
Richard 523
Richd. 397
Thomas 397, 523
Thomas (Col.) 3
Bussey, Martha 276
Bustock, Willock 92
Butler, Betty (Mrs.) 441
Edward 441
Elizabeth 258
Elizabeth (Mrs.) 276
George E. 736
James M. 736, 737
John B. 372
Mollie W. 736
Sallie E. (Mrs.) 737

Butler (cont.)
Samuel 441
Sarah 286
Thomas 276
Willie J. 736
Butt, Abi (Mrs.) 367
Ann 367
Cartwrite 367
Eliza. (Mrs.) 367
Sarah (Mrs.) 171
Solomon 367
Butterworth, Sarah (?)
139
Button, Douglas W. 693
F. W. 692
Hannah 690
Harmon 690
Helen R. 693
J. Mortimer 693
Jennie E. 693
Lula M. 693
William (Cpt.) 87
Buxton, John (Rev.) 372
Byars, Jemima 291
Mary 291, 292
Byers, Sally 118
Byfield, Annie 107
Richard 107
William 107
Byne, William 171
Byrd, (?) 20, 21, 22,
222, 228, 251, 615,
644
(?) (Col.) 505, 617
(?) (Cpt.) 237
(?) (Mrs.) 372
(?) Ann B. 643
(?) Ann R. 643
Anne Harrison 665
Arthur Virginius 643,
644
Betsey 236
C. W. 615
Carolina Virginia
(Mrs.) 643
Charles Willing 616,
643, 644
Chas. W. 615
Chas. W. (Jdg.) 616
Cordelia Willing 644
Elizabeth Hill 221
Ellen de Jarnette 644
Emily B. (Mrs.) 643
Evelyn 22, 224, 424
Evelyn (Mrs.) 17
Evelyn Taylor 424, 425,
617
Frances E. (Mrs.) 615,
616
G. J. 643, 644
George H. 662, 665
George James 643, 644
George Virginius 644
Gulielmi 16
Hannah (Mrs.) 615
Jane B. De Jarnette
644
Jane Evelyn 644
Lucy 631, 665
Maria 627, 628
Maria (Mrs.) 237
Mary 628
Mary (Mrs.) 16, 22,
372
Mary Ann 644
Mary Willing (Mrs.)
616
Otway 151

Byrd (cont.)
R. F. 644
R. W. 644
Richard W. 372, 643,
644
Richard Willing 643,
644
Richd. W. 643
Richd. Willing 644
Robert 631
Robert de Jarnette 644
Robert Fisher 643, 644
Samuel O. 615, 616
Ursula 222
Virginia Taylor 644
Wickham 665
Wilhelmina 361, 547
William 16, 17, 20,
22, 76, 221, 222,
228, 236, 237, 246,
361, 372, 628, 665
William (Col.) 222, 547
William (II) (Col.) 22
William (III) 643
William (Jr.) 21
William (Sr.) 21
Wm. 224
Wm. (Col.) 425
Bywaters, Annie R. 653
Elizabeth 654
John 654
Cabell, (?) 346, 349
Anne B. Cocke (Mrs.)
348
Cary Charles 348
Elizabeth 347
Elizabeth (Mrs.) 346,
347
Elizabeth Burks (Mrs.)
346
Elizabeth N. 171
Elizabeth Nichols 348
Francis Barraud 348
Francis Hartwell 348
George (Dr.) 172
Hannah (Mrs.) 347
Hartwell 346
Hartwell (Mrs.) 346
Joseph C. 346
Joseph Carrington 346
Juliet Calvert Bolling
(Mrs.) 348
Margaret 350
Margaret Read (Mrs.)
347
Margaret Read Venable
(Mrs.) 348
Mary Anne 347
N. Francis 348
Nathaniel Francis 348
Nicholas (Col.) 347
Nicholas (Jr.) 347,
348
Nicholas C. 347
Nicholas Carrington
347
Philip Barraud 348
Philip Barraud (Rev.)
348
Robert B. 162
Samuel Jordan (Col.)
349, 350
William 346
William (Col.) 172,
349
William (Dr.) 346,
347
William (Sr.) 347

772

Chiswell (cont.)
Polly 232
Susanna 75
Cholmeley, (?) 76
Choulyn, Margaret (?)
469
Christ, Catherine (Mrs.)
487
Henry 487
Sarah 487
Christerin, Rosina 332
Christerlin, Elisabetha
304, 323
Christian, (?) (Rev.)
210
Ann 57, 122
Ann. B. (Mrs.) 364
Archer Hunt 607
Bailey 53
Billie Payne 129
Charles 126
Charles Hunt 126
Drury 109, 119, 122,
123
George Reade 52
Henry 365, 607
Israel 52, 53, 54
J. B. 365
J. B. (Jdg.) 364
James 119
Jesse George 130
John 53, 114, 131,
158, 173
John B. (Jdg.) 364
John F. (Dr.) 364
Judith 115
Letitia 364
M. (Mrs.) 365
Martha 57
Martha (Mrs.) 52, 53,
54
Mary 114, 364
Robert 364
Sarah French (Mrs.)
607
Turner 129, 130
Will 131
Wm. 161
Christie, James 373
Christler, (?) 323, 325
Abraham 321
Absalom 321
Adam 321, 322, 323,
324
Andrew 304
Anna 322
Anna Magdalene (Mrs.)
317
Aron 323
Benjamin 321, 325
Catharine 323
Deobold 305, 321, 322
Deobold (Mrs.) 304
Dinah 325
Dorothea 304
Eleanora 323
Elias 325
Elisabeth 323
Elisabetha 320, 321,
325
Elisabetha (Mrs.) 331
Elizabeth 302, 321,
322
Elizabeth (Mrs.) 303,
305, 323, 325
Georg 317, 325, 329
George 317, 322, 329
Hanna 323

Christler (cont.)
Heinerich 303, 320,
321, 323, 325, 331
Heinrich 302, 303, 304,
305
Jemima 325
Joel 321
John Georg 317, 321,
322
John George 317, 322,
323
Jonas 322
Joseph 325
Juliana 322
Julius 321
Loocy 322
Maria 320, 321, 322,
329
Mary (Mrs.) 325
Rosina 321, 325
Susana 322
Susanna 323
Theobolt 304
William 323
Christlerin, Anna 317,
325
Elisabetha 302, 303,
321, 322
Elizabeth 298
Elizabetha 302, 303
Christopher, Elizabeth
(Mrs.) 300
Martin 300, 301
Christopherin, Elizabetha
308
Christophers, Elizabeth
(Mrs.) 300
Martin 300
Chrombohr, Maria Barbara
470
Churchill, Armistead 242
Hannah (Mrs.) 242
Clack, Ann 514
James 81, 91
Jane 91
Jane (Mrs.) 728
Mary (Mrs.) 81
William 81
Claiborn, Hannah 513
Claiborno, Augustine
512, 513, 514
Bathurst 513
Betty 359, 514
Charles Augustine 513
Cole 516
Elizabeth (Mrs.) 153
Herbert 250, 512
John (Dr.) 649
Leonard 512
Mary (Mrs.) 512, 513,
516
Philadelphia 237
Philip Whitehead 237,
238, 359
Susanna 513, 514
Thomas 649
W. C. C. 153
William 516
William Cole 516
Wm. 166, 513
Clare, (?) (Mrs.) 173
James 173
Clarendon, (?) 86
Clark, Agathy 136
Ann 115, 129, 130
Charles 136
Chiles Tyrell 136
Christopher 136

Clark (cont.)
David 136
Elias 173
Elizabeth W. 531
George Rogers 701
Hannah 139, 140, 141,
142, 143
Jane (Mrs.) 205
Joshua 136
Judith 136
Lucy 136
Martha (Mrs.) 173
Mary 273, 647
Mary Ann 729
Micajah 136, 162
Milley 136
Molly 136
Morning 136
Patricia P. 167, 695
Patricia P. (Mrs.) 167
Peter H. 527
Rachel 136
Samuel 136
William (Cpt.) 527
Wm. 647
Clarke, Elizabeth 173
Elizabeth H. (Mrs.)
157
George 539
Hannah (Mrs.) 86
John 85, 86, 157
John (Sir) 85
Mary 539
Mary Ann (Mrs.) 160
Rebecca E. (Mrs.) 173
Thomas 373
William 595, 596
William (Sir) 85
Clarkson, Elizabeth 139
Clary, Nicholas 173
Clay, (?) 702
Ann (Mrs.) 159
Henry 180
John 218
Mary 373
Mathew 159, 373
Clayborn, Sarah 128
Clayton, (?) 648
Arthur 76
Barbara (Mrs.) 648
Delphia (Mrs.) 648,
649
Eliza (Mrs.) 648
Elvy 248
George 76, 648, 649
Isabella (Mrs.) 68, 69
Jasper 76, 247
Jasper (Cpt.) 248
Jasper (Sir) 76
Johannis 68
John 76, 219, 224,
648, 649
John (Mrs.) 648
John (Sir) 76
Juliana 69, 76
Lucy 649
Mary 76, 648, 649
Prudence 76
Rebecca 76, 112
Richard Gass 648
Sally 649
Samuel 648
Temperance (Mrs.) 648
Thomas 68, 69, 76
Thomas (Dr.) 76
Will. 117
William 248
Cleaver, Granny 527

774

Corbin (cont.)
  Sylvester W. 653
  Tayloe 655
  Thomas 655
  Virginia 653
  Virginia T. 653
  William 652
  Winifred 401
Corbyn, Henrici 524
  Laetitiae 524
  Margaret 656
  Thomas 656
Corderoy, (?) 90
  Anna 90
Cordery, Edward 90
  John 401
  William 401
Corling, Ann (Mrs.) 30
  Charles 29, 30, 373
  Eliza 29, 30
  Elizabeth (Mrs.) 29
  William 29
  Wm. 29
Cornah, Helen 391
Cornick, William 373
Cornillon, (?) 154
Cornwall, John 373
Cornwallis, (?) 186
  (?) (Lord) 431
Corran, Ann (Mrs.) 373
  William 373
Cosbie, Ann Winkfield
  131
  Barbara 135
  Cha. 131
  Charles 128, 135
  Charles Scott 135
  David 125, 135
  Eliz. 135
  Elizabeth 130
  Fortunatus 135
  Garland 132
  James 135
  James Overton 128
  Judith 135
  Lucy 135
  Lucy Hawkins 131
  Nicholas 132
  Patsy 135
  Pleasants 125
  Polly 135
  Richmond 135
  Robert 135
  Sydnor 135
  Tho. 130
  William 130
  Winkfield 131
Cosby, David 119, 120,
  122, 141, 142, 143,
  144
  Elizabeth 133
  Fortunatus 118
  Garland 116
  Hickerson 130
  James 122, 144
  Jeremiah 120, 143
  Mary 130
  Minor M. 166
  William 119, 142
  Winifred 141
Cottom, (?) 501
Cotton, (?) 657
  Hanna (Mrs.) 390
  Hannah (Mrs.) 395
  Henry 657
  Jemima 657
  John 390, 395, 657
  John Ralph 657

Cotton (cont.)
  Mary 390
  Mary Jane 657
  Nathaniel 657
  Peggy 657
  Ralph 657
  Robert 657
  Sarah 657
  Susannah 657
  William 657
Couch, Samuel 251
Coulston, Charity 391
Coulter, John 595
Course, Catharine (Mrs.)
  174
Courtney, Dandridge P.
  174
  Jane (Mrs.) 161
  John 161
  Mildred (Mrs.) 153
  Philip 162, 165
  Philip (Rev.) 205
  Polly (Mrs.) 159
  Thomas 153
  Thos. 159
Cousin, Gerard B. 152
  Jenny Pope (Mrs.)
  152
Coutts, Elvira 373
  Patrick 246
  William 149
  William (Rev.) 201,
  236, 245
Coventon, Kathrine 394
  Mary (Mrs.) 394
  Nehemiah 394
  Sarah 394
Cowan, William 373, 681
Coward, Jane 2
  Samuel 2
Cowherd, Albert G. 174
Cowland, James 160
Cowley, Robert 163
Cowling, Euphan N.
  (Mrs.) 174
  Willis 174
Cowper, Rebecca (Mrs.)
  373
  Robert (Cpt.) 373
  William 373
Cox, James (Cpt.) 374
  Jane (Mrs.) 419
  John 527
  John (Cpt.) 595
  Peter 419
  R. H. (Dr.) 636
  Rebecca 119
  William 374
Coyle, John 174
  William 174
Crafford, Pelatiah 277
Craft, Armstead 527
  Emily 527
  George 527
  Philip 527
Craig, Adam 161, 253
  Adam (Mrs.) 374
  Alexander 225, 243
  Ann 374
  Anne (Mrs.) 157
  John J. 595
Craigwald, Elizabeth
  112
Cralle, Hannah Kenner
  401
  J. B. (Mrs.) 703
  John 401
  Sarah (Mrs.) 401

Crane, Harriette 630
Crank, William 257
Crannidge, Mary 277
Crawford, Bennet A. 174
  Hannah H. (Mrs.) 174
  John 244
  Mary Ann 620, 621
  Nelson 731
  William 174
  William (Dr.) 174
Crayne, David S. 527
  Ellina Ellender 527
  Jacob 527
  Jacob (Jourdan) 527
  Patsy 531
  Peggy Ann 527
Creagler, (?) 298
  Christopher 298
  Jacob 298
  Nicholas 298
  Susanna (Mrs.) 298
Creamer, Old Miss 527
Creecy, William (Lt.)
  374
Crew, John 391
  John (Jr.) 161
Crewdson, Henry 174
  Sophia (Mrs.) 174
Crickett, Robert 527
Crider, Andrew 527
  Caty (Mrs.) 527
  Ceilia (Mrs.) 527
  Daniel 527
  Daniel (Sgt.) 527
  Elizabeth 534
  Henry 527
  Jacob 527
  John 527
  Matilda 532
  Melissa 527
  Samuel 527
  Tina (Mrs.) 527
  William 527
Cridlin, W. B. 8
Crigler, (?) 298, 308
  Abraham 298, 302
  Anna 308
  Aron 298
  Catharine (Mrs.) 308
  Christopher 308
  Elisabetha 323
  Elizabeth 298, 323
  Jacob 330
  Johannes 308
  John 308
  Lewis 308
  Ludwig 308
  Margaret 298
  Nancy 321
  Rosannah 316
  William 308
Cringan, Jno. (Dr.) 161
Cringer, John (Dr.) 202
Cringhan, Jane (Mrs.)
  151
  John (Dr.) 151
Crisler, Adam 298
  Catharine 298
  Dinah 314
  Fawatt 304
  John 316
  Lewis 316
  Maria 314
  Rosanna 311
  Rosannah 309
Cristler, Ambrosius 323
  Heinerich 323
  Margaretha 323

776

Dawson (cont.)
John 175, 374
Musgrave (Rev.) 659
Thomas 58
William 151
William (Rev.) 247
Day, (?) (Col.) 175
(?) (Mrs.) 175
Ann (Mrs.) 588
Anne (Mrs.) 588
John 154, 214, 215,
258, 260, 497, 588
Thos. 216
de Bresson, Catharine
Livingston (Mrs.)
175
de Greuhm, (?) 176
de Hallend, Margaret
656
Thomas Corbyn 656
De Jarnette, Jane B.
644
de la Hay, Charles 518
De la Ware, (?) (Lord)
3
De Sear, James 162
Deadman, Susanna 234
Dean, Josiah 57
Deans, Nellie 105
Dearborn, Henry (Gen.)
175
Simon 175
Dearling, (?) 668
G. H. 668
Mary 668
Debbo, Nancy 527
Debboe, Abraham 529
America 529
Benjamin 529
Eliza 529
James 529
Joseph 528, 529
Locky (Mrs.) 529
Mellissa 529
Old Miss 528
Peggy 529
Phillip 529
Sena 528
Wyatt 529
Decatur, (?) (Mrs.) 374
Stephen (Cpt.) 374
Deer, John 309, 310
Degge, Dorothy (Mrs.)
561
John 561
Sarah (Mrs.) 561
Deiss, Anna Elisabeth
471
Matthew 471
DeJarnette, Jane B. 643
R. E. 6
R. E. (Mrs.) 6
Delander, Abraham 277
Delaware, (?) (Lord)
86, 353
Delp, (?) 302, 324
Adam 324
Conrad 331
Daniel 324, 332
Magd. (Mrs.) 331
Margaretha (Mrs.)
331
Michael 331
Rebecca 301, 324, 325
Susanna 302
Delpin, Rebecca 324,
332
Demby, Mary (Mrs.) 367

Demuth, Henry 475
Jacob 475
Margaret (Mrs.) 475
Denby, Anne 367
Edwd. 367
Denison, Caroline Bowman
(Mrs.) 365
George 365
Henry M. (Rev.) 365
Henry Mandeville (Rev.)
365
Denning, Fanny Mary 667
Jane Hester 667
Dennis, Donock 396
Elizabeth 539
George Robertson (Dr.)
1
Henry 277
Denny, Alexander P. L.
(Dr.) 176
Cynthia 611
Edward 611
James 611
James W. 611, 612
Mary (Polly) 611
Dent, John Herbert (Cpt.)
176
Denwood, Mary 391
Depp, Eleanor 139
Derbigny, Austin 155
Derrick, Behethland 260
Benjamin 260, 273
Elizabeth 263
Francis (Mrs.) 277
Katherine (Mrs.) 260
Matthew 277
Deschler, Abr. G. (Rev.)
478
Abraham G. (Rev.) 478
Ann Maria 489
Gottlieb Abraham
(Rev.) 478
Deshler, Gottlieb
Abraham (Rev.) 484
Devany, Aaron 649
Dexter, Samuel 374
Dice, Anna Elisabeth 471
Matthew 471
Dick, William 374
Dickonson, James 374
John 593
Mary (Mrs.) 374
Dickerson, Crispin 529
Ja. 135
James 135
Nancy 533
Nancy Roscow 135
Susan 534
Susanna Robinson 135
Dickeson, Ja. Cole 130
Jo. 130
Dickinson, J. F. (Gen.)
176
William 158
Wm. 176
Dickson, Beverley 254
Beverley (Jr.) 150
Henry 374
John 374
Mary (Mrs.) 374
William 374
Diether, Anna Barbara
488
Dietrick, Anna Barbara
488
Digge, Dorothy (Mrs.)
561
John 561

Digges, (?) 425, 580,
660
Alice Grymes (Mrs.)
570
Ann 582
Charles 234
Cole 227, 244, 424,
425
Dudley 88, 231, 249,
570
Dudley (Sir) 582
Edward 582
Edward (Col.) 227,
659
Elizabeth (Mrs.) 659
Lucy Brooke 659
Mary 424
Patty 249
Sarah 659
Susanna 227
Thomas 205
Thomas (Maj.) 659
William 234
Diggs, Cole 580
Edward 747
Elizabeth (Mrs.) 747
Martha C. 176
Mary 580
Porcia 747
Thomas 115
Dillard, James (Jr.)
241
L. (Dr.) 176
Lynch 529
Mildred (Mrs.) 176
Milly Ward (Mrs.) 529
Dillon, Thomas 252
Dindore, (?) (Widow) 491
Dipp, Eleanor 139
Dishman, (?) 90
Dixon, (?) 80, 108, 735
Anna 55
Anne 334
Anthony Tucker 161
Beverly 243
Edward (Cpt.) 248,
573
Elizabeth 57
Elizabeth (Mrs.) 55,
57, 79
George 374
Harry 573
John 57, 78, 79, 80,
108, 155, 161, 235,
244, 334, 735
John (Col.) 495
John (Dr.) 79
John (Rev.) 53, 334
Lucy 53
Lucy (Mrs.) 53, 78,
334
Moses 176
Rober 334
Rosanna (Mrs.) 495
Sarah (Mrs.) 161
Thomas 53, 334, 573
Thomas (Cpt.) 57
Turner 573
William 53, 55, 57
Dixson, Benjamin 529
Berry 529
Bluford 529
Frances (Mrs.) 529
George 529
Ginsey 529
Hezekiah 529
Jack 529
James 529

779

Fey (cont.)
  Charles 473
  Dorothy (Mrs.) 473
  John 481
  Susanna (Mrs.) 481
ffausett, John 396
ffenn, Andrew 396
fflybrass, Anne 396
ffoxcroft, Isaac (Lt.)
  396
ffreman, Elizabeth 396
Ffurs, Ann 390
  John 390
  Mary (Mrs.) 390
Ficklin, Benjamine 164
Field, John (Col.) 702
  Lewis 702
  Mary 295
  Mildred 702
  Susan (Mrs.) 155
  Thomas 155
Fielding, Ambrose 403
  Ann 403
  Edward 403
  Rachel 403
  Richard 403
  Sarah 403
  Thomas 403
Fields, Robert 375
Finch, Catherine 57
  Jane 85
  Thomas (Sir) 85
Fincksin, Elisabetha 332
Finder, Barbara 473
  Barbara (Mrs.) 473
  Martin 473
Finks, (?) 308
  Catharine 308
  Catherine 307, 308
  Christina 299, 300
  Elizabeth 299
  Elizabetha 302, 303
  Mary 299, 300, 303,
    308
Finley, Polly (Mrs.)
  685
Finnie, Alex. (Rev.) 517
  Alexander 234
  Alexander (Rev.) 518
  Jane 247
  Joanna (Mrs.) 247
  John Austin 517
  Nancy 250
  William (Col.) 156,
    242
Fischborn, Anna
    Catherine (Mrs.) 475
  Philip 475
Fischer, Adam 320, 321
  Bernard 329
  Bernhard 329
  Bernhardt 332
  Eva (Mrs.) 332
  Magdalina (Mrs.) 331
  Stephan 314, 325, 330
  Stephen 304, 331
Fischerin, Anna Barbara
    332
  Elisabetha 320, 332
  Eva 329
  Magd. 329, 330
  Magdalina 304
  Maria 314, 325
Fischers, (?) 305, 315
Fishback, Anna 322
  John Frederick 322
Fishburn, Anna Catherine
    (Mrs.) 475

Fishburn (cont.)
  Philip 475
Fisher, Henry C. 753
  Joseph 145
  Maddox 2
  Robert 177
  Robert (Dr.) 375
  Rose 2
Fisk, (?) 384
Fitzgerald, Edward 177
  Peter 138
Fitzhugh, (?) 659
  Alice (Mrs.) 747
  Ann (Mrs.) 522
  Ann Barbara (Mrs.)
    282
  Ann D. 747
  Ann H(arrison) 747
  Ann H. 659
  Ann Harrison 661
  Ann R. 747
  Anna Barbara (Mrs.)
    281
  Anna Harrison 659
  Anne 268, 282
  Anne Barbara (Mrs.)
    268
  Barbara 227, 268
  Barbara (Mrs.) 268, 281
  Betty 268, 286
  Cole 660
  Daniel 268, 269, 282,
    285, 747
  Dudley 659, 660
  Edward 747
  Edward D. 660
  Edward H. 660
  Elicabeth 264, 268,
    269, 283, 286
  Elizabeth (Mrs.) 495
  Elizabeth C. 747
  Elizabeth Cole 660,
    661
  George 57, 268, 284,
    659, 747
  George (Jr.) 747
  George (Mrs.) 747
  Henry 268, 269, 281,
    285, 287, 425, 659,
    747
  Henry (Col.) 268, 282,
    284, 659
  Henry (Cpt.) 282, 283
  Jane 267, 269
  John 268, 269, 281,
    286, 495, 659
  John (Maj.) 227, 268,
    281, 282
  Lettice 522
  Lucy 268, 269, 283
  Lucy (Mrs.) 268, 282,
    283
  Lucy Brooke (Mrs.) 659
  Maria 660
  Mary 747
  Mary (Mrs.) 747
  Mordica 747
  Nicholas Battaile 268,
    285
  Philip 268
  Sarah 258, 264, 268,
    269, 281, 286, 660,
    747
  Sarah (Mrs.) 268, 284,
    285, 659, 747
  Sarah B. 660
  Susanna 264, 269, 282

Fitzhugh (cont.)
  Susanna (Mrs.) 268,
    281, 282, 283
  Susannah 267, 268,
    269
  Theoderick 285
  Theodorick 268
  Thomas 268, 281, 285,
    286, 747
  Thomas (Jdg.) 599
  Thomas Knox 747
  Thomas L. 660
  Thos. 659
  Ursula (Mrs.) 268,
    284, 285
  William 252, 268, 281,
    283, 284, 285, 522,
    659, 747
  William Beverley 268
  William Beverly 284
  Wm. 285, 659
Fitzpatrick, Ben. 126
  Constantine Perkins
    126
  Eliz. 125
Fitzwhylson, (?) 251
Fuller, Bartholomew
    178
  James 178
Fulton, Alexander 178
  Elizabeth (Mrs.) 460
  James 460
  John H. 593
Fultz, Catharine (Mrs.)
    472
  George 472
Funck, Catharine (Mrs.)
    469
  Margaret 469
  Peter 469
Funk, Catharine (Mrs.)
    469
  Margaret 469
  Peter 469
Fushee, James 403
  John 403
  Sopha 403
Gaar, (?) 321
  Abraham 311, 329
  Adam 331
  Aron 329
  Benjamin 323, 329
  Catha (Mrs.) 321
  Catharine (Mrs.) 310
  Diana 329
  Diana (Mrs.) 311
  Elisabetha 304, 329
  Elisabetha (Mrs.) 331
  Elizabeth 321
  Elizabeth (Mrs.) 305
  Elizabeth Barbara
    322
  Felix 329
  Johannes 320, 329, 331
  John 320, 329
  John Adam 329, 330
  Leanna 318, 329
  Lorenz 329
  Ludwig 321
  Magd. 330
  Margaret 329
  Margaretha (Mrs.) 331
  Mary Magdalene 325
  Michael 304, 305,
    314, 315, 321, 322,
    329, 331
  Rosanna 329
  Rosina 305, 321, 322

Gaar (cont.)
  Susanna 329
Gaarin, Catharina 311
  Catharine 310
  Elisabeth 326
  Elisabetha 314
  Margaret 323
  Margaretha 320
Gabriel, (?) 499
Gadsden, Christopher
    (Gen.) 375
Gage, Alice (Mrs.) 178
  Arnold 178
Gahr, Michael 322
Gaines, Frances 421
  Harry (Maj.) 230, 320
  Sarah (Mrs.) 421
Gairdner, George 154
Gall, Catherine 488
Gallego, (?) 179
  (?) (Mrs.) 375
Gallet, Anna Maria 468
Gallohough, James 505
Gallon, John 618
Gallow, John 618
Galt, Gabriel 150, 494
  John M. 161, 243
  John M. (Cpt.) 375
  John M. (Dr.) 375
Gamble, Charlotte S.
    (Mrs.) 166, 375
  John 375
  Robert 163, 375
  Robt. 166
Gannell, Helen 335
  S. N. 335
  S. W. 335
Gantier, Francis (Mrs.)
    157
Gardner, Elizabeth
    (Mrs.) 178
  Freeman (Cpt.) 375
  William (Cpt.) 375
  Wm. 163
Garland, Barbara 139
  John 118
  Mary 117
Garnett, James I. 636
  Marie (Mrs.) 636
  Muscoe 157
  Reuben 635, 636
Garr, (?) 297, 298, 301,
    304, 305, 306, 309,
    310, 311, 314, 316,
    318, 321, 322, 323,
    325, 329
  Aaron 309
  Benjamin 298
  Dinah (Mrs.) 311
  George 309
  John C. 297
  Louis 310
  Peter 309
Garrell, Thomas 396
Garret, Susanna 133
Garrett, Anne 277
Garriott, Anna Catherine
    487
  Samuel 487
  Sarah (Mrs.) 487
Garton, Eliz 116
Gary, Wm. 165
Gaskins, Ann (Mrs.) 436
  Eliza 403
  Francis 403
  Isaac 403
  Jesse 413
  Jessie 403

Gaskins (cont.)
  John 403, 436
  Thomas 403
  William 436
Gaskinshull, Thomas 741
Gast, Peggy (Mrs.) 495
  Peter 495
Gaston, Hannah (Mrs.)
    375
  William 375
Gates, (?) (Gen.) 250
  Robert 250
Gatewood, (?) (Mrs.)
    375
  Ann (Mrs.) 375
  Philemon 375
  Sally 375
  Thomas 375
Gathright, Elizabeth
    705
Gautier, Frances (Mrs.)
    159
Gay, Betty 122
  Charles C. 163
  Elizabeth 119, 121
Gayle, John 496
Geddy, Elizabeth (Mrs.)
    44
  James 239
  Nancy 239
Gee, Henry 514
  James 517, 633
  James (Cpt.) 514
  James Henry 633
  John 517
  Lovinia N. 633
  Mary (Mrs.) 633
  Sarah 518
  William Henry 633
Geiger, Adam 473
  Anna Elisabeth 481
  Anna Maria 479
  Barbara (Mrs.) 486
  Catherine 486
  Catherine (Mrs.) 486
  Christian 467, 473,
    479, 480, 484, 486,
    488, 490, 491
  Christian (Sr.) 491
  Emilie 491
  Frederick 481, 482,
    488, 490
  Jacob 488
  John Peter 480
  Lydia 484
  Margaret 488
  Margaret (Mrs.) 473,
    479
  Susanna 490
  William 488, 489
Gemison, William 257
Genszle, (?) 317
Gentry, Eliz. 126
Geoghegan, Martha (Mrs.)
    178
George, Alexander 160
  Annie (Mrs.) 530
  Ceilie 529, 530
  Ceilie (Mrs.) 529,
    530
  Cornelius 530
  Cornelius M. 529
  Cumberland 692
  Edney 530
  Elizabeth 530
  Ellis 530
  Hugh 529, 530
  James H. 529

George (cont.)
  John 529
  Martha W. 530
  Mary 529
  Mildred 529, 530
  Nolen 530
  Sally 530
  William 530
Geradine, (?) (Mrs.) 651
Gerard, (?) (Mrs.) 375
Gerber, (?) 320
  Christoph 319, 320
  Christopher 315, 320
  Dorothea 316
  Elisabetha 319
  Freiderich 324
  Friederich 315, 316,
    319, 320
  Jacob 315, 316, 320
  Jemima 319
  Magdalen 320
  Margaretha 319
  Maria 315, 316, 319,
    320
  Maria (Mrs.) 319
  Mary 315
  Moses 319
  Nelly 319
  William 319
Gerberin, Dorothea 315
  Dorothy (Mrs.) 316
  Jacob 316
Geret, Anna Catherine
    487
  Samuel 487
  Sarah (Mrs.) 487
Gerrand, Mary 114
Geruss, Augustin 490
Geyger, Christian 477
  John 477
  Margaret (Mrs.) 477
Gholson, Thos. 165
Gibbon, James (Col.) 592
  James (Lt.) 375
  James (Maj.) 592
Gibbons, Ann (Mrs.) 375
  Hannah 272
  Thomas 375
  Thomas (Cpt.) 375
Gibbs, Hanna R. H.
    (Mrs.) 460
  Isabella 460
  John 9
  John C. (Dr.) 178
  Matthew 514
  Richard 460
  Thos. 164
  William Allen 460
Giberne, Wm. (Rev.) 697
Gibson, (?) (Mrs.) 375
  Francis 13
  Gibby 13
  Jonathn. 696
  Robert 376
  Thomas 13, 206
  William 178
  Wm. H. 178
Giese, Frederick Henry
    (Rev.) 478, 484
Giffen, James F. 746
Giffin, Louise Elizabeth
    Wallis 746
  Thomas 296
Gilbert, Eliz 114
  Revnear 376
Gilchrist, Catherine
    (Mrs.) 6
  Robert 6, 7

Goodwyn, Albert T. 48
  Albert Thweatt 48
  Amey Eppes 47
  Eliza H. 48
  Elizabeth (Mrs.) 47
  Martha T. (Mrs.) 48
  Peterson 48
  Peterson (Col.) 47, 48
  Rebecca 145
Googe, Claiborn 133
  Unie 133
Gooseley, George 153
  Mary (Mrs.) 153
Goosley, Cary 240
Gordon, (?) 23, 25, 496
  Alexander 24
  Anne 274
  Armistead C. 23
  Armistead C. (Dr.) 23
  David 24, 41
  Elizabeth 23, 24
  Elizabeth (Mrs.) 660,
    661
  Elizabeth C. 660
  Elizabeth C. (Mrs.)
    660
  Elizabeth Cole 661
  Elizabeth Cole Fitzhugh
    660
  Elizabeth Jane (Mrs)
    661
  Eloise 710
  George 23, 24
  Griffin 660
  I. Carr 376
  Jack 23
  James 24, 115, 156,
    659, 660, 661
  James (Col.) 23, 231
  James (Sir) 24
  James McCreary 660
  John 23, 56, 110,
    659, 660, 661
  Lucy 118
  Lucy (Mrs.) 659
  Lucy A. H. 661
  Lucy Ann 660
  Lucy Ann Harrison
    660
  Magdalen 24
  Maria 660
  Marjorie 24
  Martha (Mrs.) 156
  Mary 56
  Mary Jane (Mrs.) 660,
    661
  Patrick 24
  Peter 23
  Sally 660
  Samuel 24, 41, 236,
    659, 660, 661
  Samuel (Sr.) 661
  Samuel D. 661
  Samuel Douglas 661
  Sarah (Mrs.) 496
  Sarah Digges 660
  Thomas G. 660
  Thomas Griffin 661
  Thomas Griffin
    Thornton 660
  William 23, 24
  William F. 660
  Wm. F. 660, 661
  Wm. Fitzhugh 660, 661
Gorthan, John 396
Gossling, Mary 257
Gouge, Ann 556
  William (Col.) 556

Gough, Pumphrey 133
  Rolling 133
Goulding, Ann (Mrs.)
    376
  Daniel 376
Gowel, (?) (Mrs.) 179
  Christian 179
Gower, Ann (Mrs.) 434,
    450
  Easter (Mrs.) 434
  Esther (Mrs.) 450
  Frances 435, 450
  Francis 434, 435, 450
  John 434, 450
  Katharine 434
  Katherine 434, 450
  Rachel 441
  Rachel (Mrs.) 435, 450
  Sarah (Mrs.) 434, 450
  Standley 434
  Stanley 450
  Susanna 435
  Susannah 450
  Winifred 435
  Winnefred 450
Graham, (?) 665
  (?) (Col.) 662
  Caroline H. 703
  Elizabeth M. A. B.
    (Mrs.) 703
  George 703
  George Mason 703
  John 86, 703
  Mary 86
  Mary Ann Jane 703
  Richard 703
  Robert 179
  William 242
Grammer, Julianna S.
    P. (Mrs.) 179
Granberry, (?) (Mrs.)
    384
Granbery, George 376
  John 376
Granger, Gideon 179
  Jane (Mrs.) 390, 395
  John 395
  Lettuce 390
  Nicholas 390, 395
Grant, Alexander 109
  James 262
  James (Col.) 179
  Mary 277
Grantham, Uriah 179
Grantland, John 179
Grason, James 114
Gravat, Behethland 260
  Behethland (Mrs.) 260
  John 256, 260
  Ursula 260
Graves, Dolly 529
  John 530
  Josel 118
  Mary 113, 124, 128
  Nancy 306, 307
  Peyton 530
  Ralph 119
  Sally 114, 119
  Sarah 118
  Susanna 133
  Thomas 530
  Washington 530
Gravina (?) (Mrs.) 179
  Henry 179
Gray, (?) 661, 664
  Anne 661
  Arthur 351
  Arthur (Rev.) 289

Gray (cont.)
  Edwin 662
  Elizabeth 661
  Elizabeth (Mrs.) 179,
    351
  George Lewis 376
  Henry 139, 162, 205
  James 662
  Jane 662, 663
  John 396, 661
  Joseph 661, 662, 664
  Katherine S. 709
  Laura (Mrs.) 659
  Lucy 662
  Mary 661, 662, 664
  Mary Carter 557
  Nathaniel 268
  Peter 662
  Phebe (Mrs.) 162, 205
  Sarah 661, 662
  T. B. W. (Dr.) 557
  William 179, 361, 661
  Wm. 496
Grayson, (?) 662
  (?) (Mrs.) 134
  Wm. 495
Green, (?) 376, 666
  Amy 713
  Calbin 658
  Eliz. (Mrs.) 666
  Eliza Eperson 666
  Eliza Epperson 742
  Eliza. (Mrs.) 666
  Elizabeth (Mrs.) 158,
    179, 666
  Franky 743
  Grief 666
  Grief (Col.) 666, 742
  Henry 666
  Horace 713
  J. T. 179
  James W. 709
  John 179
  Joseph 179
  Marshall 666
  Marston 666
  Mary 666
  Robert 117
  Signora 666
  Thomas 666
  Thomas C. 709
  William 179, 254
Greenhow, (?) (Mrs.)
    651
  John 150, 254
  Robert 376
Greenup, Catherine S.
    (Mrs.) 160
  Chas. 160
Greenway, (?) 209
Gregory, Christina 353
  Fendall 645
  Frances 718
  James 119
  Mary (Mrs.) 238
  Roger 236, 238
  William 119, 241
Greig, (?) (Adm.) 494
  Archibald (Cpt.) 494
  James 179
Grendon, Thos. (Jr.) 21
Gresham, Ann (Mrs.) 158
  Anne (Mrs.) 179
  Burwell 205
  William 158, 179
Grey, ffrancis (Cpt.) 10
  James 390
  Katharine (Mrs.) 390

786

Hull (cont.)
Richard 404, 406, 407
Richard (Col.) 241
Richard (Jr.) 404
Sarah 404, 407
Thomas 406
William 404
Huls, (?) (Mrs.) 677
Polly 677
Humble, Michael 611,
612
Nancy 612
Hume, John 308
Sallie 308
Humphreys, (?) 5
David Carlisle 5
Margaret Finley 5
Rebecca 5
Humphries, Catherine 277
Joseph 277
Humston, William 277
Hundley, Berry R. 530
Christopher (Francis)
530
Dorcus (Mrs.) 530
Eliza Jane 530
Jesse S. 530
John 530
John B. 530
Joseph 530
Mary 530
Nancy 530
Susannah 530
William W. 530
Wyett 530
Hungerford, John P. 591
Thomas 265, 270
Hunley, Letitia 56
Hunt, Archer 607
Jeremiah 181
William 13, 14
William (Sr.) 13
Hunter, Ariana 377
Edward R. (Dr.) 377
Juliett E. 756
Margaret (Mrs.) 149,
150
Miles 150
Robert B. 377
Sally (Mrs.) 377
Hunton, James 181
Hurd, Thomas 429, 430
Hurdly, Susanna 277
Hurley, Edward 182
Hurt, Nancy 530
Rebecca 124, 125, 126
Sally 533
Hutchings, Ann (Mrs.)
377
Hutchins, Marian 713
Hutchison, Elizabeth
141, 142
George 191, 530
Hutson, David 118
Lucy 534
Hutter, Ernestine 711
Hutton, Eliza Woodside
(Mrs.) 182
Henry I. 431
James 182
Hyde, Benjamin 514
Mary (Mrs.) 514
I'Anson, Chs. Thomas
752
John (Dr.) 751
Mary 751
Mary (Mrs.) 752
Thomas 751

Inglish, Wm. 217
Ingersol, Jared 182
Ijams, Joshua M. 634
Isaacs, Isaiah 159
Irvine, Walter 160
Ingersol, Jared 182
Inglis, Mungo 74
Inglish, Dianah (Mrs.)
217
Wm. 217
Innis, Hugh 239
James 255
Irvine, Walter 160
Isaacs, Isaiah 159
Isabel, Ann 117
Susannah 128
Isham, (?) 726
Henry 9
Ishan, Daniel 390
Ishonn, Daniel 396
Izard, George (Gen.) 221
Jackson, (?) (Prs.) 591
Anna 87
George Charles 479
Lewis Marshall 702
Margaret (Mrs.) 479
Richard 182
Sarah 479
Thomas 463
Wm. 479
Wm. A. 702
Jacob, Ann (Mrs.) 388
Mary 539
Mary (Mrs.) 395
Richard 395, 539
Robert (Col.) 377
Robert C. 388
Jacobs, Allen 531
Claborn 531
Elisha 531
Elizabeth 377
Henry 531
Henry (Mrs.) 531
Hollens 531
Joseph 377
James, Alfred 182
Edward W. 367
Fleming 182
John 256
L(---) 395
Maria Ferrill 182
Rebecca Minor 182
Robert B. 162
Thruston (Maj.) 249
Jameson, (?) (Mrs.) 236
David (Col.) 500, 596
Edmund 159
Edmund (Mrs.) 159
Mary (Mrs.) 500
Sarah 277
Thomas 235, 236
Jamis, ffrances 396
Jamison, Andrew 111
Janney, Israel 182
Jaquelin, Edward 226
Molly 226
Jarratt, D. (Rev.) 49
Devereux (Rev.) 48,
49, 361
Martha (Mrs.) 49
Jarrett, Agnes 109
Jarvis, (?) 62
Lindsay 57
Jeffers, Dominick 44
Edward 44
John (Cpt.) 44
Jefferson, (?) 209
Cintha 531

Jefferson (cont.)
Elizabeth 531
Fanny 531
James (?) 674
Mortha 124, 125, 126,
127, 103, 182, 594
Mary 120, 121, 123,
124, 125, 127
Moses 674
Nancy (Mrs.) 674
Samuel (Cpt.) 531
Thomas 239, 594
Jeffries, Cornelia 654
Mary A. 654
Nanie 654
Octavius 653
Thomas 158
William A. 654
Jeffryes, Herbert (Col.)
430
Jenings, Ann 440
Edmund 88
Jenkins, Howard M. 640
Jacob 182
John 182
Jennings, Ann 459
Charles 587, 588
D. A. 700
Edmund 88
Edmund (Sir) 88
Jane (Mrs.) 587
Oscar 547
Robert 159
Sarah (Mrs.) 377
William 547, 588
Jerdone, Ann 292
Barbara (Mrs.) 291
Francis 237, 291,
292
Francis (Jr.) 291
Isabella 292
James 291, 292
John 291
Maria Ann Glanville
(Mrs.) 291
Mary 292
Mary (Mrs.) 291
Sarah 292
Sarah (Mrs.) 291
William 291, 292
Jerrat, Devreux 115
Jerrod, (?) (Mrs.) 377
Jervis, Ann (Mrs.) 54,
55, 56
Bannister 54
Betty 54
Edward 54
Elizabeth 55, 56, 57
Elizabeth (Mrs.) 53,
54, 55
Francis 53, 54, 55,
56, 57
Gawin 55
James 56
John 53, 54, 55, 56,
58
John Dixon 55
Lindsay 55
Lucy (Mrs.) 53, 54,
55, 56
Mary 53
Mary (Mrs.) 56, 58
Patty Reade 55
Sally (Mrs.) 55
Sarah (Mrs.) 53
Thomas 53
Thomas William 53
William 53, 54, 55, 56

793

Lingel, Anna Catherine
  (Mrs.) 472
  Barbara (Mrs.) 473
  Catharine 471
  Catherine 490
  Catherine (Mrs.) 476
  Jacob 467, 476
  John 473
  Margaret 479
  Paul 472
  Philip 473
Lingoe, Elizabeth 396
Linticum, Edward 531
  Elizabeth 532, 534
  Henry 531
  William 531
Lipin, Maria 315
Lips, (?) 330
Lipscomb, (?) 90, 295
  Ambrose 256
  Reuben 721
  Thomas U. 716
Lipscombe, Bernard
  (Cpt.) 185
  Roscow 153
Liptrott, John 70
Lithgow, Wm. 165
Little, Hannah 262
Littledale, Joseph 34
Littlepage, (?) 359,
  361, 379
  Elizabeth 546
  Fanny 239
  Frances (Mrs.) 359
  J. B. 159
  Judith 359
  Lewis 151
  Lewis (Gen.) 500
  Richard 358, 546
  Richard (Cpt.) 359
  Sarah (Mrs.) 358
Littleton, (?) (Col.)
  232
  Edw. 391
  Sarah 538
  Southy (Col.) 538
Livingston, Aliba 168
  Anne (Mrs.) 379
  Brackholst 185
  Chancellor 168
  John 158, 185
  John (Cpt.) 379
  Justice (Dr.) 245
  Peter V. B. (Jr.) 149
Lloyd, (?) 303
  Edward 231
Loadwick, Elizabeth 711
Lockhart, Mary (Mrs.)
  185
Loevenstein, Conrad
  467
Lofborough, Hannah 639
Loftis, Frances 112
Logan, (?) 5
  John 5
  Mary (Mrs.) 165
Lomax, Eliz. 110
  John 150, 252
  Lunsford 155, 240
London, John James 350
Long, Ann 390
  Anna Catharine 470
  Daniel 390
  Eliza (Mrs.) 390
  Henry 470
  Lucy 116
  Philip 483, 491
  William 467

Longo, Mary 391
Longworth, Millisent 458
Lord, William 258
Lorentz, Margaret 468
Loretz, Andrew 492
  Andrew (Jr.) 492
Love, Alexander 379
  Ira D. 185
  Jane (Mrs.) 495
Lovel, Samuel 531
Lovell, Samuel 531
Lovett, John 379
Lowell, William 278
Lownes, Jane (Mrs.) 185
Lowry, Ann 379
  William 379
Loyall, (?) (Mrs.) 379
  George 379
  Paul 379
Lucas, Edmund (Cpt.) 379
  Walter 10
  Wm. 10
Lucie, (?) (Mrs.) 630
Luck, Samuel 717
Lucke, Christian 481
  Elizabeth (Mrs.) 481
Luddington, Hanna 396
  Robt. 392
Ludlow, Annie L. 682
  Augustus C. (Lt.) 379
Ludlowe, Gabriel 290
  Sarah 290
Ludwell, Lucy 342
  Philip 71, 226, 230,
    342, 430, 505
  Philip (Col.) 71
  Philip (Sr.) 539
  Thomas 20
Luecke, Christian 481,
  482
  Elisabeth 482
  Elizabeth 490
  John Henry 481
Lugg, John (Rev.) 185
Lun, Elizabeth 282
Lund, Elizabeth 258,
  264, 270
  Frances 278
  Frances (Mrs.) 259
Lung, Philip 483
Lunsford, Alexr. 408
  Thomas (Sir) 86
  William 408
Lusk, Martha V. 460
  Mary 461
  Patsy 461
  Sallie 461
  William 461
Luttrell, (?) 689, 691
  B. E. 690
  B. M. 692
  B. Mortimer 693
  Burrell 689, 690
  Burrell E. 689, 690
  Burrell Edmund 689
  Burrell Edward 690
  Burrell M. 692
  C. J. 692
  Capitol L. 690
  Charles 690
  Cora J. 692
  Elizabeth Rachel 689
  Frances (Mrs.) 689
  Hannah 653, 689
  Hannah (Mrs.) 689,
    690
  Hannah B. 692
  Hannah Button 689

Luttrell (cont.)
  James W. 689
  John W. 652, 654, 689,
    691, 692, 693
  John Willis 652, 692
  Julia Francis 690
  Juliett Ann 689
  L. M. 692
  Lucie A. 690
  Lucie Marie 690
  Lucie Mary 690
  Lucy Ann 690
  Mary (Mrs.) 689
  Mary E. (Mrs.) 690
  Mary Elizabeth 690
  Mary Elizabeth (Mrs.)
    690
  Mary L. 692
  Mary Ritchie (Mrs.)
    690
  Mitcham 653
  Mitcham C. 692, 693
  Mortimer 653
  Richard 689, 690
  Richard T. 653
  Sallie A. 692
  Sally 689
  Sarah (Mrs.) 689
  Sarah Ann 653
  Sarah E. 652, 654,
    693
Lygon, Margaret (Mrs.)
  656
  William 656
Lyle, James 379
  James (Jr.) 159
Lyles, Anne (Mrs.) 379
  William Henry 379
Lyman, Elihu (Maj.) 185
Lynch, Frances (Mrs.)
  154
  Francis 185
  Hastings 154
  J. F. 185
  James Head 154
  John 185
Lyne, Wm. 162
Lyon, (?) (Mrs.) 242
  James (Dr.) 379
  Matthew 185
  Walter 242
Lyons, (?) (Jdg.) 211
  Judith (Mrs.) 152
  Peter 152, 165, 379
M'Call, James P. 185
M'Causland, Emily Jane
  379
  Marcus 379
M'Clurg, James (Dr.)
  379
  Walter 379
M'Collum, Samuel 185
M'Cormick, John 185
M'Coy, John 185
  Wm. (Gen.) 185
M'Craw, Mary G. 183
  Samuel 183
M'Credie, John 379
M'Dougal, Maria 379
M'Dowell, Jno. A. 185
M'Glassin, (?) (Maj.)
  185
M'Kenzie, Donald 186
  William 379
M'Kerlie, P. H. 738
M'Kinstry, John (Col.)
  186
M'Lein, Mary (Mrs.) 186

Muse (cont.)
 William T. 188
Mussteen, Shadrach
 (Rev.) 529
Mutler, Eliz. 110
Mutter, John 380
 Lucinda (Mrs.) 380
Myers, Elizabeth (Mrs.)
 188
 Moses 188
 Samuel 45
Myles, Alice 430
 John 430
Nadler, Christian 475
 Sebastian 475
 Sophia (Mrs.) 475
Nalle, Lucetta 295
 Martin 294
Napier, Booth 74, 134
 Booth (Jr.) 134
 Frances 74
 John 155
 Patrick 115
 Patrick (Dr.) 74
 Rene 112, 126
 Robert 74
 Sarah Garland 126
Narbes, (?) 322
 John 322
Narbow, (?) 20
Nash, Abner 149
 Agatha 454
 Agathy (Mrs.) 453
 Ann (Mrs.) 453
 Anne 447, 453
 Betty 411
 Betty (Mrs.) 454
 Caleb 369
 Eliza 453
 Elizabeth 454
 Esther (Mrs.) 273
 Fielding 408
 George 273, 411, 454
 Hanna 453
 Hannah 454
 Hannah (Mrs.) 454
 Jeremiah 454
 John 410, 411, 453,
  454
 Judith (Mrs.) 454
 Kerych 408
 Lucy (Mrs.) 411, 454
 Lydia Solley 369
 Mary (Mrs.) 410, 411,
  454
 Pitman 454
 Richard 453, 454
 Robert 273
 Sally 454
 Sarah (Mrs.) 369, 454
 Solomon 453
 Susanna 273
 Thaddeus 454
 Thomas 453
 Thos. 369
 William 410, 453,
  454
 Winifred 411
Nason, John 333
 Joyce 21
Naughton, Katherine 273
Naylor, (?) 555
 Elizabeth 273
 Leacy Ann 709
Neale, Abner 410
 Amey (Mrs.) 411
 Chro. 410
 Daniel 409

Neale (cont.)
 Elizabeth 411
 Hannah 409, 410
 James 411
 Jeane (Mrs.) 411
 John 411
 Judith 410
 Lucretia 409
 Martha (Mrs.) 411
 Mary 273
 Mary Griffin 411
 Mary Stachell 411
 Matthew 413
 Presley 411, 413
 Rebecca (Mrs.) 413
 Richard 411
 Sally Kenner 411
 Sarah 273
 Sarah Presley 411
 Shapleigh 410
 Susan (Mrs.) 411
 Thomas 411
 William 409, 411
Neaps, Anne 273
Nebulian, Elisa (Mrs.)
 394
 Elise 396
 Morice Matthews 394
 William Matthews 394
Neel, Abner 409, 410
 Christopher 409
 Chro. 409, 410
 Daniel 409, 410
 Hannah 410
 John 410
 Jon. 409
 Judith 410
 Lucke 410
 Mathew 409
 Nathan 409
 Peter 410
 Richard 409
 Rodham 409, 410
 Rodm. 409
 Shapleigh 410
 Wm. 409
Neele, Abner 410
 Mary 410
Neill, (?) 504
 Jean Harris 711
 John B. 711
 John Baldwin (Jr.)
  711
 Lewis 711
 William McDonald 711
Nelms, Abe 409
 Alice 409
 Ann 409
 Charles 409, 410
 Edw. Northern 410
 Eliz. 409
 Elizabeth 410
 Hannah 408
 Jeremiah 410
 John 408, 410
 Joshua 410
 Judith 409
 Lettie 410
 Lucretia 409
 Mary 408
 Moses 409
 Nansy 410
 Presley 410
 Richard 408, 409
 Richd. 408
 Samuel 408, 409
 Sarah 408, 410
 William 408, 409, 410

Nelms (cont.)
 Winifred 409
 Wm. 408, 409, 410
Nelson, (?) 73
 (?) (Gen.) 73
 Agnes 130
 Ann 136
 Catherine Griffin 136
 Catherine Winston 132
 Cleland (Rev.) 730
 Eleanor (Mrs.) 461
 Elizabeth 132, 136
 Frances Anderson 136
 Hephzibah 136
 Hugh 236
 Hugh (Col.) 569
 Hugh (Jdg.) 594
 Hugh Thomas 569
 James S. 461
 Jo. 130, 132, 136
 Jo. (Col.) 134, 136
 John 132, 136
 Jos. 132
 Joseph 132
 Judith (Mrs.) 569
 Judith Carter (Mrs.)
  569
 Lucy 570
 Lucy (Mrs.) 166, 571
 Lucy Eppes 136
 Maria 380
 Martha 653
 Mary 136
 Nathaniel 571
 Philip 136
 Rebecca Woodley 136
 Robert (Jdg.) 569,
  570
 S. B. B. (Mrs.) 671
 Samuel D. 461
 Sarah 132, 136
 Sarah Cary 714, 715
 Solmon Hughes 136
 Susan 570
 Thomas 89, 227, 228,
  569
 Thomas (Gen.) 569, 570
 Thomas (Gov.) 571
 Thos. (Gov.) 570
 William 73, 136, 151,
  160, 227, 236, 245
 William (Col.) 76
 William (Jr.) 236
Neselton, William 273
Nestor, George 380
Netherington, Elizabeth
 273
Neu, Eva 481
 Juliana (Mrs.) 481
 Nicholas 489
 Peter 481
Neville, John (Admiral)
 583
 Sarah 112
Nevins, David 273, 275
 Janet 273
 Janet (Mrs.) 273
 Mary 273
Nevison, (?) (Rev.) 234
Newble, Zachariah 273
Newman, Elizabeth 532
 James 273
 John 188
 Polly 532
Newport, Elizabeth 273
Newsum, William 384
Newton, (?) 550
 Agnes A. 552

806

807

Pratt, Margaret 267
  Mildred 264, 270
  Susanna 267
Precious, Matthew
  (Cpt.) 382
Preisch, August 475
  Augustin 467, 471, 475
  Augustin (Jr.) 467
  Conrad 467
  Elisabeth 475
  Elisabeth (Mrs.) 471,
    475
  Mary (Mrs.) 475
  Peter 479
Preiss, Adam 468
  Anna Catharine 468
  Anna Catharine (Mrs.)
    468
  Anna Maria 480
  Augustin 467, 468,
    488
  Catharine (Mrs.) 473
  Catherine 488
  Conrad 467, 480
  Daniel 468, 473
  Elisabeth 468, 480
  Frances 488
  Frederick 480
  Henry 468, 480
  Henry David 468
  Irene 489
  John Frederick 468
  Magdalene (Mrs.) 468
  Maria Catharine 468
  Maria Catherine 478
  Mary 488
  Michael 480
  Peter 480, 488
  Sarah 473
  Susanna 467
Prentis, Joseph 165
  Mary (Mrs.) 232
  William 232
  William (Cpt.) 190
Prescott, Mary 336
  Robert 336
Presly, (?) 415
Preston, (?) (Mrs.) 166
  Francis (Gen.) 593
  J. (Gen.) 166
  William C. 593
Prestridge, Thomasin 279
Prett, Catherine 488
Preuss, Anna Catherine
    (Mrs.) 478
  Augustin 481, 489
  Christina 481
  Conrad 481
  Frederick 478, 481
  John George 481
  John Peter 481
  Peter 481
  Sarah 478
Price, Adam 468
  Alexander Pope 155
  Ann (Mrs.) 149, 201
  Anna Catharine 468
  Anthony 263
  Augustin 467, 468,
    472
  Augustine 491
  Barbara (Mrs.) 568,
    569
  Barret 114
  Catherine (Mrs.) 382
  Conrad 467
  Elisabeth 468
  Elisabeth (Mrs.) 472

Price (cont.)
  Elisha 165
  Elizabeth T. (Mrs.)
    569
  ffrances (Mrs.) 395
  Henry 468, 480, 702
  Henry David 468
  J. D. (Rev.) 190
  James 151, 152
  James (Cpt.) 203
  James (Rev.) 382
  Jane 130, 131
  Jane (Mrs.) 161
  Jean Ballard 129
  John 139, 155, 161,
    201
  John (Cpt.) 159, 208
  John Fox 126
  John Frederick 468
  John L. 154
  John W. H. (Cpt.) 382
  Katie 127
  Leonard 114
  Magdalene (Mrs.) 468
  Maria Catharine 468
  Maria D. 568
  Martha 121
  Mary 258, 488
  Mary (Mrs.) 155, 159,
    190, 208
  Meredith 126, 127,
    129
  P. H. 568
  Peter 166, 480, 488
  Sarah D. 661
  Susanna 467
  Thomas 258, 569
  Thomas (Jr.) 569
  Thomas (Rev.) 56
  Thomas (Sr.) 568
  Walter 395
  Wilson 161
  Wm. 162
Prichard, A. M. 526, 652,
    689, 691, 692
Priddy, John 158, 190
  Margaret (Mrs.) 158,
    190
Pride, Nat. 713
  Thomas 190
Pringle, Henry 190
Prior, Henry (Mrs.) 701
Prisch, Anna Catherine
    (Mrs.) 478
  Anna Margaret (Mrs.)
    477
  Anna Maria 476, 478
  Augustin 476, 477,
    479
  Augustin (Jr.) 476,
    477, 478
  Augustine 491
  Barbara 476
  Catherine (Mrs.) 476,
    479
  Conrad 477, 479
  Elisabeth 479
  Elisabeth (Mrs.) 477,
    479
  Frederick 476, 478,
    479
  Juliana 479
  Margaret 477
  Margaret (Mrs.) 476,
    477, 478, 479
  Peter 477
  Sarah 478
Proby, Minson 382

Proby (cont.)
  Paul 382
Proctor, Will (Rev.)
    134
Prosser, John 157, 163,
    382
  Letitia (Mrs.) 148
  William 148
Proudfit, John 382
Proudlove, Pemberton
    279
Provoost, Samuel (Rev.)
    382
Pryor, (?) 76, 90
  (?) (Col.) 134
  Elizabeth 119
  J. 254
  James (Jdg.) 701
  James (Mrs.) 701
  John 119
  John (Maj.) 190
  Luke 125
  Margaret 76
  Martha 116, 130
  Mary 76
  Patty 120
  Rebecca 730
  Sally 114
  Sam 120
  Samuel 111, 120, 701
  Sarah 117
  Will 115, 120, 130,
    131
  Will (Cpt.) 119
  Will (Maj.) 121
  William 76, 125, 131
  William (Cpt.) 109,
    119
Pugh, Theophilus (Col.)
    228
Pullen, Peggy 532
  Thomas 532
Purcell, Charles 190
Purdie, (?) 76
  Alexander 235, 247,
    250
  James 250
Putnam, Rufus 190
Pynes, Frances (Mrs.)
    160
Quarles, (?) 721, 722,
    723, 724
  Aaron 722
  Ann 496
  Ann E. 723
  Ann Howell 723
  Anne Daingerfield 724
  Anne Dangerfield 725
  Bettie 720, 721
  Dorothy 721
  Dorothy (Mrs.) 720
  Eleanor Williamson
    723
  Ella Jane 724
  Frances West 723
  Francis 118
  Francis Edwin 723,
    724
  Francis West 722, 723
  George Bathurst
    Parkhill 723, 724,
    725
  Groege William 724
  H. W. 724, 725
  Henry 723
  Henry (Cpt.) 496
  Henry Francis 724
  Henry West 723, 724, 725

813

814

Ruffin (cont.)
  John (Col.) 244
  John (Jr.) 515
  Julian C. 630, 631
  Sterling 192
Rufsel(s), Janet (Mrs.)
  33
  Robert 33
Rufsels, Adam 33
  John-Adam 33
  Margaret 33
Ruh, Abraham 476, 478
  Jacob 478
  Margaret (Mrs.) 476,
  478
  Mary Magdalene 476
Runckel, Margaret 475
  Margaret (Mrs.) 475
  Peter 475
Runkel, John William
  (Rev.) 484
Runnels, Dabney 533
Rupert, Hebner (Mrs.)
  192
Rusch, Elizabeth 490
Rush, Anna Maria (Mrs.)
  479
  Benjamin (Dr.) 750
  Carl 470
  Catherine 490
  Charles 467, 468, 472
  Elisabeth (Mrs.) 472
  John 479, 491
  Maria Elisabeth (Mrs.)
  468, 470
Russell, Alexander 382
  Armistead 248
  Charles H. 1
  George W. (Cpt.) 382
  Janet (Mrs.) 156
  Mary 505
  Will. 252
  William 395, 505
Rust, Ann 455
  Benjamin 455
  Eleanor 455
  James 455
  John 455
  Metcalfe 455
  Nancy (Mrs.) 455
  Samuel 455
  Sarah 455
  Sarah (Mrs.) 455
Rutherford, (?) 23
  John (Sir) 23
Ryan, Andrew (Mrs.) 192
  Ann 123, 124
  John M. 158, 192
Ryding, Thomas 396
Ryer, Catherine 491
  Elisabeth 483
  Peter 483, 491
  Philip 483
Ryling, (?) 396
Sabella, Isabella 99
Sackrider, (?) (Dr.) 163
  Mary (Mrs.) 163
Saffell, (?) 725
Sale, (?) (Rev.) 645
Sallard, Ann (Mrs.) 559
  Charles 559
  Simon 559
Salle, Abraham 109
Salter, Ann (Mrs.) 216,
  217
  Edward 216
  Mary 216
  Sarah 216

Salter (cont.)
  Thomas 217
  William 216, 247
  Willm. 216
  Wm. 217
Samford, Samuel 418
Sampson, Ann 136, 143
  Eliz. 136
  Elizabeth 142
  Ezra (Rev.) 192
  James Johnson 136
  Jean 136
  Judith 143
  Old Stephen 136
  Richard 114
  Sarah 136, 141
  Stephen 108, 136, 138,
  141, 142, 143, 144
  Stephen (Old) 136
  Stephen (Sr.) 140
  Will 136
  William 144
Samuels, Frances (Mrs.)
  164
  Wm. 701
Sanders, Doctor 533
  James 391, 395
  Mary 391
  Presley 192
  Richard 395
  Virlinda (Mrs.) 391,
  395
Sanderson, Martha 462
Sandman, Catharina 323
Sandys, George 85
  Margaret 85
  Samuel (Sir) 85
Sanford, (?) 608
  Burr 608
  Elizabeth 608
  Jeremiah 608
  Mary 439, 459
  Priscilla (Mrs.) 608
  Vincent 608
Sansum, Sarah 117, 132
Sargeant, William Hill
  382
Stachell, Charles S. 383
Satterthwait, Joseph
  Wallace 637
Saunders, (?) 634
  Ann Madison 635
  Anna Hill 636
  Benj. 128
  Clayburn 118
  Emily Jones 635
  John 124, 128
  John (Maj.) 383
  John Jones 635
  Judith (Mrs.) 165
  Julius 118
  Lavinia Jones 635
  Lewis 383
  Lucinda Jones 635
  Lucy Waller 634, 635
  Marianne (Mrs.) 166
  Marie Walker 635
  Mary 124
  Mary (Mrs.) 162, 165
  Mary Walker 635
  Polly 243
  Reuben 635
  Reuben Walter Raleigh
  636
  Robert H. 162
  Sarah 635
  Sarah (Mrs.) 634, 635,
  636

Saunders (cont.)
  Sarah Ann Elizabeth
  636
  Susan Frances 636
  William (Col.) 634,
  635, 636
  William Alexander 635,
  636
Saurbier, Anthony 486
  Catherine (Mrs.) 486
  William 486
Savage, (?) 387
  Ann B. (Mrs.) 365
  Dorothy 396
  Elizabeth 1
  Geo. Thomas 388
  George 234
  John 391
  John (Maj.) 388
  Leah (Mrs.) 388
  Littleton 387
  Littleton (Col.) 383,
  388
  Margaret (Mrs.) 387
  Mary 388
  Mary (Mrs.) 388
  Mary William 365
  Nathaniel Littleton
  362 -
  Thomas 387
  Thomas Littleton 388
  William 365
Sawyer, Joseph 215
  Joshua 273
  Willm. 215
Sayre, Jane (Mrs.) 339
  Samuel Wm. 339
Sayus, Voncile B. 673
Scaife, John 223
Scallion, William 383
Scarborough, Edward K.
  383
Scarbrough, Edmund (Col.)
  3
  Tabitha 3
Scarbrugh, (?) (Col.) 3
  Charles (Sir) 540, 541
  Edmund 226, 541
  Edmund (Col.) 540
  Matilda 540
  Mitchell 561
  William 540
Scarlett, (?) 431
  Martin 431
Schaefer, Elizabeth 489
  George 488, 490, 491
  George (Jr.) 488
  Jacob 483, 488, 491
  John 467, 483
  John Michael 489
  Mary (Mrs.) 483
  Michael 488
  Philip 488, 490, 491
  Sarah 489
  Susanna 488, 489
Schaeffer, George 473
  John Philip 473
  Maria Elisabeth (Mrs.)
  473
Schell, Gertrude 471
Schemel, W. H. (Rev.)
  193
Scherer, Samuel 153
Scherp, Anna Elisabeth
  467, 468
  Anna Margaret (Mrs.)
  467
  John Ernst 467

817

827

Washington (cont.)
Elizabeth (Mrs.) 265,
269, 281, 282, 283,
284, 285
Ferdinand 265, 270
Frances 264, 265, 269,
270, 271, 282, 286
Frances Townshend 265,
270, 271, 286
George 151, 152, 252,
265, 269, 285, 361,
540, 730, 734
George (Gen.) 75, 199
George (Mrs.) 354
Henry 258, 264, 265,
269, 270, 281, 283,
284, 285
Henry (Cpt.) 258, 265,
270
Henry (Jr.) 258, 264,
270, 286
Jane (Mrs.) 519
John 66, 258, 262,
264, 265, 269, 270,
271, 281, 282, 283,
285, 286, 519, 520
John (Col.) 75
John (Cpt.) 258, 265,
269, 270, 283, 284
John (Maj.) 65, 75,
224
John Augustine (Col.)
613
John H. 616
Katherine 265, 269,
283
Laurence Augustine
199
Lawrence 75, 259, 261,
264, 265, 269, 270,
272, 281, 283, 284,
285, 286
Lawrence (Cpt.) 519,
520, 521
Lun 283
Lund 257, 265, 269,
270, 286
M----- (Mrs.) 258
Margaret 264, 270
Margaret (Mrs.) 265,
269, 284
Martha Dandridge
Custis (Mrs.) 356
Mary 265, 269, 270,
279, 280, 281, 285
Mary (Jr.) 258, 265,
270
Mary (Mrs.) 258, 265,
269, 270, 281, 282,
283, 28≒, 286
Mary T(ownshend?) 264
Mary T. 270
Mildred 258, 261, 264,
270, 272, 286, 519,
520
Nathaniel 258, 264,
265, 267, 269, 270,
279, 281, 285, 287
Richard 286
Robert 257, 265, 269,
270, 285
Samuel 265, 270, 548
Sarah 265, 269, 284
Susanna 265, 269, 281
Thomas 257, 265, 269,
282, 285
Thornton 265, 271
Townesend 281

Washington (cont.)
Townsend 282
Townshend 257, 258,
264, 265, 269, 270,
283, 285
W. Augustine 548
Warner 366
William 265, 269, 284
William Augustine 548
William Strother 257,
265, 270
Wm. 163
Wm. Strother 285
Waters, Sally 232
William 230
Watkins, Ann Dandridge
359
David 158, 199
Eliz. 127
Elizabeth (?) 359
Elizabeth (Mrs.) 130
Fielding Lewis 130
George 130
John 359
John Dandridge 359
Joseph 156
Mary 122, 124
Watkinson, Thos. 360
Watlington, Paul 89, 244
Watson, Abijah 534
Hilary 621
John 164
Joseph Shelton 155
Mary 111
Peter 394
Robert 394
Susannah (Mrs.) 394
W. M. 621
Watts, (?) (Dr.) 157
Jo. (Cpt.) 134
Mary 521
Richard 521
Waugh, Abner 159
James 385
John 262
Wayland, Adam 300, 301
Elizabeth 301
Maria (Mrs.) 300
Waylandin, Maria 300
Wayman, Herman 313
J. J. 692, 693
J. Maude 692
Lillian M. 693
Maude J. 693
S. L. 693
Wayne, (?) 190
(?) (Gen.) 592
Anthony (Gen.) 613
Weakley, Charles (Mrs.)
686
Weaver, (?) 301
Annie (?) 309
Catharine 303, 310
Elias 309
Elizabeth (Mrs.) 299,
303
Hannah 303
John 299, 303
Margaret 303, 311,
327
Margaret (Mrs.) 311
Matheus 303
Matthias 303
Peter 303, 310, 311,
325
W. C. (Mrs.) 145
Weavers, (?) 308
Webb, (?) 366, 750

Webb (cont.)
Amy 443
Ann 443, 459
Ann (Mrs.) 443
Barbara (Mrs.) 440,
459
Betty 440, 459
Clare (Mrs.) 444
Conrade 366
Cuthbert 444, 459
Cuthberth 440
Elizabeth 750
Elizabeth (Mrs.) 440,
459
Frances 443, 750
Frances (Mrs.) 440,
443, 444, 459
George 109, 750
George (Cpt.) 385
Georgina (Mrs.) 366
Giles 439, 440, 443,
459
Henry 366
Henry Y. 199
Horace (Mrs.) 702
Isaac 439, 440, 443,
444, 459
James 385, 439, 440,
443, 459, 750
James (Jr.) 750
James Hawks 443
John 439, 440, 443,
444, 459, 750
John Span 440, 459
John Spann 459
Kedar 385
Lucius Osborne 366
Lucy 247
Lucy (Mrs.) 366, 750
Mary 385, 440, 459,
750
Mary (Mrs.) 439, 459
Mary Ann (Mrs.) 366
Priscilla 443
Sarah 443, 444
Sarah (Mrs.) 385, 440,
459
Tabitha 440, 459
Thomas 459, 750
Thomas (?) 459
William 156, 440, 459,
750
William (Smith (Dr.)
750
Wm. 702
Wm. Smith (Dr.) 750
Webber, Ada 685
Anne 139
Wm. 161
Weber, (?) 310, 311,
325
Ambes 302
Amy 311
Anna 311
Aron 299
Barbara 299, 302, 303
Catherine 490, 491
Catherine (Mrs.) 476
Daniel 302
Diana 311
Elias 311
Elisabetha 311, 325
Elisabetha (Mrs.) 331
Elizabeth 303
Elizabeth (Mrs.) 299
Elizabetha 302
George 476
Hanna 299, 327